Intelligent Multimedia Databases and Information Retrieval:

Advancing Applications and Technologies

Li Yan
Northeastern University, China

Zongmin Ma
Northeastern University, China

Senior Editorial Director:	Kristin Klinger
Director of Book Publications:	Julia Mosemann
Editorial Director:	Lindsay Johnston
Acquisitions Editor:	Erika Carter
Development Editor:	Michael Killian
Production Editor:	Sean Woznicki
Typesetters:	Adrienne Freeland, Jennifer Romanchak, Mackenzie Snader, Milan Vracarich Jr.
Print Coordinator:	Jamie Snavely
Cover Design:	Nick Newcomer

Published in the United States of America by
Information Science Reference (an imprint of IGI Global)
701 E. Chocolate Avenue
Hershey PA 17033
Tel: 717-533-8845
Fax: 717-533-8661
E-mail: cust@igi-global.com
Web site: http://www.igi-global.com

Library of Congress Cataloging-in-Publication Data

Intelligent multimedia databases and information retrieval: advancing applications and technologies / Li Yan and Zongmin Ma, editors.
p. cm.
Includes bibliographical references and index.
Summary: "This book details the latest information retrieval technologies and applications, the research surrounding the field, and the methodologies and design related to multimedia databases"--Provided by publisher.
ISBN 978-1-61350-126-9 (hardcover) -- ISBN 978-1-61350-127-6 (ebook) -- ISBN 978-1-61350-128-3 (print & perpetual access) 1. Multimedia systems. 2. Databases. 3. Intelligent agents (Computer software). I. Yan, Li, 1964- II. Ma, Zongmin, 1965-
QA76.575.I254 2012
006.7--dc23

2011027682

British Cataloguing in Publication Data
A Cataloguing in Publication record for this book is available from the British Library.

Editorial Advisory Board

Table of Contents

Preface vii

Acknowledgment xii

Section 1

Chapter 1
Profiling User Color Perception for Image Retrieving 1
Imad El-Zakhem, Université de Reims Champagne Ardenne, France
Amine Aït-Younes, Université de Reims Champagne Ardenne, France
Herman Akdag, Université Paris 6, France
Hanna Greige, University of Balamand, Lebanon

Chapter 2
Approach of Using Texture and Shape for Image Retrieval 30
Gang Zhang, Northeastern University, China & Shenyang University of Technology, China
Zongmin Ma, Northeastern University, China
Li Yan, Northeastern University, China

Chapter 3
Mid-Level Image Descriptors 46
Jean Martinet, University of Lille, France
Ismail Elsayad, University of Lille, France

Chapter 4
An Image Retrieval Model Combining Ontology and Probabilistic Ranking 61
Lisa Fan, University of Regina, Canada
Botang Li, University of Regina, Canada

Chapter 5
Annotation of Medical Images 74
Chia-Hung Wei, Ching Yun University, Taiwan
Sherry Y. Chen, Brunel University, UK

Preface

The decreasing costs of consumer electronic devices such as digital cameras and digital camcorders, along with the ease of transportation facilitated by the Internet, has lead to a phenomenal rise in the amount of multimedia data. Now multimedia data comprising of images, audio, and video is becoming increasingly common. Given that this trend of increased use of multimedia data is likely to accelerate, there is an urgent need for providing a clear means of capturing, storing, indexing, retrieving, analyzing, and summarizing such data.

Image data, for example, is a very commonly used multimedia data. The early image retrieval systems are based on manually annotated descriptions, called text-based image retrieval (TBIR). TBIR is a great leap forward, but has several inherent drawbacks. First, textual description is not capable of capturing the visual contents of an image accurately, and in many circumstances, textual annotations are not available. Second, different people may describe the content of an image in different ways, which limits the recall performance of textual-based image retrieval systems. Third, for some images there is something that no words can convey. To resolve these problems, content-based image retrieval (CBIR) systems are designed to support image retrieval, and have been used since the early 1990s. Also, some novel approaches (e.g., relevance feedback, semantic understanding, semantic annotation, and semantic retrieval of images) have been developed in the last decade to improve image retrieval and satisfy the advanced requirements of image retrieval.

Multimedia data retrieval is closely related to multimedia data management. Multimedia data management facilitates the manipulation of multimedia data such as representation, storage, index, retrieval, maintenance, and so on. Multimedia data retrieval is the key to implementing multimedia data management on one hand. On the other hand, multimedia data retrieval should be carried out based on multimedia data representation, storage, and index, which are the major tasks of multimedia data management. Databases are designed to support the data storage, processing, and retrieval activities related to data management, and database management systems can provide efficient task support and tremendous gain in productivity is hereby accomplished using these technologies. There is no doubt that database systems play an important role in multimedia data management, and multimedia data management requires database technique support. Multimedia databases, which have become the repositories of large volumes of multimedia data, are emerging.

Multimedia databases play a crucial role in multimedia data management, which provide the mechanisms for storing and retrieving multimedia data efficiently and naturally. Being a special kind of databases, multimedia databases have been developed and used in many application fields. Many researchers have been concentrating on multimedia data management using multimedia databases. The research and development of multimedia data management using multimedia databases are receiving increasing attention. By means of multimedia databases, large volumes of multimedia data can be stored and indexed and then retrieved effectively and naturally from multimedia databases. Intelligent multimedia data retrieval systems are built based on multimedia databases to support various problem solving and decision making. Thus, intelligent multimedia databases and information retrieval is a field that must be investigated by academic researchers together with developers both from CBIR and AI fields.

The book has two focuses on multimedia data retrieval and multimedia databases, aiming at providing a single account of technologies and practices in multimedia data management. The objective of the book is to provide the state of the art information to academics, researchers, and industry practitioners who are involved or interested in the study, use, design, and development of advanced and emerging multimedia data retrieval and management with ultimate aim to empower individuals and organizations in building competencies for exploiting the opportunities of the knowledge society. This book presents the latest research and application results in multimedia data retrieval and management. The different chapters in the book have been contributed by different authors and provide possible solutions for the different types of technological problems concerning multimedia data retrieval and management.

INTRODUCTION

This book, which consists of fifteen chapters, is organized into two major sections. The first section discusses the feature and semantics of multimedia data as well as their usage in multimedia information retrieval in the first eight chapters. The next seven chapters covering database and intelligence technologies for multimedia data management comprise the second section.

First of all, we take a look at the issues of the feature and semantics of multimedia data as well as their usage in multimedia information retrieval.

Imad EL-Zakhem *et al.* concentrate on building a user profile according to his own perception of colors for image retrieving. They develop a dynamic construction of the user profile, which will increase their satisfaction by being more personalized and accommodated to their particular needs. They suggest two methods to define the perception and transform it into a profile: the first one is achieved by querying the user and getting answers and the second one is achieved by comparing different subjects and ending up by an appropriate aggregation. They also present a method recalculating the amount of colors in the image based on another set of parameters, and the colorimetric profile of the image is being modified accordingly. Avoiding the repetition of the process at the pixel level is the main target of this phase, because reprocessing each image is time consuming and not feasible.

In content-based image retrieval, different kinds of features (e.g., texture features, color features and shape features) may be used jointly, and feature integration is hereby one of crucial issues in content-based image retrieval. Gang Zhang *et al.* develop an approach of integrating shape and texture features and investigate if integration features are more discriminative than single features. Single feature extraction and description is foundation of the feature integration. They apply Gabor wavelet transform with minimum information redundancy to extract texture features, which are used for feature analyses. Fourier descriptor approach with brightness is used to extract shape features. Then both features are integrated together by weights. They make the comparisons among the integration features, the texture features, and the shape features so that the discrimination of the integration features can be testified.

The research domain of automatic image annotation and search from low-level descriptors analysis has considerably evolved in the last 15 years. Since then, this domain has reached a level of maturity where only small improvements are brought in new models and systems. Jean Martinet and Ismail Elsayad propose a classification of image descriptors, from low-level descriptors to high-level descriptors, introducing the notion of mid-level descriptors for image representation. A mid-level descriptor is described as an intermediate representation between low-level descriptors (derived from the signal) and high-level descriptors (conveying semantics associated to the image). Mid-level descriptors are built for the purpose of yielding a finer representation for a particular set of documents. They describe a number of image representation techniques from a mid-level description perspective.

There are hundreds of millions of images available on the current World Wide Web, and the demand for image retrieval and browsing online is growing dramatically. The typical keyword-based retrieval methods for multimedia documents assume that the user has an exact goal in mind in searching a set of images whereas users normally do not know what they want, or the user faces a repository of images whose domain is less known and content is semantically complicated. In these cases it is difficult to decide what keywords to use for the query. Lisa Fan and Botang Li present an approach of the user-driven ontology guided image retrieval. It combines (a) the certain reasoning techniques based on logic inside ontology and (b) the uncertain reasoning technique based on Bayesian Network to provide users the enhanced image retrieval on the Web. Their approach is for easily plugging in an external ontology in the distributed environment and assists user searching for a set of images effectively. In addition, to obtain a faster real-time search result, the ontology query and BN computation should be run on the off-line mode, and the results should be stored into the indexing record.

A large number of digital medical images have been produced in hospitals in the last decade. These medical images are stored in large-scale image databases and can facilitate medical doctors, professionals, researchers, and college students to diagnose current patients and provide valuable information for their studies. Image annotation is considered as a vital task for searching, and indexing large collections of medical images. Chia-Hung Wei and Sherry Y Chen present a complete scheme for automatic annotation on mammograms. Firstly, they present the feature extraction methods based on BI-RADS standards. This ensures that the meaning and interpretation of mammograms are clearly characterized and can be reliably used for feature extraction. Secondly, they propose the SVM classification approach to image annotation. Finally, their experimental results demonstrate that the scheme can achieve fair performance on image annotation.

Digital image storage and retrieval is gaining more popularity due to the rapidly advancing technology and the large number of vital applications, in addition to flexibility in managing personal collections of images. Traditional approaches employ keyword based indexing which is not very effective. Content based methods are more attractive though challenging and require considerable effort for automated feature extraction. Görkem Aşılıoğlu *et al.* present a hybrid method for extracting features from images using a combination of already established methods, allowing them to be compared to a given input image as seen in other query-by-example methods. First, the image features are calculated using edge orientation autocorrelograms and color correlograms. Then, distances of the images to the original image are calculated using the L1 distance feature separately for both features. The distance sets are then be merged according to a weight supplied by the user.

Disadvantages with text-based image retrieval have provoked growing interest in the development of Content-Based Image Retrieval (CBIR). In CBIR, instead of being manually annotated by text-based keywords, images are indexed by their visual content, such as color, texture, etc. Ling Shao surveys content-based image retrieval techniques on representing and extracting visual features, such as color, shape, and texture. The feature representation and extraction approaches are first classified and discussed. Then, he summarizes several classical CBIR systems which rely on either global features or features detected on segmented regions. The inefficiency and disadvantages of those narrow-domain systems are also presented. Finally, he discusses two recent trends on image retrieval, namely semantic based methods and local invariant regions based methods, and proposes directions for future work.

With the rapid growth of digital videos, efficient tools are essential to facilitate content indexing, searching, retrieving, browsing, skimming, and summarization. Sport video analysis aims to identify what excites audiences. Previous methods rely mainly on video decomposition, using domain specific knowledge and lacking the ability to produce personalized semantics especially in highlight detection. Research on suitable and efficient techniques for sport video analysis has been conducted extensively over the last decade. Chia-Hung Yeh *et al.* review the development of sport video analysis and explore solutions to the challenge of extracting high-level semantics in sport videos. They propose a method to analyze baseball videos via the concept of gap length. Use-interaction may be a solution to achieve personalization in semantics extraction. The techniques introduced can be wildly applied to many fields, such as indexing, searching, retrieving, summarization, skimming, training, and entertainment.

The second section deals with the issues of database and intelligence technologies for multimedia data management.

The last decades have witnessed a considerable rise in the amount of multimedia data. Data models and database management systems (DBMSs) can play a crucial role in the storage and management of multimedia data. Being a special kind of database systems, multimedia databases have been developed and used in many application fields. Shi Kuo Chang, Vincenzo Deufemia, and Giuseppe Polese present normal forms for the design of multimedia database schemes with reduced manipulation anomalies. They first discuss how to describe the semantics of multimedia attributes based upon the concept of generalized icons, already used in the modeling of multimedia languages. They then introduce new extended dependencies involving different types of multimedia data. Based upon these new dependencies, they define five normal forms for multimedia databases, some focusing on the level of segmentation of multimedia attributes, others on the level of fragmentation of tables. Thus a normalization framework for multimedia databases is developed, which provides proper design guidelines to improve the quality of multimedia database schemes.

Multimedia data is a challenge for data management. The semantics of traditional alphanumeric data are mostly explicit, unique, and self-contained, but the semantics of multimedia data are usually dynamic, diversiform, and varying from one user's perspective to another's. Dawen Jia and Mengchi Liu introduce a new model, titled the Information Networking Model (INM). It provides a strong semantic modeling mechanism that allows modeling of the real world in a natural and direct way. With INM, users can model multimedia data, which consists of dynamic semantics. The context-dependency and media-independency features of multimedia data can easily be represented by INM. In addition, multimedia multiple classifications are naturally supported. Based on INM, they propose a multimedia data modeling mechanism in which users can take advantage of basic multimedia metadata, semantic relationships, and contextual semantic information to search multimedia data.

With increasing use of multimedia in various domains, several metadata standards appeared these last decades in order to facilitate the manipulation of multimedia contents. These standards help consumers to search content they desire and to adapt the retrieved content according to consumers' profiles and preferences. However, in order to extract information from a given standard, user must have a pre-knowledge about this latest. This condition is not easy to satisfy due to the increasing number of available standards. Samir Amir *et al.* first give an overview about existing multimedia metadata standards and CAM4Home project initiative that covers a wide area of information related to multimedia delivery and includes multimedia content description, user preference and profile description, and devices' characteristic description. Then they relate about multimedia and generic integration issues by discussing the work done by W3C working group in order to integrate heterogeneous metadata and some generic approaches providing mapping between ontologies. They also consecrate to the illustration of the proposal of a new architecture for the multimedia metadata integration system and discuss about challenges of its realization.

Semantic characterization is necessary for developing intelligent multimedia databases, because humans tend to search for media content based on their inherent semantics. However, automated inference of semantic concepts derived from media components stored in a database is still a challenge. Ranjan Parekh and Nalin Sharda demonstrate how layered architectures and visual keywords can be used to develop intelligent search systems for multimedia databases. The layered architecture is used to extract meta-data from multimedia components at various layers of abstractions. To access the various abstracted features, a query schema is presented which provides a single point of access while establishing hierarchical pathways between feature-classes. Minimization of the semantic gap is addressed using the concept of visual keyword (VK). Semantic information is however predominantly expressed in textual form, and hence is susceptible to the limitations of textual descriptors–viz. ambiguities related to synonyms, homonyms, hypernyms, and hyponyms. To handle such ambiguities they propose a domain specific ontology-based layer on top of the semantic layer, to increase the effectiveness of the search process.

Fuzzy set theory has been extensively applied to the representation and processing of imprecise and uncertain data. Image data is becoming a kind of important data resources with rapid growth in the number of large-scale image repositories. But image data is fuzzy in nature and imprecision and vagueness may exist in both image descriptions and query specifications. Li Yan and Z. M. Ma review some major work of image retrieval with fuzzy logic in the literature, including fuzzy content-based image retrieval and database support for fuzzy image retrieval. For the fuzzy content-based image retrieval, they present how fuzzy sets are applied for the extraction and representation of visual (colors, shapes, textures) features, similarity measures and indexing, relevance feedback, and retrieval systems. For the fuzzy image database retrieval, they present how fuzzy sets are applied for fuzzy image query processing based on a defined database models, and how various fuzzy database models can support image data management.

Project portfolio management of multimedia production and use emerges today as a challenge both for the enrichment of traditional classroom based teaching and for distance education offering. In this way, Joni A. Amorim, Rosana G. S. Miskulin, and Mauro S. Miskulin intend to answer the following question: "Which are the fundamental aspects to be considered in the management of projects on educational multimedia production and use?" They present a proposal of a project management model for digital content production and use. The model, the methodology and the implementation are named EduPMO (Educational Project Management Office). The model, the methodology and the implementation should be understood as related but independent entities. This interdisciplinary investigation involves different topics, going from metadata and interoperability to intellectual property and process improvement.

Latent Semantic Analysis (LSA) or Latent Semantic Indexing (LSI), when applied to information retrieval, has been a major analysis approach in text mining. It is an extension of the vector space method in information retrieval, representing documents as numerical vectors, but using a more sophisticated mathematical approach to characterize the essential features of the documents and reduce the number of features in the search space. Anne Kao *et al.* summarize several major approaches to this dimensionality reduction, each of which has strengths and weaknesses, and describe recent breakthroughs and advances. They show how the constructs and products of LSA applications can be made user-interpretable and review applications of LSA beyond information retrieval, in particular, to text information visualization. While the major application of LSA is for text mining, it is also highly applicable to cross-language information retrieval, Web mining, and analysis of text transcribed from speech and textual information in video.

Acknowledgment

The editors wish to thank all of the authors for their insights and excellent contributions to this book and would like to acknowledge the help of all involved in the collation and review process of the book, without whose support the project could not have been satisfactorily completed. Most of the authors of chapters included in this book also served as referees for chapters written by other authors. Thanks go to all those who provided constructive and comprehensive reviews.

A further special note of thanks goes to all the staff at IGI Global, whose contributions throughout the whole process from inception of the initial idea to final publication have been invaluable. Special thanks also go to the publishing team at IGI Global. This book would not have been possible without the ongoing professional support from IGI Global.

The idea of editing this volume stems from the initial research work that the editors did in past several years. The research work of the editors was supported by the *Program for New Century Excellent Talents in University* (NCET-05-0288).

Li Yan
Northeastern University, China

Zongmin Ma
Northeastern University, China

Section 1

Chapter 1
Profiling User Color Perception for Image Retrieving

Imad El-Zakhem
Université de Reims Champagne Ardenne, France

Amine Aït-Younes
Université de Reims Champagne Ardenne, France

Herman Akdag
Université Paris 6, France

Hanna Greige
University of Balamand, Lebanon

ABSTRACT

The aim of this work is to build a user profile according to his own perception of colors for image retrieving. Images are being processed relying on a standard or initial set of parameters using the fuzzy set theory and the HLS color space (Hue, Lightness, and Saturation). We developed a dynamic construction of the user profile, which will increase his satisfaction by being more personalized and accommodated to his particular needs. We suggest two methods to define the perception and transform it into a profile; the first method is achieved by querying the user and getting answers, which will guide through the process of implementation of the profile; the second method is achieved by comparing different subjects and ending up by an appropriate aggregation. We also present a method that will recalculate the amount of colors in the image based on another set of parameters, so the colorimetric profile of the image is being modified accordingly. Avoiding the repetition of the process at the pixel level is the main target of this phase, because reprocessing each image is time consuming and turned to be not feasible.

DOI: 10.4018/978-1-61350-126-9.ch001

INTRODUCTION

Image retrieving is an important problem that can be useful in many fields (Foulloy, 1990), Hammami (2002), Hong (2000) and Le Saux (2003)). For example, in medical applications, it is important to retrieve images in order to help medical expert forecasts. Another example lies in web content detection: classification of images to determine whether they contain a lot of skin texture or not in order to detect adult and sexual contents (Hammami, 2002).

There are several works on image classification based on the determination of a similarity degree between images. This kind of classification can be done through several techniques, for example: statistical approach like Support Vector Machines (Hong, 2000; Barla, 2003; Vapnik, 1998), color and illumination features using histograms intersection (Barla, 2003; Bourghorbel, 2002) and fuzzy logic (Chen, 2002; Omhover, 2004; Vertan, 2000).

Among these Image Retrieval Systems, we distinguish at least two kinds: those that consider the histograms and those that don't. Barla et al address the problem of classifying images by exploiting color and illumination features, using histogram intersections. The histogram intersection is used as a kernel function for SVMs and allows one to classify images by similarity of histograms (Barla, 2003).

Han and Ma propose a fuzzy color histogram that permits to consider the color similarity across different bins and the color dissimilarity in the same bin (Han, 2002). Thus, as in Vertan (2000), a pixel of a given color will contribute not only to its specific bin, but its membership value will be spread to other histogram bins.

Another kind of approach is presented by Wang and Du: they propose an algorithm for indexing and retrieving images based on region segmentation, and they also compute similarities between images in order to classify them (Wang, 2000). As for Frigui, he describes a system that offers the refinement of the user query (Frigui, 2001). The user's relevance feedbacks are modeled by fuzzy sets, i.e. the user expresses his satisfaction or discontentment by assigning a label to the retrieved images. A dissimilarity based on fuzzy integrals is then used. It is a kind of supervised learning for image retrieval systems.

All the aforementioned authors work with a query image. That is not the case of Binaghi et al who use a user query expressed by crisp values of colors (Binaghi, 1994). More precisely, they provide methodological and technical solutions to compute similarities between the query and the image index. The user also has to choose the color dimension (hue, chroma or lightness), the image area covered by the referent color and the type of color distribution in the image. Thus, the user has to know exactly what he is looking for in terms of colors and color distribution in order to obtain satisfactory results. That is why we have focused on the problem of the query expression which is very simple in our case: the user can ask only for a certain tone if he wants.

The aim of this work is not to make a classical classification but to retrieve images according to their dominant(s) color(s) expressed through linguistic expressions. In this work, Images are processed using a fuzzy representation of colors based on the HLS space. The image processing consists of modeling the three dimensions of color (hue, saturation and lightness) by using fuzzy membership functions.

The standard colorimetric profile of each image is build using standard values of the membership functions. These profiles may not be accepted by all users since the perception is a subjective issue. To resolve this problem, the user is asked to build his profile, thus when retrieving images, they will be brought regarding his perception.

To avoid the reprocessing of images, we use a new approach by applying a transformation procedure on the standard colorimetric profile of the images according to user's perception. In this procedure, we use the notions of comparability and compatibility of fuzzy subsets

Figure 1. An example of a color histogram

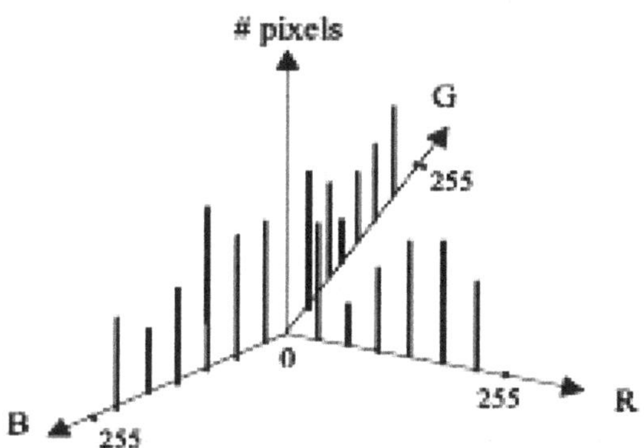

The chapter is organized as follows: after a discussion about the color representation we present in section 2 the problem of color representation with fuzzy membership functions and image processing. The global approach for building a user profile is presented in section 3. In section 4, the notions of comparability and compatibility of fuzzy subsets are presented. Finally, some statistical results are presented in section 5.

COLOR REPRESENTATION

Colors are being represented through different color spaces like the RGB, HLS, Lab etc.

The CIE (Commission Internationale de l'Eclairage) has standardized the weights of the triplet R, G,B. The intensities of the three components are additive, so that all colors accessible from an RGB basis are obtained by sums of the primary colors R, G, and B and by multiplications by nonnegative constants (CIE, 1986).

Despite its use in computer systems, the RGB color representation has some drawbacks like the poor human interpretation, the none-uniformity, etc.

The polar representation, like the HLS and HSV, uses one variable for light intensity and two variables defined on the chromatic circle, may allow a better handling of the color parameters for quantitative purposes. Many research studies took interest in the polar space color representations (Kender, 1976; Smith, 1978; Shih, 1995; Carron, 1995).

In many color-based image retrieval{XE "retrieval"} applications (CBIR), the color properties of an image are characterized by the probability distribution of the colors in the image. Based on the color space representation, many CBIR systems represent region colors by means of histograms, so that they can be stored in a simple, intuitive way.

Histograms may be represented in two-dimensional or three-dimensional spaces (Figure 1).

The color histogram remains the most popular representation of color distributions since it is insensitive to small object distortions and easy to compute. However, it is not very efficient due to its large memory requirement. Typically, a color histogram might consist of 512 bins. With such a large number of bins, the performance of current indexing techniques is reduced to a sequential scanning (Webe, 1998; Rui, 1999). To make color histogram-based image retrieval truly scalable to large image databases it is desirable to reduce the number of parameters needed to describe the histogram while still preserving the retrieval performance.

Approaches to deal with these problems include the usage of coarser histograms (Mitra, 1997; Pass, 1999), dominant colors or signature colors (Androutsos, 1999; Deng, 2001) and application of signal processing compression techniques such as the Karhunen–Loève transform, discrete cosine transform, Hadamard transform, Haar transform, and wavelets, etc. (Albuz, 2001; Berens, 1995; Hafner, 1995).

Also another drawback of histograms is that they tend to be noisy. Sometimes it is necessary to extract only relevant information from complete histograms, thus retaining reduced feature vectors. Some authors rely on extracting their Color

Figure 2. The RGB space

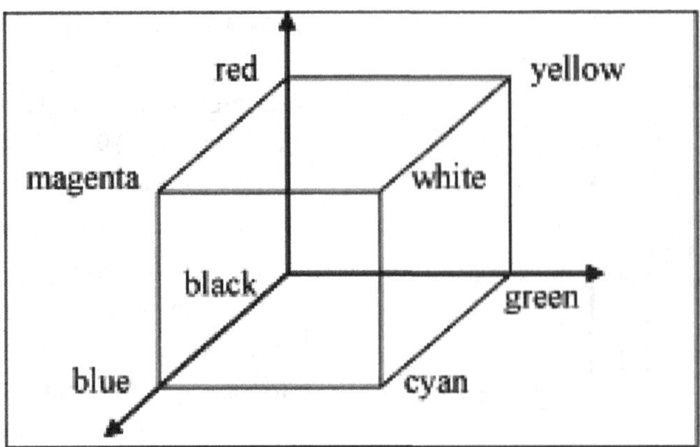

Moments or Color Sets (Diplaros, 2006; Swain, 1991; Li, 1999).

Color moments are good descriptors when the analyzed region presents a dominant color, but this technique provides confusing results when applied to mixed color regions. Color Sets can be adjusted to represent color regions, but they introduce a quantization on the original color histograms, thus, they do not adapt to the characteristics of any particular colored region.

FUZZY REPRESENTATION OF COLORS AND IMAGE PROCESSING

As we know, one of the spaces usually used to represent the color on a screen is the RGB space (Red, Green and Blue). It is a three dimensional space representing the three primary colors that usually vary from 0 to 255. The origin of this space (0, 0, 0) corresponds to the lack of color which represents the "black" color. On the other hand the point (255,255,255) corresponds to the maximum of color which represents the "white". The representation of the colors in this space gives us a cube (Figure 2).

In classification methods, this space is used in the calculation of similarity through color histogram (Swain, 1991) which represents the distribution of the pixels on the three axes (red, green, blue). However with this kind of histogram it is difficult to define a fuzzy membership degree to a given color, for example how to define in a fuzzy way a "pink"?

The RGB space is not appropriate for our problem also because three dimensions (R, G and B) are necessary to identify a color. To facilitate the color identification we choose another space that allows us to characterize a color with only one dimension: its hue. Indeed hue is enough to recognize the color, except when the color is very pale or very somber. This other space is called HLS (Hue, Lightness, and Saturation) where lightness corresponds to the quantity of "white" in the color and saturation corresponds to the light intensity of the color. The identification of color is made in two steps: first H, then L, S. The HLS space can be represented through a cylinder or a bi-cone (Figure 3).

Moreover, in practice, various models of color representation use also a "two-step" identification of color. For example, Aron Sigfrid Forsius, Pantone Matching System, RAL (*Reich-sAusschuss, für Lieferbedingungen und Gütesi-cherung*), Munsel, ISCC-NBS (*Inter-Society Color Council - National Bureau of Standards*), etc. (cf. Couwenbergh(2003)) use at first a color

Figure 3. The HLS space

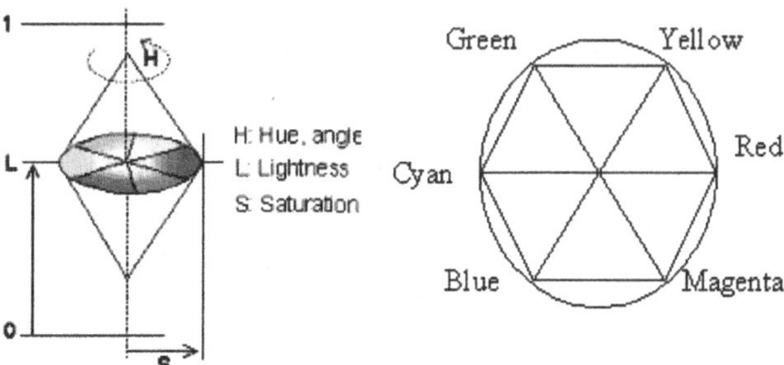

description by means of the hue then a refinement through the saturation and the lightness.

H is defined as an angle but we can also represent it in the interval [0,255] as the other components L and S. The difference between H and the other components is that its definition interval loops which means that 0 and 256 are the same points. The "pure" red (represented in RGB space by the point (255, 0, 0)) corresponds to an angle equal to 0° for *h*, a saturation *s* equal to 255 and a lightness *l* equal to 128.

For this problem, we limit ourselves to the nine fundamental colors defined by the set $\mathcal{T}$ representing a good sample of colors (dimension H):

$\mathcal{T}$ = {*red, orange, yellow, green, cyan, blue, purple, magenta, pink*}

This set corresponds to the seven colors of Newton (cf. Roire(2000)) to which we have added color pink and color cyan. Of course, this choice is not restrictive; we can modify the set of colors as desired.

Fuzzy Representation of Colors

As we have seen HLS space is convenient for our problem but it is a non UCS (uniform color scale) space (Herrera, 2001). Indeed our eyes don't perceive small variations of hue when color is green (h = 85) or blue (h = 170) while they perceive it very well with orange (h = 21) for example.

To deal with non uniformly distributed scales, authors such as Herrera and Martinez propose to use fuzzy linguistic hierarchies with more or less labels, depending on the desired granularity (Herrera, 2001). Another approach from Truck (2001) is to represent the hues with trapezoidal or triangular fuzzy subsets thanks to colors definitions from www.pourpre.com. This technique is more empirical but fits better the human perception, that is why we also use this approach.

For each color of $\mathcal{T}$ they built a membership function varying from 0 to 1 (f_t with $t \in \mathcal{T}$). If this function is equal to 1, the corresponding color is a "true color" (cf. Figure 4).

These functions were built using colors definition (www.poupre.com). For each fundamental color, the associated interval is defined according to linguistic names of colors. For example to construct f_{yellow}, we can use color "mustard" whose hue is equal to 55 and whose membership to f_{yellow} is equal to ***0.5***.

For some colors, the result gives a wide interval. It is the case for the colors "green" and "blue" which are represented by trapezoidal fuzzy subsets.

For the construction of these functions, in this article we suppose that two functions representing two successive colors have their intersection point value equal to 1/2. It means that when h corresponds to an intersection point it can be assigned to both colors with the same weight.

Figure 4. The dimension H

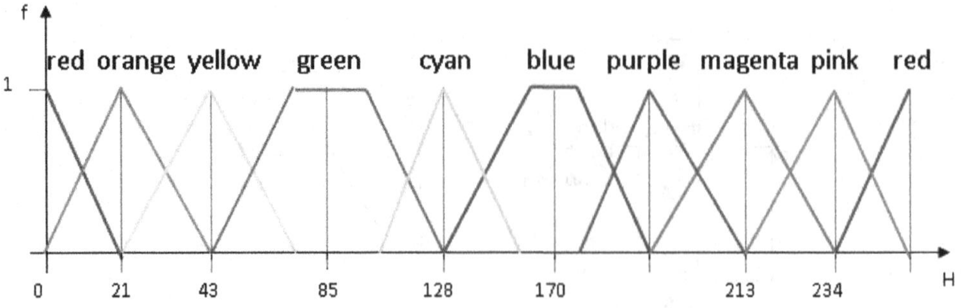

Figure 5. Trapezoidal fuzzy subset

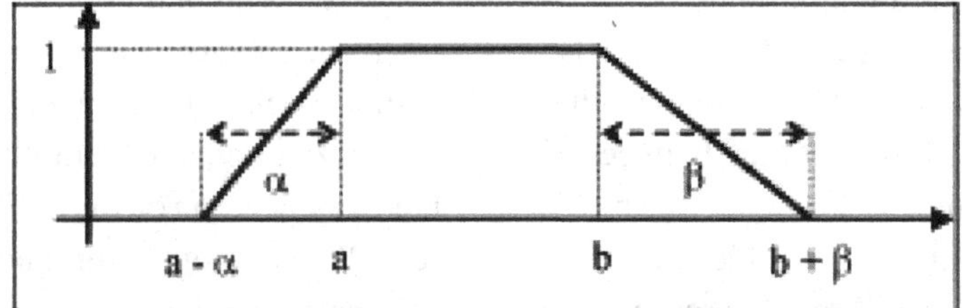

As usual (Bouchon-Meunier, 1995) we denote (a, b, α, β) a trapezoidal fuzzy subset (Figure 5). When the kernel is reduced to only one point, it is a triangular subset denoted by (a, α, β) since $a=b$.

Now we can define the membership function of any color t:

$$\forall t \in T, f_t(h) = \begin{cases} 1 & if \quad h \geq a \\ & \wedge \quad h \leq b \\ 0 & if \quad h \leq a - \alpha \\ & \wedge \quad h \geq b + \beta \\ \dfrac{h-(a-\alpha)}{\alpha} & if \quad h > a - \alpha \\ & \wedge \quad h < a \\ \dfrac{(b+\beta)-h}{\beta} & if \quad h > b \\ & \wedge \quad h < b + \beta \end{cases} \tag{1}$$

For example, for $t = orange$ we have a triangular subset with:

$$f_{orange}(h) = \begin{cases} 0 & if \quad h \geq 43 \\ \dfrac{h}{21} & if \quad h < 21 \\ \dfrac{43-h}{22} & if \quad h \geq 21 \end{cases} \tag{2}$$

For $t = green$ we have a trapezoidal subset with $(a = 75, \alpha = 22, b = 95, \beta = 33)$:

$$f_{green}(h) = \begin{cases} 1 & if \quad h \geq 75 \\ & \wedge \quad h \leq 95 \\ 0 & if \quad h \leq 43 \\ & \wedge \quad h \geq 128 \\ \dfrac{h-43}{22} & if \quad h > 43 \\ & \wedge \quad h < 75 \\ \dfrac{128-h}{33} & if \quad h > 95 \\ & \wedge \quad h < 128 \end{cases} \tag{3}$$

Figure 6. Fundamental color qualifiers

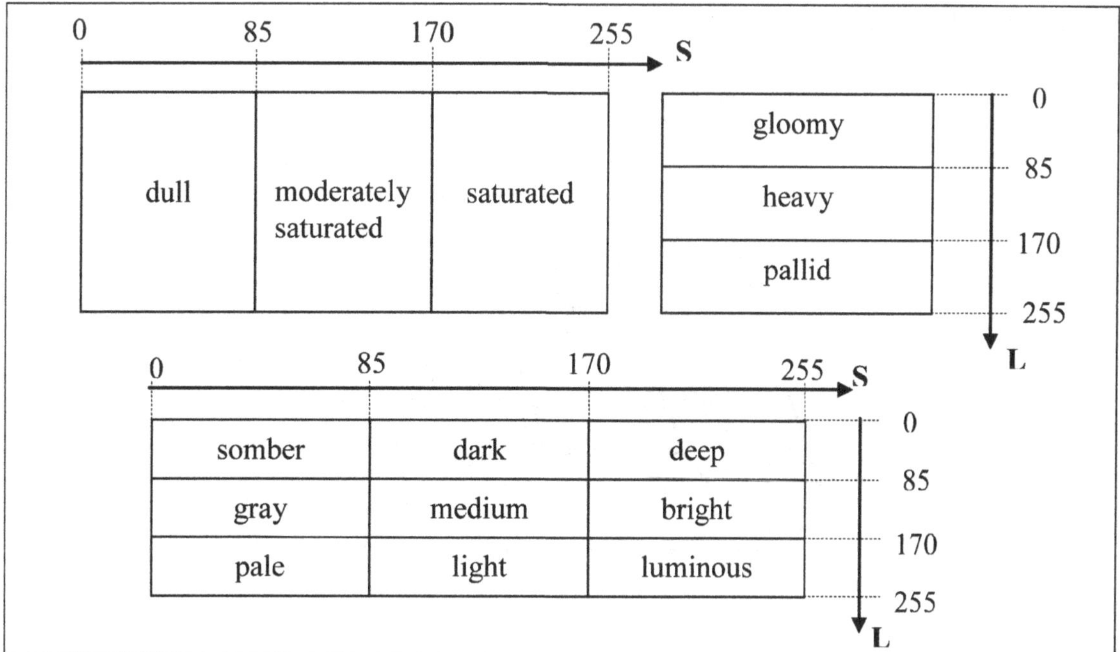

Moreover if we want to complete the modeling, it is necessary to take into account the two other dimensions *(L, S)*. A scale representing the colorimetric qualifiers is associated to each dimension. These two intervals are divided into three: the first subinterval corresponds to a low value, the second to an average value and the last to a strong value. This division gives for saturation *S*: "*dull*", "*moderately dull*" and "*saturated*"; and for lightness *L*: "*gloomy*", "*heavy*" and "*pallid*".

These two scales are then aggregated to give nine qualifiers for colors defined by the following set (Figure 6) (Aït Younes, 2007):

Q = {somber, dark, *deep, gray, medium, bright, pale, light, luminous*}.

Each element of the set Q is associated to a membership function varying between 0 and 1 ($\tilde{f}_q$ with $q \in Q$). For these functions the intersection point value is also supposed equal to 1/2 (cf. Figure 8)). Every function is represented through the set $(a, b, c, d, \alpha, \beta, \gamma, \delta)$ (Figure 7).

The membership function of any qualifier q is defined below:

$$\forall q \in Q, \tilde{f}_q(l,s) = \left\{ \begin{array}{ccc} 1 & if & a \le s \le b \\ & \wedge & c \le l \le d \\ 0 & if & s \le a-\alpha \vee s \ge b+\beta \\ & \vee & l \le c-\gamma \vee l \ge d+\delta \\ \frac{l-(c-\gamma)}{\gamma} & if & c-\gamma < l < c \\ & \wedge & \alpha l - \gamma s \le \alpha c - \gamma a \\ & \wedge & \beta l + \gamma s \le \beta c + \gamma b \\ \frac{(d+\delta)-l}{\delta} & if & d < l < d+\delta \\ & \wedge & \beta l - \delta s > \beta d - \delta b \\ & \wedge & \alpha l + \delta s > \alpha d + \delta a \\ \frac{s-(a-\alpha)}{\alpha} & if & a-\alpha < s < a \\ & \wedge & \alpha l - \gamma s > \alpha c - \gamma a \\ & \wedge & \alpha l + \delta s \le \alpha d + \delta a \\ \frac{(b+\beta)-s}{\beta} & if & b < s < b+\beta \\ & \wedge & \beta l + \gamma s > \beta c + \gamma b \\ & \wedge & \beta l - \delta s \le \beta d - \delta b \end{array} \right. \quad (4)$$

Figure 7. Trapezoidal 3-D fuzzy subset

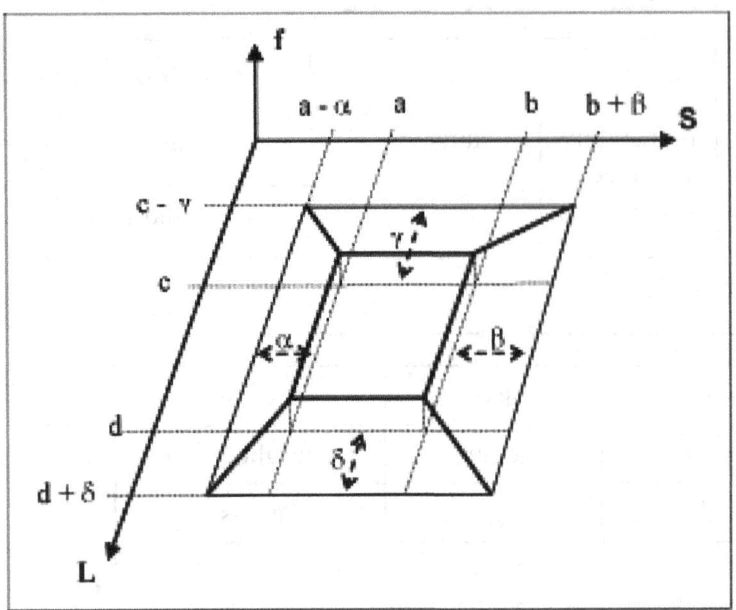

Figure 8. Dimensions L and S

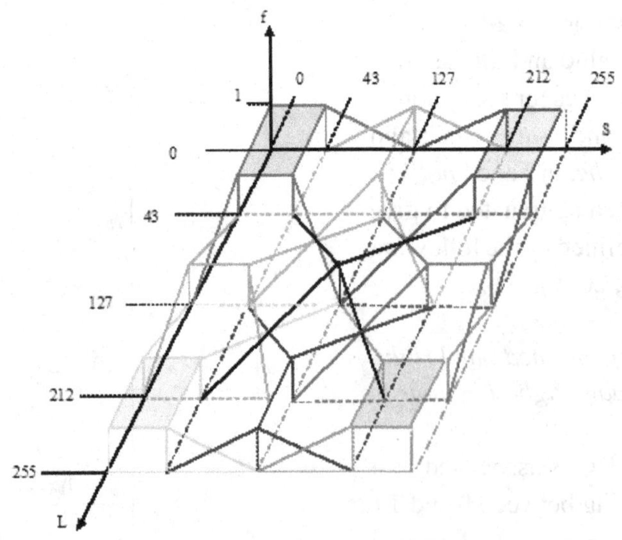

For example, for q = *somber*, we have (a = α = 0, b = 43, β = 84, c = γ = 0, d = 43, δ = 84):

$$\tilde{f}_{somber}(l,s) = \begin{cases} 1 & if \quad s \leq 43 \\ & \wedge \quad l \leq 43 \\ 0 & if \quad s \geq 127 \\ & \vee \quad l \geq 127 \\ \dfrac{127-l}{84} & if \quad 43 < l < 127 \\ & \wedge \quad l > s \\ \dfrac{127-s}{84} & if \quad 43 < s < 127 \\ & \wedge \quad l \leq s \end{cases} \tag{5}$$

We also took into account the colors black, gray and white. Fuzzy membership functions are associated to this colors (f_{black}, f_{white} and f_{gray}). These colors are completely defined through the spaces L and S. If the lightness is very low then the color is white, and a high level of the lightness means the color is black. If the saturation is very low then the color is gray. For this last color we define three qualifiers: *dark, medium* and *light* which are associated to fuzzy membership functions: $\tilde{f}_{dark}$, $\tilde{f}_{medium}$ and $\tilde{f}_{light}$ (Figure 9).

For example, for t= *black* we have (a = α = 0, b = 255, β = 0, c = γ = 0, d = 15, δ = 10):

$$f_{black}(l) = \begin{cases} 1 & if \quad l \leq 15 \\ 0 & if \quad l \geq 25 \\ \dfrac{25-l}{10} & if \quad 15 < l < 25 \end{cases} \tag{6}$$

Image Processing

Each pixel can now be categorized in one or more fuzzy classes with an associated membership degree. Thus, it is possible to compute the membership functions to the various classes (colors and qualifiers) for the whole image.

Let I be an image and $\mathcal{P}$ be the set representing the pixels of I.

Each element p of the set $\mathcal{P}$ is defined by its color coordinates (h_p, l_p, s_p). We calculate the functions $f_t(h_p)$, $\tilde{f}_q(l_p, s_p)$, $\tilde{f}_q(l_p, s_p)$ for $t \in \mathcal{T}$ and $q \in \mathcal{Q}$.

Figure 9. Black, gray and white

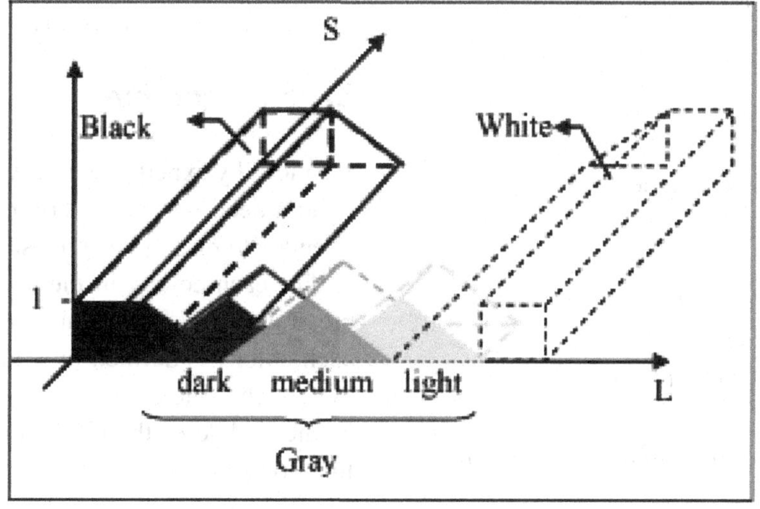

Let F_t and $\tilde{F}_{t,q}$ be the following functions, representing the membership degree of I to the classes t and (t,q):

$$\bullet \forall t \in \mathcal{T}, F_t(I) = \frac{\sum_{p \in \mathcal{P}} f_t(h_p)}{|\mathcal{P}|}$$

$$\bullet \forall (t,q) \in \mathcal{T} \times \mathcal{Q}, \tilde{F}_{t,q}(I) = \frac{\sum_{p \in \mathcal{P}} \tilde{f}_q(l_p, s_p) \times g_t(h_p)}{|\mathcal{P}|}$$

With $g_t(h_p) = \begin{cases} 0 & if\ f_t(h_p) = 0 \\ 1 & else \end{cases}$

The profile associated to the image is denoted by $[F_t(I), \tilde{F}_{t,q}(I)]$ and contains 96 elements: $|\mathcal{T}| + |\mathcal{T} \times \mathcal{Q}| + |$ {black, white, gray} $| + |$ {gray} $\times$ {dark, medium, light} $|= 9 + 81 + 3 + 3$ (Figure 10).

Because of the representation of colors in two steps (hues on the one hand, and qualifiers on the other hand), the classes follow a hierarchy: classes $C_t with t \in \mathcal{T} \cup \{black, white, gray\}$ can be considered as fathers and the classes $\tilde{C}_{c,q}$ $with$ $(c,q) \in \mathcal{T} \cup \{gray\} \times \mathcal{Q}$ as their sons.

Let us denote:

$$\bullet F^*(I) = \max_{t \in \mathcal{T}}(F_t(I))$$

$$\bullet \tilde{F}_t^*(I) = \max_{q \in \mathcal{Q}}(\tilde{F}_{t,q}(I))\ \forall t \in \mathcal{T},$$
$$and\ for\ t = gray,\ q \in \{dark, medium, light\}$$

An image I will be assigned to:

- the classes C_t if $F_t(I) \geq F^*(I) - \lambda$, $\forall t \in \mathcal{T} \cup \{black, white, gray\}$ with λ a tolerance threshold.
- the classes $\tilde{C}_{t,q}$ if $F_t(I) \geq F^*(I) - \lambda$ and ,

$$\forall (t,q) \in \mathcal{T} \times \mathcal{Q} \cup \{gray\} \times \{dark, medium, light\}$$

Thus, an image can be assigned to several classes, and it can be assigned to a subclass only if it is also assigned to its father class. For example, an image cannot be assigned to "red, bright" class ($\tilde{C}_{red,bright}$) if it is not assigned to the "red" one (C_{red}).

The standard colorimetric profile of each image is build using the standard values of the membership functions as described above. These profiles may not be accepted by all users since the perception is a subjective issue. To resolve this problem, the user is asked to build his profile, thus when retrieving images, they will be brought regarding his perception.

USER PROFILE FOR COLOR PERCEPTION

The aim is to build for each user his own membership functions of colors and qualifiers (Figure 4 and Figure 8). Starting from the initial functions defined in the previous section, we will modify the function parameters for each user.

The user is invited to build his profile by identifying himself as an expert or as a simple user. An expert user will follow a many-steps algorithm; on the other hand the task for a simple user is much more simplified. The experts profiles are built using a questionnaire while non-experts' by comparison of subjects (El-Zakhem, 2008).

Expert Algorithm

We mean by expert, the user who is interested to build a detailed colorimetric profile and who is intended to respond to a questionnaire R.

For each color i in the set T, we denote its previous by $(i-1)$ and its successive by $(i+1)$; also each color i is defined by a value m_i in the set $\mathcal{M}$. Each value in $\mathcal{M}$ corresponds to a color in T (the middle of the kernel of the membership function (Figure 4)).

Figure 10. Profile representing an image.

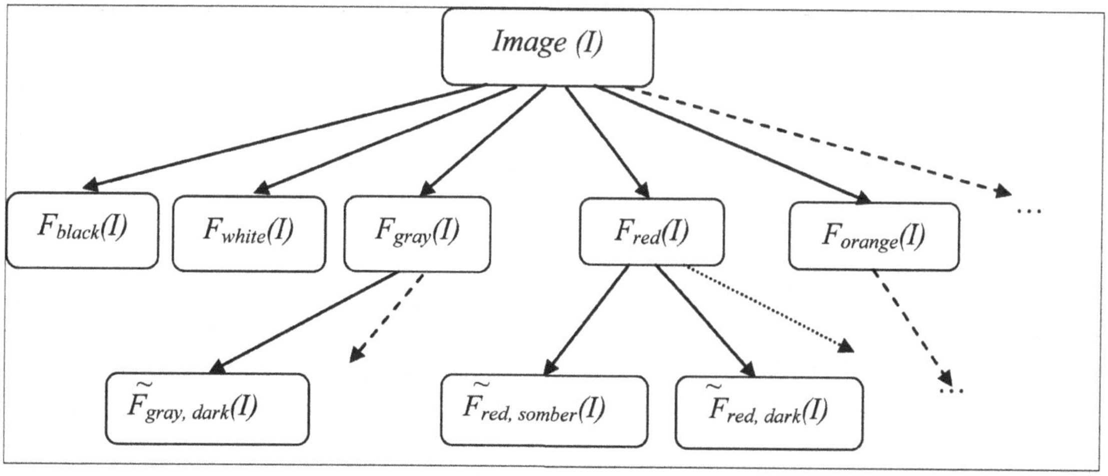

Image (I)

$F_{black}(I)$ $F_{white}(I)$ $F_{gray}(I)$ $F_{red}(I)$ $F_{orange}(I)$ …

$\tilde{F}_{gray,\ dark}(I)$ $\tilde{F}_{red,\ somber}(I)$ $\tilde{F}_{red,\ dark}(I)$ …

In order to define the user's perception of colors we have to define the hue, saturation and lightness according to the user. For the hue, we present to the user sample pictures as form of question. The answer given is in form of interval-value where the user considered that the hue in question meets well his perception. When asked about qualifiers the user is asked to use linguistic terms as in the set $\mathcal{Q}$.

The perception of color is defined on three dimensions: hue, saturation and luminance. Each of these dimensions is decomposed into a set of granules. For the hue, the set of granules is the set $\mathcal{T}$. For the luminance the set is *{gloomy, heavy, pallid}* and for the saturation the set is *{Dull, moderate, saturated}*.

Each question will be relevant to one aspect of the perception in question. For example while dealing with color perception we can say that the aspects are the saturation, hue and luminosity.

Hue Setting

- We fix the luminance and the saturation and we show for each color *"i"*, a sample picture of the deviations of colors *{i-1, i, i+1}*. For example in Figure 11, let yellow be the color *"i"*, we fix luminance to 128 and full saturation to 255 and the hue is varying from m_{i-1} until m_{i+1} where m_{i-1} corresponds to the *{orange}* color and m_{i+1} corresponds to the *{green}* color.
- The user clicks on two points a_i and b_i (or one point $a_i = b_i$) where he considers that it is the pure yellow, so these points are the kernel of the fuzzy membership function. ($\alpha_i < a_i$ and $\beta_i > b_i$)
- Updating the set of maximums $\mathcal{M}$ and set $m_i = avg(a_i, b_i)$
- To avoid having a colorless zone we set β_{i-1} of the previous color is equal to $a_{i-b} - b_{i-1}$ and $\alpha_{i+1} = a_{i+1} - b_i$.

Luminance Setting

- The user describes the zones in a sample picture by using linguistic terms like gloomy, heavy and pallid. These terms are the attributes for the luminance dimension. Thus we get five zones: black, gloomy, heavy, pallid and white as shown in Figure 12.
- Also for simplification of the algorithm, the user may only choose the heavily colored zone while the gloomy zone is set to

Figure 11. Hue of yellow color from orange to green

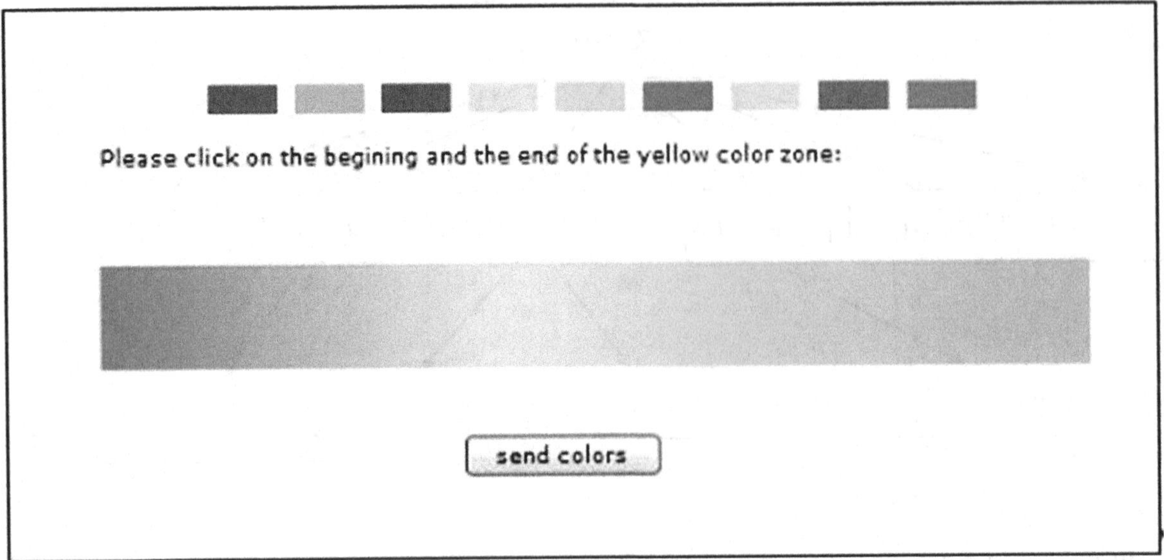

Figure 12. Five zones

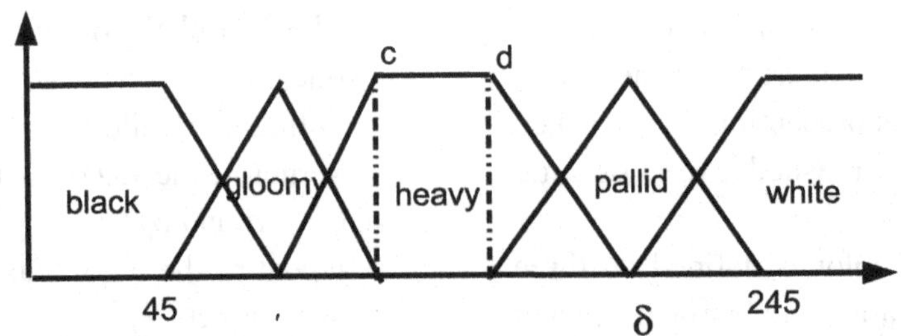

c - 45 and the pallid zone is set to *245-d*, (Figure 13).

- The setting of the luminosity is repeated with each hue or only with selected hues chosen by the user.

Saturation Setting

The maximum saturation of any color in HLS space is having a value of 255. The user has to use also linguistic terms as in the setting of luminance; these terms are dull, moderate and saturated. Figure 14 describes the three zones of saturation.

"Simple User" Algorithm

We call a *simple user* a person who is not intending to follow a complex algorithm but instead he would like to adopt an already stored profile. The user will choose to model his perception by imitating an already configured profile. In order to achieve this task; the user would like to compare different existing profiles. This can be done by showing the user the result of retrieving images according to some existing profiles. Each existing profile would bring up a different set of images from the other.

Figure 13. Three zones

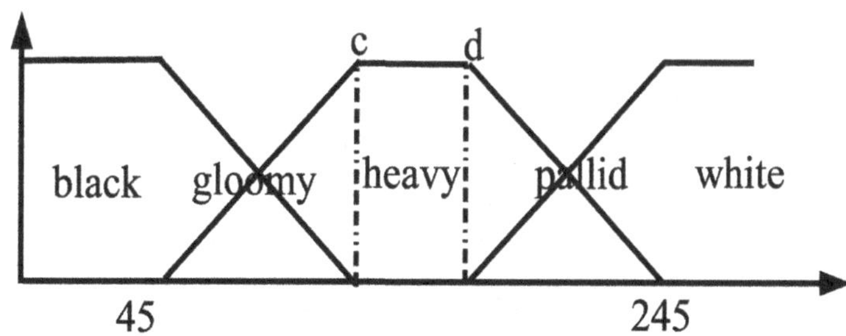

Figure 14. Saturation dimension

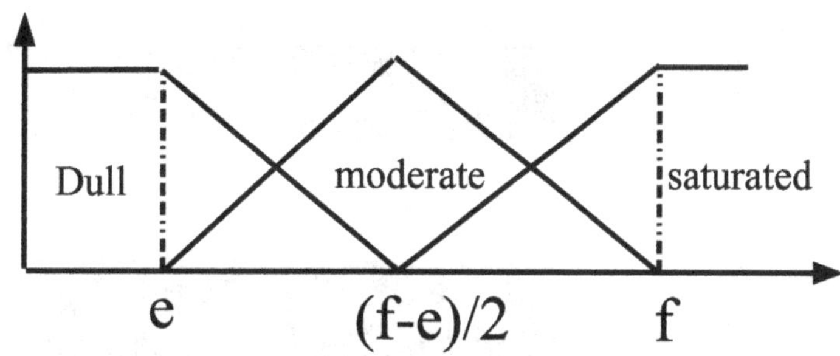

These sets must be displayed on the same screenshot. The effect of luminance, brightness, contrast, quality of light, topic of experience, physical and mental and emotional state of the user, quality of the display, are shown processed and evaluated at the same moment, and their effect on the perception is being ignored and mutually neglected. In each set, the images are selected regarding to their dominant color. Figure 15 shows an example of 4 sets of images according to 4 profiles of experts regarding to the dominant color cyan.

Since perception is very subjective we do not expect that the user perception matches completely with one of the experts' profiles. Thus the user will give a satisfaction degree for each set of images which are close to his perception. These satisfaction degrees are linguistic terms which are easy to use but less precise. We can limit to the use of 5 linguistic terms distributed on the interval from 0 to 1.

For example: very weak (0 to 20%), weak (20 to 40%), average (40 to 60%), good (60 to 80%), very good (80 to 100%). Keeping in mind that at the low level, the base of each set chosen is a fuzzy membership function of the color being modeled. So, in order to build a new fuzzy function reflecting the perception of the user, the user will choose 2 sets of images which considers close to his perception and we have to aggregate the 2 fuzzy functions and to take into consideration the satisfaction degrees.

We suppose that these two satisfaction degrees will be at least equal to "average"" (≥50) (Unbalanced linguistic term set (Herrera, 2007)).

The problem is reduced to an aggregation problem of two fuzzy functions taking into account the weight given for each function. Figure 16 refers to 2 fuzzy functions with respective weights 90% and 70%.

In this example, we can notice that the user is more satisfied with the expert 2. The fuzzy

Figure 15. Different sets of cyan images according to 4 experts

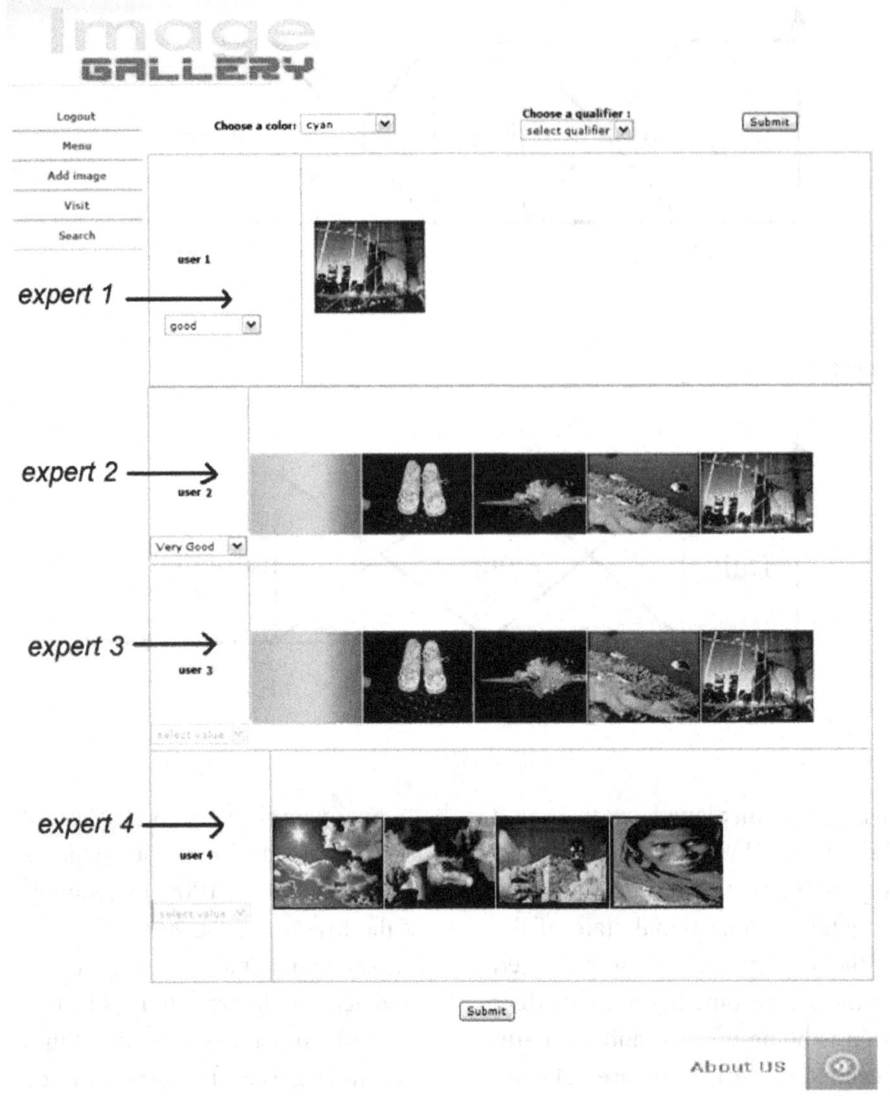

function representing the perception of expert 2 is shifted to the right comparing it with the fuzzy function representing the perception of the expert 1.

We suppose that the satisfaction increasing is due to the moving on the right of the expert 1 fuzzy subset. To build a representative fuzzy subset for the user perception we have to emphasize this moving. The fuzzy subset for the user perception should be on the right of the expert 2 fuzzy subset as shown Figure 16.

This approach can be summarized as follows:

1. The user choose a color
2. Showing to the user the result of retrieving images, according to some existing profiles.
3. The user choose the 2 best sets of images which are close to his perception

Figure 16. Two fuzzy functions and the expected result of their aggregation

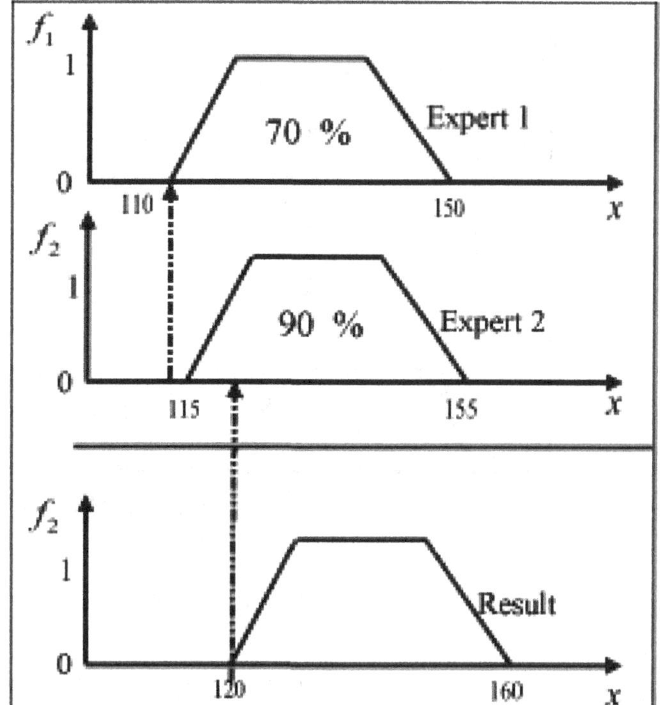

4. The user gives a satisfaction degree for each set of images
5. Aggregation of the two fuzzy subsets associated to these sets

We recall that *T* is the set of the 9 fundamental colors Of Newton:

T={red, orange, yellow, green, cyan, blue, purple, magenta, pink}

For each user u_k the membership function of each hue $t_j \in T$ is defined by: $f_{t_j}^{u_k}(h)\ \forall\ t_j \in T$

Definition 1

Let $e_i \in \mathcal{E}$ be an expert, and the set of all experts. Let $\mathcal{SI}_{e_i}(t_j)$ be the set of all images with a dominant color t_j *according to the perception of the expert* e_i

The user chooses the 2 best sets of images and gives a satisfaction degree for each set: $w_{1,j}^k$ and $w_{2,j}^k$ with $w_{1,j}^k \geq w_{2,j}^k$

The fuzzy subset defined by the expert e_1 *for the hue* t_j *is given by the function* $f_{t_j}^{e_1}$ denoted by the quadruplet $(a_{1,j}, b_{1,j}, \alpha_{1,j}, \beta_{1,j})$, and the fuzzy subset defined by the expert e_2 *for the hue* t_j *is given by the function* $f_{t_j}^{e_2}$ denoted by the quadruplet $(a_{2,j}, b_{2,j}, \alpha_{2,j}, \beta_{2,j})$

Definition 2

Let D_L *be the difference between the positions of the middles of segments* $[(a_{1,j} - \alpha_{1,j},0),(a_{1,j}, 1)]$ *and* $[(a_{2,j} - \alpha_{2,j},0),(a_{2,j}, 1)]$ *as shown inFigure18.*

$$D_L = a_{1,j} - a_{2,j} - \frac{\alpha_{1,j} + \alpha_{2,j}}{2} \quad (7)$$

Figure 17. Two fuzzy functions according to 2 experts

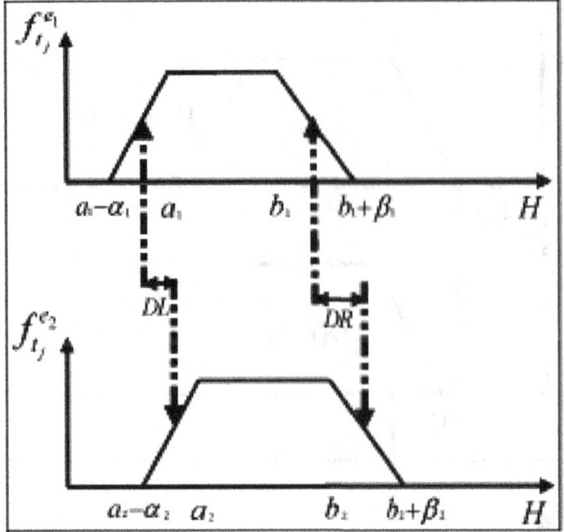

Let D_R be the difference between the positions of the middles of segment:

$[(b_{1,j}, 1), (b_{1,j} + \beta_{1,j}, 0)]$ *and* $[(b_{2,j}, 1), (b_{2,j} + \beta_{2,j}, 0)]$

$$D_R = b_{1,j} - b_{2,j} + \frac{\beta_{1,j} - \beta_{2,j}}{2} \quad (8)$$

To build the fuzzy subset representing the user perception, we have to emphasize the moving (left and right) between $f_{t_j}^{e_1}$ and $f_{t_j}^{e_2}$.

This movement will also depend on the missing satisfaction $(100 - w_{1,j}^k)$

Definition 3

Let δl_j^* and δr_j^* the left and right translation attributes

$$\Rightarrow \begin{cases} \delta l_j^* = D_L \times \dfrac{100 - w_{1,j}^k}{w_{1,j}^k - w_{2,j}^k} \\ \delta r_j^* = D_R \times \dfrac{100 - w_{1,j}^k}{w_{1,j}^k - w_{2,j}^k} \end{cases} \quad (9)$$

Definition 4

Let M_L and M_R two translation modifiers (Bouchon-Meunier, 2001):

$$\bullet M_L(f_{t_j}(x)) = f_{m_L(t_j)}(x) = Max(0, Min(1, \phi_L(x))) \quad (10)$$

$$With: \phi_L(x) = \begin{cases} \dfrac{x - a - \delta l_j + \alpha}{\alpha} & If \quad x \leq a + \delta l_j \\ \dfrac{-x + b + \delta l_j + \beta}{\beta} & If \quad x > a + \delta l_j \end{cases}$$

and ϕ_L a nondecreasing function for $x \leq a + \delta l_j$, *and non increasing function for* $x > a + \delta l_j$

$$\bullet M_R(f_{t_j}(x)) = f_{m_R(t_j)}(x) = Max(0, Min(1, \phi_R(x))) \quad (11)$$

With

$$\phi_R(x) = \begin{cases} \dfrac{x - a - \delta r_j + \alpha}{\alpha} & If \quad x \leq a + \delta r_j \\ \dfrac{-x + b + \delta r_j + \beta}{\beta} & If \quad x > a + \delta r_j \end{cases}$$

Figure 18. Different cases of fuzzy subsets comparison

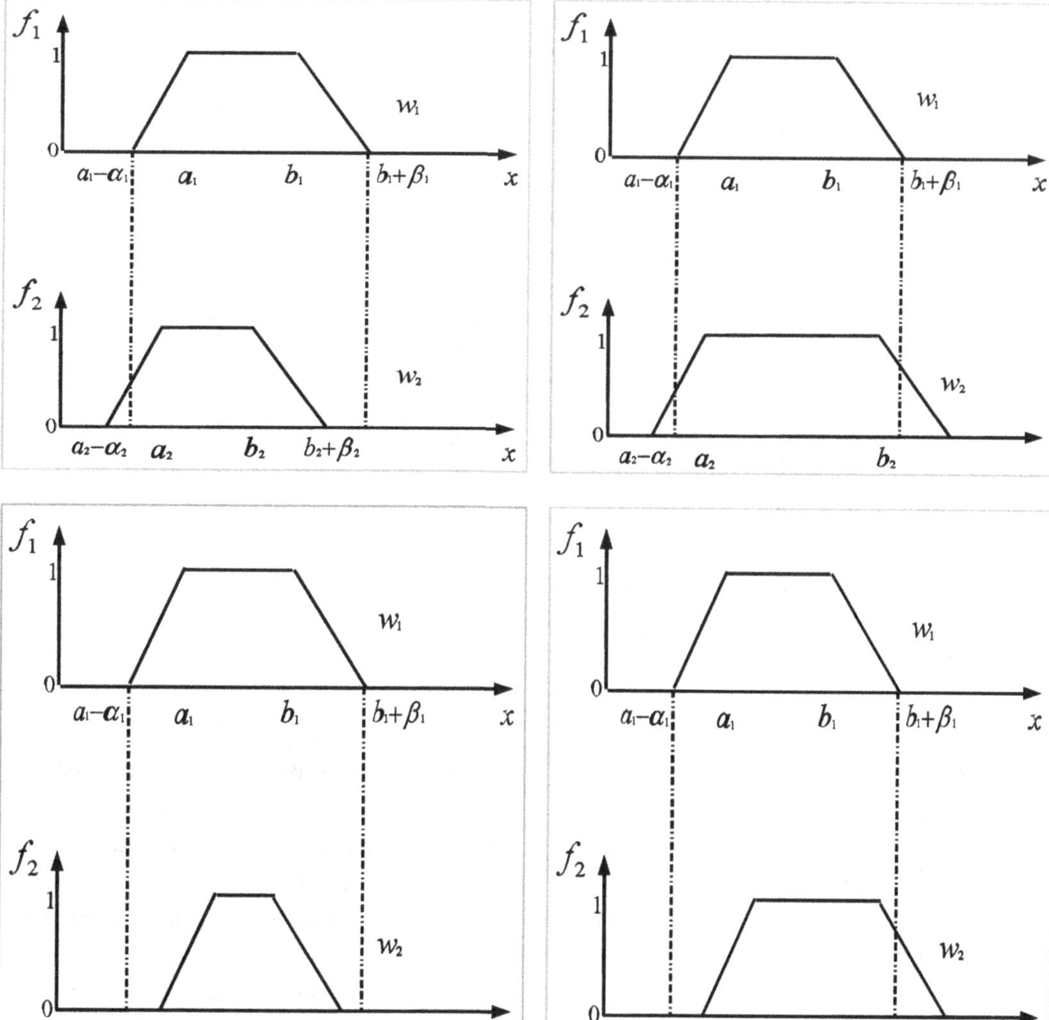

To determine the function representing the perception of the user u_k of the color t_j, we apply the two modifiers to the function $f_{t_j}^{e_1}$:

$f_{m_L(t_j)}^{e_1}(h) = M_L(f_{t_j}^{e_1}(h))$, shown in Figure 19 in red line.

$f_{m_R(t_j)}^{e_1}(h) = M_R(f_{t_j}^{e_1}(h))$, shown in Figure 19 in blue line.

The result is obtained by aggregating these two subsets:

$$f_{t_j}^{u_k}(h) = f_{m_L(t_j)}^{e_1}(h)\ \mathcal{OP}\ f_{m_R(t_j)}^{e_1}(h)$$

The operator $\mathcal{OP}$ is an intersection or union operator; its value depends on the translation attributes δl_j and δr_j as follows:

Figure 19. Result of aggregation after applying left and right translation modificators

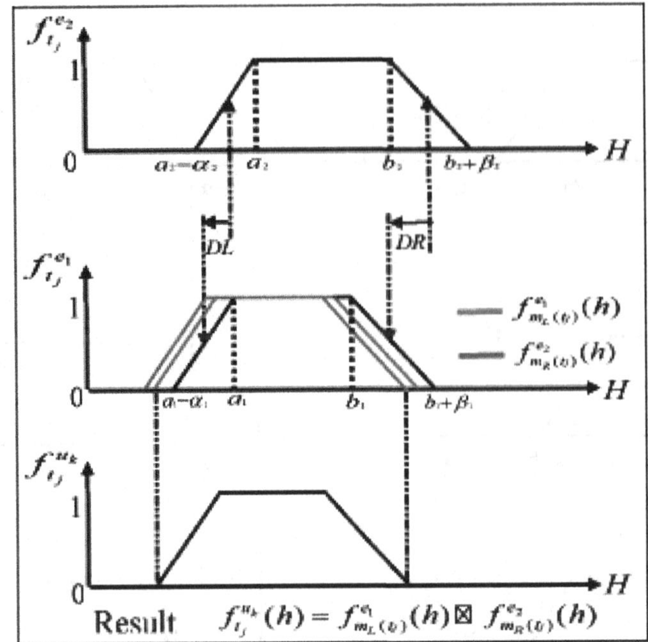

$$\mathcal{OP} \Rightarrow \begin{cases} if \delta l \times \delta r \geq 0 \\ \quad if \delta l > \delta r \\ \quad \mathcal{OP} = \cap \\ \quad\quad else \\ \quad \mathcal{OP} = \cup \\ \quad\quad else \\ \quad if \delta l > 0 \\ \quad \mathcal{OP} = \cap \\ \quad\quad else \\ \quad \mathcal{OP} = \cup \end{cases} \qquad (12)$$

In the case of Figure 19 the operator $\mathcal{OP}$ in an intersection operator as represented in the third fuzzy function of Figure 19.

Global Procedure for the User Perception Modeling

The fuzzy subsets representing different colors are adjacent, and then any change of a color representation will have an influence on the adjacent colors.

If we want to have a coherent system, the modifications must respect some constraints:

- The standard profile is assigned to the user.
- To avoid empty areas, a modification on a hue representation causes a modification on the adjacent hue representation
- If a hue representation is modified, only the emphasis of this modification will be allowed.

The global approach for building the profile can be defined as follows.

1. Initialization:

$\bullet f_{t_j}^{u_k} = f_{t_j}^{standard}(h), \quad \forall t_j \in \mathcal{T}$

$\bullet \delta l_j = \delta r_j = 0, \quad \forall t_j \in \mathcal{T}$

2. Choosing a hue $t_j \,/\, t_j \in \mathcal{T}$
3. $\mathcal{T} = \mathcal{T} - t_j$

4. Showing the $\mathcal{SI}_{e_i}(t_j)$. with $\mathcal{SI}_{e_i}(t_j)$ the set of images with a dominant color t_j according to the expert e_i perception
5. The user choose the 2 best sets of images which are close to his perception, and give a satisfaction degree for each one: $w_{i,j}^{k}$
6. Calculating the δ:

$$\begin{cases} \delta l_j = Max(\delta l_j^*, \quad a_{j-1} - b_{j-1}) \\ \delta r_j = Min(\delta r_j^*, \quad b_{j+1} - a_{j+1}) \end{cases} \text{ and } \delta l_j + a_j \leq \delta r_j + b_j$$

$$\Rightarrow \begin{cases} \delta l_j = Min(\delta r_j^* + b_j - a_j, \quad Max(\delta l_j^*, \quad a_{j-1} - b_{j-1})) \\ \delta r_j = Max(\delta l_j^* + a_j - b_j, \quad Min(\delta r_j^*, \quad b_{j+1} - a_{j+1})) \end{cases}$$

7. Calculating the $f_{t_j}^{u_k}(h) = f_{m_L(t_j)}^{e_1}(h) \quad \mathcal{OP} \quad f_{m_R(t_j)}^{e_1}(h)$
8. Modification of $f_{t_{j-1}}^{u_k}$ and of $f_{t_{j+1}}^{u_k}$:

$$\begin{cases} \delta l_{j-1} = 0 \\ \delta r_{j-1} = \delta l_j \end{cases}$$

$$\begin{cases} \delta l_{j+1} = \delta r_j \\ \delta r_{j+1} = 0 \end{cases}$$

$$\Rightarrow \begin{cases} f_{t_{j-1}}^{u_k}(h) = f_{m_L(t_{j-1})}^{u_k}(h) \quad \mathcal{OP} \quad f_{m_R(t_{j-1})}^{u_k}(h) \\ f_{t_{j+1}}^{u_k}(h) = f_{m_L(t_{j+1})}^{u_k}(h) \quad \mathcal{OP} \quad f_{m_R(t_{j+1})}^{u_k}(h) \end{cases}$$

9. Feedback
   - Showing the $\mathcal{SI}_0(t_j)$, with $\mathcal{SI}_0(t_j)$ the set of images with a dominant color t_j according to the perception of the user u_k ($f_{t_j}^{u_k}(h)$).
   - determining the satisfaction degree of the user for this set of images: $w_{0,j}^{u_k}$
     - if $w_{0,j}^{u_k} > w_{1,j}^{u_k}$ then:
     - back to step 6 with $\begin{cases} f_{t_j}^{e_2} = f_{t_j}^{e_1} \quad et \quad w_{2,j}^{u_k} = w_{1,j}^{u_k} \\ f_{t_j}^{e_1} = f_{t_j}^{u_k} \quad et \quad w_{1,j}^{u_k} = w_{0,j}^{u_k} \end{cases}$
     - if $w_{0,j}^{u_k} < w_{1,j}^{u_k}$ then:
     - back to step 7 with $f_{t_j}^{e_1} = f_{t_j}^{u_k}$ and

$$\begin{cases} \delta l_j = -\delta l_j \times \dfrac{100 - w_{0,j}^{u_k}}{(100 - w_{0,j}^{u_k}) + (100 - w_{1,j}^{u_k})} \\ \delta r_j = -\delta r_j \times \dfrac{100 - w_{0,j}^{u_k}}{(100 - w_{0,j}^{u_k}) + (100 - w_{1,j}^{u_k})} \end{cases}$$

10. back to step 1

RETRIEVING IMAGES

Once the user has set his values for the hues and the qualifiers, he would browse the database and search for images. As explained before, the images are processed using the standard values, and the user has built his profile representing his perception. Our approach avoids the reprocessing of images by applying a transformation procedure on the standard colorimetric profile of the images according to user's perception.

In this procedure, we use the notions of comparability and compatibility of fuzzy subsets.

Comparability

Two fuzzy subsets are called comparable if they are close enough to each others. If the subsets are totally different so we consider that the subsets are not comparable. The degree of comparability between 2 subsets will range from 0 (too far or independent) to 1 (too close). Using the notion of comparability with colors we are interested in comparable colors. Thus, a certain color is said comparable to its adjacent colors (Figure 20).

Figure 20. Example of non-comparable and comparable subsets

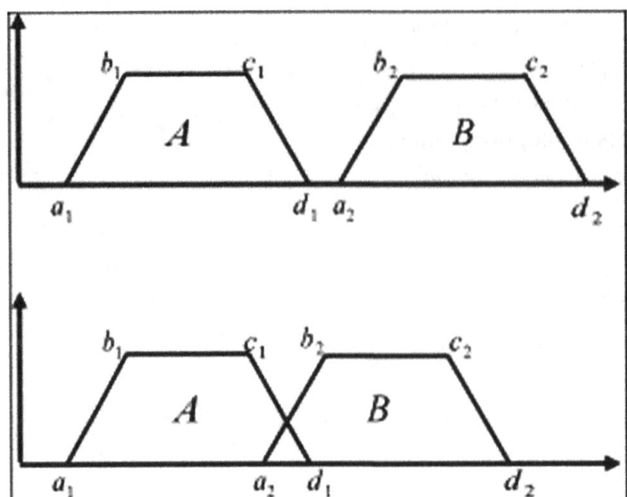

The fuzzy membership function is defined by a trapezoid schema and by the four points *(a, b, c, d)*. The degree of comparability of the subset *B* to set the subset *A* is shown in Equation (13).

All the subsets which are close to the subset *A* will form Γ(*A*)

So we denote:

$$B \in \Gamma(A) \quad \text{if} \quad \gamma(A,B) \geq 0$$

Considering a new color $t_{i_{new}}$ and an initial color t_i, we can write:

$$t_i \in \Gamma(t_{i_{new}}) \quad \text{iff} \quad \gamma(t_{i_{new}}, t_i) > 0$$

Compatibility

A certain image is characterized as blue if one of its dominant colors is blue, in other words, the image is blue if its membership degree in the blue color is high enough or simply it passed over a fixed threshold.

The same image would not characterized as blue according to another user, or, if the settings of blue color (the values of *a, b, c, d*) have been changed. Let's suppose that originally an image *I* has a degree *d* of membership in the color *c*, this degree *d* will vary if the setting of the color *c* will change. If we want to get the new degree d_{new}, the only way that gives the exact result is to reprocess the image *I* pixel by pixel.

Our approach will avoid this long process and it simulates the variation of the initial settings of colors by some arithmetic calculations.

Exhibit 1.

$$\gamma(A_1, A_2) = Max\left[\frac{f_{A_1}(a_2) + f_{A_1}(b_2) + f_{A_2}(c_1) + f_{A_2}(d_1)}{4} ; \frac{f_{A_1}(c_2) + f_{A_1}(d_2) + f_{A_2}(a_1) + f_{A_2}(b_1)}{4}\right] \quad (13)$$

Figure 21. Notion of compatibility

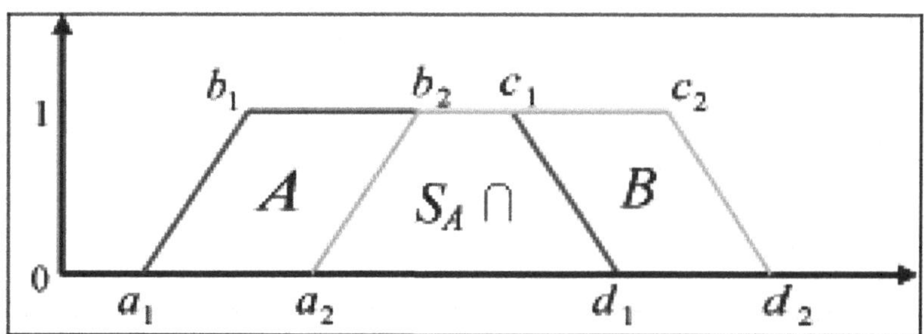

The problem is similar to the problem of system variation. For an image *I*, we will recalculate its colorimetric profile into a new n-dimensional system. The new system is defined according to each user's perception of colors.

Once we set the comparability degree of each new subset, only subsets with a degree of comparability greater than a fixed threshold are selected; therefore we will be able to define a compatibility degree only if the comparability degree is greater than the threshold; this is because when dealing with color in HLS space a deviation is accepted until some limit beyond this limit the new color will be more adherent to the next color (Couwenbergh, 2003; Boust, 2003). In other words, its membership in the next color will be greater than the membership in the initial old color. We should always keep in mind that colors are adjacent and there is no empty partition corresponding to 'no color' in the hue diagram.

We denote the comparability degree

$$\Phi(B, A) = \frac{S_A \cap S_B}{S_A} \tag{14}$$

Where S_A is the surface of the initial trapeze *A* and S_B is the surface of new trapeze *B* being compared to S_A (Figure 21).

Since we are dealing with a fuzzy membership function so the coordinate of the points *b* and *c* is 1 and the coordinate of *a* and *d* is 0

$$S_A = \frac{b_1 - a_1}{2} + c_1 - b_1 + \frac{d_1 - c_1}{2}$$

$$S_B = \frac{b_2 - a_2}{2} + c_2 - b_2 + \frac{d_2 - c_2}{2}$$

It is obvious that $\phi(B,A) \neq \phi(A,B)$

Hue Compatibility

Let's consider an initial color t_i represented by a fuzzy membership function *f* and by the points a_1, b_1, c_1, d_1, the new color $t_{i_{new}}$ represented by a fuzzy membership function f_{new} and by the points a_2, b_2, c_2, d_2.

We have six possible models of compatibility between t_i and $t_{i_{new}}$. 3 of them when $t_{i_{new}}$ is on the right of t_i as shown in Figure 23, and 3 when $t_{i_{new}}$ is on the left of t_i as shown in Figure 24. The intersection of the segments $[a_1, b_1]$ and $[c_2, d_2]$ is the point *P* with coordinate x_p and y_p.

$$\Phi(B, A) = \begin{cases} \dfrac{(x_p - a_2) \times y_p}{S_1} & if \quad b_1 \wedge c_1 < b_2 \\ \dfrac{(x_p - a_1) \times y_p}{S_1} & if \quad b_2 \wedge c_2 < b_1 \\ \dfrac{b_2 - a_2}{2} + c_1 - b_2 + \dfrac{d_1 - c_1}{2} & if \quad (b_1 < b_2) \wedge (b_2 < c_1 < c_2) \\ \dfrac{b_1 - a_1}{2} + c_2 - b_1 + \dfrac{d_2 - c_2}{2} & if \quad (b_2 < b_1) \wedge (b_1 < c_2 < c_1) \\ \dfrac{b_2 - a_2}{2} + c_2 - b_2 + \dfrac{d_2 - c_2}{2} & if \quad b_1 < b_2 < c_2 < c_1 \\ \dfrac{b_1 - a_1}{2} + c_1 - b_1 + \dfrac{d_1 - c_1}{2} & if \quad b_2 < b_1 < c_1 < c_2 \end{cases} \tag{15}$$

Figure 22. The function of a modified color along with the standard

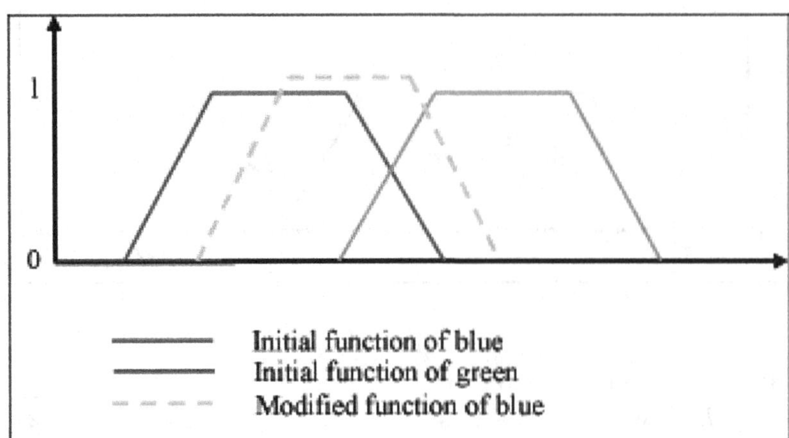

Figure 23. New subset on the right of the initial

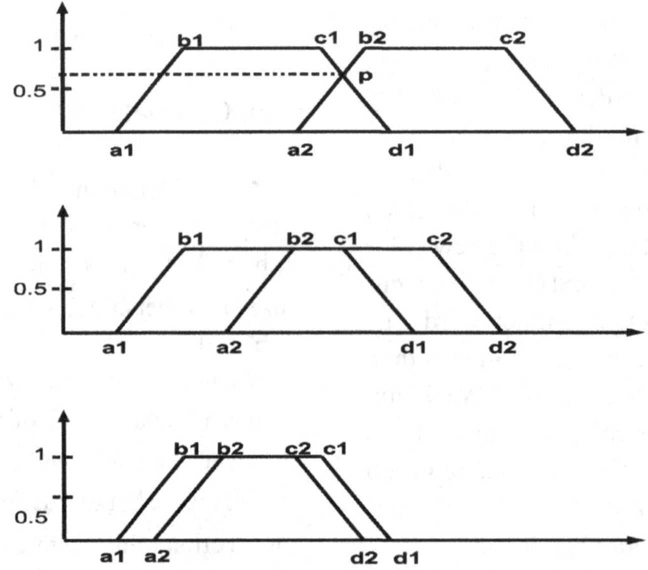

The coordinate of *p* are:

$$x_p = \frac{d_i b_j - a_j c_i}{b_j - a_i + d_i - c_i}$$

$$y_p = \frac{d_i - a_j}{b_j - a_i + d_i - c_i}$$

According to the above equations, the new inserted color will affect more then or one fuzzy function, and less then or 3 fuzzy functions. Thus the new profile of the image will be recalculated and the adjacent values of the color in question will vary too. For example in Figure 22, the new blue is between the old blue and old green, the membership of the image to the new color blue will be:

Figure 24. New subset on the left of the initial

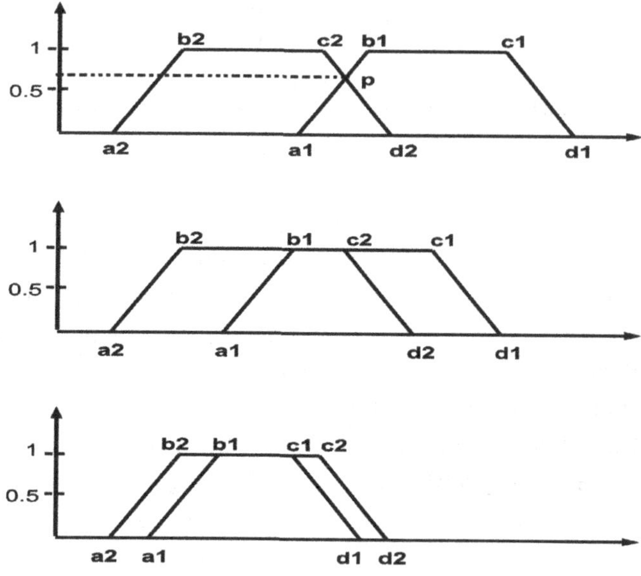

$$F_{B_{new}}(I) = \Phi(B_{new}, B_s) \times F_{B_s}(I) + \Phi(B_{new}, G_s) \times F_{G_s}(I) \quad (16)$$

B_S is the standard function of blue, G_S is the standard function of Green, B_{new} is the new function of blue. The general function is given as follows:

$$F_{t_{i_{new}}}(I) = \sum_{t_i \in \Gamma(t_{i_{new}})} \Phi(t_{i_{new}}, t_i) \times F_{t_i}(I) \quad (17)$$

Assuming that the qualifiers which depend on the dimensions L and S remain the same, and then we still have the same values for the 9 qualifiers and only the functions on the dimension H are modified, so we can always write:

$$\forall (t_i, q_j) \in T \times Q, \quad \tilde{F}_{t_{i_{new}}, q_j} = \sum_{\forall (t_i) \in \Gamma(t_{i_{new}})} \Phi(t_{i_{new}}, t_i) \times \tilde{F}_{t_i q_j}(I) \quad (18)$$

Qualifier Comparability

The same reasoning done above with the dimension hue is intended to be done with the other two dimensions, the saturation and lightness. Each hue is being described by the qualifiers so for each hue $t_{i_{new}}$ we calculate $\tilde{F}_{t_{i_{new}}, q_{j_{new}}}$

Assuming that the qualifiers depending on the dimension saturation will be modified then we have to calculate the new hue qualified according to saturation in function of the old hue qualified according to saturation, so the equation is:

$$\tilde{F}_{t_{i_{new}}, q_{j_{n1}}} = \sum_{\forall (q_j) \in \Gamma_s(q_{j_{n1}})} \Phi(q_{j_{n1}}, q_j) \times \tilde{F}_{t_{i_{new}} q_j}(I) \quad (19)$$

with $q_{j_{n1}}$ the modified qualifier on the dimension S

Taking into consideration the above equation, we will calculate the new hue and the new saturation together in function of the new lightness we can write:

$$\tilde{F}_{t_{new}, q_{j_{n2}}} = \sum_{\forall (q_{j_{n1}}) \in \Gamma_L(q_{j_{n2}})} \Phi(q_{j_{n2}}, q_{j_{n1}}) \times \tilde{F}_{t_{new} q_{j_{n1}}}(I) \quad (20)$$

with $q_{j_{n2}}$ the modified qualifier on the dimension L

Γ_L compatibility for lightness (L)

Γ_S compatibility for saturation (S)

We can demonstrate that the order of calculation of the new saturation and the calculation of the new lightness has no effect (El Zakhem, 2007). The same results are reached by any order of calculation.

STATISTICAL RESULTS

For this kind of research, a comparison with the other similar works is usually welcome. But this is a hard task for several reasons. First, most of the research includes an image query which we don't, as we focus on a simple color query. Secondly, the image databases are usually not the same. Indeed, some authors use texture databases (Binagui, 1994; Frigui, 2001) while some others use Comstock database (Vertan, 2000), or Common Color Dataset (Han, 2002), et cetera. However, authors like Omhover et al (cf. Omhover(2004)) propose their software online (http://strict.lip6.fr}) which is very convenient for a comparison. But they use an image query and they compare not only colors but also shapes in the image, which can't be compared to our method. That is why we only propose a performance study of our software.

As Salton and McGill proposed in Salton(1983) the performance of a software can be evaluated in two steps:

1. Response time: it represents the time elapsed between the user query and the software response. For all the works using an image query, this information is important. However in our work the image processing is done before the image retrieval.
2. Recall and precision: Images are considered either relevant or not relevant, and retrieved or not retrieved according to a request (Table 1).

Recall measures the ability of the software to retrieve all relevant images:

Table 1. Performance of a software

	Relevant	Not Relevant
Retrieved	RR correctly retrieved	R-NR falsely retrieved
Not Retrieved	NR-R missed	NR-NR correctly rejected

Table 2. The validation results

	Relevant	Not Relevant
Retrieved	897 correctly retrieved	103 falsely retrieved
Not Retrieved	164 missed	/ correctly rejected

$$\text{Recall} = \frac{\text{relevant retrieved}}{\text{all relevant}} = \frac{\text{RR}}{\text{RR} + \text{NRR}} \quad (21)$$

And precision measures the ability to retrieve only relevant images:

$$\text{Precision} = \frac{\text{relevant retrieved}}{\text{all retrieved}} = \frac{\text{RR}}{\text{RR} + \text{RNR}} \quad (22)$$

First of all, the choice of image database is important to validate the software. We have used a colored image database containing a description of the images by keywords, like "the color": the ImageBank (http://creative.gettyimages.com/imagebank/). The two rates presented were calculated (according to ImageBank).

On a total of 1000 images we have obtained the following results:

- 85% for the first rate (recall)
- 89 \% for the second (precision) (cf. table 1 and table 2)

The reason why 103 images are not well-classified and 164 images are not selected is due to the subjectivity of the classification of Image-Bank (IB) experts.

Indeed, IB experts usually associate at most two color-keywords. Moreover, the naming of the colors is very subjective:

For example, an expert may call a *dark pink* what another expert may call a *magenta*. This perception also depends a lot on the neighboring colors in the image: e.g. a *yellow* on a black background may not be perceived the same way than a *yellow* on a white background.

For example, for the color green all the images relevant according to ImageBank are presented in Figure 25. The Figure 26 presents the green images selected by our software. The image (20) were not retrieved by our software (missed) and

Figure 25. Green images according to ImageBank

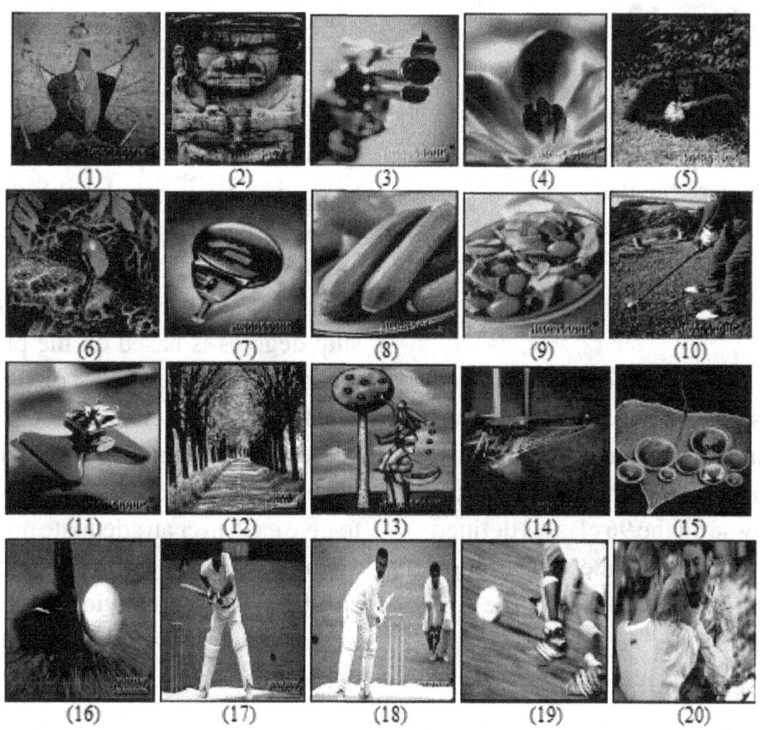

Figure 26. Green images retrieved by our software

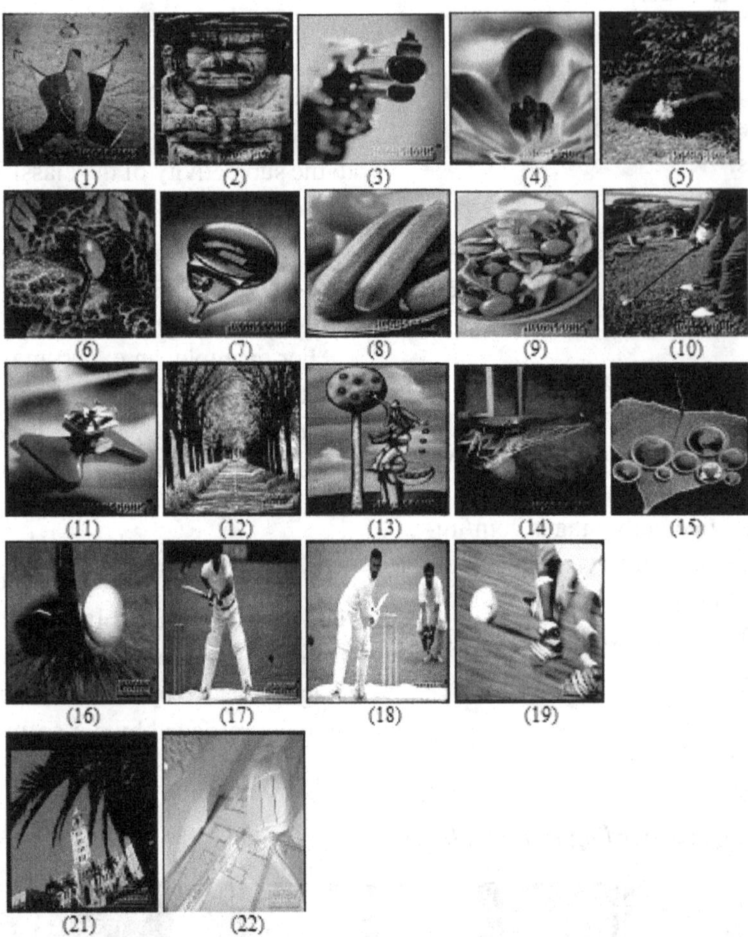

the images (21) and (22) were falsely retrieved (according to the IB classification).

CONCLUSION

In this work we have developed an approach that permits to classify images according to their dominant color(s) and giving satisfactory results. For the image extraction from the database, it is not necessary to browse all the 96 classes defined in section 2. We can make a first selection through the fundamental colors and then look at the corresponding son classes to refine the query.

We also developed an algorithm that would compute the new membership degrees if we move from the initial set of colors and qualifiers to another set which fits better the user's perception of colors. The computation of the new membership degrees is based on the profile constructed in the initial phase and not on the original images.

Building a user profile based on the user's perception is the main target of this chapter. Since the perception of colors is very subjective, we try to give each user an adequate profile by following a simple method and using a user-friendly tiny software. Users are divided into groups; there are the experts who want to get a profile suiting 100 percent their perceptions and going into exhaustive details, some other users who would prefer not going so deep into details. This dynamic approach for user profile construction will increase the user's satisfaction and will not only affect the image retrieving domain but all themes that rely on subjectivity and perceptions. Our ongoing work will introduce a feedback process to improve the user profile construction.

REFERENCES

Aït Younes, A., Truck, I., & Akdag, H. (2007). Image retrieval using fuzzy representation of colors. *Soft Computing - A Fusion of Foundations. Methodologies and Applications, 11*(3), 287–298.

Albuz, E., Kocalar, E., & Khokhar, A. A. (2001). Scalable color image indexing and retrieval using vector wavelets. *IEEE Transactions on Knowledge and Data Engineering, 13*(5), 851–861. doi:10.1109/69.956109

Androutsos, D., Plataniotis, K. N., & Venetsanopoulos, A. N. (1999). A novel vector-based approach to color image retrieval using a vector angular-based distance measure. *Computer Vision and Image Understanding, 75*(1-2), 46–58. doi:10.1006/cviu.1999.0767

Barla, A., Odone, F., & Verri, A. (2003). Histogram intersection kernel for image classification. *Proceedings of the International Conference on Image Processing (ICIP03),* (pp. 513-516).

Berens, J., Finlayson, G. D., & Gu, G. (2000). Image indexing using compressed colour histogram. *IEE Proceedings. Vision Image and Signal Processing, 147*(4), 349–353. doi:10.1049/ip-vis:20000630

Bouchon-Meunier, B. (1995). *La Logique Floue et ses Applications*. Addison Wesley.

Bouchon-Meunier, B., & Marsala, C. (2001). Linguistic modifiers and measures of similarity or resemblances. *Proceedings of IFSA/NAFIPS 2001,* (pp. 2195-2199), Vancouver, Canada.

Bourghorbel, S., Boujemaa, N., & Vertan, C. (2002). Histogram-based color signatures for image indexing. *Proceedings of Information Processing and Management of Uncertainty in Knowledge-Based Systems,* IPMU 2002.

Boust, C., Chahine, H., Vièenot, F., Brettel, H., Ben Chouikha, M., & Alquié, G. (2003). Color correction judgments of digital images by experts and naive observers. *Proceedings of PICS, 2003*, 4–9.

Carron, T. (1995). *Segmentations d'images couleur dans la base Teinte-Luminance-Saturation: Approche numérique et symbolique*. Thèse de Doctorat, Université de Savoie.

Chen, Y., & Wang, J. Z. (2002). A region-based fuzzy feature matching approach to content-based image retrieval. *IEEE Transactions on Pattern Analysis and Machine Intelligence, 24*(9), 1252–1267. doi:10.1109/TPAMI.2002.1033216

Commission Internationale de l'Eclairage (CIE). (1986). *Colorimetry*, 2nd ed. Vienna, Austria: CIE Publication.

Couwenbergh, J. P. (2003). *Guide complet et pratique de la couleur*. Paris, France: Eyrolles.

Deng, Y., Manjunath, B. S., Kenney, C., Moore, M. S., & Shin, H. (2001). *An* efficient color representation for image retrieval. *IEEE Transactions on Image Processing, 10*(1), 140–147. doi:10.1109/83.892450

Diplaros, A., Gevers, T., & Patras, I. (2006). Combining color and shape information for illumination-viewpoint invariant object recognition. *IEEE Transactions on Image Processing, 15*(1), 1–11. doi:10.1109/TIP.2005.860320

El-Zakhem, I., Aït Younes, A., Truck, I., Greige, H., & Akdag, H. (2007). *Color image profile comparison and computing.* ICSOFT 2007 2nd International Conference on Software and Data Technologies, (pp. 228-231), Barcelona, Spain.

El-Zakhem, I., Aït Younes, A., Truck, I., Greige, H., & Akdag, H. (2008). *Mapping personal perception into user profiles for image retrieving.* 8th International FLINS Conference on Computational Intelligence in Decision and Control, (pp. 393-398). Madrid, Spain.

Foulloy, L. (1990). *Du contrôle symbolique des processus: Démarche, outils, exemples.* Ph.D. Thesis, Université Paris XI.

Hafner, J., Sawhney, H. S., Equitz, W., Flickner, M., & Niblack, W. (1995). Efficient color histogram indexing for quadratic form distance functions. *IEEE Transactions on Pattern Analysis and Machine Intelligence, 17*(7), 729–736. doi:10.1109/34.391417

Hammami, M., Chen, L., Zighed, D., & Song, Q. (2002). Définition d'un modèle de peau et son utilisation pour la classification des images. *Proceedings of MediaNet, 2002*, 187–198.

Han, J., & Ma, K. K. (2002). Fuzzy color histogram and its use in color image retrieval. *IEEE Transactions on Image Processing, 11*(8), 944–952. doi:10.1109/TIP.2002.801585

Herrera, F., Herrera-Viedma, E., & Martinez, L. (2008). A fuzzy linguistic methodology to deal with unbalanced linguistic term sets. *IEEE Transactions on Fuzzy Systems, 16*(2), 354–370. doi:10.1109/TFUZZ.2007.896353

Herrera, F., & Martinez, L. (2001). A model based on linguistic two-tuples for dealing with multigranularity hierarchical linguistic contexts in multiexpert decision-making. *IEEE Transactions on Systems, Man and Cybernetics. Part B, 31*(2), 227–234.

Hong, P., Qi, T., & Huang, T. S. (2000). Incorporate support vector machines to content-based image retrieval with relevance feedback. *Proceedings of IEEE International Conference on Image Processing,* (pp. 750-753).

Kender, J. (1976), *Saturation, hue and normalized color: Calculation, digitization effects, and use*. Master's Thesis, Dept. of Computer Science, Carnegie-Mellon University.

Le Saux, B. (2003). *Classification non exclusive et personnalisation par apprentissage: Application à la navigation dans les bases d'images.* Ph.D. Thesis, INRIA, France.

Li, Z., Zayane, O. R., & Tauber, Z. (1999). Illumination invariance and object model in content-based image and video retrieval. *Journal of Visual Communication and Image Representation, 10*, 219–244. doi:10.1006/jvci.1998.0403

Manjunath, B. S., Ohm, J. R., Vasudevan, V. V., & Yamada, A. (2001). Color and texture descriptors. *Transactions on Circuits and Systems for Video Technology, 11*(6), 703–715. doi:10.1109/76.927424

Mitra, M., Huang, J., & Kumar, S. R. (1997). Combining supervised learning with color correlograms for content-based image retrieval. *Proceedings of Fifth ACM Multimedia Conference.*

Omhover, J. F., Detyniecki, M., & Bouchon-Meunier, B. (2004). A region-similarity-based image retrieval system. [Perugia, Italy.]. *Proceedings of IPMU, 04*, 1461–1468.

Pass, G., & Zabih, R. (1999). Comparing images using joint histograms. *Multimedia Systems, 7*(3), 234–240. doi:10.1007/s005300050125

Roire, J. (2000). *Les noms des couleurs*. Pour la science, Hors série, no. 27.

Rui, Y., Huang, T. S., & Chang, S. F. (1999). Image retrieval: Current techniques, promising directions, and open issues. *Journal of Visual Communication and Image Representation*, *10*(1), 39–62. doi:10.1006/jvci.1999.0413

Salton, G., & McGill, M. J. (1983). *Introduction to modern information retrieval.* McGraw-Hill.

Shih, T. Y. (1995). The reversibility of six geometric color spaces. *Photogrammetric Engineering and Remote Sensing*, *61*(10), 1223–1232.

Smith, A. R. (1978). Color gammet transform pairs. *Computer Graphics*, *12*(3), 12–19. doi:10.1145/965139.807361

Swain, M. J., & Ballard, D. H. (1991). Color indexing. *International Journal of Computer Vision*, 7(1), 11–32. doi:10.1007/BF00130487

Truck, I., Akdag, H., & Borgi, A. (2001). A symbolic approach for colorimetric alterations. [Leicester, England.]. *Proceedings of EUSFLAT, 2001*, 105–108.

Truck, I., Akdag, H., & Borgi, A. (2001). Using fuzzy modifiers in colorimetry. *Proceedings of the 5th World Multiconference on Systemics, Cybernetics and Informatics, SCI 2001,* (pp. 472-477), Orlando, Florida, USA.

Vapnik, V. (1998). *Statistical learning theory.* New York, NY: John Wiley and Sons.

Vertan, C., & Boujemaa, N. (2000). Embedding fuzzy logic in content based image retrieval. *Proceedings of the 19th International Meeting of the North American Fuzzy Information Processing Society NAFIPS 2000* (pp. 85-90). Atlanta, USA.

Wang, J. Z., & Du, Y. (2001). Scalable integrated region-based image retrieval using IRM and statistical clustering. *Proceedings of the ACM and IEEE Joint Conference on Digital Libraries,* (pp. 268-277), Roanoke, VA.

Weber, R., Schek, H., & Blott, S. (1998). A quantitative analysis and performance study for similarity search methods in high-dimensional spaces. *Proceedings of 24th VLDB, 1998,* (pp. 194–205).

Chapter 2
Approach of Using Texture and Shape for Image Retrieval

Gang Zhang
Northeastern University, China & Shenyang University of Technology, China

Zongmin Ma
Northeastern University, China

Li Yan
Northeastern University, China

ABSTRACT

Feature integration is one of important research contents in content-based image retrieval. Single feature extraction and description is foundation of the feature integration. Features from a single feature extraction approach are a single feature or composite features, whether integration features are more discriminative than them or not. An approach of integrating shape and texture features was presented and used to study these problems. Gabor wavelet transform with minimum information redundancy was used to extract texture features, which would be used for feature analyses. Fourier descriptor approach with brightness was used to extract shape features. Then both features were integrated in parallel by weights. Comparisons were carried out among the integration features, the texture features, and the shape features, so that discrimination of the integration features can be testified.

INTRODUCTION

Ever since the 1970s, the further development has been made in content-based image retrieval. The basic idea of content-based image retrieval is to extract and describe the discriminative features from an image, and use these features to index the image. Then similarity measure is used for indexes to locate the same or similar images in an image database. Feature extraction and description is one of important components in content-based image retrieval, and is used to extract a set of discriminative features from an image to describe the content in the image. How these features are described and organized effectively is emphasized to describe the content in the image better. Furthermore, it will affect similarity measure directly. Currently, low level visual features are usual, and

DOI: 10.4018/978-1-61350-126-9.ch002

can be divided into texture features, shape features, color features, etc. According to low level visual features, the feature extraction and description approaches can be divided into texture feature extraction and description approaches (Haralick *et al*, 1973; Won *et al*, 2002; Wu *et al*, 2000; Jhanwar *et al*, 2004; Shi *et al*, 2005), shape feature extraction and description approaches (Zhang & Lu, 2002; Mokhtarian & Bober, 2003; Teague, 1980; Xin *et al*, 2007), color feature extraction and description approaches (Swain *et al*, 1991), etc. As being carried out for single feature, these approaches are called single feature extraction and description approach.

Texture and shape features are the commonly used low level visual features. Texture can describe the details of object surface, and shape can describe the contour of object effectively. That texture and shape are used together can describe the features of the image more effectively. Usually, texture feature extraction and description approaches can be divided into structure approaches, statistic approaches, model approaches, and transform approaches (Materka & Strzelecki, 1998). Gabor wavelet transform is one of commonly used transform approaches. The discovery of orientation-selective cells in the primary visual cortex of monkeys almost 40 years ago and the fact that most of the neurons in this part of the brain are of this type triggered a wave of research activity aimed at a more precise, quantitative description of the functional behavior of such cells (Hubel & Wiesel, 1974). Gabor wavelet transform is a computational model which simulates the principle of operation of these cells. Its basic idea is to use Gabor function as mother wavelet to compute a set of wavelets where each wavelet captures energy of specific frequency and direction in a window. Then energy is used for texture features to index an image. Texture features which are invariant to direction and scale can be extracted and described by the invariance of Gabor function to rotation and of wavelet transform to scale. The wavelet function set from the transformation of mother wavelet forms a set of non-orthogonal basis in Gabor wavelet transform approach, which means that redundancy information are involved in computation of texture features in the feature extraction and description (Arivazhagan *et al*, 2006). To reduce the redundancy information, a set of orthogonal wavelet function basis is introduced into Gabor wavelet transform approach (Manjunath *et al*, 2000; Ro *et al*, 2001). The Gabor wavelet transform approach is of minimum information redundancy, and used for the texture feature extraction and description in the chapter.

Shape feature extraction and description approaches can usually be divided into contour-based and region-based approaches (Zhang & Lu, 2004). Fourier descriptor approach is one of important contour-based approaches. Its basic idea is to use the boundary pixels of object to compute shape signature. Fourier transform is used for these shape signatures to compute Fourier coefficients. Then the Fourier coefficients which are invariant to translation, scale, rotation, and change of initial point are used for shape features. The merits of Fourier descriptor approach (Zhang & Lu, 2003; Kauppinen *et al*, 1995) are as followed. First, the effect of noise and change of boundary on shape feature extraction and description is reduced effectively by analyzing shape in frequency domain. Second, Fourier descriptor approach has low computation. Third, the features from Fourier descriptor approach is a compact description, and easy to be normalized. Besides, simple similarity measure can be used for feature matching. Fourth, the system which uses Fourier descriptor approach has better retrieval performance compared to the systems using many shape feature extraction approaches. In recent years, some modified versions are presented to improve the performance of Fourier descriptor approach further. Zhang *et al* transform an image from Cartesian coordinate system to Polar coordinate system. Then Fourier transform is used for the transformed image to improve the performance of Fourier descriptor approach (Zhang & Lu, 2002). Kunttu *et al* use

Fourier transform for the images of different scales to compute image signatures (Kunttu *et al*, 2006). When computing the Fourier coefficients, these approaches usually use the coordinates of boundary pixels of object only. In the previous work, it is found that the performance of Fourier descriptor approach can be improved further if the brightness of boundary pixels of object is also introduced into the computation of Fourier coefficients (Zhang *et al*, 2008). The Fourier descriptor approach is used for the shape feature extraction and description in the chapter.

An object usually contains several features in an image, so the feature integration has received more and more attention in recent years. Its basic idea is to compute more discriminative features by integrating several features. Feature integration approaches can be categorized into serial integration and parallel integration approaches according to whether the features are used in order. Kumar *et al* uses discrete cosine transform to extract the texture features of hand, and uses the shape properties, i.e., perimeter, eccentricity, palm width, and etc, to describe the shape features of hand. Then the texture and shape features are used for personal recognition (Kumar & Zhang, 2006). Using the integration features for image retrieval, the approach doesn't use the shape and texture features in order. So the feature integration approach is called parallel integration approach. Zhang *et al* use Fourier descriptor approach for texture primitives of an image to extract the shape features. The features are used to group the texture primitives. Gabor wavelet transforms are used for each group of texture primitives to extract the texture features. Then these texture features are used for image retrieval (Zhang *et al*, 2008). Using the integration features for image retrieval, the approach uses the shape and texture features in order. So the feature integration approach is called serial integration approach.

Single feature extraction and description approach is usually carried out for the whole image, and an image usually contains diverse information. So the features from single feature extraction and description approaches are a single feature, or composite features, and whether the integration features are more discriminative than the features or not. An approach of using texture and shape for image retrieval was proposed for these problems. Features from Gabor wavelet transform approach with minimum information redundancy are used for features analyses. Then they are integrates with the features from Fourier descriptor approach with brightness to compute integration features. Discrimination of the integration features are testified by comparing with the features from Gabor wavelet transform with minimum information redundancy and Fourier descriptor approach with brightness.

GABOR WAVELET TRANSFORM WITH MINIMUM INFORMATION REDUNDANCY

Gabor Wavelet Transform Approach

Gabor wavelet transform can be regarded as the wavelet transform whose mother wavelet is Gabor function (Arivazhagan *et al*, 2006). A Gabor wavelet is also a complex planar wave restricted by 2-D Gaussian envelope. Aside from scale and orientation, the only thing that can make two Gabor wavelets differ is the ratio between wavelength and the width of the Gaussian envelope. Every Gabor wavelet has a certain wavelength and orientation, and is then convolved with an image to estimate the magnitude of local frequencies of that approximate wavelength and orientation in the image. The Gabor wavelets can be considered as a class of self-similar functions. Let $\psi(x, y)$ be the mother Gabor wavelet, then this self-similar filter set is obtained by appropriate dilations and rotations of the mother wavelet.

Suppose that $f(x, y)$ denotes an image of size $M \times N$. Then its discrete Gabor wavelet transform can be denoted as

Figure 1. 5×6 Gabor filters in polar coordinate system

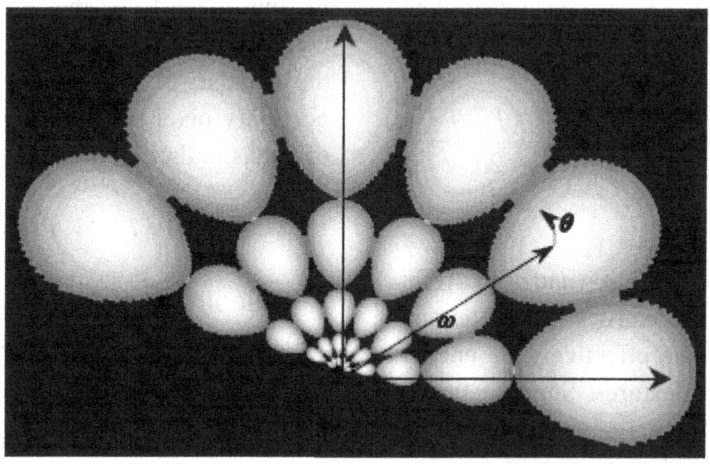

$$G_{pq}(x,y) = \sum_s \sum_t f(x-s, y-t)\psi^*_{pq}(s,t) \tag{1}$$

Here s, t are the filter mask size variables, and p, q are the scale and direction values respectively. Also ψ^*_{pq} is the complex conjugate of ψ_{pq}, which is a self-similar function generated from the dilation and rotation of the mother wavelet ψ.

$$\psi^*_{pq}(x, y) = a^p\, \psi(x', y') \tag{2}$$

Here a is the factor of scale and greater than 1. Also $p = 0, 1 \ldots P\text{-}1$ and $q = 0, 1 \ldots Q\text{-}1$ respectively. P and Q are the total number of scales and directions. $x' = a^p (x \cos\theta + y \sin\theta)$ and $y' = a^p (-x \sin\theta + y \cos\theta)$ where $\theta = q\,\pi/ Q$.

$$\psi(x,y) = \left(\frac{1}{2\pi\sigma_x\sigma_y}\right)\exp\left(-\frac{1}{2}\left(\frac{x^2}{\sigma_x^2} + \frac{y^2}{\sigma_y^2}\right)\right)\exp(2\pi j W x) \tag{3}$$

Here W defines the frequency bandwidth of Gabor filter. It has been found in neurophysiology that $W = 0.5$ is completely consistent with visual system of human (Zhang *et al*, 2008). σ_x and σ_y are constants of Gaussian envelope along x and y axles in time domain respectively.

As the wavelet functions from the transformation of Gabor function forms a set of non-orthogonal basis, redundancy information are involved in the computation of texture features.

Gabor Wavelet Transform with Minimum Information Redundancy

Suppose that $f(x, y)$ denotes an image of size $M \times N$. Gabor wavelet transform with orthogonal wavelet function basis (Ro et al, 2001) is used the image to extract and describe texture features.

The image $f(x,y)$ is transformed from the spatial domain to the frequency domain. The normalized frequency domain is partitioned along the redial direction and angular direction according to the psychophysical research results. The 6 divisions are carried out at intervals of $\pi/6$ along the angular direction and the 5 octave divisions are carried out along the redial direction. The sub-bands in the frequency domain are called feature channels. Gabor wavelet transform is used for each feature channel to extract and describe the texture features. The 5×6 Gabor filters in polar coordinate system is shown in Figure 1.

Suppose that $G_{s,r}(\omega,\theta)$ denotes Gabor function at s-th redial index and r-th angular index, then $G_{s,r}(\omega,\theta)$ can be denoted as

$$G_{s,r}(\omega,\theta)=\exp[\frac{-(\omega-\omega_s)^2}{2\sigma^2_{\omega_s}}]\cdot\exp[\frac{-(\theta-\theta_r)^2}{2\sigma^2_{\theta_r}}] \quad (4)$$

Here, the parameter ω_s, θ_r, $\delta_{\omega s}$, and $\delta_{\theta r}$ can refer to (Ro *et al*, 2001). Energy can describe the texture information in an image effectively, so energy is used as the texture features. Suppose that e_i denotes the energy information from the feature channel $i = 6\times s + r + 1$, then e_i can be denoted as

$$e_i=\log[\sum_{\omega=0+}^{1}\sum_{\theta=0°+}^{360°}[G_{s,r}(\omega,\theta)\cdot|\omega|\cdot F(\omega,\theta)]^2] \quad (5)$$

Here, the parameter $|\omega|$ is Jacobian term between Cartesian and Polar frequency coordinates. $F(\omega, \theta)$ is Fourier transform of the image $f(x, y)$. As the frequency domain is divided into 30 feature channels, the dimension of the texture feature vector is 30. Suppose that TD denotes the texture feature vector, then TD can be denoted as

$$\mathrm{TD} = \{e_1, e_2, \ldots, e_{30}\} \quad (6)$$

FOURIER DESCRIPTOR APPROACH WITH BRIGHTNESS

Fourier Descriptor Approach

The main steps of Fourier descriptor approach (Zhang *et al*, 2003) are as follows. First, the boundary pixels are computed. Second, shape signature function are used. Finally, the Fourier coefficients are computed.

Suppose that $f(x, y)$ denotes a gray image of size $M \times N$. After having been transformed into the binary image, Canny edge detector is used for the image to extract the edge pixels. Then boundary tracing algorithm is used to compute the boundary pixel set. Suppose that P denotes the boundary pixel set and PN denotes the number of pixels in the set, then the P can be denoted as

$$\mathrm{P} = \{(x(t), y(t)) \mid t \in [1, PN]\} \quad (7)$$

Centroid distance approach is used for the set P to compute shape signatures. Suppose that (x_0, y_0) denotes the centroid of object in the image, then x_0 and y_0 can been denoted as respectively

$$x_0=\frac{1}{PN}\sum_{i=1}^{PN}x_i, \cdot y_0=\frac{1}{PN}\sum_{i=1}^{PN}y_i \quad (8)$$

Then the distance from each pixel in the set P to the centroid is computed. Suppose that $r(t)$ denotes the distance from the t-th pixel in the set P to the centroid, then $r(t)$ can be denoted as

$$r(t)=([x(t)-x_0]^2+[y(t)-y_0]^2)^{1/2}, t = 1, \ldots, PN \quad (9)$$

Discrete Fourier transform is used for $r(t)$. Suppose that a_n denotes the transform coefficients, then a_n can be denoted as

$$a_n=\frac{1}{PN}\sum_{t=1}^{PN}r(t)\exp(\frac{-2j\pi nt}{PN}), n = 0, 1, \ldots, PN\text{-}1 \quad (10)$$

The first Fourier transform coefficient a_0 is used to normalize all the Fourier transform coefficients. Then the phase information is ignored and magnitudes are kept in the coefficients. Suppose that b_n denotes the normalized Fourier transform coefficients whose phase information has been ignored, then b_n can be denoted as

$$b_n = | a_n / a_0 | \quad (11)$$

Here b_n (n = 1, ..., PN-1) are invariant to translation, scale, rotation, and change of initial point. Then b_n are used for the Fourier descriptors. As the centroid distance is a function of real value, only half Fourier descriptors are different. Suppose that SD denotes the shape feature vector, then SD can be denote as

$$SD = \{b_i \mid i \in [1, PN/2 - 1]\} \quad (12)$$

For the purpose of computation simplification, only k Fourier descriptors are used to form shape feature vector. The parameter k can be determined by experiments.

Fourier Descriptor with Brightness

To improve the discrimination of the shape features computed from the Fourier descriptor approach further, Fourier descriptor approach with brightness is proposed. After the boundary pixels are computed, the centroid distance approach is used to compute the shape signatures. Then Fourier transforms are used for the shape signatures with brightness of the boundary pixels as weights, so that the shape features can be computed.

Suppose that $f(x, y)$ denotes a gray image of size $M \times N$. After $f(x, y)$ is transformed into a binary image, the Canny edge detector and boundary tracing are used for the binary image to compute the coordinates of boundary pixels of shape. Suppose that BN denotes the number of boundary pixels, BP denotes the boundary pixel set, then BP can be denoted as

$$BP = \{(x(t), y(t), val(t)) \mid t \in [1, BN]\} \quad (13)$$

Then the centroid distance signature function is used for BP to compute the shape signatures. Suppose that (x_c, y_c) denote the centroid of pixels in BP, then x_c and y_c can be denoted as respectively

$$x_c = \frac{1}{N}\sum_{t=1}^{BN} x(t) \text{ and } y_c = \frac{1}{N}\sum_{t=1}^{BN} y(t) \quad (14)$$

Suppose that $r(t)$ denotes the distance of t-th boundary pixel to the centroid (x_c, y_c), then $r(t)$ can denoted as

$$r(t) = ([x(t) - x_c]^2 + [y(t) - y_c]^2)^{1/2}, t = 1, \ldots, BN \quad (15)$$

The discrete Fourier transform is used for $r(t)$ to compute the Fourier coefficients with the brightness of boundary pixels in the formula (13) as weights. Suppose that a_n denote the Fourier coefficient, then a_n can be denoted as

$$a_n = \frac{1}{BN}\sum_{t=1}^{BN} val(t) * r(t) * \exp\left(\frac{-2j\pi nt}{BN}\right), n = 0, \ldots, BN\text{-}1 \quad (16)$$

Here, $\varphi(t) = val(t) * r(t)$ is called centroid distance signature function with brightness. Then the first Fourier coefficient a_0 is used to normalize all Fourier coefficients. The phase information is ignored, but the magnitudes of the coefficients are kept. This makes these coefficients invariant to translation, rotation, scale, and change of start point. Suppose b_n(n = 1, ..., PN-1) denote the Fourier coefficients which are invariant to translation, rotation, scale, and change of start point, then b_n can be denoted as

$$b_n = |a_n / a_0| \quad (17)$$

Here, b_n(n = 1, ..., PN-1) are used as the shape feature. Then the first k shape features which can rebuild the centroid distance signature function with brightness approximately are used to form the shape feature vector and k is from the experimental results. Suppose that SD denotes the shape feature vector of image $f(x, y)$, then SD can be denoted as

$$SD = \{b_i \mid i \in [1, k]\} \quad (18)$$

IMAGE RETRIEVAL USING TEXTURE AND SHAPE FEATURES

Feature extraction and description, similarity measure, and performance evaluation of system are three elementary components in image retrieval. Three elementary components, which will be used in the chapter, will be demonstrated as followed.

Extraction and Description of Integration Features

Suppose that TD denotes the texture feature vector computed from Gabor wavelet transform with minimum redundancy, and SD denotes the shape feature vector computed from Fourier descriptor approach with brightness. Then the texture and shape features are integrated in parallel by weights. Suppose that FD denotes the integration feature vector of image $f(x, y)$, the parameters w_1 and w_2 denote the contributions of shape and texture features on the integration features respectively, then FD can be denoted as

$$FD = \{TD(w_1)\ SD(w_2)\} \tag{19}$$

Here the parameters w_1 and w_2 can be computed by domain knowledge, priori knowledge, or statistic approaches. Here re-weighting approach (Wu *et al*, 2005) is used to compute w_1 and w_2. First, the parameters w_1 and w_2 are set as 0.5 respectively. After one retrieval, the positive and negative samples are used to modify w_1 and w_2. After two sequential modification, if the difference of two-time w_1 and w_2 are less than preset threshold, then re-weighting ends to reduce convergence time.

Similarity Measure

Here weighted Euclidean distance is used for similarity measure. Suppose that FD(q), SD(q), and TD(q) denote the integration feature vector, shape feature vector, and texture feature vector of a sample image q respectively, FD(i), SD(i), and TD(i) denote the integration feature vector, shape feature vector, and texture feature vector of image i in the image database respectively, and $w = \{w_1, w_2\}$ denotes weight coefficient set, then the weighted Euclidean distance can be denoted as

$$D(FD(q), FD(i)) = \left[w_1 \sum_{c_1=1}^{k} \left[SD_{c_1}(q) - SD_{c_1}(i) \right]^2 + w_2 \sum_{c_2=1}^{30} \left[TD_{c_2}(q) - TD_{c_2}(i) \right]^2 \right]^{1/2} \tag{20}$$

Here $SD_{c1}(q)$ denotes c_1-th element of shape feature vector of the sample image q. $TD_{c2}(q)$ denotes c_2-th element of texture feature vector of the sample image q. $SD_{c1}(i)$ denotes c_1-th element of shape feature vector of the image i in the image database. $TD_{c2}(i)$ denotes c_2-th element of texture feature vector of the image i in the image database.

Performance Evaluation Approach

To analyze the performance of system using the texture and shape features, retrieval precision and recall are introduced (Zhang *et al*, 2007). Suppose that N denotes the number of retrieved images at a time, N' denotes the number of retrieved relevant images at a time, N'' denotes the number of relevant images in an image database, then retrieval precision P and recall R can be denoted as respectively

$$P = N' / N \text{ and } R = N' / N'' \tag{21}$$

EXPERIMENTS AND ANALYSES

Works are carried out from three aspects. First, Features from a single feature extraction approach are analyzed. Second, the parameter k is computed in the formula (18). Third, comparisons are carried out among the integration features, the texture features from Gabor wavelet transform with minimum information redundancy (Ro *et al*, 2001), and the shape features from Fourier descriptor approach (Zhang & Lu, 2003).

Experimental image database contains 3000 MRI images in which cervical vertebra images, cervical disc images and Lumbar Disc images are 1000 respectively. Moreover, these images are gray images of size 481 × 481. Test codes are compiled by Matlab, and the machine configuration for test is Intel(R) Celeron(R) mainboard, 1.60GHZ CPU main frequency, and 256MB memory.

FEATURES FROM A SINGLE FEATURE EXTRACTION APPROACH

It is proposed that the features from a single feature extraction and description approach can be composite features in the early psychophysical research results (Petkov & Kruizinga, 1997). Here the features from Gabor wavelet transform with minimum information redundancy are used for feature analyses. The 5 images only with dominant shape features are selected from the image database. Gabor wavelet transform approach with minimum information redundancy is used for each image to extract and describe the texture features. The 5 images and their texture feature values are shown in Figure 2.

It can be found from Figure 2 that the values of texture features aren't zero although these images only contain shape information. This means that the features from Gabor wavelet transform with minimum information redundancy aren't a single feature, but composite features.

Computation of *k*

The 60 images are selected from the image database. Let $k = \{x \mid x \in [5, 60] \text{ and } x \bmod 5 = 0\}$, the original and rebuilt centroid distance signature function with brightness is computed for each image. Experimental results show that the rebuilt centroid distance signature function with brightness is similar to the original when $k \geq 10$. So $k = 10$ is used in the subsequent experiments.

Discrimination of Integration Features

Two test image sets are formed from the image database. Each test set contains 30 images, in which there are 10 cervical vertebra images, 10 cervical disc images, and 10 lumbar disc images. In the first test set, 6 images are basic images. Then each basic image is deformed by 3 kinds of transformation, including 2 rotations, 1 scaling, and 1 translation (See Figure 3 (a)). In the second test set, 30 images are selected as basic images (See Figure 3 (b)).

Extraction and description of integration features are carried out for each image of each test image set. Weighted Euclidean distance is used to measure similarity between images. Then retrieval precision and recall are used to measure the performance of system using the integration features. For the purpose of comparisons, Gabor wavelet transform with minimum information redundancy is used to extract and describe texture features for each image, and Fourier descriptor approach is used to extract and describe shape features for each image. Euclidean distance is used to measure similarity between images. Retrieval precision and recall are used to measure the performance of systems using the texture and shape features respectively.

The 9 images are selected as sample images for the first test image set. The 3 test results are shown in Figure 4. The first image on the left is selected as a sample image for query. The images on the right are the pre-8 retrieved images when the systems using the features from Gabor wavelet transform with minimum information redundancy, those from Fourier descriptor approach, and the integration features are used respectively.

The curves of retrieval precision and recall of the systems which use the features from Gabor wavelet transform with minimum information

Figure 2. 5 images and their feature values

	(1)	(2)	(3)	(4)	(5)
1	1	1	1	1	1
2	0.7431	0.7592	0.9067	0.8873	0.7511
3	0.4042	0.1386	0.8568	0.4889	0.0335
4	0.547	0.0483	0.3246	0.2192	0
5	0.2661	0	0.0006	0.0003	0
6	0	0	0	0	0
7	0.888	0.934	0.7863	0.8226	0.9358
8	0.6352	0.7978	0.8812	0.8145	0.6875
9	0.5877	0.2425	0.6863	0.4626	0.011
10	0.7342	0.1053	0.4619	0.3196	0
11	0.4404	0	0.0142	0.0022	0
12	0	0	0	0	0
13	0.4908	0.7651	0.6506	0.6368	0.8044
14	0.4493	0.7577	0.7573	0.7191	0.5574
15	0.6783	0.373	0.77	0.492	0.0007
16	0.8146	0.1687	0.6195	0.4877	0
17	0.5153	0.0002	0.1797	0.1084	0
18	0.0001	0	0	0	0
19	0.5508	0.6919	0.6467	0.6308	0.7302
20	0.6061	0.6789	0.6255	0.6952	0.4848
21	0.5997	0.5402	0.6552	0.6297	0.0002
22	0.6762	0.3082	0.6204	0.6213	0
23	0.3579	0.0042	0.2332	0.2244	0
24	0	0	0	0	0
25	0.5969	0.4866	0.5845	0.5445	0.6553
26	0.5679	0.5449	0.5409	0.5677	0.419
27	0.5499	0.5466	0.5667	0.5945	0.0001
28	0.4801	0.4567	0.5161	0.5563	0
29	0.16	0.151	0.1812	0.2189	0
30	0	0	0	0	0

(1)

(2)

(3)

(4)

(5)

Figure 3. Two test image sets

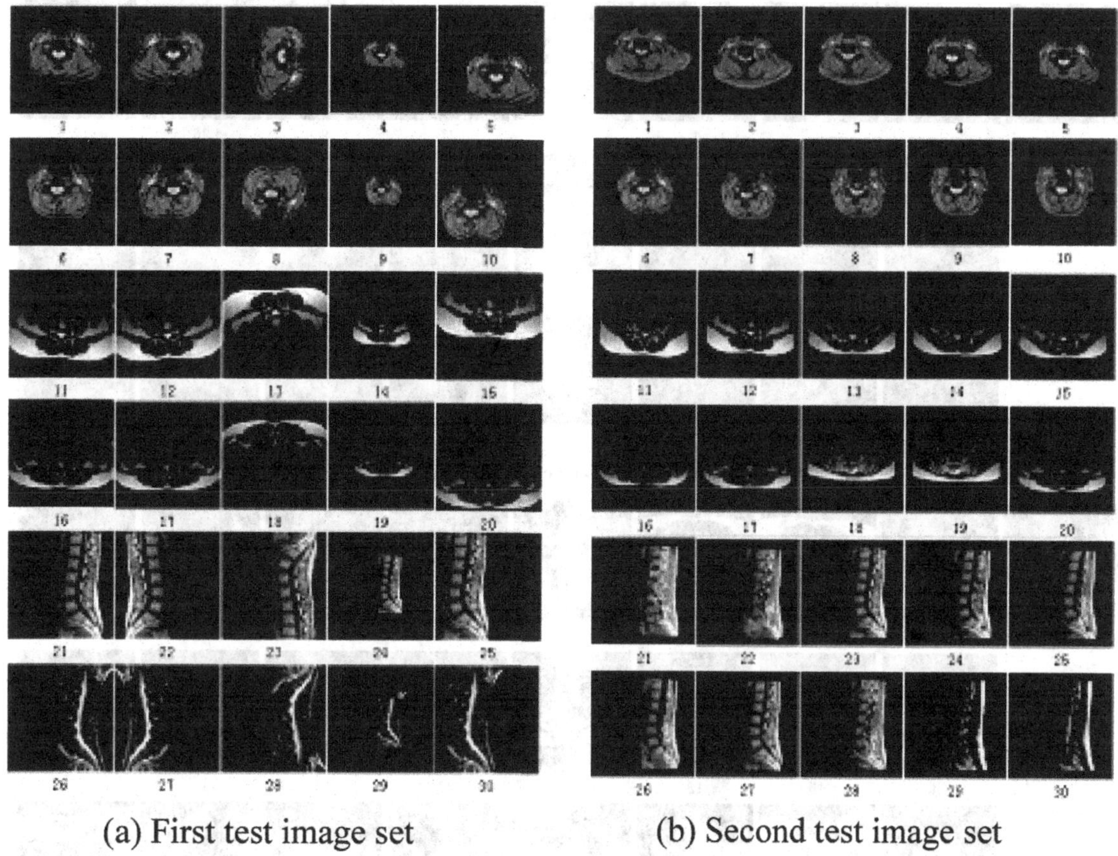

(a) First test image set (b) Second test image set

redundancy, those from Fourier descriptor approach, and the integration features respectively are shown in Figure 5. The horizontal axes of the curves denote images, in which the first three images are the cervical disc images, the middle three are lumbar disc images, and the last three are cervical vertebra images. The ordinate axes of the curves denote the retrieval precision and recall, respectively. Here "◆", "■" and "▲" are used to denotes the retrieval precision and recall of the systems which use the features from Gabor wavelet transform with minimum information redundancy, those from Fourier descriptor approach, and the integration features, respectively.

It can be found from Figure 4 and Figure 5 that the system using the integration features has better retrieval performance as a whole. However, the retrieval performance of systems using the features from Gabor wavelet transform with minimum information redundancy and Fourier descriptor approach respectively are better than that of system using the integration features sometimes. It is found by analyses that the used weights w_1 and w_2 are not optimal in order to reduce convergence time.

The 9 images are selected as sample images for the second test image set. The 3 test results are shown in Figure 6. The first image on the left is selected as a sample image for query. The images on the right are the pre-8 retrieved images when the systems using the features from Gabor wavelet transform approach with minimum

Figure 4. Three test results for first test image set

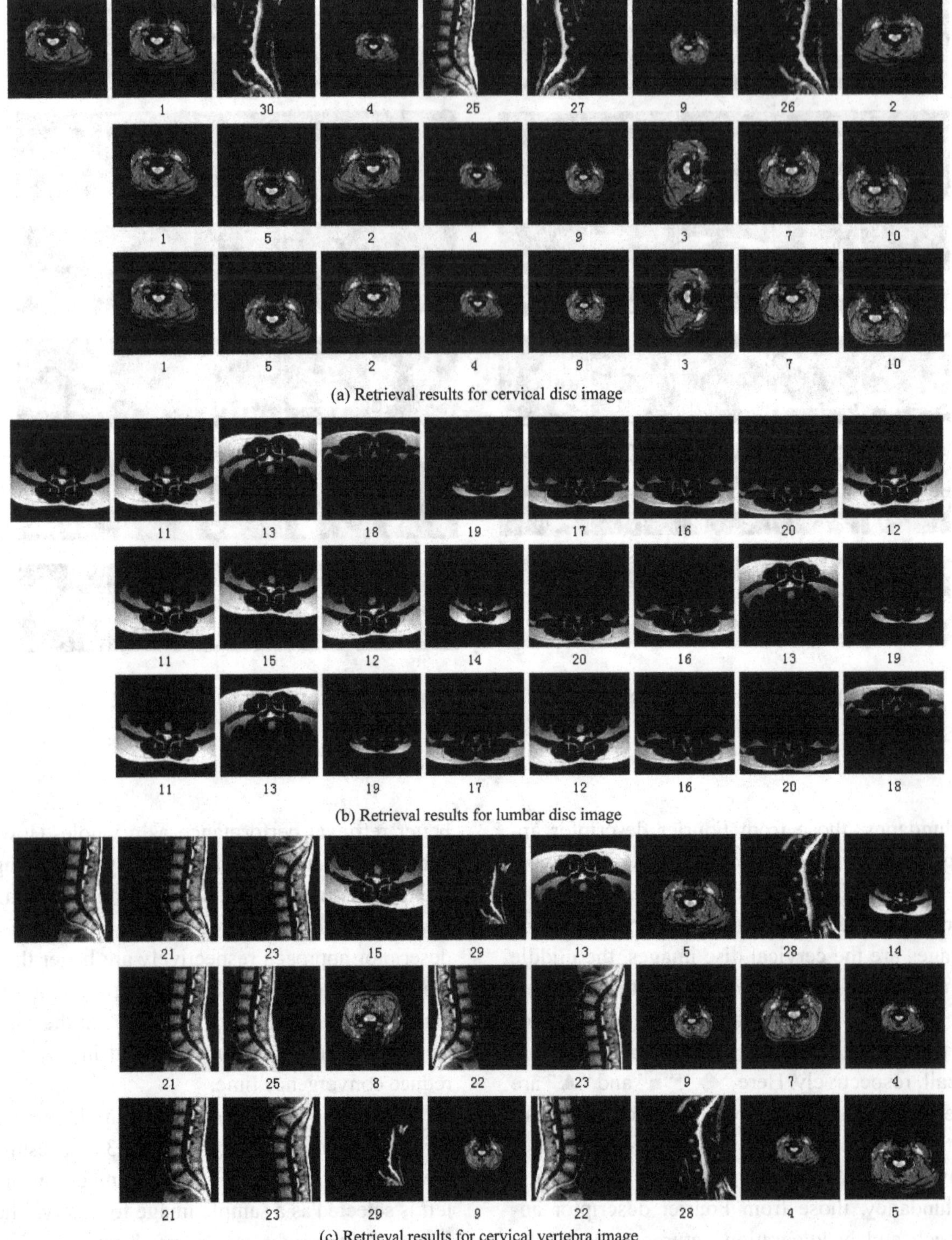

(a) Retrieval results for cervical disc image

(b) Retrieval results for lumbar disc image

(c) Retrieval results for cervical vertebra image

Figure 5. Retrieval precision and recall curves for first test set

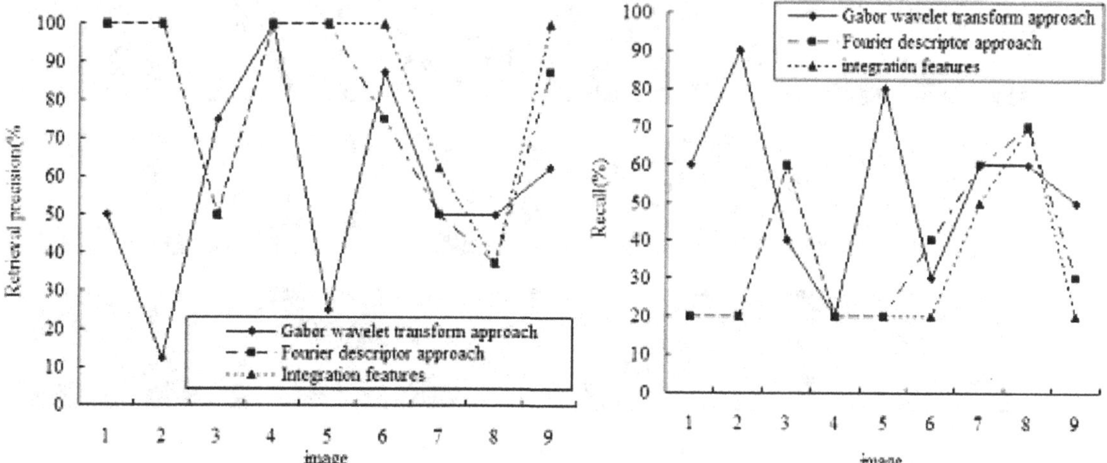

information redundancy, those from Fourier descriptor approach, and the integration features are used respectively.

The curves of retrieval precision and recall of the systems which use the features from Gabor wavelet transform approach with minimum information redundancy, those from Fourier descriptor approach, and the integration features respectively are shown in Figure 7. The horizontal axes of the curves denote images, in which the first three images are the cervical disc images, the middle three are lumbar disc images, and the last three are cervical vertebra images. The ordinate axes of the curves denote the retrieval precision and recall, respectively. Here "◆", "■" and "▲" are used to denotes the retrieval precision and recall of the systems which use the features from Gabor wavelet transform approach with minimum information redundancy, those from Fourier descriptor approach, and the integration features, respectively.

It can be found from Figure 6 and Figure 7 that the system using the integration features has better retrieval performance as a whole.

CONCLUSION

An approach of using texture and shape for image retrieval is presented. The approach uses the Gabor wavelet transform with minimum information redundancy to extract texture features, which are used for feature analyses. Fourier descriptor approach with brightness is used to extract shape features. Then the texture and shape features are integrated in parallel by weights. The following conclusions are drawn by experiments. First, the features from a single feature extraction and description approach are composite features. Second, the integration features are more discriminative as a whole.

FUTURE RESEARCH DIRECTIONS

In the latter work, the following works will be carried out. First, texture information and shape information will be separated from an image. Second, single feature will be extracted from the separated information. Third, serial integration will be attempted.

Figure 6. Three test results for second test image set

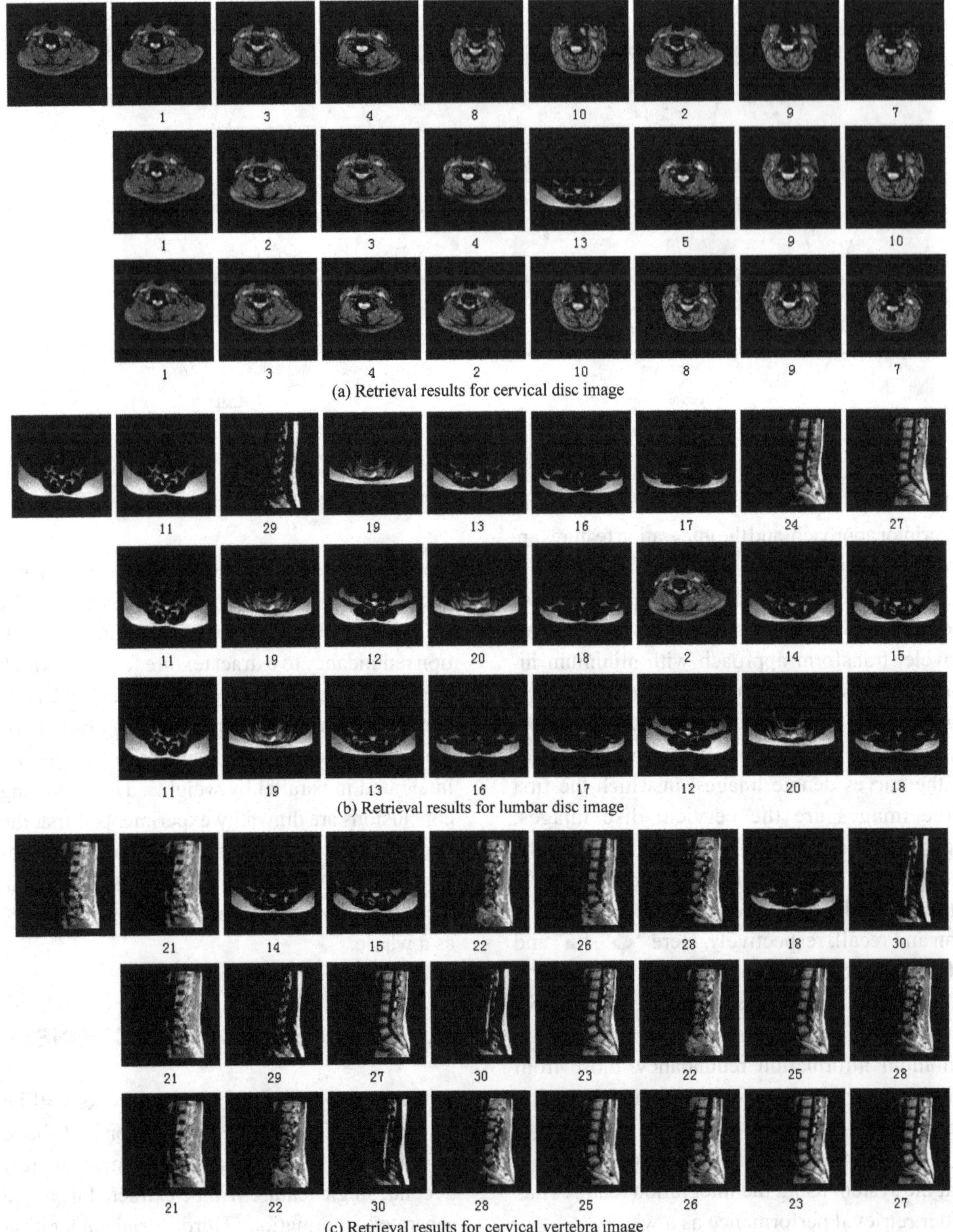

(a) Retrieval results for cervical disc image

(b) Retrieval results for lumbar disc image

(c) Retrieval results for cervical vertebra image

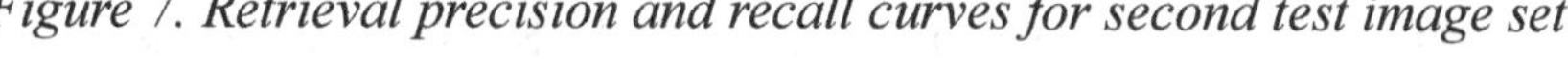

Figure 7. Retrieval precision and recall curves for second test image set

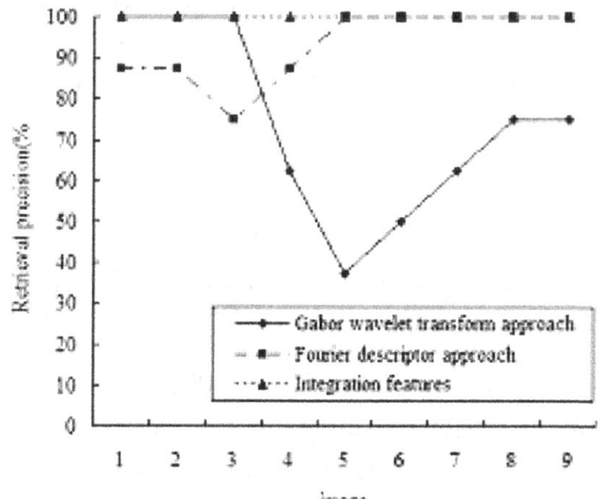

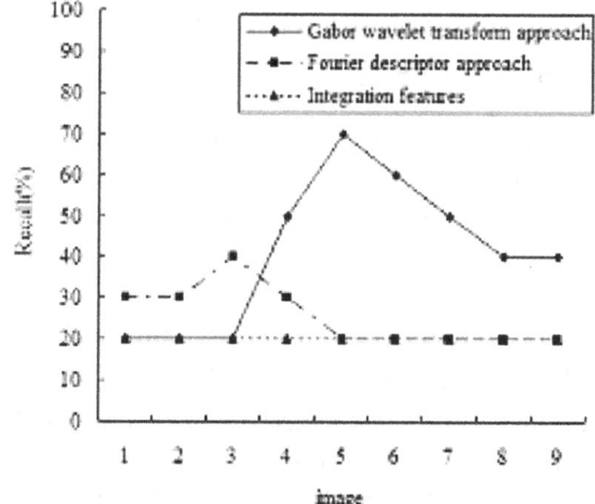

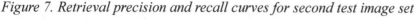

REFERENCES

Arivazhagan, S., Ganesan, L., & Priyal, S. P. (2006). Texture classification using Gabor wavelets based rotation invariant features. *Pattern Recognition Letters*, *27*(16), 1976–1982. doi:10.1016/j.patrec.2006.05.008

Haralick, R., Shanmugan, K., & Dinstein, I. (1973). Texture feature for image classification. *IEEE Transactions on Systems, Man, and Cybernetics*, *SMC-3*(6), 610–621. doi:10.1109/TSMC.1973.4309314

Hubel, D. H., & Wiesel, T. N. (1974). Sequence regularity and geometry of orientation columns in the monkey striate cortex. *The Journal of Comparative Neurology*, *158*(3), 267–293. doi:10.1002/cne.901580304

Jhanwar, N., Chaudhuri, S., Seetharaman, G., & Zavidovique, B. (2004). Content based image retrieval using motif cooccurrence matrix. *Image and Vision Computing*, *22*(14), 1211–1220.

Kauppinen, H., Seppanen, T., & Pietikainen, M. (1995). An experimental comparison of autoregressive and Fourier-based descriptors in 2D shape classification. *IEEE Transactions on Pattern Analysis and Machine Intelligence*, *17*(2), 201–207. doi:10.1109/34.368168

Kumar, A., & Zhang, D. (2006). Personal recognition using hand shape and texture. *IEEE Transactions on Image Processing*, *15*(8), 2454–2461. doi:10.1109/TIP.2006.875214

Kunttu, I., Lepistö, L., Rauhamaa, J., & Visa, A. (2006). Multiscale Fourier descriptors for defect image retrieval. *Pattern Recognition Letters*, *27*(2), 123–132. doi:10.1016/j.patrec.2005.08.022

Liu, C. J., & Wechsler, H. (2001). A shape- and texture-based enhanced fisher classifier for face recognition. *IEEE Transactions on Image Processing*, *10*(4), 598–608. doi:10.1109/83.913594

Manjunath, B. S., Wu, P., Newsam, S., & Shin, H. D. (2000). A texture descriptor for browsing and similarity retrieval. *Signal Processing Image Communication*, *16*(1-2), 33–43. doi:10.1016/S0923-5965(00)00016-3

Materka, A., & Strzelecki, M. (1998). *Texture analysis methods-a review (Tech. Rep. No. COST B11)*. Brussels, Belgium: Technical University of Lodz, Institute of Electronics.

Mokhtarian, F., & Bober, M. (Eds.). (2003). *Curvature scale space representation: Theory, applications, and Mpeg-7 standardization*. Norwell, MA: Kluwer Academic Publishers.

Petkov, N., & Kruizinga, P. (1997). Computational models of visual neurons specialized in the detection of periodic and aperiodic oriented visual stimuli: Bar and grating cells. *Biological Cybernetics*, *76*(2), 83–96. doi:10.1007/s004220050323

Ro, Y. M., Kim, M., Kang, H. K., Manjunath, B. S., & Kim, J. (2001). MPEG-7 homogeneous texture descriptor. *ETRI Journal*, *23*(2), 41–51. doi:10.4218/etrij.01.0101.0201

Shi, Z. P., Hu, H., Li, Q. Y., Shi, Z. Z., & Duan, C. L. (2005). Texture spectrum descriptor based image retrieval. *Journal of Software*, *16*(6), 1039–1045. doi:10.1360/jos161039

Swain, M. J., & Ballard, D. H. (1991). Color indexing. *International Journal of Computer Vision*, *7*(1), 11–32. doi:10.1007/BF00130487

Teague, M. R. (1980). Image analysis via the general theory of moments. *Journal of the Optical Society of America*, *70*(8), 920–930. doi:10.1364/JOSA.70.000920

Won, C. S., Park, D. K., & Park, S. J. (2002). Efficient use of Mpeg-7 edge histogram descriptor. *ETRI Journal*, *24*(1), 23–30. doi:10.4218/etrij.02.0102.0103

Wu, H., Lu, H. Q., & Ma, S. D. (2005). A survey of relevance feedback techniques in content-based image retrieval. *Chinese Journal of Computers*, *28*(12), 1969–1979.

Wu, P., Manjunath, B. S., Newsam, S., & Shin, H. D. (2000). A texture descriptor for browsing and similarity retrieval. *Signal Processing Image Communication*, *16*(1-2), 33–43. doi:10.1016/S0923-5965(00)00016-3

Xin, Y. Q., Pawlak, M., & Liao, S. (2007). Accurate computation of zernike moments in polar coordinates. *IEEE Transactions on Image Processing*, *16*(2), 581–587. doi:10.1109/TIP.2006.888346

Zhang, D. S., & Lu, G. J. (2002). Shape-based image retrieval using generic Fourier descriptor. *Signal Processing Image Communication*, *17*(10), 825–848. doi:10.1016/S0923-5965(02)00084-X

Zhang, D. S., & Lu, G. J. (2003). A comparative study of curvature scale space and Fourier descriptors for shape-based image retrieval. *Journal of Visual Communication and Image Representation*, *14*(1), 41–60. doi:10.1016/S1047-3203(03)00003-8

Zhang, D. S., & Lu, G. J. (2004). Review of shape representation and description techniques. *Pattern Recognition*, *37*(1), 1–19. doi:10.1016/j.patcog.2003.07.008

Zhang, G., Ma, Z. M., & Deng, L. G. (2007). Directed filter for dominant direction fuzzy set in content-based image retrieval. In *Proceedings of the 2007 ACM Symposium on Applied Computing*. (pp. 76-77). Seoul, Republic of Korea: ACM Press.

Zhang, G., Ma, Z. M., & Deng, L. G. (2008). Texture feature extraction and description using fuzzy set of main dominant directions of variable scales in content-based medical image retrieval. In *Proceedings of the 2008 ACM Symposium on Applied Computing* (pp. 1760-1761). Fortaleza, Brazil: ACM Press.

Zhang, G., Ma, Z. M., Tong, Q., He, Y., & Zhao, T. N. (2008). Shape feature extraction using Fourier descriptors with brightness in content-based medical image retrieval. In *Proceedings of the Fourth International Conference on Intelligent Information Hiding and Multimedia Signal Processing*. (pp. 71-74). Harbin, China: IEEE Computer Society.

Zhang, Z. Y., Shi, Z. P., Shi, Z. W., & Shi, Z. Z. (2008). Image retrieval based on contour. *Journal of Software, 19*(9), 2461–2470. doi:10.3724/SP.J.1001.2008.02461

ADDITIONAL READING

Andrysiak, T., & Choras, M. (2005). Image retrieval based on hierarchical Gabor filters. *International Journal of Applied Mathematics and Computer Science, 15*(4), 471–480.

Duan, L. J., Gao, W., Zeng, W., & Zhao, D. B. (2005). Adaptive relevance feedback based on Bayesian inference for image retrieval. *Signal Processing, 85*(2), 395–399. doi:10.1016/j.sigpro.2004.10.006

Fang, Y. C., Wang, Y. H., & Tan, T. N. (2004). Improving face detection through fusion of contour and region information. *Chinese Journal of Computers, 27*(4), 482–491.

Fogel, I., & Sagi, D. (1989). Gabor filters as texture discriminator. *Biological Cybernetics, 61*(2), 103–113. doi:10.1007/BF00204594

Hung, M. H., Hsieh, C. H., & Kuo, C. M. (2006). Similarity retrieval of shape images based on database classification. *Journal of Visual Communication and Image Representation, 17*(5), 970–985. doi:10.1016/j.jvcir.2005.09.002

Lin, H. C., Chiu, C. Y., & Yang, S. N. (2003). Finding textures by textual descriptions, visual examples, and relevance feedbacks. *Pattern Recognition Letters, 24*(14), 2255–2267. doi:10.1016/S0167-8655(03)00052-7

Saha, S. K., Das, A. K., & Chanda, B. (2007). Image retrieval based on indexing and relevance feedback. *Pattern Recognition Letters, 28*(3), 357–366. doi:10.1016/j.patrec.2006.04.005

Wang, Y. H., Fan, W., & Tan, T. N. (2005). Face recognition based on information fusion. *Chinese Journal of Computers, 28*(10), 1657–1663.

Wei, C. H., Li, C. T., & Wilson, R. (2005). A content-based method to medical image database retrieval. In Ma, Z. M. (Ed.), *Database Modeling for Industrial Data Management* (pp. 258–292). Hershey, PA: Idea Group publishing. doi:10.4018/978-1-59140-684-6.ch009

Zhang, G. Ma, Z. M., Cai, Z. P., & Wang, H. L. (2007). Texture Analysis Using Modified Computational Model of Grating Cells in Content-based Medical Image Retrieval. In *Proceedings of International Conference on Medical Imaging and Informatics* (pp. 184-191). Beijing: Middlesex University Press.

Zhang, G., Ma, Z. M., Deng, L. G., & Cai, Z. P. (2007). Oriented Filter Based on Dominant Directions in Content-based Image Retrieval. *Journal of Northeastern University, 28*(7), 978–981.

Zhao, H. T., Yu, D. J., Jin, Z., & Yang, J. Y. (2003). A shape- and texture-based face recognition. *Journal of Computer Research and Development, 40*(4), 538–543.

Chapter 3
Mid-Level Image Descriptors

Jean Martinet
University of Lille, France

Ismail Elsayad
University of Lille, France

ABSTRACT

We present in this chapter a classification of image descriptors, from the low level to the high level, introducing the notion of intermediate level. This level denotes a representation level lying between low-level features – such as color histograms, texture or shape descriptors, and high-level features – semantic concepts. In a chain of process point of view, mid-level descriptors represent an intermediate step or stage between low and high level, dedicated to specific tasks such as annotation, object detection/recognition, or similarity matching. After introducing a definition for the three different levels, we review a number of approaches making use of such intermediate levels. We namely focus on different approaches making an analogy with text processing, by adapting and applying standard text processing techniques to image indexing.

INTRODUCTION

In typical Content-Based Information Retrieval (CBIR) systems, it is always important to select an appropriate representation for documents (Baeza-Yates & Ribeiro-Neto 1999). Indeed, the quality of retrieval results depends on the quality the internal representation of the content. Classical models of information retrieval usually consider that a document is described by a set of descriptors. In text retrieval for instance, the descriptors take the form of representative index terms, that are keywords extracted from the collection.

When considering visual documents, the problem of the *semantic gap* arises. The notion of semantic gap has been defined a decade ago by Smeulders et al. (2000) as the lack of coincidence between the information that one can extract from the visual data and the interpretation that the same data have for a user in a given situation. In the case of images, because of the distance between the raw signal (i.e. the pixel matrix) and its interpretation,

DOI: 10.4018/978-1-61350-126-9.ch003

it is difficult to automatically extract an accurate semantic content representation of their content. Traditional automatic annotation techniques extract information from *low-level descriptors* (or *low level features*) to infer information about corresponding *high-level descriptors*. Note that although the two notations (*descriptor* and *feature*) are similar and can be assimilated, we preferably use the more general notation descriptor instead of feature in this chapter because of its dedication to indexing.

Because the step from the low level to the high level is not straightforward, many techniques make use of several chains of processes, in order to extract and refine the information incrementally. We call *mid-level descriptors* the result of such intermediate processes that help narrowing the semantic gap. The main target of techniques using such mid-level descriptors could be, for instance, to improve the results quality of a patch classifier (e.g. based on Support Vector Machines) by defining and using mid-level descriptors as an input, as compared using with only low-level descriptors.

The objective of this chapter is to introduce the emerging concept of *mid-level descriptors*, by identifying existing approaches making use of such descriptors, which illustrates and supports the proposed classification of descriptors. We review some of the widely used approaches in visual document indexing using such descriptors.

The remainder of the chapter is organized as follows. We introduce in the following section some definitions of the different levels of description of images. Then we review a number of approaches in image indexing, from the proposed *mid-level description* perspective. We namely explore an analogy between text and image, which is widely used in image indexing. We also introduce other *mid-level* descriptors like image epitomes and spatial data mining. We conclude this chapter by giving the main trends for the future of this research domain.

BACKGROUND

The notion of intermediate level (or mid-level) descriptor is not new. For instance, Luo & Savakis (2001) proposed the use of a Bayesian network for integrating knowledge from low-level to mid-level features for indoor/outdoor classification of images. The network integrates low-level features (color and texture) and so-called mid-level features (external knowledge about sky and grass) using a single classification engine. Mylonas et al. (2007) have also used some mid-level descriptors. Their work aims at improving both image segmentation and labeling of materials and simple objects at the same time, with obvious benefits for problems in the area of image understanding. The novelty of the proposed idea lies on blending well-established segmentation techniques with mid-level features. ARG (Attributed Relational Graphs) were used as mid-level descriptors in their approach, so that images can be described as structured sets of individual objects, thus allowing a straightforward mapping to a graph structure. We provide below process-oriented definitions of low-, high-, and mid-level descriptors. Figure 1 shows a schematic description of the situation each level of description.

Definition 1: Low-Level Descriptor

A low-level descriptor is a continuous or discrete numeric or symbolic measurement that is computed directly from the signal (e.g. image pixels), locally in a (part of a) document. Low-level descriptors (LLD) include usual color histograms, texture and shape descriptors. They qualify measurements operated directly from the signal, in a straightforward manner, involving neither external knowledge/learning process, nor global statistical analysis of other documents. For instance, the local binary pattern (LBP) operator and the Scale-Invariant Feature Transform (SIFT) feature (Lowe, 2004) are considered low-level descriptors.

Figure 1. Schematic description of the situation of mid-level descriptors

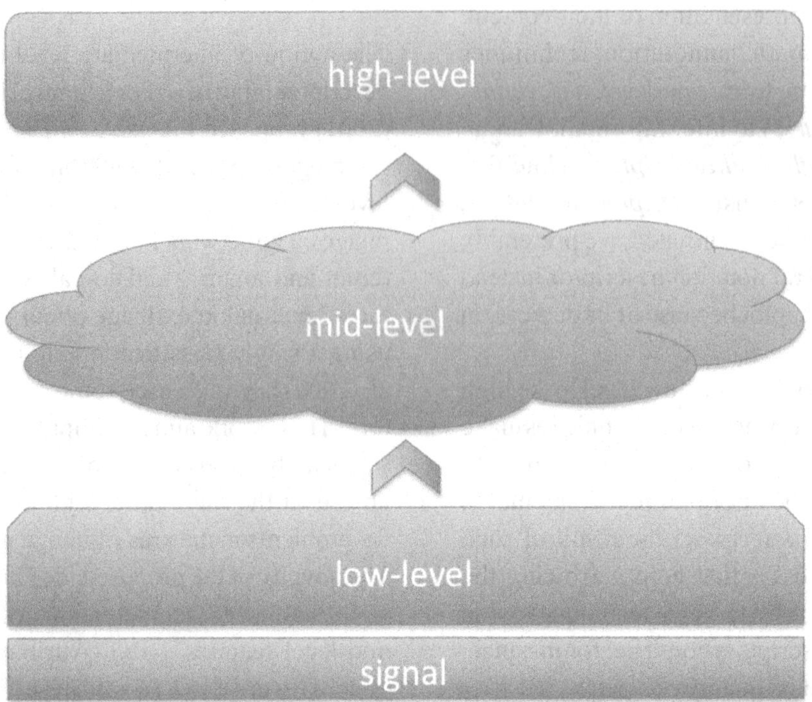

A low-level descriptor is defined to capture a certain visual property an image, either globally for the entire image or locally for a given group of pixels. The most commonly used features include those reflecting color, texture, shape, and salient/interest points in an image. In a global extraction, features are computed to capture the overall characteristics of the image. For instance, in a color layout approach, the image is divided into a small number of sub-images and the average color components (e.g., red, green, and blue intensities) are computed for every sub-image. The overall image is thus represented by a vector of color components where a particular dimension of the vector corresponds to a certain sub-image location.

Definition 2: High-Level Descriptor

A high-level descriptor is a piece of human-interpretable semantic information describing a (part of a) document. High-level descriptors (HLD) represent semantics of the document, such as a set of keywords, or a text description. They represent the ultimate goal of annotation, indexing, high-level concept detection, or more generally automatic generation of semantic descriptors.

Most of the automatic indexing methods intend to make the system learn a *correspondence model* between LLD and HLD. Once this correspondence model is learnt, the system is able to generate some HLD from a given set of LLD, that is to say, the system is able to infer semantics from descriptors directly extracted from the signal, such as a color histogram. For instance, the result of an image classifier that categorizes images between *indoor* and *outdoor* is considered a high-level descriptor. In the same way, the result of a face recognition module that outputs the name of a given face is also consider a high-level descriptor.

Between those widely agreed two levels of representation, we introduce the classification of *mid-level descriptors* (MLD) that participate in narrowing the *semantic gap*. They are intermediate descriptors built on top of LLDs, possibly after a learning process, with the finality of both facilitating the generation of HLD and enhancing their quality.

Definition 3: Mid-Level Descriptor

A mid-level descriptor is a continuous or discrete numeric or symbolic measurement obtained after a global (i.e. collection-wise) analysis of low-level descriptors, possibly by applying supervised or unsupervised learning methods on a subset of documents in the collection, and possibly involving the use of external knowledge.

Given this definition, while MLDs can serve as an input for other MLDs or for HLDs, only LLFs are connected to MLDs. Besides, an SVM image patch classifier, for instance, can be seen either as an MLD or a HLD, depending on the *type* of the output (conveying semantics or not).

A sound choice of descriptors is crucial to build a meaningful representation of visual documents from a database, dedicated to specific tasks such as annotation, object detection/recognition, or similarity matching. The proposed definition of mid-level descriptors is closely related to the notion of *modality* in a multimedia document. A modality is defined as an *application-dependent abstraction of a signal* that may serve as an input of a process in an early stage (Martinet & Satoh, 2007). A modality is characterized by its properties, such as the embedding medium, the structure, and the extraction process. Note that this definition of modality is different from the one adopted in the domain of Human-Computer Interactions, that is to say a communication channel such as the olfactory, taste, auditory, tactile and visual channels.

Figure 2 gives an example where the output of a face detector module is connected to the input of a face recognizer module. While the first module is considered a MLD taking some LLD as inputs, the second module is considered a HLD because its output conveys semantics.

After having defined the different levels of descriptors in this section, we review in the next section a number of approaches in text and visual document indexing and search that make use – explicitly or not – of mid-level descriptors. Indeed, most of the image representation techniques rely on intermediate descriptors to improve the representation.

MID-LEVEL PERSPECTIVE FOR TEXT PROCESSING AND RETRIEVAL

Historically, mid-level descriptors have been first defined for text representation. In this section, we review some text representation techniques that fall into our categorization of mid-level descriptors, namely the dimension reduction techniques for representation, the language models for text retrieval and classification, and the phrase-based representation scheme for text documents.

Dimension Reduction and Latent Topic Models as MLD for Representation

Dimension reduction techniques in document description are statistical methods that allow reducing the dimensionality by selecting most representative dimensions in a space. They have been widely used in document representation to both reduce the processing complexity in a lower dimension space, and to increase the quality of the representation by ignoring dimensions that are found either not relevant in a given data set, or redundant because highly correlated to other dimensions. Most of the dimension reduction techniques produce an intermediate representation, which is a lower dimension space where descriptors and documents are projected. Points in this space are viewed as mid-level descriptors.

Figure 2. Example of mid-level descriptors extracted from different modalities

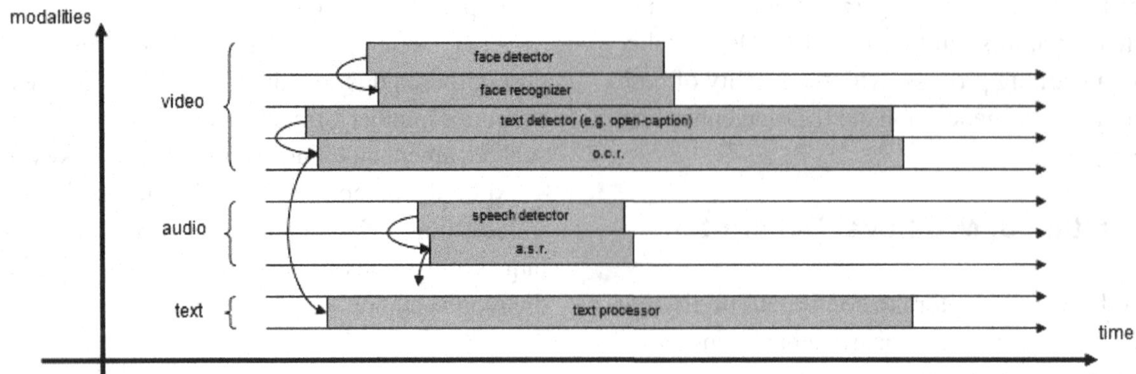

We describe below two popular dimension reduction techniques that are the Principal Component Analysis and the Latent Semantic Analysis.

Principal component analysis (PCA) involves a mathematical procedure that transforms a number of possibly correlated variables into a smaller number of uncorrelated variables called *principal components*. The first principal component accounts for as much of the variability in the data as possible, and each succeeding component accounts for as much of the remaining variability as possible.

Latent Semantic Indexing (LSI) is an indexing and retrieval method that is based on a singular value decomposition that identifies patterns in the relationships between the terms and concepts contained in an unstructured collection of text. LSI is based on the principle that words that are used in the same contexts tend to have similar meanings. A key feature of LSI is its ability to extract the conceptual content of a body of text by establishing associations between those terms that occur in similar contexts.

LSI is the application of Latent Semantic Analysis (LSA) to document indexing. LSA is usually based on a term-document matrix that describes the occurrences of terms in documents. It is a sparse matrix whose rows correspond to terms and whose columns correspond to documents. The terms are typically not stemmed because LSA can intrinsically identify the relationship between words and their stem forms. A typical example of the weighting of the elements of the matrix is *tf-idf* (term frequency–inverse document frequency): the element of the matrix is proportional to the number of times the terms appear in each document, where rare terms are up-weighted to reflect their relative importance. LSA transforms the occurrence matrix into a relation between the terms and some concepts, and a relation between those concepts and the documents. Thus the terms and documents are indirectly related through the concepts. LSI can be used to compare the documents in the concept space (data clustering, document classification). Moreover, it can be used to find similar documents across languages, after analyzing a base set of translated documents (cross language retrieval). In addition, it can play a role in translating a query of terms into the concept space, and find matching documents.

Experiments reported in text document retrieval and categorization using such statistical preprocessing steps yields representations enabling to obtain better results than using raw text (Baeza-Yates & Ribeiro-Neto, 1999). The intermediate representation schemes given by PCA and LSI fall into our categorization of MLD, in the sense that they are built from raw documents and they enable a representation that is closer to the semantic space.

Language Modeling as MLD for Classification

Language models (Ponte & Croft, 1998) have been successfully used in text retrieval. Graphical models, such as Latent Dirichlet Allocation (LDA) (Blei et al., 2003) and Correspondence LDA have been applied to the image annotation problem (Blei & Jordan, 2003). LDA is a generative probabilistic model of a corpus, and more precisely a three-level hierarchical Bayesian model. The basic idea is that documents are represented as random mixtures over latent topics, where each topic is characterized by a distribution over words. Blei & Jordan (2003) proposed a Correlation LDA, which is an extension of LDA, to relate words and images. This model assumes that a Dirichlet distribution can be used to generate the mixture of latent factors. This mixture of latent factors is then used to generate words and regions. The EM algorithm is used to estimate the parameters of this model. The experiment results shown in Blei & Jordan (2003) indicate that LDA yields a lower *perplexity* in text document representation and collaborative filtering than with a standard bag-of-word approach (a lower perplexity score indicates a better generalization performance), and also the models yields a better accuracy in document classification tasks. Here again, the intermediate representation given by the Bayesian modeling, which is built after an analysis of the document set, is classified as an MLD in the proposed classification of descriptors.

Text Phrases as MLD for Retrieval

Inspired by data mining techniques, some text processing techniques analyze text collections in order to detect words frequently occurring together, and build so-called *text phrases* for document indexing and retrieval. A text phrase is a group of words functioning as a single unit in the syntax of a sentence. According to the definition of the different levels of descriptors provided in this chapter, a visual phrase is considered a mid-level descriptor.

Association Rules in Text Processing

Association rules are popular in sales transactions analysis (Agrawal et al. 1993), especially for market basket analysis. Consider a supermarket with a large collection of items. Typical business decisions that the management of the supermarket has to make include what to put on sale, how to design coupons, how to place merchandize on shelves in order to maximize the profit. Analysis of past transaction data – using association rules – is a commonly used approach in order to improve the quality of such decisions. Questions such as "if a customer purchases product A, how likely is he to purchase product B?" and "What products will a customer buy if he buys products C and D?" are answered by association finding algorithms.

Discovering Phrases by Mining Association Rules Over Words

Given a set of documents D, the problem of mining association rules is to discover all rules that have support and confidence greater than some pre-defined minimum support and minimum confidence. Although a number of algorithms are proposed improving various aspects of association rule mining, A priori by Agrawal et al. (1994) remains the most commonly used algorithm. Haddad et al. (2000) have applied association rules to text analysis. Their work aims at extracting the terminology from a text corpus by using patterns applied after a morphological analysis. The terminology is structured with automatically extracted dependencies relations. This extracted terminology enables a more precise description of the documents.

Association rules have been used subsequently for discovering relevant patterns in several types of data, namely to extract phrases from text. The use of phrases has been successfully applied to document indexing, clustering and retrieval (Jing et al.1994, Hammouda et al. 2004). An approach called Phrase Finder is proposed to construct collection-dependent association thesauri automatically using large full text document collections. The association thesaurus can be accessed through natural language queries in INQUERY, an information retrieval system based on the probabilistic inference network. The main idea is to build this description with phrases after finding some statistical associations between individual words in the collection.

TEXT PROCESSING TECHNIQUES ADAPTED TO IMAGE REPRESENTATION

There are theoretical similarities between natural languages and visual language. Natural languages consist of words, and visual language consists of visual words. In natural languages, there are grammars, which restricts the words distribution and order. In an image, when divided into patches, there exist some constraints about how the patches are combined together to form meaningful objects. Indeed, a random combination of patches or pixels does not construct a meaningful image. This section starts by developing an analogy between text and image, and then demonstrates how image annotation can benefit from text processing techniques, in the form of building mid-level descriptors.

Analogy Between Text and Image Documents

Text retrieval systems generally employ a number of standard steps in the processes of indexing and searching a text collection (Baeza-Yates & Ribeiro-Neto, 1999). The text documents are first parsed into words. Second, the words are represented by their stems: for example "walk", "walking" and "walks" would be represented by the stem "walk". Third, a stop list is used to filter very common words out, such as "the" and "an", which occur in most documents and are therefore not discriminating for a particular document. In the popular Vector Space Model, for instance, a vector represents each document, with components given namely by the frequency of occurrence of the words in the document. The search tack is performed by comparing the query vector to the document vectors, and by returning the most similar documents, i.e. the documents with the closest vectors, as measured by angles.

Visual Words in Images

The analogy with visual documents considers that an image is composed of *visual words* with a given topology. A visual word is a local segment in an image, defined either by a region (image patch or blob) or by a reference point together with its neighborhood. Since multimedia documents usually have a spatial-temporal structure, they can be segmented space-wise and time-wise in fundamental units (Cees et al. 2005), in order to represent a piece of information within a window. For instance, a video stream can be segmented temporally, by selecting portions of the video stream between consecutive key-frames. The key-frames can be further segmented spatially by selecting regions, visterms (Jeon et al. 2004, Quelhas et al. 2005, Quelhas et al. 2007), SIFT-bags (Zhou et al. 2008) or blobs (Carson et al. 1999) ideally corresponding to real world objects. An audio stream can be partitioned into small segments of a given duration, from which features such as energy, tone, pitch, or fundamental frequency can be extracted. The text stream arising from OCR/ASR process can also be segmented into characters, words, or syntagms (sequence of words in a particular syntactic relationship to one another).

Figure 3. Analogy between image and text document in semantic granularity (from Zheng et al. 2006)

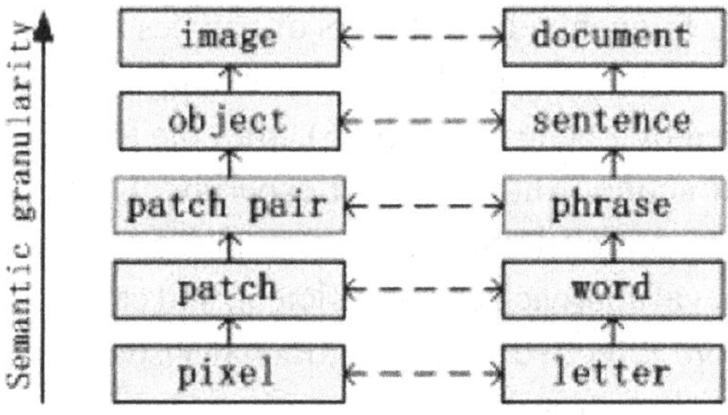

The space-time segmentation process of a multimedia stream results in elementary perceptual representations from each modality such as key-frame regions, audio samples, or character strings. These individual objects are named *perceptual objects*, as opposed to conceptual objects (Martinet & Satoh 2007), which cannot be derived directly from the data since an interpretation is necessary. For images, perceptual objects are assimilated to visual words.

Images are particular arrangements of different pixels in a 2D space, while text documents are particular arrangements of different letters in 1D space. Figure 3 shows the possible semantic granularities of an image and a text document, and analogies between their constituent elements. For Zheng et al. (2006), pixels are equated to letters, patches to words, patch pairs to phrases, objects to sentences.

While a *letter* is the smallest unit in a text document, a pixel (considered a *visual letter*) is the smallest unit of the visual document. A *visual word* in an image is viewed as set of visual letters: it can be a square patch, or a blob extracted by a segmentation algorithm. Considering the variance of pixels within a local patch, the number of different patches is huge even if the patch size is small. Therefore, local patches are to be properly quantized into a limited number of visual words, typically via clustering, in order to form a visual vocabulary. This step can be assimilated to the stemming part of text processing.

Spatial Relations in 2D Data

One fundamental difference between text and image is that while a text is 1D linear sequence of letters, an image is a 2D matrix of pixel. The word's order and distance in the text can be taken into account to refine the representation. In the same way, taking into account the distance between visual words and their topology can greatly enhance the quality of the representation.

However, most approaches only utilize the occurrence of image features in classification, while ignoring the spatial relation between them, which might provide additional information to help image classification. Carneiro & Jepson (2004) have used semi-local spatial constraints to which allow a sound grouping of feature matches, therefore successfully reducing the number of false positives in similarity matching.

Visual Language Models as MLD for Image Indexing

Sivic et al. (2005), Wang et al. (2006), and Bosch et al. (2007) have used pLSA in the context of images, applied to scene classification. These techniques are used to automatically discover image categories in a collection, by computing latent concepts in images from the co-occurrences of visual words in the collection. Wu et al. (2007) also proposed a visual language modeling method for content-based image classification. This method proposes to build visual language models for image classification, which capture both co-occurrence and spatial proximity of local image features. This approach first segments images into patches, then maps each patch into a visual word. It also assumes that each visual word is only conditionally dependent on its neighbors. Based on a collection of training images for a given category, the spatial correlation of visual words is modeled as the conditional probability by using statistical language modeling algorithms. Given a novel image, its label is determined by estimating its likelihood given a category. Authors have compared their *trigram* approach (one visual word is conditionally dependant on two of his neighbors, the whole forming a word triple) with pLSA and LDA on a classification task with Caltech and Corel datasets, and found an increase of 39% in accuracy with pLSA, and an increase of 28% in accuracy compared with LDA.

Other approaches include Tirilly et al. (2008), who proposed a language modeling approach for image categorization. Their approach is based on probabilistic Latent Semantic Analysis (pLSA) – as well as on geometric properties of the keypoints – to eliminate *useless* visual words. Besides, they integrate spatial relations between visual words to overcome the problem of loosing the spatial information of visual words.

Visual Phrases as MLD for Image Representation and Retrieval

The analysis of visual words occurrences and configurations allows detecting frequently occurring patterns. Zheng et al. (2006) made the analogy between image retrieval and text retrieval, and proposed a visual phrase-based approach to retrieve images containing desired objects. Visual phrases are defined as pairs of adjacent local image patches, and are constructed using data mining techniques. They provide methods for constructing visual phrases from images and for encoding the visual phrases for indexing and retrieval purposes.

In this approach, SIFT descriptors are used to extract and describe salient local patches in each image and each local patch is represented by a 128-dimenstional feature vector. Different local patches are vector quantized into visual words using a clustering algorithm. Clustering different local image patches can find its counterpart in text retrieval, where each word is transformed using *case folding* and *stemming* techniques before being indexed, for the purpose of effective and efficient retrieval. Once the visual words are defined, visual phrases are extracted by detecting frequent adjacent pairs of patches across the collection. Figure 4 shows an example of image used by Zheng et al. (2006), after the local patch extraction. Authors report experiments showing that demonstrate that visual phrase-based retrieval approach can be efficient, and can be 20% more effective than a traditional visual bag-of-words approach.

Adaptation of Association Rules to Extract Visual Phrases

Martinet & Satoh (2007) share the same objective as Zheng et al. (2006) of designing a higher level of description for representing documents. However, while Zheng et al. (2006) consider adjacent pairs of patches, the approach of Martinet & Satoh (2007) is more general in two ways. First, they consider not only adjacent words, but also all the words co-occurring in the same *context*. A context is defined based on the notion of *space-time windows* in multimedia documents, which includes a temporal dimension, as shown Figure 5. Second, the method they proposed handles sets of items, which is more general than just pairs. In that way, they can represent the relations between visual words in a more general way.

They adapt the definition of association rules to the context of perceptual objects, for merging strongly associated objects, in order to get a more compact representation of the data. The building of the phrase representation is done by iteratively *merging* objects pairs corresponding to frequently occurring patterns, that is to say objects that have been discovered involved in strong association rules. A rule is evaluated as strong, if its confidence exceeds a *confidence threshold* and its support exceeds a *support threshold* (see Figure 5).

Figure 4. An example of image after local patch extraction by SIFT. The circles denote the extracted local patches (from Zheng et al. 2006).

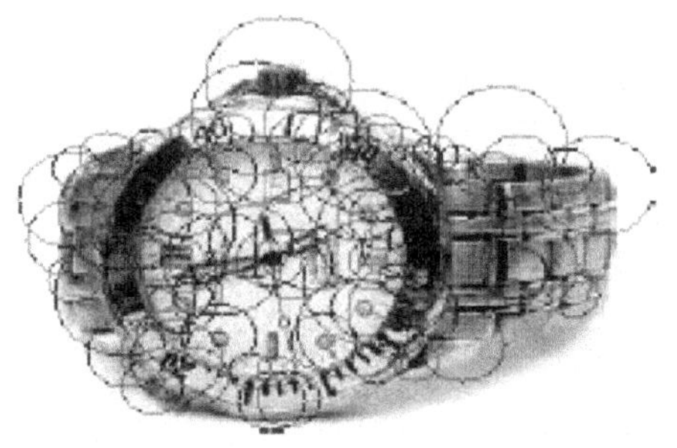

The basis behind this merging process lies in the assumption that frequently occurring patterns of objects inside a space-time window are likely to represent parts of higher-level conceptual objects. Indeed, neighboring image objects frequently occurring in a given configuration are likely to belong to the same physical object, and consequently they are likely to have the same conceptual interpretation. By merging objects involved in strong rules, the obtained representation is likely to be both more compact and more meaningful regarding the data set to be represented. Experiments reported by Martinet & Satoh (2007) show that the new representation space of visual phrases enables a better separation of documents, that is to say that index terms in the new space have a higher discriminative power, and consequently is likely to yield a more precise search.

Association Rules Applied to Spatial Databases

With a huge amount of spatial data collected by satellite telemetry systems, remote-sensing systems, regional sales systems and other data collection tools, it is a crucial to develop tools for discovery of interesting knowledge from large spatial databases.

Figure 5. Example of representation of two rules. The upper representation shows a high confidence rule, and the lower representation shows a lower confidence rule. Only the support of Y is changed between the two cases (from Martinet & Satoh, 2007).

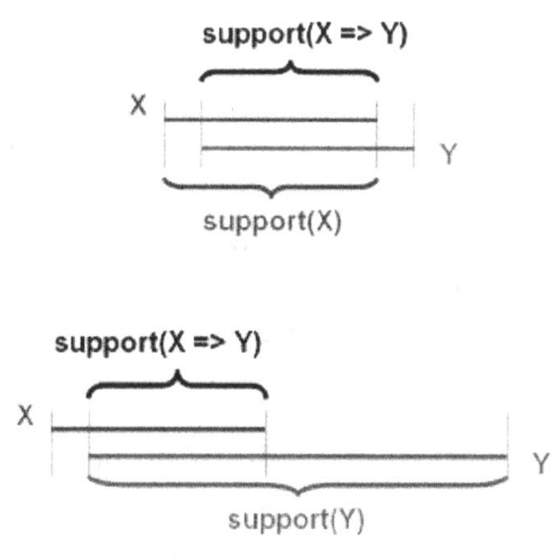

A spatial database is a database that is optimized to store and query data related to objects in space, including points, lines and polygons. While typical databases can understand various numeric and character types of data, additional functionality needs to be added for databases to process spatial data types. These are typically called *geometry* or *feature*. A spatial association rule is a rule indicating certain association relationships among a set of spatial and possibly non-spatial predicates, indicating that the patterns in the rule have relatively frequent occurrences in the database and strong implication relationships. For example, a rule like "*most big cities in Canada are close to the Canada-U.S. border*" is a spatial association rule. Reported works show that useful and interesting association rules can be discovered efficiently in large spatial databases. With the rapid progress of research into data mining and data warehousing in recent years, many data mining and data warehousing systems have been developed for mining knowledge in relational databases and data warehouses. Spatial data mining is a subfield of data mining that deals with the extraction of

Figure 6. Example of multimedia stream containing two media (or modalities), and objects are represented with discovered relations. The relations can be possibly between objects inside a modality (e.g. text-text) or across modalities (text-image) (from Martinet & Satoh, 2007).

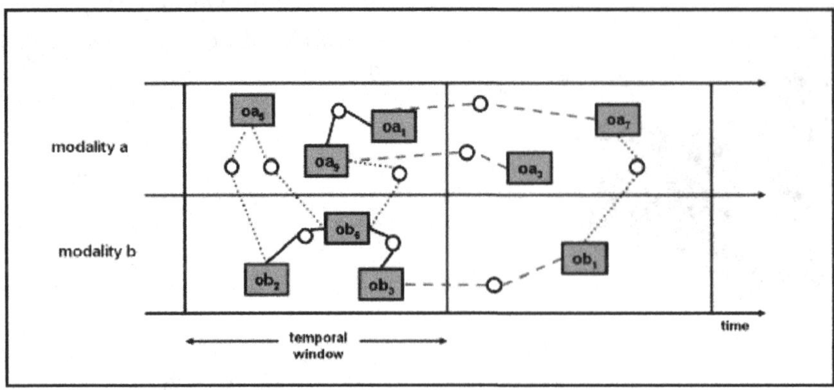

implicit knowledge, spatial relationships, or other interesting patterns not explicitly stored in spatial databases (Han. et al., 1997, Zeitouni, 2002).

OTHER EXAMPLE OF MLD: IMAGE AND VIDEO EPITOMES

A natural image can take a significant amount of resources while processed by a modern computer, although it might appear straightforward to human at the first glance. The reason is that an image usually contains much redundant information which can be easily filtered out by a human brain, but it turns out to be hard for a computer. Therefore, it is useful to have a condensed version of the image, or a summary of a sequence of highly correlated images. One would like the representation to take as few resources as possible, while preserving information sufficient for achieving the goals of indexing, search and display. Furthermore, this representation is preferably to be visually informative.

Color histograms and templates are two extremes in describing an image. The first one only summarizes the color information, and loses the spatial arrangement of images. There have been great efforts to incorporate spatial information into the color histogram. The color coherence method proved to be successful in applications such as image indexing and retrieval. But they are not visualized representations. Methods based on templates and basis functions do maintain the geometrical properties of an image, but they suffer from large deformations in shape. They are too rigid to tolerate variations. In order to jointly analyze and synthesize data, patch-based probability models are introduced by Jojic et al. (2003). These models, called "epitomes", compile patches drawn from input images into a condensed image. In image processing, an epitome is a condensed digital representation of the essential statistical properties of ordered datasets, such as matrices representing images, audio signals, videos, or genetic sequences.

Although much smaller than the original data, the epitome contains many of the smaller overlapping parts of the data with much less repetition and with some level of generalization. The first use of epitomic analysis was performed on image textures and was used for image parsing. In this sense an image epitome is a condensed intermediate representation (that is to say a MLD) of the original image, statistically built from the patches. It has been successfully used for image compression, indexing and search. The epitome

Figure 7. Video epitomes training (from Cheung et al. 2007)

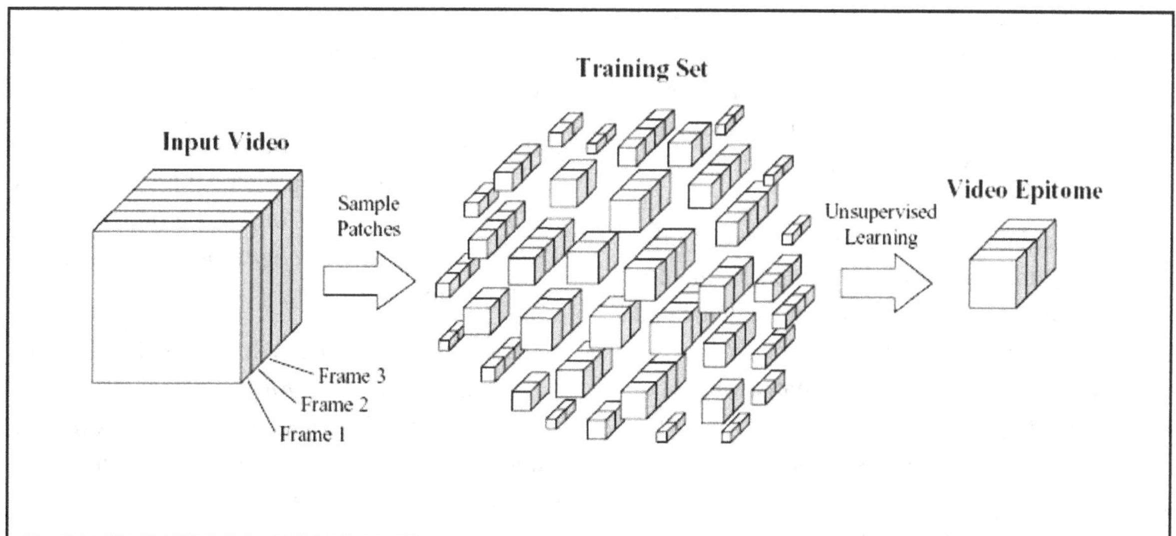

model has also been applied to videos. Filling in missing parts of a video, removing objects from a scene and performing video super-resolution are examples of tasks in which the video epitome has proven useful. Figure 7 outlines the procedure used to learn a video epitome as introduced by Cheung et al. (2007). Viewing the input video as a 3D space-time volume, a large number of 3D training patches are drawn from the video. The learning algorithm is used to compile these patches into an "epitome" – a video that is smaller in both space and time, but contains many of the spatial and temporal patterns in the original input video.

They derive the epitome learning algorithm by specifying a generative model, which explains how the input video can be generated from the epitome (in the opposite direction shown in the figure). The advantages of specifying a generative model is that the model is more adaptive than a non-generative technique, and it can be used as a sub-component in other systems. Here is introduced a 3D model of video similar to the 2D epitome model described in Jojic et al. (2003).

CONCLUSION AND FUTURE RESEARCH DIRECTIONS

This chapter proposes a classification of descriptors, from low-level descriptors to high-level descriptors, introducing the notion of *mid-level descriptors* for image representation. A mid-level descriptor is described as an intermediate representation between low-level descriptors (derived from the signal) and high-level descriptors (conveying semantics associated to the image). Mid-level descriptors are built for the purpose of yielding a finer representation for a particular set of documents. We have described a number of image representation techniques from a mid-level description perspective.

The research domain of automatic image annotation and search from low-level descriptors analysis has considerably evolved in the last 15 years, since QBIC (Flickner et al. 1995), one of the first such systems was released. Since then, this domain has reached a level of maturity where only small improvements are brought in new models and systems. Most of the approaches described in this chapter are based on visual words, which constitute a major step in image annotation.

This representation opens the way to massively apply text processing and language modeling techniques to image processing.

We believe that further significant improvement in general image search and annotation in the future can be only reached by the use of external sources of knowledge (such as context, or ontological descriptions), or by restricting the application domain. One way to restrict the application domain is to learn and build dedicated and meaningful representation schemes for a given database, which require complex statistical global analyses of the data.

The question will then arise of how general this methodology can be. That is to say, researchers could for instance estimate for a database the gain in representation quality of using a representation scheme built with another database. Designing such general approaches a challenge for the next step in multimedia annotation and retrieval.

REFERENCES

Agrawal, R., Imielinski, T., & Swami, A. (1993). Mining association rules between sets of items in large databases. In *Proceedings of the International Conference on Management of Data* (pp. 207–216). ACM Press.

Agrawal, R., & Srikant, R. (1994). Fast algorithms for mining association rules. In *Proceedings of International Conference on Very Large Data Bases* (pp. 487-499). VLDB.

Baeza-Yates, R., & Ribeiro-Neto, B. (1999). *Modern information retrieval*. ACM Press.

Blei, D. M., & Jordan, M. I. (2003). Modeling annotated data. In *Proceedings of the 26th Annual International Conference on Research and Development in Information Retrieval* (pp. 127-134). SIGIR '03. ACM Press.

Blei, D. M., Ng, A. Y., & Jordan, M. I. (2003). Latent dirichlet allocation. *Journal of Machine Learning Research, 3*, 993–1022.

Bosch, A., Zisserman, A., & Munoz, X. (2006). Scene classification via pLSA. In *Proceedings of European Conference on Computer Vision* (pp. 517-530).

Carneiro, G., & Jepson, A. (2004). Flexible spatial models for grouping local image features In *Proceedings of the Conference on Computer Vision and Pattern Recognition* (pp. 747-754). IEEE Computer Society.

Carson, C., Thomas, M., Belongie, S., Hellerstein, J., & Malik, J. (1999). *Blobworld: A system for region-based image indexing and retrieval*. In Third International Conference on Visual Information Systems. Springer.

Cees, G., Snoek, M., & Worring, M. (2005). Multimodal video indexing: A review of the state-of-the-art. *Multimedia Tools and Applications, 25*(1), 5–35. doi:10.1023/B:MTAP.0000046380.27575.a5

Cheung, V., Frey, B. J., & Jojic, N. (2005). Video epitomes. In [Los Alamitos, CA: IEEE Computer Society.]. *Proceedings of the Conference on Computer Vision and Pattern Recognition, 1*, 42–49.

Flickner, M., Sawhney, H., Niblack, W., Ashley, J., Huang, Q., & Dom, B. (1995). Query by image and video content: The QBIC system. *IEEE Computer. Special Issue on Content Based Retrieval, 28*(9), 23–32.

Haddad, H., Chevallet, J.-P., & Bruandet, M.-F. (2000). *Relations between terms discovered by association rules*. In 4th European Conference on Principles and Practices of Knowledge Discovery in Databases PKDD'2000, Workshop on Machine Learning and Textual Information Access.

Hammouda, K. M., & Kamel, M. S. (2004). Efficient phrase-based document indexing for web document clustering. In *IEEE Trans. on Knowledge and Data Engineering* (pp. 1279–1296). IEEE Computer Society.

Han, J., Koperski, K., & Stefanovic, N. (1997). GeoMiner: A system prototype for spatial data mining. In *Proceedings of International Conference on Management of Data* (pp. 553–556). ACM SIGMOD'97, ACM Press.

Jeon, J., & Manmatha, R. (2004). Using maximum entropy for automatic image annotation. In *Proceedings of the Third International Conference Image and Video Retrieval* (pp. 24-32). CIVR. Springer.

Jing, Y., & Croft, B. W. (1994). An association thesaurus for information retrieval. In *Proceedings of RIAO-94, 4th International Conference Recherche d'Information Assistee par Ordinateur* (pp. 146-160). New York, US.

Jojic, N., Frey, B. J., & Kannan, A. (2003). Epitomic analysis of appearance and shape. In *Proceedings of the Conference on Computer Vision and Pattern Recognition*. IEEE Computer Society.

Lowe, D. (2004). Distinctive image features from scale-invariant keypoints. *International Journal of Computer Vision, 60*(2), 91–110. doi:10.1023/B:VISI.0000029664.99615.94

Luo, J., & Savakis, A. (2001). Indoor versus outdoor classification of consumer photographs using low-level and semantic features. In *Proceedings of International Conference ion Image Processing,* vol. 2, (pp. 745–748). ICIP'01. IEEE Computer Society.

Martinet, J., & Satoh, S. (2007). *A study of intra-modal association rules for visual modality representation.* In International Workshop on Content-Based Multimedia Indexing, (pp. 344–350). CBMI. IEEE Computer Society.

Mylonas, P., Spyrou, E., & Avrithis, Y. (2007). High-level concept detection based on mid-level semantic information and contextual adaptation. In *Proceedings of the Second International Workshop on Semantic Media Adaptation and Personalization* (SMAP), (pp. 193-198). Washington, DC: IEEE Computer Society.

Ponte, J., & Croft, W. B. (1998). A language modeling approach to information retrieval. In *Proceedings of the 21st Annual International ACM SIGIR Conference on Research and Development in Information Retrieval* (pp. 275-281). SIGIR'98. ACM Press.

Quelhas, P., Monay, F., Odobez, J.-M., Gatica-Perez, D., & Tuytelaars, T. (2007). A thousand words in a scene. [IEEE Computer Society.]. *Transactions on Pattern Analysis and Machine Intelligence, 29*(9), 1575–1589. doi:10.1109/TPAMI.2007.1155

Quelhas, P., Monay, F., Odobez, J. M., Gatica-Perez, D., Tuytelaars, T., & Van Gool, L. (2005). Modeling scenes with local descriptors and latent aspects. *In Proceedings of the Tenth IEEE International Conference on Computer Vision.* IEEE Computer Society.

Sivic, J., Russell, B. C., Efros, A. A., Zisserman, A., & Freeman, W. T. (2005). Discovering object categories in image collections. In *Proceedings of the International Conference on Computer Vision.* (pp. 370-377). ICCV. IEEE Computer Society.

Smeulders, A. W. M., Worring, M., Santini, S., Gupta, A., & Jain, R. (2000). Content-based image retrieval at the end of early years. *IEEE Trans. on PAMI,* 1349-1380.

Tirilly, P., Claveau, V., & Gros, P. (2008). Language modeling for bag-of-visual words image categorization. In *Proc. Int. Conf. on Content-based Image and Video Retrieval.*

Wang, B., Li, L., Li, M., & Ma, W.-Y. (2006). Large-scale duplicate detection for Web image search. In *Proceedings of International Conference on Multimedia and Expo* (pp. 353-356). IEEE Computer Society.

Wu, L., Li, M., Li, Z., Ma, W., & Yu, N. (2007). Visual language modeling for image classification. In *Proceedings of the International Workshop on Workshop on Multimedia Information Retrieval* (pp. 115-124). MIR '07. ACM Press.

Zeitouni, K. (2002). *A survey of spatial data mining methods databases and statistics point of views*. Hershey, PA: IRM Press.

Zheng, Q. F., Wang, W. Q., & Gao, W. (2006). Effective and efficient object-based image retrieval using visual phrases. In *Proceedings of the 14th Annual ACM International Conference on Multimedia* (pp. 77-80). ACM Press.

Zhou, X., Zhuang, X., Yan, S., Chang, S. F., Johnson, M. H., & Huang, T. S. (2008). SIFT-bag kernel for video event analysis. In *Proceeding of the 16th ACM International Conference on Multimedia*, (pp. 229-238). MM '08. ACM Press.

ADDITIONALREADING SECTION

Datta, R., Joshi, D., Li, J., & Wang, J. Z. (2008). Image Retrieval: Ideas, Influences, and Trends of the New Age. *ACM Computing Surveys*, *40*, 1–60. doi:10.1145/1348246.1348248

Lafon, S., & Lee, A. B. (2006). Diffusion Maps and Coarse-Graining: A Unified Framework for Dimensionality Reduction, Graph Partitioning, and Data Set Parameterization. *IEEE Transactions on Pattern Analysis and Machine Intelligence*, *28*(9), 1393–1403. doi:10.1109/TPAMI.2006.184

Smeulders, A.W.M., Worring, M., Santini, S., Gupta, A., & Jain, R. (2000). Content-based image retrieval at the end of early years. *IEEE Trans. on PAMI*, 1349-1380.

Zhang, J., Marszałek, M., Lazebnik, S., & Schmid, C. (2007). Local Features and Kernels for Classification of Texture and Object Categories: A Comprehensive Study. *International Journal of Computer Vision*, *73*(2), 213–238. doi:10.1007/s11263-006-9794-4

KEY TERMS AND DEFINITIONS

Association Rule: a rule required to satisfy a user-specified minimum support and a user-specified minimum confidence at the same time.

Clustering: The assignment of a set of observations into subsets (called clusters) so that observations in the same cluster are similar in some sense. Clustering is a method of unsupervised learning, and a common technique for statistical data analysis.

High-Level Descriptor: A high-level descriptor is a piece of human-interpretable semantic information describing a (part of a) document. High-level descriptors (HLD) represent semantics of the document, such as a set of keywords, or a text description.

Low-Level Descriptor: A low-level descriptor is a continuous or discrete numeric or symbolic measurement, which is computed directly from the signal (e.g. image pixels), locally in a (part of a) document.

LSI: Latent Semantic Indexing is an indexing and retrieval method that uses a mathematical technique called singular value decomposition to identify patterns in the relationships between the terms and concepts contained in an unstructured collection of text.

Mid-Level Descriptor: A mid-level descriptor is a continuous or discrete numeric or symbolic measurement obtained after a global (i.e. collection-wise) analysis of low-level descriptors, possibly by applying supervised or unsupervised learning methods on a subset of documents in the collection, and possibly involving the use of external knowledge.

Modality: application-dependent abstraction of a signal that may serve as an input of a process in an early stage.

Visual Word: An analogy can then be made between the words of a text and the regions of an image, and between phrases and so.

Chapter 4
An Image Retrieval Model Combining Ontology and Probabilistic Ranking

Lisa Fan
University of Regina, Canada

Botang Li
University of Regina, Canada

ABSTRACT

The demand for image retrieval and browsing online is growing dramatically. There are hundreds of millions of images available on the current World Wide Web. For multimedia documents, the typical keyword-based retrieval methods assume that the user has an exact goal in mind in searching a set of images whereas users normally do not know what they want, or the user faces a repository of images whose domain is less known and content is semantically complicated. In these cases it is difficult to decide what keywords to use for the query. In this chapter, we propose a user-centered image retrieval method based on the current Web, keyword-based annotation structure, and combining ontology guided knowledge representation and probabilistic ranking. A Web application for image retrieval using the proposed approach has been implemented. The model provides a recommendation subsystem to support and assist the user modifying the queries and reducing the user's cognitive load with the searching space. Experimental results show that the image retrieval recall and precision rates are increased and therefore demonstrate the effectiveness of the model.

DOI: 10.4018/978-1-61350-126-9.ch004

INTRODUCTION

With the development of the Internet and database techniques, Information Retrieval (IR) has become very popular (Ricardo, B.Y. & Berthier, R.N., 1999). As a powerful form of delivering information, multimedia data are frequently used in many applications. Techniques for effectively dealing with multimedia databases are useful and in demand. During the past decade, online image retrieval has become one of the most popular topics on the Internet. The number of images available in online repositories is growing dramatically. For example, Flickr.com is hosting more than 50 million member-submitted images on their website (Terdiman, D., 2009), and Google claims that they have indexed more than 880 millions images since 2004 (Google, 2009). It is expected that the number of images found in personal collections, publications and archives will continue to grow at an exponential rate. Given the recent explosion of interest in social networking, largely driven by Myspace, Facebook and YouTube, one can expect to see image searching playing a very important role in the future. As a result, the demand for efficient and effective image retrieval, searching, and browsing methods will also increase significantly. Demand will come from users in various domains, including medicine, publishing, architecture, crime prevention, and fashion.

Image retrieval is a human centered task. Images are created by people and are ultimately retrieved and used by people for human related activities. The typical method of image retrieval using mostly by the industry is to create a keyword-based query interface above the media indexing database (Agosti & Smeaton, 1996). There are two major problems in keyword-based image retrieval. The first one is the retrieval quality problem from the search result. The keyword annotation of image documents has low capability to analyze semantic relations among keywords, such as synonym, homonym and antonym. Taking the topics of images as an example, it is nearly impossible to include all the synonyms of the topic keywords in the annotation for every image. The reality is that if the images are annotated with keywords having same meanings with users input but in different terms, those images are not able to be retrieved by the keyword-based retrieval system. The second problem is that keyword-based search methods always assume that users have the exact searching goal in their minds (Hyvonen, Saarela & Viljanen, 2003). However, in the real world application, the case is that users normally do not know what they want. Most of them only hold a general interest to explore the images, and have a vague knowledge about the domain topic. As a result, a recommendation or a support subsystem, helping users to modify their queries, is needed.

Semantic Web technologies have been expected to improve the quality of information retrieval on the Web (Berners-Lee, Hendler & Lassila, 2001) & (Berners-Lee). In this paper, we proposed a hybrid model which is using a Web Ontology-based reasoning component and combining Bayesian Network model to improve the quality of image retrieval. Our proposed method returns more query keywords as recommendations which are semantically related to the user input keywords so that it can assist the users to explore more relevant images.

RELATED WORK

Image Retrieval is a large and active research area of computer and information science. A summary review of the literature shows an exceptionally active community of researchers in this area. Smeulders et al. reviewed more than 200 research papers prior to 2000 (Smeulders, Worring, Santini, Gupta & Jain, 2000). Rui et al. have summarized more than 100 research papers (Rui, Huang & Chang, 1999). Recently, Datta et al. have surveyed about 300 papers, mostly published between 2000 and 2007 (Datta, Joshi, Li & Wang, 2008).

Keyword-Based and Content-Based Image Retrieval

Traditionally, there are two main research approaches in the area of image retrieval: text based and content based. Text-based image retrieval can be traced back to the late 1970s. In such systems, images are either annotated with text, or text surrounding the images is analyzed to produce a set of keywords referring to the image. The images can be retrieved by matching text-based queries with the keywords. This approach is to create a set of keywords as metadata to describe the images and then associate it to the image document. As a result, it is also called keyword annotation. Based on the keyword annotations, the system can apply keyword-based information retrieval techniques to search the images (Long, Zhang & Feng, 2003). Searchers try to analyze the text around image to improve the Web Image retrieval. However, huge amount of the images on Web, such as personal uploaded photo gallery, still lack the adequate text description. Two disadvantages to this approach are that a considerable level of human labor is required for manual annotation and annotation tends to be inaccurate due to the subjectivity of human perception (Sethi & Coman, 2001). That is, different people may perceive the same image content differently. The perception subjectivity and annotation impreciseness may cause unrecoverable mismatches later in the retrieval processes.

In order to overcome the disadvantages of text-based retrieval, content-based image retrieval (CBIR) was introduced. It is an important alternative and complement to traditional text-based image searching and can greatly enhance the accuracy of the information returned. Most proposed CBIR techniques automatically extract low-level features (i.e., color, texture, shapes of objects and special layout) to measure the similarities among images by comparing the feature differences (Shi, Xu & Han, 2007). However, an obvious semantic gap exists between what user-queries represent based on the low-level image features and what the users think. To bridge this semantic gap, researchers have investigated techniques that retain some degree of human intervention either during input or search, thereby utilizing human semantics, knowledge, and recognition ability effectively for semantic retrieval. Among various techniques in narrowing the semantic gap, a relevance feedback mechanism has been identified as an especially helpful tool to provide a significant performance boost in CBIR systems (Rui, Huang, Ortega & Mehrotra, 1998). There are two types of limitations with the current content-based methods that employ user feedback. Firstly, since our understanding of human vision is limited, we may not have a correct set of image features to begin with. Therefore, perception models based on those features will not be adequate to specify user feedback. Secondly, selecting several images several times at each session will not provide enough data to train a complex model. Attempts (Aslandogan et al, 1997), (Hunter, 2001), (Liu, Chia & Chan, 2004) also have been made to validate ontology in practice to bridge the semantic gap. The need of a machine understandable representation of multimedia content descriptions is addressed. In (Liu, Chia & Chan, 2004), an image retrieval web service is set up. The essential part is a three level ontology which associates the image content and human understandable concept. But all the concepts are still built from low level. The current techniques for reducing the semantic gap have been reviewed by Liu et al. (Liu, Zhang, Lu & Ma, 2007).

A number of efficient content-based image retrieval systems have been presented in the last few years. For example, a database perspective of image annotation and retrieval has been studied by Carneiro, G. & Vasconcelos, N. (2005). (Garneriro & Vasconcelos, 2005); a statistical approach of automatic linguistic indexing model was presented by Li, J. & Wang, J. Z. (2003). (Li & Wang, 2003); a machine learning approach is applied to study ancient art was presented by Li, J. & Wang, J. (2004). (Li & Wang, 2004). However, in the scenarios of the online Web image retrieval, content-based approach is still hard to meet the requirements of immediate response of retrieval result to users. Features input, such as color, shape and texture, is still not suitable and realistic for most of the online users. Furthermore, it is difficult for the systems to deal with the features such as human emotions and perceptions of the images. There is a trend toward making use of both the textual information obtained from the Web and the visual content of images. Our research on image retrieval is consistent with this research direction. In our study, we realized that both keyword-based and content-based approach is hard to solve the semantic problem. A solution is to incorporate the Ontology technology into image retrieval.

Ontology-Based Image Retrieval

With the advent of Semantic Web technology, information retrieval is able to widely be benefited from this ambitious technology which is being expected as the next generation of Internet. When searching information on the Web, it is very common that there are numerous different terms representing the same meaning of certain online resources. A solution to this problem is to provide a third part component of information collection, Ontology (Davies, Fensel & Harmelen, 2003). Ontology is playing a key role as the core element of knowledge representation on the Semantic Web for machine understanding. Basically, Ontology consists of vocabularies and their relations to describe the existing things around us in the world. Some effort has been made for image retrieval using Semantic Web techniques, for example the case study of a view-based image search method using semantic annotation and retrieval from Hyvonen, E., Saarela, S., & Viljanen, K. (2003). Nevertheless, applying semantic annotation to the existing image resources will encounter the same difficulty with realizing the whole Semantic Web vision. Benjamins has pointed out that too little semantic content are available on the current Web, and shifting the current keyword annotation of the current Web content onto semantic annotation is also a big challenge (Kant & Mamas, 2005). In order to discover an approach widely available for the existing content, our study is focusing on utilizing Ontology techniques and improving the reusability of the keyword annotation.

A successful image retrieval method should have a recommendation system to assist users to find what they actually need. To compute the relevance of the recommendations, however, the logic-based Ontology technology lacks the capability to support plausible reasoning (Costa, Laskey & Laskey, 2005) & (Benjamins et al, 2002). Because the propositions are either true or false, the kind of classical tradition of monotonic deductive reasoning can only answer the "Yes" or "No" questions. For instance, if a user makes a query with the keyword "Car," but the system only contains the index of the documents with the keywords "Vehicle" and "Honda Civic". By looking up into the Ontology, the machine is able to understand that the concept "Car" is a subclass of the concept "Vehicle," and "Honda Civic" is an instance of the class "Car". Which is closer to the user's query? From the pure logic-based approach, it can hardly answer the question without the totally matched result. Therefore, a method combining Ontology and Bayesian Network technologies to support uncertain reasoning for the retrieval system is proposed.

Bayesian Network

Bayesian Network (BN) has become a very popular topic of uncertain reasoning in the artificial intelligent community, and it has been applied to various research areas, such as medical diagnosis program, knowledge expert support system, classification and information retrieval etc. (Pearl, 1998). Inspired by the BN model for information retrieval from Ribeiro-Neto, B., Silva, I., & Muntz, R. (2000), we built up a BN model for computing the relevance ranking of the neighbours of the input concept in the Ontology graph.

In the latest URSW05 workshop, some researchers preferred adding probabilistic extension into Ontology to enable the uncertain reasoning capability within Ontology, for instance the extension to OWL for representing particular Bayesian Network model (Ding & Peng, 2004). Web Ontology is designed for representing and sharing knowledge in a distributed environment through Internet but uncertain reasoning models are usually application-independent. As a result, our proposed method prefers running the BN inference after the reasoning from Ontology. In this model, the Ontology is serving as the source providing extend metadata for the BN Computation.

THE ONTOLOGY GUIDED IMAGE RETRIEVAL MODEL

In general, the process of our approach for image retrieval can be divided into three phases. *Phase one* is that once the system acquires the input keyword *k* from the user, it will try to look for the target images, which are annotated with the same keywords. If the target images record is found from the database, it will return the hits of those images. Otherwise, it requests to proceed for the second retrieval step, sending the keywords set to the Ontology reasoner.

In *phase two*, the Ontology reasoner is trying to find all the neighboring information of the input keyword. The keyword *k* is retrieved inside the Ontology, by the Ontology reasoner; which relies on the rule-based inference technique. The reasoner will look up the conceptual graph to find the matched node which represents the concept *k*. If the matched node is not found, the reasoner will return an empty set. If the matched node denoted as *k'* is found then *k'* will be marked.

k' is taken as an input parameter in the Ontology reasoner again. At the same time, we set the following rules for the reasoner.

- If *k'* is a class entity in the graph, then the reasoner will return all of its properties $P = \{p_1,p_2,...p_i\}$, values of those properties $V = \{v_1,v_2,...,v_i\}$, instance $I = \{i_1,i_2,...,i_i\}$, subclasses $SB = \{sb_1,sb_2,...sb_i\}$, super classes $SP = \{sp_1,sp_2,...sp_i\}$ and equivalence classes $E = \{e_1,e_2,...,e_i\}$.
- If *k'* is a property entity in the graph, then the reasoner will return all of its related classes $C = \{c_1,c_2,...,c_i\}$, the values of this property in its property domain $V = \{v_1,v_2,...,v_i\}$.
- If *k'* is an instance of specific classes in the graph, then the reasoner will return all of those classes $Cl = \{cl_1,cl_2,...,cl_3\}$.

Collecting all of the above nodes and denoting the set as *N*, the reasoner send *N* back to the retrieval system. To avoid extra computation time for the ranking, the retrieval system filters out some of the elements in the set *N*, which are not included in the indexing database, and then we have a smaller set *N'*.

The third step, as shown on Figure 1, after the nodes selection process, the nodes set *N'* will be passed to the BN model for relevance computation. In order to construct the BN model, we need to define what role the BN computation is playing in our hybrid image retrieval model. When the Ontology reasoner returns a set of corresponding nodes set *N'* to the query keyword *k*, those nodes are all the neighbors of the original query keyword (Figure 2). However, sent from the Ontology reasoner which is based on the rule-based inference engine, the returning nodes have no ranking order for relevance. Thus, the BN model is used for computing the relevance from each returning node to the query keyword *k* for providing ranking of images collection.

Let $P_i(U)$ be jpd of the all the relevance factors of the node N'_i corresponding to the concept *k'* corresponding to the input keyword. Because $P_i(U)$ is a jpd, we can have the notion, $0 \leq P_i(U) \leq 1.0$. It is possible that there are many variables

Figure 1. The retrieval procedure of our hybrid method

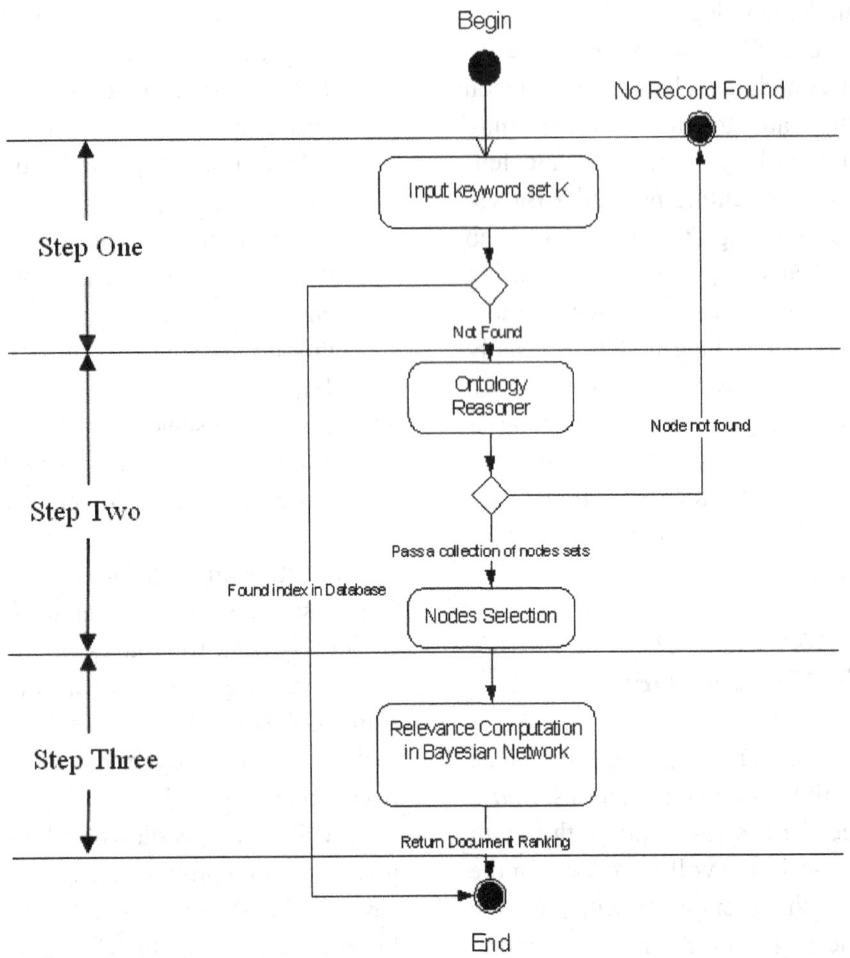

for the problem domain, so that the whole jpd table $P_i(U)$ is too large to be obtained.

Therefore, we need to find out the conditional independencies (CIs) among the variables of this jpd. To understand the meaning of the relevance between the return node and the input keyword, we can also call the relevance between node N'_i and k' semantic distance, because Ontology defines the semantics of the vocabularies. If the semantic distance is shorter, it means the node is more relevant to the concept k'. If $P_i(X) = 1.0$, we can claim that N'_i is exactly what user queried. Otherwise, if $P_i(X) = 0.0$, it means that N'_i is irrelevant to the user's query.

In other words, if the value of the probability of $P_i(X)$ is closer to 1.0, it indicates the semantic distance of node N'_i is shorter than the one whose value is closer to 0.0.

Because $P_i(U)$ represents how relevant it is between the returning node N'_i and the concept node k' to the original query keyword, we can define the variables as follows.

- *sb*: N'_i is a subclass of node k';
- *sp*: N'_i is a super class of node k';
- *i*: N'_i is an instance of node k';
- *e*: N'_i is an equivalence class of node k';
- *p*: N'_i is one of the properties of node k';

Figure 2. The neighboring information of the concept k' in the hierarchical structure graph of the ontology

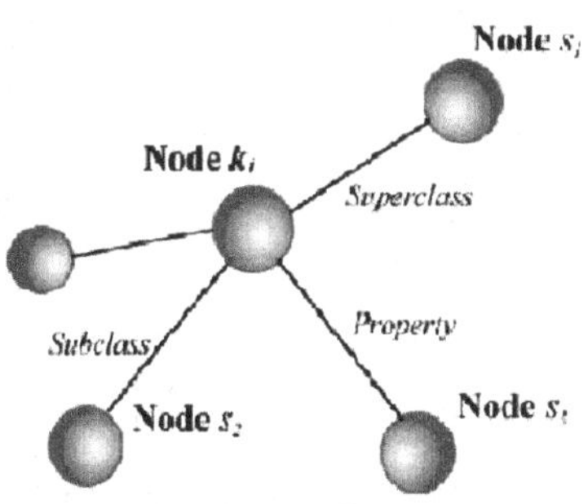

- *Pr*: *k'* is a property entity in the Ontology;
- *In*: *k'* is a instance entity in the Ontology;
- *Cl*: *k'* is a class entity in the Ontology;
- *v*: N'_i is a value of *k'*, if *k'* is a property entity in the Ontology;
- *c*: N'_i is a class of *k'*, if *k'* is a instance entity or a property entity.

All the above variables are binary, having a domain $D = \{Yes, No\}$. Because the probability $P(n)$ is that we expect to compute, therefore, in the next step, we need to define the CIs for this BN model.

Assume that we are the knowledge experts in ontology constructions. The CIs of the nodes extracted from ontology can be defined. Once we have *k'*, we will know if it is a class, property, or instance entity in the Ontology. As a result, we can acquire $P(Cl|\text{Pr},In)$. If *k'* is a property entity in the Ontology, then we have $P(v,c|\text{Pr})$. If *k'* is an instance entity, we have $P(c|In)$.

If a node is a subclass of node k_i, it indicates that it is impossible to be a super class of the node k_i. Then we can write it as $P(sb|sp)$. If a node is an equivalence class of node k_i, it indicates that it is not either a subclass or super class of the node k_i. Then we have $P(sb,sp|e)$. When the original concept node k_i takes different value, for example, as a class entity or a property entity, the return nodes' set will be different.

Figure 3. The DAG of our relevance model

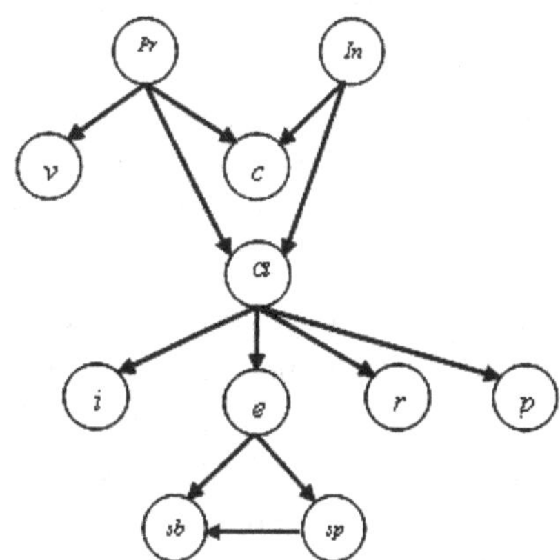

Consequently, we can obtain another conditional probability table (CPT), $P(i,r,e,p|k)$. All the CPTs can be listed as follows.

$P(Cl|\text{Pr},In)$
$P(v,c|\text{Pr})$
$P(c|In)$
$P(n|sb,sp,i,r,e,p)$
$P(i,r,e,p|Cl)$
$P(sb|sp)$
$P(sb,sp|e)$

According to the above CPTs, we can draw the DAG as shown in Figure 3.

According to the DAG, we can simplify the jpd into small tables, as follows $P(U) = P(\text{Pr}) \times P(In) \times P(v|\text{Pr}) \times P(c|\text{Pr},In) \times P(Cl|\text{Pr},In) \times P(i,e,r,p|Cl) \times P(sb,sp|e) \times P(sb|sp)$ (1)

Once we have the whole $P(U)$ equation (1), the values of CPT tables are ready to be assigned for the initialization work. Once the Ontology reasoner returns the set N' of nodes, we can obtain the values of the variables of *k, e, sb, sp, i, r,* and *p*. Post those values as evidences to the BN network, propagating by the HUGIN (Jensen, Lauritzen & Olesen, 1990) or Shafer & Shenoy (1990) method. Then the probability $P(n)$ can be queried.

Using this method for computing all the returning nodes, the ranking factors are obtained for each node.

With these factors, the system can retrieve the related images' documents from the index database. After sorting the images by the relevance, eventually, the system can have a descending order of the images' list of the retrieval result.

The set of returned concepts with the relevance can be served as query keywords of recommendations to the users on top of the search result, because those keywords are the neighbors of the input query keyword, and are semantically related to users query. This recommendation system can help users address the problem that they have an unclear search goal in mind. A simple and long ranked list of retrieval result can not satisfy the need of the users. Lots of researchers have proposed to provide a better organized search result. For example, online search result clustering. For the reason that the amount of the online images growing amazingly every day, the search result may return hundreds or thousands of images to the users. Since we used our approach to increase the recall rate, thus, our recommendations with keywords assisting users to find the desired images can be viewed as a search result categorization consisting of clusters of the meaningful keywords.

IMPLEMENTATION AND DISCUSSION RESULTS

We have implemented our hybrid retrieval model by combining Ontology and BN techniques into a Web application. The experiment demonstrates some promising results. In our experiment, a query with the keyword "car" is input into the search system. The images annotated with keywords, such as "automobile" or "Honda," which are the equivalent to "car" or a brand name of "car," are shown in Figure 4.

In this implementation application, all the images are stored in a local web site and indexed with keywords in a local database. We assume that all the images are annotated well with keywords representing the topics of those images.

The reason that we set this assumption is that one of the purposes in this research project is to reuse the existing resource of annotation on the Web without any modification or attachment to it. The architecture of our application is shown in Figure 5.

The Ontology reasoning component here serves as a Web service. The reason we wrap the Ontology reasoner logic into a SOAP XML Web service is that we have considered that the Ontology can be possibly selected from a remote online Ontology provider, such as WordNet (WordNet) Ontology, and SOAP XML Web Services have been considered as efficient choices for remote information access crossing platform and organizational boundaries. In the experiment from our application, we finished our programming with the help of the existing research and tools of Semantic Web and Bayesian Networks. For instance, we implemented a demo Ontology in Ontology Web Language (OWL) using a Java Ontology APIs, Jena, from HP research lab (McGuinness & Harmelen, 2004) & (McBride, 2000). Our Bayesian Network computation model was constructed and inferred by the MSBNx (Microsoft Bayesian Network Toolkit) from Microsoft research (Microsoft Bayesian Network Toolkit).

There are 210 images in our local image library, and 18 different keywords annotating the images, stored in database. There is an indexing database for all the image resources running in our system as well. In this experiment, all the images are stored in the local Web site. First of all, this application provides both Ontology & BN based search and Keyword-based search methods. Secondly, each related keyword returned from the Ontology reasoner was ranked by the semantic distance between the original input keyword node and the returned concept node from Ontology.

The shorter the semantic distance between two nodes, the higher position the image will be put on

Figure 4. A screenshot of the search result from a query "car"

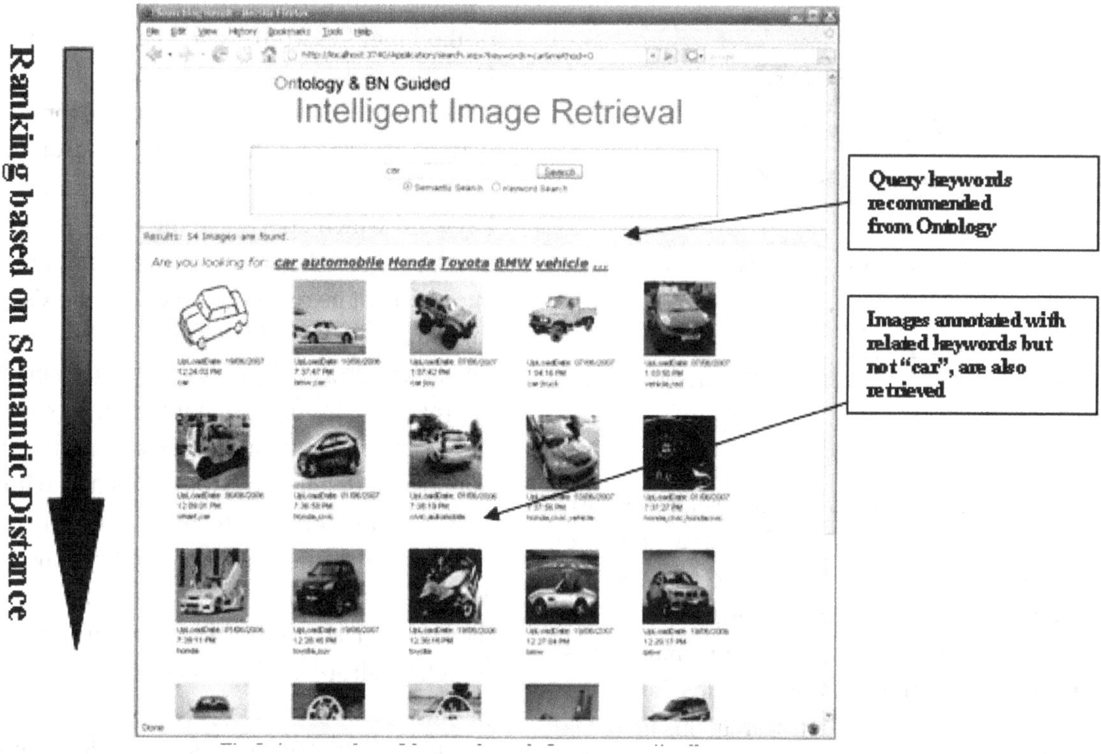

Figure 5. The architecture of our retrieval system

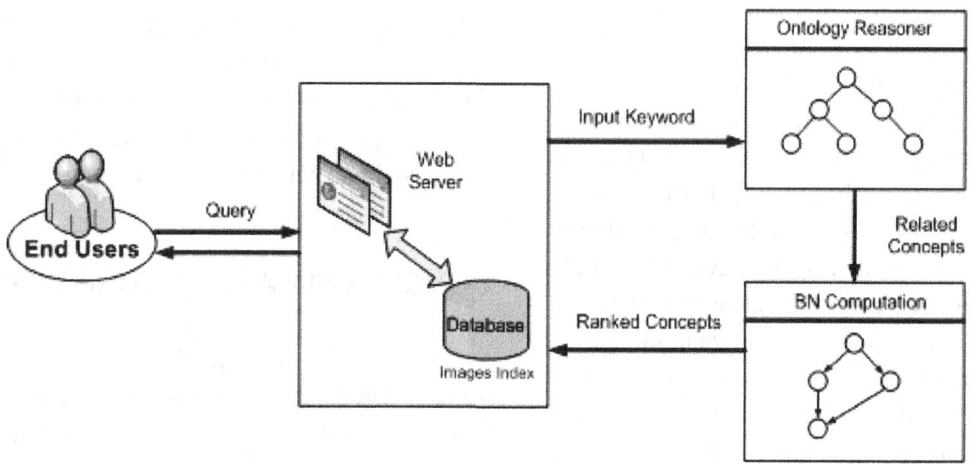

Figure 6. A detailed view of one return image item

the search result ranking. The Bayesian Network model plays a critical key role in the semantic distance computation. Figure 6 shows the detail information from the search result.

In this example, an image of a vehicle is annotated with the only keyword "vehicle". If using the classical keyword match search, this image is not able to be retrieved. In our experiment, the query keyword "car" is input into our system. After the Ontology reasoning, keyword "vehicle" is returned as the super class of concept "car" in the conceptual graph. "vehicle" is passed into the BN computation as evidence in the BN belief network model, defined earlier. Then, after the network propagation, a relevance probability of "vechicle," also called semantic distance value, is sent back to the main process.

The comparison results of using different retrieval methods for one simple query, "car," is listed in Table 1. According to the experiment data from the table, there are only 15 images which are directly annotated with the keyword, "car," and 39 images with other related keywords, such as "vehicle," "honda civic," and "automobile". The recommendation system works as planned and the recommendations from the search result contain the recommended image resources for users to navigate the search result. Take an example from the search in Figure 4, those recommended keywords, such as "automobile," "honda" and "toyota," are the neighboring nodes of the input keyword, "car," generated from the Ontology reasoning.

The recall rates of our search approach are mainly affected by the Ontology reasoning, because, if the Ontology does not contain the concept keyword which appears in the image annotation and represents the topic of the images, those images will not be retrieved. In others words, under this situation, the recall rates are lowered. Another factor to affect the recall rate of our proposed approach is the image annotation. However, at the beginning of our implementation, we assumed that all the images are well annotated with keywords representing topics. Therefore, our experiment result is not affected by this factor. With the assumption in our experiment, it is indicated that all the retrieved records from the search result are relevant to the user's query, since the keywords of those retrieved records are semantically relevant to the query keyword and ranked with relevance rate. Table 2 shows the recall rates of the two retrieval methods from our experimental data.

To sum up, the experimental data has shown that the Ontology & BN based method returned far more related records from the images library. Furthermore, the search result of our method not only covers the one from the keyword-based search, but also provides semantic recommendation for the end users to navigate around the result set of images, to solve the problem that users do not have the exact search goal in their minds.

CONCLUSION AND FUTURE WORK

In this chapter, we have presented an approach of the user-driven Ontology guided image retrieval. It combines (a) the certain reasoning techniques based on logic inside Ontology and (b) the uncertain reasoning technique based on Bayesian Network to provide users the enhanced image

Table 1. The comparison of two methods

Approach	Description	Providing Semantics Recommendation	Numbers of Images in Search Result
Ontology & BN based Retrieval	Using Ontology for semantic reasoning, and BN for ranking computation	Yes	39
Keyword-based Retrieval	Find matched keyword in the indexing database	No	18

retrieval on the web. More significantly, our approach is for easily plugging in an external Ontology in the distributed environment and assists user searching for a set of images effectively. In addition, to obtain a faster real-time search result, the Ontology query and BN computation should be run on the off-line mode, and the results should be stored into the indexing record.

Although our retrieval method has shown that it can retrieve more images than the keyword-based method, there are still some problems that we found from our experiment. The returned concepts from the Ontology reasoner are ranked relying on their basic relations inside Ontology with the original input keyword. For example, a brand name, "Honda," and model name, "Civic," both are the values of the properties of the concept, "car". Which one is closer to the user query? Our model still cannot answer this sort of precise question in semantics. This will be studied in our future research work. We are also going to apply a large scale remote Ontology into our system, such as WordNet. And searching a larger scale image library will be considered. User profile oriented recommendations should take into consideration in our future works since users have different search experience, search strategies and knowledge about the domain topics. Personalized user recommendations would serve better the user's individual goals.

Table 2. The recall rates of two methods

	Recall Rate
Our Retrieval Method	92%
Keyword-based Retrieval	20%

REFERENCES

Agosti, M., & Smeaton, A. (1996). *Information retrieval and hypertext.* New York, NY: Kluwer.

Aslandogan, Y. A., Their, C., Yu, C. T., Zou, J., & Rishe, N. (1997). *Using semantic contents and Wordnet in image retrieval. SIGIR* (pp. 286–295). ACM.

Benjamins, V. R., Centreras, J., Corcho, O., & Gomez-Perez, A. (2002). *Six challenges for the Semantic Web.* ISWC2002

Berners-Lee, T. (1998). *Semantic Web road map.* World Wide Web consortium. Retrieved from http://www.w3.org/ DesignIssues/ Semantic.html

Berners-Lee, T., Hendler, J., & Lassila, O. (2001). The Semantic Web. *Scientific American.*

Carneiro, G., & Vasconcelos, N. (2005). A database centric view of semantic image annotation and retrieval. *Proceedings of ACM Conference on Research and Development in Information Retrieval.*

Costa, P. C. G., Laskey, K. B., & Laskey, K. J. (2005). *PR-OWL: A Bayesian ontology language for the Semantic Web*. URSW`05

Datta, R., Joshi, D., Li, J., & Wang, J. Z. (2008). Image retrieval: Ideas, influences, and trends of the new age. *ACM Computing Surveys, 40*(2).

Davies, J., Fensel, D., & Harmelen, F. V. (2003). *Towards the Semantic Web - Ontology-driven knowledge management*. Wiley.

Ding, Z., & Peng, Y. (2004). A probabilistic extension to ontology language OWL. *Proceedings of the 37th Hawaii International Conference on System Sciences*.

Google. (2004). *Google achieves search milestone with immediate access to more than 6 billion items*. Retrieved from http://www.google.com/ press/ pressrel/ 6billion.html

Hunter, J. (2001). Adding multimedia to the Semantic Web: Building an MPEG-7 ontology. In I. F. Cruz, S. Decker, J. Euzenat, & D. L. McGuinness (Eds.), *Proceedings of the International Semantic Web Working Symposium*, (pp. 261-283).

Hyvonen, E., Saarela, S., & Viljanen, K. (2003). *Intelligent image retrieval and browsing Semantic Web techniques – A case study*. The International SEPIA Conference.

James, Z., & the Wang Research Group. (n.d.). *Research on intelligent media annotation*. Pennsylvania State University. Retrieved from http:// wang.ist.psu.edu/ IMAGE/

Jensen, F. V., Lauritzen, S. L., & Olesen, K. G. (1990). *Bayesian updating in causal probabilistic network by local computation*.

Kant, S., & Mamas, E. (2005). *Statistical reasoning – A foundation for Semantic Web reasoning*. URSW`05.

Li, J., & Wang, J. (2003). Automatic linguistic indexing of pictures by a statistical modeling approach. *IEEE Transactions on Pattern Analysis and Machine Intelligence, 25*(9).

Li, J., & Wang, J. (2004). Studying digital imagery of ancient paintings by mixtures of stochastic models. *IEEE Transactions on Image Processing, 13*(3), 340–353. doi:10.1109/TIP.2003.821349

Liu, S., Chia, L. T., & Chan, S. (2004). Ontology for nature scene image retrieval. *Lecture Notes in Computer Science, 3291*, 1050–1061. doi:10.1007/978-3-540-30469-2_14

Liu, Y., Zhang, D., Lu, G., & Ma, W. Y. (2007). A survey of content-based image retrieval with high-level semantics. *Journal of the Pattern Recognition Society, 40*, 262–282. doi:10.1016/j.patcog.2006.04.045

Long, F., Zhang, H., & Feng, D. D. (2003). Fundamentals of content-based image retrieval. In Feng, D., Siu, W. C., & Zhang, H. J. (Eds.), *Multimedia information retrieval and management-Technological fundamentals and applications*. Springer.

McBride, B. (2001). *Jena: Implementing the RDF model and syntax specification*. Retrieved from http://www.hpl.hp.com/ personal/ bwm/ papers/ 20001221-paper

McGuinness, D. L., & Harmelen, F. V. (2004). *OWL Web ontology language overview*. W3C. Retrieved from http://www.w3.org/ TR/ owl-features/

Microsoft. (n.d.). *Bayesian network toolkit*. Retrieved from http://research.microsoft.com/ adapt/ MSBNx/

Pearl, J. (1998). *Probabilistic reasoning in intelligent systems: Networks of plausible inference* (pp. 1–20). Morgan Kaufmann.

Ribeiro-Neto, B., Silva, I., & Muntz, R. (2000). Bayesian network models for information retrieval. In Crestani, F., & Pasi, G. (Eds.), *Soft computing in information retrieval: Techniques and applications* (pp. 259–291). Springer.

Ricardo, B. Y., & Berthier, R. N. (1999). *Modern information retrieval. ACM Press*. Addison-Wesley.

Rui, Y., Huang, T., Ortega, M., & Mehrotra, S. (1998). Relevance feedback: A power tool for interactive content-based image retrieval. *IEEE Trans. On Circuit and Systems for Video Technology, 5,* 644-656.

Rui, Y., Huang, T. S., & Chang, S. F. (1999). Image retrieval: Current techniques, promising directions and open issues. *Journal of Visual Communication and Image Representation, 10*, 39–62. doi:10.1006/jvci.1999.0413

Sethi, I. K., & Coman, I. L. (2001). Mining association rules between low-level image features and high-level concepts. *Proceedings of the SPIE Data Mining and Knowledge Discovery, 3*, 279–290.

Shafer, G. R., & Shenoy, P. P. (1990). Probability propagation. *Annals of Mathematics and Artificial Intelligence, 2*(1-4), 327–351. doi:10.1007/BF01531015

Shi, D. C., Xu, L., & Han, L. Y. (2007). Image retrieval using both color and texture features. *Journal of China University of Posts and Telecommunications, 14*(1), 94–99. doi:10.1016/S1005-8885(08)60020-5

Smeulders, A. W., Worring, M., Santini, S., Gupta, A., & Jain, R. (2000). Content-based image retrieval at the end of the early years. *IEEE Transactions on Pattern Analysis and Machine Intelligence, 22*(12), 1349–1380. doi:10.1109/34.895972

Terdiman, D. (2009). Tagging gives Web a human meaning. *CNET News*. Retrieved from http://news.cnet.com/ Tagging- gives- Web- a- human- meaning/ 2009- 1025_ 3- 5944502.html

Veltkamp, R., & Tanase, M. (2000). Content-based image retrieval systems: A survey. (Technical Report UU-CS-2000-34), Utrecht University.

WordNet. (n.d.). *Software*. Retrieved from http://www.cogsci. princeton.edu/ ~wn/

Chapter 5
Annotation of Medical Images

Chia-Hung Wei
Ching Yun University, Taiwan

Sherry Y. Chen
Brunel University, UK

ABSTRACT

Automatic image annotation is a technique that automatically assigns a set of linguistic terms to images in order to categorize the images conceptually and provide means for effectively accessing images from databases. This chapter firstly introduces fundamentals and techniques of automatic image annotation to give an overview of this research field. A case study, which describes the methodology for annotating mammographic lesions, is then presented. This chapter is intended to disseminate the knowledge of the automatic annotation approaches to the applications of medical image management and to attract greater interest from various research communities to rapidly advance research in this field.

INTRODUCTION

In the last decade, a large number of digital medical images have been produced in hospitals. Such digital medical images include X-ray, computed tomography (CT), magnetic resonance imaging (MRI), functional magnetic resonance imaging (fMRI), magnetic resonance spectroscopy (MRS), magnetic source imaging (MSI), digital subtraction angiography (DSA), positron emission tomography (PET), ultrasound (US), nuclear medical imaging, endoscopy, microscopy, scanning laser ophtalmoscopy (SLO), and so on. These medical images are stored in large-scale image databases and can facilitate medical doctors, professionals, researchers, and college students to diagnose current patients and provide valuable information for their studies. Due to the increasing use of digital medical images, there is a need to develop advanced information retrieval techniques, which can improve the effectiveness of browsing and searching of large medical image databases. Among various advanced information retrieval techniques, image annotation is considered as a prerequisite task for image database management (Hersh, 2009). If images are manually annotated

DOI: 10.4018/978-1-61350-126-9.ch005

with text, keyword-based search can be used to retrieve the images. However, manual annotation suffers from the following limitations, especially in massive image databases (Feng, Siu, & Zhang, 2003).

- Manual annotations require too much time and are expensive to implement. As the number of media in a database grows, it becomes infeasible to manually annotate all attributes of the image content. For instance, annotating a 60-minute video containing more than 100,000 still images consumes a vast amount of time and expense.
- Manual annotations fail to deal with the discrepancy of subjective perceptions. When people perform image annotation, they provide the different description with their different subjective perceptions. Furthermore, the same annotators may have different subjective perceptions as time evolves;
- It is difficult to provide concrete description for some image contents. For example, the shape of organs in medical images is too complex to describe.

In an attempt to addressing these limitations, automatic image annotation is necessary for efficient image retrieval. Automatic image annotation is a hot topic in the areas of multimedia, information retrieval, and machine learning. To correspond to this trend, this chapter presents an image annotation scheme, which includes mammographic feature extraction and a supervised classification approach to mammogram annotation. The rest of the chapter is organized as follows: Section 2 reviews the methods of visual features and classification in medical images. Section 3 presents a case study, which describes the methodology of annotation for digital mammograms. Section 4 discusses potential research issues in the future research agenda. The last section concludes this chapter.

LITERATURE REVIEW

Visual Features

Automatic image annotation refers to a technique that automatically assigns a set of linguistic terms to images in order to categorize the images conceptually and provide means for effectively accessing images from databases (Deselaers, Deserno, & Muller, 2007). To make computers automatically assign linguistic terms to images, the region of interests in images need to be represented from corresponding visual features. Visual features, also called low-level features, are objectively derived from the images rather than referring to any external semantics (Feng et al., 2003). As the visual features extracted from the images should be meaningful for image seekers, the visual features used in the image retrieval systems are mainly divided into three groups: color, shape, and texture.

Color

Color, one of the most frequently used visual features for content-based image retrieval, is considered as a powerful descriptor that simplifies object identification (Gonzalez & Woods, 2002). Several color descriptors have been developed from various representation schemes, such as color histograms (Ouyang & Tan, 2002), color moments (Yu, Li, Zhang, & Feng, 2002), color edge (Gevers & Stokman, 2003), color texture (Guan & Wada, 2002), and color correlograms (Moghaddam, Khajoie, & Rouhi, 2003). For example, color histogram, which represents the distribution of the number of pixels for each quantized color bin, is an effective representation of the color content of an image. The color histogram can not only easily characterize the global and regional distribution of colors in an image, but also be invariant to rotation about the view axis.

For the retrieval of medical images, color allows images to reveal many lesion characteristics (Tamai, 1999). Color also plays an important role in morphological diagnosis (Nishibori, Tsumura, & Miyake, 2004). Color medical images are usually produced in different departments and by various devices. For example, color endoscopic images are taken by a camera that is put into the hollow organs of the body, such as stomachs and lungs. A common characteristic of such images is that most colors are made of various stains, though fine variations of natural colors are crucial for diagnosis. Nishibori (Nishibori, 2000) pointed out that problems in color medical images include inaccurate color reproduction, rough gradations of color, and insufficient density of pixels. Therefore, the effective use of the various color information in images includes absolute color values, ratios of each tristimulus color, differences in colors against adjacent areas, and estimated illumination data. In addition, many medical images are represented in gray level. For this kind of gray level images, content-based image retrieval can only consider color as a secondary feature because gray levels provide limited information about the content of an image. For specific purposes, some gray level images have pseudo-color added to enhance specific areas, instead of gray level presentation. Since pseudo-colors are artificially added to facilitate the human to observe the images, the pseudo-colors may not represent the same meaning for different users. Such pseudo-color processing increases difficulties in image annotation and retrieval.

Shape

Shape is one of the most important features in describing an image. People can easily identify different images and classify them into different categories solely from the outline of an object in a given image. As shape can convey some kind of semantic information which is meaningful to human recognition, it is used as a distinctive feature for the representation of an image object. In general, two large categories of shape descriptors can be identified: contour-based shape descriptors and region-based shape descriptors (Feng et al., 2003). Contour-based descriptors emphasize the closed curve that surrounds the boundary of an image object. The curve can be described by numerous models, including chain codes, polygons, circular arcs, and boundary Fourier descriptors. In addition, a boundary can be described by its features, for instance, inflection points. Region-based shape descriptors usually refer to the shape descriptions that are derived using all pixel information within the closed boundary of an image object. The region can be modeled in different ways, such as collections of primitives (rectangles, disks, etc.), and deformable templates.

In some medical images, shape is the most important feature to describe pathologies in medical images. For example, spine X-ray images are represented in grey scale and provide little information in terms of texture for the anatomy of interest. The vertebra shape is the most important feature that describes various pathologies in spine X-ray images. In mammograms, round masses usually indicate a well defined smooth edge which is often benign whereas stellate masses, characterized by a set of rays emanating from the centre in different directions, imply indistinct margins which are more often malignant. One of the challenges is that, while the differences between normal and pathological conditions are subtle, the shapes of the same type of pathology exhibit greater variations. Therefore, it is difficult to select a proper shape representation method that not only represents anatomical structures, but also retains enough information for similarity measure.

Texture

Texture representation in image retrieval can be used for at least two purposes (Sebe & Lew, 2002). First, an image can be considered to be a mosaic that consists of different texture regions. These regions can be used as examples to search and retrieve similar areas. Second, texture can be employed for automatically annotating the content of an image. For example, the texture of an infected skin region can be used for annotating regions with the same infection. Textural representation approaches can be classified into statistical approaches and structural approaches (Sebe et al., 2002). Statistical approaches analyze textural characteristics according to the statistical distribution of image intensity. Approaches in this category include gray level co-occurrence matrix, fractal model, Tamura feature, Wold decomposition, and so on (Feng, Siu, & Zhang, 2003). Structural approaches characterize texture by identifying a set of structural primitives and certain placement rules.

If medical images are represented in gray level, texture becomes a crucial feature, which provides indications about scenic depth, the spatial distribution of tonal variations, and surface orientation (Tourassi, 1999). For example, abnormal symptoms on female breasts include calcification, architectural distortion, asymmetry, masses, and so forth. All of those reveal specific textural patterns on the mammograms. However, selection of texture features for specifying textural structure should take account of the influences from the modulation transfer function on texture (Veenland, Grashuis, Weinans, Ding, & Vrooman, 2002). As the intensifying screens are used to enhance the radiographs, the blurring effect also changes texture features. In other words,, spatial resolution, contrast, and sharpness are all reduced in the output. Low resolution and contrast result in difficulties in measuring the pattern of tissue and structure of organs (Majumdar et al., 1998). Thus, radiographs are required to perform image enhancement in order to improve contrast, and sharpness. In addition, radiographs obtained from different devices may be present in different grayscale ranges so normalization can be performed to adjust their grayscale ranges to the same one.

Classification of Retrieval Methods

Controlled Vocabularies

Keyword-based search may be the most familiar way for users to retrieve information from the collections. In such a way, images collected in the database should be annotated for their semantics in advance. In query submission, the retrieval system has to assist users in constructing controlled terms from a thesaurus or lexical resources. However, users may submit different words to describe the same contents or objects, thereby decreasing the performance of image retrieval systems. One of the solutions is to use a set of controlled vocabulary to serve a bridge between image annotation and query formulation. There are number of medical domain thesaurus available, such as MeSH, eHealth Thesaurus, and NDAD Thesaurus. MeSH, the Medical Subject Headings, is a set of controlled vocabulary of medical subject terms and used by the National Library of Medicine for indexing articles for the MEDLINE database and cataloging other databases (Nelson, Johnston, & Humphreys, 2001); the eHealth Thesaurus is a guide to the subject terms assigned to organize the eHealth Literature Catalogue records (Wyatt & Sullivan, 2005); The NDAD Thesaurus is a subject index of the catalogues and administrative histories on the UK National Digital Archive of Datasets (NDAD) web site (Ashley, 2004).

Supervised Classification Approaches

If a set of controlled vocabulary is used to annotate image content, such an image annotation task can be seen as a problem of supervised classification. i.e., a set of known examples can be used to develop a classifier or a model for predicting unknown data (Tsai & Hung, 2008). Those class labels correspond to the words contained in the controlled vocabulary. Due to the nature of image annotation, various supervised classification approaches have been proposed to achieve the task. For instance, Vailaya, Figueiredo, Jain, & Zhang (Vailaya, Figueiredo, Jain, & Zhang, 2001) employed three Bayes classifiers to perform three-stage classification on scenery images. Ghoshal, Ircing, & Khudanpur (Ghoshal, Ircing, & Khudanpur, 2005) developed hidden Markov models and chose the optimal ones for two different image datasets COREL and TRECVID, respectively. For annotation of home photos, Lim, Tian, & Mulhem (Lim, Tian, & Mulhem, 2003) designed a three-layer feed-forward neural network to learn 26 categories, each contains color and texture features from the partitioned regions of photos. To annotate architectural objects, such as buildings, towers, bridges, Iqbal and Aggarwal (Iqbal & Aggarwal, 2002) extracted their shape features and then applied a *k*-NN approach for image classification. Other approaches to image annotation can refer to (Tsai et al., 2008).

AN EXAMPLE: ANNOTATION OF MAMMOGRAPHIC IMAGES

Framework of Image Annotation

The framework of mammogram annotation shown in Figure 1 is divided into classifier training and image annotation. In the classifier training stage, we firstly proposed the feature extraction methods of mammographic lesions based on BI-RADS standards. The methods are then used to extract image features to train classifiers of individual lesions. The development and training of classifiers is called the classifier training stage. At the image annotation stage, those trained classifiers are applied to classify the lesions presented in the mammograms. Those mammograms associated with specific lesion classes can be tagged with the names of lesions. The crucial components of the annotation framework are the mammographic feature extraction method and the classification approach, which are described in the following sections.

Mammogram Dataset

The mammogram dataset used in this work was obtained from the Digital Database for Screening Mammography (DDSM), which freely available for download at http://marathon.csee.usf.edu/Mammography/Database.html. The major advantage of using a public database is that it allows reproduction of the results and comparison with other studies. Another advantage is that the DDSM includes cases that are representative for a screening population (Varela, Timp, & Karssemeijer, 2006). The DDSM consists of 2,620 cases, available in 43 volumes. A case is a collection of mammograms and information corresponding to one mammography exam of one patient. The mammograms in each case include a craniocaudal (CC) and mediolateral oblique (MLO) view of each breast. A volume is a collection of cases collected together for purposes of ease of distribution. The DDSM database provides the chain codes of the suspicious regions and metadata of each abnormality using the BI-RADS lexicon and contains associated ground truth information about the locations of abnormalities, which were indicated by at least two experienced radiologists. Metadata include the date of study and digitization, the breast density and assessment categories, a subtlety rating, the type of pathology and detailed categorization of the nature of the perceived abnormality. With these chain codes, the outlines of the abnormalities can be identified, enabling us to crop the regions of interests (ROIs) from a full sized mammograms.

Visual Feature Extraction

BI-RADS Standards

The Breast Imaging Reporting and Data System (BI-RADS) (American College of Radiology, 2003) was developed by the American College of Radiology to enable standardised classification for evaluating the morphology of breast lesions and

Figure 1. A framework of mammogram annotation

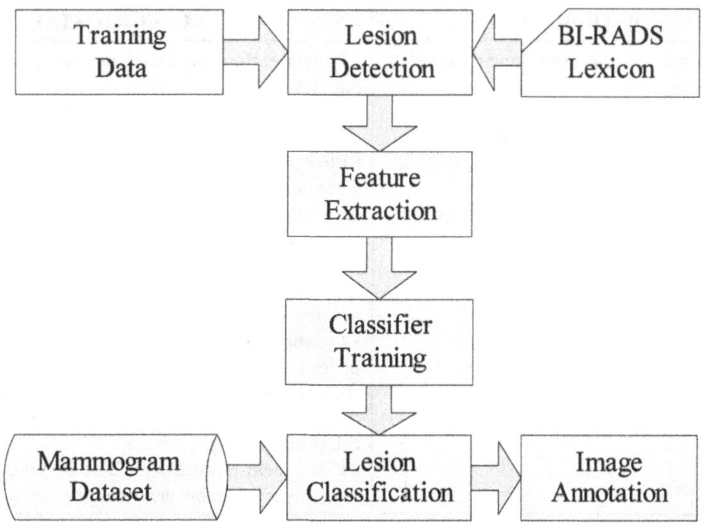

the categorisation of the findings in an unambiguous report. Since the BI-RADS lexicon has been widely used by physicians and radiologists for interpreting mammograms (Baker, Kornguth, & Floyd, 1996; Berg, Campassi, Langenberg, & Sexton, 2000; Muhimmah et al., 2006; Sampat et al., 2006), the proposed mammogram retrieval system aims to automatically assess the mammographic lesions based on their definitions specified in the BI-RADS. According to BI-RADS, masses are characterised based on shape, margin and density while calcifications are described by type and distribution. The definitions of those pathological characteristics used to interpret mammographic abnormalities in this study are listed in Table 1.

Detection and Segmentation of Calcifications

Mammograms, like most radiographs, differ essentially from general images, in the sense that they are limited to exposure dose of X-ray. The exposure dose of X-ray is kept as low as possible for patient's safety (Veenland et al., 2002). Low exposure dose of X-ray often result in low contrast in mammograms. As a result, the contrast between the areas of calcification and their backgrounds is usually limited and, depending on the imaging equipment and the image capturing conditions, the dynamic range of grey scales in different mammograms may vary significantly. To compensate for these issues, histogram equalisation needs to be performed first on all the mammograms. As the size of the mammogram (i.e., ROI) is smaller, histogram equalisation can produce better outcome to enhance the quality of images.

Before extracting calcification features, detection and segmentation of calcified spots on the mammograms is performed in order to obtain segmented mammograms, which clearly describe the distributions of calcification and types of individual calcified spots. It is observed that calcifications usually appear as spots which are the brightest objects when compared to other breast tissues. The method (Wei & Li, 2006) in Equation (1) is proposed to detect and segment calcified spots from mammograms. Denoting the (i,j) -th pixel of a mammogram g as $g(i,j)$ the response $r(i,j)$ of $g(i,j)$ to the spot detector D can be defined as

Table 1. The classification of masses and calcifications in BI-RADS

CALCIFICATION DISTRIBUTION	CALCIFICATION TYPE
• **Clustered (Grouped):** Multiple calcifications occupy a small volume (less than 2 cc) of tissue. • **Linear:** Arrayed in a line that may have branch points. • **Segmental:** Deposits in a duct and its branches raising the possibility of multifocal breast cancer in a lobe or segment of the breast. • **Regional:** Calcifications scattered in a large volume of breast tissue. • **Diffuse (Scattered):** Calcifications are distributed randomly throughout the breast.	• **Punctate:** Round or oval, less than 0.5 mm with well defined margins. • **Amorphous:** Often round or "flake" shaped calcifications that are sufficiently small or hazy in appearance. • **Pleomorphic:** These are usually more conspicuous than the amorphic forms and are neither typically benign nor typically malignant irregular calcifications with varying sizes and shapes that are usually less than 0.5 mm in diameter. • **Round and Regular:** They are usually considered benign and when small (under 1 mm), they frequently are formed in the acini of lobules. • **Lucent Centre:** These are benign calcifications that range from under 1 mm to over a centimetre or more. These deposits have smooth surfaces, are round or oval, and have a lucent centre. The "wall" that is created is thicker than the "rim or eggshell" type of calcifications. • **Fine Linear Branching:** These are thin, irregular calcifications that appear linear, but are discontinuous and under 0.5 mm in width.

Source from BI-RADS

Figure 2. Filter mask used to detect calcified spots

-1	-1	-1
-1	8	-1
-1	-1	-1

$$r(i,j)=\begin{cases}0 & \text{, if } g(i,j)<T\\ \sum_{x=1}^{X}\sum_{y=1}^{Y}D(x,y)\cdot g(i+x-\frac{X+1}{2},j+y-\frac{Y+1}{2}) & \text{, if } g(i,j)\geq T\end{cases} \quad (1)$$

where X and Y are the numbers of rows and columns of spot detector D. The Laplace operator, as shown in Figure 2, is applied to serve as spot detector D to detect calcified spots. The threshold T is defined as

$$T=\alpha\cdot\mu+(1-\alpha)\cdot M \quad (2)$$

where μ and M are the mean and maximum grey scales of the mammogram and α determines where between the mean and maximum the threshold T should lie. To avoid picking up noise and misleading information in the detection process, a priori knowledge that calcified spots are usually brighter than the backgrounds is introduced to form the threshold T for considering the brightness variation in individual mammograms. In Equation (2), if α is set to 0.5, this will take the average of the mean and maximum as the threshold. The spot detectors will skip those pixels with their grey scale lower than the threshold T by setting their corresponding responses to 0.

Without the self-adaptability to the set of α, 0.5 is the best suitable value in this study to detect calcification spots and avoid picking up noise in mammograms. A self-adaptability method for the parameter α will be proposed in future to tune the optimal value against the variation of each mammogram. Two segmentation results of linear and diffuse distributions are shown in Figure 3 and Figure 4, respectively. Once calcified spots have been detected, the resulting output can be used to calculate its calcification features, which are described in the following three sections.

Figure 3. Segmentation of a calcification mammogram. (a) A calcification mammogram with linear distribution. (b) The segmented mammogram.

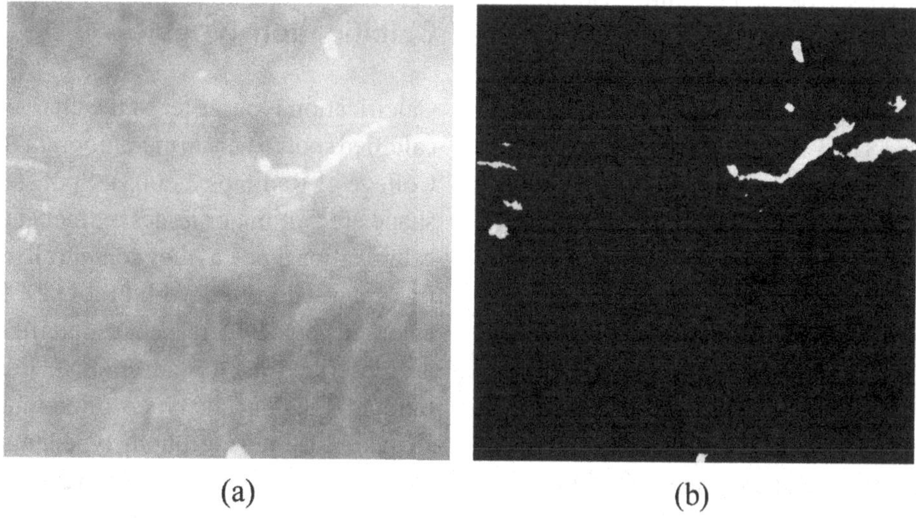

(a) (b)

Figure 4. Segmentation of a calcification mammogram. (a) A calcification mammogram with diffuse distribution. (b) The segmented mammogram.

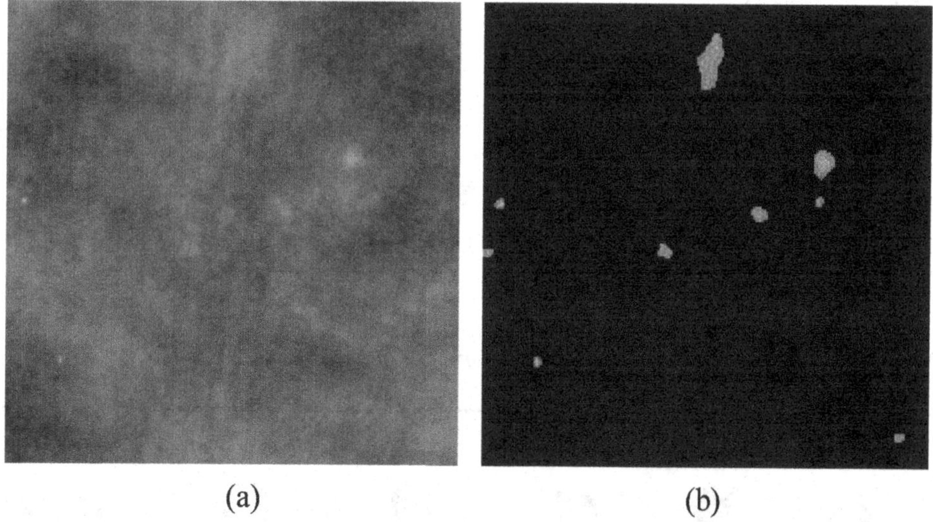

(a) (b)

Feature Extraction of Calcifications

According to BI-RADS, calcification is characterised by type and distribution. Type refers to the characteristics of individual calcified spots, such as shape, margin, and density. Distribution refers to characteristics of all the calcified spots in a mammogram considered together, such as the spread range and density of calcification and the arrangement of the calcified spots (American College of Radiology, 2003) As both type and distribution are taken into consideration together, this will result in diverse calcification lesion categories (see Table 1), each seen as a particular lesion. To provide a visual interpretation of this, a pictorial representation of the two calcification characteristics based on their definitions in Table 1 is shown in Figure 5. More specifically, Figure 5 shows the schematic representation of pathological characteristics of calcifications described in Table 1. From Figure 5 and Table 1, it can be found that the calcification features used in El-Naqa, Yang, Galatsanos, Nishikawa, & Wernick (El-Naqa, Yang, Galatsanos, Nishikawa, & Wernick, 2004) only measure the distribution pattern of calcifications, and ignore the type of individual calcified spots. Furthermore, the study does not take account of linear distribution and segmental distribution in the description of distribution patterns.

Four calcification mammograms with different lesions are shown in Figure 6. The mammogram in Figure 6(a) is considered punctate and clustered calcification because the calcified spots are oval shape and group together. The shape of individual calcified spots and the pattern of the whole distribution in Figure 6(b) both show a linear pattern so the lesion is considered fine-linear branching and linear calcification. Calcified spots in Figure 6(c) with varying sizes and shapes are thought as the plemorphic and segmental calcification. With round and small spots in appearance, Figure 6(d) is considered the amorphous and clustered calcification mammogram.

Calcification Types

Calcification types refer to the characteristics of calcified spots found in mammograms (American College of Radiology, 2003). Spot size and spot shape are two major issues extracted to describe calcification types, as they contain all the information required in this work (Table 2). In Table 1, calcified spots with respect to calcification types are described as "round or oval, less than 0.5 mm" for the punctate type, "often round or flake shaped" for the amorphous type, "malignant irregular calcifications with varying sizes and shapes that are usually less then 0.5 mm in diameter".

Calcification Distribution

Calcification distributions in mammograms refer to the characteristics all the calcified spots in a mammogram considered together (American College of Radiology, 2003). In Table 1, the calcification distribution are described as "calcifications occupy a small volume of tissue" for a clustered distribution, "arrayed in a line" for a linear distribution, and "scattered in a large volume of breast

Figure 5. Pictorial representation of the calcification characteristics

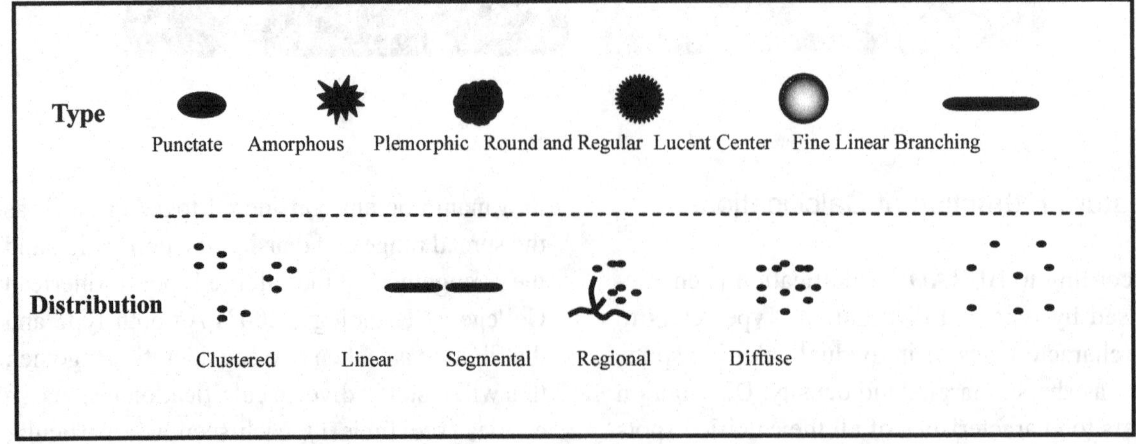

tissue" or "distributed randomly throughout the breast" for a diffuse distribution. With the above description for calcification distributions, the six distribution features (El-Naqa et al., 2004) used in this work are as follows (Table 3).

This study also takes the problem of false positive detection of calcified spots into account. Since most calcification mammograms contain a lot of calcified spots, some features will not be affected by the appearance of a few of false positive spots. For example, we can apply the generalised orders of magnitude to calculate the number of calcified spots. However, if the number of false positive is too many, some features may affect the effectiveness of our system performance. Hence, how to deal with the issue will be one of our future works.

SVM CLASSIFICATION

Suppose a set of training data belonging to two separate classes are given $D=\{(x_i, y_i), i = 1,\ldots, l\} \subset X \times R$ where X denotes the space of input image

Figure 6. Examples of calcification characteristics. (a) Punctate and clustered calcification; (b) Fine-linear branching and linear calcification; (c) Plemorphic and segmental calcification; (d) Amorphous and clustered calcification.

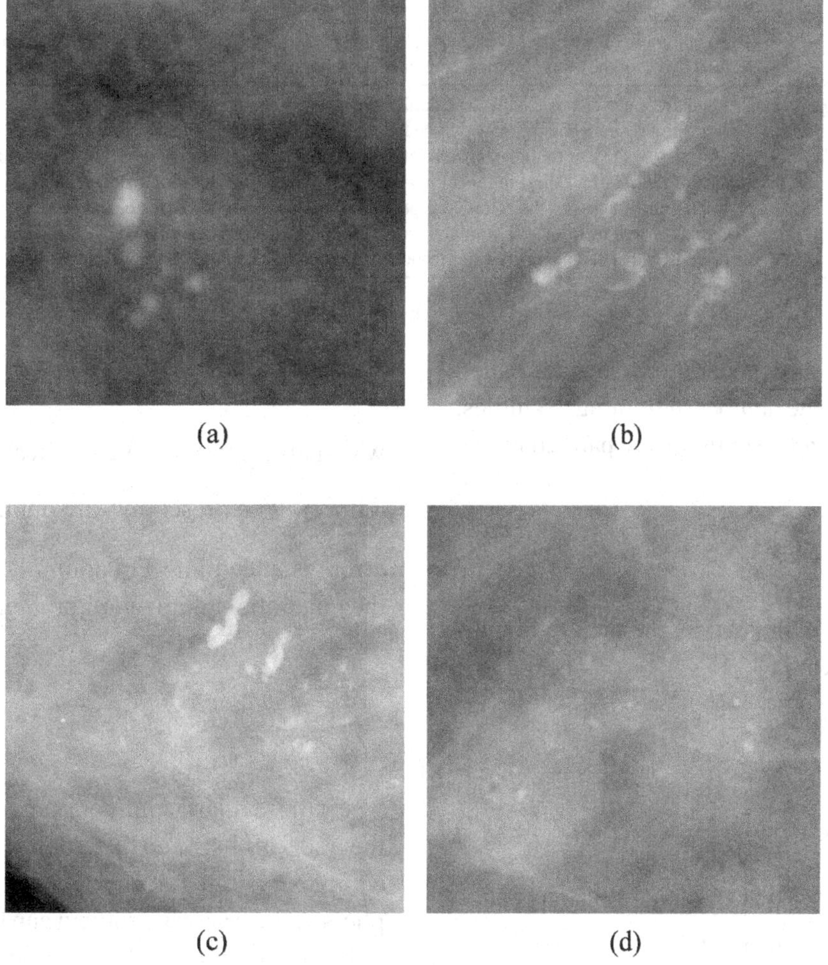

Table 2.

Spot Size:	All calcified spots are first found from the segmentation results, and then the average size of all the calcification spots is computed.
Spot Shape:	Individual spot shapes are described by the first 15 Zernike moments.

Table 3.

Brightness of Calcifications:	This is the average pixel value of the all pixels inside the calcified spots.
Number of Calcified Spots:	When a small number of calcified spots are found in a mammogram, all the detected spots are normally taken into consideration for the distribution characteristic. However, when a large number of spots appear in a mammogram, the significance of each spot in a particular category is reduced. To make approximate comparisons, the number of calcified spots can be represented in generalised orders of magnitude, an estimate measure of quantity expressed as a power of 10. Therefore, the number of spots is computed according to $n=10\cdot log_{10}(number)$, where *number* and *n* are the actual number of spots and the value representing the feature in this work.
Dispersion of Calcifications:	Dispersion is defined as a measure of the spatial property of being scattered about over an image area, represented by the 15 Zernike moments of the binary image directly transformed from the segmented mammogram. As the segmented mammogram only preserves the calcified spots and removes the underlying breast tissue, the feature extracted from a segmented mammogram directly reflects the calcification distribution.
Contrast of Calcifications:	This is the ratio between the average pixel value of calcified spots and that of their surrounding regions, formed by using the morphological 'dilation' operation with a circular structuring element.
Diffuseness of Calcifications:	This feature, inter-distance between calcified spots, is computed as follows: 1) A segmented mammogram is transformed into a binary image where the pixels corresponding to the centres of the individual spots are set to 1 and all the rest of the pixels are set to 0; 2) A Delaunay triangulation is next applied to connect the centres of the calcified spots in this binary image. The resulting shape of a Delaunay triangulation expresses the spatial diffuseness of the calcified spots in a binary image; 3) To describe the resulting shape of this triangulation and facilitate the similarity comparison, the average mean and standard deviation of the inter-distance between neighbouring calcification spots is computed based on this triangulation.

features, $y\in\{1,-1\}$ denotes the associated label, and l represents the number of training examples. The set of data can be optimally separated by the hyperplane

$$f(x)=(w,x)+b. \tag{3}$$

This can be expressed as the quadratic optimization problem [1]

$$\min_{w,b}\frac{1}{2}\|w\|^2,$$

$$\text{subject to } y_i((w^T x_i)+b)\geq 1, \forall\, i=1,\ldots,l. \tag{4}$$

Then, slack variables ξ_i are introduced to relax the hard-margin constraints

$$y((w,x_i)+b)\geq 1-\xi_i, i=1,\ldots,l, \xi_i\geq 0, \tag{5}$$

which allows for some classification errors. The term $\sum_{i=1}^{l}\xi_i$ representing the number of training errors is added into Equation (4) to reformulate the quadratic optimization problem

$$\min_{w,b,\xi}\frac{1}{2}\|w\|^2+C\sum_{i=1}^{l}\xi_i \tag{6}$$

where the regularization constant $C>0$ determines the trade-off between the empirical error and the complexity term. As introducing Lagrange multipliers α, the primary problem can be transformed to its dual problem, which is easier to solve.

For nonlinearly separate data, SVM maps the input data into a higher dimensional space through an underlying nonlinear mapping $\phi(\cdot)$ and then finds an optimal hyperplane in the feature space. However, the computation of $\phi(x_i)\cdot\phi(x_j))$ is intractable to work directly in the feature space. To circumvent the problem, the function $K(x_i,x_j)=\phi(x_i)\cdot\phi(x_j))$ is applied to yield the inner products in feature space. Any function that satisfies Mercer's conditions can perform the implicit mapping. The kernel function is used to avoid explicitly computing features ϕ Therefore, the optimal α^* can be obtained by the following equation

$$\alpha^* = \arg\max_{\alpha} -\frac{1}{2}\sum_{i-1}^{l}\sum_{j-1}^{l}\alpha_i\alpha_j y_i y_j K(x_i,x_j) - \sum_{k-1}^{l}\alpha_k \qquad (7)$$

where $K(x,x')$ is the kernel function performing the nonlinear mapping from the input space into a high dimensional feature space. Those examples $i \notin sv$ (support vector) for which $\alpha_i = 0$ are ignored. As α is determined, b^* and w^* can obtained to find the hyperplane. This study considers three of kernel functions: radial basis functions (RBF), polynomial, and splines kernels.

Probabilistic Scaling

Suppose y_i and f_i are the desired output and the actual output of SVM of data element i, respectively. In the binary class case, the output of the whole training data set is sigmoid, and can be interpreted as the probability of class 1. The logistic likelihood produces the cross-entropy error

$$E = -\sum\left[y_j \log f_j + (1-y_j)\log(1-f_j)\right] \qquad (8)$$

which represents the negative log likelihood. To apply the output of SVM for logistic regression, y_i is transformed into the probabilistic value t_i with $0 \le t_i \le 1$, which is transformed from

$$t_i = \frac{y_i + 1}{2}. \qquad (9)$$

The parametric model proposed in [2] can fit the posterior $P(y=1|x)$. The *a-posteriori* probability P_i of the class membership is computed using two parameters λ and η in Equation (10).

$$p_i = \frac{1}{1+\exp(\lambda f_i + \eta)}. \qquad (10)$$

The optimal parameters λ^*,η^* are determined by minimizing the negative log likelihood of the training data

$$\min F(t_i, p_i) = -\sum_i t_i \log(p_i) + (1-t_i)\log(1-p_i)$$

$$\text{where } p_i = \frac{1}{1+\exp(\lambda f_i + \eta)}. \qquad (11)$$

To find the optimal parameter set $v^* = [\lambda^*,\eta^*]$, the problem is solved by Newton's method. Newton's method is a numerical optimization method that finds a minimum of a function $F : \Re^n \to \Re^2$ by approaching it with a convergent series of approximations. The search starts in an initial point and computes the step toward the next point. The termination test will be performed for minimization until the minimum is found. The Newton's method based on the 2nd order Taylor series of cost function can be represented as

$$F(V_0 + \Delta V) = F(V_0) + g\Delta V + \frac{1}{2}\Delta V^T H \Delta V + O(\|\Delta V\|^3)$$

$$\approx F(V_0) + g\Delta V + \frac{1}{2}\Delta V^T H \Delta V \qquad (12)$$

where g is the gradient of F,

$$g \equiv \nabla F = \begin{bmatrix} \frac{\partial F}{\partial \lambda} \\ \frac{\partial F}{\partial \eta} \end{bmatrix} \tag{13}$$

and H is the Hessian matrix

$$H \equiv F'' = \begin{bmatrix} \frac{\partial^2 F}{\partial \lambda^2} & \frac{\partial^2 F}{\partial \lambda \partial \eta} \\ \frac{\partial^2 F}{\partial \eta \partial \lambda} & \frac{\partial^2 F}{\partial \eta^2} \end{bmatrix}. \tag{14}$$

Since V_0 represents a given value to variable V in the function $F(V_0+\Delta V)$, Equation (10) can be substituted by

$$G(\Delta V) = F(V_0+\Delta V) \tag{15}$$

The minimum of the function $G(\Delta V)$ is given when its derivative $G'(\Delta V) = 0$.

$$G'(\Delta V) = g + H\Delta V = 0$$

$$\Rightarrow \Delta V = -(H^{-1}g) \tag{16}$$

where ΔV determines the step size toward the next point. The optimal parameter set can be obtained as

$$V^* = V_{final-1} + \Delta V_{final} \tag{17}$$

Therefore, Equation (10) can be used to compute the *a-posteriori* probability P_i of the class membership for each image in the database.

PERFORMANCE EVALUATION

Since the image annotation is seen as a classification problem, we tested our algorithm on classification of characteristics of calcification lesions for the DDSM database. In calcification lesions, distribution characteristics are divided into five categories, including "clustered", "linear", "segmental", "regional", and "diffuse" categories. Type characteristics are classified into "punctuate", "amorphous", "pleomorphic", "round and regular", "lucent centre", and "fine linear branching". In performance measurement, the classification accuracy rates for the dataset were computed by comparing the assigned class and actual class. The classification accuracy rate is the number of correct classifications divided by the total number of classification. Table 4 lists the experimental results of classification obtained using the proposed SVM algorithm and Bayes classification. The experimental results show that the average rate of the proposed algorithm is higher than that of Bayes classification. Among the distribution categories, the proposed algorithm can achieve the highest accuracy on the "clustered" category in distribution characteristic and "pleomorphic" category type characteristic, respectively. Apart from the classification performance, the results can also be explained from the effectiveness of feature extraction. Those features extracted for describing calcification distribution are more effective than those used for type characteristic. Since calcified spots are too small, it is very difficult to precisely describe the characteristics of individual spots. This indicates that the accuracy rates for distribution characteristics are better than those for type characteristics.

FUTURE RESEARCH ISSUES

Although automatic annotation for medical images has been an active research field and reasonable progress has been made in past years, many research issues remain open. This section will address some of the issues on the future research agenda.

Table 4. Classification accuracy rates obtained using the proposed SVM algorithm and Bayes classification

Characteristic of Calcification Lesion	Proposed	Bayes
Distribution Characteristic		
Clustered	87%	80%
Linear	80%	81%
Segmental	83%	75%
Regional	81%	78%
Diffuse	77%	72%
Type Characteristic		
Punctate	78%	68%
Amorphous	79%	70%
Pleomorphic	83%	77%
Round and Regular	75%	78%
Lucent Centre	72%	65%
Fine Linear Branching	80%	76%
Average Accuracy	79.5%	74.5%

Standard Controlled Vocabulary

Controlled vocabulary plays a vital role in the task of medical image annotations because controlled vocabulary can not only allow users to specify their queries from a list of predefined words, but also simplify the complexity of image annotation. Although several medical thesaurus resources have been created for medical use, standard controlled vocabulary for each type of medical image still needs to be recognized by the medical professionals. In addition, standard controlled vocabulary should contain precise definitions of vocabulary and their characteristics.

User Interaction

Human intervention during the training stage can greatly improve the performance on image annotation. Relevance feedback is a powerful technique used for facilitating interaction between the user and the annotation algorithm. The research issue includes the learning algorithms, which can dynamically update the weights embedded in the query object to model the high-level semantics and perceptual subjectivity.

Standard Evaluation Test-Bed

Standard evaluation test-beds should be constructed for the comparison between different annotation algorithms. The difficulty in creating evaluation test-beds is that evaluation test-beds need to include distinct categories and the number of the total images should be great, like actual image databases. In addition, the information about lesion details should also be provided.

CONCLUSION

Image annotation is considered as a vital task for searching, and indexing large collections of medical images. This chapter presents a complete scheme for automatic annotation on mammograms. Firstly, we present the feature extraction methods based on BI-RADS standards. This ensures that the meaning and interpretation of mammograms are clearly characterized and can be reliably used for feature extraction. Secondly, we propose the SVM classification approach to image annotation. Finally, our experimental results demonstrate that the scheme can achieve fair performance on image annotation.

REFERENCES

American College of Radiology. (2003). *The ACR Breast Imaging Reporting and Data System (BI-RADS)* (4th ed.). Reston, VA: American College of Radiology.

Ashley, K. (2004). The preservation of databases. *Vine, 34*, 66–70. doi:10.1108/03055720410551075

Baker, J. A., Kornguth, P. J., & Floyd, C. E. Jr. (1996). Breast imaging reporting and data system standardized mammography lexicon: Observer variability in lesion description. *AJR. American Journal of Roentgenology, 166*, 773–778.

Berg, W. A., Campassi, C., Langenberg, P., & Sexton, M. J. (2000). Breast imaging reporting and data system: Inter- and intraobserver variability in feature analysis and final assessment. *AJR. American Journal of Roentgenology, 174*, 1769–1777.

Deselaers, T., Deserno, T. M., & Muller, H. (2007). Automatic medical image annotation in ImageCLEF 2007: Overview, results, and discussion. *Pattern Recognition Letters, 29*, 1988–1995. doi:10.1016/j.patrec.2008.03.001

El-Naqa, I., Yang, Y., Galatsanos, N. P., Nishikawa, R. M., & Wernick, M. N. (2004). A similarity learning approach to content-based image retrieval: Application to digital mammography. *IEEE Transactions on Medical Imaging, 23*, 1233–1244. doi:10.1109/TMI.2004.834601

Feng, D., Siu, W. C., & Zhang, H. J. (2003). *Multimedia information retrieval and management: Technological fundamentals and applications*. Berlin, Germany: Springer.

Gevers, T., & Stokman, H. (2003). Classifying color edges in video into shadow-geometry, highlight, or material transitions. *IEEE Transactions on Multimedia, 5*, 237–243. doi:10.1109/TMM.2003.811620

Ghoshal, A., Ircing, P., & Khudanpur, S. (2005). Hidden Markov models for automatic annotation and content-based retrieval of images and video. In *Proceedings of the 28th International ACM SIGIR Conference on Research and Development in Information Retrieval* (pp. 544-551).

Gonzalez, R. C., & Woods, R. E. (2002). *Digital image processing*. Upper Saddle River, NJ: Prentice Hall.

Guan, H., & Wada, S. (2002). Flexible color texture retrieval method using multi-resolution mosaic for image classification. In *Proceedings of the 6th International Conference on Signal Processing* (pp. 612-615).

Hersh, W. (2009). *Information retrieval: A health and biomedical perspective*. New York, NY: Springer.

Iqbal, Q., & Aggarwal, J. K. (2002). Retrieval by classification of images containing large man-made objects using perceptual grouping. *Pattern Recognition, 35*, 1463–1479. doi:10.1016/S0031-3203(01)00139-X

Lim, J.-H., Tian, Q., & Mulhem, P. (2003). Home photo content modeling for personalized event-based retrieval. *IEEE MultiMedia, 10*, 28–37. doi:10.1109/MMUL.2003.1237548

Majumdar, S., Kothari, M., Augat, P., Newitt, D. C., Link, T. M., & Lin, J. C. (1998). High-resolution magnetic resonance imaging: Three dimensional trabecular bone architecture and biomechanical properties. *Bone, 22*, 445–454. doi:10.1016/S8756-3282(98)00030-1

Moghaddam, H. A., Khajoie, T. T., & Rouhi, A. H. (2003). A new algorithm for image indexing and retrieval using wavelet correlogram. In . *Proceedings of the International Conference on Image Processing, 2003*, 497–500.

Muhimmah, I., Oliver, A., Denton, E. R. E., Pont, J., Perez, E., & Zwiggelaar, R. (2006). Comparison between Wolfe, Boyd, BI-RADS and Tabar based mammographic risk assessment. In *Proceedings of the 8th International Workshop on Digital Mammography* (pp. 407-415).

Nelson, S. J., Johnston, D., & Humphreys, B. L. (2001). Relationships in medical subject headings . In Bean, C. A., & Green, R. (Eds.), *Relationships in the organization of knowledge* (pp. 171–184). New York, NY: Kluwer Academic Publishers.

Nishibori, M. (2000). Problems and solutions in medical color imaging. In *Proceedings of the Second International Symposium on Multi-Spectral Imaging and High Accurate Color Reproduction* (pp. 9-17).

Nishibori, M., Tsumura, N., & Miyake, Y. (2004). Why multi-spectral imaging in medicine? *Journal of Imaging Science and Technology, 48*, 125–129.

Ouyang, A., & Tan, Y. P. (2002). A novel multi-scale spatial-color descriptor for content-based image retrieval. In *Proceedings of the 7th International Conference on Control, Automation, Robotics and Vision* (pp. 1204-1209).

Sampat, M. P., Whitman, G. J., Stephens, T. W., Broemeling, L. D., Heger, N. A., & Bovik, A. C. (2006). The reliability of measuring physical characteristics of spiculated masses on mammography. *The British Journal of Radiology, 79*, S134–S140. doi:10.1259/bjr/96723280

Sebe, N., & Lew, M. S. (2002). Texture features for content-based retrieval . In Lew, M. S. (Ed.), *Principles of visual information retrieval* (pp. 51–85). London, UK: Springer.

Tamai, S. (1999). The color of digital imaging in pathology and cytology. In *Proceedings of the First Symposium of the "Color" of Digital Imaging in Medicine* (pp. 61-66).

Tourassi, G. D. (1999). Journey toward computer-aided diagnosis: Role of image texture analysis. *Radiology, 213*(2), 407–412.

Tsai, C.-F., & Hung, C. (2008). Automatically annotating images with keywords: A review of image annotation systems. *Recent Patents on Computer Science, 1*, 55–68. doi:10.2174/1874479610801010055

Vailaya, A., Figueiredo, A. T., Jain, A. K., & Zhang, H.-J. (2001). Image classification for content-based indexing. *IEEE Transactions on Image Processing, 10*, 117–130. doi:10.1109/83.892448

Varela, C., Timp, S., & Karssemeijer, N. (2006). Use of border information in the classification of mammographic masses. *Physics in Medicine and Biology, 51*, 425–441. doi:10.1088/0031-9155/51/2/016

Veenland, J. F., Grashuis, J. L., Weinans, H., Ding, M., & Vrooman, H. A. (2002). Suitability of texture features to assess changes in trabecular bone architecture. *Pattern Recognition Letters, 23*, 395–403. doi:10.1016/S0167-8655(01)00172-6

Wei, C.-H., & Li, C.-T. (2006). Calcification descriptor and relevance feedback learning algorithms for content-based mammogram retrieval. In *Proceedings of the 8th International Workshop on Digital Mammography 2006* (pp. 307-314).

Wyatt, J. C., & Sullivan, F. (2005). E-health and the future: Promise or peril? *British Medical Journal*, *331*, 1391–1393. doi:10.1136/bmj.331.7529.1391

Yu, H., Li, M., Zhang, H.-J., & Feng, J. (2002). Color texture moments for content-based image retrieval. In . *Proceedings of the International Conference on Image Processing*, *2002*, 929–932. doi:10.1109/ICIP.2002.1039125

Chapter 6
A Hybrid Approach to Content-Based Image Retrieval

Görkem Aşılıoğlu
TOBB ETÜ, Turkey

Emine Merve Kaya
TOBB ETÜ, Turkey

Duygu Sarıkaya
TOBB ETÜ, Turkey

Shang Gao
University of Calgary, Canada

Tansel Ozyer
TOBB ETÜ, Turkey

Jamal Jida
Lebanese University, Lebanon

Reda Alhajj
University of Calgary, Canada & Global University, Lebanon

ABSTRACT

Digital image storage and retrieval is gaining more popularity due to the rapidly advancing technology and the large number of vital applications, in addition to flexibility in managing personal collections of images. Traditional approaches employ keyword based indexing which is not very effective. Content based methods are more attractive though challenging and require considerable effort for automated feature extraction. In this chapter, we present a hybrid method for extracting features from images using a combination of already established methods, allowing them to be compared to a given input image as seen in other query-by-example methods. First, the image features are calculated using Edge Orientation Autocorrelograms and Color Correlograms. Then, distances of the images to the original image will be calculated using the L1 distance feature separately for both features. The distance sets will then be merged according to a weight supplied by the user. The reported test results demonstrate the applicability and effectiveness of the proposed approach.

DOI: 10.4018/978-1-61350-126-9.ch006

INTRODUCTION

Due to the rapid development of the internet and the world-wide web, multimedia information and visual data has become more common than ever. Moreover, with the ease of access to image databases and the increase in the availability of multimedia information, the need for efficient image retrieval has become a matter of concern. The widespread technologies of today let us browse the visual data related to its text content; that is, its corresponding tag. Although the available text based search engines are in high demand, they are not always sufficient; merely depending on the textual information and indexing is hardly satisfactory in terms of availability, accuracy and effectiveness. Some of the drawbacks with the methods used for indexing can be viewed as: (i) they do not conform to a standard description language; (ii) they are inconsistent; (iii) they are subjective; and (iv) they are time consuming (Idris & Panchanathan, 1997). In order to meet the needs of the users and overcome the drawbacks of the methods based on textual information and indexing, content based image retrieval (CBIR) has been the point of focus in many recent research efforts, especially since the early 90s.

The large number of diversified image resources had bottlenecked efficient image retrieval methods. For instance, if images from last century (black and white) and contemporary news media are mixed together and stored in a database, difficulties arise when multiple criteria are required to retrieve a set of similar images. The hybrid approach for CBIR is therefore advantageous due to the complex nature of images with current technologies. By using hybrid retrieval criteria, images are more accurately retrieved and compared.

The development of automated CBIR systems has been an attractive research area due to its wide range of applications in critical fields like bioinformatics and medical imaging, space images, personal collections, homeland security, etc. There are many CBIR approaches described in the literature, e.g., (Chang & Jay Kuo, 1993; Howarth & Ruger, 2004; Kubo et al. 2003; Smith & Chang, 1996; Sun & Ozawa, 2003); the two papers (Veltkamp & Tanase, 2000; Zachary & Iyengar, 1999) include good surveys of CBIR systems. Moreover, various instances of hybrid methods are present in the literature. For instance, Gebara and Alhajj (2007) introduced a combination method using data mining techniques; feature-based methods are presented in (Howarth & Ruger, 2004; Ziou et al., 2009), where hybridized features can be used to generate CBIR systems; an automated system is covered in (Smith & Chang, 1996) with hybridized methodology.

Some of the known systems could be briefly mentioned as follows. QBIC (Niblack et al., 1993) is one of the most-well known and earliest content-based image retrieval systems. The VIR Image Engine (Bach et al., 1996), developed by Virage Inc., is similar to QBIC in the sense that it supports querying by color, shape, layout and texture. Multimedia Analysis and Retrieval System (MARS) (Huang et al., 1996) project was started at the University of Illinois to develop an effective multimedia database management system. Photobook (Pentland, et al., 1994) project was developed at MIT and uses the features of the images for comparison. In WBIIS (Wang et al., 2001), Wang et al. developed an image retrieval system using Daubechies wavelet transformation. In SIMPLICITY (Wang et al., 2001), Wang et al. developed an image retrieval system in which they developed different image features for different image types. WaveQ (Gebara & Alhajj, 2007) which was developed earlier at the University of Calgary is another CBIR system using Wavelets to narrow down the search to a single cluster. Then, the similar images are retrieved from the closest cluster.

The problem may be roughly defined as follows. Given a query image, the term CBIR represents the process of retrieving related images from a collection of images on the basis of image features such as color, texture and shape. The tools, methods and algorithms used originate from fields such as pattern recognition, computer vision, signal processing, neural networks and statistics. Achieving higher accuracy is always the concern especially in vital application like medical image processing, homeland security, remote monitoring, etc. Extracting the best descriptive features is the main challenge in the process.

The shape feature is one of the major key attributes when used for characterizing an object, because the human eye sees images as composed of individual objects, which can be basically best characterized by their shapes (Zhang & Lu, 2001). Face recognition, image preprocessing, space exploration, computer vision, fingerprint identification, handwriting analysis, medical diagnosis, meteorology and manufacturing are among areas which benefit from the shape feature while CBIR is in use. There are many proposed methods to accomplish the content based retrieval by shape features such as Transform methods, Fourier transform (Zhang & Lu, 2001), Neural networks methods, region based methods that use moment descriptors. Shape retrieval focuses on three primary points: shape representation, shape similarity measure and shape indexing (Zhang & Lu, 2001).

Color histograms are widespread in CBIR based on the color feature. They are based on the color distribution in an image. They are easy to implement and are efficient, moreover they are insensitive to small changes in camera viewpoint and angles (Pass & Zabih, 1996). Thus, they could be considered practical. However, they do not include any spatial information, and are therefore liable to false positives. This problem creates an obstacle for usage in large databases. Moreover, the histogram is not robust to large appearance changes (Huang et al., 1997).

Image clustering has been the main focus of many recent research efforts. Assuming that every object has an associated value on every dimension, most previous clustering models have focused on grouping objects with similar values on a subset of dimensions (Yang et al., 2002). Thus, they lack the adequacy to capture consistency among objects in an image. Therefore, clustering methods to capture coherence by a subset of objects on a subset of features, while allowing non-existing attribute values, are being offered (Yang et al., 2002).

In this paper, we introduce a hybrid method with the help of a combination of already established methods. First, the shape and color features of the images are to be calculated using Edge Orientation Autocorrelograms and Color Correlograms, respectively. Then, the features will be compared to a given image, calculating the distance of the original image to the given image separately for both features. After all the images had their distances calculated to the given image, the distances will be sorted and ranked in a single list by merging the two separate distance lists according to the weight specified by the user. The conducted experiments produced good results on non-texture images with single and multiple objects.

The rest of this paper is organized as follows. Section 2 presents the implementation of the proposed approach. Section 3 covers all components of the proposed hybrid approach. Section 4 reports experimental results. Section 5 is conclusions and future work.

Implementation Overview of Proposed Method

We aim to create a system which is easy to use by considering the diversity of the users. With the widespread usage of computers and other handhold electronic devices, it is necessary to have the system flexible enough to be smoothly and effectively used even by those who have little knowledge of the computer technology. Further, we emphasize the accuracy in this study, and thus the time-effectiveness is a secondary concern. Our system should support as many image file extensions as needed. Also, it should be extensible for future usage and contributions.

Features and Benefits

The system provides the necessary features to meet the needs of the users who wish to use it for CBIR; that is, the current implementation is intended to serve both causal users and professional. It providing for basic needs of casual users who are mostly interested in retrieving images from a large database, personal collection or publicly available collections. It also meets the needs of professional who are interested in conducting targeted search to retrieve images that match a given query image in scientific experiments or for security purposes like to track a terrorist suspect.

The proposed solution gives users the opportunity to specify the influence of each feature. In other words, it allows the users to choose how much each feature affects the retrieved results. For instance, the users may choose to disable the color or edge features as required; users are also able to dictate how much they affect the result they retrieve.

Used Techniques and Technologies

The proposed solution has been presented as a desktop application, written in C#.NET. We developed the system on Visual C # 2008 Express Editions. In the rest of this section, we describe how each feature is adequately handled by the system.

A color correlogram demonstrates how the spatial correlation of pairs of colors changes according to the distance (Huang et al., 1997). This is essential in guiding the process for detecting the components in a given image.

The shape detection is computed with the help of the edge orientation autocorrelograms. The Sobel Operator is used for our edge detection algorithm. It is effective enough to serve the target as demonstrated in the test results reported in this paper.

Edge detection refers to algorithms that intend to identify the points where the image brightness changes dramatically; that is, discontinues. The change in brightness indicates a change from one part of the image into another. The Sobel Operator computes the gradient of the image intensity, showing how dramatically the image changes at that point, hence demonstrating the resemblance of that point of the edge to be detected (Sobel & Feldman, 1973).

Fundamentally, an edge orientation autocorrelogram characterizes an image feature at which edges are classified on their orientations and correlation between their neighbor edges. Consequently, it keeps track of the continuous edges and lines of images while major shape properties are also investigated and kept. The obstacles that may normally arise while using CBIR (such as scaling and rotation changes in the viewpoint) are dealt with by using normalization (Mahmoudi et al., 2003). The effectiveness of normalization is very feasible from the conducted testing.

PREVIOUS AND PROPOSED WORK

Color Correlograms

A color correlogram is a method for comparing images. It takes into account the spatial information of the color pixels in an image; hence it produces better methods than simple color histograms and the similar methods that do not use this information. We prefer to use this method for two reasons: (1) it yields good results, performing fairly well when there are images of the same place but with different lighting, zooming, etc, (2) it is not difficult to compute and doesn't take too much time or memory (Huang et al., 1997).

When calculating the correlogram, let us assume we have an image that is n x n pixels and call the image I. The correlogram looks at the positions of colors relative to each other in an image. It is basically a table in which each entry has three properties: the source pixel, a pixel of the color we are searching for, and the probability of finding the target pixel. This probability can be calculated using the following formula (Huang et al., 1997):

$$\gamma_{c_i,c_j}^{(k)}(I) \triangleq Pr_{p_1 \in Ic_i, p_2 \in I}[p_2 \in I_{c_3} \mid |p_1 - p_2| = k]$$

Here i and j are elements of the set {1, 2,..., m}, where m signifies the number that the colors in the image are quantized into, therefore c_i shows the ith color in this space. We show the pixels as p, so that p_1 is the source pixel (the pixel having the color i) and p_2 is the pixel we are looking for. We must keep in mind that:

$$|p_1 - p_2| = \{\max(|x_1 - x_2|, |y_1 - y_2|)\}$$

In the above equation, x and y represent the coordinates of a point p in the image. One other thing to note here is the distance that we have use in the search. This method chooses a fixed d that defines the correlogram, which means that d is the maximum distance that will be searched. In this method, we search for every k that is between 1 and d. Choosing this value is significant because as d gets larger, the memory requirements will increase, but if d is too small, the quality of the procedure will decrease (Huang et al., 1997).

The calculation of the above probability is done using histograms. We know that the probability of a pixel's color in an image being c is equal to the number of times the color occurs in the image divided by the number of pixels in the image. This can be formalized as shown below:

$$h_{c_i}(I) \triangleq n^2 \bullet \Pr_{p \in I}[p \in I_{c_i}]$$

To compare two images (for this example, I and J) with each other to find out how similar they are, the following two formulas are used:

$$|I - J|_{h,L_1} \triangleq \sum_{i \in [m]} |h_{c_i}(I) - h_{c_i}(J)|$$

$$|I - J|_{\gamma,L_1} \triangleq \sum_{i,j \in [m], k \in [d]} |\gamma_{c_i,c_j}^{(k)}(I) - \gamma_{c_i,c_j}^{(k)}(J)|$$

While working with these equations, we must keep in mind that although these show that every color is equally important, the importance can be changed if necessary, to provide better results (Huang et al., 1997).

Edge Detection

The shape detection part of the proposed hybrid system is employed using edge orientation autocorrelograms, which require an edge detection method to be applied to the image first. As recommended by the authors of (Sobel & Feldman, 1973), we have used the Sobel Operator for our edge detection algorithm, followed by the algorithm of the edge orientation autocorrelogram.

Edge Detection with the Sobel Operator

The Sobel Operator can be defined as a discrete differentiation operator. It computes an approximation of the gradient of the image intensity function. For every point in the image, the Sobel operator returns the corresponding gradient vector, or the norm of this vector. Simply put, the operator calculates the gradient of the image intensity at each point, showing how 'abruptly' or 'smoothly' the image changes at that point, thus pointing out the likeliness of that point in the image being an edge (Sobel & Feldman, 1973).

Mathematically, the Sobel operator can be described as two 3 x 3 kernels which are convolved with the original image to calculate an approximation of the derivatives. Convolution can be defined as a mathematical operator which takes two functions and creates a third function which represents the amount of overlap between the two original functions. If our original image is O, the horizontal derivative result image is R_x, and the vertical derivative result image is R_y, the application of the convolution operator can be shown with the following equations (Sobel & Feldman, 1973):

$$R_X = \begin{bmatrix} +1 & 0 & -1 \\ +2 & 0 & -2 \\ +1 & 0 & -1 \end{bmatrix} * O$$

$$R_y = \begin{bmatrix} +1 & +2 & +1 \\ 0 & 0 & 0 \\ -1 & -2 & -1 \end{bmatrix} * O$$

where * denotes the 2-dimensional convolution operation. Then, the gradient's magnitude is calculated as follows.

$$R = \sqrt{R_x^{\ 2} + R_y^{\ 2}}$$

Also, the direction of the gradient can be calculated as an angle using the following formula:

$$\theta = \tan^{-1}\left(\frac{R_y}{R_x}\right)$$

Edge Orientation Autocorrelogram

Basically, an edge orientation autocorrelogram defines an image feature where edges are classified on their orientations and the correlation between their neighbor edges. Thus, it incorporates information of continuous edges and lines of images and describes major shape properties of images. Using normalization against scaling and rotation, and natural properties of edge detection, this technique can tolerate translation, scaling, color, illumination and viewing position variations (Mahmoudi et al., 2003).

The first step of generating an edge orientation autocorrelogram is edge detection, which is detailed in the previous section. The algorithm follows edge detection by a simple thresholding operation to single out prominent edges and create a binarized image. Then, the edges are segmented into n uniform, 5-degree segments.

The fourth step in the algorithm is to generate a distance set which shows the distances from the current edge that is used in calculating the correlation; it is apparent that nearby edges have high correlation. Mahmoudi et al. have described four members set to be used in the algorithm presented in their paper, containing only odd numbers, following the logic that if the information of an even numbered pixel is needed, it can be obtained from an odd numbered pixel around it.

The final stage of the algorithm involves the actual computation of the edge orientation autocorrelogram. The correlogram is a matrix with n rows and d columns, where any element of the matrix indicates the number of similar edges with a certain distance between them. Two edges with k pixel distances apart are said to be similar if the absolute values of the difference between their orientations and amplitudes are less than an angle and an amplitude threshold value.

The generated feature vector is then normalized to tolerate scaling, illumination and rotation. The normalization procedures are quite simple; detailed descriptions can be found in (Mahmoudi et al., 2003).

Combining the Methods

The two methods described above have been combined with the following approach.

First, features of the images are calculated using the edge orientation autocorrelogram and the color correlogram method. The features are separately stored in an image property structure.

Querying the database of images is done by example. The features of the query image are extracted using the method detailed above. The features of the query image are compared to the features of the database images using the L1 distance method.

The L1 distance is the absolute value of component-wise difference between two objects. Given objects $x = (x_1, x_{2,\ldots,} x_n)$ and $y = (y_1, y_{2,\ldots,} y_n)$, the L1 distance d is defined as:

Figure 1. General workflow of the hybrid method for CBIR

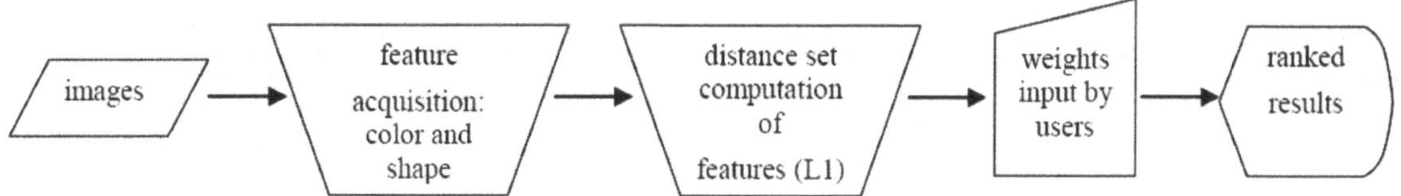

$$d = \sum_{i=1}^{n} | x_i - y_i |$$

The total distance is calculated separately for the two features; then combined according to their weights. To do that, the distance sets of both the edge orientation autocorrelogram and the color correlogram will be statistically normalized between 0 and 1. After that, the distance sets will be multiplied by the user supplied weight. The weights can be set by users according to image properties, i.e., users can customize the importance between color and shape of query images. For example, if the query image is monotone, the user can completely ignore the color component from the feature set, or may decide that the shape of images is more important than color, which is often the case when the image pool is large containing both colored and black & white images from various resources.

Then, the total distance between images will be calculated by adding the distance sets together.

The images will then be ranked, the image from the database with the smallest distance will be ranked as the first image; the other images follow the same suit. The method is expected to produce better results than both edge oriented autocorrelogram and color correlogram, given a proper weight for a proper set of images. The formal approach is symbolized in Figure 1.

EXPERIMENTAL RESULTS

Database

Our first experiment was done with the 1000 image database used in (Li & Wang, 2003) and (Wang et al., 2001). The images consist of 256 x 384 pixel sized color photographs. Every hundred images in this set is a cluster by itself, composed of similar photographs, such as tribal scenes, flowers, food photos, horses, nature, etc. The goal within this data set was to find images within the 100-image cluster that the query image belongs to within the first five ranks of reported results. Our second experiment was with 30 images, where each image has an existing counterpart which has to be discovered by the algorithm.

Limitations

Within the bounds of the experiment, all tested images are resized to 200 x 200 pixels to reduce the runtime cost of the algorithms. Even then, analyzing the features of a single image takes roughly 90 seconds on a 2.2 GHz Athlon 64, mainly due to our un-optimized algorithm and serial execution. However, this should not an issue because accuracy is the main target in this research; it would be possible to speed up the process by running in a more powerful computing environment.

Table 1.

	True	False
Actual True	True Positive (TP)	False Negative (FN)
Actual False	False Positive (FP)	True Negative (TN)

Features

72 color buckets are considered for color correlogram calculation, using the RGB color space. The images are converted to grayscale for edge orientation autocorrelogram calculation. Any edge with a magnitude of under 25 is discarded during the edge detection phase of the edge orientation autocorrelogram. The distance set used in both edge detection autocorrelograms and color correlograms is D = {1, 3, 5, 7}. The merging ratio for the first database is 30% edge orientation autocorrelogram versus 70% color correlogram. We discovered by experimenting that this is an ideal ratio for color photographs. However, a 50% ratio for each feature worked best for the second experiment, where objects were the central focus of the photographs. These ratios were discovered through the use of a training set, which was a sample group of images (5 from every cluster), which the algorithm was tested on. The training images were not used as the query images in the experiment, but were left in the database to provide noise.

Queries

There are no specific queries designed to use with the first database; 20 images at random are chosen, two from every cluster, and the images ranking in the top ten are checked to see if they returned images from the same cluster. For the second database, the rank of the correct image is checked to see if it was successful.

Results

The experiment indicated that the algorithm achieved 85% success rate in the first part of the experiment, which is to say on average, almost eight images in the top ten ranked images will be semantically related to the query image. The failures were often minor, such as mistaking the sea for the similarly colored and textured sky. Beaches, tribal people and mountains ranked the worst among the data sets, while dinosaurs, buses and ruins provided excellent results. This difference in results between different sets can be attributed to the color complexity of the photos. The second experiment showed that, even when spread out among unrelated images, the merged algorithm can find the answer to the query within the top five ranked images at worst. On average, the images show up in the second place. Both of the experiments were tried with only one feature instead of a merge. On both experiments, the average success rate was significantly decreased up to 15% loss in accuracy, compared to our hybrid approach.

To further demonstrate the effectiveness of the proposed method, we provide the related *precision* and *recall* statistics. To define precision and recall, the normally utilized contingency matrix is shown below (Table 1):

Based on the contingency matrix, precision is defined as:

$$\text{precision} = \frac{TP}{TP + FP}$$

and recall is defined as:

Figure 2. Precision and recall statistics for the proposed method

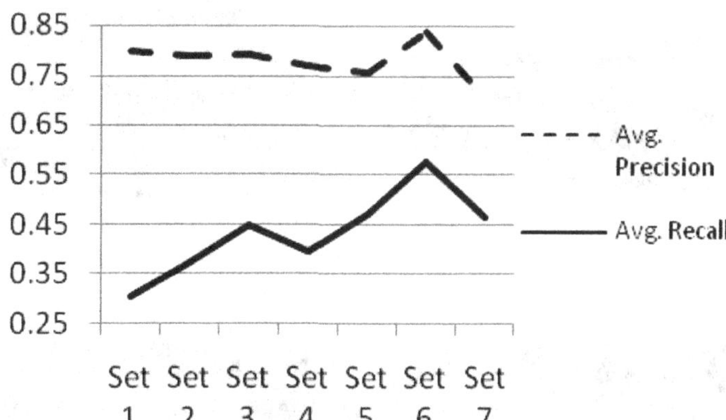

$$\text{recall} = \frac{TP}{TP + FN}$$

In other words, precision is the fraction of retrieved images that are relevant to ranked results, whereas recall is the fraction of the images that are relevant to the query that are successful retrieved within top ranked results.

To illustrate the effectiveness of CBIR, we randomly choose 7 data sets from 1000 images, each containing 10 images; we take top 10 ranked results to compute precision and recall. The test outcome can be positive (correctly retrieved) or negative (incorrectly/not retrieved) and the related entries in the contingency matrix are interpreted as follows:

- **TP:** Selective images are correctly retrieved (within top ranked results).
- **FP:** Visually invisible images, such as pure black and over-exposure images, or irrelevant images from the original data set that are incorrectly identified by top ranked results.
- **FN:** Selective images that are not retrieved (within top ranked results).

The results are plotted in Figure 2.

From precision and recall statistics, we can see that the general precision of retrieval is satisfactory, provided that only 10 ranked results are considered; and recall is low as expected, because the 1000 images are clustered in the experimental setting, leading to a potentially large number of relevant images for difererent query images.

To compare the hybrid approach with single methods, we change the weights assigned to distance sets in order to adjust the importance between color correlogram and edge orientation autocorrelogram. For example, if we want to ignore the color correlogram we set the weight to 0 and set the weight of edge orientation autocorrelogram to 1. We randomly select images from the original data set and retrieved similar images. Our findings are described below:

1. For colored images with 2 or more objects (such as several people celebrating together), the hybrid approach accuracy improves approximately 17%, compared with method that only uses the color correlogram.
2. For monotone images (such as snow in the mountain), the average improvement of using single color correlogram is not significant.
3. If we only use edge orientation autocorrelogram, some color-rich pictures can be

Figure 3. An example of a good match

Figure 4. An example of a bad match

mistakenly retrieved as expected results for queries. However, with our current implementation, which converts colored images to grayscale, this effect is not significant (it reports approximately 3% improvement for certain images on average).

Comparison

When we compare our hybrid method to the other methods, including plain Color Correlograms, Edge Orientation Autocorrelograms or previous work like Color Coherence Vectors (Pentland et al., 1994), we see that our method performs better than any of these methods. Given the same data sets, plain Color Correlograms and Edge Orientation Autocorrelograms achieved 59% and 44% success rates, respectively, in the first experiment, and could report a correct answer within the first 5 related images for the second experiment. An implementation of the color coherence vector method yielded 52% for the first experiment, and results within the first 5 related images for the second experiment. Clearly, the proposed hybrid method surpasses all these algorithms when they are used solely. However, it should also be noted that while our method is better on average, there are some types of images it stutters at, and one of these other methods may be more suited for such image. For example, EOACs excel at the comparison of object-only images, while CCs find similar color features better than CCV or histograms. Our method addresses this concern by allowing users to specify the weights of the included methods. Fine tuning the weights can lead to near perfect results with almost all images. However, this fine tuning requires human expertise for better tune up. We are currently looking at some approaches to automate the whole process if possible, though finding appropriate values for the contribution of each attribute is challenging. Finally, some of the good and bad matched images are displayed in Figure 3, 4, 5, 6, and 7.

CONCLUSION AND FUTURE WORK

In this paper, we presented several CBIR algorithms and proposed a way to combine them in order to create a more effective system of image retrieval than its subsystems (parts). We have demonstrated that the combinations of the algo-

Figure 5. An example of single object matching

Figure 6. An example of a good first match

Figure 7. An example of a good match

rithms will surpass the results presented by the originals, albeit at a small level.

The implementation has been coded using C#.NET as its framework enables us to provide an easily extendable solution, as well as allows us to create a more presentable application rather than a flat testbed. To remove the burden of having to re-code simple image tasks such as resizing or iterating through the pixels of an image, we have opted to use the open source AForge framework (http://code.google.com/p/aforge/).

This study provides a base for further studies and improvements. Since the basic idea of this paper itself is to combine several content-based image retrieval algorithms and techniques to get better results, it encourages further studies to adapt new algorithms and techniques as well as adding new features resulting in better outcomes and more efficiency.

Finally, it is worth mentioning that throughout this study, a few clustering algorithms and techniques have been attempted including k-means algorithm (Alsabti et al., 1998; Arthur & Vassilvitskii, 2007). After testing these techniques and algorithms and not experiencing the expected outcomes in the end, it is later decided that more advanced clustering or segmentation algorithms should be implemented in the future. It is considered that Graph Partitioning Active Contours (GPAC) for Image Segmentation (Sumengen & Manjunath, 2006), which basically focuses on the active contours and curves rather than only the colors, could be a sufficient way to satisfy the clustering / segmentation needs for our study. GPAC introduces a new type of diverse segmentation cost mechanisms and related active contour methods which mainly focus on pairwise resemblance of the pixels, which allows for discrimination of the foreground and the background parts of the photo, thus allowing us to apply our algorithm to just the foreground or the background, giving us better results.

REFERENCES

AForge. (n.d.). *Framework*. Retrieved from http://code.google.com/p/aforge/

Alsabti, K., Ranka, S., & Singh, V. (1998). An efficient K-means clustering algorithm. *In Proc. 1st Workshop on High Performance Data Mining.*

Arthur, D., & Vassilvitskii, S. (2007). K-means++: The advantages of careful seeding. *Proceedings of the Eighteenth Annual ACM-SIAM Symposium on Discrete Algorithms,* (pp. 1027-1035).

Bach, J., Fuller, C., Gupta, A., Hampapur, A., Gorowitz, B., & Humphrey, R. … Shu, C. (1996). Virage image search engine: An open framework for image management. In *Proceedings of the SPIE Conference on Storage and Retrieval for Image and Video Databases IV*, (pp. 76–87).

Chang, T., & Jay Kuo, C. C. (1993). Texture analysis and classification with tree structured wavelet transform. *IEEE Transactions on Image Processing, 2*(3), 429–441. doi:10.1109/83.242353

Gebara, D., & Alhajj, R. (2007). *Waveq: Combining wavelet analysis and clustering for effective image retrieval.* 21st International Conference on Advanced Information Networking and Applications Workshops, 1, (pp. 289–294).

Howarth, P., & Ruger, S. (2004). Evaluation of texture features for content-based image retrieval. In *Proc. of International Conference on Image and Video Retrieval*, (pp. 326–334).

Huang, J., Kumar, S. R., Mitra, M., Zhu, W. J., & Zabih, R. (1997). Image indexing using color correlograms. *Proceedings of the 1997 Conference on Computer Vision and Pattern Recognition (CVPR '97),* pp. 767.

Huang, T. S., Mehrotra, S., & Ramchandran, K. (1996). Multimedia analysis and retrieval system (mars) project. In *Proceedings of 33rd Annual Clinic on Library Application of Data Processing - Digital Image Access and Retrieval.*

Idris, F., & Panchanathan, S. (1997). Review of image and video indexing techniques. *Journal of Visual Communication and Image Representation, 8*(2), 146–166. doi:10.1006/jvci.1997.0355

Kubo, M., Aghbari, Z., & Makinouchi, A. (2003). Content-based image retrieval technique using wavelet-based shift and brightness invariant edge feature. *International Journal of Wavelets, Multresolution, and Information Processing, 1*(2), 163–178. doi:10.1142/S0219691303000141

Li, J., & Wang, J. Z. (2003). Automatic linguistic indexing of pictures by a statistical modeling approach. *IEEE Transactions on Pattern Analysis and Machine Intelligence*, *25*(9), 1075–1088. doi:10.1109/TPAMI.2003.1227984

Mahmoudi, F., Shanbehzadeh, J., Eftekhari-Moghadam, A. M., & Soltanian-Zadeh, H. (2003). Image retrieval based on shape similarity by edge orientation autocorrelogram. *Pattern Recognition*, *36*, 1725–1736. doi:10.1016/S0031-3203(03)00010-4

Niblack, W., Barber, R., Equitz, W., Flickner, M., Glasman, E., & Petkovic, D. … Taubin, G. (1993). The qbic project: Querying images by content using color, texture, and shape. In *Proceedings of the SPIE Conference on Storage and Retrieval for Image and Video Databases*, (pp. 173–187).

Pass, G., & Zabih, R. (1996). Histogram refinement for content-based image retrieval. *Proceedings of the 3rd IEEE Workshop on Applications of Computer Vision*, (p. 96).

Pentland, A., Picard, R., & Sclaroff, S. (1994). Photobook: Tools for content based manipulation of image databases. In *Proceedings of the SPIE Conference on Storage and Retrieval for Image and Video Databases II.*

Sklansky, J. (1978). Image segmentation and feature extraction. *IEEE Transactions on Systems, Man, and Cybernetics*, *8*, 237–247. doi:10.1109/TSMC.1978.4309944

Smith, J. R., & Chang, S. F. (1996). VisualSEEk: A fully automated content-based image query system. *ACM International Conference Multimedia*, (pp. 87–98).

Sobel, I., & Feldman, G. (1973). A 3x3 isotropic gradient operator for image processing. In Duda, R., & Hart, P. (Eds.), *Pattern classification and scene analysis* (pp. 271–272). John Wiley and Sons.

Sumengen, B., & Manjunath, B. S. (2006). Graph partitioning active contours (GPAC) for image segmentation. *IEEE Transactions on Pattern Analysis and Machine Intelligence*, *28*(4), 509–521. doi:10.1109/TPAMI.2006.76

Sun, Y., & Ozawa, S. (2003). Semantic-meaningful content-based image retrieval in wavelet domain. In *Proc. of the 5th ACM SIGMM International Workshop on Multimedia Information Retrieval*, (pp. 122–129).

Veltkamp, R. C., & Tanase, M. (2000). *Content-based image retrieval systems: A survey*. (Technical report, UU-CS-2000-34).

Wang, J., Li, J., & Wiederhold, G. (2001). Simplicity: Semantics-sensitive integrated matching for picture libraries. *IEEE Transactions on Pattern Analysis and Machine Intelligence*, *23*(9), 947–963. doi:10.1109/34.955109

Yang, J., Wang, W., Wang, H., & Yu, P. (2002). Delta-clusters: Capturing subspace correlation in a large data set. *Proceedings of the 18th International Conference on Data Engineering*, (p. 517).

Zachary, J. M., & Iyengar, S. S. (1999). Content based image retrieval systems. In *Proceedings of the IEEE Symposium on Application-Specific Systems and Software Engineering and Technology*, (pp. 136–143).

Zhang, D., & Lu, G. (2001). A comparative study on shape retrieval using Fourier descriptors with different shape signatures. *Proceedings of the Second IEEE Pacific Rim Conference on Multimedia: Advances in Multimedia Information Processing*, (pp. 855-860). October 24-26.

Zhang, M., & Alhajj, R. (2010). Effectiveness of naq-tree as index structure for similarity search in high-dimensional metric space. *Knowledge and Information Systems*, *22*(1). doi:10.1007/s10115-008-0190-y

Ziou, D., Hamri, T., & Boutemedjet, S. (2009). A hybrid probabilistic framework for content-based image retrieval with feature weighting. *Pattern Recognition*, *42*(7), 1511–1519. doi:10.1016/j.patcog.2008.11.025

KEY TERMS AND DEFINITIONS

CBIR: It is the acronym for content based image retrieval. Given a query image, It finds the visually similar images.

Color Correlograms: Color correlogram is the spatial pairwise color correlation according to distance.

Edge Detection: Edge detection is a problem to find object boundaries in image analysis.

Edge Orientation Autocorrelogram: It defines an image feature where edges are classified on their orientations and the correlation between their neighbor edges.

Sobel Operator: Discrete differentiation operator in edge detection.

Chapter 7
A Survey on Feature Based Image Retrieval Techniques

Ling Shao
University of Sheffield, UK

ABSTRACT

In this chapter, we review classical and state of the art Content-Based Image Retrieval algorithms. Techniques on representing and extracting visual features, such as color, shape, and texture, are first presented. Several well-known image retrieval systems using those features are also summarized. Then, two recent trends on image retrieval, namely semantic based methods and local invariant regions based methods, are discussed. We analyze the drawbacks of current approaches and propose directions for future work.

INTRODUCTION

With the rapid growth of the Internet, a huge number of images are produced and stored every day. The need to retrieve relevant images from a huge and growing database is shared by many groups, including radiologists, journalists, librarians, photographers, historians, and database engineers. Most existing Image Retrieval systems are text-based. Traditionally, Images are first annotated using text, and then text-based Database Management Systems are used to perform Image Retrieval. However, the content in an image is often not well captured using words, which results in erroneous or inaccurate annotation. Furthermore, manually annotating millions of images is a time-consuming and tedious task. Another drawback of text-based image retrieval results from the subjectivity of human perception, i.e. for the same image content, different people may perceive it differently.

Disadvantages with text-based image retrieval have provoked growing interest in the development of Content-Based Image Retrieval (CBIR).

DOI: 10.4018/978-1-61350-126-9.ch007

That is, instead of being manually annotated by text-based keywords, images are indexed by their visual content, such as color, texture, etc. The performance of a CBIR system is highly dependent on the distinctiveness and robustness of the visual features extracted from an image.

The remainder of this chapter is organized as follows. In Section 2, visual feature representation and extraction is discussed. Feature extraction is the basis of Content-Based Image Retrieval. Features discussed include color, texture, shape and spatial layout. An overview of a number of commercial and research CBIR systems is presented in Section 3. In Section 4, recent work in CBIR is reviewed. Finally, the conclusion is drawn in Section 5.

VISUAL FEATURE REPRESENTATION AND EXTRACTION

The representation of visual features in images is a fundamental issue in Content-Based Image Retrieval. Computer vision and pattern recognition algorithms provide the means to extract numerical descriptors which give a quantitative measure to such features. The features employed in most CBIR techniques include: color, texture, local shape and spatial layout. The following is a brief description of some current methods for extracting such features and the similarity measures between such features.

Color Representation

Color is one of the most widely used visual features in Image Retrieval. It is relatively easy to compute and is independent of image size and orientation. The perception of color is dependent on the chromatic attributes of images. From a physical point of view, color perception is dependent on the spectral energy distribution of the electromagnetic radiation that strikes the retina. From the psychological point of view, color perception is related to several factors, including color attributes (brightness, chromaticity and saturation), surrounding colors, color spatial organization, the viewing surround, the observer's memory/knowledge/experience, etc (Bimbo, 1999).

Several ways have been proposed for representing color. The RGB color representation is a reasonable choice when there is little variation in the recording or in the perception, since the representation is designed to match the cone color channels of the eye. An image expressed as (R, G, B) makes most sense for processing digitized paintings, photographs and trademarks, where the planar images are taken in frontal view under standard conditions. The use of opponent color representations (Swain and Ballard, 1991) makes a substantial improvement to the RGB color representation. The employment of opponent color axes (R-G, 2B-R-G, R+G+B) has the advantage of isolating the brightness information on the third axis. The first two (chromatic) axes can be down-sampled, since humans are more sensitive to brightness than to chroma. The CMY (Cyan, Magenta, Yellow) color representation is usually used for color printing (Sharma, 2003). They are the complements of Red, Green and Blue, and are called subtractive primaries since they are obtained by subtracting light from white. The HSV (Hue, Saturation, Value) representation is often used because of its invariant properties (Gonzalez and Woods, 2002). For example, the hue is invariant under camera rotation and illumination changes, so is more suitable for image retrieval.

Color histograms are one of the most commonly used color feature representations in Image Retrieval. They are obtained by discretizing image colors and identifying the proportion of pixels within an image having specific values. The color histogram of a circular image region is invariant to camera rotation, because rotation does not change the proportion of pixels that have particular color intensity levels inside the circular region. Zoom also does not affect the color histogram of an image region, if the scale of that region is selected properly. However, color histograms are sensitive to illumination variations, because illumination changes have a shifting effect on histograms. The use of normalized RGB through their sum, or only using the Hue and Saturation components of the Color representation can largely resolve such lighting sensitivity problems (Hashizume et al., 1998). Only using color histograms is usually not effective for image retrieval, because images containing very different content could result in similar color histograms.

Some alternative color feature representations are proposed for utilizing the spatial relations between color pixels, e.g. color constants (Worring and Gevers, 2001), color signatures (Kender and Yeo, 1998) and blobs (Chang et al., 1997).

Color features can be compared using common similarity measures between feature vectors. For example, the similarity between color histograms can be evaluated by computing the L_1 or L_2 distance between them. The L_1 or L_2 distances D_1 and D_2 respectively between a query image histogram $\mathbf{H}(Q)$ and the histogram of a test image in the database $\mathbf{H}(T)$ are defined as follows:

$$D_1(Q,T) = \sum_{i=1}^{n} | \mathbf{H}(Q_i) - \mathbf{H}(T_i) | \quad (1)$$

$$D_2(Q,T) = \left(\sum_{i=1}^{n} (\mathbf{H}(Q_i) - \mathbf{H}(T_i))^2 \right)^{1/2} \quad (2)$$

where i represents the index in the histogram bin. If two images are similar, the distances tend to be small.

There are also some similarity measures that are specific for comparing color features. Swain and Ballard (1991) proposed Histogram Intersection as a similarity measure for Color Histograms. The Histogram Intersection between a query image and an image in the database is defined as:

$$HI(Q,T) = \frac{\sum_{i=1}^{n} \min(\mathbf{H}(Q_i), \mathbf{H}(T_i))}{\sum_{i=1}^{n} \mathbf{H}(T_i)} \quad (3)$$

The value of $HI(Q,T)$ ranges from 0 to 1, with 1 being the Histogram Intersection of two same images, and zero when they are highly dissimilar.

Niblack et al. (1993) presented a technique for comparing the histograms between similar but not identical colors. In order to reduce the indexing dimension, the 256 most significant colors are first extracted from the RGB color space. The distance measure between two images is then defined as:

$$D(Q,T) = (\mathbf{H}(Q) - \mathbf{H}(T))^T \mathbf{W}(\mathbf{H}(Q) - \mathbf{H}(T)) \quad (4)$$

where $\mathbf{W}$ is a weighting matrix representing the extent to which the histograms bins are perceptually similar to each other. $W_{i,j}$ is estimated according to the Euclidean distance $d_{i,j}$ between colors i and j in the Munsell color space (Munsell, 1912):

$$W_{i,j} = (1 - d_{i,j} / \max(d_{i,j})) \quad (5)$$

The Color Correlogram, proposed by Huang et al. (1997), is another popular approach for image color comparison. This method describes the global distribution of local spatial correlation of colors. A Color Correlogram of an image is a table indexed by color pairs, where the k-th entry for (i, j) specifies the probability of finding a pixel of color j at a distance k from a pixel of color i in the image. The Color Correlogram of an image I can be defined as follows:

$$CC_{i,j}^{k}(I) = P(I(p_1) = i, I(p_2) = j \| p_1 - p_2 |= k) \quad (6)$$

where p denotes a pixel in the image, and $I(p)$ represents the color of pixel p. Color Correlograms are more effective in discriminating images than Color Histograms, since they capture the spatial correlations of colors in an image.

Texture Representation

Texture refers to the visual patterns which are perceptually homogenous, but for which the individual elements that comprise the pattern carry little information. Texture has both a statistical and a structural (repetition) aspect. It contains important structural information about surfaces and their relationship to the surrounding environment. Periodicity, smoothness, coarseness, regularity and degree of complexity are some of attributes of a texture. Scale is also a critical property of texture, because a textured region may appear textureless when it is observed at a different scale.

Although texture is an accepted visual concept, a precise definition of texture tends to be intangible. Ballard and Brown (1982) state: "The notion of texture admits no rigid description, but a dictionary definition of texture as 'something composed of closely interwoven elements' is fairly apt." A texture is usually represented by numerical measures that are derived from texture features in either the space or frequency domain. Statistical and structural representations are the two widely used measures for describing the texture of an image region.

Due to the periodicity property of texture, auto-correlation can be used as a texture representation that describes the spatial size of grey-level primitives. The lag k auto-correlation function of an image region R can be defined as:

$$AC(I_R,k) = \frac{\sum_{i\in R}(I(i)-\mu_R)\cdot(I(i-k)-\mu_R)}{\sum_{i\in R}(I(i)-\mu_R)^2} \quad (7)$$

where $I(i)$ indicates the intensities of the image region, and μ_R the average of the intensities in R. The auto-correlation value of a coarse texture decreases slowly with distance, while the auto-correlation value of a fine texture decreases rapidly with distance.

The co-occurrence matrix (Haralick et al., 1973) can be used as a texture feature that describes the spatial relationships between grey-levels. Each element in the matrix $P_D(i, j)$ represents the probability of two pixels having the grey-levels of i and j at a given distance D. The co-occurrence matrix can be defined as follows:

$$P_D(i,j) = P(\mathrm{I}(p_1) = i, \mathrm{I}(p_2) = j \,\big|\, |p_1 - p_2| = D) \quad (8)$$

where P is probability, and p_1 and p_2 denote the locations in the grey-level image **I**. The distance D is defined in polar coordinates, with discrete length and orientation. The dimension of the co-occurrence matrix is N x N, if the image **I** has N grey values. Some attributes of these co-occurrence probabilities have been used to characterize the properties of a texture region. These attributes are defined as follows:

$$energy = \sum_{i,j} P^2(i,j) \quad (9)$$

$$contrast = \sum_{i,j} (i-j)^2 P(i,j) \quad (10)$$

$$entropy = -\sum_{i,j} P(i,j)\log_2 P(i,j) \quad (11)$$

$$homogeneity = \sum_{i,j} \frac{P(i,j)}{1+|i-j|} \quad (12)$$

The co-occurrence matrix method is not suitable for textures composed of large patches, because it does not consider the primitive shape of the texture.

Textures can also be represented by fractal properties such as fractal dimension. Fractal dimension characterizes the coarseness of the texture surface. Fractal dimension can be estimated using various methods, such as spatial correlation estimator, Fourier estimator, surface estimator, box counting, and blanket estimator. Freeborough (1997) compared several fractal dimension estimation methods and concluded that Fourier based estimation correlates more closely with the true fractal dimension than all other methods.

Textures can also be represented in the frequency domain by analyzing the power spectral density function. Since the coarseness of textures is dependent on the spatial periodicity, the spectral energy of coarse textures tends to be concentrated at low spatial frequencies, and the spectral energy of fine textures is concentrated at high spatial frequencies.

A texture representation based on texture energy is called a texture signature. Texture energy was proposed by Laws (1980) using 12 basis functions. 12 new images are first obtained by convolving the original image with each of the 12 basis functions. Then each of these images is transformed into an energy image by replacing each pixel in the convolved image by an average of the above values in a window centered on that pixel. Therefore, each pixel in the original image is represented by a multi-dimensional feature vector, which is dependent on the 12 texture energy images. Texture signatures can be extracted from the multi-dimensional space of the texture feature vectors. The similarity between a query texture and a target texture can be evaluated by computing the correlation between their texture signatures.

The structural representation of texture assumes that texture is constructed from texture primitives according to certain placement rules. Voorhees and Poggio (1987) and Blostein and Ahuja (1989) used Laplacian of Gaussian functions for filtering the image to extract texture elements. Fu (1982) proposed a method that regards the texture image as texture primitives arranged according to a placement rule, which is defined by a tree grammar. A texture is then described as a string in the language defined by the grammar, where the symbols are the texture primitives.

The similarity between texture feature representations is usually evaluated using distance measures, such as Euclidean distance and Mahalanobis distance.

Shape Representation

Similar to texture, shape is a widely understood concept but difficult to define formally. Marshall (1989) defined shape as a function of position and direction of a connected curve within a two-dimensional field. Shape representations of an object are usually based on a set of attributes extracted from the boundary and interior of the shape. Attributes can either describe the global form of the shape, such as its area, compactness and the major axis orientation, or local elements such as interesting points and corners. Generally, shape representations can be divided into two types: region based (internal) and boundary based (external). The former describes the internal region enclosed by the object contour, whereas the latter characterizes the external boundary of the object. Both the boundary based and region based shape representations can be further divided in spatial and transform domain methods. The latter covers techniques that are based on mathematical transforms, such as Fourier and Wavelet transforms.

The use of moment invariants is one of the most popular methods for describing the internal region of a shape in the spatial domain. The moments of a region R are defined as:

$$M_{pq} = \sum_{(x,y)\in R} x^p y^q f(x,y) \tag{13}$$

where $f(x, y)$ is the image and (p+q) indicates the order of the moment. The moments can be normalized to be invariant under transformations such as translation, rotation and scaling. A set of functions, called moment invariants, were proposed by Hu (1962) based on the above moments. Hu's moment invariants have been employed by numerous researchers in object recognition and image retrieval.

The internal region of an object's shape can also be described in the transform domain using some of the coefficients of their 2D discrete Fourier transform. The 2D discrete Fourier transform of a function $f(x, y)$ defined over the set $\{0,1,\ldots,M-1\}\times\{0,1,\ldots,N-1\}$ can be expressed as follows:

$$F(m, n) = \sum_{x=0}^{M-1}\sum_{y=0}^{N-1} f(x,y)e^{-2\pi j(mx/M+ny/N)} \tag{14}$$

With this representation, shape similarity is evaluated in the transform domain. Therefore, translation of $f(x, y)$ results in a change of phase of $F(m, n)$. Rotation and scaling of $f(x, y)$ result in substantial changes in $F(m, n)$, i.e. the rotation of $f(x, y)$ results in equivalent rotation in $F(m, n)$, and the scaling of $f(x, y)$ with the factor a results in scaling of $F(m, n)$ with the factor $1/a$. To overcome this, Marshall [37] proposed to repeat shape matching at multi-scales and multi-rotations.

Wavelets can be used as another method for describing the internal region of a shape in the transform domain. The advantage of using wavelets for shape representation is that they allow the shape region to be described from coarse to detail. For example, Haar's wavelets were used by Jacobs et al. (1995) in a multi-resolution image retrieval algorithm.

Boundary based representations can be obtained by extracting those pixels that comprise the boundary of the object shape. Since the total number of boundary pixels may be large, usually only the more perceptually significant points are selected. Chain encoding is a simple way of linking such boundary points. A grid is superimposed on the boundary in such a way that boundary points coincide with grid intersections. The points are linked by horizontal, vertical and diagonal line segments which represent eight directions and which are numbered from 0 to 7. In this way, the approximated curve to the object shape is encoded by a string of numbers. This method is usually sensitive to irregularities of the shape boundary, because irregular boundaries result in chain encoding being very sensitive to noise. Low-pass filtering is usually needed before chain encoding is applied.

Histogram of edge directions (Jain and Vailaya, 1996; Gevers and Smeulders, 1998) is a popular global boundary based shape representation in the spatial domain. Edge detectors, such as Sobel operator or Canny detector (1986), are first applied on the image to extract the edges and their directions. A histogram is then generated on the quantized directions of the edges. The use of histogram makes the approach translation invariant, and the scale invariance is realized by normalizing the histogram with the number of edge points in the image. One disadvantage of the method is that histograms are not rotation invariant. To overcome this, Jain and Vailaya (1996) proposed to smooth the histograms to reduce their sensitivity to rotation. A histogram can be also constructed on the curvature of all the boundary pixels (Sonka et al., 1998).

"Shape context" introduced in (Belongie et al., 2001) is another well-known boundary based shape representation in the spatial domain. A set of discrete points sampled from the outlines of a shape is used to represent the shape. The shape context of a reference point is described by a histogram of the relative positions of the remaining points of the shape. Two matching techniques are proposed by Mori et al. (2001): one using a small number of representative shape contexts, and the other based on vector quantization of shape contexts feature space.

The Fourier Descriptors (Gonzalez and Woods, 2002) are one of the major representations for describing the boundary of a shape in the transform domain. If the shape boundary is sampled with a constant step size at *N* locations, the Fourier Descriptors can be obtained by applying the discrete Fourier transform on the boundary curve as follows:

$$\mathbf{FD}(k) = \frac{1}{N}\sum_{n=0}^{N-1} z(n)e^{-j2\pi nk/N} \tag{15}$$

where $z(n)$ represents the complex boundary curve. The Fourier Descriptors are independent of the starting point of the sampling. Rotation and scaling invariance is made by an improvement proposed by Rui et al. (1996). Similarly, shape boundaries may be also represented by Wavelet Descriptors (Chuang and Kuo, 1996). Hough transform (Hough, 1962) has also been used for shape representation (Chan and Sandler, 1992).

In shape representation of the spatial domain, similarity is measured as a distance in a multi-dimensional feature space. Distance measures, e.g. Euclidean distance and Mahalanobis distance, are used for calculating the similarity between shape feature representations. The methods are usually sensitive to shape distortions, and there is no guarantee that human perception of closeness corresponds to the topological closeness in feature space. In transformation based shape representation, similarity measures are more robust to shape distortions, and are more tolerant to partial occlusions, because spectral information represents the main character of the shape.

Spatial Relationships

Spatial relationships between entities such as points, lines, regions, and objects can be classified, according to their geometric concepts, into directional relationships and topological relationships. Relative directions such as left of, right of, above or below are used in directional relationships. In order to define directions, a reference orientation must be established. The reference entity can be objects inside the image or an external frame. Topological relationships utilize concepts from set theory between close entities, e.g. containment, overlapping, adjacency and disjunction.

The representation of spatial relationships can be divided into object-based structures and relational structures. Object-based structures combine spatial relationships with the visual information about each entity (Hoiem et al., 2004). A space partitioning technique that enables a spatial entity to be located in space is needed. Object-based representations include Grids, Quadtrees and R-Trees (Li, 1998). Relational structures separate spatial relationships from the visual information about those entities (Benn and Radig, 1984). Relational structure representations consider entities in the image to be symbols. Among the relational representations, 2D Strings, proposed by Chang and Liu (1984), is one of the most popular methods. A 2D String is a two-dimensional symbolic string constructed from the symbolic image. RS-Strings, introduced by Huang and Jean (1996), is another approach for relational structure representation.

Image retrieval according to spatial relationships is performed by matching the query representation against the spatial structures representing spatial knowledge in the images.

Content-Based Image Retrieval Systems

Many Content-Based Image Retrieval systems have emerged with the development of Internet and digital image databases. This section surveys some well-known image retrieval systems: some of them are commercial systems; others are for the purpose of research/demonstration. Since each of the systems is renowned and influential, the survey is presented in a sequential way and the overall discussion of all the cited systems is drawn at the end of the section. For each system, the features extracted using techniques discussed in the previous section are first reviewed, then the similarity measures and the methods how the retrieval results are presented are summarized. For more comprehensive reviews of classical CBIR systems, please refer to (Veltkamp and Tanase, 2000; Smuelders et al., 2000; Antani et al., 2002).

QBIC

QBIC is one of the most famous commercial image retrieval systems and was developed by IBM (Niblack et al., 1993). The features used include color, texture and shape. The color features consist of the 3D average color vector of a segmented object or the whole image in RGB, YIQ, Lab and Munsell color space, and a 256-dimensional RGB color histogram. The texture features computed are the coarseness, contrast, and directionality attributes. The shape features extracted include shape area, circularity, eccentricity, major axis orientation and a number of moment invariants. These shape features are extracted for all the object contours, semi-automatically detected in the database images. The features extracted from the whole image are easily affected by differing backgrounds and object occlusions. The accuracy of segmented objects is highly dependent on the segmentation algorithms.

QBIC supports queries based on example images, user constructed sketches and selected color and texture patterns. The color and texture pattern are chosen from a sampler.

The color distance between a query image and a database image is a weighted Euclidean distance, where the weights are the inverse standard deviation for each component over the samples in the database. The average color distance and the quadratic histogram distance are used for matching two color histograms. The texture and shape distances are both weighted Euclidean distances between feature vectors.

Virage

Virage Image Engine is another commercial Content-Based Image Retrieval system developed by Virage corporation (Bach et al., 1996). Features are built upon five abstract data types: global values and histograms, local values and histograms, and graphs. Color, texture and shape features can be extracted based on these primitives. The use of global features and features detected on segmented regions also hinders the generality of the retrieval system.

The similarity measure between images is the combination of similarity scores computed using the distance functions defined for each primitive. These individual scores are combined using a set of weights in a way characteristic to the application. The overall score is then stored in a score structure, which allows a quick recomputation of the score for a new set of weights.

The Virage Image Engine provides a number of facilities for image insertion, image query, weight adjustment for re-query, inclusion of keywords, support for several popular image file formats, and support for queries by sketch.

VisualSEEK

VisualSEEK is developed by the Image and Advanced Television Lab, Columbia University (Smith and Chang, 1996). Each image in the database is first decomposed automatically into regions of equally dominant colors. Color and shape features are then extracted from these regions. The Color Set which is extracted using the back-projection technique is used as the color feature. Shape features computed include the region centroid, region area, and the width and height of the minimum bounding rectangle of the region. A query is to find the images that contain the most similar arrangements of similar regions. The decomposition of image regions of equally dominant colors makes the system limited to certain image types with distinctive colors.

For matching of two images, the similarity measures of the color and shape features are first computed independently. The color set similarity is defined as $S(c_q, c_t)=(c_q - c_t)^t A(c_q - c_t)$, where c_q, c_t are two color sets and A is the color similarity matrix. The Euclidean distance is used as the distance between the centroids of regions, while the distance of area between two regions is the absolute value of the difference. The distance between the minimum bounding rectangles of two regions is calculated using the L_2 metric. The total distance between two regions is the weighted sum of the four distances above.

NETRA

NETRA is developed by the Department of Electrical and Computer Engineering, University of California, Santa Barbara (Ma and Manjunath, 1999). Images are first segmented into regions of homogeneous colors, and color, texture, shape and spatial location features are extracted from these regions. Color is represented by a color codebook of 256 colors which are quantized from the RGB color space. The color feature vector is then defined as $f_c = (c_0, p_0, \ldots, c_n, p_n)$, where c_i indicates the index into the color codebook, and p_i the fraction of that color in the region. The texture feature vector is represented by the means and standard deviations of the amplitudes of Gabor decomposition of the image region: $f_t = (\mu_{0,0}, \ldots, \mu_{s,k}, \sigma_{0,0}, \ldots, \sigma_{s,k})$, where s indicates the number of scales, and k the number of directions. The shape is represented by three feature vectors: f_K, which is based on the curvature; f_R, which is based on the centroid distance; and f_Z, which is based on the complex coordinate function. The homogeneous color based region segmentation technique makes the algorithm not applicable for images dominated by textures or structures.

The distance between two color feature vectors is the weighted Euclidean distance in RGB space. The distance between two texture feature vectors is calculated using the L_1 metric. The Euclidean distance is used for the distance between two shape feature vectors.

Photobook

Photobook is developed by the Vision and Modelling Group, MIT Media Laboratory, Cambridge (Pentland et al., 1996). Three types of image content, namely faces, 2D shapes and textures, are represented by features. Faces are represented by the eigenvectors of a covariance matrix as an orthogonal coordinate system of the image space. Texture features, which are viewed as homogeneous 2D discrete random fields, are expressed as the sum of three orthogonal components using Wold decomposition. The three components correspond to periodicity, directionality and randomness. Shape features are extracted from the feature points on the silhouette of the segmented region. These feature points are then used as nodes in building a finite element model of the shape. The eigenvectors are then computed from the shape model to determine a feature point correspondence between this new shape and some average shape. The system still relies on the robustness of the region segmentation, which is highly content dependent.

The distance between two eigenimage representations is calculated using the L_2 metric. Two shape features are compared by computing the amount of strain energy needed to deform one shape to match the other.

PicToSeek

PicToSeek was developed by the Intelligent Sensory Information Systems group, University of Amsterdam (Gevers and Smeulders, 2000). Images are represented by feature vectors which are the combination of color and shape invariants. Color models are proposed independent of the object geometry, object pose, and illumination change. Shape invariant features are then computed from the color invariant edges. For image search, PicToSeek uses the k-nearest neighbor classifier. PicToSeek collects images on the Internet and catalogues them into various image styles and types. Then, the invariant color and shape features are extracted to produce a high-dimensional image index for automatic image retrieval. The color and shape invariants are not robust for background confusion and object cluttering.

PicToSeek allows for image search by visual browsing through the precomputed image catalogue, query by pictorial example and query by image features. The retrieval process is conducted in an interactive, iterative manner guided by the user with relevance feedback.

CIRES

CIRES (Iqbal and Aggarwal, 2002) was presented by the Computer and Vision Research Centre, the University of Texas at Austin. The system combines structure, color and texture for retrieving images in digital libraries. Structure is extracted via hierarchical perceptual grouping principles, which construct lower-level image features, such as edges, into a meaningful higher-level interpretation. An approach for color analysis is used for mapping all colors in the color space into a fixed color palette. Texture feature is extracted using a bank of even-symmetric Gabor filters. The similarity measure of structure and texture is calculated using the Euclidean distance. Histogram intersection measure is used for color. Again, the global features used make the system unpractical for images containing different objects with cluttering.

Most of the aforementioned Content-Based Image Retrieval systems use color and texture features, some use shape features, and only very few use spatial relationships. One feature type only works for images dominated by that feature, e.g. texture features are most suitable for images with manifest textures. The frequencies of usage reflect the accuracy and effectiveness of these features. The more accurate and more reliable the features can be extracted, the easier it is to use the features in the right way. All the above systems attempt to combine various features, such as color, texture and shape, into a composite feature vector, which results in high dimensionality and low performance. However, separate features don't have the discriminative power to retrieve images in general, because the variety of image types in a real-life image database is enormous. Another drawback of the available CBIR systems is that the features are extracted from segmented regions, which makes the systems vastly dependent on the accuracy of the segmentation algorithm used. Unfortunately, segmentation methods are usually designed for particular image classes, but not for any images in general. Those classical image retrieval systems can therefore only be used for narrow-domain image databases, which contain certain image types, but will perform poorly for broad-domain image databases, which contains an extensive variety of image types.

RECENT DEVELOPMENTS IN CBIR

In this section, recent advances in CBIR are reviewed. Most of the techniques cited have not been developed into commercial systems yet. There are two major trends in CBIR. The first trend is image retrieval using semantics. The purpose is to bridge the gap between low level features and semantic meanings. The second trend is using local invariant regions for image retrieval. The following discussed techniques are grouped according to the two trends.

Semantic Based Methods

Vogel and Schiele (2004) presented a method for natural scene retrieval based on the semantic classification of typical regions in an image.

The combination of scene classes in an image can be used to construct the semantic concepts of the image. The frequency of the occurrence of various semantic concepts is then used to retrieve scene categories.

Schober et al. (2005) described a semantic image retrieval technique utilizing logical reasoning about the semantic contents of the image. The method consists of two parts: training and analysis. An expert first models a domain dependent entity and trains it by assigning typical image regions to concepts of the domain. Features of the assigned regions are automatically extracted and the knowledge base is extended to map the feature values to the concepts. An image can be semantically classified by using the concepts of the extracted regions.

Yang and Hurson (2005) proposed a hierarchical semantic based indexing scheme to facilitate content-based image retrieval in ad hoc networks. This search scheme employs a hierarchical structure to organize image data based on their semantic contents. First-order logic expressions are used for the representation of image content, and the content-related mobile nodes are grouped into clusters, which reduce the search cost of content-based image retrieval. This search scheme is also scalable to large network sizes and large number of data objects.

A semantic repository modeling method for image databases was introduced in (Zhang et al., 2004). The semantic model uses a visual dictionary to represent different feature types, such as color, texture or shape. A classification tree is trained by images with known labels from the visual dictionary. A semantic graph structure is employed to demonstrate the relationships between the semantic repositories.

Duygulu and Vural (2001) developed an algorithm for multi-level image segmentation, based on the concept of uniformity tree, where each node corresponds to a homogeneous region according to the closed colors in the color palette at any level of the uniformity tree. Therefore, a stack of segmented images is obtained with different levels of detail. Semantic image retrieval can then be carried out based on the uniformity tree. In (Duygulu et al., 2002), they described an approach for object recognition, where image regions are associated with words. Images are first segmented into regions, which are classified into a variety of feature types. A mapping between region types and concepts is then learned using an expectation maximization technique.

Bringing out semantic meanings from an image in a database still remains a challenging problem. The available approaches are limited to small sets of semantic concepts. They are not sophisticated enough to deal with semantic retrieval in a broad domain.

Local Invariant Regions Based Methods

The first influential image retrieval algorithm using local invariant regions was introduced by Schmid and Mohr (1997). The invariant regions that are invariant to rotation, translation and scaling are detected around Harris corner points (1988). Differential greyvalue invariants are used to characterize the detected invariant regions in a multi-scale way to ensure invariance under similarity transformations and scale changes. Semi-local constraints and a voting algorithm are then applied to reduce the number of mis-matches.

Van Gool et al. (2001) described a method for finding occurrences of the same object or scene in a database using local invariant regions. Both geometry-based and intensity-based regions are employed. The geometry-based regions are extracted by first selecting Harris corner points (1988) as 'anchor points' then finding nearby edges detected by Canny's detector (1986) to construct invariant parallelograms. The intensity-based regions are defined around local extrema in intensities. The intensity function along rays emanating from a local extremum is evaluated. An invariant region is constructed by linking those points on the rays where the intensity function reaches extrema. Color moment invariants introduced in (Mindru et al., 1998) are adopted as region descriptor for characterizing the extracted regions. A voting process is carried out by comparing the descriptor vectors of the query and test images to select the most relevant images to the query. False positives are further rejected using geometric and photometric constraints.

An image retrieval technique based on matching of distinguished regions is presented in (Obdrzalek and Matas, 2002). The distinguished regions are the Maximally Stable Extremal Regions introduced in (Matas et al., 2002). An extremal region is a connected area of pixels that are all brighter or darker than the pixels on the boundary of the region. Local invariant frames are then established on the detected regions by studying the properties of the covariance matrix and the bi-tangent points. Correspondences between local frames are evaluated by directly comparing the normalized image intensities. Matching between query and database images are then done based on the number and quality of established correspondences.

Sivic et al. (2003, 2004) proposed a search engine like algorithm for objects in video materials which enables all shots containing the same object as the query to be retrieved. Regions are first detected by the Harris affine detector (Mikolajczyk and Schmid, 2002) and maximally stable extremal region detector (Matas et al., 2002). Each region is then represented by a 128 dimensional invariant vector using SIFT descriptor (Lowe, 1999). Vector quantization is applied on the invariant descriptors so that the technology of text retrieval can be employed. In (Sivic and Zisserman, 2004), they further developed a method for obtaining the principal objects, characters and scenes in a video by measuring the reoccurrence of spatial configurations of viewpoint invariant features.

A specific human face image retrieval approach using local salient regions (Shao et al., 2007) was proposed by Shao and Brady (2006). The salient regions are the locally most informative regions which are highly repeatable under various viewpoint and illumination variations. Therefore, those salient regions are potentially more suitable for image indexing and retrieval. Similarity measures based on normalized correlation are used to match query images and images in the database. In (Shao & Brady, 2006), the authors further extend the algorithm to apply on object category retrieval. Generalized color moment invariants (Mindru et al., 2004) are adopted to be the region descriptor and a voting mechanism is used to search for the most similar category to the query.

The utilization of local regions makes image retrieval robust to occlusions, cluttering and changes in the background. The invariance of the detected regions and the region description enables the algorithms to be robust under viewpoint and illumination variations.

CONCLUSION

This chapter surveys content-based image retrieval techniques. The feature representation and extraction approaches are first classified and discussed. Then, we review several classical CBIR systems which rely on either global features or features detected on segmented regions. The inefficiency and disadvantages of those narrow-domain systems are also presented. Finally, two recent trends in image retrieval research are discussed and analyzed.

The existing image retrieval systems can only be used for narrow-domain image databases, which contain certain image types, but will perform poorly for broad-domain image databases, which contains an extensive variety of image types. This has created a need for CBIR algorithms which have the capability to retrieve images in general either semantically or query based.

REFERENCES

Antani, S., Kasturi, R., & Jain, R. (2002). A survey on the use of pattern recognition methods for abstraction, indexing and retrieval of images and video. *Pattern Recognition, 35*(4), 945–965. doi:10.1016/S0031-3203(01)00086-3

Bach, J., Fuller, C., Gupta, A., Hampapur, A., Gorowitz, B., & Humphrey, R. … Shu, C. (1996). Virage image search engine: An open framework for image management. *Proceedings of the SPIE, Storage and Retrieval for Image and Video Databases,* San Jose, USA, (pp. 76-87).

Ballard, D. H., & Brown, C. M. (1982). *Computer vision*. Englewood Cliffs, NJ: Prentice-Hall, Inc.

Belongie, S., Malik, J., & Puzicha, J. (2001). Matching shapes. *Proceedings of the IEEE International Conference on Computer Vision*, Vancouver, Canada, (pp. 454-461).

Benn, W., & Radig, B. (1984). Retrieval of relational structures for image sequence analysis. *Proceedings of the 10th International Conference on Very Large Data Bases*, Singapore, (pp. 533-536).

Bimbo, A. D. (1999). *Visual information retrieval*. San Francisco, CA: Morgan Kaufmann.

Blostein, D., & Ahuja, N. (1989). Shape from texture: Integrating texture-element extraction and surface estimation. *IEEE Transactions on Pattern Analysis and Machine Intelligence, 11*(12), 1233–1251. doi:10.1109/34.41363

Canny, J. (1986). A computational approach to edge detection. *IEEE Transactions on Pattern Analysis and Machine Intelligence, 8*(6), 679–698. doi:10.1109/TPAMI.1986.4767851

Chan, C. K., & Sandler, M. D. (1992). A neural network shape recognition system with Hough transform input feature space. *Proceedings of the International Conference on Image Processing and its Applications*, Maastricht, The Netherlands, (pp. 197-200).

Chang, S. F., Chen, W., Meng, H. J., Sundaram, H., & Zhong, D. (1997). Videoq: An automated content based video search system using visual cues. *Proceedings of the 5th ACM International Multimedia Conference*, Seattle, USA, (pp. 313-324).

Chang, S. K., & Liu, S. H. (1984). Picture indexing and abstraction techniques for pictorial databases. *IEEE Transactions on Pattern Analysis and Machine Intelligence, 6*, 475–484. doi:10.1109/TPAMI.1984.4767552

Chuang, G. C. H., & Kuo, C. C. J. (1996). Wavelet descriptors of planar curves: Theory and applications. *IEEE Transactions on Image Processing, 5*(1), 56–70. doi:10.1109/83.481671

Duygulu, P., Barnard, K., de Freitas, N., & Forsyth, D. (2002). Object recognition as machine translation: Learning a lexicon for a fixed image vocabulary. *Proceedings of European Conference on Computer Vision* (ECCV), Copenhagen, Denmark, (pp. 97-112).

Duygulu, P., & Vural, F. (2001). Multi-level image segmentation and object representation for content based image retrieval. *Proceedings of SPIE Electronic Imaging, Storage and Retrieval for Media Databases*, San Jose, USA, (pp. 460-469).

Freeborough, P. A. (1997). A comparison of fractal texture descriptors. Proceedings of the 8th British Machine Vision Conference, Essex, UK.

Fu, K. S. (1982). *Syntactic pattern recognition and applications*. New Jersey: Prentice-Hall.

Gevers, T., & Smeulders, A. (1998). Image indexing using composite color and shape invariant features. *Proceedings of the 6th International Conference on Computer Vision*, Bombay, India, (pp. 576-581).

Gevers, T., & Smeulders, A. W. M. (2000). PicToSeek: Combining color and shape invariant features for image retrieval. *IEEE Transactions on Image Processing, 9*, 102–119. doi:10.1109/83.817602

Gonzalez, R. C., & Woods, R. E. (2002). *Digital image processing*. Prentice Hall Press.

Gool, L., Tuytelaars, T., & Turina, A. (2001). Local features for image retrieval . In Veltkamp, R. C., Burkhardt, H., & Kriegel, H. P. (Eds.), *State-of-the-art in content-based image and video retrieval* (pp. 21–41). Kluwer Academic Publishers.

Haralick, R. M., Shanmugam, K., & Dinstein, I. (1973). Textural features for image classification. *IEEE Transactions on Systems, Man, and Cybernetics, 3*(6), 610–621. doi:10.1109/TSMC.1973.4309314

Harris, C., & Stephens, M. (1988). A combined corner and edge detector. *Proceedings of the 4th Alvey Vision Conference*, Manchester, UK, (pp. 147-151).

Hashizume, C., Vinod, V. V., & Murase, H. (1998). Robust object extraction with illumination-insensitive color descriptions. *Proceedings of the IEEE International Conference on Image Processing*, Chicago, USA, (pp. 50-54).

Hoiem, D., Sukthankar, R., Schneiderman, H., & Huston, L. (2004). Object-based image retrieval using the statistical structure of images. *Proceedings of the IEEE Computer Society Conference on Computer Vision and Pattern Recognition*, Washington DC, USA, (pp. 490-497).

Hough, P. V. C. (1962). *Method and means for recognizing complex patterns*. (U.S. Patent: 3069654).

Hu, M. (1962). Visual pattern recognition by moment invariants. *IEEE Transactions on Information Theory, 8*(2), 179–187. doi:10.1109/TIT.1962.1057692

Huang, J., Kumar, S. R., Mitra, M., Zhu, W., & Zabih, R. (1997). Image indexing using color correlograms. *Proceedings of IEEE Conference on Computer Vision and Pattern Recognition*, San Juan, Puerto Rico, (pp. 762-768).

Huang, P. W., & Jean, Y. R. (1996). Spatial reasoning and similarity retrieval for image database-systems based on RS-Strings. *Pattern Recognition, 29*(12), 2103–2114. doi:10.1016/S0031-3203(96)00048-9

Iqbal, Q., & Aggarwal, J. (2002). CIRES: A system for content-based retrieval in digital image libraries. *Proceedings of the International Conference on Control, Automation, Robotics and Vision*, Singapore, (pp. 205-210).

Jacobs, C. E., Finkelstein, A., & Salesin, D. H. (1995). Fast multiresolution image querying. *Proceedings of the 22nd Annual Conference on Computer Graphics*, Los Angeles, USA, (pp. 277-286).

Jain, A. K., & Vailaya, A. (1996). Image retrieval using color and shape. *Pattern Recognition, 29*(8), 1233–1244. doi:10.1016/0031-3203(95)00160-3

Kender, J., & Yeo, B. (1998). Video scene segmentation via continuous video coherence. *Proceedings of the IEEE Computer Society Conference on Computer Vision and Pattern Recognition*, Santa Barbara, USA, (pp. 367-373).

Laws, K. I. (1980). *Textured image segmentation*. Ph.D. dissertation, Department of Engineering, University of Southern California.

Li, C. (1998). Multimedia and imaging databases. *IEEE Communications Magazine, 36*(2), 28–30. doi:10.1109/MCOM.1998.648745

Lowe, D. G. (1999). Object recognition from local scale-invariant features. *Proceedings of the 7th International Conference on Computer Vision*, Kerkyra, Greece, (pp. 1150-1157).

Ma, W. Y., & Manjunath, B. S. (1999). NeTra: A toolbox for navigating large image databases. *Multimedia Systems*, *7*, 184–198. doi:10.1007/s005300050121

Marshall, S. (1989). Review of shape coding techniques. *Image and Vision Computing*, *7*(4), 281–294. doi:10.1016/0262-8856(89)90032-2

Matas, J., Chun, O., Urban, M., & Pajdla, T. (2002). Robust wide baseline stereo from maximally stable extremal regions. *Proceedings of the British Machine Vision Conference*, Cardiff, UK.

Mikolajczyk, K., & Schmid, C. (2002). An affine invariant interest point detector. *Proceedings of the 6th European Conference on Computer Vision*, Copenhagen, Denmark, (pp. 128-142).

Mindru, F., Moons, T., & Gool, L. (1998). Color-based moment invariants for the viewpoint and illumination independent recognition of planar color patterns. *Proceedings of International Conference on Advances in Pattern Recognition*, (pp. 113-122).

Mindru, F., Tuytelaars, T., Gool, L., & Moons, T. (2004). Moment invariants for recognition under changing viewpoint and illumination. *Computer Vision and Image Understanding*, *94*, 3–27. doi:10.1016/j.cviu.2003.10.011

Mori, G., Belongie, S., & Malik, J. (2001). Shape contexts enable efficient retrieval of similar shapes. *Proceedings of the IEEE Computer Society Conference on Computer Vision and Pattern Recognition*, Hawaii, USA, (pp. 723-730).

Munsell, H. (1912). A pigment color system and notation. *The American Journal of Psychology*, *23*, 236–244. doi:10.2307/1412843

Niblack, W., Barber, R., Equitz, W., Flickner, M., Glassman, E., Petkovic, D., & Yanker, P. (1993). *The QBIC project: Querying images by content using colour, texture and shape. Proceedings of SPIE 1908* (pp. 173–187). Storage and Retrieval for Image and Video Databases.

Obdrzalek, S., & Matas, J. (2002). Local affine frames for image retrieval. *Proceedings of the International Conference on Image and Video Retrieval*, London, UK, (pp. 318-327).

Pentland, A., Picard, R. W., & Sclaroff, S. (1996). Photobook: Content-based manipulation of image databases. *International Journal of Computer Vision*, *18*(3), 233–254. doi:10.1007/BF00123143

Rui, Y., She, A. C., & Huang, T. S. (1996). Modified Fourier descriptors for shape representation – A practical approach. *Proceedings of the 1st International Workshop on Image Databases and Multimedia Search*, Amsterdam, The Netherlands.

Schmid, C., & Mohr, R. (1997). Local greyvalue invariants for image retrieval. *IEEE Transactions on Pattern Analysis and Machine Intelligence*, *19*(5), 530–535. doi:10.1109/34.589215

Schober, J., Hermes, T., & Herzog, O. (2005). PictureFinder: Description logics for semantic image retrieval. *Proceedings of the IEEE International Conference on Multimedia and Expo*, Amsterdam, Netherlands, (pp. 1571-1574).

Shao, L., & Brady, M. (2006). Specific object retrieval based on salient regions. *Pattern Recognition*, *39*(10), 1932–1948. doi:10.1016/j.patcog.2006.04.010

Shao, L., & Brady, M. (2006). Invariant salient regions based image retrieval under viewpoint and illumination variations. *Journal of Visual Communication and Image Representation*, *17*(6), 1256–1272. doi:10.1016/j.jvcir.2006.08.002

Shao, L., Kadir, T., & Brady, M. (2007). Geometric and photometric invariant distinctive regions detection. *Information Sciences*, *177*(4), 1088–1122. doi:10.1016/j.ins.2006.09.003

Sharma, G. (2003). *Digital color imaging handbook*. CRC Press.

Sivic, J., Schaffalitzky, F., & Zisserman, A. (2004). Efficient object retrieval from videos. *Proceedings of the 12th European Signal Processing Conference*, Vienna, Austria.

Sivic, J., & Zisserman, A. (2004). Video data mining using configurations of viewpoint invariant regions. *Proceedings of the IEEE Conference on Computer Vision and Pattern Recognition*, Washington DC, USA, (pp. 488-495).

Smith, J. R., & Chang, S. F. (1996). VisualSEEK: A fully automated content-based image query system. *Proceedings of ACM Multimedia*, Boston, USA, (pp. 87-98).

Smuelders, A., Worring, M., Santini, S., Gupta, A., & Jain, R. (2000). Content-based image retrieval at the end of early years. *IEEE Transactions on Pattern Analysis and Machine Intelligence*, *22*, 1349–1380. doi:10.1109/34.895972

Sonka, M., Hlavac, V., & Boyle, R. (1998). *Image processing, analysis and machine vision*. International Thomson Computer Press.

Swain, M. J., & Ballard, D. H. (1991). Color indexing. *International Journal of Computer Vision*, *7*, 11–32. doi:10.1007/BF00130487

Veltkamp, R. C., & Tanase, M. (2002). Content-based image retrieval systems: A survey. (Technical Report, UU-CS-2000-34), Department of Computer Science, Utretch University.

Vogel, J., & Schiele, B. (2004). Natural scene retrieval based on a semantic modeling step. *Proceedings of Conference on Image and Video Retrieval* (CIVR), Dublin, Ireland, (pp. 207-215).

Voorhees, H., & Poggio, T. (1987). Detecting textons and texture boundaries in natural images. *Proceedings of the 1st International Conference on Computer Vision*, London, UK, (pp. 250-258).

Worring, M., & Gevers, T. (2001). Interactive retrieval of color images. *International Journal of Image and Graphics*, *1*(3), 387–414. doi:10.1142/S0219467801000244

Yang, B., & Hurson, A. (2005). Ad hoc image retrieval using hierarchical semantic-based index. *Proceedings of IEEE International Conference on Advanced Information Networking and Applications*, Taiwan, (pp. 629-634).

Zhang, R., Zhang, Z., & Qin, Z. (2004). Semantic repository modeling in image database. *Proceedings of IEEE International Conference on Multimedia and Expo*, Taipei, Taiwan, (pp. 2079-2082).

Chapter 8
Extracting Sport Video Semantics:
Research and Applications

Chia-Hung Yeh
National Sun Yat-sen University, Taiwan

Wen-Yu Tseng
National Sun Yat-sen University, Taiwan

Yu-Dun Lin
National Sun Yat-sen University, Taiwan

Chih-Chung Teng
National Sun Yat-sen University, Taiwan

ABSTRACT

Recent developments in video content analysis contribute to the emergence of multimedia database management. With the rapid growth of digital videos, efficient tools are essential to facilitate content indexing, searching, retrieving, browsing, skimming, and summarization. Sport video analysis has attracted lots of research attention because of its entertainment applications and potential commercial benefits. Sport video analysis aims to identify what excites audiences. Previous methods rely mainly on video decomposition, using domain specific knowledge. Research on suitable and efficient techniques for sport video analysis has been conducted extensively over the last decade. However, several longstanding challenges, such as semantic gap and commercial detection, are still waiting to be resolved. This chapter reviews research on sport video analysis and investigates the potential applications and future trends of sport video analysis.

DOI: 10.4018/978-1-61350-126-9.ch008

INTRODUCTION

Rapid developments of digital video processing technologies and communication infrastructure, along with the increase of bandwidth, enable the easy access, editing, and distribution of video contents. More and more digital videos are now available for entertaining, commercial, educational, and other purposes. As videos become important sources of everyday knowledge, one of the major problems that we face nowadays is the ways to manage the explosive amounts of videos generated everyday effectively, promoting high-quality modes of life and consumer technology.

Multimedia and communication technologies have become maturer after their rapid development for almost half of a century. Digital technologies are now widely applied to speech, audio, video, and graphics in various commercial applications. Furthermore, the availability of broadband wired/wireless infrastructures and new technologies, such as peer-to-peer networking, has changed the distribution and exchange of digital media. In this new era, research has shifted its focus from technology development to novel applications.

Content-based video analysis aims at organizing videos into systematic structures so that their semantic contents can be effectively represented by still images, video clips, graphical representations, and textual descriptors (Manjunath, 2000, 2002; Chang, 2001). Significant audio and visual cues are used as the foundation for video presentation. Suitable and effective techniques for video content analysis have been studied and developed extensively over the last decade. Due to the content variations of each of the videos, the style and extent selected vary greatly and no standard can be found, which should be included and excluded for content-based video analysis. Furthermore, the ways to extract the semantic meaning of videos are generally known to be an open and challenging problem (Chang, 1997; Li, 2006; Rui, 1998; Yeh, 2005).

Sport video analysis has drawn many researchers' attention because of its commercial potentials in the entertainment industry. Audience rating is an indicator of aforementioned factors. Increasing audience rating and attracting advertisement are the top priorities of TV broadcasters. Therefore, American broadcasters such as ESPN, ABC, FOX and other local media try their best to attract audience attention by providing desirable broadcasting, charming anchors, high definition videos, and etc. Sport video analysis belongs to one of the content-based video analyses. Sport videos tend to be well-structured due to similar filming techniques used in a sport game; therefore, they could be analyzed. One goal of sport video analysis is to extract the underlying semantic content. However, different from textual information, the wide range of semantics appeared in multiple modes in a sport video. Extracting semantics accurately and concisely still poses an ongoing challenge for research community. The expectations of the users encourage the investigation of this growing area. This chapter provides an overview of major developments in sport video analysis. We discuss semantic approaches to sport videos understanding and the trend of this field. In particular, several important research issues are discussed, including commercial detection, playfield detection, highlight extraction, and etc. Potential applications are also suggested. This chapter aims to discuss sport video analysis. The rest of this chapter is organized as follows: we first examine sport video filming and discuss commercial detection in broadcast TV programs, an essential step for broadcast video processing. Then, several sport video filming techniques are introduced. Research issues of sport video analysis; including playfield detection, highlight exaction and object tracking/reorganization, are discussed. Finally, concluding remarks and future trend of sport video analysis are given.

Figure 1. Camera-mounted positions in baseball field

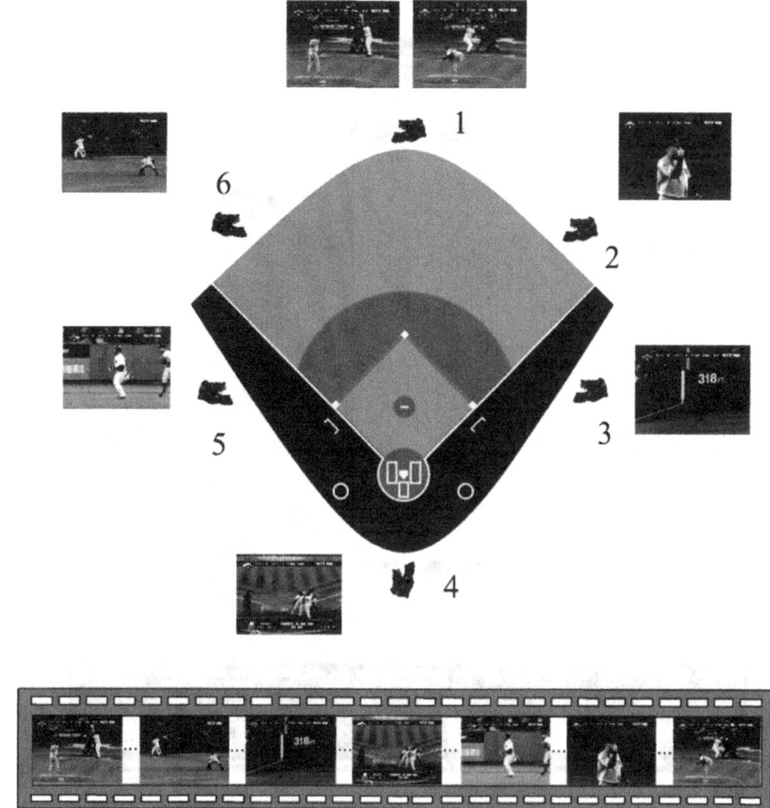

SPORT VIDEO FILMING

Sport videos consist of audio and visual information. Visual information is captured through different cameras mounted in the playfield. Therefore, shots in a sport video have different camera distances and shooting angles. Previous researches show that sport video has its own syntactic structure with respect to game rules and presentation. Though shots in sport video of a particular sport differ from one game to another, these shots are often directed in certain ways. The reason is that most shots could be taken by cameras mounted at similar places or locations, with similar field coverage and shooting angles.

Take baseball games as an example, a baseball video can be segmented into several representative shots, including pitching view, catch view, close-up view, running view, and audience view. There are at least 6 Electronic Field Production (EEP) cameras placed around a baseball field as showed in Figure 1. These cameras provide full coverage of the baseball field and record all events happening in the field. Figure 1 illustrates an event of a two-base hit with one runner scored. The pitcher pitches the ball and the batter hits a line-drive double to the left field, at the same time the runner scores from the second base. Then the manager comes out to make a mound visit. This event is captured by cameras 1, 4, 3, 5, 2, 6, and back to 1 consecutively.

Figure 2 shows the camera-mounted position in tennis field. In this figure, one player hits a serve and the receiver makes a good return and earns a point. Cameras 1, 5, 3, 2, 4, 3, and back to 1 takes these shots in sequence. From the above

Figure 2. Camera-mounted positions in tennis court

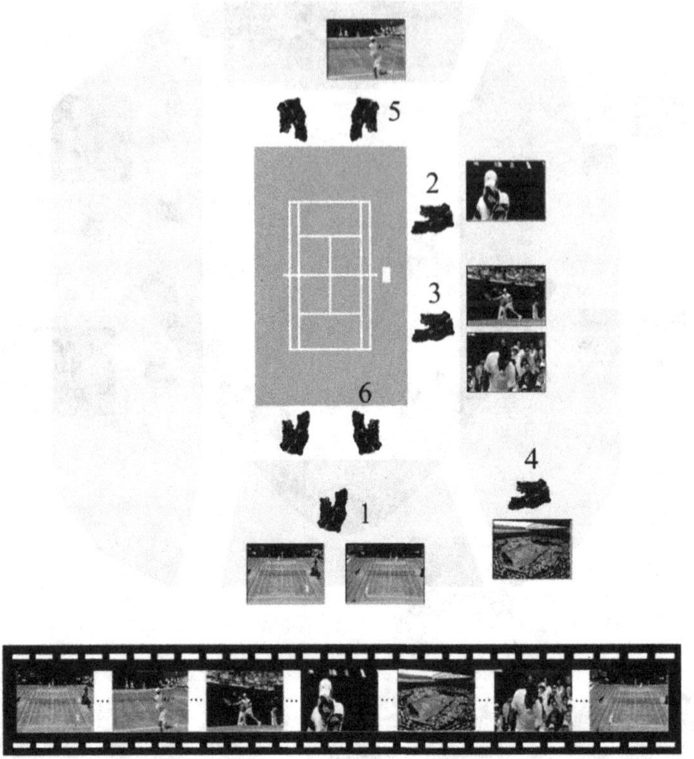

observation, we conclude that sport videos are made of a sequence of shots. A Shot, recording a continuous action in temporal and spatial, is a basic element in video, which is composed of consecutive frames taken by a single camera. A series of shot transitions constructs an event. Due to syntactic structure and the temporal relation of shots, sport videos can be analyzed to further capture their high-level semantics.

SPORT VIDEO ANALYSIS

Hundreds of digital TV sport channels can be recorded for future playbacks and millions of sport video clips available from the Internet for streaming and/or file download. To manage these sport videos effectively, it is important to develop automatic techniques for indexing, searching, browsing, editing, summarizing, skimming, and abstracting.

Commercial Detection

Commercials appear in broadcast TV programs and are inter-mixed with general programs, occupying up to 20% of the total broadcast time. Although commercials bring significant revenues for most privately owned TV companies, it is quite annoying to be interrupted by commercials when watching games. The detection and removal of commercials are essential to video content analysis, making content analysis algorithms more efficient. Therefore, the separation of commercials is the first step to TV program process, such as sport video analysis for content management.

Figure 3. Structure of a TV program (a) with black frames and (b) without black frame

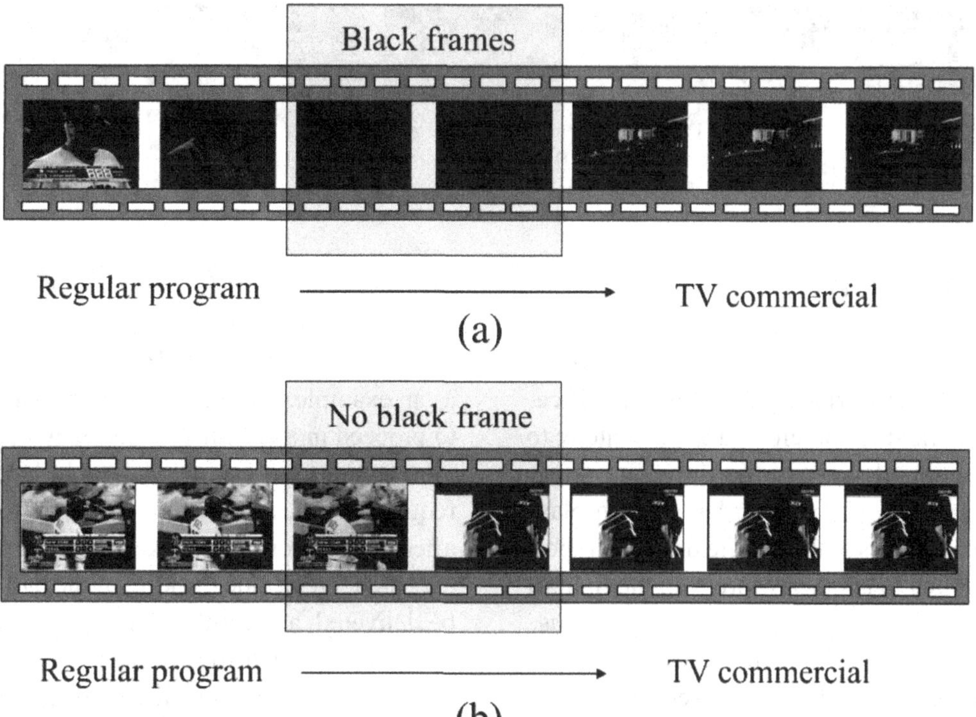

Furthermore, this technology can also be adopted by advertisement companies to verify their contracts on commercials broadcasted times.

Several methods and patents have been proposed to deal with commercial detection problems. The most straightforward method is using black frames as an "activity" detector to identify commercials (Blum, 1992). Figure 3 shows the structure of TV program with/without black frames. However, because each nation holds different regulations, not all TV stations use black frames to flag commercial breaks. In Lienhart's work (Lienhart, 2001), monochrome frames, scene breaks, and two "action" indicators (i.e. edge change ratio and motion vector length) are used to detect commercials. In (Marlow, 2001), the rate of shot cuts is used to identify commercials; shorter average shots show a higher probability to be commercials. In (Duygulu, 2004), two important characteristics of commercials, multiple-time repeat and distinctive color/audio, are observed to distinguish commercials from regular programs. Zhang et al. proposed a learning-based TV commercial detection scheme. Six basic visual and five audio features are extracted from each shot, and a set of context-based features are derived from these basic features. Then, a SVM classifier is applied to identify each shot as commercial or regular program (Hua, 2005). Chang et al. transformed the problem of commercial detection to infer the optimal sequence through the duration model as global characteristics (Mizutani, 2005). SVM classifiers are employed to distinguish between commercial and program segments based on their local characteristics. The proposed method captures both global-local characteristics to finalize decision. However, due to the variations of filming techniques and the styles of commercials, the detection and removal of commercials are still a challenging problem.

Figure 4. Various playfields

Playfield Detection

Playfield is one of major settings of sport videos. Figure 4 shows various playfields. Identification of playfield is, therefore, a good strategy to decompose sport videos efficiently for further semantic analysis. Each sport has its own playfield and the colors of the playfields of each sport vary from one to another. Moreover, the light of playfields may change as time goes by because a sport game lasts for several hours, often with different lighting conditions. Kuo et al. proposed a color-based GMMs (Gaussian Mixture Model) model to segment the grass and soil of baseball fields, which can extract different kinds of fields efficiently with low error rate (Kuo, 2008). Chang et al. first defined two states of soccer games, play and break (Xie, 2004). The dominant color ratio is detected through HSV (Hue-Saturation-Value) color space, and motion intensity is calculated from each macroblock. Finally, HMM (Hidden Markov Model) is used to classify play and break. In (Jiang, 2004), the authors also used GMM to describe the sample clustering in the feature space, and the proper parameter through such training is obtained to match target statistics. Then, region-growing operation is employed to screen out the playfield from the background.

Highlight Detection

Highlights are often required when broadcasting. Highlight extraction aims to provide fast browsing techniques, determining the key moments of an extraneous sport game such as "NBA 10 TOP play" and "MBL TOP 5 plays." Highlight detection aims at providing a digested version from a long sport game. Taking baseball games as an example, the audience waits for the games to proceed most of time when many interviews, introductions, and commercials took place. Time is required for the next batter to walk up to the plate after the previous hitter exchanges signals with the catcher to decide the kind of the ball going to be delivered, and for the change of inning when both teams switch from offense to defense and vice versa. Exciting events, such as home runs, scoring, and double play, take place sparsely in baseball games. Highlight detection could help extract those exciting moments and skip those waiting times.

Existing sport highlight detection methods can be categorized into detection via content and detection via external information. In (Rui, 2000), only audio features are used to detect highlights, along without visual features. Through manual observation, crowd cheer, scoreboard display and change in direction are used to develop three models for highlight detection in (Nepal, 2001). Identifying what interests the audience, (Hanjalic, 2003) used motion activity, density of cuts, and audio energy to derive a function for detecting exciting scenes. Chang's research (Chang, 2002) observed that most highlights in baseball games composed of a special type of scene shots that reveal context transition. The authors used field descriptor, edge descriptor, and the amount of grass, camera motion, and player height to train four Hidden Markov Models (HMM) for four kinds of highlights. With the aim of extracting highlights for soccer programs, Chao et al. used Dynamic Bayesian Network (DBN) (Chao, 2005). Eight features (i.e. close-up view, audience region, replay, gate, board, referee, and audio) are employed to train DBN to capture desired events, penalty kick event, corner kick event, and card event for soccer programs. Tian et al. (Duan, 2003) propose a mid-level framework to connect low-level audiovisual processing and high-level semantic analysis for various kinds of sports. The proposed system can be applied to event detection, highlight extraction, summarization, and personalization of sports video.

Xu et al. proposed a generic framework for sport event detection, combining the analysis and alignment of web-casting text and broadcast sports videos (Xu, 2003). Web-casting text has complete and accurate time information of events. Therefore, events in sports videos can be captured by aligning the time tag of web-casting text and the event moment of broadcast sports videos. However, not all broadcast programs are available in the form of web-casting texts. Without event time information on the internet, video content analysis is still needed for many recorded sports videos. Hsu et al. proposed a novel representation method based on likelihood models through the integration of audio-motion cues (Cheng, 2006). The proposed models measure the "likeliness" of low-level audio features and the motion features to a set of predefined audio types and motion categories, respectively. Finally, a hidden Markov model (HMM) is employed to model and detect the transition of semantics representation for highlight segment extraction. Chu et al. proposed a framework to detect events in baseball videos and develop several practical applications (Chu, 2008). Rule-based decision and model-based decision are used to detect semantic events explicitly. Practical applications include the automatic generation of box score, automatic game summarization, and automatic highlight generation.

Although sport video highlight extraction has been studied extensively, it is tough to define what the "highlight" of each sport and for each audience. The major difficulty lies in the semantic representation of what human recognizes as "highlights." In soccer games, "goal scene" is generally considered as highlights while appears more attractive because it is one of the most difficult ball skills to master. Therefore, the ways to define highlights and to extract their semantics from sport videos are still a challenging research issue.

Scoreboard Reorganization

Superimposed caption, such as score box, contains different kinds of information, and capture significant events in sport games when it takes place. Figure 5 shows examples of some score boxes in baseball videos. The limitation of most highlight detection systems mentioned above is that they are unable to detect the exact high-level semantics, including inning change, score and strike out. Superimposed caption provides crucial information for the understanding of sport videos. Chang et al. proposed an event summarization system using superimposed caption text detection and recognition (Zhang, 2002). The proposed system combines video text with camera view recognition to accurately detect the various types of high-level semantic events in baseball videos. Hsieh et al. proposed a scoreboard detection and reorganization system to acquire the accurate information from different kinds of scoreboards (Hung, 2008). The proposed system consists of two steps: location and reorganization processes. With the integration of scoreboard caption and shot transition, encouraging performance can be achieved for event-based video summarization and retrieval systems. In (Chu, 2008), the authors proposed a caption feature extraction method for text and symbol reorganization. Text information includes the number of scores, and symbol information indicates base occupation and the number of outs. The change of scores, outs, and base-occupation situation are considered together in event detection. Caption information is very

Figure 5. Various score boxes in baseball videos

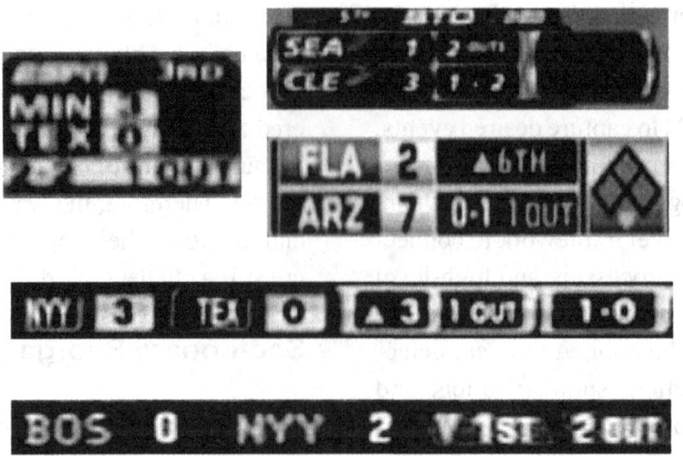

helpful for sport video analysis; however, each TV broadcast station has its own scoreboard styles and it is tough to have a robust and generic method that could be applied to all kinds of scoreboards.

Object Tracking

Object tracking enhances the performance of sport video analysis, enrich the experience of sport game watching, as well as provide insightful information, such as tactic analysis, for sport player training. Xiong et al. used a visual object detection algorithm to detect most frequently appeared scenes in sports programs by identifying objects such as soccer goalposts and baseball catcher (Xiong, 2005). Given that these objects are always the focus of sport highlights, the authors used these objects and audio features in the highlight extraction of sports programs. In (Yu, 2003), the authors proposed a trajectory-based algorithm for the automatic detection and tracking of balls in soccer videos. The proposed method draws the trajectory of the ball as time goes by and this information improves play-break analysis, high-level semantic event detection, as well as the detection and analysis of basic actions and team ball possession. In (Zhu, 2008), the authors analyzed sport videos from tactics' instead of the audience's perspective. The proposed method extracts tactic information and recognizes the tactic patterns from goal events in soccer videos. Chu et al. proposed a method to track ball trajectory through single view pitching scenes based on Kalman filter (Chu, 2006). The detected results, namely, trajectory, can be applied to either entertainment or game analysis. In (Li, 2008), Lin et al. proposed a method to recognize five baseball pitch types of baseball videos. The proposed method models the temporal behavior of pitch type using HMMs. Figure 6 shows an example of ball tracking in baseball videos. Ball tracking is still challenging due to the variations of ball appearances over frames. The variations come from its sizes, shapes, colors, and velocity, which change irregularly over frames. There are many other moving objects that make similar situation as baseballs in sport videos. Moreover, the balls are relative smaller than other objects and often merged with lines and are immersed in the backgrounds.

Pitching Shot Extraction and Its Semantic Distribution Analysis

Baseball games have temporal syntactic structures because of the game rules. All events occur

Figure 6. Examples of ball tracking in baseball videos

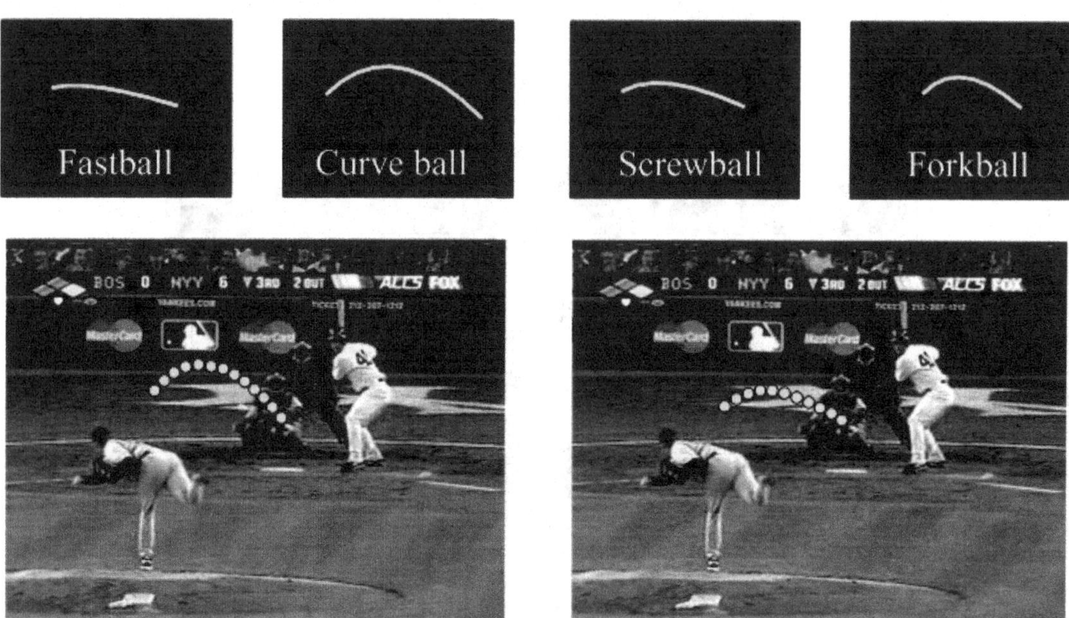

Figure 7. Example of occurrence of the highlight between two pitching shots

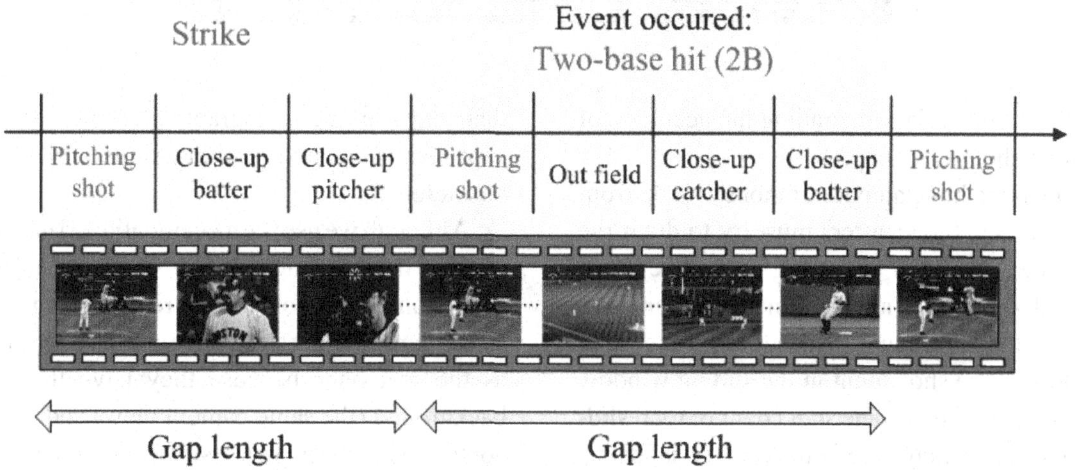

between two adjacent pitching scenes. In this chapter, we propose a method to extract high-level semantics of baseball videos from different perspective. The distance between two consecutive pitching shots is called "gap length" and the scene between two pitching shots is called "pitching scene" (Yeh, 2009). Figure 7 shows the highlight occurred between two pitching shots. The gap length implies semantic information. Despite its simplicity, the gap length gives considerable semantic information for each baseball video. However, most recorded broadcasting videos

Figure 8. Flowchart of the proposed pitching-shot extraction

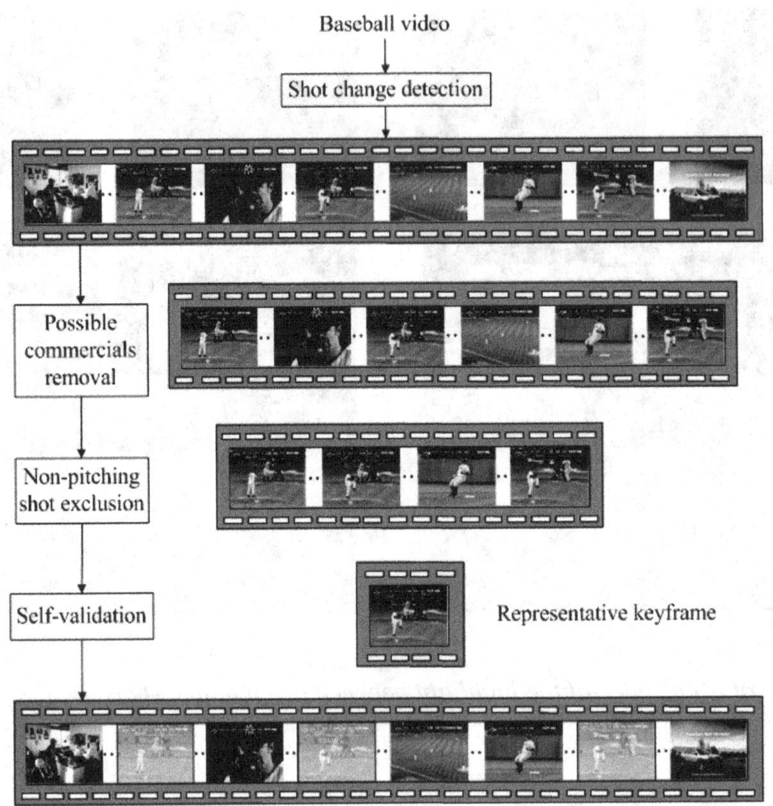

contain commercials, degrading the accuracy of pitching shot detection.

Given the huge amount of money made from commercials, broadcasters must try to dram the audience's attention to the high frequency shot cut and short shot interval. In this regard, we observe the shot count distribution in a sliding window. If the shot count in the sliding window is larger than the average shot count of total sliding window, it may belong to commercial shots. Through this process, most of commercials are removed. Although we do exclude commercials, there are still a large number of non-pitching shots remaining such as runner close-ups, pitcher close-ups, batter close-ups, catch overview, and audience. Therefore, we try to exclude non-pitching shots by calculating the average histogram difference within each shot and the average histogram difference of total shots. Then, those shots larger than the average histogram difference of total shots could be non-pitching shots and should be excluded.

Although we use the aforementioned methods to filter the non-pitching shots, more than 50% of the candidate shots are not real pitching shots. These non-pitching shots have similar histograms as the real ones because they have the same background (the same camera view) and similar content. Therefore, we use self-validation method to obtain a dominate cluster which contains pitching shots. First, we select the center frame of each candidate pitching shots as its keyframe. Second, we calculate the differences of each keyframe to others. Then, the summation of the differences is regarded as a criterion for pitching-shot similarity. The keyframe with the minimum difference is selected as the representative keyframe. This representative keyframe is used to filter out the

Figure 9. Gap length distribution of five baseball videos

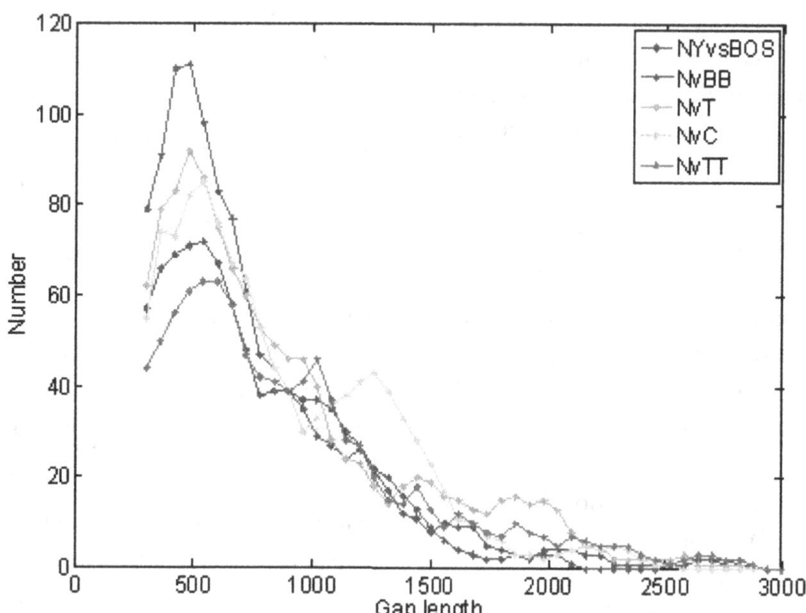

non-pitching shots. Figure 8 shows the flowchart of the proposed pitching shot extraction method.

Through the pitching-shot extraction, temporal syntactic structures of baseball videos can be obtained. Here, the scene between two pitching shots is called as pitching scene which may contains highlight events. The gap length of each pitching scene can be calculated. Five MLB baseball videos recorded from the cable TV are used to simulate the proposed algorithm as showed in Figure 9. (NY: New York Yankees; BOS: Boston Red Sox; BB: Baltimore Orioles; T: Texas Rangers; C: Cleveland Indians; TT: Toronto Blue Jays). The length of each baseball game is about 3 hours. The gap length distribution of baseball videos implies the type of that baseball game such as pitcher's duel or slugfest; therefore it can be used for searching and retrieving. The applications of gap length distribution can be further studied for baseball video semantic analysis.

CONCLUSION

This chapter reviews the development of sport video analysis and explores solutions to the challenge of extracting high-level semantics in sport videos. We also propose a method to analyze baseball videos via the concept of gap length. The techniques introduced can be wildly applied to many fields, such as indexing, searching, retrieving, summarization, skimming, training and entertainment. Though previous work contributes to these different areas greatly, they extract a limited range of semantics in sport videos, lacking the ability to produce personalized semantics especially in highlight detection. Because of the lack of user-oriented information, these techniques lack the ability to produce personalized semantics especially in highlight detection. Use-interaction may be a solution to achieve personalization in semantics extraction. Aiming overcome different types of sports and develop significant applications, sport video analysis continues to be a hot research field.

Nowadays ball tracking techniques plays an important role in the entertainment industsry. In combination with computer vision and image processing techniques, techniques proposed are already applied to virtual environment and TV broadcast enhancement. For example, QuesTec [http://www.questec.com/] develops virtual three-dimensional replay environment, SuperVision system, for a baseball game. Instant replays can be shown immediately, displaying any number of pitches, ball trajectory, movement, ball speed and plate-location etc. Video game product is another promising research topic. Actions captured in the playfield provide sufficient information for video game development. Developing practical game-play and creating a realistic experience, as you are there, still need long-lasting efforts.

REFERENCES

Blum, D. W. (1992). *Method and apparatus for identifying and eliminating specific material from video signals*. (US patent 5,151,788).

Chang, P., Han, M., & Gong, Y. (2002). *Extract highlights from baseball game video with hidden Markov models*. International Conference on Image Processing, (pp. I-609-I-612).

Chang, S. F., Puri, A., Sikora, T., & Zhang, H. J. (2001). Introduce to the special issue on MPEG-7. *Circuits and Systems for Video Technology*, *11*, 685–687. doi:10.1109/TCSVT.2001.927419

Chang, S. F., Smith, J. R., Beigi, M., & Benitez, A. (1997). Visual information retrieval from large distributed on-line repositories. *Communications of the ACM*, *40*, 63–71. doi:10.1145/265563.265573

Chao, C. Y., Shih, H. C., & Huang, C. L. (2005). *Semantics-based highlight extraction of soccer program using DBN*. International Conference on Acoustics, Speech, and Signal Processing, (pp. 1057-1060).

Cheng, C. C., & Hsu, C. T. (2006). Fusion of audio and motion information on HMM-based highlight extraction for baseball games. *Multimedia*, *8*, 585–599. doi:10.1109/TMM.2006.870726

Chu, W. T., Wang, C. W., & Wu, J. L. (2006). *Extraction of baseball trajectory and physics-based validation for single-view baseball video sequences*. International Conference on Multimedia and Expo, (pp. 1813-1816).

Chu, W. T., & Wu, J. L. (2008). Explicit semantic events detection and development of realistic applications for broadcasting baseball videos. *Multimedia Tools and Applications*, *38*, 27–50. doi:10.1007/s11042-007-0145-4

Duan, L. Y., Xu, M., Chua, T. S., Tian, Q., & Xu, C. S. (2003). *A mid-level representation framework for semantic sports video analysis*. ACM International Conference on Multimedia, (pp. 33-44).

Duygulu, P., Chen, M.-Y., & Hauptmann, A. (2004). *Comparison and combination of two novel commercial detection methods*. International Conference on Multimedia and Expo, (pp. 27-30).

Hanjalic, A. (2003). *Generic approach to highlights extraction from a sport video*. International Conference on Image Processing, (pp. 1-4).

Hanjalic, A. (2003). *Multimodal approach to measuring excitement in video* (pp. 289–292). International Conferences on Multimedia and Expo.

Hanjalic, A., & Zhang, H. J. (1999). An integrated scheme for automated video abstraction based on unsupervised cluster-validity analysis. *Circuits and Systems for Video Technology*, *9*, 8. doi:10.1109/76.809162

Hua, X.-S., Lu, L., & Zhang, H.-J. (2005). *Robust learning-based TV commercial detection*. International Conference on Multimedia and Expo.

Hung, M. H., & Hsieh, C. H. (2008). Event detection of broadcast baseball videos. *Circuits and Systems for Video Technology*, *18*, 1713–1726. doi:10.1109/TCSVT.2008.2004934

Jiang, S., Ye, Q., Gao, W., & Huang, T. (2004). *A new method to segment playfield and its applications in match analysis in sports video*. ACM International Conference on Multimedia, (pp. 292-295).

Kuo, C. M., Hung, M. H., & Hsieh, C. H. (2008). *Baseball playfield segmentation using adaptive Gaussian mixture models.* International Conference on Innovative Computing Information and Control.

Li, C. C., Chou, S. T., & Lin, C. W. (2008). Statistical pitch type recognition in broadcast baseball videos. *Proceedings of the International Conference of Computer Vision & Graphic Image Processing.*

Li, Y., Lee, S. H., Yeh, C. H., & Kuo, C.-C. J. (2006). Techniques for movie content analysis and skimming. *IEEE Signal Processing Magazine*, *23*, 79–89. doi:10.1109/MSP.2006.1621451

Lienhart, R., Kuhmnch, C., & Effelsberg, W. (2001). *On the detection and recognition of television commercials*. International Conference on Multimedia Computing and Systems, (pp. 509-516).

Manjunath, B. S., Huang, T., Teklap, A. M., & Zhang, H. J. (2000). Guest editorial introduction to the special issue on image and video processing for digital libraries. *Image Processing*, *9*, 1–2. doi:10.1109/TIP.2000.817594

Manjunath, B. S., Salembier, P., & Sikora, T. (2002). *Introduction to MPEG-7. John Wiley & Sons*. England: LTD.

Marlow, S., Sadlier, D. A., McGerough, K., O'Connor, N., & Murphy, N. (2001). *Audio and video processing for automatic TV advertisement detection*. Irish Signals and Systems Conference, (pp. 25-27).

Mizutani, M., Ebadollahi, S., & Chang, S.-F. (2005). *Commercial detection in heterogeneous video streams using fused multi-modal and temporal features*. International Conference on Acoustics, Speech, and Signal Processing, (pp. 157-160).

Nepal, S., Srinivasan, U., & Reynolds, G. (2001). Automatic detection of "Goal" segments in basketball. *Proceedings of the 9th ACM International Conference on Multimedia*, (pp. 261-269).

Rui, Y., Gupta, A., & Acero, A. (2000). Automatically extracting highlights for TV baseball programs. *Proceedings of the ACM International Conference on Multimedia*, (pp. 105-115).

Rui, Y., Huang, T. S., & Mehrotra, S. (1998). Constructing table-of-content for video. *ACM Journal of Multimedia Systems*, *7*, 359–368. doi:10.1007/s005300050138

Xie, L., Xu, P., Chang, S. F., Divakaran, A., & Sun, H. (2004). Structure analysis of soccer video with domain knowledge and hidden Markov models. *Pattern Recognition Letters*, *25*, 767–775. doi:10.1016/j.patrec.2004.01.005

Xiong, Z., Radhakrishnan, R., Divakaran, A., & Huang, T. S. (2005). *Highlights extraction from sports video based on an audio-visual marker detection framework*. International Conference on Multimedia and Expo, (pp. 29-32).

Xu, C., Wang, J., Li, Y., & Duan, L. (2006). Live sports event detection based on broadcast video and Web-casting text. *Proceedings of the ACM International Conference on Multimedia*, (pp. 221-230).

Yeh, C. H., Kuo, C. H., & Liou, R. W. (2009). Movie story intensity representation through audiovisual tempo analysis. *Multimedia Tools and Applications*, 205–228. doi:10.1007/s11042-009-0278-8

Yeh, C. H., Lee, S. H., & Kuo, C.-C. J. (2005). Content-based video analysis for knowledge discovery . In Chen, C. H., & Wang, P. S. P. (Eds.), *Handbook of pattern recognition and computer vision* (3rd ed.). World Scientific Publishing Co. doi:10.1142/9789812775320_0029

Yeh, C. H., & Teng, C. H. (2009). *Statistical understanding of broadcast baseball videos from the perspective of semantic shot distribution.* Computer Vision & Graphic Image Processing.

Yu, X., Xu, C., Leong, H. W., Tian, Q., Tang, Q., & Wan, K. W. (2003). *Trajectory-based ball detection and tracking with applications to semantic analysis of broadcast soccer video.* ACM International Conference on Multimedia, (pp. 11-20).

Zhang, D., & Chang, S. F. (2002). Event detection in baseball video using superimposed caption recognition. *ACM International Conference on Multimedia*, (pp. 315-318).

Zhu, G., Xu, C., Zhang, Y., Huang, Q., & Lu, H. (2008). *Event tactic analysis based on player and ball trajectory in broadcast video.* International Conference on Content-based Image and Video Retrieval, (pp. 515-524).

KEY TERMS AND DEFINITIONS

Pitching Shot: Every baseball events start from a pitcher throwing the ball. Consequently the pitching shot is the basic element to our proposed algorithm.

Gap Length: The distance between two consecutive pitching shots.

Section 2

Chapter 9
Normal Forms for Multimedia Databases

Shi Kuo Chang
University of Pittsburgh, USA

Vincenzo Deufemia
Università di Salerno, Italy

Giuseppe Polese
Università di Salerno, Italy

ABSTRACT

In this chapter we present normal forms for the design of multimedia database schemes with reduced manipulation anomalies. To this aim we first discuss how to describe the semantics of multimedia attributes based upon the concept of generalized icons, already used in the modeling of multimedia languages. Then, we introduce new extended dependencies involving different types of multimedia data. Such dependencies are based on domain specific similarity measures that are used to detect semantic relationships between complex data types. Based upon these new dependencies, we have defined five normal forms for multimedia databases, some focusing on the level of segmentation of multimedia attributes, others on the level of fragmentation of tables.

INTRODUCTION

In the last decade multimedia databases have been used in many application fields. The internet boom has increased this trend, introducing many new interesting issues related to the storage and management of distributed multimedia data. For these reasons data models and database management systems (DBMSs) have been extended in order to enable the modeling and management of complex data types, including multimedia data. Researchers in this field have agreed on many characteristics on which to base the classification of multimedia DBMSs (MMDBMS). Some of them are (Narasimhalu, 1996):

- The data model for representing multimedia information. This should provide effective means to represent relationships among media types.

DOI: 10.4018/978-1-61350-126-9.ch009

- The indexing techniques used to enable content based retrieval of multimedia information.
- The query language. This should allow to efficiently express complex characteristics of data to be retrieved, like multimedia data.
- The clustering techniques on multimedia information to enhance its retrieval.
- Support for distributed multimedia information management.
- Flexible architectures.

The latter is a critical point, because multimedia information systems are in continuous evolution. Thus, it is important that the architectures of MMDBMSs be flexible enough to be extensible and adaptable to future needs and standards. A conspicuous number of MMDBMS products have been developed. Examples include CORE (Wu *et al.*, 1995), OVID (Oomoto & Tanaka, 1993), VODAK (Lohr & Rakow, 1995), QBIC (Flickner *et al.*, 1995), ATLAS (Sacks-Davis *et al.*, 1995), etc., each providing enhanced support for one or more media domains among text, sound, image, and video. At the beginning, many DBMS producers would preferably rely on the object-oriented data model to face the complexity of multimedia data, but there have also been examples of MMDBMSs based on the relational data model and on specific, non-standard data models. However, in order to facilitate the diffusion of multimedia databases within industrial environments researchers have been seeking solutions based on the relational data model, possibly associated to some standard design paradigm, like those used with traditional relational DBMSs (RDBMSs). Extensible relational DBMSs have been an attempt in this direction. Such DBMSs store object data using the Binary Large Object (BLOB) data type (IBM, 1995). BLOBs store arbitrarily large objects in a database and allow an object to have complex metadata which may be interrogated using a general query interface.

In the last years DBMS vendors have produced extended versions of relational DBMSs (Rennhackkamp 1997), with added capabilities to manage complex data types, including multimedia. In particular, these new products extend traditional RDBMSs with mechanisms for implementing the concept of object/relational universal server. In other words, they provide means to enable the construction of user defined Data Types (UDT), and Functions for manipulating them (UDF). New standards for SQL have been created, and SQL3 (Elmasri & Navathe, 2003) has become the standard for relational DBMSs extended with object oriented capabilities. The standard includes UDTs, UDFs, LOBs (a variant of BLOBS), and type checking on user defined data types, which are accessed through SQL statements. Early examples of extensible RDBMSs include Postgres (Stonebraker & Kemnitz, 1995), IBM/DB2 version 5 (Davis, 1999), Informix (Rennhackkamp, 1997), and ORACLE 8 (Oracle, 1999).

More recent projects address the needs of applications for richer semantic content. Most of them rely on the MPEG-standards MPEG-7 and MPEG-21. MPEG-7 (Kosch, 2003) is an XML-based multimedia meta-data standard, which proposes description elements for the multimedia processing cycle from the capture, analysis/filtering, to the delivery, and interaction. MPEG-21 (Kosch, 2003) is the standard defining an open multimedia framework that will cover the entire multimedia content delivery chain encompassing content creation, production, delivery, personalization, consumption, presentation and trade. MARS realizes an integrated multimedia information retrieval and database management system, that supports multimedia information as first-class objects suited for storage and retrieval based on their semantic content (Chakrabarti *et al.*, 2000). Multimedia Data Cartridge is a system extension of the Oracle 9i DBMS providing a multimedia query language, access to media, processing and optimization of queries, and indexing capacities relying on a multimedia database schema derived from MPEG-7 (Kosch *et al.*, 2005).

The normalization of multimedia databases needs to account for many new issues as opposed to alphanumeric databases. Many different types of complex data need to be analyzed. In this chapter we describe a general purpose framework to define normal forms in multimedia databases. The framework applies in a seamless way to images as well as to all the other different media types. The semantics of multimedia attributes are defined by means of generalized icons (Chang, 1996), previously used to model multimedia languages in a visual language fashion. In particular, generalized icons are here used to derive extended dependencies, which are parameterized upon the similarity measure used to compare multimedia data. Based on these new dependencies, we define five normal forms aiming to reach a suitable partitioning of multimedia data, and to derive database schemes that prevent possible manipulation anomalies. As a practical application, in the paper we show how to use our framework for normalizing multimedia databases used in e-learning applications. In particular, we apply our normal forms to transform the database schema in order to make it suitably accessible from different client devices, including PDAs and other mobile devices, each with different multimedia and bandwidth capabilities. This problem frequently occurs in multimedia database applications, since they are often used in a distributed scenario, in which it has to be guaranteed a suitable quality of service even if accessing the multimedia databases through clients with limited capabilities. Finally, based on the e-learning example, we provide some experimental data to validate the proposed framework.

BACKGROUND

As MMDBMSs technology has started becoming more mature, the research community has been seeking new methodologies for multimedia software engineering. Independently from the data model underlying the chosen MMDBMS, multimedia software engineering methodologies should include techniques for database design, embedding guidelines and normal forms to prevent anomalies that might arise while manipulating multimedia data. In the literature we find some new normalization techniques extending traditional normal forms for relational databases (Santini & Gupta, 2002) (Arenas & Libkin 2004) (Vincent *et al.*, 2004). However, many of them focus on specific domains, and no general purpose normalization framework for multimedia is provided. In particular, the technique in (Santini & Gupta, 2002) focuses on the normalization of image databases by partitioning images so as to enhance search and retrieval operations. To this sake the technique aims to define dependencies among image features, which suggest the designer how to efficiently map them into a database schema. The techniques in (Arenas & Libkin 2004) (Vincent *et al.*, 2004) focus on the normalization of XML documents.

SEMANTICS OF MULTIMEDIA ATTRIBUTES

Before discussing dependencies and normal forms for multimedia databases we need to define the semantics of multimedia attributes.

A dependency is a property of the semantics of attributes. Database designers use their understanding of the semantics of attributes to specify functional dependencies among them (Elmasri & Navathe, 2003). As we know, other than alphanumeric data, multimedia databases can store data types, such as text, sound, image, and video, which are characterized by complex structures and semantics. Prime versions of MMDBMSs provided a new data type for storing complex data, namely BLOB. This storage technique yielded some problems, because BLOBs are non-interpreted byte streams, hence the DBMS has no knowledge concerning their structure and the content of their components. It can only see them as atomic data types. Although inefficient, the simple structure of the BLOB data type makes it general enough to model most of the complex data types used in multimedia databases. Thus, a better solution should at least allow us to model and manipulate all the different complex data types that might be needed in multimedia computing. This is why some RDBMS vendors have aimed to develop extensible RDBMSs, that is, RDBMSs extended with new complex data types, together with added capabilities to let developers define and implement their own data types, and the corresponding manipulation functions.

Beyond the storage strategy used for the different media types, we define a framework to model their semantics so as to be able to derive functional dependencies between them. To this sake, we have exploited the framework of generalized icons (Chang, 1996), which are dual objects (x_m, x_i), with a logical part x_m, and a physical part x_i. They can be used to describe multimedia objects such as images, sounds, texts, motions, and videos. A generalized icon for modeling images is like a traditional icon, whereas those for modeling sounds, texts, motions, and videos are earcons, ticons, micons, and vicons, respectively. For all of them we denote the logical part with x_m, whereas the physical parts will be denoted with x_i for icons, x_e for earcons, x_t for ticons, x_s for micons, and x_v for vicons. The logical part x_m always describes semantics, whereas x_i represents an image, x_e a sound, x_t a text, x_s a motion, and x_v a video. Furthermore, a multicon is a generalized icon representing composite multimedia objects (Arndt *et al.*, 1997). Thus, a multicon will also be a dual object, where the logical part represents the semantics of the combined media. Generalized icons can be combined by means of special icon operators. The latter are dual objects themselves, where the logical part is used to combine the logical parts x_m of the operand icons, whereas the physical part is used to combine their physical parts x_i. For instance, by applying a temporal operator to several icons and an earcon we might obtain a vicon, with the physical part representing a video, and the logical part describing the video semantics.

In our framework we associate a generalized icon to each complex attribute, using the logical part to describe its semantics, and the physical part to describe the physical appearance based upon a given storage strategy. The logical parts of generalized icons will have to be expressed through a semantic model. Conceptual graphs are an example of formal semantic model that can be used to describe logical parts of generalized icons (Chang, 1996). Alternatively, the designer can use frames, semantic networks, or visual CD forms (Chang *et al.*, 1994).

As an example, choosing a frame based representation, an image icon representing the face of a person may be described by a frame with attributes describing the name of the person, the colors of the picture, objects appearing in it, including their spatial relationships. A vicon will contain semantic attributes describing the images of the video photograms, the title of the video, the topic, the duration, temporal relationships, etc. Similarly, semantic attributes in an earcon might be used to describe the title of the sound, if any, the genre, the singer (in case it is a song), the sampling rate, etc.

Based on the specific domain of the multimedia database being constructed, the designer will have to specify the semantics of simple and complex attributes according to the chosen semantic model. Once s/he has accomplished this task, the generalized icons for the multimedia database are completely specified, which provides a semantic specification of the tuples in the database.

As an example, to describe semantics in a database of singers we might use attributes name, birthday, genre, as alphanumeric attributes, and picture as an icon representing the singer picture, one or more earcons to represent some of his/her songs, and one or more vicons to represent his/her video clips. A tuple in this database describes information about a specific singer, including his/her songs and video clips. This provides a complete semantic specification of the tuple.

EXTENDED DEPENDENCIES

In traditional relational databases a functional dependency is defined as a constraint between two sets of attributes from the database (Codd, 1972). Given two sets of attributes X and Y, a functional dependency between them is denoted by X→Y. The constraint says that, for any two tuples t_1 and t_2, if t_1[X] = t_2[X], then t_1[Y] = t_2[Y]. This concept cannot be immediately applied to multimedia databases, since we do not have similar simple and efficient methods to compare multimedia attributes. In other words, we need a method for defining equalities between groups of attributes involving complex data types.

Generally speaking, the matching of complex attributes needs to be an approximate match. In fact, the problem of comparing complex data for equality resembles the problem of retrieval from multimedia databases, where the query is entered by sketching or composing an object belonging to the same media type of the one being retrieved. Then, by using a specific indexing and retrieval technique (Arndt *et al.*, 1997), it is possible to retrieve a set of objects from the database that are similar to the query objects. Thus, it is also possible to select the most similar object, since the objects in the answer set are ranked according to a certain degree of similarity.

We follow a similar criterion to define extended functional dependencies for multimedia databases. This means that we can extend the definition of dependency by selecting a specific similarity function and thresholds to perform approximate comparisons of complex data types. Thus, the functional dependencies change if we use different similarity functions. As a consequence, we enrich the notation used for functional dependencies to include symbols representing the chosen similarity function. Before this, in what follows we introduce some basic concepts of the relational model and of similarity theory (Santini & Jain, 1999).

In the relational model the database is viewed as a set of relations of time-varying content. A multimedia database is formed by one or more relations of the form R(x_1: X_1,..., x_n: X_n), where X_1,...,X_n are data types, and x_i is the name of the *i*-th field or column of the relation R. The union of two sets of attributes X and Y is written as XY. An instance of R, that is, its content at a given time is defined as a subset of the Cartesian product $X_1 \times \ldots \times X_n$. This instance can be represented as a relation having as rows (named *tuples*) the elements of the subset of $X_1 \times \ldots \times X_n$, and as columns the attributes of R. If R = {X_1,..., X_n} is a database scheme, then we write *attr*(R) for $\cup_{i=1..n} X_i$. If *t* is a tuple of this relation (i.e., an element in an instance of R), then *t*[A] denotes the value of this tuple in the A-column; *t*[A] is called the A-value of *r*. A schema consists of a set of relations, where each relation is defined by its attribute sets, and some semantic constraints. In this chapter we restrict our attention to constraints which can be expressed as multimedia functional dependencies (MFDs).

Tuples of a relation can be compared by means of a set of relevant features Φ. For instance, images can be compared using attributes like color, texture, shape, etc.; audio data can be compared using loudness, pitch, brightness, bandwidth, and harmonicity. The values of each feature $F \in \Phi$ belong to a domain $D = dom(F)$.

The similarity between two elements *x* and *y* in a tuple is based on distance measures or, equivalently, on similarity functions, defined on feature spaces that we assume to be metric spaces. In the following, we will always refer to metric distance functions, but it should be understood that the same considerations apply to similarity function, given the symmetry between distance and similarity functions (Santini & Jain, 1999).

In particular, given two elements *x* and *y* belonging to a given data type X, we consider distance functions of type d: $D^2 \rightarrow [0,1]$, such that for each $v_x, v_y \in D$ $d(v_x, v_y)$ returns the distance of x from y with respect to the feature space D. In what follows we indicate such distance with $d(x, y)$ for any two elements x, y: X. Moreover, given a data type X, we denote with D(X) the set of distance functions defined on X, and with X_d the feature space on which the distance function d is defined.

In order to evaluate the similarity between the multimedia objects of two tuples we introduce a *tuple distance function*, which summarizes the results produced by the different distance functions applied to the elements of the tuples. In particular, given a relation $R(z_1{:}Z_1,\ldots, z_n{:}Z_n)$, if $x=(x_1,\ldots, x_n)$ and $y=(y_1,\ldots, y_n)$ are two tuples of R, then $\varpi(x, y) = g(d_1(x_1, y_1),\ldots, d_n(x_n, y_n))$ measures the distance between x and y, where $d_i \in D(Z_i)$ and g: $[0,1]^n \rightarrow [0,1]$ is a monotone aggregation function that combines the n scores to derive an overall score. Aggregation functions should satisfy the triangular norm properties, that is, the conservation, monotonicity, commutativity, and associativity properties. There are several aggregation functions defined in fuzzy logic literature (Fagin, 1996), among which the *min* function is the most commonly used. Notice that if n=1 then $\varpi(x, y)= d_1(x, y)$. Given a set of data types X, we denote with TD(X) the set of tuple distance functions defined on X.

Definition 1. Let $R(z_1{:}Z_1,\ldots, z_n{:}Z_n)$, ϖ be a tuple distance function on R, t be a maximum distance threshold, $x=(x_1,\ldots, x_n)$ and $y=(y_1,\ldots, y_n)$ be two tuples in R, we say that x is *similar* within t to y with respect to ϖ, denoted with $x \cong_{\omega(t)} y$, iff $\varpi(x, y) \leq t$.

Now we are ready to introduce the notion of functional dependency for multimedia databases, named *type-M functional dependency*.

Definition 2. (*type-M functional dependency*) Let R be a relation with attribute set U, and X, Y $\subseteq$ U. $X_{g1(t')} \rightarrow Y_{g2(t'')}$ is a *type-M functional dependency* (MFD) relation if and only if for any two tuples t1 and t2 in R that have $t1[X] \cong_{g1(t')} t2[X]$, then $t1[Y] \cong_{g2(t'')} t2[Y]$, where $g_1 \in TD(X)$ and $g_2 \in TD(Y)$, whereas t' and $t'' \in [0,1]$ are thresholds.

This means that the features used by g_2 on Y depend on the features used by g_1 on X; or, alternatively, the values of the features used by g_1 on X component imply the range of values for the features used by g_2 on Y component. Notice that given a distance function d_1 and a threshold t, $x_1 \cong_{d1(t)} x_2$ and $x_2 \cong_{d1(t)} x_3$ does not imply $x_1 \cong_{d1(t)} x_3$, as shown in Figure 1. However, we can state that $x_1 \cong_{d1(2t)} x_3$. In general, if $X_{d1(t')} \rightarrow Y_{d2(t'')}$ holds then for any two tuples t1 and t2 that have $t1[X] \cong_{d1(kt')} t2[X]$, then $t1[Y] \cong_{d2(kt'')} t2[Y]$, with $k \in R$. Thus, given an element x belonging to a data type X, the equivalent class of x respect to a distance function $d \in D(X)$ and a threshold $t \in [0,1]$ is defined as $[x]_{\cong d(t)} = \{y \in X \mid y \cong_{d(t)} x\}$. Similarly, for a tuple $x=(x_1,\ldots, x_n)$ of a relation $R(z_1{:}Z_1,\ldots, z_n{:}Z_n)$, the equivalent class of x respect to a tuple distance function ϖ is defined as $[x]_{\cong\varpi(t)} = \{(y_1,\ldots, y_n) \mid y_i \cong_{di(ti)} x_i$, with $y_i \in Z_i$, $d_i \in D(Z_i)$, $t_i \in [0,1]$ for $1 \leq i \leq n$ and $\varpi(x,y)= g(d_1(x_1,y_1),\ldots, d_n(x_n,y_n))\}$.

As an example, if we define a functional dependency between attributes FINGERPRINT and PHOTO of police database, and use the fingerprint matching function FINGERCODE for comparing digital fingerprint [JPH00], and the similarity technique used by QBIC for comparing photo images, we would write as follows

$$\text{FINGERPRINT}_{FINGERCODE(t')} \longrightarrow \text{PHOTO}_{QBIC(t'')}$$

This constraint says that for any two tuples t_1 and t_2 such that t_1[FINGERPRINT] is considered similar within the threshold t' to t_2[FINGERPRINT] by the FINGERCODE, then t_1[PHOTO] is considered similar within the threshold t'' to t_2[PHOTO] by the QBIC. Given the semantics of the FINGERPRINT attribute it is expectable that a designer will fix the value of t' close to zero.

From definition 2 it is clear that $X_I \rightarrow Y_{s2}$ is a type-M dependency relation where I is the identity relation and s_2 is a tuple distance function. In particular, $X_I \rightarrow Y_I$ is a type-M dependency

Figure 1. Relationships among tuples on domains X_{d1} and Y_{d2}

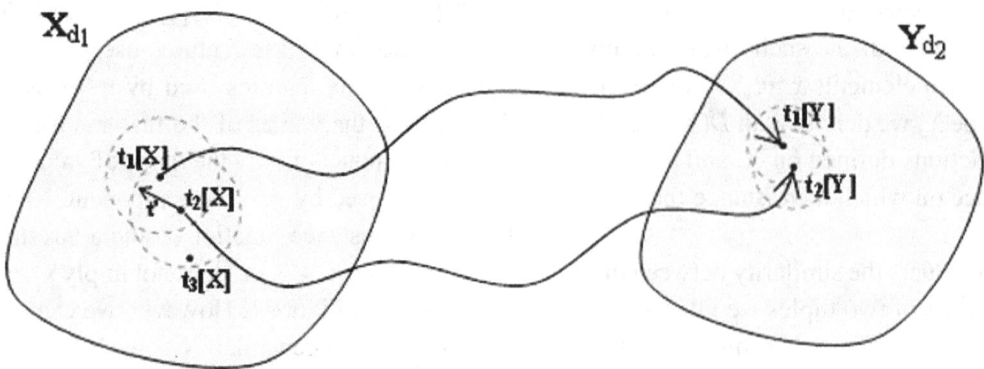

relation. In other words if we use identity relations as distance functions, we can regard any dependency relation as a type-M dependency relation. Therefore, some of the type-M normal forms we define in this chapter will be identical to the usual normal forms, as long as we use identity relations as distance functions. In the following we omit the tuple distance function from the MFDs when this corresponds to the identity relation.

As an example, in a multimedia database of songs, suppose SONG is an attribute storing the earcon for a song, and GENRE is an attribute storing the genre of the song stored in SONG. It might be the case that SONG implies the attribute GENRE, yielding an MFD. Thus, given two tuples t_1 and t_2, if the two earcons t_1[SONG] and t_2[SONG] are considered similar according to a distance function s_1, then also their genre should be similar. We write

$$\text{SONG}_{s1} \longrightarrow \text{GENRE}$$

if every time t_1[SONG] is considered similar to t_2[SONG] according to the similarity technique s_1 then also t_1[GENRE] = t_2[GENRE], where GENRE is an alphanumeric attribute, for which we use the identity relation, whereas SONG is an earcon. However, as it can be imagined, the distance function used heavily affects the functional dependencies. In fact, a distance function might consider two songs similar only because they have a similar title, which would not imply they have the same genre. This is why the distance function has to be explicitly represented in the notation.

As for classical dependency relations, the existence of certain MFDs in a relation implies the existence of others. Inference rules are means to construct these implicit dependencies. In the following we define inference rules for MFDs. Given a MFD $X_{g1(t1)} \rightarrow Y_{g2(t2)}$, we denote with *Dist*($g_1$, X) the sequence of distance functions applied by g_1 on X. Moreover, given two functions $g_1 \in TD(X)$ and $g_2 \in TD(Y)$ we define $g_1 \bullet_h g_2(x,y) = h(g_1(x), g_2(y))$ with h triangular norm aggregation function.

1. The *reflexive rule* $XY_{g1(t1)} \rightarrow Y_{g2(t2)}$ holds if *Dist*(g_1, Y)=*Dist*(g_2, Y) and $t_2 \geq t_1$. That is, the reflexive rule holds if the distance functions used by g_1 and g_2 on the attributes in Y are the same, and the threshold for g_2 is greater than the one for g_1.
2. The *augmentation rule* $\{X_{g1(t1)} \rightarrow Y_{g2(t2)}\} \models XZ_{g3(t3)} \rightarrow YZ_{g4(t4)}$, holds if *Dist*($g_1$, X) = *Dist*($g_3$, X), *Dist*($g_2$, Y) = *Dist*($g_4$, Y), *Dist*($g_3$, Z) = *Dist*($g_4$, Z), $t_3 \geq t_1$ and $t_4 \geq t_2$.
3. The *transitive rule* $\{X_{g1(t1)} \rightarrow Y_{g2(t2)}, Y_{g2(t3)} \rightarrow Z_{g3(t4)}\} \models X_{g1(t5)} \rightarrow Z_{g3(t6)}$, holds if $t_2 \leq t_3$, $t_1 \leq t_5$, and $t_4 \leq t_6$.

4. The *decomposition rule* $\{X_{g1(t1)} \rightarrow YZ_{g2(t2)}\} \models X_{g1(t1)} \rightarrow Y_{g3(t2)}$, holds if *Dist*$(g_2, Y) =$ *Dist*(g_3, Y).
5. The *union rule* $\{X_{g1(t1)} \rightarrow Y_{g2(t2)}, X_{g1(t3)} \rightarrow Z_{g3(t4)}\} \models X_{g1(t5)} \rightarrow YZ_{g4(t6)}$, where $g_4 = g_2 \bullet g_3$, $t_5 = \max\{t_1, t_3\}$ and $t_6 = t_2 + t_4$.
6. The *pseudotransitive rule* $\{X_{g1(t1)} \rightarrow Y_{g2(t2)}, WY_{g3(t3)} \rightarrow Z_{g4(t4)}\} \models WX_{g5(t5)} \rightarrow Z_{g4(t4)}$, holds if *Dist*$(g_1, X) =$ *Dist*(g_5, X), *Dist*$(g_2, Y) =$ *Dist*(g_3, Y), *Dist*$(g_3, W) =$ *Dist*(g_5, W), $t_3 \geq t_2$ and $t_5 = t_1 + (t_3 - t_2)$.

Definition 3. (*type-M multivalued dependency*) Let R be a multimedia relation with attribute set U, and $X, Y \subseteq U$. $X_{g1(t')} \twoheadrightarrow Y_{g2(t'')[g3(t''')]}$ is a *type-M multivalued dependency* (MMD) relation if and only if for any two tuples t1 and t2 in R such that $t1[X] \cong_{g1(t')} t2[X]$, there also exist in R two tuples t3 and t4 with the following properties:

- $t3[X], t4[X] \in [t1[X]]_{\cong g1(t')}$
- $t3[Y] \cong_{g2(t'')} t1[Y]$ and $t4[Y] \cong_{g2(t'')} t2[Y]$
- $t3[R - (XY)] \cong_{g3(t''')} t2[R - (XY)]$ and $t4[R - (XY)] \cong_{g3(t''')} t1[R - (XY)]$.

Where $g_1 \in TD(X)$, $g_2 \in TD(Y)$ and $g_3 \in TD(R-(XY))$, whereas t', t'' and t''' $\in [0,1]$ are thresholds.

Because of the symmetry in the definition, whenever $X_{g1(t1)} \twoheadrightarrow Y_{g2(t2)[g3(t3)]}$ holds in R, so does $X_{g1(t1)} \twoheadrightarrow [R - (XY)]_{g3(t3)[g2(t2)]}$.

An MMD $X_{g1(t1)} \twoheadrightarrow Y_{g2(t2)[g3(t3)]}$ in R is called a *trivial MMD* if (a) $Y \subseteq X$ or (b) $X \cup Y = R$. An MMD that satisfies neither (a) nor (b) is called a *non trivial MMD*.

Similarly to multimedia functional dependencies (MFDs), we can define inference rules for MMDs.

1. $X_{g1(t1)} \twoheadrightarrow Y_{g2(t2)[g3(t3)]} \models X_{g1(t1)} \twoheadrightarrow [R-(XY)]_{g3(t3)[g2(t2)]}$, where $g_1 \in TD(X)$, $g_2 \in TD(Y)$, $g_3 \in TD(R-(XY))$, and $t_1, t_2, t_3 \in [0,1]$.
2. If $X_{g1(t1)} \twoheadrightarrow Y_{g2(t2)[g3(t3)]}$ and $W \supseteq Z$ then $WX_{g4(t1)} \twoheadrightarrow YZ_{g5(t2)[g6(t3)]}$ where *Dist*$(g_4, W) =$ *Dist*$(g_5, Z) = I$, *Dist*$(g_1, X) =$ *Dist*(g_4, X), and *Dist*$(g_2, Y) =$ *Dist*(g_5, Y).
3. $\{X_{g1(t1)} \twoheadrightarrow Y_{g2(t2)[g3(t3)]}, Y_{g2(t2)} \twoheadrightarrow Z_{g4(t4)[g5(t5)]}\} \models X_{g1(t1)} \twoheadrightarrow (Z-Y)_{g6(t4)[g7(t7)]}$ where *Dist*$(g_3, Z-Y) =$ *Dist*$(g_4, Z-Y) =$ *Dist*$(g_6, Z-Y)$ and $g_7 \in TD(R-(Z-Y))$.
4. $X_{g1(t1)} \rightarrow Y_{g2(t2)} \models X_{g1(t1)} \twoheadrightarrow Y_{g2(t2)[g3(t3)]}$.
5. If $X_{g1(t1)} \twoheadrightarrow Y_{g2(t2)[g3(t3)]}$ and there exists W with the properties that (a) $W \cap Y = \emptyset$, (b) $W_{g4(t4)} \rightarrow Z_{g5(t5)}$, and (c) $Y \supseteq Z$, then $X_{g1(t1)} \rightarrow Z_{g5(t5)}$.

Given a set D of MFDs and MMDs specified on a relation schema R, we can use the inference rules to infer the set of all dependencies D^+ that will hold in every relation instance of R that satisfies D.

In order to present the notion of multimedia join dependency we need to introduce the multimedia operations of projection and join. Given a relation r over a multimedia relation R(X), a subset Y of X, a tuple distance function $g \in TD(Y)$, and a threshold t, the *multimedia projection* of R on Y respect to $g(t)$, denoted with $\pi_{Y,g(t)}(R)$, is defined by

$$\pi_{Y,g(t)}(R) = \{ v(Y) \mid v \in r \text{ and } g(v, w) \leq t \text{ for each tuple } w \text{ in } u[Y]\}$$

Note that the duplicate elimination is performed according to the function g and the associated threshold t. Obviously, if $t = 0$ then $w = v$, and the tuple distance function g corresponds to exact matching for the particular features it considers.

Let R(X,Y) and S(Y,Z) be multimedia relations where X, Y, and Z are disjoint sets of attributes, $g \in TD(Y)$ be a tuple distance function, and t be a threshold. The *multimedia join* of R and S respect to $g(t)$, denoted with $R \bowtie_{g(t)} S$, is the relation defined by

$$R \bowtie_{g(t)} S = \{(x,y,z,k) \mid (x,y) \in R, (y', z) \in S \text{ with } y \cong_{g(t)} y', \text{ and } k = g(y,y')\}$$

That is, the multimedia join is created by linking tuples of R with tuples of S that have similar values, within a threshold t respect to a function g, for all the attributes that are common to the two multimedia relations. The parameter k is introduced in the joined tuples, and represents a fuzzy value describing their degree of similarity.

Notice that the multimedia join raises many new issues and problems. In fact, we have higher probability to generate spurious tuples due to false alarms. Moreover, false dismissals lead to a new type of manipulation anomaly, not existing in traditional alphanumeric databases, namely the problem of *dismissed tuples*. These are tuples that should have been generated as a result of the multimedia join, but indeed they were discarded because a false dismissal occurred.

In the following we give the definition of Type-M join dependency.

Definition 4. (*type-M join dependency*) Let R be a relation on U, and $\{X_1,\dots,X_n\} \subseteq U$, with the union of X_i's being U. If $R = \Pi_{X1,g1(t1)}(R) \bowtie_{g1(t1)} \Pi_{X2,g2(t2)}(R) \bowtie_{g2(t2)} \dots \bowtie_{gn-1(tn-1)} \Pi_{Xn,I}(R)$, we say that R satisfies a *Type-M Join Dependency* (MJD), denoted by $\bowtie_{[g1(t1),\dots,gn-1(tn-1)]}[X_1,\dots, X_n]$, where $g_i \in TD(X_i \cap X_{i+1})$ and $t_i \in [0,1]$ for each $1 \leq i \leq n-1$.

An MVD is a special case of an MJD. An MVD $X_{g1(t1)} \rightarrow\!\!\!\rightarrow Y_{g2(t2)[g3(t3)]}$ for a relation on R is the MJD $\bowtie_{[g1(t1)\cdot g2(t2),g1(t1)\cdot g3(t3)]}(XY, X(R-Y))$.

In the following we provide some inference rules to infer MJDs. Let $S=\{X_1,\dots,X_n\}$ and $R=\{Y_{n+1},\dots,Y_m\}$.

1. $\emptyset \models \bowtie_{[g(t)]}[X]$, for any finite set of attributes X, and with $g \in TD(X)$, $t \in [0,1]$.
2. $\bowtie_{[g1(t1),\dots,gn-1(tn-1)]}[S] \models \bowtie_{[g1(t1),\dots,gn-1(tn-1),gn(tn)]}[S, Y]$ if $Y \subseteq$ ***attr***(S) and $g_n \in TD(Y)$.
3. $\bowtie_{[g1(t1),\dots,gn-1(tn-1),gn(tn),gn+1(tn+1)]}[S, Y, Z] \models \bowtie_{[g1(t1),\dots,gn(tn)\cdot gn+1(tn+1)]}[S, YZ]$.
4. $\{\bowtie_{[g1(t1),\dots,gn-1(tn-1),gn(tn)]}[S,Y], \bowtie_{[gn+1(tn+1),\dots,gm-1(tm-1)]}[R]\} \models \bowtie_{[g1(t1),\dots,gn-1(tn-1),gn(tn),gn+1(tn+1),\dots,gm-1(tm-1)]}[S, R]$ if Y = ***attr***(R).
5. $\bowtie_{[g1(t1),g2(t2)]}[S, YA] \models \bowtie_{[g1(t1),g2(t2)]}[S, Y]$ if $A \notin$ ***attr***(S).

NORMAL FORMS IN MULTIMEDIA DATABASES

In traditional alphanumeric databases normal forms are used to derive database schemes that prevent manipulation anomalies (Elmasri & Navathe, 2003). Similar anomalies can arise in multimedia database. Thus, a multimedia database designer should take all the precautions at database design time to avoid such anomalies. As an example, let us consider the following relation of an Art Exhibition multimedia database schema, with some MFDs associated to its attributes:

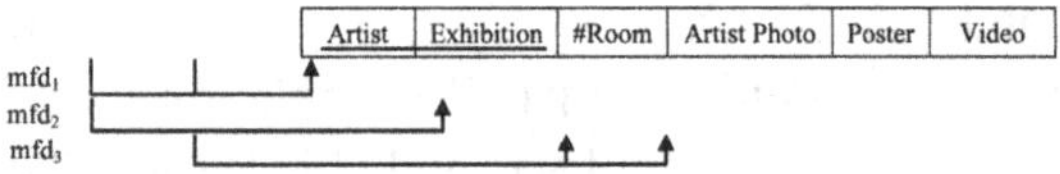

It is easy to imagine how the schema of such relation will yield manipulation anomalies, because it mixes together too many types of information. In fact, if we delete an exhibition from the database, we might lose an artist's data, such as his/her photo. Moreover, in order to perform such operation we need to perform deletion across all the tuples referring to that exhibition, because the relation schema yields duplication of information regarding an exhibition. If we are willing to insert an artist's picture, without knowing data of an exhibition, we have to leave some blank attributes, one of which belongs to the primary key. In order to avoid such anomalies, we should have stored information about exhibitions separately from those of artists.

Other types of anomalies arise from the fact of grouping to many multimedia data in the same multimedia attribute. For instance, the soundtrack of a video might be useful for different queries and multimedia presentations, hence we need to store the video and its soundtrack as two separated multimedia attributes, together with synchronization information to coordinate their combination. Thus, we need to segment the vicon associated to the video. Synchronization information can be stored as metadata or as special relations, depending on the specific MMDBMS technology used.

In this section we present five normal forms for multimedia databases. They are based on the M-type dependencies defined above. Therefore, their results depend upon the distance functions used to derive dependencies, and can be used to derive multimedia database schemes without potential manipulation anomalies. Moreover, the application of a normal form itself might need a specific manipulation function, such as a segmentation function, to handle a specific media type.

Our first normal form for multimedia attributes (1MNF) regards the granularity of multimedia attributes. We say that a multimedia database schema is in *first multimedia normal form* (1MNF) if each attribute A has the type of number, string or elementary generalized icon. For instance, image attributes can be decomposed in a certain number of k image components, which will be stored as separated attributes. In this case, the application of the normalization process is based on a specific segmentation function. This normalization process can also be applied to composite multimedia objects to decompose them into elementary generalized icons, which will be stored in separate attributes. For instance, as seen above, we might have a vicon attribute and might want to separate sounds from images. Again, the application of these normal forms requires the availability of specific segmentation function. Moreover, as said above the decomposition of a composite multimedia attribute may require the storing of additional data structures to enable the reconstruction of the original attribute format. In particular, such data structure should store the relations between the different attribute components.

We say that a multimedia database schema is in *second multimedia normal form* (2MNF) if it is in 1MNF and each non prime attribute A is fully dependent on the primary key. In case there is a partial dependency of A from a subset $\{k_i,\ldots, k_j\}$ of key attributes, then the designer can decide to normalize the schema by splitting the original schema R into two sub-schemes $R_1 = R - T$ and $R_2 = \{k_i,\ldots, k_j\} \cup T$, where $T = \{A\} \cup \{B_i \mid B_i \in R, \{k_i \ldots k_j\}_{s1} \rightarrow B_{is2}\}$. For brevity, in the following we omit the threshold from the similarity expressions.

As an example, let us analyse the MFDs and the normal forms of the relation schema from the art exhibition multimedia database seen above.

{Artist, Exhibition}→#Room is a full dependency, but {Artist, Exhibition} → ArtistPhoto$_{d1}$ and {Artist, Exhibition} → {Poster, Video}$_{d2}$ are partial dependencies because of mfd$_2$ and mfd$_3$, respectively. These MFDs lead to the decomposition of the relation into the following three relations, each of which is in 2MNF.

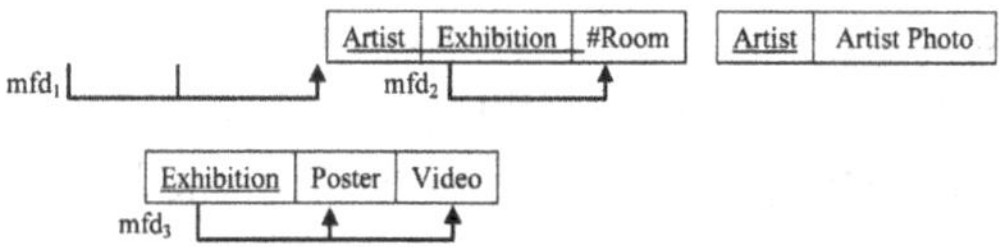

We say that a multimedia database schema R is in *third multimedia normal form* (3MNF) if it is in 2MNF and the non prime attributes are not mutually dependent. Equivalently, we can say that whenever a MFD $X_{s1} \rightarrow A_{s2}$ holds in R, either (a) X is a superkey of R, or (b) A is a prime attribute of R.

As an example, let us consider the following simple multimedia relation:

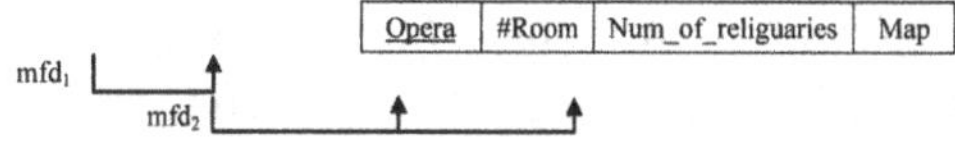

The dependency mfd$_2$ violates 3MNF because #Room is not a superkey of the relation, and Num_of_Religuaries and Map are not prime attribute. We can normalize the relation schema by decomposing it into the following two 3MNF relation schemas. We construct the first relation by removing the attributes violating 3MNF, namely Num_of_Religuaries and Map, from the original relation, and placing them with #Room into the second relation.

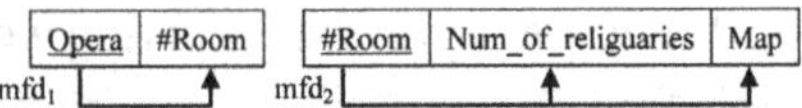

From the discussion so far we notice that the normal forms we define are characterized by the specific distance functions used to derive functional dependencies. As an example, let us consider the following simple multimedia database schema:

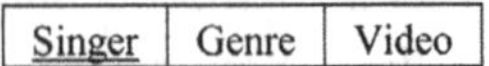

Each tuple in this simple database contains the name of a singer, his/her genre, and a set of his/her video. A designer might first decide to apply traditional first normal form to the attribute *Video*, since this is a multivalued attribute. Thus, the new schema will be as follows:

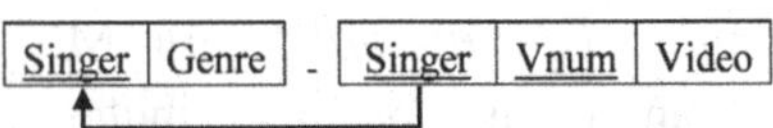

where the video have been stored in a separate relation, with a foreign key *Singer* on the original table, since there is a 1 to N relationship between singers and their video. Notice that we needed to add a new attribute *Vnum* on the new relation to form a key. The new attribute is a serial number to distinguish the different videos of a singer.

At this point, there might be the need to apply our first normal form to separate each video into three components, namely a song title, a vicon for the video itself, and an earcon for the background song. Thus, the second relation will be as follows,

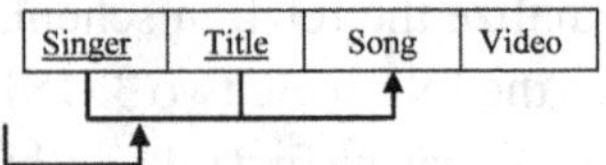

The extraction of the title attribute made the *Vnum* attribute useless, hence we eliminated it, and made the pair of attributes (*Singer, Title*) the new primary key. We can reasonably imagine a scenario in which three similarity functions s_1, s_2 and s_3 generate the following dependencies:

$\{\text{Singer, Title}\}_{s1} \rightarrow \text{Song}_{s2}$

$\text{Song}_{s2} \rightarrow \text{Video}_{s3}$

The second dependency violates 3MNF, because the attribute *Song* is not a primary key, nor *Video* is a prime attribute. In order to normalize such relation schema we need to separate the *Song* and *Video* attributes to form a third relation. However, the designer might decide to limit the splitting of tables due to efficiency issues.

Iteratively transforming a database schema to put it in 1MNFs may cause the introduction of MMDs. Such undesirable dependencies can be detected by the following multimedia normal form. We say that a multimedia database schema R is in *fourth multimedia normal form* (4MNF) with respect to a set of multimedia dependencies D if, for every nontrivial MMD $X_{g1(t1)} \twoheadrightarrow\!\!\!\!\!\rightarrow Y_{g2(t2)[g3(t3)]}$ in D^+, X is a superkey for R. In case there is a nontrivial MMD $X_{g1(t1)} \twoheadrightarrow\!\!\!\!\!\rightarrow Y_{g2(t2)[g3(t3)]}$ in D^+ with X not superkey for R, then the designer can decide to normalize the schema by splitting the original schema R into two sub-schemes $R_1 = (X \cup Y)$ and $R_2 = (R - Y)$.

As an example, let us consider the following simple multimedia relation:

The multivalued dependency mmd_1 violates 4MNF because Exhibition is not a superkey of the relation. We can normalize the relation schema by decomposing it into the following two 4MNF relation schemas.

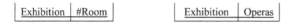

Exhibition	#Room

Exhibition	Operas

Finally, a multimedia database schema R that is in *fifth multimedia normal form* (5MNF) guarantees the lossless join properties, and prevents the problem of dismissed tuples. Formally, we say that R is in 5MNF with respect to a set D of MFDs, MMDs, and MJDs if, for every nontrivial type-M join dependency $⧖_{[g1(t1),\ldots,gn\text{-}1(tn\text{-}1)]}(X_1,\ldots, X_n)$ in D^+, every X_i is a superkey for R.

Normalizing Multimedia Databases for E-Learning Applications

In this section we describe the design process of multimedia databases for e-learning applications. Such applications should provide facilities to let students access multimedia documents through the web, by using different clients (laptop, tablet, PDA, etc.), which might have different multimedia and bandwidth capabilities. Figure 2 shows a typical screen of an e-learning application, where a video is played on the left side, and slides are browsed synchronously with the video on the right side. Students might access this site not only by using different client devices, but also connections with different bandwidth, such as modems, ADSL, GPRS, etc. Thus, the normalization process of multimedia databases underlying this type of applications should be structured in a way to guarantee a suitable trade off between QoS and hardware capabilities.

Figure 2. A typical distance learning application displayed on Tablet PC with a GPRS connection

Let us suppose that the database designer has produced a database schema including the following relation, and that the tuple distance functions s/he has used yield the multimedia functional dependencies mfd_1, mfd_2.

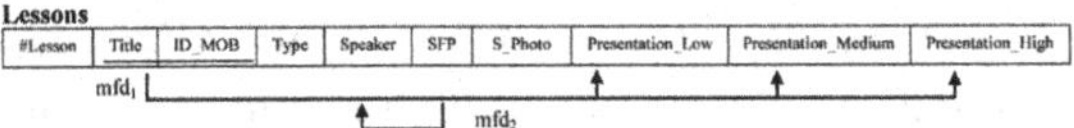

Each tuple in this relation contains the sequential number of a lesson, its title, the identifier of the associated multimedia objects, the lesson type (i.e., lecture, seminary, laboratory, etc.), the name of the speaker with its fingerprint (SFP) and its photo, and the multimedia presentations. The latter are stored in three different quality formats to suite different student access facilities. Let us also suppose that in this application the multimedia presentations of a lesson are multicons including the video of the lecturer, the associated audio, and the slides presented by the lecturer. In this early sketch of the database schema *Lessons* relation stores such presentations as a single tuple. However, due to possible limited bandwidth of some students' connections, we might need to decompose the whole presentation into simpler components so that each student might view only those supported by its devices. Moreover, in order to have these components readily accessible we need to store them separately into the database, together with meta data representing synchronization information necessary to recompose them. To this aim, we apply the first normal form to separate each presentation into three components, namely a micon for the slides, a vicon for the video itself, and an earcon for the speech component. Let us suppose that we have the same audio and the same slides for the three different quality formats, hence we will use one micon and one earcon for all of them, yielding a total number of 5 attributes instead of 9, as shown by the following relation.

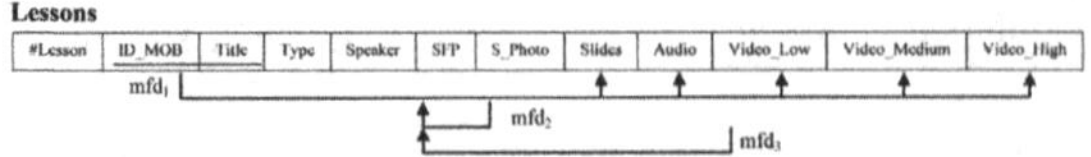

Such a schema already highlights some inefficiency. In fact, if the same lesson is offered in two different languages, we will use two tuples that only differ in the speaker and the audio components, but they share the same video. This schema might entail manipulation anomalies. In fact, if we want to replace the video component with a new one we need to perform this operation on two tuples (this is even worst if the same lesson is offered into more than two languages). Moreover, when deleting a lesson we lose the associated multimedia objects which might be useful for other lessons. For example, we might want to use the multimedia contents describing a binary tree both in a *Data Structure* lesson and a *Programming* lesson.

These anomalies occur because we have grouped different media components in the same multimedia object and heterogeneous information in the same relation. The first problem can be solved by applying our 1MNF, whereas the second can be solved by applying our 2MNF and 3MNF.

The functional dependency mfd_1 reveals that the relation schema *Lessons* is not in 2MNF. The application of our normalization rule leads to the following relation schemes:

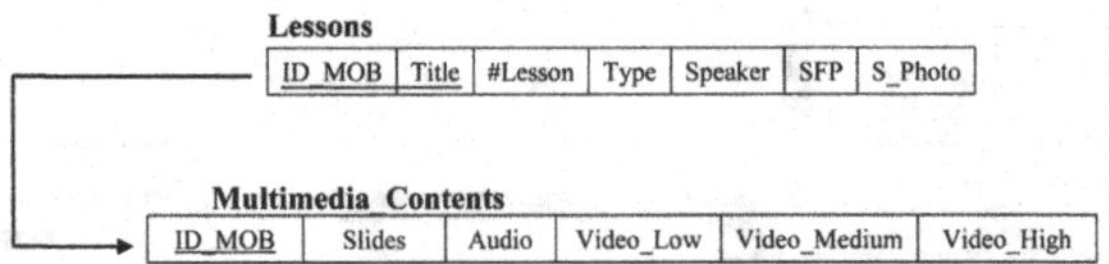

Notice that the attribute *ID_MOB* in the relation *Lessons* is a foreign key pointing to the multimedia presentation associated to a lecture.

The functional dependencies mfd_2 and mfd_3 reveal a violation of 3MNF. Thus, applying our normalization rule would lead to the following database schema.

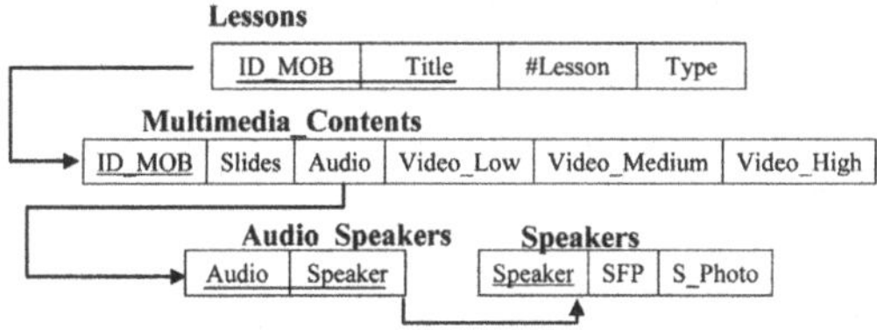

However, when normalizing databases the designer always makes some efficiency considerations before splitting relations. In our case, given that the attribute audio does not carry additional information we might remove the relation audio and introduce a direct foreign key from the relation *Multimedia_Contents* to the relation *Speakers*, yielding the following schema.

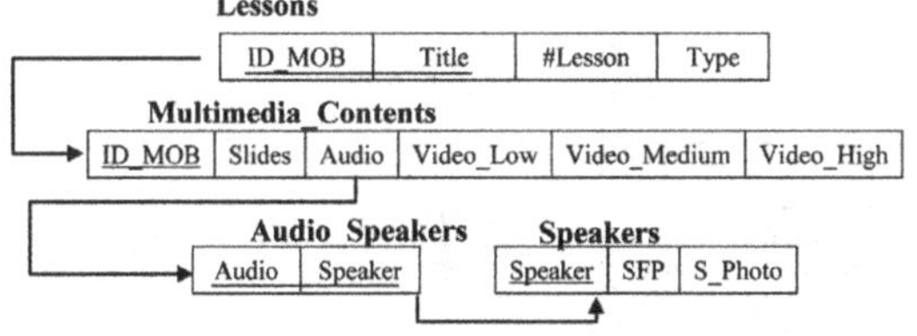

The MFD $\{SFP\}_{\text{FINGERCODE}} \rightarrow \{Speaker\}$ does not violate the 3MNF because now *Speaker* is a prime attribute.

At this point we might notice that the same set of slides can be used by different lecturers, and that some of them might be useful for constructing different lessons. However, if we delete a lesson we lose all of them. This happens because in the schema shown above they are grouped together in a single attribute, which violates the 1MNF. Thus, we might store each single slide in a separate relation, together with additional slide information, such as slide comment. Given that a single slide might be used in more than one lecture, and that a single lecture uses many different slides, we have a many to many relationship between lessons and slides, yielding the following normalized schema:

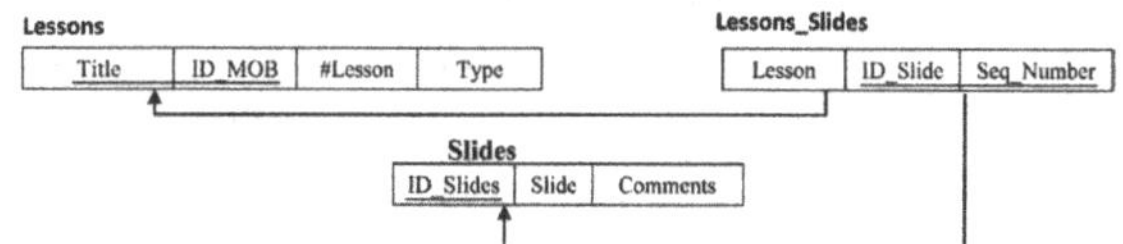

To highlight the benefits of the normalization framework we collected data to compare access performances of the normalized database with respect to the initial database schema. In particular, we performed simulation experiments on a multimedia database consisting of twelve lessons, two instructors and thirty students. We have divided the students into two groups based on the connection bandwidth they could use: dial up connection (56kbps) and ADSL connection (640kbps). Then, we have performed several simulations by varying the mix of the two groups of students accessing the multimedia database simultaneously. For each simulation we have estimated the minimum, average, and maximum access time needed by each group of students to access the lessons. Such parameters have always been computed twice, once on the initial database schema (whose size is of 178 Mb) and once on the normalized schema (whose size is of 163 Mb). In particular, the tuple selected from the initial Lessons schema has two types of presentations: the Presentation Low attribute of 4.35 Mb and the Presentation High attribute of 11 Mb, whereas the tuple selected from the normalized schema has an Audio attribute of 1.27 Mb, a Slide attribute of 0.5 Mb, a Video Low attribute of 2.63 Mb and a Video High attribute of 9.70 Mb.

The results of the simulation are summarized in Figure 3. It can be easily noticed that even for relatively small multimedia attributes the normalized multimedia database provides better access performances. Moreover, with the non-normalized database it strangely happened that we gained worse average performances by increasing the number of students with high connection bandwidth. More precisely, we have observed that 20 students with ADSL connections represent the

Figure 3. Simulation results

Non-Normalized Database

	Student's group mix		*Access Times*		
	$56kbps$	$640kbps$	*Min*	*Avr*	*Max*
Simulation 1	30	0	6.26	14.75	28.99
Simulation 2	20	10	2.97	8.09	16.89
Simulation 3	10	20	3.27	6.88	21.39
Simulation 4	0	30	4.40	8.45	12.29

Normalized Database

	Student's group mix		*Access Times*		
	$56kbps$	$640kbps$	*Min*	*Avr*	*Max*
Simulation 1	30	0	1.90	5.09	12.84
Simulation 2	20	10	1.09	4.97	9.64
Simulation 3	10	20	1.76	3.98	7.38
Simulation 4	0	30	1.15	3.74	7.78

Figure 4. Histogram showing average access performances

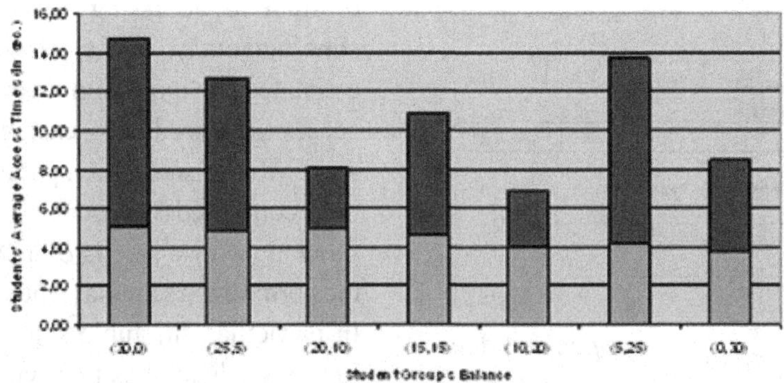

threshold from which the performances of the DBMS get worse in the execution of the queries. This is mainly due to the fact that the database has to serve more requests simultaneously, hence it has some loss of performance, whereas in other cases requests from slow connections can be served later. On the other hand, we have observed that the normalized database allows more than 20 fast connections before starting losing performances.

The histogram in Figure 4 shows how the average access time to the multimedia lessons changes by varying the "mix" of the two groups of students. Other than lower average access times, the normalized database also shows smaller variations across different mix of students with respect to the non-normalized one.

These performance gaps increase when the database contains bigger multimedia attributes. To this end we have performed further simulations to monitor the average access time with bigger multimedia objects. In particular, we have considered a non-normalized database of 869 Mb whose normalized version is of 788Mb. Figure 5 shows performances gained on an entry of a non-normalized (normalized, resp.) database containing a Presentation High (Video High, resp.) attribute of 61 Mb (59.7 Mb, resp.).

Figure 5. Performances comparison on a large multimedia object

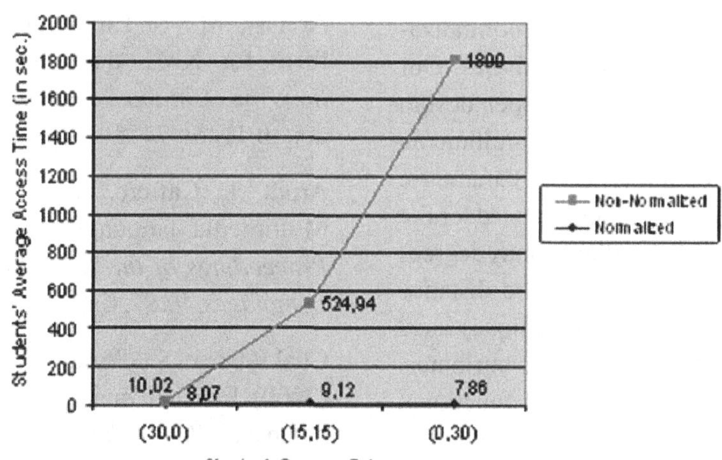

In conclusion, we have shown that in the presented e-learning application context the normalization process can bring benefits not only in terms of reduced manipulation anomalies, but also in terms of access performances. Thus, our approach provides a multimedia database designer with a mean to evaluate and improve the quality of the database schema that in many circumstances can result into enhanced performances.

FUTURE RESEARCH DIRECTIONS

Since the multimedia dependencies and multimedia normal forms depend upon the tuple distance functions, by imposing additional constraints on tuple distance functions we can introduce more restricted multimedia dependencies and multimedia normal forms. This makes the proposed framework very flexible to accommodate the requirements of different applications. For example, to support gesture languages in a virtual classroom for e-learning applications we can introduce different tuple distance functions to classify gestures as similar or dissimilar, leading to different protocols for gesture languages supported by the same underlying multimedia database. Furthermore other normal forms can be introduced if we explore deeper certain application domains such as e-learning.

Another important issue regards the normalization of multimedia databases in adaptive multimedia applications, where a media data may be replaced/combined/augmented by another type of media for people with different sensory capabilities. To this end, the normalization process yields a partitioning of the database that facilitates the management of adaptiveness.

However, multimedia applications rarely use multimedia components separately. Thus, an extensive partitioning of the database might lead to an increased overhead when joining multimedia components for a given presentations. This can be unacceptable for some application domains, such as web-based applications. Thus, for multimedia database applications we particularly stress the importance of reaching a suitable compromise between normalization and efficiency. This means that in a good design practice a designer should always be able to decide the right extent of partitioning according to the efficiency requirements in the context of the specific application.

CONCLUSION

In this chapter we have proposed a normalization framework for multimedia databases. Our goal here it has been to derive proper design guidelines to improve the quality of multimedia database schemes. The framework is parametric with respect to the distance functions used for the different media domains, and allows many degrees of normalization, depending upon the distance function and the segmentation techniques used to decompose complex multimedia attributes. In practice, the detection of type-M functional dependencies might not be a simple activity. In fact, by following the traditional approach of alphanumeric relational databases, the designer could detect type-M functional dependency based on his/her knowledge. However, multimedia data are much more complex than alphanumeric data. Moreover, the existence of thresholds might yield this into a subjective activity. Alternatively, in order to reduce subjectivity, the detection of type-M dependencies could be accomplished by finding feature correlations, which is a problem widely analyzed in the literature. To this regard, several techniques have been proposed, such as principal component analysis (PCA), independent component analysis (ICA), and so on. They are all based on training sets, and aim to identify independent features for indexing, querying, and retrieve multimedia data based on their contents. Thus, after performing this type of analysis the designer knows which are the features that are not independent, meaning that there must be some dependencies between them. This is a valuable information for designers to start characterizing the dependencies and to begin the normalization process. However, the approaches of feature selection cannot suggest whether the multimedia database and the application programs need to be redesigned upon the addition of new features.

REFERENCES

Arenas, M., & Libkin, L. (2004). A normal form for XML documents. *ACM Transactions on Database Systems*, *29*(1), 195–232. doi:10.1145/974750.974757

Arndt, T., Cafiero, A., & Guercio, A. (1997). Multimedia languages for teleaction objects. *Proceedings of the IEEE Symposium on Visual Languages, VL97*, Capri Isle, Italy, (pp. 322-331).

Chakrabarti, S., Porkaew, K., & Mehrotra, S. (2000). Efficient query refinement in multimedia databases. *Proceedings of the IEEE International Conference on Data Engineering*, San Diego, California, USA, (p. 196).

Chang, S. K. (1996). Extending visual languages for multimedia. *IEEE MultiMedia*, *3*(3), 18–26. doi:10.1109/93.556536

Chang, S. K., Polese, G., Orefice, S., & Tucci, M. (1994). A methodology and interactive environment for iconic language design. *International Journal of Human-Computer Studies*, *41*, 683–716. doi:10.1006/ijhc.1994.1078

Codd, E. F. (1972). Further normalization of the database relational model . In Rusum, R. (Ed.), *Data base systems* (pp. 33–64). Prentice Hall.

Davis, J. (1999). *IBM/DB2 universal database: Building extensible, scalable business solutions*. Retrieved from http://www.software.ibm.com/data/pubs/papers

Elmasri, R., & Navathe, S. B. (2003). *Fundamentals of database systems* (4th ed.). Addison-Wesley.

Fagin, R. (1996). Combining fuzzy information from multiple systems. In *Proc. 15th ACM Symp. Principles of Database Systems*, Montreal, Canada (pp. 216-226).

Flickner, M., Sawhney, H., Niblack, W., Ashley, J., Huang, Q., & Dom, B. (1995). Query by image and video content: The QBIC system. *IEEE Computer, 28*(9), 23–32.

IBM. (1995). *DATABASE 2 SQL reference - For common servers*. (Part No. S20H-4665-00).

Kosch, H. (2003). *Distributed multimedia database technologies supported by MPEG-7 and MPEG-21*. CRC Press. doi:10.1201/9780203009338

Kosch, H., Böszörmenyi, L., Döller, M., Libsie, M., Kofler, A., & Schojer, P. (2005). The life-cycle of multimedia metadata. *IEEE MultiMedia, 12*(1), 80–86. doi:10.1109/MMUL.2005.13

Narasimhalu, A. D. (1996). Multimedia databases. *Multimedia Systems, 4*(5), 226–249. doi:10.1007/s005300050026

Oomoto, E., & Tanaka, K. (1993). OVID: Design and implementation of a video-object database system. *IEEE Transactions on Knowledge and Data Engineering, 5*(4), 629–643. doi:10.1109/69.234775

Oracle. (1999). *Oracle 8iTM release 2 features overview*. November 1999. Retrieved from http://www.oracle.com

Rennhackkamp, M. (1997). Extending relational DBMSs. *DBMS Online, 10*(13).

Sacks-Davis, R., Kent, A., Ramamohanarao, K., Thom, J., & Zobel, J. (1995). Atlas: A nested relational database system for text applications. *IEEE Transactions on Knowledge and Data Engineering, 7*(3), 454–470. doi:10.1109/69.390250

Santini, S., & Gupta, A. (2002). Principles of schema design for multimedia databases. *IEEE Transactions on Multimedia, 4*(2), 248–259. doi:10.1109/TMM.2002.1017737

Santini, S., & Jain, R. (1999). Similarity measures. *IEEE Transactions on Pattern Analysis and Machine Intelligence, 21*(9), 871–883. doi:10.1109/34.790428

Stonebraker, M., & Kemnitz, G. (1995). The POSTGRES next-generation database management system. *Communications of the ACM, 34*, 78–92. doi:10.1145/125223.125262

Vincent, M. W., Liu, J., & Liu, C. (2004). Strong functional dependencies and their application to normal forms in XML. *ACM Transactions on Database Systems, 29*(3), 445–462. doi:10.1145/1016028.1016029

Wu, J. K., Narasimhalu, A. D., Mehtre, B. M., Lam, C. P., & Gao, Y. J. (1995). CORE: A content-based retrieval engine for multimedia Information System. *Multimedia Systems, 3*(1), 25–41. doi:10.1007/BF01236577

Chapter 10
Towards a Dynamic Semantic and Complex Relationship Modeling of Multimedia Data

Dawen Jia
Carleton University, Canada

Mengchi Liu
Carleton University, Canada

ABSTRACT

Multimedia data is a challenge for data management. The semantics of traditional alphanumeric data are mostly explicit, unique, and self-contained, but the semantics of multimedia data are usually dynamic, diversiform, and varying from one user's perspective to another's. When dealing with different applications in which multimedia data is involved, great challenges arise. We first introduce a novel data model called Information Networking Model (INM), which can represent the dynamic and complex semantic relationships of the real world. In this chapter, we show how to use INM to capture dynamic and complex semantics relationship of multimedia data. Using INM, we present a multimedia modeling mechanism. The general idea of this novel mechanism is to place the multimedia data in a complex semantic environment based on the real world or application requirements, and then users can make use of both contextual semantics and multimedia metadata to retrieve the precise results they expect.

INTRODUCTION

Multimedia data has become more and more ubiquitous. The application potential of multimedia information retrieval is extensive, particularly in fields as *Art and Culture*, *Medical*, *Personal* and the *Web*. Compared with traditional pure alphanumeric data, multimedia data is inherently different. First, as the name implies, multimedia data refers to media data in a variety of types, such as image, video, audio, text etc. Different types of media have different characteristics. Secondly, the semantics of traditional pure alphanumeric data are usually explicit, unique and self-contained

DOI: 10.4018/978-1-61350-126-9.ch010

but the semantics of media data such as images, videos etc. can vary from one user's perspective to another's. Dealing with alternate applications in which multimedia data is involved presents great challenges.

In past decades, content-based multimedia retrieval is one of the most challenging areas in the multimedia data management field (Datta, Li & Wang, 2005; Petkovic & Jonker, 2003; Sebe, Lew, Zhou, Huang & Bakker, 2003; Yoshitaka, 1999). People focus on key problem called semantic gap (Smeulder, Worring, Santini, Gupta & Jain, 2000). Content-based multimedia retrieval relies on technologies, such as image processing, automatic feature extraction, object recognition and speech recognition, to extract semantic contents of single type of media data automatically. Research of content-based multimedia retrieval focuses on extracting internal structures and semantics of single medium data. (Datta, Joshi, Li & Wang, 2008; Petkovic & Jonker, 2003; Sebe, Lew, Zhou, Huang & Bakker, 2003).

In the database community, researchers have been devoted to presenting, indexing and querying multimedia data. They also improve existing data models, such as the relational model and object-oriented models, to represent temporal and spatial features of multimedia data. Until now, the most popular approaches to modeling multimedia data include: (1) extending the object-oriented data model (e.g. Djeraba, Hadouda & Briand, 1997; Henrich & Robbert,2001 ;Li, Ozsu &Szafron, 1997), (2) extending the object-relational model (Melton & Eisenberg, 2001), (3) MPEG-7 standard for multimedia metadata management (e.g. Doller,Renner &Kosch,2007; Manjunath, Salembier &Sikora, 2002).

The research mentioned above mainly focuses on extracting or modeling semantics and structures in single medium; relatively little progress has been made in modeling the semantic relationships between different types of media and enhancing the data models to manage multimedia data application management.

In this chapter, we first introduce Information Networking Model and discuss how the dynamic features of multimedia data can be modeled with INM. Then we present a novel multimedia data modeling mechanism. The general idea of this mechanism is to place the multimedia data in a complex semantic environment based on the real world or application requirements, and then we can make use of both contextual semantics relationships and multimedia metadata to retrieval the precise results we expect. Our approach has the following features and benefits:

1. It is easy to model the dynamic semantic nature of multimedia data, that is, the same media data in different contextual environment or from different points of view may have totally different explanations. With INM, multiple classifications of multimedia data are naturally supported.
2. It can simplify the design of multimedia application systems since the characteristics of objects, and complex relationships between objects, can be modeled in a simple and intuitive way.
3. A powerful query language has been designed for our model so that we can make use of both contextual semantics and multimedia metadata to form rich semantic query expressions to find the precise results we expect, and a user-friendly navigation can be easily implemented.
4. Compared with the content-based retrieval technique, our approach is complementary for multimedia data management and has the potential to deal with many different applications in which multimedia data involved.
5. Multimedia data can be shared easily so long as we place the multimedia data in the different contextual semantic environment.

Our research in this chapter neither deals with single modal content-based multimedia semantic extraction, nor models the temporal and spatial structure of single type of media data. We focus on modeling relationships between different modal of media data; and modeling the relationships between multimedia data and their contextual environment.

The rest of the chapter is organized as follows: first, we introduce the background of our research. Then we elaborate Information Networking Model and show how to obtain great benefits of modeling multimedia data with Information Networking Model. Lastly, we provide an insight of the future research directions and conclusion about our work.

BACKGROUND

Information modeling of the real world has been a lengthy and tedious work as there is no natural one-to-one correspondence between the two worlds. It is mainly limited by the available technologies. In the past, various data models have been the primary focus of research to simplify this task.

The most well-known and widely used data model is the relational data model in the field of data management (Codd, 1970). Its main attraction is that it is built around a simple and natural mathematical structure – the relation. However, since the data is scattered in different relations, it is hard to represent the semantic information explicitly with the relational model, especially the complex semantic relationship between relations. The object-oriented data model is more expressive than the relational model, and can express the semantic relationship between objects. However, object-oriented databases display serious shortcomings in their flexibility and ability to model both the many-faceted nature and dynamic nature of real-world entities, since the object-oriented data model only deals with static classification of objects. In order to enrich the semantic expression and overcome the shortcomings of the object-oriented data model, various object role models have been proposed to captures evolutionary aspects of real-world objects (Albano, Bergamini & Grsini, 1991; Cabot & Ravent´os, 2004; Dahchour, Pirotte & Zim´anyi, 2002; Peng & Kambayashi, 1995; Wieringa, Jonge & Spruit, 1995). In object role models, object classes and role classes are separated and an object can play several roles. Roles concern new responsibilities, facets or aspects of objects. Role classes can be organized hierarchically and can have property inheritance as well to deal with the dynamic classification of objects. The main problem with the object role model is that it just focuses on expressing elementary relationships of objects.

In our view, real world objects have various natural and complex relationships with each other. Via these relationships, objects play various roles, and then demonstrate corresponding properties that can be classified. Existing data models oversimplify and ignore the complex relationships. They focus on the roles that the objects play, as well as the properties of these roles. Finally, objects and roles are hierarchically classified. As a result, they can only provide a partial model of the real world and fail to provide one-to-one correspondence between the real world and the corresponding information model. To solve these problems, a novel data model called Information Networking Model (INM for short) has been proposed (Liu & Hu, 2009). It allows us to model the semantic relationship of the real world in a direct and natural way and represent not only static but dynamic and context-dependent information regarding objects.

For multimedia data management, it is stated in (Li, Yang, & Zhuang, 2002): "In the database community, however, although a great number of publications have been devoted to the presentation, indexing, annotation, and querying of multimedia, relatively little progress has been achieved on the semantic modeling of multimedia, which is of primary importance to various multimedia applications." (p. 729). The traditional data models have limited power in modeling the complex semantics of the real world. They also indicated that most existing data models are unable to capture precisely the semantic aspect of multimedia, which features two unique properties: *context-dependency* and *media-independency.* Each existing retrieval technique can deal with only a single type of information by queries, and therefore none of them are applicable to the retrieval of multi-model information. They then proposed a novel view mechanism called "MultiView" to model the dynamic aspect of multimedia data. However, MultiView can only solve the dynamic problem and it cannot model the complex contextual relationship.

Raymond K. Wong (1999) extended the role model "DOOR" to deal with multimedia data. With the role model, Wong only solved the dynamic problem of multimedia data. As discussed in the introduction section, our model is better than the role model.

Multimedia data prevails, especially in web-based applications. Content-based multimedia retrieval may only help little with many application systems in which multi-types media data is involved, such as social network websites (e.g. Facebook, MySpace). In these applications, users' profiles, photos, videos, notes and relationships between users, etc., should be managed. Those websites haven't provided rich query functions or navigation ability for the user to search multimedia data. Many web multimedia search engines such as Microsoft Live Search, Google Image and Yahoo Search only provide low level metadata, such as size of file, resolution of an image etc. to filter the search results. The technologies that can offer users the ability of multi-aspect multimedia searches are in high demand.

INFORMATION NETWORKING MODEL

Information about the real world has various complex relationships. Each entity in the real world may play different roles or have different interpretation in different environments. A person can be both an employee and a student at a university. Some movie stars also direct movies and vice versa for directors who make appearances in films. That means the role of objects in the real world is not static, unique or isolated; instead it is dynamic, diversified and contextual. Traditional relational models fall short in expressing complex semantics of the real world, whereas object-oriented models cannot capture the dynamic nature since an object has a unique identity and can only belong to one class. To solve the dynamic modeling problem, several role models have been proposed but they fail to model the complex relationships between objects in the real world. Information Networking Model (INM) is a novel model to represent complex semantic, dynamic and complex relationships of the real world in a natural and direct way (Liu & Hu, 2009). Below is an introduction to its core concepts followed by an in depth illustration of how it may be applied in a real life context.

Core Concepts

INM supports all the existing features of object-oriented data models such as class, object, inheritance and bidirectional relationship...etc. Meanwhile, INM has many novel features to represent complex semantic relationships between objects to reflect the dynamic, contextual and many-faceted aspect of real world object in a natural and direct way.

Role Relationship

An object class in INM is the same as a class in an object-oriented data model, which is used to present the static aspects of real world objects. The key feature of INM is the introduction of *role relationships*. The role relationship connects two types of respective classes, the *source class* and the *target class*. The connection is directed from the source class to the target class. Suppose two object classes, *C* and *C*□, are connected from *C* to *C*□ by the role relationship *r*. If o and o□, which are the instances of C and *C*□, are connected by *r* respectively, it is referred to as *o□ plays the role r in the context of o.* For instance, assuming there are two object classes: *Movie* and *Person. Actor* would be a role relationship connecting *Movie* to *Person. If Braveheart* is an instance of the object class *Movie,* any actor in the movie Braveheart is connected with the instance *Braveheart* by the role relationship *Actor,* which means this person plays the role *Actor* in the context of *movie Braveheart.*

Role relationship has the following features: (1) it can have *context-based attributes*. The person who plays the role *Actor* in a movie can have attribute *CharacterName,* then we call *CharacterName* a context-based attribute; (2) role relationships can be organized hierarchically. For example, *Writer* can have role sub-relationships: *ScreenplayWriter* and *NovelWriter*. Role sub-relationships can inherit or override attributes from role super-relationship; (3) a role relationship induces a *role relationship class* as a sub-class of its target class. With the role relationship *actor* connecting the class *Movie* and the class *Person,* a role relationship class *Actor(Movie)* is induced. It is a sub-class of *Person* whose instances are all movie actors.

Context-Dependent Information

A role relationship connecting the source class and the target class is directed. INM uses *context relationships* to represent inverse relationships from the target class to the source class. Furthermore, it uses *identification* to denote further semantic explanation of a role relationship under its corresponding context relationship. For example, we can define the context relationship *ActsIn* to inversely relate the target class *Person* and the source class *Movie.* In addition, the identification *Filmography* for the role relationship *Actor* is used to denote the *Filmography* of an instance of *Person* as the *Actor* in a certain *Movie.* INM automatically generates *context-dependent information* for the target class instance. Context-dependent information combines context relationships, identification and context attributes. Mel Gibson is an actor of movie Braveheart and the character he plays in the movie is William Wallace. With INM, *Braveheart* and *MelGibson* are instances of the object class *Movie* and the object class *Person* respectively, and they are connected by the role relationship *Actor*. If we define the context relationship *ActsIn* and the identification *Filmography* for the role relationship *Actor*, INM will automatically generate the context-dependent information of the instance *MelGibson* as follow: *ActsIn: Braveheart[Filmography: Actor[@CharacterName: "William Wallace"]].*

Case Study

To clearly illustrate the core concepts of INM and compare its modeling mechanism with role models more intuitively, consider a film industry information modeling scenario.

A movie involves various kinds of people such as actors, actresses and a director(s). In the movie Braveheart, Mel Gibson is both a director and an actor. Sophie Marceau performed the character Princess Isabelle in the movie Braveheart and performed the character Anna Karenina in the movie Anna Karenina. With role models, we can define *Person* as an object class with attribute *Birthday. Actor*, *Actress* and *Director* are the roles of *Person*. All these roles have the attribute *Movie*. *Actor* and *Actress* have the other attribute *Character.* The schema and the instance are shown in Figure 1.

The main problem with role models is that they focus on the roles of objects independently rather than the roles of the objects in their contexts, especially in the relationships between objects. As a result, information regarding a real world object has to be scattered in several instances: an object instance and several role instances to deal with the dynamic nature of objects during their lifetime.

In INM, we treat *Movie* and *Person* as object classes, *Actor, Actress* and *Director* as role

Figure 1. Modeling in role model

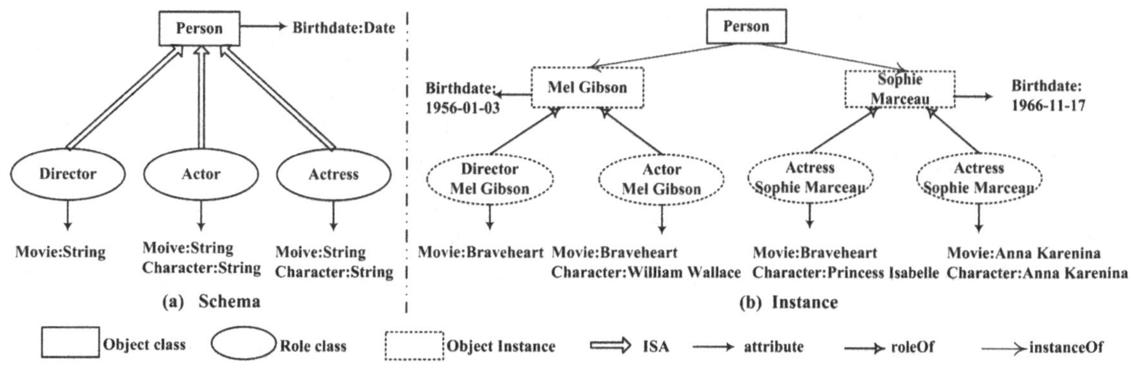

Figure 2. Modeling in information networking model

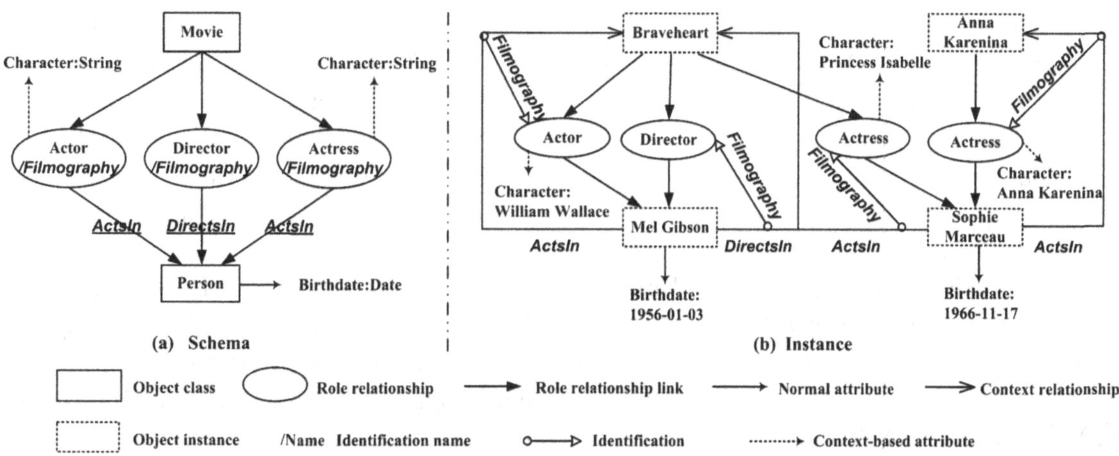

relationships connecting the object classes *Movie* and *Person*. *Figure 2* is the equivalent representation of *Figure 1* with INM. The object classes *Movie* and *Person* are respectively called the source class and the target class of the corresponding role relationships. The role relationships *Actor* and *Actress* have the same context relationship *ActsIn.* The role relationship *Director* has the context relationship *DirectIn.* They all have identification *Filmography*. As shown in *Figure 2*, Mel Gibson's filmography includes the *director* and *actor* of the *movie* Braveheart, and Sohpie Marceau's filmography includes the *actress* of the *movie* Braveheart and the *actress* of the *movie* Anna Karenina.

In comparison with the existing data model, INM has the following features:

1. We treat *Actor* and *Director* as the role relationships from *Movie* to *Person* rather than the subclasses or the role classes of *Person* independently.
2. All the information regarding real world objects are grouped in one instance, such as an instance of *Director* and *Actor* identified with *Mel Gibson,* rather than scattered in several instances: one object instance *Mel Gibson* and several role instances of *Director* and *Actor*.
3. Context-dependent information is automatically generated in the target class and

contains context relationship information, identification information and context attribute values. For example, *ActsIn:Braveheart[Filmography:Actor[@CharacterName:William Wallace]]* and *DirectsIn:Braveheart[Filmography:Braveheart.Director]* are both the context-dependent information in the instance of *Mel Gibson*.

4. Role relationships may have hierarchy. In Figure 2, role relationship *Actor* could have *LeadingRole* and *SupportingRole* as its sub-relationship; they are role sub-relationships. *LeadingRole* and *SupportingRole* inherit the attribute *Character* and their target class is *Person* as well.
5. Role relationship induces role relationship class as a sub-category of its target class. In *Figure 2*, three role relationship classes will be induced: *Actor(Movie), Director(Movie)* and *Actress(Movie)*. They are three sub-categories of the class *Person. Mel Gibson* belongs to both *sub-category Actor(Movie) and sub-category Director(Movie).*

SEMANTIC MULTIMEDIA DATA MODELING

We have introduced the features of multimedia data and INM in preceding sections. In this section, we will elaborate the advantages of our approach in multimedia data management.

Modeling the Dynamic Features of Multimedia Data

The fact that the semantics of multimedia data is dynamic, diversified and contextual leads to a significant challenge of multimedia data retrieval. Qing Li, Jun Yang, and Yueting Zhuang (2002) stated the semantics of multimedia data, which features *context-dependency* and *media-independency,* is of vital importance to multimedia applications.

Context-dependency refers that the semantic interpretations of multimedia objects, such as still images or document files, much depend on the contextual environment. The contextual environment implies the three aspects: the purposes of media objects, context where media objects are presented and the other data that interacts with the media objects. Considering the following example, in Figure 3 (a) and (b), the leftmost images are the logo image of Linux named *Tux*. When it is in the contextual environment of logo image, as shown in Figure 3 (a), the meaning of "logo image" is manifest. When the same image is placed in Figure 3 (b), the meaning of "animal" is suggested. Moreover, when a media object presents in different contextual environment, it may acquire the different context-based properties. For example, as a logo image, Tux can be described by "designer" and "usedTime", whereas as an animal, it has attributes like "name", "category" and "habitat".

Now we show how to use INM-based solution to model the dynamic semantics of Image *Tux*. As depicted in Figure 4, *Software*, *ContextDefault* and *Image* are three object classes. *Logo* is a role relationship between *Software* and *Image* with context-based attributes *designer* and *usedTime*, which means that an image is a software logo and the logo is designed by the *designer* and used during *usedTime*. *Animal* is a role relationship between *ContextDefault* and *Image*. It has the context-based attributes *Name*, Category and *Habitat* which means an image plays the role of animal and need to be described by attributes Name, Category, and Habitat. (*ContextDefault* is a system default object class and ContextObject is the default instance of *ContextDefault. ContextDefault* is used as the source class of the role relationships which don't have specific context). As we learned from previous section, two role relationship classes *Logo(software)* and *Animal* will be generated automatically for object class *Image* as its sub-classes. Image instances belong to different role relationship classes described

Figure 3. (a) Tux in the context of logo (b) Tux in the context of animal

Figure 4. Modeling the dynamic features of multimedia data

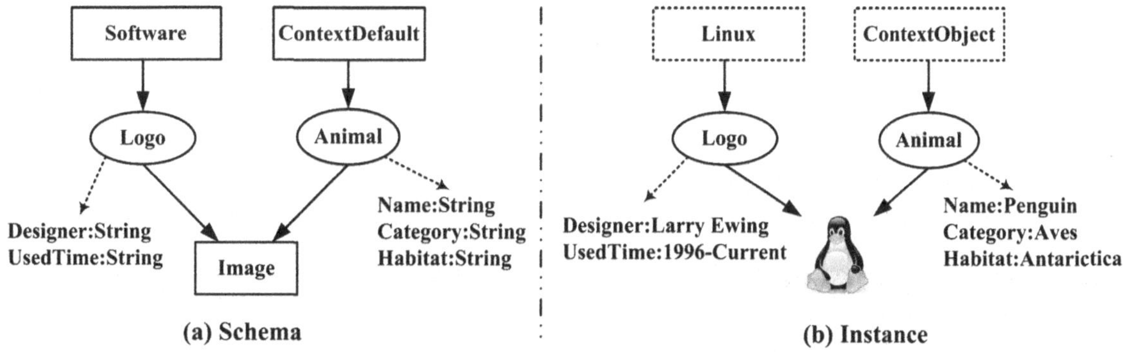

by different attributes. An Image instance belonging to multiple role relationship classes will be described by all the attributes with the context information. That's how INM supports multiple classifications of multimedia data in a natural way.

The other issue is *media-independency* which means media object of different types may suggest the similar or related semantic meaning. For example, there are a picture of penguin and a video of lion. Though the two objects belong to different media, they all contribute to interpret the same concept "animal" and therefore can be described with the same set of properties, such as "name", "category" and "habitat". Figure 5 is an extension of Figure 4, which presents a solution based on INM. As depicted in Figure 5, both object class *Image* and *Video* are the target classes of role relationship *Animal*, therefore both of them can described by the context-based attributes *Name*, *Category* and *Habitat* defined in role relationship *Animal*.

Now we use INM-based database language to model the sample in Figure 4 and Figure 5.

Schema Definition

A class schema is mainly made up of three parts:

1. "Class" as a declaration of an object class;
2. Class name: as shown in Exhibit 1, all bold type words are the name of the object class;

Figure 5. Solution of the media-independency feature of multimedia data

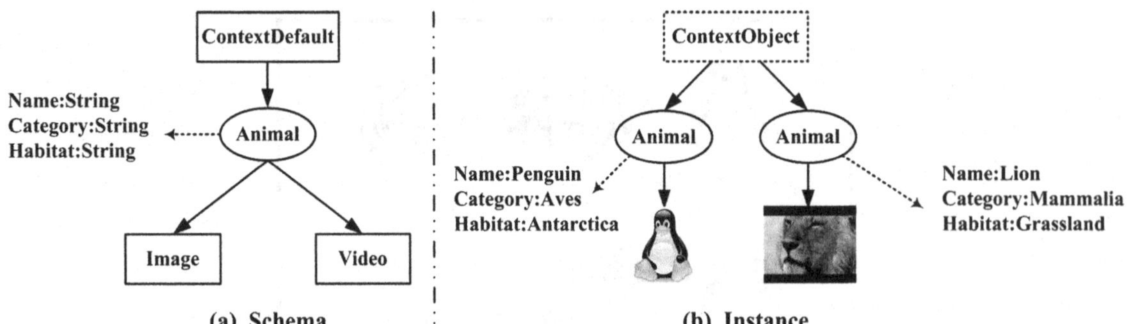

Exhibit 1.

```
Class Image[@imageData:oid];
Class Video[@videoData:oid];
Class Software[
        Logo[ r-based(@designer:String,
                              @usedTime:String)]:Image]];
Class reuse ContextDefault[
                              Animal[ r-based@name:String,
                                                  @category:String,
                                                  @
habitat:String):Image|Video]];
```

3. Class body: Class body is in a bracket and made up of attributes, role relationships and their target object classes and relations with other classes.

As shown in Exhibit 1, the attribute start with the symbol "@" and the type of the attributes must be given. Role relationship name is shown as the italics, and key word "r-based" indicates the role attributes.

Here, we create three classes: Image, Video and Software (*ContextDefault* is a system default class and already exist in system, therefore, when we need to redefine it, we use the key word "re-use", and the old elements will be retained in the new definition).

Data Insertion

In Exhibit 2, we insert an image object *Tux*, a video object *LionLive* and a software object *Linux*. We use function *LargeObject_import* to insert the large object data. As shown in Figure 4 (b), *ContextObject* is the default instance of Class *ContextDefault*, and when we insert some data in *ContextObject*, it can be omitted in the data manipulation language.

Data Query Language

A new query language *named Information Networking Model Query Language (INMQL)* is designed. First, a simple introduction of some key symbols in *INMQL* will be given. Then we use some examples to explain how *INMQL* works.

Exhibit 2.

```
Insert Image Tux[@imageData:LargeObject_import('file_address')];
Insert Video LionLive[@videoData:LargeObject_import('file_address')];
Insert Software Linux[
                                    Logo:Tux[ @designer:"Larry Ewing",
                                                 @usedTime:"1996-Current"]];
Insert Contextdefault [
                                    Animal:Image.Tux[ @name:"Penguin",
                                                           @category:"Aves",
                                                           @
habitat:"Antartica"],
                                    Animal:Video.LionLive[ @name:"Lion",
                                                                  @
category:"Mammalia",
                                                                  @
habitat:"Grassland"]];
```

1. Single value variable: *$X*.
2. *$X* is a variable that match one attribute value or object instance at a time, but the query results are always a set at a time. Like SQL, select *X* from .... *X* matches one at a time but the result may have many. (e.g. As shown in Figure 6, example (1)(2), Software $X means $X is the instance of class *Software* and *Image* $X=Tux means $X is the instance *Tux* of class *Image*.)
3. Wildcard character "*": * is a wildcard character. If we an object class instance is assigned to variable *$X*, we can use "construct *$X**" to construct all content of the instance. (e.g. As shown in Figure 6 (example 1, 2), the result is the whole object but not just the object name.);
4. Path expressions: slash (/) and double slashes (//). The path expressions here are similar with XPath in XML. Slash (/) stands for parent-child relationship and slashes (//) stands for ancestor-descendant relationship.
5. Construct result: using the key word "*construct*". Symbol "<>" is used for constructing group result. As shown in Figure 6 (example 3), the result is grouped as pair of animal name and animal video data.

INM-Based Multimedia Data Modeling Mechanism

Besides the dynamic feature, multimedia data is diversity, which means multimedia have different types of media data. Most research only focus on the contend-based multimedia retrieval which addresses single media processing. On the other side, multimedia data is prevailing and content-based multimedia retrieval may help little with many application systems that multiple types of media data is involved, such as the social network websites (e.g. Facebook, MySpace). In these applications, users' profiles, photos, videos, notes and relationships between users, etc., should be managed. In this section, we will propose a complementary mechanism compared with the content-based retrieval technique for multimedia data. Our mechanism focuses on the semantic relationship between external semantic environment and multimedia data. The general idea of

Figure 6. Sample queries

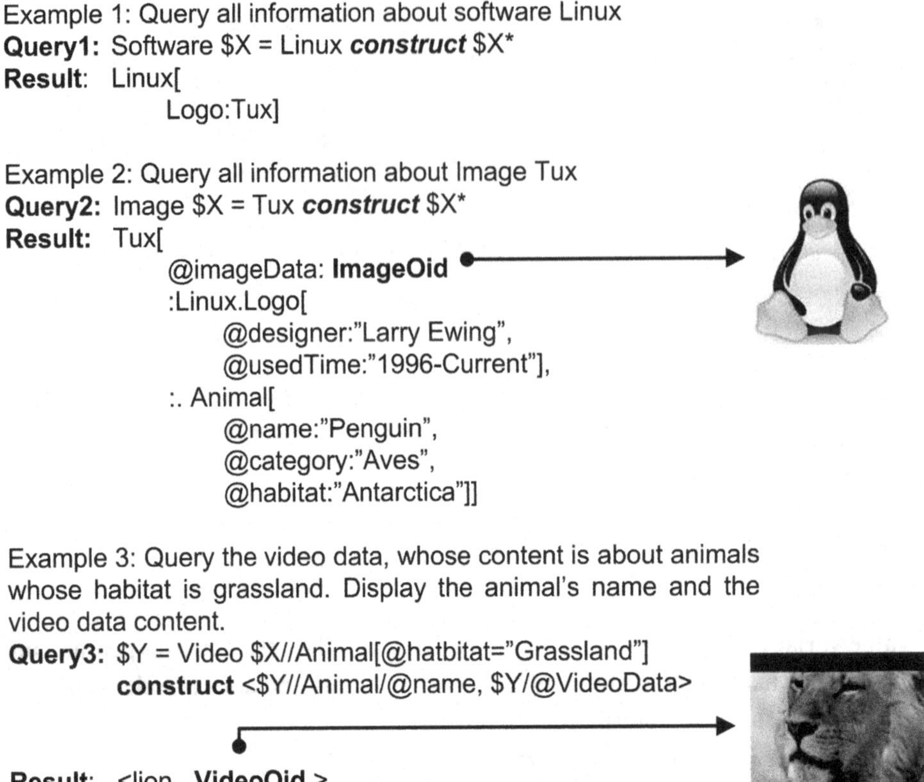

this novel mechanism is to place the multimedia data in a complex semantic environment based on the real world modeling or users' requirements, and then users can make use of both contextual semantics and multimedia metadata to retrieval the precise results they expect.

Example 1: Query all information about software Linux
Query1: Software $X = Linux construct $X*
Result: Linux[
Logo:Tux]
Example 2: Query all information about Image Tux
Query2: Image $X = Tux construct $X*
Result: Tux[
@imageData: ImageOid
:Linux.Logo[
@designer:"Larry Ewing",
@usedTime:"1996-Current"],
:. Animal[
@name:"Penguin",
@category:"Aves",
@habitat:"Antarctica"]]
Example 3: Query the video data, whose content is about animals whose habitat is grassland. Display the animal's name and the video data content.
Query3: $Y = Video $X//Animal[@hatbitat="Grassland"]
construct <$Y//Animal/@name, $Y/@VideoData>
Result: <lion, VideoOid >

Multimedia Structure Modeling

Multimedia data has different types, such as video, audio, image etc., and these types have their own relationships. To well manage multimedia data, we need to organize all kinds of multimedia data properly.

First, we model multimedia based on their taxonomic hierarchy structure. As shown in Figure 7 (a), object class *Multimedia* has all common attributes used to describe multimedia data. Different types of multimedia data, such as video, image and document, are modeled as the subclasses of class *Multimedia* and inherit all its attributes. For example, object class *PDF* inherit all the attribute form both class *Multimedia* and class *Document*, and it also has the specific attribute *Pages* which present how many pages a *PDF* document contains. These attributes are mainly the metadata about multimedia files. These metadata are not only used to describe the features of multimedia data, and more importantly they help us to browse, filter and retrieve the multimedia data. Metadata can be extracted from multimedia files or added manually. Many web multimedia search engines such as Microsoft Live Search, Google Image and Yahoo Search use this way to search the multimedia data. Besides the low level metadata, such as size of file, resolution of an image etc., semantic annotation is also very important for multimedia retrieval. The famous websites like YouTube,

Figure 7. (a) Multimedia hierarchy structure (b) Multimedia internal relations

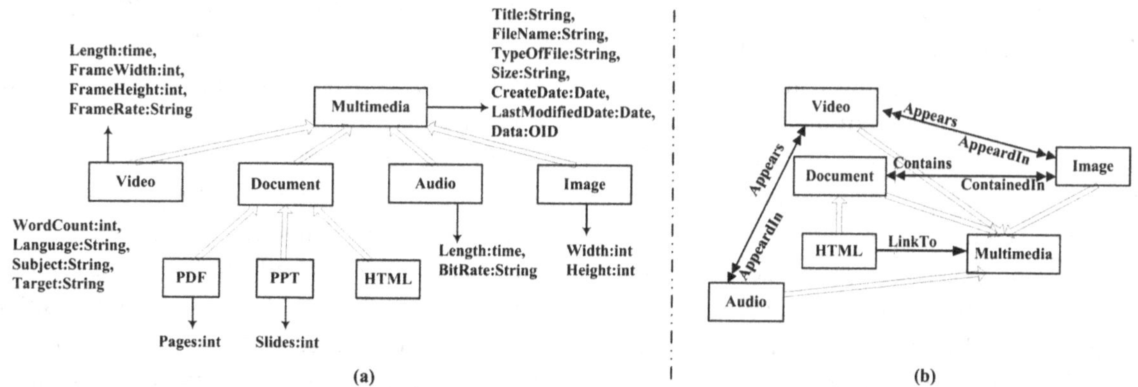

Flickr and MySpace provide a mechanism that offer users the ability to add tags to multimedia data, thereby enabling the data to be classified, searched and filtered.

Secondly, we can model the relations between different media types, as depicted in Figure 7 (b). Besides the hierarchy relationship, there are many other relations among different media types. For example, a video object is made up of many still image objects, so there is a relationship between object class Video and object class Image. We can define the relation from Video to Image as *Appears* and the inverse relation from Image to Video as *AppeardIn*, vice versa. The relationships between different media can be bidirectional or mono-directional. In Figure 9, just relation *LinkTo* is mono-directional, which presents an html file contain the hyperlink linking to other objects. The relation is heritable. If there is a relation names *R* from object class *A* to object class *B*, then *A* has the relation *R* with all subclasses of *B*. Such as in Figure 9, HTML can link to any kinds of media data. With these relations, we can find different media data in a navigation way. Moreover, we can use these relations to construct more meaningful query.

Context-Based Multimedia Semantic Modeling

The general idea of our context-based multimedia semantic modeling is to place the multimedia data in a complex semantic environment based on the real world modeling or users' requirements. There are three steps:

First, we model the multimedia data, which includes the hierarchy structure of multimedia data and relations in different types of media data. Secondly, we model the semantic application environment based on the real world application requirements. Lastly, we build the relationships between the semantic application environment and multimedia data.

We take the movie database as the example. A movie can be related to many types of multimedia data. The digital movie file, trailer, features and movie clips are the video data. A movie may contain many songs are audio data. The film stills, posters of a movie are image data. Besides these multimedia data, a movie itself contains a lot of information, such as cast, director, writer, genre, plot, awards etc. A typical online database to provide information about movies is IMDb (Internet Movie Database). IMDb mainly provides the descriptive information about movies, except for some photos and a few videos. On the other hand, if you search the video data in Google

Video or Microsoft Live Search, you can only use some simple keywords and then the system will return thousands of related results. User can filter the results with the basic metadata such as the duration or resolution of the video. Now the question is how we combine the two approaches and then we can take advantages of both. With the metadata information, we can filter multimedia data by their size, type and semantic tags. Then with the contextual information, we can search multimedia data not only use the simple tags or basic metadata, but use the rich semantic contextual information.

As shown in Figure 8, we take movie database as the example to elaborate INM-based multimedia modeling mechanism. For the movie database modeling, we may need to store the movie video data like trailers, features etc., songs as the audio data, and posters as image data. The first step is modeling the *multimedia data layer*, which includes the hierarchical structure of multimedia data, the basic metadata attributes and relations in different types of media data. Here we give a simplified view of this layer. A full schema was given in Figure 7 but it is changeable, depending on the application requirements. The second step is constructing the *semantic application layer* based on the natural features of movies. Besides the multimedia features, a movie has connections with many other objects. INM allows us to directly model the real world based on its organizational structure, so data modeling process can be greatly simplified. In the last step, we built the *semantic relationship layer* which modeled the relationships between *semantic application Layer* and *multimedia data layer* with role relationships. We can use the role relationships to represent the semantics of media data in a particular contextual environment. For example, an image can be a film still of a movie, and we can define context based attributes *castName* and *character* to stand for the name of the casts and their character name respectively. As mentioned in previous section, an image file can be of different interpretations with different perspectives and in different context. What we need to do is just building the different relationship between object classes in *semantic application layer* and object classes in *multimedia data layer.*

As elaborated in the paper (Liu & Hu, 2009), INM supports even more complicated relationships. With these rich semantic relationships, we can construct very powerful queries using INMQL with concise syntax to get precise results. This takes advantage of all basic metadata, semantic relationships and contextual semantics based on our modeling mechanism. Moreover, powerful semantic navigation functions can be easily implemented.

FUTURE RESEARCH DIRECTIONS

Ramesh Jain (2008) mentioned that "Multimedia researchers should be using content and context synergistically for bridging the semantic gap". In this chapter, we focused on the contextual semantics of multimedia application data management. Although we discussed multimedia structure modeling (including the basic multimedia metadata and relationship between different media types), the real complex audiovisual content that MPEG-7 describes is not involved in the chapter. The multimedia content that adheres to MPEG-7 is mainly organized with XML format. Many research publications have been devoted to mapping, indexing, and query MPEG-7 multimedia metadata in DBMS. As we presented, our *Information Networking Model* is more powerful and natured to model the semantic relationship of the real world than existing models. It also provides a more powerful query mechanism, so I believe it can do better to manage MPEG-7 than existing DBMSs. Next, we have the following research work to continue. First, we will improve INM itself, in ways such as reasoning ability, based on the application requirements; we will go on to perfect our contextual based modeling

Figure 8. INM-based multimedia application modeling

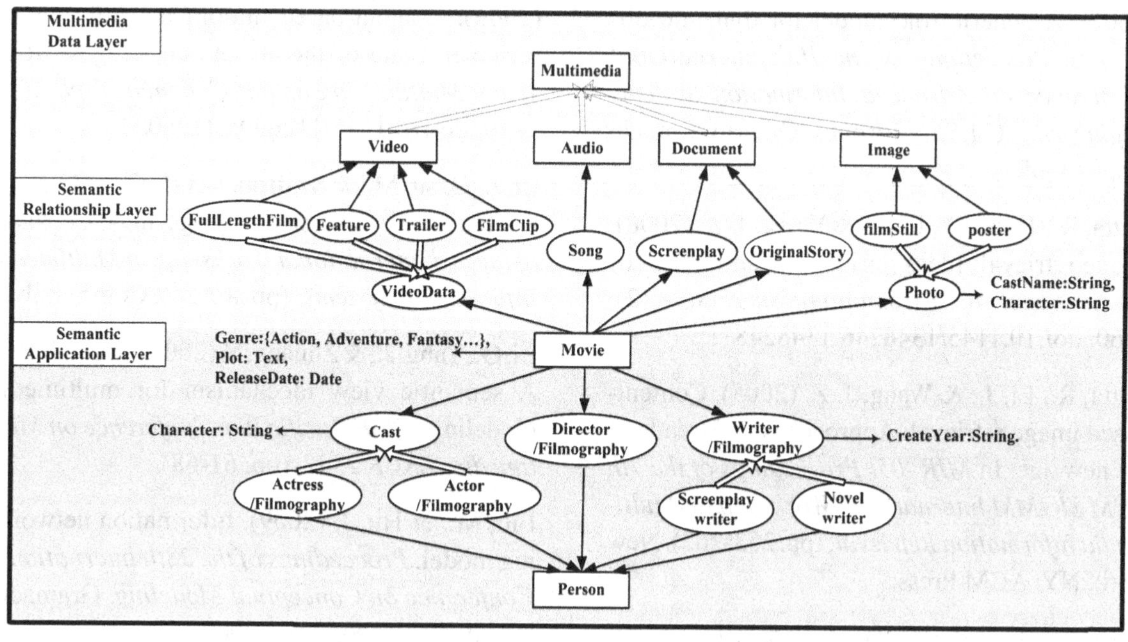

mechanism and to find more multimedia application cases that can be well supported with our approaches. Second, we try to figure out how to model multimedia semantic content with INM. In this regard, we need to figure out how to manage XML with INM. Finally, we can look to combine both content and context, producing a two-sided multimedia data retrieval system.

CONCLUSION

In this chapter, we have introduced a new model titled the Information Networking Model. It provides a strong semantic modeling mechanism that allows us to model the real world in a natural and direct way. With INM, we can model multimedia data which consists of dynamic semantics. The context-dependency and media-independency features of multimedia data can easily be represented by INM. In addition, multimedia multiple classifications are naturally supported. Based on INM, we proposed a multimedia data modeling mechanism in which users can take advantage of basic multimedia metadata, semantic relationships and contextual semantic information to search multimedia data.

REFERENCES

Albano, A., Bergamini, R., Ghelli, G., & Orsini, R. (1993). An object data model with roles. In *Proceedings of the 19th International Conference on Very Large Data Bases (VLDB)*, Dublin, Ireland. (pp. 39–51).

Cabot, J., & Ravent'os, R. (2004). Roles as entity types: A conceptual modelling pattern. In *Proceedings of the 23rd International Conference on Conceptual Modeling(ER)*, Shanghai, China. 69–82

Codd, E. F. (1970). A relational model of data for large shared data banks. *Communications of the ACM, 13*(6), 377–397. doi:10.1145/362384.362685

Dahchour, M., Pirotte, A., & Zim'anyi, E. (2002). A generic role model for dynamic objects. In *Proceedings of the 10th International Conference on Advanced Information Systems Engineering(CAiSE),* Toronto, Ontario, Canada (pp. 643–658).

Datta, R., Joshi, D., Li, J., & Wang, J. Z. (2008). Image retrieval: Ideas, influences, and trends of the new age. *ACM Computing Surveys, 40*(2), 1–60. doi:10.1145/1348246.1348248

Datta, R., Li, J., & Wang, J. Z. (2005). Content-based image retrieval: Approaches and trends of the new age. In *MIR '05: Proceedings of the 7th ACM SIGMM International Workshop on Multimedia Information Retrieval*, (pp. 253-262). New York, NY: ACM Press.

Djeraba, C., Hadouda, K., & Briand, H. (1997). Management of multimedia scenarios in an object-oriented database system. *Multimedia Tools and Applications, 4*(2), 97–114. doi:10.1023/A:1009634430444

Doller, M., Renner, K., & Kosch, H. (2007). *Introduction of an MPEG-7 query language*. International Conference on Digital Information Management, 1, (pp. 92-97).

Henrich, A., & Robbert, G. (2001). POQLMM: A query language for structured multimedia documents. In *Proceedings 1st International Workshop on Multimedia Data and Document Engineering,* (pp. 17–26).

Hull, R., & King, R. (1987). Semantic database modeling: Survey, applications, and research issues. *ACM Computing Surveys, 19*(3), 201–260. doi:10.1145/45072.45073

Jain, R. (2008). Multimedia information retrieval: Watershed events. *Proceedings of the ACM First International Conference on Multimedia Information Retrieval*, (pp. 229-236).

Lew, M. S., Sebe, N., Djeraba, C., & Jain, R. (2006). Content-based multimedia information retrieval: State of the art and challenges. *ACM Trans. Multimedia Comput. Commun. Appl., 2*(1), 1–19. doi:10.1145/1126004.1126005

Li, J., Ozsu, M., & Szafron, D. (1997). MOQL: A multimedia object query language. In *Proceedings of the 3rd International Workshop on Multimedia Information Systems*, (pp. 19-28). Como, Italy.

Li, Q., Yang, J., & Zhuang, Y. (2002). MediaView: A semantic view mechanism for multimedia modeling. *IEEE Pacific Rim Conference on Multimedia, LNCS 2532,* (pp. 61-68).

Liu, M., & Hu, J. (2009). Information networking model. *Proceedings of the 28th International Conference on Conceptual Modeling.* Gramado, Brazil, LNCS, Springer 2009.

Manjunath, B. S., Salembier, P., & Sikora, T. (2002). *Introduction to MPEG-7: Multimedia content description interface*. Wiley & Sons.

Melton, J., & Eisenberg, A. (2001). SQL multimedia and application packages (SQL/MM). *SIGMOD Record, 30*(4), 97–102. doi:10.1145/604264.604280

Peckham, J., & Maryanski, F. J. (1988). Semantic data models. *ACM Computing Surveys, 20*(3), 153–189. doi:10.1145/62061.62062

Peng, Z., & Kambayashi, Y. (1995). Deputy mechanisms for object-oriented databases. In *Proceedings of the Eleventh International Conference on Data Engineering (ICDE),* Taipei, Taiwan, (pp. 333–340).

Petkovic, M., & Jonker, W. (2003). Content-based video retrieval: A database perspective. *Proceedings of the First ACM Conference on Multimedia Systems and Applications*. Springer.

Sebe, N., Lew, M. S., Zhou, X., Huang, T. S., & Bakker, E. (2003). The state of the art in image and video retrieval. In *Proceedings of the International Conference on Video Retrieval (CIVR)*.

Smeulders, A. W. M., Worring, M., Santini, S., Gupta, A., & Jain, R. (2000). Content-based image retrieval at the end of the early years. *IEEE Transactions on Pattern Analysis and Machine Intelligence, 22*(12), 1349–1380. doi:10.1109/34.895972

Su, J. (1991). Dynamic constraints and object migration. In *Proceedings of the 17th International Conference on Very Large Data Bases (VLDB)*, Barcelona, Catalonia, Spain, (pp. 233–242).

Wieringa, R. J., Jonge, W. D., & Spruit, P. (1995). Using dynamic classes and role classes to model object migration. *Theory and Practice of Object Systems, 1*(1), 61–83.

Wong, R. (1999). Heterogeneous multifaceted multimedia objects in DOOR/MM: A role-based approach with views. *Journal of Parallel and Distributed Computing, 56*(3), 251–271. doi:10.1006/jpdc.1998.1522

Yoshitaka, A., & Ichikawa, T. (1999). A survey on content-based retrieval for multimedia databases. *IEEE Transactions on Knowledge and Data Engineering, 11*(1), 81–93. doi:10.1109/69.755617

KEY TERMS AND DEFINITIONS

Context-Based Multimedia Retrieval: The information retrieval methods rely on the contextual environment rather than the semantic content of the multimedia data itself.

Context-Dependency: The semantics of multimedia data are not only determined by the multimedia data themselves, but also the contextual environment that they are associated with.

Contextual Environment: The contextual environment is composed of three aspects: the purposes of the media objects, the context in which media objects are presented and the other data that interacts with the media objects itself.

Information Networking Model: A novel database model focuses on modeling the complex relationship of real world information. It can model complex relationships between objects, between objects and relationships, and between relationships. It supports context-dependent representation and access to object properties as well as providing one-to-one correspondence between the real world and the corresponding information model in a simple, natural and direct manner.

Media-Independency: Different types of multimedia data, such as images, videos and text, may share similar semantic meaning and require a common set of properties to describe them.

Multimedia Multiple Classifications: A multimedia object can belong to several different categories simultaneously. A category is a collection of objects with common semantics and can be described by common attributes.

Chapter 11
Towards a Unified Multimedia Metadata Management Solution

Samir Amir
University of Sciences and Technologies of Lille (USTL– Lille1), France

Ioan Marius Bilasco
University of Sciences and Technologies of Lille (USTL– Lille1), France

Md. Haidar Sharif
University of Sciences and Technologies of Lille (USTL– Lille1), France

Chabane Djeraba
University of Sciences and Technologies of Lille (USTL– Lille1), France

ABSTRACT

With increasing use of multimedia in various domains, several metadata standards appeared these last decades in order to facilitate the manipulation of multimedia contents. These standards help consumers to search content they desire and to adapt the retrieved content according to consumers' profiles and preferences. However, in order to extract information from a given standard, a user must have a pre-knowledge about this latest. This condition is not easy to satisfy due to the increasing number of available standards. In this chapter, we introduce some of the main de facto multimedia standards that cover the description, by means of metadata, of the content and of the use context (profiles, devices, networks...). We discuss then the benefits of proposing an integrated vision of multimedia metadata standards through the usage of a generic multimedia metadata integration system, and we expose the challenges of its implementation.

INTRODUCTION

Nowadays, with the vast expansion of the World Wide Web, several standards (such as MPEG-7(Chang, 2001), MPEG-21(Pereira, 2001), TV-Anytime (TV-Anytime Forum, 2003), etc.) have appeared for enhancing the retrieval, the usage and the delivery of multimedia data over a variety of channels (Web, TV, mobile). Those standards introduce descriptions of the content itself and of the context in which the content was created or for which the content was designed. We call these descriptions *metadata* as they bring new knowledge about the content and the context

DOI: 10.4018/978-1-61350-126-9.ch011

seen as regular *data*. The metadata presented in various multimedia standards describe different kinds of multimedia contents (e.g., video, image, audio, etc.), devices consuming or transmitting these contents (e.g., networks, TV, mobile, etc.), services processing or dealing with them (e.g., search, adaptation, etc.) and finally environment of user consuming these contents (e.g., user profile, user preference, etc.).

The first category of metadata presented here above, which is about content, can be found in multimedia standards such as (MPEG-7, Dublin Core (Weibel, 1998) or TV Anytime), as well as in different ongoing research projects such as the one defended by the *CAM4Home Consortium*[1] which proposes a dedicated content description schema called *CAM Core Metadata* (ITEA2-CAM4Home, 2008). This kind of metadata provides explicit knowledge about the features of the content (genre, appearing concepts, etc.) and about the physical properties of the content (required bandwidth, required decoders, file size, resolution, etc.). This knowledge improves the search processes as it enriches the signal-based characterization of content, with explicit knowledge closer to user criteria (such as, meaning-full keywords). The content-related metadata can also be used in order to propose adequate adaptation processes as, depending on the type of content, specific techniques might apply better.

The last three categories presented above are about the context in which the delivery of multimedia content takes place. Standards such as MPEG-21, CC/PP (Klyne, 2004) or description schemes like CAM Supplementary Metadata schema proposed by the *CAM4Home Consortium*[1] cover context-related information. These metadata offer knowledge that can also be injected in search, retrieval and delivery processes. While doing search, systems could benefit from the information about the user access device in order to propose content that are compatible. While doing delivery, systems can interpret the capacity of the access device and the capacity of the delivery network and it can use this information in order to adapt by simplifying accordingly the content (doing transcoding or transrating for videos, doing resolution reduction for images, doing filtering for complex documents such as web pages, etc.).

Considering the current state of art with regard to multimedia content and context descriptions, standards and consortium initiatives, taken all together, cover fairly well all aspects of the multimedia delivery problem. However, in order to take advantage of these entire standards one must have a strong and a very diversified pre-knowledge about a part or all of them. Besides the specific encoding proposed by each solution, those standards that are often created by specific multimedia communities (such as Multimedia Pictures Experts Groups – MPEG[2], World Wide Web Consortium - W3C[3], Dublin Core – DC[4], CAM4HOME Consortium – C4H[5],...) have led to the availability of multiple terminological and syntactical resources in numerous domain of multimedia. These different types of metadata are encoded using existing description languages (e.g., XML Schema (Thompson, 2009) for MPEG-7 and TV-Anytime or RDF Schema (Brickley, 2004) for CAM Core Metadata and CAM Supplementary Metadata), different vocabularies and different ontologies depending on the community that has created them. These multimedia contents can also be enriched by other kind of metadata such as consumers' annotations (e.g., comments, social tags, etc.) which is free text added by consumers having different point of view and different understanding about multimedia content.

Dealing with knowledge from multiple independent metadata standards is one of the most important challenges in multimedia domain due to the semantic heterogeneity of information as mentioned here above. The creation, the delivery and the consumption of rich multimedia experiences between different entities in multimedia community (e.g., multimedia content consumers, commercial content providers, simple producer, etc.) requires that each of these entities must be able to interpret all metadata standards used by the community. However this requirement is not easy to satisfy due to numerous standards which appeared and will appear in multimedia community.

An important prerequisite solution for this problem is to establish interoperability between the various metadata representations. This can be done by defining a framework for mapping and converting between the different metadata representations. The framework described in this chapter is a multimedia metadata integration system we planned to integrate as part of CAM4Home project to achieve both syntactical and semantic interoperability between different multimedia metadata standards used by multimedia community.

This chapter first gives an overview about existing multimedia metadata standards and CAM4Home project initiative (introduced above) that covers a wide area of information related to multimedia delivery and includes multimedia content description, user preference and profile description and devices characteristic description. Then we relate about multimedia and generic integration issues by discussing the work done by W3C working group in order to integrate heterogeneous metadata and some generic approaches providing mapping between ontologies (Kalfoglou, 2002) (Doan, 2002) (Doan, 2000).

The second part of the chapter is consecrated to the illustration of the proposal of a new architecture for the multimedia metadata integration system and discuss about challenges of its realization. We first deal with the homogenization of different encoding styles (XML Schema, RDF Schema, and OWL (McGuinness, 2004)). Then we propose a solution for semantic disambiguation of metadata descriptions by explicitating the meaning of a concept with regard to its definition context. Several meanings can be associated with the same concept and a (definition) context-based filtering process is proposed. Finally, we expose the validation of mappings suggested by semantic proximity measured between concepts after the disambiguisation phase. We use the expressive power of Description Logic (Baader, 2003) in order to describe assumption on the possible mapping. The validation is proven or invalidate by using a version of Tableau algorithm (Baader, 2001).

Multimedia Metadata Standards

In this section we briefly present some standards and consortium initiatives related to content description (MPEG-7, TV-AnyTime, CAM Core Metadata model) and context description (MPEG-21, CC/PP, CAM Supplementary Metadata model (Bilasco, 2010)). The aim of this section is twofold. It allows unfamiliar reader to get acquainted with these standards and it also illustrates the heterogeneity of multimedia metadata encoding using specific community semantics and using specific schema languages (XML Schema and RDF Schema). We start by presenting the content-related metadata standards.

Content-Related Metadata Standards

We have selected in this section three XML Schema based standards (MPEG-7, TV-Anytime and Dublin Core) as well as a description schema designed within the CAM4Home project that is defined using RDF Schema.

We have chosen three XML Schema based standards in order to differentiate between standards with a very complex structural organization such as MPEG-7 composed of hundreds of descriptors defined by inheritance and yielding complex compositions, light-weight standard such as Dublin Core having moreover a simple and linear structure and a small set of concepts and intermediate with regard to schema complexity such as TV-Anytime. The choice of TV-Anytime is also guided by the fact that the TV community that is slightly different from MPEG community, and we are interested in how similar concepts were brought in standards by different communities having different cultural backgrounds.

We have selected XML Schema based standards and RDF Schema in order to illustrate the heterogeneity that can arouse with respect to the underlying specification schema languages and the need of migrating these underlying schema languages to a common format.

MPEG-7

From the standardization efforts of the Working Group *Moving Picture Experts Group* (MPEG) emerged in 2001 the MPEG-7 specifications. MPEG-7 is a standard that covers the semantic description of media resources. Although the descriptors proposed in MPEG-7 specifically cover the multimedia resources of type audio and video, MPEG-7 is extensible and can include other types of media. MPEG-7 provides a series of audio-visual description tools that are grouped into the following categories: descriptors (D), description schemas (DS) and description definition language (DDL).

A descriptor is a unit of indexing features describing the primary visual, audio or object semantic. The description schemes, which are high-level descriptors, include several D and other DS on structured and semantic units. The DDL defines the syntax for creating new DS. Since DDL is derived from XML Schema, DDL allows the extensibility of the MPEG-7 (Bilasco, 2005).

DS defined in MPEG-7 currently cover the following categories: visual description (VDS), audio description (ADS) and structural description of multimedia content (MDS). VDS and ADS describe the physical, logical or semantic structure of multimedia document. These structures are built using the DS offered by MDS. Figure 1 shows a fragment of MPEG-7 standard specification corresponding to the structural definition of the *VideoSegment*Type that is part of the MDS scheme. The construction of mapping between several standards must take into account the eventual lexical proximity (such as synonymies) between label names (such as *VideoSegment*) as well as the specificities of each underlying definition language. By examining the XML Schema fragment presented in Figure 1 we can observe that the *VideoSegment*Type is an extension of a generic *Segment*Type and it is composed by a sequence of properties corresponding to other instances of the MPEG-7 Structural (MDS) and Visual DS (VDS). Each property has a given cardinality. All these information constitutes the context of the *VideoSegment* type definition. This kind of information must be taken into account during the mapping process as it would allow the filtering among "false friends" mapping candidates.

TV-Anytime

TV-Anytime Forum is an association of organizations which seeks to develop specifications to enable audio-visual and other services based on mass-market high volume digital storage in consumer platforms. They have promoted a homonym standard, TV-Anytime which is a multimedia metadata standard that allows consumers to select and acquire content of interest.

TV-Anytime standard facilitates user browsing, selection and acquisition of content independently from their system of distribution, even if they are enhanced TV, interactive TV (ATSC, DVB, DBS and others) or Internet. TV-Anytime standard is a specification linking the creators and content providers to consumers. TV-Anytime allows the access to different views, versions or editions of a particular topic and it gives a short description for contents. User is able to add personal metadata, as annotation, comments, tags which can be useful for search services. To ensure compatibility, TV-Anytime has adopted a common representation format for the exchange of metadata. The adopted representation format is XML Schema.

The definition of the ProgramInformation-Type is presented in the TV-Anytime fragment shown in Figure 2. The structural organization of this concept is notably less important than the

Figure 1: Example of MPEG-7 description scheme: Definition of VideoSegmentType

```
<complexType name="VideoSegmentType">
 <complexContent>
  <extension base="mpeg7:SegmentType">
   <sequence>
    <choice minOccurs="0">
     <element name="MediaTime" type="mpeg7:MediaTimeType"/>
     <element name="TemporalMask" type="mpeg7:TemporalMaskType"/>
    </choice>
    <choice minOccurs="0" maxOccurs="unbounded">
     <element name="VisualDescriptor" type="mpeg7:VisualDType"/>
     <element name="VisualDescriptionScheme"
              type="mpeg7:VisualDSType"/>
     <element name="VisualTimeSeriesDescriptor" type="mpeg7:VisualTimeSeriesType"/>
    </choice>
    <element name="MultipleView" type="mpeg7:MultipleViewType" minOccurs="0"/>
    <element name="Mosaic" type="mpeg7:MosaicType" minOccurs="0" maxOccurs="unbounded"/>
    <choice minOccurs="0" maxOccurs="unbounded">
     <element name="SpatialDecomposition" type="mpeg7:VideoSegmentSpatialDecompositionType"/>
     <element name="TemporalDecomposition"
              type="mpeg7:VideoSegmentTemporalDecompositionType"/>
     <element name="SpatioTemporalDecomposition"
              type="mpeg7:VideoSegmentSpatioTemporalDecompositionType"/>
     <element name="MediaSourceDecomposition"
              type="mpeg7:VideoSegmentMediaSourceDecompositionType"/>
    </choice>
   </sequence>
  </extension>
 </complexContent>
</complexType>
```

Figure 2. Example of TV-Anytime specification: Program information type

```
<complexType name="ProgramInformationType">
   <sequence>
    <element name="BasicDescription" type="tva:BasicContentDescriptionType"/>
    <element name="OtherIdentifier" type="mpeg7:UniqueIDType" minOccurs="0"
             maxOccurs="unbounded"/>
    <element name="AVAttributes" type="tva:AVAttributesType" minOccurs="0"/>
    <element name="MemberOf" type="tva:BaseMemberOfType" minOccurs="0"
             maxOccurs="unbounded"/>
    <element name="DerivedFrom" type="tva:DerivedFromType" minOccurs="0"/>
    <element name="EpisodeOf" type="tva:EpisodeOfType" minOccurs="0"/>
    <element name="PartOfAggregatedProgram" type="tva:CRIDType" minOccurs="0"/>
    <element name="AggregationOf" type="tva:AggregationOfType" minOccurs="0" />
   </sequence>
  <attribute name="programId" type="tva:CRIDType" use="required"/>
  <attributeGroup ref="tva:fragmentIdentification"/>
  <attribute name="metadataOriginIDRef" type="tva:TVAIDRefType"use="optional"/>
  <attribute ref="xml:lang" default="en" use="optional"/>
</complexType>
```

VideoSegment type of MPEG-7 presented in the previous section. No inheritance information about eventual parents is provided. The properties are defined by a single sequence construct with no alternative constructs. The mapping of this concept to other concepts in other standards would be more straightforward than the mapping of a VideoSegment, however ambiguities might arise as many "mapping" candidates could be identified if less constraints on the structure are defined.

Dublin Core

The Dublin Core (Weibel, 1998) is one of the more compact metadata standards which have very simple structure. It is used to describe information

Figure 3. Example of Dublin Core specification

```
<xs:element name="title" substitutionGroup="any"/>
<xs:element name="creator" substitutionGroup="any"/>
<xs:element name="subject" substitutionGroup="any"/>
<xs:element name="description" substitutionGroup="any"/>
<xs:element name="publisher" substitutionGroup="any"/>
<xs:element name="contributor" substitutionGroup="any"/>
<xs:element name="date" substitutionGroup="any"/>
<xs:element name="type" substitutionGroup="any"/>
<xs:element name="format" substitutionGroup="any"/>
<xs:element name="identifier" substitutionGroup="any"/>
<xs:element name="source" substitutionGroup="any"/>
<xs:element name="language" substitutionGroup="any"/>
<xs:element name="relation" substitutionGroup="any"/>
<xs:element name="coverage" substitutionGroup="any"/>
<xs:element name="rights" substitutionGroup="any"/>
```

resources. It defines conventions for describing things online in ways that make them easy to find. Officially it contains fifteen elements (title, creator, subject, description, publisher, contributor, date, type, format, identifier, source, language, relation, coverage, and rights).

The Dublin Core is already used to describe digital materials such as video, sound, images, text, and composite media, like web pages. These fifteen elements were deliberately made simple so that non-library catalogers could provide basic information for resource discovery. Because of its simplicity, the Dublin Core has been used with other types of materials, and for applications demanding increased complexity. Its design, which allows for a minimum set of shareable metadata in the Open Archive Initiative-Protocol for Metadata Harvesting, prove its efficiency as thousands of projects worldwide, use the Dublin Core for cataloging, or collecting data from the Web. Figure 3 shows the fifteen elements of Dublin Core standard which are encoded using XML Schema.

The structural and the linguistic simplicity of Dublin Core make it very easy for the mapping. Its semantic is clearly described, calling only external resources without any need to take into account the structure of the concept, is sufficient to link between proprieties defined in other schemas and those specified in the Dublin Core standard.

CAM4Home Core Metadata

CAM4Home Core Metadata is a part of the CAM4Home Metadata model proposed by the CAM4Home Consortium in order to deal with multimedia content in the era of Web, TV and mobile convergence. The objective of the CAM4Home consortium is to create a metadata enabled content delivery framework to allow end users and commercial content providers to create and deliver rich multimedia experiences. These multimedia experiences are based on a novel concept of collaborative aggregated multimedia. The Collaborative Aggregated Multimedia (CAM) refers to aggregation and composition of individual multimedia contents (called objects) into a content bundle that may include references to content based services and can be delivered as a semantically coherent set of content and related services over various communication channels. The consortium develops one common metadata framework for CAM content that can be applied for both personal and commercial applications and is interoperable with relevant standard metadata and content representation technologies.

CAM4Home Core Metadata is part of the CAM4Home Metadata Framework and offers complete descriptions of the structure and behavior of core CAM entities which are necessary to represent and manipulate simple or aggregated multimedia content. CAM Core Metadata

Figure 4. RDF-S definitions of concrete classes and properties

```
01: <rdfs:Class rdf:about="&core;CAMElementMetadata"  rdfs:label="core:CAMElementMetadata">
02:  <rdfs:subClassOf rdf:resource="&abstract;ContentFeatureContainer"/>
03: </rdfs:Class>
04: <rdf:Property rdf:about="&core;title rdfs:label="core:title">
05:  <rdfs:domain rdf:resource="&core;CAMElementMetadata"/>
06:  <rdfs:subPropertyOf rdf:resource="&abstract;simpleFeatureMetadata"/>
07:  <rdfs:range rdf:resource="&xsd;string"/>
08: </rdf:Property>
09: <rdfs:Class rdf:about="&core;AppearingConcept"  rdfs:comment="A class for representing an
                      AppearingConcept"   rdfs:label="core:AppearingConcept">
10:  <rdfs:subClassOf rdf:resource="&abstract;ContentFeatureMetadata"/>
11: </rdfs:Class>
12: <rdf:Property rdf:about="&core;hasAppearingConcepts " rdfs:label="core:hasAppearingConcepts">
13:  <rdfs:range  rdf:resource="&core;AppearingConcept"/>
14:  <rdfs:domain rdf:resource="&core;MultimediaElementMetadata"/>
15:  <rdfs:subPropertyOf rdf:resource="&abstract;hasFeatureMetadata"/>
16: </rdf:Property>
```

supports the representation of a wide variety of Multimedia content in CAM Objects: downloadable applications, software services, images, video, etc. Specific metadata is attached to different types of Multimedia entities. This metadata describes both the content file or service deployment method and the actual content or service that is provided. This metadata model also describes the mechanisms by which CAM Bundles aggregate CAM Objects.

A fragment of the CAM4Home Core Metadata specification done using RDF Schema is shown in Figure 4. The example illustrates the generic RDF Schema templates for introducing simple and structured core metadata constructs to specialize the abstract concepts into concrete metadata elements. Any simple metadata used for content feature description is directly associated as a property which specializes the simpleFeatu rePropertyrdf:property (lines 06-08 in Figure 4). Any structured metadata used for content feature description extends the ContentFeatureMetadata class (lines 9-11 in Figure 4). It is associated with a given concrete feature container by introducing a property that links the container and the newly created structured metadata. A naming convention has been adopted in order to make the property name reflect the metadata construct they are introducing. Complex properties use *has* prefix before the actual class name. In the example shown in Figure 4, hasAppearingConcept is a complex property in that it uses another class definition in the metadata model (the AppearingConcept class).

The main difference with the XML Schema based standards is that the class definition can be done in separate places over an RDF Schema document as well as for XML Schema language all knowledge about a concept is contained within the main definition of the concept (xsd:complexElement). For instance, all properties of a concept are defined independently (line 04-08 for core: title and line 12-16 for core: hasAppearingConcept). Hence there is a need to have a global approach in describing the complete definition of a concept and not considering only a local approach (with regard to the specification document definition). Another specificity of RDF Schema is that it may introduce refined type of composition. In XML Schema world, each property of a complex element can be seen *isPartOf* relation. However, this might not always apply. In RDF Schema properties can be typed and hence more elaborate relation can be transposed without any loss of information into the RDF Schema descriptions.

Context-Related Metadata Standards

In the previous section we introduced some metadata standards related to the description of multimedia content. The previous section offered a view on how different encoding technologies impact on the structure and the organization of metadata standards. In the following we discuss some metadata standards which introduce concepts for characterizing the delivery context. The aim of this section is to illustrate how different communities (MPEG, CAM4Home and W3C) perceive and models through metadata the delivery context. In all the standards which we present here after (respectively MPEG-21, CAM4Home Supplementary Metadata, CC/PP) concepts like user device, access network, environmental context and theirs properties are represented using various constructs depending on the encoding scheme considered.

MPEG-21

MPEG-21 *Multimedia Framework* proposes solutions for the use of multimedia resources across a wide variety of networks and access devices. To achieve this, MPEG-21 addresses the standardization of content management, reuse content in new contexts of use, protection of rights of privacy of consumers and providers of multimedia content, etc. MPEG-21 is built on top of the family of MPEG standards (MPEG-1, MPEG-2, MPEG-4, MPEG-7) drawing particularly on MPEG-4 regarding the dissemination of information and MPEG-7 semantic description for content.

MPEG-21 is organized into several parts that can evolve independently. Each part covers one of the aspects related to the management and dissemination of multimedia information. To date, there are twelve parts which make up the platform MPEG-21, among which the *Digital Item Adaptation (DIA). Authors* in (Vetro, 2005) define sets of tools for describing the environment of use and properties of media resources which can affect the diffusion process (terminals, networks, users profile and preferences).

The fragment of MPEG-21 DIA presented in Figure 5 illustrates the specification of the TerminalCapabilities (lines 1 to 09 in Figure 5), InputOutputCapabilities concept specification (lines 10 to 20 in Figure 5) that embeds together with audio information and DisplayCapabilities of the device (lines 21-30 in Figure 5) such as resolution or type of display device, etc. Hence we have a four level description for introducing characteristics of a device seen as a terminal giving user access to content.

In the following paragraph we will discuss how the same concept Device or Terminal is modeled and encoded with the metadata initiative of the CAM4Home consortium.

CAM4Home Supplementary Metadata

CAM4Home Supplementary Metadata is a part of the CAM4Home Metadata model proposed by the CAM4Home Consortium that was briefly introduced in the previous section.

CAM Supplementary Metadata schema provides information required to enable interoperability of the platform services and supplement the Core metadata. CAM Supplementary Metadata provides the structures for profiling of users, communities, devices, network and platform services. For each one of these entities several profiles can be associated in order to support time-dependant (in the morning, in the afternoon) and usage-dependent (at home, at work) characteristics.

A fragment of the schema describing the device profiles and device-related metadata within the CAM4Home Supplementary Metadata schema is shown in Figure 6. A first rdf:property construct introduces the hasC4HDeviceProfile property (lines 1-4 in Figure 6) that links C4HDeviceProfile description to a given C4HDevice. Further on, the hasDeviceCapabilities property (defined by lines 5-8 in Figure 6) attaches a DeviceCapabilitiesDescription to a given C4HDeviceProfile. Other descriptions not included in this fragment such as software or hardware description can be attached to a C4HDeviceProfile in order to describe a specific device configuration. The

Figure 5. Example of MPEG-21 DIA specification of TerminalCapabilities and DisplayCapabilities

```
<complexType name="TerminalCapabilitiesType">
 <complexContent>
  <extension base="dia:DIAUsageEnvironmentBaseType">
   <sequence>
    <element name="TerminalCapabilities" type="dia:TerminalCapabilitiesBaseType minOccurs="0"
     maxOccurs="unbounded"/>
   </sequence>
  </extension>
 </complexContent>
</complexType>
        .....
<complexType name="InputOutputCapabilitiesType">
 <complexContent>
  <extension base="dia:TerminalCapabilitiesBaseType">
   <sequence>
    <element name="Display" type="dia:DisplayCapabilitiesType"  minOccurs="0"
     maxOccurs="unbounded"/>
    <element name="AudioOut"  type="dia:AudioOutputCapabilitiesType" minOccurs="0"/>
    <element name="UserInteractionInputSupport" type="dia:UserInteractionInputSupportType "
     minOccurs="0"/>
   </sequence>
  </extension>
 </complexContent>
</complexType>

<complexType name="DisplayCapabilitiesType">
 <complexContent>
  <extension base="dia:DIABaseType">
   <sequence>
    <element name="Resolution" type="ResolutionType" minOccurs="0" maxOccurs="unbounded"/>
    <element name="DisplayDevice"type="mpeg7:ControlledTermUseType"  minOccurs="0"
     maxOccurs="unbounded"/>
   </sequence>
  </extension>
 </complexContent>
</complexType>
```

DeviceCapabilitesDescription (lines 13-15 in Figure 6) is composed of Display Capabilities descriptions (lines 13-23 in Figure 6), Audio Capabilities description and Browser Capabilities (not included in the fragment). Properties such as display Size (lines 16-19 in Figure 6) and type Of Display (lines 20-23 in Figure 6) describe the display capabilities of a device.

From a logical point of view, many similarities can be observed between the MPEG-21 DIA TerminalCapabilities and C4HDevice descriptions. DeviceCapabilitiesDescription (from CAM4Home) element could be partially mapped onto the TerminalCapabilities (from MPEG-21 DIA) element. DisplayCapabilities concept is available in both specification, however they encoding is quite different with regard to the labels used for introducing display-related properties (e.g. displaySize in CAM4Home vs. Resolution in MPEG-21 DIA) and the way the properties are encoded (e.g. displaySize as a string vs. Resolution as a complex element having a vertical and horizontal resolution components).

However, the MPEG-21 DIA addresses the issue of characterizing a wide variety of access devices. The CAM4Home project only considered a small set of devices such as 3G mobiles phones, TV set-top boxes, laptop and desktop computers.

A fine grain analysis of MPEG-21 DIA and CAM4Home Supplementary Metadata suggests that the CAM4Home Supplementary Metadata can be partially mapped on a subset of MPEG-21 DIA descriptions. A coherent metadata integration approach should be able to identify similarities like the one we have presented above by going beyond the logical structure imposed by XML Schema

Figure 6. Example of CAM4Home supplementary specification of Device and DisplayCapabilities

```
<rdf:Property rdf:about="&supplementary;hasC4HDeviceProfile" ...>
  <rdfs:domain rdf:resource="&supplementary;C4HDevice"/>
  <rdfs:range rdf:resource="&supplementary;C4HDeviceProfile"/>
</rdf:Property>
<rdf:Property rdf:about="&supplementary;hasDeviceCapabilities" ...>
  <rdfs:range rdf:resource="&supplementary;C4HDeviceCapabilitiesDescription"/>
  <rdfs:domain rdf:resource="&supplementary;C4HDeviceProfile"/>
</rdf:Property>
<rdf:Property rdf:about="&supplementary;hasDisplayCapabilities" ...>
  <rdfs:domain rdf:resource="&supplementary;C4HDeviceCapabilitiesDescription"/>
  <rdfs:range rdf:resource="&supplementary;DisplayCapabilities"/>
</rdf:Property>
<rdfs:Class rdf:about="&supplementary;DisplayCapabilities" ...>
  <rdfs:subClassOf rdf:resource="&abstract;DeviceMetadata"/>
</rdfs:Class>
<rdf:Property rdf:about="&supplementary;displaySize" ...>
  <rdfs:domain rdf:resource="&supplementary;DisplayCapabilities"/>
  <rdfs:range rdf:resource="xsd:string"/>
</rdf:Property>
<rdf:Property rdf:about="&supplementary;typeOfDisplay" ...>
  <rdfs:domain rdf:resource="&supplementary;DisplayCapabilities"/>
  <rdfs:range rdf:resource="xsd:string"/>
</rdf:Property>
```

or RDF Schema constructs. The computation of partial mappings between parts of the metadata specifications seems also to be very useful when considering specifications having complex structures like the ones exhibited by MPEG-21 DIA.

CC/PP

As part of a framework for adaptation and contextualization of content, a format; called CC/PP that can describe the possibilities of a user agent (Web browser, modem, etc.) was proposed by W3C. The CC/PP is a language based on profile description. Each CC/PP profile is a description of the possibilities of access device and user preferences that can be used to guide the adaptation of contents.CC/PP is based on RDF, which was developed by the W3C as a language for describing metadata. RDF provides a basic framework for the scalability of CC/PP vocabulary, through the usage of XML namespaces.

CC/PP Profile contains attributes and values which are processed by a server to determine the most appropriate form of a media resource relative to this profile. It is structured to enable a client and/or an intermediate server to describe their capabilities by referring: a) a standard profile, accessible to origin server or other sender and b) a smaller set of properties outside the standard profile, but understood by both parties. CC/PP profile is structured in a hierarchy with 2 levels with a number of components, each component having at least one or more attributes.

The main difference with the previous standards is that CC/PP specifications provide only very few predefined concepts (Profile, Component, Property, Structure and Attribute). A profile is composed of one or several components. Components are described either using CC/PP natives' properties such as CC/PP structures and CC/PP attributes or using properties defined by external schemas. The CC/PP standard was conceived as a generic approach for describing any kind of client profiles. Constructing the mapping between other standards and CC/PP should be envisioned in a new way as CC/PP is more over a container (having a structure that conforms the profile-component pattern) of descriptions. When mapping CC/PP to other standards we should take into account the RDF Schema included in CC/PP description through specific XML namespaces. For CC/PP-related the mapping one should

Figure 7. CC/PP profile definition using a specific namespace for component properties

```
01: <rdf:RDF xmlns:rdf="http://www.w3.org/1999/02/22-rdf-syntax-ns#"
        xmlns:ccpp="http://www.w3.org/2002/11/08-ccpp-schema#">
02:   <rdf:Description rdf:about="http://www.example.com/profile#MyProfile">
03:     <cpp:component>
04:       <rdf:Description rdf:about="http://www.example.com/profile#TerminalHardware">
05:         <!-- TerminalHardware properties here -->
06:       </rdf:Description>
07:     </ccpp:component>
08:     <ccpp:component>
09:       <rdf:Description rdf:about="http://www.example.com/profile#TerminalSoftware">
10:         <!-- TerminalSoftware properties here -->
11:       </rdf:Description>
12:     </ccpp:component>
13:     <ccpp:component>
14:       <rdf:Description rdf:about="http://www.example.com/profile#TerminalBrowser">
15:         <!-- TerminalBrowser properties here -->
16:       </rdf:Description>
17:     </ccpp:component>
18:   </rdf:Description>
19: </rdf:RDF>
```

consider the instances of CC/PP profiles and the mapping will be done among the RDF Schema associated with the XML namespaces. So, here we have to consider a specific schema mapping process driven by instances.

For instance, the CC/PP fragment in Figure 7 introduces three components: TerminalHardware (lines 3-7), TerminalSoftware (lines 8-12) and TerminalBrowser (lines 13-17). These components where defined as belonging the http://www.example.com/profile namespace. Hence, if one considers mapping the fragment in 7 onto other standards, one should compute a mapping between the RDF Schema corresponding to the http://www.example.com/profile namespace and the given standard.

EXISTING METADATA INTEGRATION SOLUTIONS

In the previous chapter we introduced some multimedia standards and we briefly discussed some issues that can arise while trying to compute mapping between existing multimedia standards, usually characterized by highly complex schema introduced numerous concepts and inter- or intra-concepts relations.

In the following, we briefly discuss some solutions available in the current state-of-art that addressed the problem of multimedia metadata integration, Afterwards, we discuss the W3C initiative, called Ontology for Media Object (WonSuk, 2009), that opens the way to providing specific mapping solutions closely related to *de facto* multimedia standards as those presented in the previous section. This section shows also some works done in order to semi-automatically map between heterogeneous descriptions structured as generic ontologies.

The problem of integrating heterogeneous multimedia metadata interested researcher this last decade. (Garcia, 2005) proposed a framework to integrate three different music ontologies. He used the generated MPEG-7 OWL ontology as an upper-ontology (mediated schema) to integrate other music metadata (MusicBrainz schema, Simac music ontology and a music vocabulary to describe performances). This music metadata are mapped manually to MPEG-7 ontology. (Hunter, 2003) proposed a core top-level ontology for the integration of information from different domains. A core top-level is an extensible ontology that expresses the basic concepts that are common across a variety of domains and media types and that can provide the basis for specialization into domain-specific concepts and vocabularies. It allows the construction of well-defined mappings between several domain-specific knowledge representations (i.e., metadata vocabularies).

Some other frameworks have been proposed to integrate multimedia metadata (Doerr, 2003) (Tsinaraki, 2004) (Troncy, 2003). However, these frameworks are limited and cover usually a small number of standards. The Ontology for Media Object mentioned previously is, at our knowledge, the framework that considers the integration of the largest number of metadata standards. Moreover, all exiting works, including Ontology for Media Object are based on manual mapping which requires experts having deep knowledge about each considered standard and, hence, an important time for the acquiring the knowledge and processing hundreds of metadata definitions. A semi-automatic framework for mapping between different formats of metadata facilitates the integration process; this is the reason that drove us to propose a new framework described later in this book chapter. Our solution is inspired by the existing generic ontology matching approaches. We have studied these approaches in order to select the most adequate approach for multimedia metadata (Amir, 2009).

Ontology for Media Object (W3C)

In order to enhance the integration of heterogeneous metadata, since 2008 a new W3C working group has been working at the definition of a new system called *Ontology and API for Media Object* (WonSuk, 2009). The ontology obtained following the integration process is expected to support cross-community data integration of information related to multimedia content on the Web. The API will provide read access and potentially write access to media objects, relying on the definitions from the ontology.

The *Ontology for Media Object* addresses the inter-compatibility problem by providing a common set of properties to define the basic metadata needed for media objects and the semantic links between their values in different existing vocabularies. It aims at circumventing the current proliferation of video metadata formats by providing full or partial translation and mapping between the existing formats. The ontology is to be accompanied by an API that provides uniform access to all elements defined by the ontology, which are selected elements from different formats. Table 1 shows a part of the mapping result between some multimedia metadata standards (METS, LOM2.1, CableLabs 1.1, YouTube and TV-Anytime) and a set of mediated ontology properties (API).

Notwithstanding the efforts of *Ontology for Media Object* working group, we think that the integration could benefit from the existing approaches to find a semi-automatic semantic mapping between a common set of properties which a mediator between user and metadata standards. At the given time, the W3C working group constructs the mapping manually.

Currently the W3C Working Group considers standards such as: Dublin Core, EXIF (EXIF, 2004), ID3 (ID3, 1999), IPTC (IPTC, 2008), Media RSS (Media RSS, 2008), MPEG-7 and XMP (XMP, 2008). The manual mapping is more precise then the semi-automatic one, but the first one is hard to realize for large standards and need to be updated manually after each modification or addition of new properties.

In order to deal with this problem, and to link semi-automatically proprieties and concepts over various multimedia standards we are working in order to design and implement a multimedia metadata integration system described in the next section.

Ontology Metadata Mapping

A mapping is a sort of alignment between ontology constructs as defined in (Kalfoglou, 2002). That is, given two ontologies, one should be able to map concepts found in the first ontology onto the ones found in the second one. Several

Table 1. A fragment of mapping table (Ontology for Media Object)

Standards API	METS	LOM 2.1	*CableLabs 1.1*	*YouTube*	TV-Anytime
contributor	metsHdr/agent	contribute	Actors Actors_Display Advisories Director	credit@role	CreditsList/CreditsItem + role
language	X	language	Languages	media:content@lang	Language, CaptionLanguage, SignLanguage
copyright	Copyright	X	Provider	copyright	DRMDeclaration / CopyrightNotice
format	X	format	Encrypting_System_Info Encryption Encryption_Algorithm Encryption_Date Encryption_Key_Block Encryption_Time Encryption_Time Audio_Type	content@type	AVAttributes
genre	ImageDescription, INAM	Learningresourcetype	Genre Category	content@medium	Genre

mapping algorithms have been proposed during the last few years, each of them has been implemented for a specific domain. Several surveys (Kalfoglou, 2003) (Shvaiko, 2005) (Rahm, 2001) about different existing method for ontologies mapping show that their applicability depend on utilization domain.

When doing ontology mapping, some authors focus only on syntax and structure (Doan, 2002) (Doan, 2000) others use specific semantics associated with concepts in the ontology and some of them extract information from instances (Madhavan, 2001) to give more precision during schema mapping operation.

Kalfoglou and Schorlemmer (Kalfoglou, 2002) developed an automatic method for ontology mapping, IF-Map, based on the Barwise-Seligman theory of information flow. Their method built on the proven theoretical ground of Barwise and Seligman's channel theory, provides a systematic and mechanized way for deploying it on a distributed environment to perform ontology mapping among a variety of different ontologies. They consider a mapping between two ontologies as a logic informorphism and they apply tools based channel theory to establish the semantic mapping.

Doan et al. (Doan, 2002) developed a system, GLUE, which employs machine learning techniques to find mappings. Given two ontologies, for each concept in one ontology, GLUE finds the most similar concept in the other ontology using probabilistic definitions of several practical similarity measures. It exploits information about the concept instance such as the frequencies of words in the text, instance names, the value formats, or the characteristics of value distributions. GLUE is an interesting approach and is applicable to semi-structured metadata such as those defined by XML Schema that implies a tree structure. However, it does not take into consideration the type of relationship between concepts. All mappings are considered as equivalence relationships.

Structural and syntactic solutions such Cupid (Madhavan, 2001) can be applied with success for semi-structured metadata but it does not offer a

Figure 8. Metadata multimedia integration system architecture

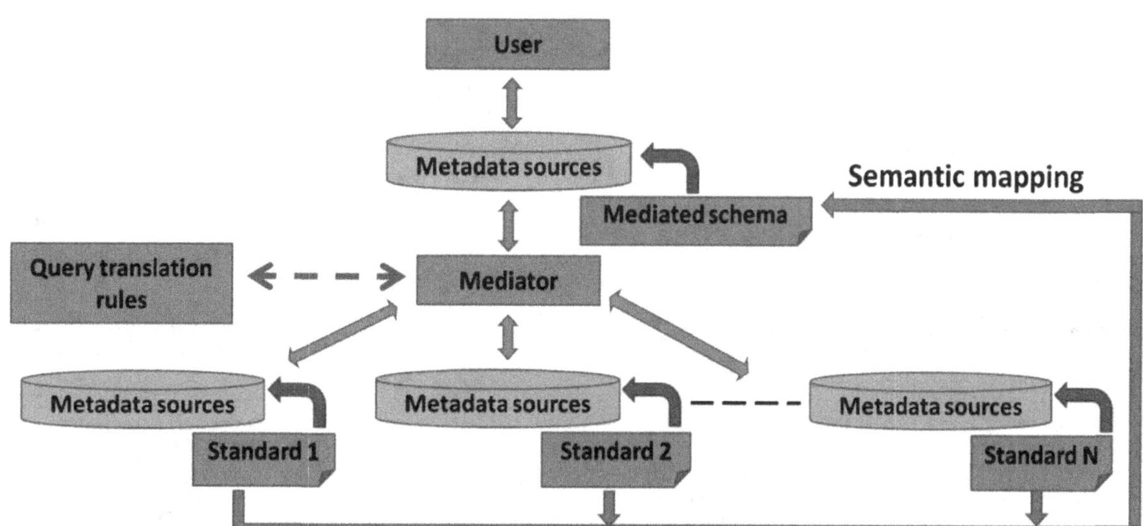

good mean to resolve heterogeneity problem that can arise while considering semantic resources.

Nevertheless, some of these approaches are purely semantic and give interesting results in specific domain depending on the complexity of semantic and structure of resources. In the next section we will present the approach that we consider it as a compatible with the complexity of multimedia metadata and it is applicable for our suggested framework.

MULTIMEDIA METADATA INTEGRATION SYSTEM

Firstly, we present the overview of our approach. Secondly, we discuss some issues and solutions regarding the homogenization of schema languages used before illustrating how we envision computing mappings between various concepts using formal tools such as Description Logic (Baader, 2003).

Overview of the Approach

Figure 8 shows the general architecture of multimedia metadata integration system. This system helps users to interpret metadata encoded by external formats (other than the one adopted as the mediated format). The specification of external formats is done by other communities which use different technologies to encode multimedia contents and contexts. The user of the integration system is not able de understand the meaning of this external metadata if it does not have a pre-knowledge about it. The framework described below is a solution to deal with this problem. It allows user to access existing metadata requiring knowledge only about the mediated schema.

With a view to making a good understanding of the role of this framework, we present in Figure 9 an integrated mapping which we are experimenting within the CAM4HOME ITEA2 project. Figure 9 shows a fragment of CAM4Home metadata model (that plays the role of the mediated schema) mapped to two other metadata standard (DIG35 and MPEG7) fragments. The role of mapping consists of facilitating the access

Figure 9. Example of CAM4Home metadata fragment mapped to DIG35 and MPEG7

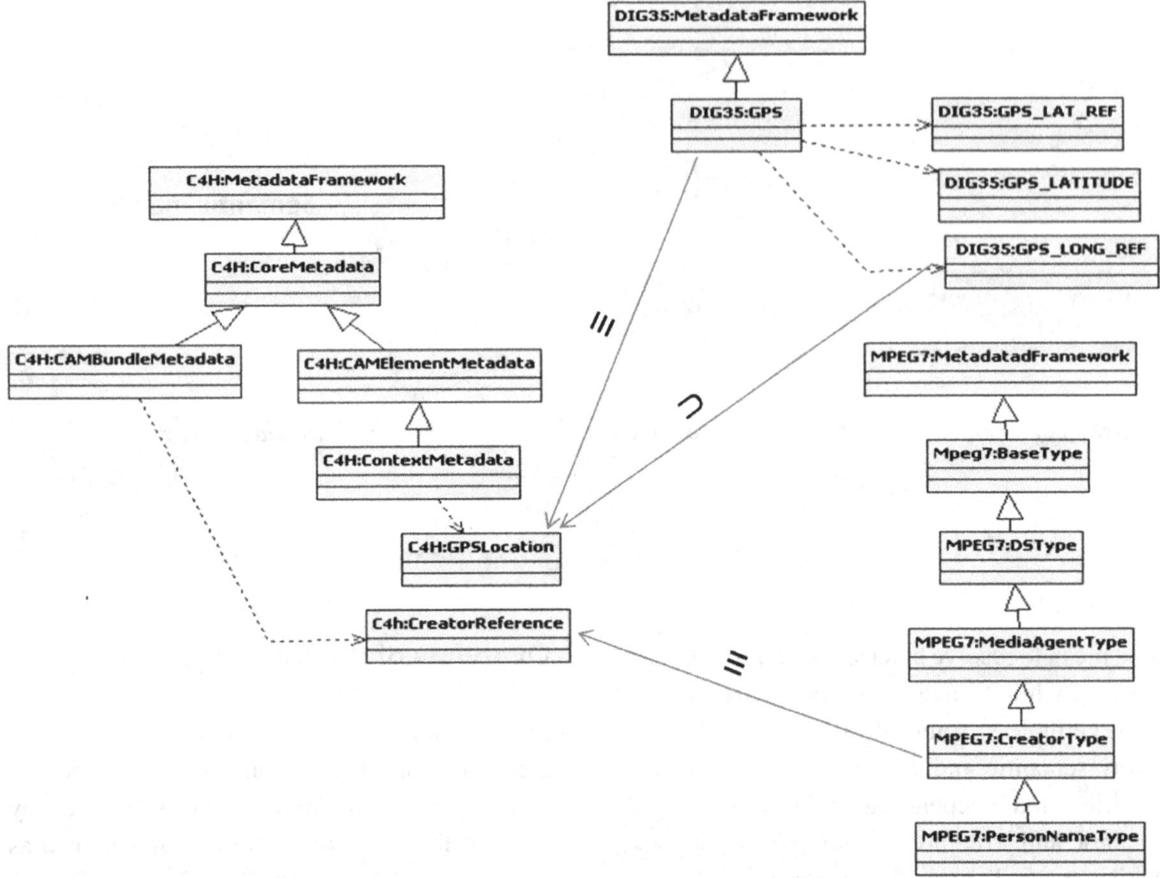

to information of users regardless of the encoding used by external standards. For instance, if a CAM4HOME user asks the following query *get c4h:CreatorReference of MediaObject#1* and if this information is not natively available in CAM-4HOME format, the integration system exploits existing mapping in order to rewrite queries and to retrieve metadata from MPEG-7. Hence, the user does not have to look by itself for equivalent queries tailored for MPEG-7 constructs. The integration system must find the equivalence relationship between concepts in the mediated schema and external metadata standards considered for integration.

The framework that we present here enables the construction of single *virtual integrated metadata* sources that regroups information required by services or users dealing with metadata. With this framework user does need any pre-knowledge about all standards to be able to interpret their meaning. End-user requests metadata from virtual integrated metadata source which is the interface between end user and all available metadata resources.

Virtual integrated metadata interpreter sends the query to metadata source mediator which will use translation rules to transform the query so it matches the available metadata sources containing the metadata corresponding to the query. Translation rules are defined according to the semantic mapping done between the mediated schema and different schemas describing metadata standards.

Finally, metadata sources mediator translates query results via rules back language used by virtual integrated metadata source. The solution we propose follows a Local As View approach. As each source is integrated independently of the other, the system is flexible and does not require recomputing all mappings when a new standard is integrated. In contrast to Local As View, adding, deleting, updating one standard integrated in the system requires a total change of mapping because the properties of the mediated schema elements were extracted according to the global mapping previously done.

To implement the framework described here above, four main challenges have to be taken into consideration:

1. Syntactic heterogeneity due to the diversity of existing description language. This kind of heterogeneity is resolved by the homogenization of all standards to a unique format able to express all semantics available in each standard. The conversion must capture all semantics in original schemas.
2. Finding the semantic alignment between mediated schema and metadata multimedia standards. This step is done after the homogenization.
3. Query translation rules definition according to the complex alignment done between mediated schema and metadata standards.
4. Identification of all information encoded by different metadata format and describing a given multimedia object.

In the following we will only talk about two first challenges which are described in the next sections.

Multimedia Metadata Homogenization

Homogenization is a necessary stage to implement our suggested framework. (Kalfoglou, 2003) consider that a common representation language is often necessary in order to create a semantic mapping between heterogeneous resources. Therefore, the challenge at this stage of the work is to specify a set of translation rules to convert between different encoding schema languages (XML Schema, RDF Schema, OWL).This step must be done with a minimum loss of structural and semantic information.

Several research works have been done during the last few years in order to resolve heterogeneity problem. Some of them focus on the syntactic level of resources to resolve semantic ambiguity (Chaudhri, 1998). Others have showed that using different syntax or structure formalization is source of various errors when transforming a representation into another (Bowers, 2000).

Since the appearance of XML, several multimedia standards have adopted XML to describe their metadata (MPEG-7, TV-Anytime, MPEG-21, IEEELOM (LOM, 2002), SCORM (SCORM, 2004), etc.). However, XML Schema provides support for explicit structural, cardinality and datatyping constraints, but offers little support for the semantic knowledge necessary to enable flexible mapping between metadata domains. RDF schema has appeared to cope with XML Schema semantic limitations (Antoniou, 2008). It provides support for rich semantic descriptions but provide limited support for the specification of local usage constraints. Finally, OWL appeared as extension of RDF Schema, it allows maximum semantic expressiveness. These three description languages mentioned previously cover a large amount of multimedia metadata standards (Hausenblas, 2007). For this reason we will restrict our study to them within the integration framework we plan to implement.

In order to implement our suggested framework we chose to use OWL-DL (McGuinness, 2004) which is sub-language of OWL as a common language. OWL-DL has a sufficient expressiveness for all types of multimedia metadata. Besides, existing mapping approaches based on logic description methods cannot be applicable to OWL-Full ontology which is sometimes undecidable.

In order to convert XML Schema to OWL several approaches have been proposed during the last few years to alleviate the lack of formal semantics in XML documents by converting this latest to OWL ontology. Authors in (Matthias, 2004) made a conversion only between XML Schema and OWL without considering XML instance metadata, (Battle, 2004) has proposed an approach to convert XML document to OWL ontology using XML Schema. If this latest is not available they generate it from XML data instance. Bohring et al. (Bohring, 2005) proposed a framework for converting a single XML instance document to an OWL model. Authors in (Garcia, 2005) used an approach called XSD2OWL to transform an XML Schema into a set of OWL ontologies.

Authors of XSD2OWL introduced an adjustment to first versions of XSD2OWL in order to alleviate some lacks relative to some implicit semantic after the conversion of XML Schema into OWL ontology. The XSD2OWL produces three ontologies: one describing the domain concepts of the XML Schema, a second one describing the user-defined value types used by the XML Schema and finally a third one, keeping track of the structure information (position of properties in complex elements descriptions). The latest ontology is necessary as all syntactic information (like the order of properties) is lost when passing to OWL encodings. The XSD2OWL mapping has been successfully applied to the MPEG-7 XML Schemas producing a MPEG-7 Ontology. The result got from this conversion is interesting from our point of view. However, the ontology produced is OWL-Full which is undecidable.

We think that the XS2OWL algorithm described in (Chrisa, 2007) is more suitable for the homogenization step as it responds to the following requirements: It outputs OWL-DL ontologies, which gives us the opportunity to use inference based on description logic to find semantic mapping. It conserves all structural information which can be used for the mapping. Besides, the XS2OWL model and its implementation has been successfully applied to several *de-facto* multimedia standards (IEEE LOM, MPEG-21, MPEG-7 and others) and its results showed that the captured semantics is similar with the manually created one.

Concerning the conversion from RDF Schema to OWL, we know that OWL is an extension of RDF Schema. OWL inherits and extends RDF Schema characteristics. Therefore, any document which is valid according to RDF Schema is valid as an OWL-Full ontology. However, this condition is not always satisfied for OWL-DL (Patel-Schneider, 2004). For this reason we must distinguish between OWL-Full and OWL-DL. Besides, the ontology result must be syntactically compatible with the result of XS2OWL algorithm mentioned before.

Before presenting in detail the method for computing mappings between concepts in various multimedia metadata standards, we recall the main conclusion of the homogenization step. A common schema description language is needed for computing coherent mappings. OWL-DL, notably due to its decidability feature, was selected for playing the role of common schema description language within the integration framework. XS2OWL tool will be used to convert XML Schema to OWL-DL. A tool for converting RDF Schema to OWL-DL will be developed within the framework.

Semantic Method for Multimedia Metadata Mapping

The mapping process is a two step process. The first one consists in associating explicit meaning to concepts issued from various standards created by communities having specific backgrounds. The explicit meanings are defined with regard to a neutral external semantic resource. In the following, we use WordNet to do explicitation. However other resources such as DBpedia (Auer, 2008) or YAGO (Suchanek, 2008) can be

Figure 10. (a) Mediated schema (on the left-side), (b) fragment of DIG35 (DIG35, 2002) standard ontology

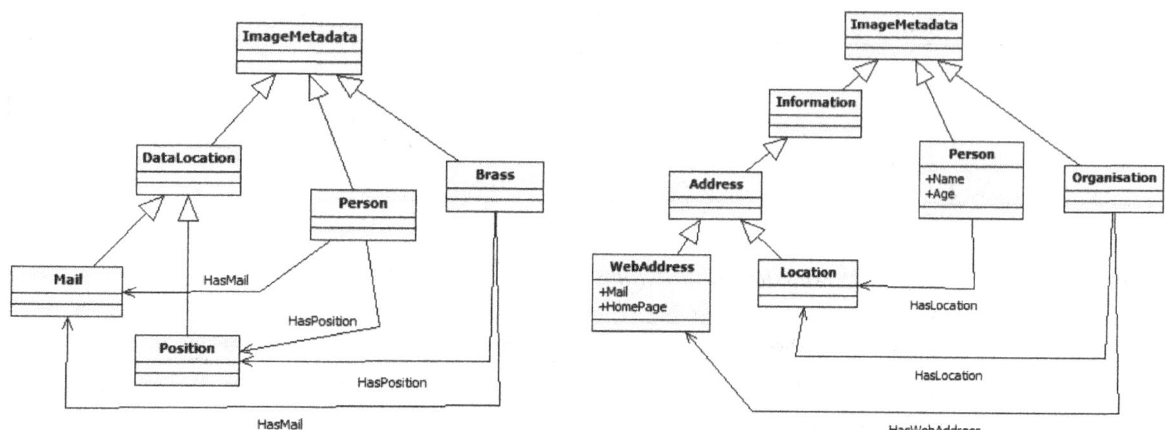

considered as external resources in order to increase the neutrality of the explicitation process.

Multimedia Metadata Explicitation

Because of the richness of natural language, different multimedia ontologies maybe use different terminologies to denote the same concept. The explicitation of concept meanings is a necessary step to offer adequate solution for facing the linguistic heterogeneity (Bouquet, 2003). Explicitation is done by giving all possible interpretations of each concept via an external resource which contain a set of synonyms for each concept.

We use WordNet (Fellbaum, 1998) as an external resource for explicitation. WordNet is an on-line lexical reference system developed at Princeton University. It consists of synonym sets called synsets, and each synset represents a single distinct concept. For instance, the right-hand side of Figure 10 is a part of DIG35 standard ontology created manually. The explicitation of the embedded Organization concept is represented by seven synsets returned by WordNet: (Organization#1∪ …∪Organization#7).

Each synset corresponds to a specific meaning of the Organization concept. For instance, the Organization#1synset contains words (sister terms, hyponyms, etc) related to the notion of *a group of people who work together*. For instance, the Organization#1synset contains words (sister terms, hyponyms, etc) related to the notion of *an organized structure for arranging or classifying*.

Concepts explicitation is a necessary step because it gives to each concept all possible interpretations for it. However, concepts explicitation can also result in a wide enlargement of the field of meaning of concepts. The selection of pertinent classes of words considered (sister terms, hyponyms, etc.) for each synset is an open issue. Sense filtering is a needful operation which allows the selection of the real meaning of concept. In order to select the real meaning of a given concept C on the hierarchy H, sense filtering operation uses, n neighbors of C $(C_{1,}\ldots_{,} C_{l})$ with regard to the hierarchy H. Other resources can be also helpful for sense filtering operation (e.g. extraction of semantic from documentation, user comment, and social tags for instance).

Mapping Discovering Using DL

Notwithstanding the existing approaches for ontology mapping, DL based techniques are more appropriate for that, since they rely on the explicit and formal semantics represented by ontologies. When used for comparing ontologies, they ensure that the original semantics of resources is

Table 2. DL axioms and corresponding set relations

DL Axioms		Set relations
$C1 \subseteq C2$	⇔	$C1 \cap \neg C2$ is unsatisfiable.
$C1 \supseteq C2$	⇔	$C2 \cap \neg C1$ is unsatisfiable.
$C1 \equiv C2$	⇔	$C1 \cap \neg C2$ is unsatisfiable and $C2 \cap \neg C1$ is unsatisfiable.
$C1 \perp C2$	⇔	$C1 \cap C2$ is unsatisfiable.

Table 3. WordNet relations vs. subsumption axioms

Relations in WordNet	Subsumption axioms
$term_1$ *meronym* $term_2$	$term_1 \subseteq term_2$
$term_1$ *holonym* $term_2$	$term_2 \subseteq term_1$
$term_1$ *hyponym* $term_2$	$term_1 \subseteq term_2$
$term_1$ *hypernym* $term_2$	$term_2 \subseteq term_1$

preserved. Besides, DL provides an explicit and a formal interpretation of concepts (Amir, 2009).

A valid semantic mapping between two concepts C_1 and C_2 belonging, respectively, to ontologies O1 and O_2 is a logical relationship (⊆- left subsumption, ⊇-right subsumption, ≡ - equivalence and ⊥- disjointness -). This logical relationship can be computed starting from the explicitation results obtained from external resource and depending on the nature of the relationship it must satisfy one one of the operations shown in Table 2

In order to do inference between concepts, the relationships between concepts in mediated schema and multimedia metadata standards is computed by using the explicitation results provided by external resource. The results are transformed to the axioms as the premises of inference. To obtain this kind of axioms we analyze the relationship within the synsets provided by WordNet. WordNet organizes terms based on the semantic relations of them. So these relations are the origin of the generation of axioms. The table here bellows shows the transformation of relations of terms from WordNet to corresponding **subsumption** axioms.

Once the axiom is obtained by analyzing the retrieved WordNet synsets, we use Tableau algorithm that can be easily applied to DL as illustrated in (Baader, 2001). The Tableau algorithm establishes the relationships between concepts by observing one of the four conditions of satisfaction mentioned above, which corresponds to the axiom to be validated.

Tableau algorithm belongs to a class of algorithms that use subsumption expansion in order to prove the satisfability of a relation (e.g. $C1 \subseteq C2$). The Tableau algorithm expands each ontology concept by considering the subsumption axioms deduced from WordNet relations. Then it tries to prove the satisfiability of the considered relation by verifying the coherence of the set relations as indicated in Table 2. The relation itself can be seen as a *complex* concept (C) that is defined by the associated set relations.

The algorithm exhaustively applies **tableau rules** which decompose the syntactic structure of this *complex* concept in order to construct a so-called ***completion tree***. Each node (x) of a *completion* is labeled with a concept set $L(x) \subseteq sub(C)$ where sub(C) is a set of sub-concepts composing the concept C. Each edge $<x, y>$ is

Figure 11. Tableau algorithm expansion rules

$\cap$ - rule: if (1) $(C_1 \cap C_2) \in L(x)$
(2) $\{ C_1, C_2 \} \not\subset L(x)$
then $L(x) \rightarrow L(x) \cup \{ C_1, C_2 \}$
$\cup$ - rule: if (1) $(C_1 \cup C_2) \in L(x)$
(2) $\{ C_1, C_2 \} \cap L(x) = \perp$
then $L(x) \rightarrow L(x) \cup \{ C \}$ for some $C \in \{ C_1, C_2 \}$
$\exists$ - rule: if (1) $\exists S.C \in L(x)$
(2) x has no S-neighbor y with $C \in L(y)$
then create a new node y with $L(\langle x, y \rangle) = S$
and $L(y) = \{ C \}$
$\forall$ - rule: if (1) $\forall S.C \in L(x)$
(2) there is an S-neighbor y of x with $C \notin L(y)$,
then $L(y) \rightarrow L(y) \cup \{ C \}$

labeled by $L(\langle x, y \rangle) = R$ for some role R occurring in *sub(C)*, where the *sub(C)* is the set of sub-concepts of *C*.

The expansion rules are illustrated in Figure 11. The algorithm terminates when the graph is complete (no further inference is possible) and returns "mapping satisfiable", or when contradiction have been revealed and return in this case "mapping unsatisfiable"; see (Baader, 2001) for details. This contradiction is called a clash and means that for some concepts C, $\{ C_1, \neg C_2 \} \subseteq L(x)$. This means that the concept C_1 and the negation of concept C_2 co-occurs and hence the subsumption relation is unsatisfiable.

In the following we illustrate how Tableau algorithm can be used to validate a mapping between two concepts belonging to two different schemas. We use a fragment of the DIG35 standard and the mediated schema proposed in Figure 10.

Firstly, we start to extract the logic formula for each concept in two schemas (Bouquet, 2003), this step is done after concepts explicitation step (see Figure 12).

Secondly, we apply the sense filtering operations on available synsets. The aim of this filtering is to identify which one of the synsets is closer to the meaning of the concept in the ontology where he was initially defined. Hence, the sense filtering operation is taking into account the context of the source ontology by examining the neighboring concepts. For instance, if we consider the DIG-35 fragment considered, synsets associated with the Organization concept but containing terms which are not at all related with at least one of neighboring concepts: location, address or image will be left out. Same filtering can be applied to the Brass concepts in the mediated schema.

In the current example, the Organization#3 and Brass#3 synsets are the result of filtering operations. Both synsets refer to "the persons (or committees or departments etc.) who make up a body for the purpose of administering something". As they are belonging to the same synset then they can be represented by the same label, which means that there is an equivalence relationship between the two atomic concepts according to WordNet. However, this is not always true when considering complex structures because the meaning of a given atomic concept depends also on its hierarchy in the schema. Therefore, this relationship is considered as an axiom and has to be validated.

Figure 12. Logic formula extracted

$$C_1 = C\ (\text{Organization}) =$$

$$(\text{Organization\#1} \cup \ldots. \cup \text{Organization\#8}) \cap$$

$$\forall \text{HasLocation}.(\text{Location\#1} \cup \ldots. \cup \text{Location\#4}) \cap$$

$$\forall \text{HasWebAddress}.((\text{Web\#1} \cup \ldots. \cup \text{Web\#7}) \cap$$

$$(\text{Address\#1} \cup \ldots. \cup \text{Address\#8})) \cap$$

$$(\text{Image\#1} \cup \ldots. \cup \text{Image\#9}).\ (1)$$

$$C_2 = C\ (\text{Brass}) =$$

$$(\text{Brass\#1} \cup \ldots. \cup \text{Brass\#7}) \cap$$

$$\forall \text{HasPosition}.(\text{Position\#1} \cup \ldots. \cup \text{Position\#16}) \cap)\ (2)$$

$$\forall \text{HasMail}.(\text{Mail\#1} \cup \ldots. \cup \text{Mail\#5}) \cap (\text{Image\#1} \cup \ldots. \cup \text{Image\#9})$$

Table 4. List of concept and relations

C_{11}= (Organization#3)
C_{12} = (Location#1 ∪ .... ∪ Location#4)
C_{13}= (Web#1 ∪ .... ∪ Web#7)
C_{14} = (Address#1 ∪ .... ∪ Adress#8)
C_{15} = (Image#1 ∪ .... ∪Image#9)
C_{21}= (Brass#3)
C_{22}= (Posotion#1 ∪ .... ∪ Position#16)
C_{23} = (Mail#1 ∪....∪Mail#5)
R_1= HasLocation, R_2= HasWebAddress, R3= HasPosition, R_4= HasMail

The axiom stating that C_1 and C_2 are equivalent is explicitated here below:

$C_1 \equiv C_2 \Leftrightarrow C_1 \cap \neg C_2$ is unsatisfiable and $C_2 \cap \neg C_1$ is unsatisfiable.

To compute the validity of the axiom we introduce new concepts and relations starting from (1) and (2) equations. We also restrain the number of synsets corresponding the filtering applied to the mapped concepts (see C_{11} and C_{21} concept sets). The list of concept and relations are presented in Table 4.

Since Organization#3 and Brass#3 belong to the same synset according to WordNet, they can be represented by the same label $C_{11.}$ However, this is not necessary mean that the mapping is validated. We have to validate or invalidate the axiom by testing the satisfaction of the corresponding DL-axiom (from Table 2). Hence (1) and (2) equations become:

$$C_1 = C_{11} \cap \forall R_1.\ C_{12} \cap \forall R_2.\ (C_{13} \cap C_{14}) \cap C_{15}$$

$$C_2 = C_{11} \cap \forall R_3.\ C_{22} \cap \forall R_4.\ C_{23} \cap C_{15.}$$

We apply the De Morgan's law to transform the concepts to negation normal form

$$\neg C_2 = \neg C_{11} \cup \exists R_3.\ \neg C_2 \cup \exists R_4.\ \neg C_{23} \cup \neg C_{15}$$

The tableau algorithm initializes a tree T which contains initially only one node x0 labeled with the following concept set: L(x0) = {C1 ∩ ¬C2}, called the root node. The Tableau rules showed in Figure 11 in order to extend L(x0).If tableau algorithm returns unsatisfiable for C1 ∩¬C2 as well as for the second tree computed starting from the concept set C2 ∩¬C1, then the axiom C1≡ C2 can be considered as a valid mapping.

In order for the Tableau algorithm to expand rules in a coherent manner we need to consider equally the explicitation of relations and related concepts involved in the equations. Hence, this solution exhibits a recursive behavior. Currently, we are working on studying the depth of the recursion tree to consider. At the leaf levels, we only consider the mapping provided by WordNet synset comparisons without verifying the equivalence (or partial subsumption) by using Tableau algorithm. For the current experience, we have applied to all relations and related concepts the mapping obtained following the WordNet synset comparison. The results obtained from WordNet show that R_1 maps on R_3 and R_2 (partially) maps on R_3. Under this assumption, the Tableau algorithm validates the mapping of C_1 and C_2.

FUTURE RESEARCH DIRECTIONS

We described in the previous sections some existing tools which can be used to integrate heterogeneous multimedia metadata. We have shown DL characteristics and its advantages to discover a mapping between mediated multimedia metadata ontologies. Since DL is monotonic, we also consider getting other semantic resources involved especially in the explicitation process. They allow enriching schema semantic, sense filtering, enhancing semantic mapping between concepts. An external resource does not mean necessary thesaurus such WordNet but any kind of information that can be extracted from other corpus (e.g., user comment, social tags, documentation provided by communities that have created multimedia metadata standards, etc). Since these corpuses contain fuzzy information, we consider testing other methods based fuzzy logic or probabilistic approaches for discovering semantic mapping.

CONCLUSION

This paper has given an overview of multimedia metadata heterogeneity problems and discussed issues related to an integration system based on DL. We have shown how to homogenize different metadata format in order resolve syntaxic heterogeneity of existing schema description languages. Homogenization is achieved by translating all schema specifications (done mainly in XML Schema or RDF Schema) to OWL-DL. Homogenization methods that preserve the structural information of originals schemas and that capture source schema implicit semantics were presented. We have migrated all schema description to OWL-DL as this ontology language fits well with metadata semantics representation and it supports description logic reasoning. DL is a powerful logical framework issued from the domain of knowledge representation which exhibits high expressiveness constructs. In order to facilitate the mapping between concepts, the precise meaning of concepts within the given context must be first explicitated. The explicitation is done via external resources in order to give all possible interpretation of concepts in schemas. As we have shown before, explicitation is a necessary operation; it must be done in order to select the real meaning of each concept. Since all these steps are done, the mapping can be considered as a DL axiom which must satisfy some conditions. Conditions validation can be tested using Tableau algorithm and its rule-based extension mechanism.

ACKNOWLEDGMENT

This work was kindly supported by the ITEA2 CAM4HOME project.

REFERENCES

Advanced Distributed Learning (ADL) Technical Team. (2004). *Sharable content object reference model (SCORM)*. Retrieved April 2004, from http://www.adlnet.org/ Technologies/scorm/ default.aspx

Amir, S. (2009). Un système d'intégration de métadonnées dédiées au multimédia. *In Informatique des Organisations et Systèmes d'Information et de Décision* (pp. 490-492). Toulouse, France.

Amir, S., Bilasco, I. M., & Djeraba, C. (2009). *A semantic approach to metadata management in sensor systems* (pp. 112–119). Paris, France: Cognitive Systems with Interactive Sensors.

Antoniou, G., & Harmelen, F. V. (2008). *A Semantic Web primer* (2nd ed.). Cambridge, MA: The MIT Press.

Auer, S., Bizer, C., Kobilarov, G., Lehmann, J., Cyganiak, R., & Ives, Z. (2008). DBpedia: A nucleus for a Web of open data. In *International Semantic Web Conference: LNCS 4825,* (pp. 722-735).

Baader, F., Calvanese, D., McGuinness, D. L., Nardi, D., & Patel-Schneider, P. (2003). *The description logic handbook, theory, implementation, and applications*. Cambridge University Press.

Baader, F., & Sattler, U. (2001). An overview of tableau algorithms for description logics. In *Studia Logica, 69*(1), 5-40. Springer.

Battle, S. (2004). *Round-tripping between XML and RDF.* In the 3rd International Semantic Web Conference.

Bilasco, I. M., Amir, S., Blandin, P., Djeraba, C., Laitakari, J., Martinet, J., ... Zhou, J. (2010). Semantics for intelligent delivery of multimedia content. *SAC ACM.*

Bilasco, I. M., Gensel, J., Villanova-Oliver, M., & Martin, H. (2005). On indexing of 3D scenes using MPEG-7. *Proceedings of the 13th ACM Conference on Multimedia,* (pp. 471-474).

Bohring, H., & Auer, S. (2005). Mapping XML to OWL ontologies. *LeipzigerInformatik-Tage, volume 72 of LNI,* (pp. 147-156). GI Publisher.

Bouquet, P., Serafini, L., & Zanobini, S. (2003). Semantic coordination: A new approach and an application. *International Semantic Web Conference, LNCS 2870*, (pp. 130-145).

Bowers, S., & Delcambre, L. (2000). Representing and transforming model-based information. *First Workshop on the Semantic Web at the Fourth European Conference on Digital Libraries*. (pp. 18-20). Lisbon, Portugal.

Brickley, D. (2004). *RDF vocabulary description language 1.0: RDF schema*. Retrieved February 10, 2004, from http://www.w3.org/TR/ rdf-schema/

Chang, S. F., Sikora, T., & Puri, A. (2001). Overview of the MPEG-7 standard. *IEEE Transactions on Circuits and Systems for Video Technology, 11*, 688–695. doi:10.1109/76.927421

Chaudhri, V. K., Farquhar, A., Fikes, R., Karp, P. D., & Rice, J. P. (1998). OKBC: A programmatic foundation for knowledge base interoperability. In *Proceedings of the 15th National Conference on Artificial Intelligence and of the 10th Conference on Innovative Applications on Artificial Intelligence,* (pp. 600-607). AAAI Press.

Chrisa, T., & Stavros, C. (2007). Interoperability of XML schema applications with OWL domain knowledge and Semantic Web tools. In *On the Move to Meaningful Internet Systems, OTM2007, Part I, LNCS 4803*, (pp. 850–869).

DIG35. (2002). *Metadata standard for digital images*. Retrieved June 2002, from http://xml.coverpages.org/ dig35.html

Doan, A., Madhavan, J., Domingos, P., & Halevy, A. (2002). *Learning to map between ontologies on the Semantic Web.* In the 11th International World Wide Web Conference, (pp. 662-673), Hawaii, USA.

Doan, A. H., Domingos, P., & Levy, A. (2000). *Learning source descriptions for data integration.* In the Workshop at the Conference of the American Association for Artificial Intelligence, (pp. 81–92).

Doerr, M., Hunter, J., & Lagoze, C. (2003). Towards a core ontology for information integration. *Journal of Digital Information*, *4*(1).

Fellbaum, C. (1998). *WordNet: An electronic lexical database*. Cambridge: The MIT Press.

Garcia, R., & Celma, O. (2005). *Semantic integration and retrieval of multimedia meta-data.* In the 5th International Workshop on Knowledge Markup and Semantic Annotation (pp. 69-80).

Hausenblas, M. (2007). *Multimedia vocabularies on the Semantic Web*. Retrieved July 2007, from http://www.w3.org/2005/ Incubator/mmsem/ XGR-vocabularies-20070724/

Hunter, J. (2003). Enhancing the semantic interoperability of multimedia through a core ontology. *IEEE Trans. on Circuits and Systems for Video Technology*, *13*, 49–58. doi:10.1109/ TCSVT.2002.808088

ID3. (1999). *Developer information*. Retrieved September 2007, from http://www.id3.org/ Developer_Information

IPTC. (2008). *Standard photo metadata*, June 2008. Retrieved June 2008, from http://www.iptc.org/ std/ photometadata/2008/ specification/ IPTC-PhotoMetadata-2008.pdf

ITEA2-CAM4Home. (2008). *Collaborative aggregated multimedia for digital home.* Retrieved May 2008, from http://www.cam4home-itea.org/

Kalfoglou, Y., & Schorlemmer, M. (2002). *Information-flow-based ontology mapping*. In the 1st International Conference on Ontologies, Databases and Application of Semantics, (pp. 98-127). Irvine, CA.

Kalfoglou, Y., & Schorlemmer, M. (2003). Ontology mapping: The state of the art. *The Knowledge Engineering Review*, *18*(1), 1–31. doi:10.1017/ S0269888903000651

Klyne, G., Reynolds, F., Woodrow, C., Ohto, H., Hjelm, J., Butler, M. H., & Tran, L. (2004). *Composite capability/preference profiles (CC/PP): Structure and vocabularies 1.0.* W3C recommendation. Retrieved January 2004, from http:// www.w3.org/ TR/ CCPP-struct-vocab/

Madhavan, J., Bernstein, P. A., & Rahm, E. (2001). *Generic schema matching with Cupid.* In the 27th International Conference on Very Large Data Bases, (pp. 49-58).

Matthias, F., Christian, Z., & David, T. (2004). *Lifting XML schema to OWL*. In the 4th International Conference of Web Engineering, (pp. 354-358).

McGuinness, D. L., & Harmelen, F. V. (2004). *OWL Web ontology language overview*. Retrieved February 2004, from http://www.w3.org/ TR/ owl-features

Patel-Schneider, P. F., Hayes, P., & Horrocks, I. (2004). *OWL Web ontology language semantic and abstract syntax.* W3C recommendation. Retrieved February 2004, from http://www.w3.org/ TR/owl-semantics/

Pereira, F. (2001). The MPEG-21 standard: Why an open multimedia framework? Springer. *Interactive Distributed Multimedia Systems, LNCS, 2158*, 219–220. doi:10.1007/3-540-44763-6_23

Rahm, E., & Bernstein, P. A. (2001). A survey of approaches to automatic schema matching. *The VLDB Journal, 10*(4), 334–350. doi:10.1007/s007780100057

Shvaiko, P., & Euzenat, J. (2005). A survey of schema-based matching approaches. *Journal on Data Semantics, 5*(1), 146–171.

Suchanek, F., Kasneci, G., & Weikum, G. (2008). Yago - A large ontology from Wikipedia and WordNet. *Elsevier Journal of Web Semantics, 6*(3), 203–217. doi:10.1016/j.websem.2008.06.001

Thompson, H. S., Mendelsohn, N., Beech, D., & Maloney, M. (2009). *W3C xml schema definition language (XSD) 1.1 part 1: Structure*. W3C candidate recommendation, April 2009. Retrieved April 2009, from http://www.w3.org/TR/xmlschema11-1/

Troncy, R. (2003). *Integrating structure and semantics into audio-visual documents*. In the 2nd International Semantic Web Conference, (pp. 566-581).

Tsinaraki, C., Polydoros, P., & Christodoulakis, S. (2004). *Integration of OWL ontologies in MPEG-7 and TVAnytime compliant semantic indexing*. In the 16th International Conference on Advanced Information Systems Engineering, (pp. 299 - 325).

TV-Anytime Forum, Metadata Working Group. (2003). *Metadata specification version 1.3*. Retrieved March 2003, from ftp://tva:tva@ftp.bbc.co.uk/Specifications/COR3_SP003v13.zip

Vetro, A., & Timmerer, C. (2005). Digital item adaptation overview of standardization and research activities. *IEEE Transactions on Multimedia, 7*(3), 418–426. doi:10.1109/TMM.2005.846795

Vocabulary Workspace, E. X. I. F. (2004). *RDF schema.* Retrieved December 2003, from http://www.w3.org/ 2003/12/exif/

WG12: Learning Object Metadata. (2002). *Learning object metadata standard.* Retrieved December 2002, from http://ltsc.ieee.org/wg12/

Weibel, S. Kunze, J., Lagoze, C., & Wolf, M. (1998).*Dublin Core metadata for resource discovery*. Retrieved April 1998, from http://www.ietf.org/ rfc/rfc2413.txt

Won Suk, L., Burger, T., Sasaki, F., & Malaise, V. (2009). *Use cases and requirements for ontology and API for media object 1.0.* W3C Working Group.

XMP. (2008). *Specification, part 2.* Retrieved January 2008, from http://www.adobe.com/devnet/ xmp/pdfs/XMPSpecificationPart2.pdf

Yahoo. Media RSS Module. (2008). *RSS 2.0 module*. Retrieved January 2004, from http://video.search.yahoo.com/ mrss

ENDNOTES

1 www.cam4home-itea.org

2 www.mpeg.org

3 www.w3.org

4 www.dublincore.org

5 www.cam4home-itea.org

Chapter 12
Abstractions in Intelligent Multimedia Databases:
Application of Layered Architecture and Visual Keywords for Intelligent Search

Ranjan Parekh
Jadavpur University, India

Nalin Sharda
Victoria University, Australia

ABSTRACT

Semantic characterization is necessary for developing intelligent multimedia databases, because humans tend to search for media content based on their inherent semantics. However, automated inference of semantic concepts derived from media components stored in a database is still a challenge. The aim of this chapter is to demonstrate how layered architectures and "visual keywords" can be used to develop intelligent search systems for multimedia databases. The layered architecture is used to extract meta-data from multimedia components at various layers of abstractions. While the lower layers handle physical file attributes and low-level features, the upper layers handle high-level features and attempts to remove ambiguities inherent in them. To access the various abstracted features, a query schema is presented, which provides a single point of access while establishing hierarchical pathways between feature-classes. Minimization of the semantic gap is addressed using the concept of "visual keyword" (VK). "Visual keywords" are segmented portions of images with associated low- and high-level features, implemented within a semantic layer on top of the standard low-level features layer, for characterizing semantic content in media components. Semantic information is however predominantly expressed in textual form, and hence is susceptible to the limitations of textual descriptors – viz. ambiguities related to synonyms, homonyms, hypernyms, and hyponyms. To handle such ambiguities, this chapter proposes a domain specific ontology-based layer on top of the semantic layer, to increase the effectiveness of the search process.

DOI: 10.4018/978-1-61350-126-9.ch012

INTRODUCTION

Over the last couple of decades a number of multimedia applications such as: digital photo albums, computer based training, games and entertainment, online galleries, medical applications, and information kiosks have led to the growth of large repositories of digital media. Muller (2004) states that "The Radiology Department of the University Hospital of Geneva alone produced more than 12,000 images a day in 2002" (p. 1).

In this scenario a fast and efficient search and retrieval mechanism from these repositories assumes a fundamental importance, as a repository without a retrieval mechanism is comparable to a library without a catalog – even though all the information is present, it is practically inaccessible to somebody with a specific search criteria.

Therefore, the issue of having a multimedia repository that can be searched efficiently has become of paramount importance, in other words, "The question we now need to answer is how to build a multimedia database around a multimedia repository" (Baral, 1998, p. 38).

Otherwise, "Much similarly to the case of books in a library that have not been indexed, information stored in a multimedia archive that cannot be searched, identified, and accessed easily is practically unavailable" (Wallace, 2006, p. 34).

Earliest attempts in building multimedia repositories amenable to search and retrieval has been though textual annotations. However, many drawbacks to this approach soon became apparent; some of these include:

- It requires manual annotation and processing, hence it becomes time consuming.
- Search results are dependent on exact matching of text strings, hence the presented results are not complete.
- Search efficiency is limited by subjective nature of textual descriptions; hence it can lead to false and missed matches.
- Support for Query-by-Example (QBE) is not possible; hence the user needs to be good at formulating the query.

To overcome these limitations the research community focused on Content Based Storage and Retrieval (CBSR) techniques, in which features are extracted directly from the media files by automated algorithms, and used as metadata for their subsequent search and retrieval. A number of research prototype systems have been developed, for example: QBIC (Niblack, 1993), CORE (Wu, 1995), PhotoBook (Pentland, 1996), VisualSEEK (Smith, 1996), and the Digital Library Project (DLP) of the University of California (Belongie, 1997).

However, there are still a number of unresolved research issues, such as the following three:

Compatibility: Various systems developed independently are potentially incompatible with each other. Therefore, there is a need for integration with a uniform approach and a single point of access. However, this is not easy as pointed out by Liu (2001, p. 235): "Since each kind of multimedia data … has its own characteristics, it is very difficult to develop a uniform method for content-based retrieval." How to achieve a single point of access is also not fully resolved, as articulated by

Wallace (2006, p. 34): "The development of single points of access, providing common and uniform access to their data, despite the efforts and accomplishments of standardization organizations, has remained an open issue …"

Layered Architecture: Since multimedia metadata can belong to various levels of abstractions, there is a need for a layered or hierarchical approach to data analysis for a better understanding of media content. Comaniciu (2002, p. 603) points out that: "To improve performance, the execution of low-level tasks should be task driven i.e. supported by independent high level information."

One of the most widely used multimedia metadata standard is MPEG-7, however, "currently, the biggest shortcoming for MPEG-7 is that it cannot present the multimedia document in different layers and in different granularities." (Jianfeng, 2003, p. 414).

Semantic Gap: One of the important issues in most programming and information processing paradigms is that of bridging the semantic gap between the user's thought process and the computing systems' formalization. According to Deruyver (2005, p. 213) "... obtaining a correct (semantic) segmentation remains an open problem for many images of real life."

Furthermore, "The process by which perceptual and interpretive matter in an image is recognized, is as yet, an incompletely understood cognitive phenomenon" (Enser, 2005, p. 180).

This work tries to address these three issues by proposing a layered architecture for a multimedia database system with a content based mechanism for characterizing, searching and retrieving multimedia content at various abstraction levels, while using a single access point.

The objectives of this chapter are to report on the following issues:

1. Results of meta-research, including literature review on the evolution of multimedia databases and search methodologies.
2. An expose of layered architectures for multimedia databases.
3. Investigate effective means of characterizing semantic entities in media files by automatically generating textual captions.
4. Demonstrate how Visual Keywords can be used to automatically characterize semantic entities in images, as well as their spatial positions.
5. Outline details of an ontology-based layer to remove ambiguities related to textual descriptors.

MULTIMEDIA DATABASE LAYERED ARCHITECTURE

A number of layered architectures of multimedia databases have been proposed in literature. Some two-layer systems have been proposed to create a separation between the physical storage and the low-level (structural) features. The next level of abstraction has been built with the help of three-layered systems to handle high-level (semantic) features.

Related Work

Some early systems, such as, CORE, PhotoBook, and DLP focused only on text and images, with no support for audio and video. In later systems semantic features for audio and video were discussed; however, in these systems, the semantic descriptors are frequently typed by human annotators (Kosch, 2001; Wallace, 2006).

Content-based methods for automatically inferring semantic content have been proposed in recent years (Jianfeng, 2004). The main problem with such systems is that although information at the structural layer is expressed in terms of low-level feature vectors, information at the semantic layer is predominantly textual in nature. Consequently, these systems are susceptible to the limitations of textual descriptors; viz. different textual terms can have the same meaning (synonyms), while the same term can have multiple meanings in different contexts and domains (homonyms). Also, implicit relationships between different terms may not be clear unless explicitly defined, such as with hyponyms and hypernyms (a hyponym is a word or phrase that includes similar semantic range as included within another word, called its hypernym). These issues have been recognized by many authors, nonetheless, thus far, they have relied on domain experts to resolve such conflicts, as articulated by Jianfeng (2004, p. 38) "... there may be different explanations to

Figure 1. Multimedia database (MMDB) layered architecture

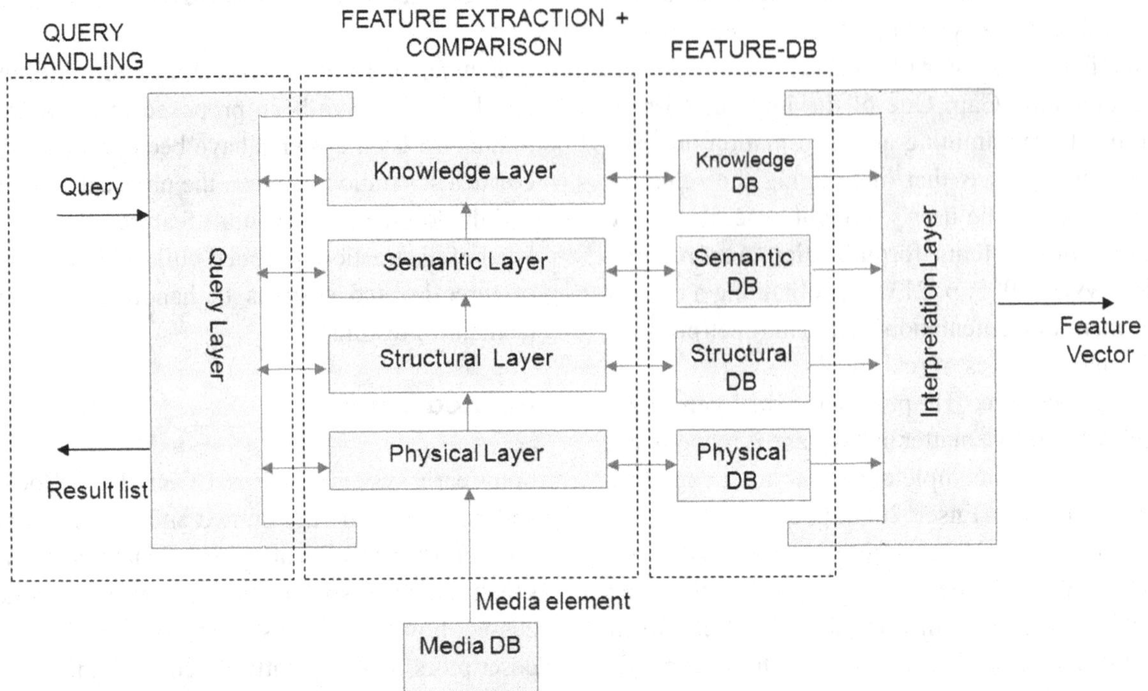

the one multimedia document. Only the experts can resolve these ambiguities."

One of the main contributions of the current work is to resolve these issues by proposing an ontology-based Knowledge-Layer above the Semantic-Layer, to provide knowledge disambiguation functions in a semi-automated manner. This Knowledge-Layer (along with an associated Knowledge-Database) acts as an interface between the Semantic-Layer (along with the associated Semantic-Database) and external domain-specific ontology files. Whenever the query engine with a search term associated with the Semantic-Layer fails to produce a hit, it transfers control to the Knowledge-Layer. The Knowledge-Layer looks up the term in a relevant ontology file and tries to find an association with related terms in the Semantic-Database. On finding such associations, it stores the same in the Knowledge-Database. A resubmission of the query to the Knowledge-Database subsequently produces a hit.

Proposed Architecture

Figure 1 depicts the proposed layered architecture. The major structural components of the proposed Multimedia Database (MMDB) consists of the media repository or media database (Media-DB) containing the media files; a feature extraction block containing algorithms for the extraction of features from the media files in an automated way; a feature database (Feature-DB) for storing the features; and a query handling block for accepting the queries from the user and forwarding them to a comparator, to compare the query features with the stored features in the Feature-DB. Based on the similarity criteria specified by the user, in conjunction with the query, a result list is generated and fed back to the query interface for the user to see, and to subsequently modify the query, if necessary.

The four functional database layers are depicted within the Feature Extraction + Comparison block shown in Figure 1. The main functions of each of these layers are as follows:

- Physical Layer handles physical file attributes like file-extension, file-size, file-creation-date
- Structural Layer handles low-level features like color, texture, loudness, pitch
- Semantic Layer handles high-level features like identifying 'sky', 'rock', 'speech', 'music'
- Knowledge layer is used for disambiguation of high-level information like differentiating between 'rock' in geology and 'rock' in music
- Query layer accepts queries from the user, splits them into sub-queries for the different layers and then hands over each to the corresponding layer

The Feature-DB stores the features corresponding to each abstraction level in different sub-units. The layers interact with the separate databases within the Feature-DB to obtain individual responses to the sub-queries. The responses from individual layers are then compiled by the Query Layer and fed back to the user as the Result List. The Interpretation layer combines the features from each layer into a combined Feature Vector, to provide a computer recognizable interpretation of the media content.

In general, a media component **M** kept in the Media-DB can be represented as a set of features corresponding to each layer, mapped to the location **L** of the physical file, as depicted in equation (1)

$$\mathbf{M} = \{\mathbf{F}_{physical}, \mathbf{F}_{structural}, \mathbf{F}_{semantic}, L\} \qquad (1)$$

HANDLING DATABASE QUERIES

The Query layer handles the queries input by the user and transforms these into sub-queries suitable for each layer. Details of this query splitting method are not covered in this chapter; however the following important points can be articulated related to query formulation.

Nature of Queries

Queries to the Physical-DB are textual in nature and might involve logical operators. A typical example would be: "Find ALL images of type 'JPG' OR 'GIF' which have been created within 7 days AND which are less than 1 MB in file size". Such a query involves file-extensions (JPG, GIF), creation-date (current date minus 7), file-size (> 1 MB), connected together by logical operators (OR, AND).

Queries to the Structural-DB might involve both textual and non-textual parameters, as well as some similarity criteria. For example, "Find 8-bit images having dimensions 400 by 300 and having color content 80% or more similar to the query image Q1". The textual parameters (bit-depth, height, width) can be directly passed to the comparator while the non-textual part (query image Q1) would need to pass through the feature extraction block to extract the color information, represent it suitably (e.g. by a 256-level histogram) before being fed to the comparator for comparison with the information stored in the database using a pre-defined norm (e.g. Euclidean distance).

Queries to the Semantic-DB would involve high-level concepts and their spatial orientations, for example, "Find images having sky at the top and car on road below". Such queries when fed to the Semantic Layer, would entail a lookup in the Semantic-DB which contains associations between the images stored in the database and the semantic entities contained in them (e.g. sky, road, car). To answer such a query the Semantic-DB would need to undergo a training phase to associate low-level features with high-level concepts.

Since semantic concepts are human abstractions, they frequently do not contain fixed or absolute definitions, rather the definitions keep changing based on the context e.g. a 'car' might have different physical parameters like size, shape, color; the 'sky' can be clear, with clouds, overcast, can be blue, white, grey, orange, red or black in color. To take care of all these variations, external domain specific knowledge-bases (KB) are coupled to the Semantic-Layer during the population phase (Figure 2a). A modular design of the database enables the context specific variations to be handled by the external knowledge-bases, rather than by the core database itself; e.g. a 'car' knowledge-base (KB) can train the database to recognize different types of cars.

Sometimes the query term to the Semantic-DB might have different meanings under varying contexts. This might involve synonyms – different terms having the same meaning e.g. "automobile" in the query and "car" in the database; homonyms – same term having different meanings e.g. "bank" of a river and "bank" for storing money; hyponyms – single terms whose meanings are encompassed by broader terms called hypernyms e.g. "bee", "wasp", "butterfly" are all types of "flying insects". To handle such ambiguities, the Knowledge Layer uses external ontology files to compare the search term and derive a more appropriate variant suitable for the specific context (Figure 2b).

The current work focuses only on the higher layers i.e. Semantic-Layer and Knowledge-Layer. Details of how these higher layers work are explained in detail in subsequent sections of the chapter.

Single Point of Access

The layered database architecture forms the basis for a layered query schema which enables the user to access the various features from a single access point (Figure 3 and Figure 4). While the nodes depict the media, feature and content types, the branches show the hierarchical percolation path of the queries across various abstraction levels. In this chapter since the focus is on semantic features, we only depict the relevant portions of the query framework; however, the model is general enough to accommodate parameters for the lower level features as well. Also, for the sake of brevity, only image features are discussed, although the database has been designed to accommodate both audio and video.

The user accesses the database at the top, marked as "Feature-DB", by specifying the requirements using an interactive interface, and at each level the corresponding valid options for the lower levels are provided to the user; and the user makes the most appropriate selection. The "Feature Class" level (A-A) reflects the layers of the database: Physical, Structural, Semantic and Knowledge.

For each feature class, the "media type" can be image, audio or video. For each media type, the "feature type" may be high-level or low-level. For each feature type, the "content type" can be selected, e.g. for media-type "image" valid content-types are "color", "texture" "shape" etc. Each content-type is defined in terms of specific attributes used to describe it along with the actual data-types. For the sake of generalizing the model, the actual attributes and data types have been omitted, as they will vary across implementations. The query framework also takes into account the fact that a media-type may be described by both textual attributes (e.g. high-level feature-type) and non-textual attributes (e.g. low-level feature-type); and comparators incorporated within the database layers will invoke the proper comparison metric to generate the result list.

Result Integration

A query submitted to the database might have different components that need to be handled

Figure 2. External information sources: (a) Knowledge-bases provide context specific information via the Semantic-Layer (b) Ontology files helps in disambiguation of information via the Knowledge-Layer

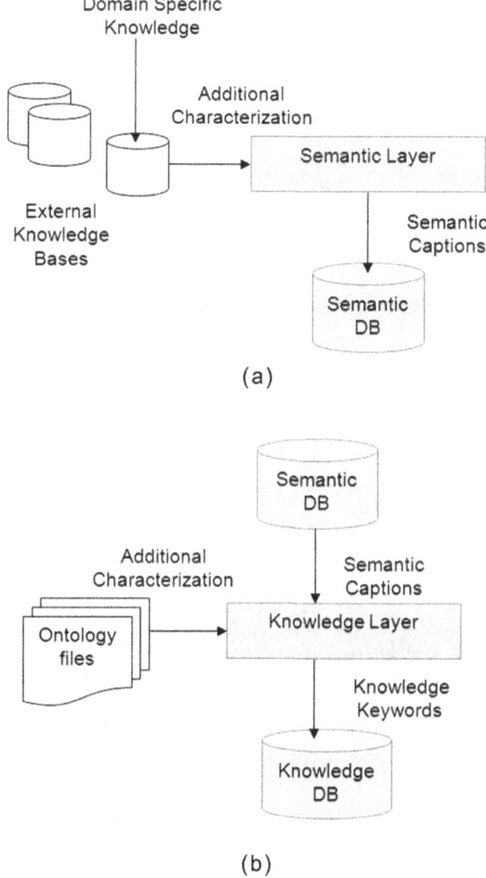

separately by each layer. The Query Layer collects the individual results from each of the layers and combines them into a single result list, which is displayed for the user to view. Each layer generates an individual result list based on the part of the query handled by it. The Query Layer then computes an intersection of the individual result lists to arrive at the final result list.

Consider the query, "Find all JPG images created within 1 month, having dimensions 800 by 600, having color combination 80% or more similar to the query image Q1, and having entities 'sky' at top, and 'vehicles' on 'road' at bottom". Based on the actual encoding of the query, the Query Layer splits the query into different components to be handled by the different layers.

- The Physical Layer produces a list of all JPG images created within 1 month. The Structural Layer creates a second list of all images having dimensions 800 by 600 and having color combinations 80% or more than that of the specified query image.
- The Semantic Layer creates a third list of all images having 'sky' at top and 'vehicles' on 'road'. To do so it looks up the semantic captions in the Semantic-DB having terms 'sky', 'road', 'vehicle' in them. These terms have been previously inserted in the Semantic-DB during the population phase by obtaining definitions of these terms from external knowledge-bases (e.g. car-KB, scenery-KB).
- The Semantic Layer trims the third list to keep only those items having sky at 'top' and road at 'bottom'.
- Finally the Knowledge Layer reads in the semantic captions 'sky', 'road', 'vehicle' and attempts to find other terms semantically associated with these terms in the Knowledge-DB.

During the population phase the Knowledge Layer would have used external ontological files to find such terms before storing them in the Knowledge-DB associated with the original term e.g. 'vehicle' might be associated with terms 'car' and 'automobile'. During the retrieval phase, the Knowledge Layer creates a fourth result list of images containing all these associated terms. The Query Layer generates an intersection of the four individual result lists so as to prepare a final result list containing all the items common in the individual lists.

Figure 3. Query schema for images in the semantic layer

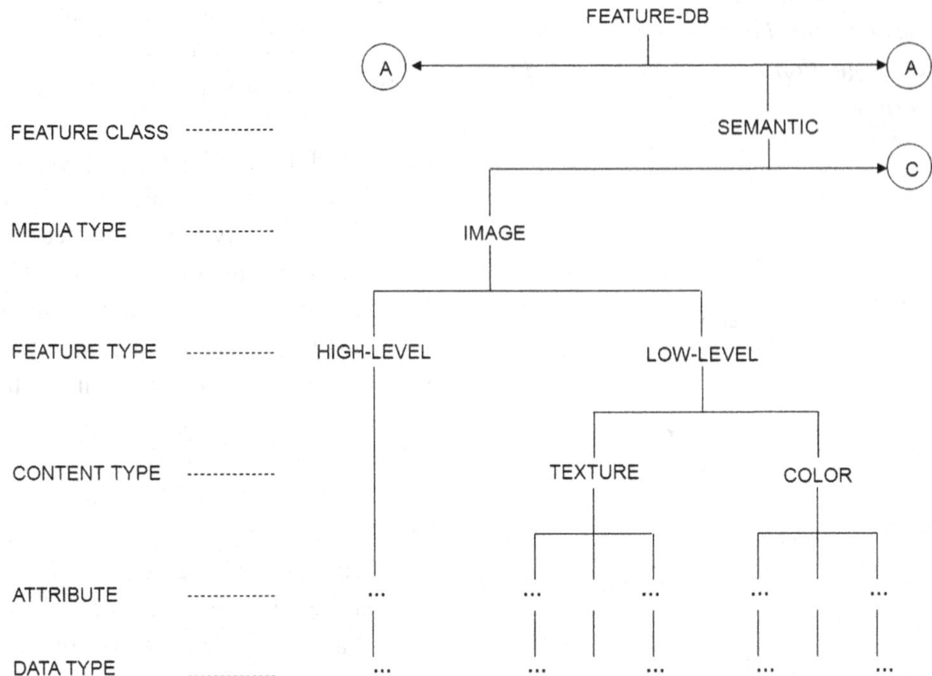

Figure 4. Query schema for the audio in the semantic layer & the knowledge layer

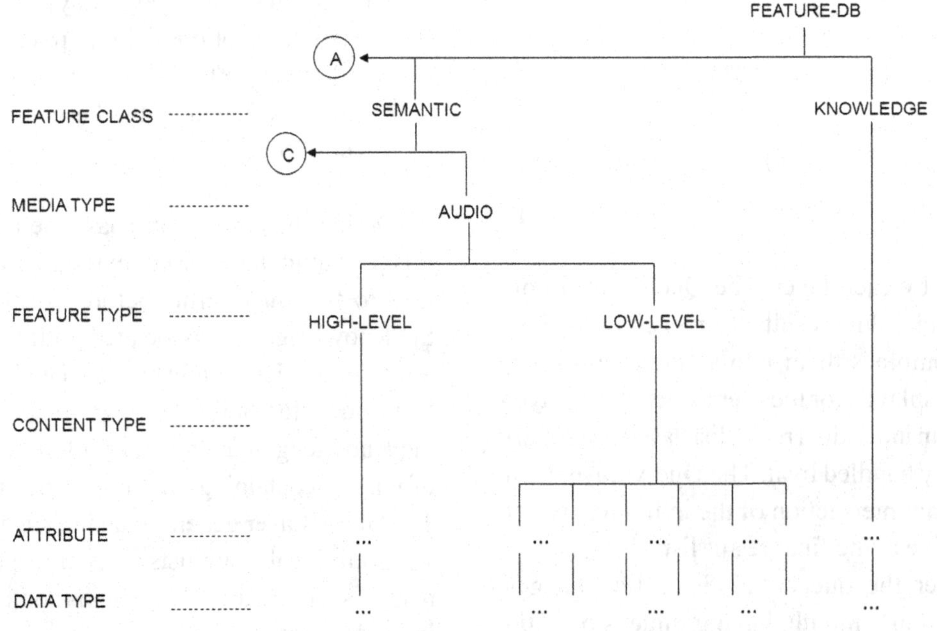

CHARACTERIZATION OF SEMANTIC ENTITIES: THE SEMANTIC LAYER

One of the objectives of this work is to investigate effective means of characterizing semantic entities in media files by automatically generating textual captions. Semantic characterization is necessary because humans tend to search for media content based on their inherent semantics

. However, automated inference of semantic concepts from media components is a challenge for the CBSR research community. This is firstly because an automated system cannot directly understand high-level concepts; it can only read in low-level features. This is referred to as the problem of "semantic gap" to indicate the fundamentally different ways in which humans and machines process information. Thus, the system needs to be explicitly trained to associate low-level features with high-level concepts, so as to infer inherent semantics

This brings the second problem into focus – semantic entities are based on human abstractions and fixed characterizations do not always exist, and when they do, they may not apply universally because they vary depending on the context or the domain. Moreover, semantic objects in general cannot be characterized by simple homogeneity criteria e.g. uniform color or uniform motion

. Hence it is generally difficult to recognize semantics using an automated procedure. However, even where this is possible, acceptable accuracy is still restricted to specific domains.

Concept of Visual Keywords

The current work uses a concept of Visual Keywords to automatically characterize semantic entities in images, as well as their spatial positions. Visual Keywords (VKs) are segmented portions of images along with associated low-level features and high-level descriptors.

Consider the natural scenery image shown in Figure 5. How would one describe the contents of this image? A possible and acceptable description could be: Sky at the top, grass at the bottom, water in the middle-right region, rock in the middle-left region. The description is seen to employ descriptors such as color and texture to define entities like sky, water, grass, rock etc. and spatial descriptors like top, bottom, left, right, middle to define their relative orientations. This observation motivates the use of Visual Keywords – just as in a textual document individual characters have no associated semantics, but they can combine to form meaningful words; similarly, this work investigates the possibility of using a collection of structural units to provide meaningful interpretation of the semantic entities. These structural units, along with their associated meaning are referred to as Visual Keywords.

A Visual Keyword is characterized at three different levels: first, it is a segmented portion of an image; therefore, it contains pixel-based information; second, it relates to low-level features containing color and texture representations; third, it has a high-level meaning expressed in terms of a semantic textual label or caption.

RELATED WORK

Earlier research work on understanding semantics of multimedia content attempts to categorize entire images into classes and scenes, such as: natural / artificial (Torralba, 1999), indoor / outdoor, city / landscape (Vailaya, 1999), natural / man-made (Bradshaw, 2000), scenery such as beach, mountain (Hsu, 2000).

Viitaniemi (2006) attempted to recognize 10 semantic classes of objects such as bicycle, bus, car, cat, and cow etc. However, the dataset used in this work contained only a single dominant object per image. Moreover, only the presence of the object is detected, no information about the spatial orientation of the object within the image is analyzed.

Figure 5. Natural scenery image

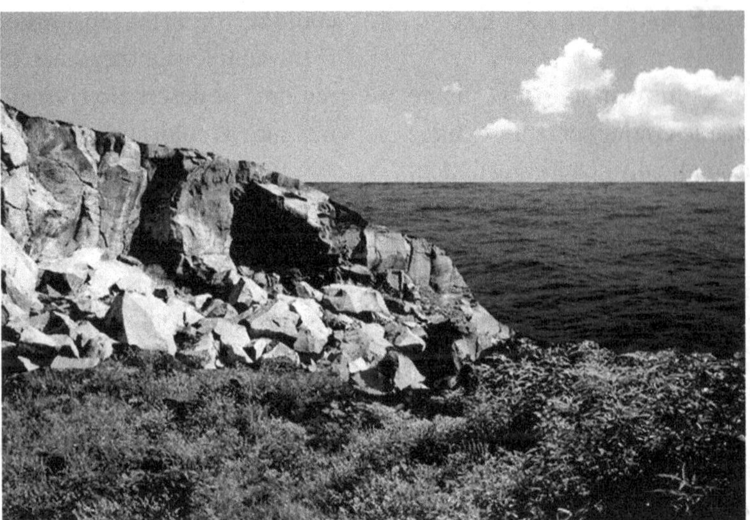

Kaick (2006) groups images into meaningful clusters having similar entities, done by using region matching; e.g. all images having trees or water. However, no semantic meaning is imposed on the matched clusters, with the result that retrieval is based on matching regions by low-level features, not by high-level queries.

The concept of visual keywords for characterization of visual media has already been proposed in literature. Zhao et al. (2001) use the term to define a set of simple geometrical shapes used for retrieval from a dataset of trademark images, using neural networks. In this work, the concept of "visual keyword" is discussed solely from the perspective of shape comparisons; however, no semantic meaning is attached to them. Hence comparisons are restricted to the low-level features.

Lim (1999) proposes visual keywords as coherent units of a visual document functioning as unique visual tokens. The meanings of these visual tokens are abstracted using a three-layer architecture comprising: pixel-feature layer, type evaluation map, and spatial aggregation map. However, since the higher-order semantic structure is abstracted using a pure probabilistic model, Latent Semantic Analysis (LSA), which represents each word as a single point in space, does not handle hypernyms and homonyms effectively, because each word can have different meanings in different contexts. Moreover, the probabilistic rank assigned to each word may not have interpretable meaning in natural language, e.g. two words having similar ranks do not always have similar meanings. Furthermore, it has been shown (Hofmann, 1999) that the probabilistic model of LSA does not match observed data; i.e. while LSA assumes a Gaussian model, in reality a Poisson distribution is observed.

To rectify this, Monay et al. (2003) use a Probabilistic LSA (PLSA) model for semantic annotations, but with rather simple images, which have one central object coded with only RGB based color information to interpret the semantic content.

Wu et al. (2007) denote a set of clustered key-points extracted from images as visual keywords. Semantic textual terms are attached to an entire image or video frame as a whole, with the result that each image becomes associated with a large number of key-terms (approximately 100 in the examples shown). Furthermore, this paper does not give any indication of how individual objects within an image are identified or their spatial orientation is detected. Moreover, the textual terms are not filtered to identify the occurrences of synonyms, homonyms and hypernyms.

Generation of Visual Keywords

In our architecture Visual Keywords (VKs) have a more holistic connotation, which incorporates the various capabilities included in the upper functional layers of the MMDB Layered Architecture shown in Figure 1.

The process for generating these VKs is depicted in Figure 6, as a sequence of four steps, expounded in the following.

Step-I: Image Segmentation: The first step in building up a repository of Visual Keywords is image segmentation (Figure 6). In this work we do not segment images into regions by color and texture, because such segmentations are often unreliable, as photographic images usually contain a large number of varying colors and textures. Moreover, a poor segmentation can result in incongruent regions for further similarity matching. In this work an image is first scaled to standard dimensions and then partitioned into non-overlapping rectangular regions using a grid pattern. This avoids the need for color/texture segmentation and clustering, and also reduces computational load. Furthermore, these grid partitions automatically provide spatial information by the virtue of their spatial location within the image.

An image **I** is segmented into a collection of n partitions, the i-th partition being denoted as P_i (equation 2):

$$\mathbf{I} = \bigcup_{n} \mathbf{P}_i \tag{2}$$

Step-II: Supervised Selection: In this step some (m) or all (n) partitions, which are rich in semantics, are selected in a supervised manner, and added to a collection of VKs. These VKs are represented as rectangular blocks of standard dimensions. The j-th VK is denoted as ${}^{V}\mathrm{K}_j$. The image is represented as a collection of VKs (equation 3):

$$\mathbf{I} = \bigcup_{m} {}^{V}\mathbf{K}_j, \quad m \le n \tag{3}$$

Step-III: Feature Extraction **:** Low-level features, color and texture, are extracted from the VKs in an automated manner. Color is mapped onto the HSV color space: hue (H), saturation (S), value (V), while texture is mapped onto a CGM texture space: contrast (C), homogeneity (G) and mean (M). The quantization scheme of H:S:V is 360:100:100 is used, while a set of four normalized symmetrical GLCMs (Grey Level Co-occurrence Matrix) computed along four directions: horizontal ($\theta = 0°$ and $180°$), vertical ($\theta = 90°$ and $270°$), right diagonal ($\theta = 45°$ and $225°$) and left diagonal ($\theta = 135°$ and $315°$) with a distance offset d=1, and are used to capture texture information. If $P_{i,j}$ represents the element (i,j) of the normalized symmetrical GLCM, and N the number of grey levels, then C,G,M are defined as in equations (4), (5), (6):

$$C = \sum_{i,j=0}^{N-1} P_{i,j}(i-j)^2 \tag{4}$$

$$G = \sum_{i,j=0}^{N-1} \frac{P_{i,j}}{1+(i-j)^2} \tag{5}$$

$$M = M_i = \sum_{i,j=0}^{N-1} iP_{i,j} = M_j = \sum_{i,j=0}^{N-1} jP_{i,j} \tag{6}$$

A VK (${}^{V}\mathrm{K}$) is represented as a set of color-based features (${}^{V}\mathrm{K}_C$) and texture-based features (${}^{V}\mathrm{K}_T$) as depicted in equations (7) and (8):

$${}^{V}\mathrm{K}=\{{}^{V}\mathrm{K}_C, {}^{V}\mathrm{K}_T\} \tag{7}$$

Figure 6. Generation of visual keywords

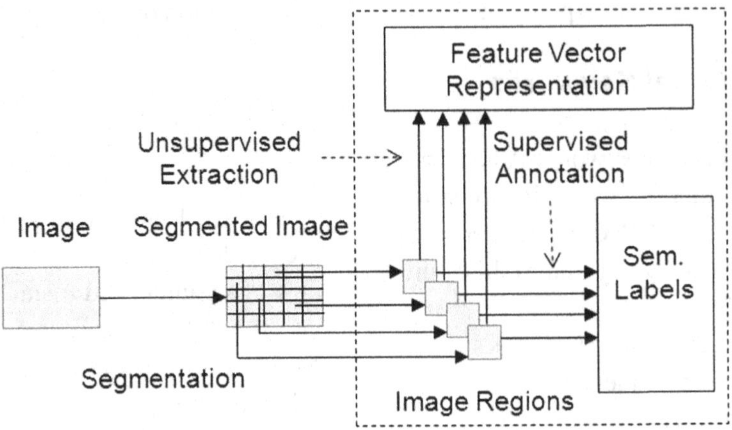

where

$$^{V}K_{C}=\{H,S,V\},\ ^{V}K_{T}=\{C,G,M\} \tag{8}$$

Step-IV: Semantic Characterization: A VK is also mapped to a semantic entity (ε) through a textual label, or caption (equation 9):

$$^{V}\mathbf{K} \rightarrow \varepsilon \tag{9}$$

An image $\mathbf{I}_i$ is subsequently represented as a collection of VKs $^{V}K_{k,i}, \forall k$ and hence as a set of semantic entities, $\varepsilon_{k,i}, \forall k$ where $\varepsilon_{k,i}$ denotes the k-th entity for the i-th image (equation 10)

$$\mathbf{I}_i = \bigcup_{\forall k} {}^{V}\mathbf{K}_{k,i} = \bigcup_{\forall k} \varepsilon_{k,i} \tag{10}$$

The collection of images that are mapped to the semantic entities they contain, are stored in the Semantic Database (Sem-DB) (equation 11).

$$\text{Sem-DB} : \bigcup_{\forall i} \left\{ \mathbf{I}_i = \bigcup_{\forall k} \varepsilon_{k,i} \right\} \tag{11}$$

Generation of External Knowledgebase

Step-V: A semantic entity ε_k can in turn be represented as a collection of VKs $^{V}K_{i,k}, \forall k$, used to represent it and hence to a collection of low-level features (equation 12).

$$\varepsilon_k = \bigcup_{\forall i} {}^{V}\mathbf{K}_{i,k} = \bigcup_{\forall i} \{ {}^{V}\mathbf{K}_C, {}^{V}\mathbf{K}_T \}_{i,k} \tag{12}$$

The collection of all such semantic entities mapped to their corresponding low-level features are stored in the VK-Knowledgebase (VK-KB) (equation 13).

$$\text{VK-KB} : \bigcup_{\forall k} \left\{ \varepsilon_k = \bigcup_{\forall i} ({}^{V}\mathbf{K}_C, {}^{V}\mathbf{K}_T)_{k,i} \right\} \tag{13}$$

Querying the Semantic Database

Two types of queries can be answered by the database. The easier of the two accepts the name of a semantic entity and finds images containing it. This involves a simple lookup in the Semantic-Database. The Semantic-Database contains a mapping between image IDs and entities they contain (equation 11).

For a specific entity name included in the query, all images containing this entity are retrieved. The more difficult query type involves providing a test image and asking the database to determine its semantic content. This involves segmenting the image, and comparing each segment to the set of VKs representing each semantic entity. This segmentation also provides information about the spatial position of the inferred entity. The test image is segmented into a number of rectangular non-overlapping partitions (equation 2). From each partition, low-level features are computed and expressed in terms of color and texture. For the j-th partition $\mathbf{P}_j$ we have (equation 14):

$$\mathbf{P}_j = \{\mathbf{P}_{C,j}, \mathbf{P}_{T,j}\} \tag{14}$$

Each partition is compared to all the entities stored in the VK Knowledgebase to determine the probability of its content belonging to a specific entity ε_k. The difference between the j-th partition and all the tested entities can be denoted as (equation 15):

$$\mathbf{P}_j \sim \bigcup_{\forall k} \boldsymbol{\mu}_k \tag{15}$$

Essentially this implies (from equation 12) a comparison of this partition with a collection of i-th VK of the k-th entity, for all values of i and k (equation 16):

$$\mathbf{P}_j \sim \bigcup_{\forall k}(\bigcup_{\forall i} {}^{V}\mathbf{K}_{i,k}) \tag{16}$$

The difference between the j-th partition and the i-th VK of the k-th entity can be denoted as follows, where ω_1 and ω_2 are appropriate scaling factors (equation 17):

$$d_{j,i,k} = \mathbf{P}_j \sim {}^{V}\mathbf{K}_{i,k} = \omega_1(\mathbf{P}_{C,j} \sim {}^{V}\mathbf{K}_{C,i,k}) + \omega_2(\mathbf{P}_{T,j} \sim {}^{V}\mathbf{K}_{T,i,k}) \tag{17}$$

Equation (17) denotes that the color and texture information of each partition is compared with that of each VK to compute the difference between them.

Color is represented in the HSV color space – which is visualized as a cone inside the coordinates of a point, representing a specific color, it is given by $\{sv\cos(2\pi h), sv\sin(2\pi h), v\}$, where $0<=h,\ s,\ v <=1$. The difference between two colors x and y is therefore (Exhibit 1).

Texture values are compared according to the Euclidean norm in the CGM texture space (equation 19):

$$d^T_{x,y} = \sqrt{(C_x - C_y)^2 + (G_x - G_y)^2 + (M_x - M_y)^2} \tag{19}$$

Exhibit 1.

$$d^C_{x,y} = \sqrt{\{s_x v_x \cos(2\pi h_x) - s_y v_y \cos(2\pi h_y)\}^2 + \{s_x v_x \sin(2\pi h_x) - s_y v_y \sin(2\pi h_y)\}^2 + \{v_x - v_y\}^2} \tag{18}$$

The difference $D_{j,k}$ between the j-th partition and the k-th entity is the mean difference between the partition and all entity VKs (equation 20), where N_k is the number of VKs representing the k-th entity:

$$D_{j,k} = \frac{1}{N_k} \sum_{i=1}^{N_k} d_{j,i,k} \qquad (20)$$

A partition is tagged with a semantic label x corresponding to semantic entity ε_x based on the minimum difference i.e. if the difference between the j-th partition and the k-th entity, $\forall k$, is the minimum for entity x (equation 21):

$$\mathbf{P}_j \rightarrow \varepsilon_x, \text{ if, } \min(\bigcup_{\forall k} D_{j,k}) = D_x \qquad (21)$$

Spatial Zones

To determine spatial position of the detected entities, the image is divided into 9 spatial zones: top-left (TL), top-center (TC), top-right (TR), middle-left (ML), middle-center (MC), middle-right (MR), bottom-left (BL), bottom-center (BC) and bottom-right (BR), as shown in Figure 7. These spatial zones are defined by grouping relevant partitions. Each spatial zone is tagged with a semantic label based on the maximum occurring entity within the spatial zones. A spatial zone may be tagged with multiple labels if the probability of occurrences of multiple entities within the zone have similar values.

For example if we consider the entire image to be segmented into 10 by 10 partition cells, as shown in Figure 7, numbered sequentially from left to right and top to bottom, the Top-Left spatial zone is a collection of the following nine cells: 1, 2, 3, 11, 12, 13, 21, 22, 23, while the Top-Center zone is made of the following twelve cells: 4, 5, 6, 7, 14, 15, 16, 17, 24, 25, 26, 27.

Figure 7. Spatial zones

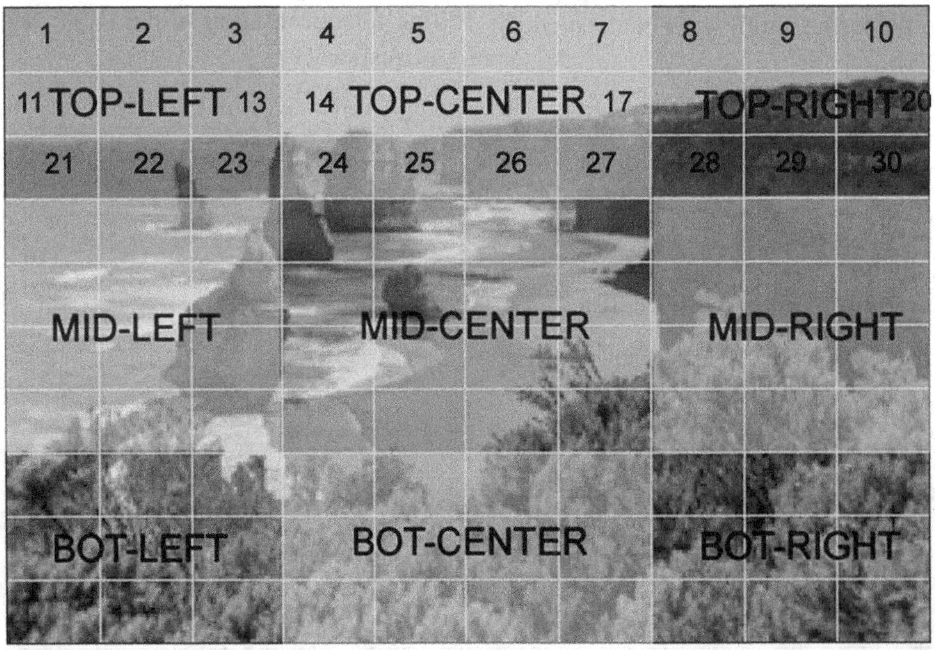

Experimentations and Results

A total of 100 natural scenery images downloaded from the Washington University Image Database available at http://www.cs.washington.edu/research/imagedatabase/groundtruth have been used for experimentation. A set of 25 images have been used as the training set. Regions containing useful semantics are segmented as part of a supervised training process. Figure 8 depicts the training set images and Figure 9 depicts samples of VKs "sky", "water", "rock" and "tree" extracted from them.

These images have standard dimension of 600 x 400 pixels, while each VK is of size 60 x 40. A total of 100 VKs for each entity are extracted and used for training purposes. Low-level features color and texture are extracted from these. Average color features are plotted in the Hue-Saturation-Value (H-S-V) space while texture features are plotted in the GLCM combined feature space of contrast, homogeneity and mean (C-H-M).

Figure 10 shows colour plot for 100 VKs each of entities "tree", "rock", "sky" and "water" with color features represented in the H-S plane. Some salient observations are as follows:

- The 'tree' VKs mostly cluster in the yellow-green region (60° to 90°), and can be differentiated from both 'sky' and 'water'

Figure 8. Training set images

Figure 9. Samples of visual keywords (VKs)

Figure 10. Color plots of hue-saturation for VKs of (a) tree (b) rock (c) sky (d) water

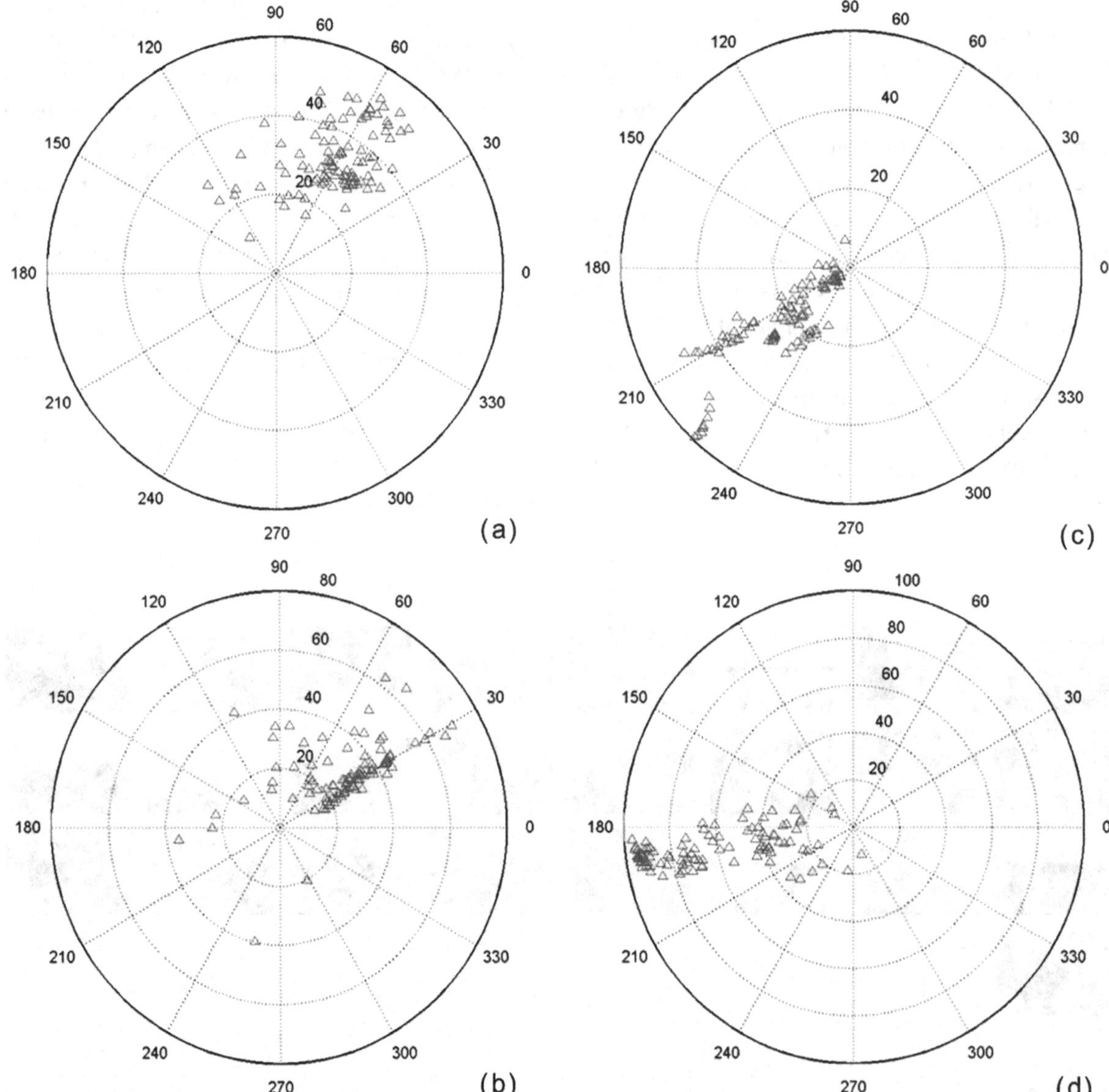

VKs which occupy the blue region (180° to 240°).

- The 'rock' VKs on the other hand are located closer to the 'tree' VKs, mainly clustering along the red-yellow (30° to 60°) region.
- Entities which have similar color patterns like 'sky' and 'water' are discriminated by using their texture patterns.
- Figure 11 shows the widely different texture plots of GLCM contrast and GLCM homogeneity of 'sky' and 'water'. 'Sky' is more homogeneous than 'water' due to the presence of ripples and waves in the latter, which however increases its contrast more.

Low-level features of VKs of each entity are now tagged with a semantic label to generate the

Figure 11. Texture plots for VKs of sky and water of (a) GLCM contrast (b) GLCM homogeneity

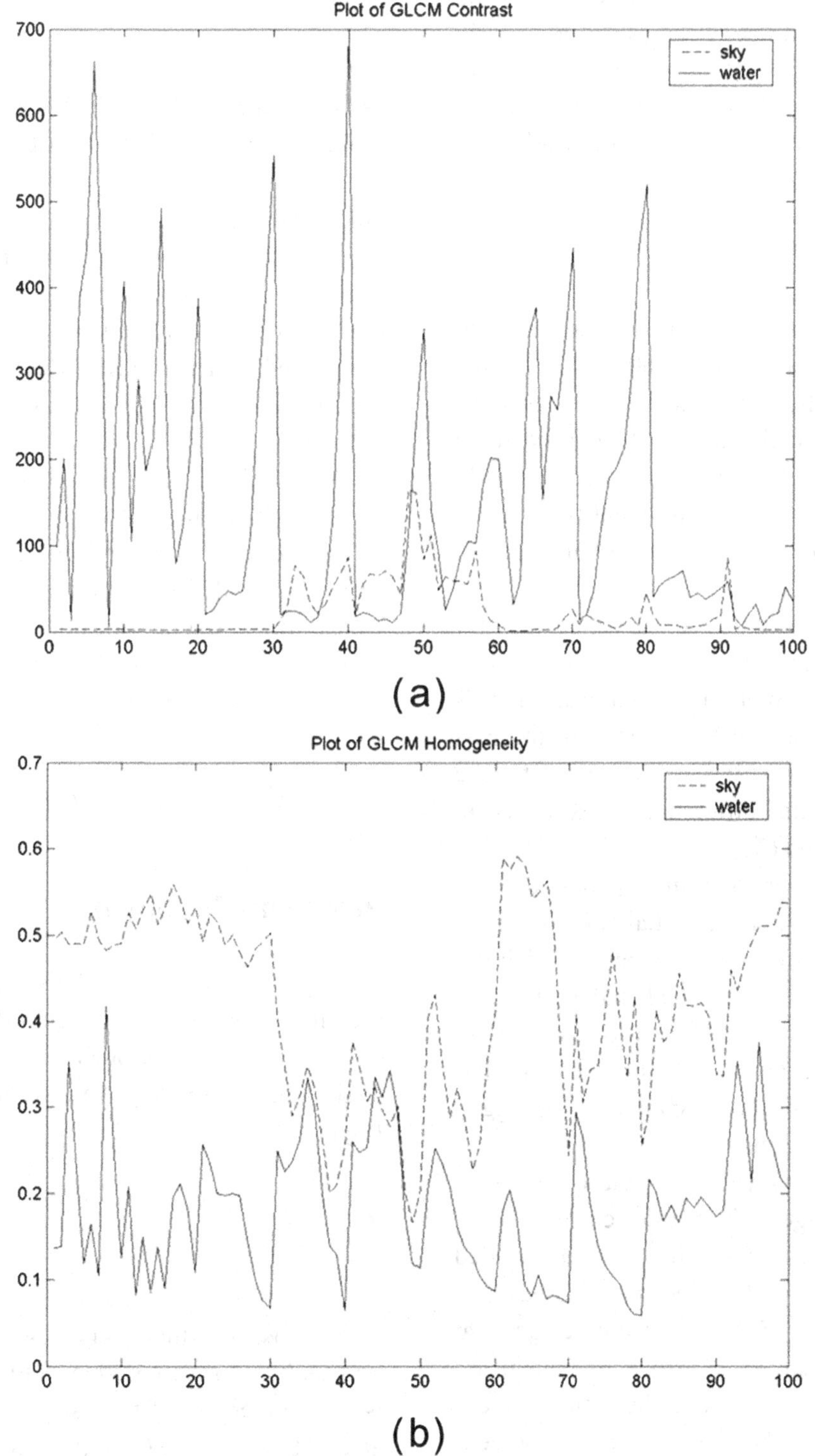

VK-Knowledgebase (VK-KB), as described in equation (13). Entries in the VK-KB are of the following form, where ε represents a specific entity name (e.g. 'sky', 'tree' etc.) associated with a collection of hue (Hu), saturation (Sa), value (Va), contrast (Co), homogeneity (Ho), mean (Me) values (equation 22):

$$\varepsilon=\{Hu,Sa,Va,Co,Ho,Me\} \quad (22)$$

The test set consists of 75 images, each scaled to standard dimensions of 600 x 400 and partitioned into 10 × 10 cells, so as to make each partition-cell (henceforth called simply 'cell') the same dimension as a VK. The images predominantly contain natural scenery-based entities: 'sky', 'water', 'tree' and 'rock'. The test images are shown in Figure 12.

Each cell is compared to the set of VKs for each entity, as explained in equations (15) to (19). The difference between each cell and an entity is computed, and the cell is tagged with the best matching entity, which corresponds to the minimum computed difference, as explained in equations (20) and (21).

Cells are then grouped into spatial zones as shown in Figure 7, and a spatial zone is tagged with the caption of a semantic entity which occurs most often within it, based on the frequency of the tags of the individual cells of the zone. In case multiple entities occur with same or similar (within 10%) abundance, a spatial zone is tagged with multiple captions.

Table 1 shows a set of sample calculations for four test images. The entities corresponding to the minimum computed difference are shaded as are the correctly identified spatial zones. For example in image 45 the brown colored grass at the bottom has led to an erroneous conclusion of the occurrence of 'rock' in the bottom zones.

Table 2 depicts the number of correctly identified spatial zones in the test images. Out if 675 zones, 586 have been correctly identified, i.e. 87%. It is to be noted that although the training procedure is supervised, the tagging of image zones with semantic captions is automated.

DISAMBIGUATION FOR SEMANTIC ENTITIES: THE KNOWLEDGE LAYER

Once the semantic entities are derived using the Semantic Layer, further characterization is necessary to remove any ambiguities generated due to synonyms, hypernyms and homonyms, as mentioned earlier. The Knowledge-Layer is used to remove such ambiguities in association with ontology files.

An ontology is a vocabulary of terms and precise specification of what those terms mean. In this work, an ontology can be thought of as a set of concept definitions, categorizing things that exist or may exist in some domain. Symbolically it is represented as a collection of entries along with associated terms (equation 23):

$$\Theta=\bigcup_{p} E_p=\bigcup_{p}\{e_1,e_2,\ldots,e_k\}_p \quad (23)$$

Providing Synonyms

Synonyms are provided by the Semantic Database. It contains a mapping between images and entity captions, as per equation (10) and depicted once again in equation (24). An example is shown in Figure 13:

$$\mathbf{I}_i \rightarrow \bigcup_{k} \varepsilon_{k,i} \quad (24)$$

Suppose a textual query posed to the Semantic Database fails to produce a hit, i.e. the query is not an element of the list of captions associated with the image (equation 25):

Figure 12. Test images

Table 1. Sample calculations for characterization of spatial zones

Image	Entity	TL	TC	TR	ML	MC	MR	BL	BC	BR
26	Sky	0.1849	0.2037	0.1847	0.3503	0.3519	0.3679	0.4728	0.4840	0.4888
	Tree	0.5226	0.5195	0.5162	0.4940	0.4739	0.4682	0.5011	0.5080	0.4843
	Water	0.4284	0.4488	0.4164	0.1662	0.1760	0.1723	0.1666	0.1778	0.1728
	Rock	0.4440	0.4357	0.4418	0.5311	0.5090	0.5084	0.5741	0.5828	0.5643
	Caption	**S**	**S**	**S**	**W**	**W**	**W**	**W**	**W**	**W**
Image	Entity	TL	TC	TR	ML	MC	MR	BL	BC	BR
28	Sky	0.2407	0.2185	0.2249	0.2779	0.3472	0.2530	0.5721	0.6297	0.5717
	Tree	0.5681	0.6517	0.6546	0.3989	0.3455	0.4976	0.1644	0.2148	0.1723
	Water	0.3703	0.4236	0.4113	0.3222	0.3656	0.3866	0.4581	0.4586	0.4658
	Rock	0.5435	0.5987	0.6073	0.3926	0.3687	0.4625	0.2721	0.3566	0.2705
	Caption	**S**	**S**	**S**	**S**	**S/T**	**S**	**T**	**T**	**T**
Image	Entity	TL	TC	TR	ML	MC	MR	BL	BC	BR
31	Sky	0.2815	0.2565	0.4751	0.2240	0.3915	0.5318	0.4555	0.5009	0.5133
	Tree	0.7157	0.6837	0.4081	0.4434	0.3220	0.2513	0.2962	0.3397	0.2098
	Water	0.4370	0.4093	0.3922	0.2914	0.4012	0.5078	0.5229	0.6017	0.5252
	Rock	0.6773	0.6465	0.4837	0.4213	0.3204	0.2510	0.2225	0.2433	0.1875
	Caption	**S**	**S**	**T/W**	**S**	**T/R**	**T/R**	**R**	**R**	**R**
Image	Entity	TL	TC	TR	ML	MC	MR	BL	BC	BR
45	Sky	0.2724	0.2915	0.3017	0.4919	0.4806	0.5005	0.5565	0.5582	0.5375
	Tree	0.4585	0.4107	0.3565	0.3025	0.2886	0.2795	0.2322	0.3367	0.2550
	Water	0.4293	0.4101	0.3647	0.4410	0.4454	0.4231	0.5415	0.6216	0.5576
	Rock	0.4012	0.3730	0.3375	0.3148	0.2973	0.3170	0.2456	0.2777	0.2317
	Caption	**S**	**S**	**S**	**T**	**T/R**	**T**	**T/R**	**R**	**T/R**

Table 2. Number of correctly identified spatial zones in test images

1	2	3	4	5	6	7	8	9	10	11	12	13	14	15
8	8	8	7	8	9	7	7	8	9	6	8	8	9	8
16	17	18	19	20	21	22	23	24	25	26	27	28	29	30
8	9	9	8	8	8	8	7	7	8	9	8	9	5	6
31	32	33	34	35	36	37	38	39	40	41	42	43	44	45
8	7	7	8	8	9	9	9	8	7	9	8	9	8	5
46	47	48	49	50	51	52	53	54	55	56	57	58	59	60
9	8	8	8	6	7	7	8	8	9	8	8	8	6	6
61	62	63	64	65	66	67	68	69	70	71	72	73	74	75
8	8	9	9	8	7	9	8	8	9	6	5	9	8	7

Figure 13. Image of 'car' along with captions

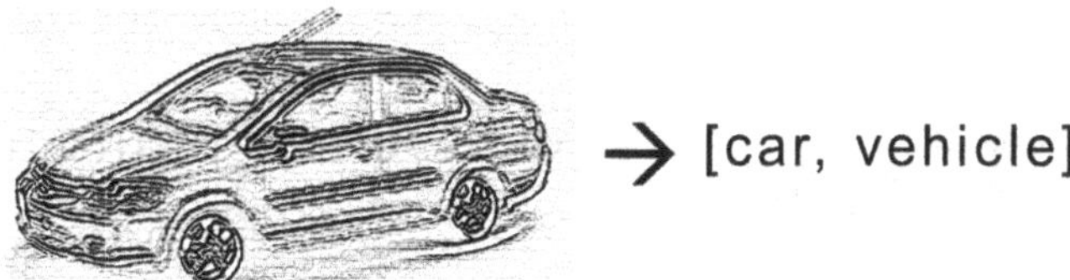

$$Q \notin \bigcup_{k} \varepsilon_{k,i} \tag{25}$$

e.g.

automobile∉[car, vehicle]

Let an entry E_p in an ontology file be mapped with a number of synonyms, e_j, j=1,2,3,… (equation 26):

$$E_p=\{e_1,e_2,\ldots,e_n\} \tag{26}$$

e.g.

automobile=[car, van]

The Knowledge layer searches the ontology file to check whether the query matches with an entry there. Suppose a match is found, as depicted in equation (27):

$$Q==E_p \tag{27}$$

The Knowledge layer retrieves the synonyms and checks whether they match an entry in the Semantic-DB. This would provide a link between the ontology and Semantic-DB. Suppose there is a match, i.e. one of the synonyms is an element of the list of captions associated with the image (equation 28):

$$e_j \in \bigcup_{k} \varepsilon_{k,i} \tag{28}$$

e.g.

car∈[car, vehicle]

The Knowledge Layer associates the ontology term with the image and adds it to the Knowledge-DB along with existing terms, i.e. the image $\mathbf{I}_i$ now gets mapped to a new term from the ontology file E_p in addition to its existing semantic captions (equation 29). This is illustrated in Figure 14:

$$\mathbf{I}_i \rightarrow \left\{ \bigcup_{k} \varepsilon_{k,i}, E_p \right\} \tag{29}$$

A resubmission of the original query to the Knowledge-DB subsequently produces a hit, i.e. the query finds a match within the semantic captions associated with the images, extended by the additional information from the ontology file (equation 30)

$$Q \in \left\{ \bigcup_{\forall k} \varepsilon_{k,i}, E_p \right\} \tag{30}$$

e.g.

automobile∈[car, vehicle, automobile]

Implicit Relationships

Sometimes the captions associated with the images and the search term, are related to each other as hypernym-hyponym pairs i.e. they have implicit semantic relationships instead of just being syn-

Figure 14. Image of 'car' along with added captions

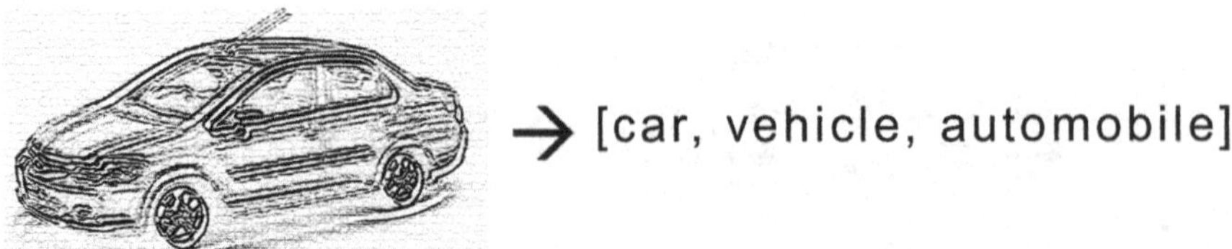

onymous. In those cases the ontology file serves to provide the proper hypernyms to resolve the meaning of the query term and generate meaning responses from the database system.

Let an entry E_q (hypernym) in the ontology file be associated with related terms (hyponyms), e_j, j=1,2,3,... (equation 31):

$$E_q=\{e_1,e_2,\ldots,e_n\}_q \quad (31)$$

e.g.

flying_insect=[bee, wasp, butterfly, mosquito]

The Semantic Database contains a mapping between images and its captions as before, (equation 32). An example is shown in Figure 15.

$$\mathbf{I}_1 \rightarrow \bigcup_{k_1} \varepsilon_{k_1} \; \mathbf{I}_2 \rightarrow \bigcup_{k_2} \varepsilon_{k_2} \quad (32)$$

Suppose a textual query posed to the Semantic Database fails to produce a valid hit, i.e. the search terms is not an element of the list of captions associated with the images (equation 33):

$$Q \notin \bigcup_{k_1} \varepsilon_{k_1} \; Q \notin \bigcup_{k_2} \varepsilon_{k_2} \quad (33)$$

e.g.

flying_insect∉[bee] flying_insect∉[wasp]

The Knowledge layer searches the ontology file to check whether the query matches with an entry there. Suppose a match is found, (equation 34):

$$Q==E_q \quad (34)$$

e.g.

flying_insect==flying_insect

The Knowledge layer retrieves the related terms and checks whether they match with an entry in Semantic-DB. Suppose there are valid matches, i.e. specific ontology terms (hyponyms) is an element of the list of captions associated with the images (equation 35):

$$e_1 \in \bigcup_{k_1} \varepsilon_{k_1} \; e_2 \in \bigcup_{k_2} \varepsilon_{k_2} \quad (35)$$

Figure 15. Images of 'bee' and 'wasp' along with captions

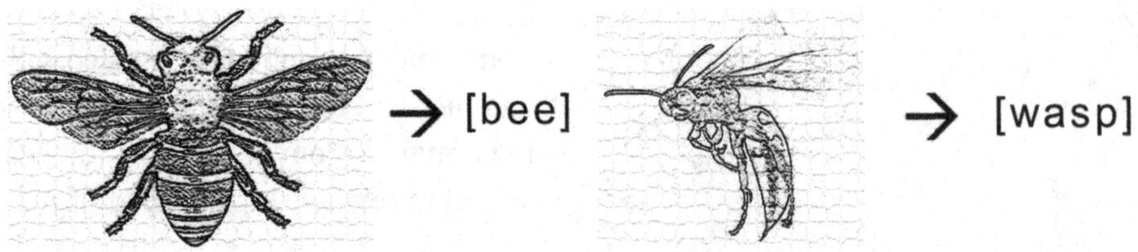

Figure 16. Images of 'bee' and 'wasp' along with added captions

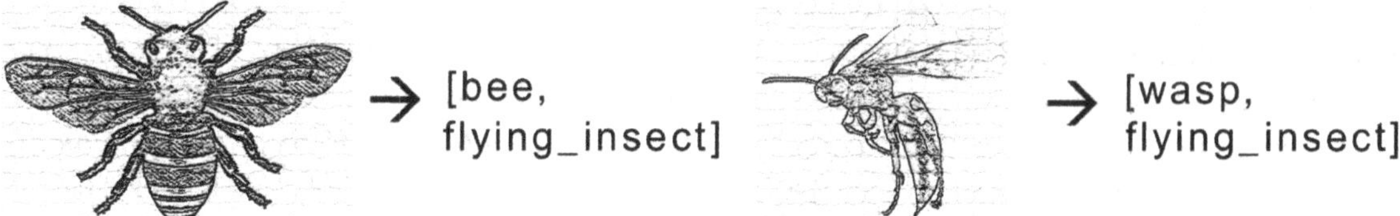

e.g.

bee ∈ [bee] wasp ∈ [wasp]

It associates the ontology term (hypernym) with the image and adds to the Knowledge-DB along with existing terms, (equation 36). The idea is illustrated in Figure 16.

$$\mathbf{I}_1 \rightarrow \left\{ \bigcup_{k_1} \varepsilon_{k_1}, E_p \right\} \mathbf{I}_2 \rightarrow \left\{ \bigcup_{k_2} \varepsilon_{k_2}, E_p \right\} \tag{36}$$

A resubmission of the original query to the Knowledge-DB produces hits, i.e. now the search terms is an element of the modified list of captions including the term from the ontology file (equation 37):

$$Q \in \left\{ \bigcup_{k_1} \varepsilon_{k_1}, E_p \right\} Q \in \left\{ \bigcup_{k_2} \varepsilon_{k_2}, E_p \right\} \tag{37}$$

e.g.

flying_insect∈[bee, flying_insect] flying_insect∈[wasp, flying_insect]

Therefore, if the search term does not directly match with the image captions nor is synonymous with them, but is an altogether different term semantically related to them as hypernym-hyponym pairs, then the Knowledge Layer of the database resolves the meaning using the following steps:

- It first checks whether the search term matches with a hypernym entry in an associated ontology file.
- If it does then the corresponding hyponym terms are checked to find out if they match with any of the image captions in the Semantic-DB. If they do, it implies that the captions of the image are related in meaning to the hyponyms in the ontology file.
- The corresponding hypernym is then retrieved from the ontology file and added to the image captions before being stored in the Knowledge-DB.
- A subsequent search in the Knowledge-DB would produce a response as the added hypernym term has already been found to match with the search term. The corresponding image is retrieved and displayed in the result list.

CONCLUSION AND FUTURE RESEARCH DIRECTIONS

The present work proposes a layered architecture of multimedia databases and focuses in more detail on the characterization and search methodologies pertaining to semantic content. The proposed layered architecture is used to extract meta-data from multimedia components at various layers of abstractions. The lower layers handle file attributes (physical layer) and low-level features (structural layer), while the upper layers handle high-level features (semantic layer) and attempts to remove ambiguities inherent in them (knowledge layer).

To access the various abstracted features, a query schema is presented. The schema provides a single point of access while establishing hierarchical pathways between feature-classes (e.g. structural, semantic), media-type (e.g. image, audio), feature-type (e.g. high-level, low-level), content-type (e.g. color, texture), attributes and data-types. An interactive interface prompts the user to input relevant parameters and options at each level, as the query percolates through the abstraction layers.

Minimization of the semantic gap is addressed using the concept of "Visual Keywords" (VKs), which are segmented portions of images along with associated low-level and high-level features. The semantic layer auto-annotates image regions by utilizing information kept in previously trained semantic knowledge bases. Ambiguities in the annotations are then resolved using domain specific ontology files. Experimentation with natural scenery images has shown the proposed technique to be effective.

Although the VKs are domain dependent, the proposed framework allows them to be customized for different visual domains. For the sake of brevity, this paper deals only with image search and retrieval, however the framework is extensible to other media types like audio and video. Moreover the architecture is scalable, additional features can be added to the search schema without changing its basic structure.

Future research will involve translating the ontological definitions into appropriate technical specifications and standardized structures. Careful consideration is also required to choose the most appropriate ontology specification system. Further research should also focus on developing encoding techniques to be used at the Query Layer, such that user queries can be split it into their components suitable for the four functional layers of the proposed model.

REFERENCES

Baral, C., Gonzalez, G., & Son, T. (1998). Conceptual modeling and querying in multimedia databases. *Multimedia Tools and Applications*, *7*(1), 37–66. doi:10.1023/A:1009670119569

Belongie, S., Carson, C., Greenspan, H., & Malik, J. (1997). *Recognition of images in large databases using a learning framework* (Tech. Rep. No. CSD-97-939), University of California, Berkeley, CS Dept.

Bradshaw, B. (2000). Semantic based image retrieval: A probabilistic approach. *Proceedings of ACM Conference on Multimedia*, (pp. 167-176).

Cominiciu, D., & Meer, P. (2002). Mean shift: A robust approach towards feature space analysis. *IEEE Transactions on Pattern Analysis and Machine Intelligence*, *24*(5), 603–619. doi:10.1109/34.1000236

Deruyver, A., Hode, Y., Leammer, E., & Jolion, J. M. (2005). Adaptive pyramid and semantic graph – Knowledge driven segmentation . In Brun, L., & Vento, M. (Eds.), *Lecture Notes in Computer Science, 3434* (pp. 213–222).

Enser, P. G. B., Sandom, C. J., & Lewis, P. H. (2005). Surveying the reality of semantic image retrieval . In Bres, S., & Laurini, R. (Eds.), *Lecture Notes in Computer Science, 3736* (pp. 177–188).

Hofmann, T. (1999). *Probabilistic latent semantic indexing*. In 22nd Annual International SIGIR Conference on Research and Development in Information Retrieval (SIGIR '99) (pp. 35-44)

Hsu, W., Chua, T. S., & Pung, H. K. (2000). Approximating content based object level image retrieval. *Multimedia Tools and Applications*, *12*, 59–79. doi:10.1023/A:1009692213403

Jianfeng, Y., Yang, Z., & Zhanhuai, L. (2003). *A hierarchical method to describe multimedia content.* In 5th International Conference on Computational Intelligence and Multimedia Applications (pp. 413-418).

Jianfeng, Y., Yang, Z., & Zhanhuai, L. (2004). *A multimedia document database model based on multi-layered description supporting complex multimedia structural and semantic contents.* In 10th International Multimedia Modelling Conference (pp. 33-39).

Kosch, H., Tusch, R., Boszormenyi, L., Bachlechner, A., Hofbauer, C., Riedler, C., et al. Hanin, C. (2001). *SMOOTH - A distributed multimedia database system.* In 27th International VLDB Conference, (pp. 713-714).

Lim, J.-H. (1999). *Learnable visual keywords for image classification.* In 4th ACM International Conference on Digital Libraries, (pp.139-145)

Liu, C. C., Hsu, J. L., & Chen, A. L. (2001). Efficient near neighbour searching using multi-indexes for content-based multimedia data retrieval. *Multimedia Tools and Applications, 13*(3), 235–254. doi:10.1023/A:1009601513674

Monay, F., & Perez, D. G. (2003). *On image auto-annotation with latent space models.* In 11th ACM International Conference on Multimedia, (pp. 275-278)

Muller, H., Michoux, N., Bandon, D., & Geissbuhler, A. (2004). A review of content-based image retrieval systems in medical applications – Clinical benefits and future directions. *International Journal of Medical Informatics, 73*(1), 1–23. doi:10.1016/j.ijmedinf.2003.11.024

Niblack, C. W., Barber, R., Equitz, W., Flickner, M. D., Glasman, E., & Petkovic, D. … Taubin, G. (1993). The QBIC project: Querying images by content using color, texture and shape. *Storage and Retrieval for Image and Video Databases, vol. 1908*, (pp. 173-187). Bellingham, WA: SPIE.

Pentland, A., Picard, R. W., & Sclaroff, S. (1996). Photobook: Content based manipulation of image databases. *International Journal of Computer Vision, 18*(3), 233–254. doi:10.1007/BF00123143

Smith, J. R., & Chang, S. F. (1997). Querying by color regions using the VisualSEEK content based visual query system . In Maybury, M. (Ed.), *Intelligent multimedia information retrieval* (pp. 23–41). CA: AAAI Press.

Torralba, A., & Oliva, A. (1999). *Semantic organization of scenes using discriminant structural templates.* In International Conference on Computer Vision (pp. 1253-1258).

Vailaya, A., Figueiredo, M. A. T., Jain, A. K., & Zhang, H. J. (1999). *Content based hierarchical classification of vacation images.* In IEEE Conference on Multimedia Computing and Systems: vol. 1, (pp. 518-523).

van Kaick, O., & Mori, G. (2006). *Automatic classification of outdoor images by region matching.* In 3rd Canadian Conference on Computer and Robot Vision, (pp. 9-16)

Viitaniemi, V., & Laaksonen, J. (2006). Techniques for still image scene classification and object detection . In Kollias, S. (Eds.), *Lecture Notes in Computer Science, 4132* (pp. 35–44).

Wallace, M., Atahnasiadis, T., Avrithis, Y., Delopoulus, A. N., & Kollias, S. (2006). Integrating multimedia archives: The architecture and the content layer. *IEEE Transactions on Systems, Man, and Cybernetics, 36*(1), 34–52. doi:10.1109/TSMCA.2005.859184

Wu, J. K., Narasimhalu, A. D., Mehtre, B. M., Lam, C. P., & Gao, Y. J. (1995). CORE: A content-based retrieval engine for multimedia information systems. *ACM Multimedia Systems*, *3*(1), 25–41. doi:10.1007/BF01236577

Wu, X., Zhao, W.-L., & Ngo, C.-W. (2007). *Near-duplicate keyframe retrieval with visual keywords and semantic context*. In 6th ACM International Conference on Image and Video Retrieval (CIVR 2007) (pp.162-169)

Zhao, T., Tang, L. H., Ip, H. H. S., & Qi, F. (2001). Visual keyword image retrieval based on synergetic neural network for Web-based image search. *Real-Time Systems*, *21*, 127–142. doi:10.1023/A:1011147421401

Chapter 13
Fuzzy Logic for Image Retrieval and Image Databases:
A Literature Overview

Li Yan
Northeastern University, China

Z. M. Ma
Northeastern University, China

ABSTRACT

Fuzzy set theory has been extensively applied to the representation and processing of imprecise and uncertain data. Image data is becoming an important data resource with rapid growth in the number of large-scale image repositories. However, image data is fuzzy in nature, and imprecision and vagueness may exist in both image descriptions and query specifications. This chapter reviews some major work of image retrieval with fuzzy logic in the literature, including fuzzy content-based image retrieval and database support for fuzzy image retrieval. For the fuzzy content-based image retrieval, we present how fuzzy sets are applied for the extraction and representation of visual (colors, shapes, textures) features, similarity measures and indexing, relevance feedback, and retrieval systems. For the fuzzy image database retrieval, we present how fuzzy sets are applied for fuzzy image query processing based on a defined database models, and how various fuzzy database models can support image data management.

INTRODUCTION

Very large collections of images are growing rapidly due to the advent of cheaper storage devices and the Internet. For example, satellites send tens of images of earth each second and these images are stored in huge databases for future retrieval. The rapid growth in the number of large-scale image repositories in many domains such as medical image management, multimedia libraries, document archives, art collections, geographical information systems, law enforcement agencies, and journalism has brought about the need for

DOI: 10.4018/978-1-61350-126-9.ch013

efficient and effective content-based image retrieval mechanisms.

Finding an image from a large set of images is an extremely difficult problem. One solution is to label images manually, but this is very expensive, time consuming and infeasible for many applications. Furthermore, the labeling process depends on the semantic accuracy in describing the image. Therefore many content based image retrieval (CBIR) systems are developed to extract low-level features for describing the image content. For an overview of content based image retrieval, ones can refer to some recent survey papers, for example, (Müller, Michoux, Bandon and Geissbuhler, 2004), (Datta, Joshi, Li and Wang, 2008) and (Shandilya and Singhai, 2010).

In real-world applications, information is often imprecise or uncertain (Parsons, 1996). Many sources can contribute to the imprecision and uncertainty of data. It has been pointed out that in the future, we need to learn how to manage data that is imprecise or uncertain, and that contains an explicit representation of the uncertainty (Dalvi and Suciu, 2007). As pointed in (Gokcen, Yazici and Buckles, 2000), image data is fuzzy in nature and in content-based retrieval this property creates some problems such as:

1. Descriptions of image contents usually involve inexact and subjective concepts. For the diversity of image contents, different people would have different understandings and descriptions.
2. Usually imprecision and vagueness exist in descriptions of the images and in some of the visual features. The descriptions, which is associated with each stored image so as to retain the important visual characteristics, are generally imprecise and quantization of visual features (object features) can also be vague.
3. User's needs to image retrieval may be naturally fuzzy. User may specify linguistic qualifiers for his/her retrieval specification and preference.
4. Finite set of recognizable feature values by human is a restricted subset of what the image actually may have.

Due to subjectivity of human perception, imprecision and vagueness exist in both image descriptions and query specifications, which usually impair a definite decision about the satisfaction of a query. To overcome this limit, it is needed to introduce a score, and quantify the degree of truth, by which the available description permits a decision about a given query. It is true in image retrieval that user is not only looking for an exact match but also looking for the nearest matches. Some previous studies have been done on applying fuzzy processing techniques to CBIR. Among them, some tried to define an efficient way of fuzzy query processing and similarity computation between the query and images in the database, and some worked on the limited values of visual properties and defined representation systems for that task (Gokcen, Yazici and Buckles, 2000).

Databases are designed to support the data storage, processing, and retrieval activities related to data management. Nowadays rapid advances in computing power have brought opportunities for databases in emerging applications such as multimedia, knowledge engineering, geographic information systems, and etc. Image databases can be viewed as controlled collections of images. It is desired by users that image databases manage a great amount of image data and provide fast query resolution. Currently some researchers tried to apply advanced database technology to support image data management. It is noted that while some work has been done on fuzzy content-based image retrieval, working on fuzzy query processing based on a defined database model and fuzzy image database models are emerging.

In this chapter, we review two aspects of existing work in area of image retrieval with fuzzy logic. The first one is the fuzzy content-based image retrieval, and we review some major work of the application of fuzzy sets in the extraction and representation of visual (colors, shapes, textures) features, similarity measures and indexing, relevance feedback, and retrieval systems. The second one is the fuzzy image database retrieval, and we review some major work of the application of fuzzy sets in fuzzy image query processing based on a defined database models and some major work of various fuzzy database models in image data management.

The remainder of the chapter is organized as follows. Section 2 discusses information imprecision and uncertainty as well as fussy set theory. The issues that fuzzy sets are applied for the extraction and representation of visual (colors, shapes, textures) features, similarity measures and indexing, relevance feedback, and retrieval systems are investigated in Section 3. Section 4 presents how fuzzy sets are applied for fuzzy image query processing based on a defined database models and how various fuzzy database models can support image data management. Section 5 concludes this chapter.

IMPERFECT INFORMATION AND FUZZY SET THEORY

Imprecise and Uncertain Information

There have been some attempts to classify the various possible kinds of imperfect information. *Inconsistency*, *imprecision*, *vagueness*, *uncertainty*, and *ambiguity* are five basic kinds of imperfect information in database systems (Bosc and Prade, 1993).

- Inconsistency is a kind of semantic conflict, meaning the same aspect of the real world is irreconcilably represented more than once in a database or in several different databases. Information inconsistency usually comes from information integration (DeMichiel, 1989).
- Intuitively, the imprecision and vagueness are relevant to the content of an attribute value, and it means that a choice must be made from a given range (interval or set) of values but we do not know exactly which one to choose at present. In general, vague information is represented by linguistic values.
- The uncertainty is related to the degree of truth of its attribute value, and it means that we can apportion some, but not all, of our belief to a given value or a group of values. The random uncertainty described with probability theory is not considered here.
- The ambiguity means that some elements of the model lack complete semantics leading to several possible interpretations.

Generally several different kinds of imperfection can co-exist with respect to the same piece of information. Imprecision, uncertainty, and vagueness are three major types of imperfect information. And fuzzy sets introduced by Zadeh (1965) have been widely used for the quantification of imprecision and uncertainty.

Fuzzy Sets and Possibility Distributions

Based on the classification of imperfect information, different types and sources of imperfect information have been investigated (Morrissey, 1990; Parsons, 1996). Many of the existing approaches dealing with imprecision and uncertainty are based on the theory of fuzzy sets (Zadeh, 1965) and possibility distribution theory (Zadeh, 1978).

Let U be a universe of discourse. A fuzzy value on U is characterized by a fuzzy set F in U. A membership function

$$\mu_F: U \rightarrow [0, 1]$$

is defined for the fuzzy set F, where $\mu_F(u)$, for each $u \in U$, denotes the degree of membership of u in the fuzzy set F. Thus the fuzzy set F is described as follows:

$$F = \{\mu_F(u_1)/u_1, \mu_F(u_2)/u_2, ..., \mu_F(u_n)/u_n\}$$

When the membership function $\mu_F(u)$ above is explained to be a measure of the possibility that a variable X has the value u, where X takes values in U, a fuzzy value is described by a possibility distribution π_X (Zadeh, 1978).

$$\pi_X = \{\pi_X(u_1)/u_1, \pi_X(u_2)/u_2, ..., \pi_X(u_n)/u_n\}$$

Here, $\pi_X(u_i)$, $u_i \in U$ denotes the possibility that u_i is true. Let π_X and F be the possibility distribution representation and the fuzzy set representation for a fuzzy value, respectively.

FUZZY SETS AND CONTENT-BASED IMAGE RETRIEVAL

A content-based image retrieval (CBIR) system is typically divided into off-line feature extraction and online image retrieval (Wei, Li and Wilson, 2005). In off-line extraction, the contents of images are extracted and described as features. In online image retrieval, the user can submit a query specification to the retrieval system for searching desired images. In order to improve the efficiencies of searching images, indexing methods are usually used in the retrieval system for feature sets. Also user can provide relevance feedback to the retrieval system in order to get better search results. It should be noted that typical content-based image retrieval systems need to handle the inherent uncertainty in feature representation, spatial relation models, similarity measures, indexing methods, and relevance feedback. Fuzzy set theory can effectively be used for this purpose. Applying fuzzy processing techniques to the CBIR systems has been extensively studied in the literature.

Fuzzy Logic in Feature Extractions and Representations for Image Retrieval

In a CBIR system, visual features in images generally include color features, texture features and shape features. Color features are among the most important features used in image retrieval. First of all, let us focus on applications of fuzzy logic in extraction and representation of color features in the CBIR systems.

Fuzzy Logic for Color Features

In (Seaborn, Hepplewhite and Stonham, 1999), a color space for content based image retrieval is presented, which is based upon psychophysical research into human perception. The proposed color space provides both the ability to measure similarity and determine dissimilarity, using fuzzy logic and psychologically based set theoretic similarity measurement. These properties are shown to be equal or superior to conventional color spaces.

Focusing on the possible embedding of the uncertainty regarding the colors of an image into histogram-type descriptors, Vertan and Boujemaa (2000) propose a color histogram approach. They define various fuzzy color histograms following a taxonomy that classifies fuzzy techniques as crude fuzzy, fuzzy paradigm based, fuzzy aggregational and fuzzy inferential. Finally a class of similarity distances is defined based on fuzzy logic operations.

In (Liang, Zhai and Chavel, 2002), an application of fuzzy relations in fuzzy set theory is proposed to the measure of color identity, where a membership function is used as a measure of the similarity, and a fuzzy-match of two colors is defined by the α-cut fuzzy relation. Also a fuzzy-search process of color histograms is developed to save from massive unnecessary calculations.

In (Han and Ma, 2002), a color histogram representation, called fuzzy color histogram (FCH), is presented by considering the color similarity of each pixel's color associated to all the histogram bins through fuzzy-set membership function. An approach for computing the membership values based on fuzzy-means algorithm is developed. The proposed FCH is further exploited in the application of image indexing and retrieval.

In (Younes, Truck and Akdag, 2005), a software system for image indexing and retrieval is presented. The classification proposed there is based on the dominant color(s) of the images. The process consists in assigning a colorimetric profile to the image in HLS (Hue, Lightness, Saturation) space. First, the definition of hue is done thanks to a fuzzy representation to take into account the non-uniformity of colors distribution. And then, lightness and saturation are represented through linguistic qualifiers also defined in a fuzzy way. Finally, the profile is built through fuzzy functions representing the membership degree of the image to different classes. In order to improve the performances i.e. to define more accurate profiles, zones of pixels, instead of pixels individually are considered. Those zones can be constructed thanks to an edge detection algorithm. A sample of pixels is chosen inside a zone to determine the color of the zone. According to the detected dominant colors, such a software system may be used to classify indoor/outdoor images or harmonious/disharmonious images.

Each color space in color image histograms consists of three components leads to 3-dimensional histograms. The procedure of projecting the 3D histogram onto one single-dimension histogram is called histogram linking. In (Konstantinidis, Gasteratos and Andreadis, 2005), a fuzzy linking method of color histogram creation is proposed based on the L*a*b* color space and provides a histogram which contains only 10 bins. The histogram creation method in hand is assessed based on the performances achieved in retrieving similar images from a widely diverse image collection.

In (Chamorro-Martínez, Sánchez, Prados-Suarez and Soto-Hidalgo, 2006), a fuzzy approach for dealing with imprecision in the image color description is presented. The notion of fuzzy dominant color is introduced on the basis of a definition of fuzzy HIS color space. Based on the dominant fuzzy colors, inclusion and resemblance query operators are used for flexibly retrieving images by means of color linguistic labels. In (Chamorro-Martínez, Sánchez and Soto-Hidalgo, 2008), fuzzy naturals-based histograms on fuzzy color spaces are introduced. In the proposed approach, histograms are fuzzy probability distributions on a fuzzy color space, where the fuzzy probability is calculated as the quotient between a fuzzy natural number and the number of pixels in the image, the former being a fuzzy (non-scalar) cardinality of a fuzzy set. This approach to histograms avoids the well-known disadvantages of the ordinary sigma-count as an estimation of the probability. It is illustrated that the potential application of the proposal by applying it to the problem of dominant color selection.

To assign a colorimetric profile to the image in HLS (Hue, Lightness, Saturation) space, in (Younes, Truck and Akdag, 2007), a definition of hue is presented using a fuzzy representation that takes into account the non-uniformity of color distribution. Lightness and saturation are represented through linguistic qualifiers also defined in a fuzzy way. The profile is built through fuzzy functions representing the membership degree of the image to different classes. Thus, the query for image retrieval is a pair (hue, qualifier). Finally the user can re-define the fuzzy representation of Hue, Lightness and Saturation, according to his own perception while looking for a match between the query and the profiles for the query for the retrieval.

In (Bhoyar and Kakde, 2009), two different approaches to color binning and subsequent JNS (Just Not the Same) color histogram computation are discussed. The first approach is based on a Neural Network Color Classifier trained using error back prorogation training algorithm. The second approach is based on heuristically designed fuzzy classifier using fuzzy if-then rules for classifying color pixels into one of the eleven JNS colors. Color signatures for images in the database are obtained using both the methods. Then a fuzzy set theoretic approach is proposed to describe and extract the fuzzy color semantics that attempt to reduce the semantic gap between the low-level visual features and the high-level semantic features. Five linguistic variables are used to represent the image color semantics providing a flexible query scheme that is able to effectively represent vagueness in human color perception.

Fuzzy Logic for Texture Features

Kulkarni and Verma (2003) present a fuzzy logic based approach for the interpretation of texture queries. Tamura feature extraction technique is used to extract each texture feature of an image in the database. A term set on each Tamura feature is generated by a fuzzy clustering algorithm to pose a query in terms of natural language. The query can be expressed as a logic combination of natural language terms and tamura feature values. The performance of the technique was evaluated on Brodatz texture benchmark database.

For the problem of imprecision in texture description, Chamorro-Martínez, Galán-Perales, Sánchez and Prados-Suarez (2006) propose a methodology to represent texture concepts by means of fuzzy sets. They model the concept of "coarseness", the most extended in texture analysis, relating representative measures of this kind of texture (usually some statistic) with its presence degree. To obtain these "presence degrees" related to human perception, they propose a methodology to collect assessments from polls filled by human subjects, performing an aggregation of these assessments by means of OWA operators. Using as reference set a combination of some statistics, the membership function corresponding to the fuzzy set "coarseness" is modeled as the function which provides the best fit of the collected data. In (Chamorro-Martínez and Martínez-Jiménez, 2010), a method to adapt the fuzzy sets that models the "coarseness" texture property according to different coarse-fine perceptions is proposed. The membership functions associated to these fuzzy sets are obtained on the basis of the human assessments given by a pool, which represent the average coarse-fine perception degree. The user's particular perception about coarseness fineness and the changes in perception influenced by the image context are taken into account to adapt the models. The membership functions are automatically adapted by means of a transformation of functions on the basis of the new coarse-fine perception.

Fuzzy Logic for Shape Features

Chanussot, Nystrom and Sladoje (2005) extend the shape signature based on the distance of the boundary points from the shape centroid, to the case of fuzzy sets. The analysis of the transition from crisp to fuzzy shape descriptor is first given in the continuous case. They analyze two methods for calculating the signature of a fuzzy shape, derived from two ways of defining a fuzzy set: first, by its membership function, and second, as a stack of its α-cuts. The first approach is based on measuring the length of a fuzzy straight line by integration of the fuzzy membership function, while in the second one we use averaging of the shape signatures obtained for the individual α-cuts of the fuzzy set. The two methods, equivalent in the continuous case for the studied class of fuzzy shapes, produce different results when adjusted to the discrete case. A statistical study, aiming at characterizing the performances of each method in the discrete case, is done.

Also there are some works on applying fuzzy logics for the extractions and representations of several features (e.g., color and shape features, color and texture features, and even color, texture and shape) simultaneously. This chapter does not discuss these works further.

Fuzzy Logic in Similarity Measures and Indexing for Image Retrieval

After features (colors, shapes, textures) of images in database are extracted and represented, features of the query specification are compared with features of the image database to determine which images match correctly (similar) with the given features. The matching process is based on similarity measure between query image and images in databases.

Color features are among the most important features used in image retrieval and direct histogram comparison is the most commonly used technique in measuring color similarity of images. In (Chaira and Ray, 2005), a scheme for fuzzy similarity based strategy is presented to retrieve an image from a library of color images. A gamma membership function, derived from the Gamma distribution, is hereby proposed to find the membership values of the gray levels of the histogram. The presented image retrieval scheme is with some popular vector fuzzy distance measures using a gamma membership function for finding the membership values of the gray levels, and the matching function is evaluated to select the appropriate retrieval mechanism.

In (Chien and Cheng, 2002), an image segmentation scheme is proposed based on fuzzy color similarity measure to segment out meaningful objects in an image according to human perception. The proposed method first defines a set of fuzzy colors based on the HLS color coordinate space. Each pixel in an image is represented by a set of fuzzy colors that are the most similar colors in the color palette selected by human. Then, a fuzzy similarity measure is developed for evaluating the similarity of fuzzy colors between two pixels. Adjacent pixels are recursively merged to form meaningful objects by the fuzzy similarity measure until there is no similar color between adjacent pixels.

In (Gadi, Benslimane, Daoudi and Matusiak, 1999), the Fourier-based shape descriptions are used and the images are represented by an N-dimensional feature vectors. The similarity measure is calculated for each component of the features vectors. Each pair of images has N similarity measures. The global similarity measure is obtained by two methods: using a fuzzy If-Then rule; considering each similarity measure obtained between two components as an opinion and then the global similarity measure consists in choosing a global opinion from the all.

Based on fuzzy similarity metrics, Tolias, Panas and Tsoukalas (1999) present an image retrieval system, which uses shape and color information to generate a 2630 byte long information vector that describes the shape and color distribution in the image. This information is generated by the application of the Discrete Wavelet Transform to the YIQ colorspace and picking the appropriate information by quantization of the Y channel coefficients and using fuzzy linguistics variables for color description. The information vectors that correspond to the images in a given database are used for the queries. Queries are carried out using the Generalized Tversky Index, a similarity index that is based on human similarity perception, which has been developed by the authors. Different retrieval results are calculated for shape and color; a final data fusion process takes place to provide the overall results.

In (Omhover, Detyniecki, Rifqi and Bouchon-Meunier, 2004), the fuzzy similarity measures in the context of a CBIR system are introduced, which leads to the observation of an invariance in the ranking for different similarity measures. Then an explanation to this phenomenon and a larger theory about order invariance for fuzzy similarity measures is proposed. A definition for equivalence classes is introduced based on order conservation between these measures. Then the consequences of this theory on the evaluation of document retrieval by fuzzy similarity are investigated.

Since a feature vector of an image is usually in the multi-dimensional space (Fonseca and

Jorge, 2003), retrieval of an image with multi-dimensional feature vector needs fast execution of search operations. At this point, indexing dimensional feature sets is very useful and helpful for image retrieval.

In (Vereb, 2003), a two-layer content-based image retrieval model is described. The model has a prefilter indexing function, based on a possible class hierarchy of the images to be stored. Based on this hierarchical indexing some typified queries can be introduced. The δ distance function used in the queries can be defined by a fuzzy algorithm based on the cut operation and the fuzzy logical connectives. This approach is called cut-and-or-not.

In (Zhang, Zhang and Yao, 2003), a indexing and retrieval methodology, called PicSearcher, is described, which integrates color, texture and shape information for content-based image retrieval in online image databases. This methodology applies unsupervised image segmentation to partition an image into a set of regions, then fuzzy color histogram as well as fuzzy texture and shape properties of each region is calculated to be part of their signatures. The fuzzification procedures resolve the recognition uncertainty stemming from color quantization and human perception of colors. At the same time, this unified fuzzy scheme incorporates the segmentation-related uncertainties into the retrieval algorithm. Then an adaptive and effective measure for the overall similarity between images is developed by integrating properties of all the regions in the image.

Fuzzy Logic in Relevance Feedback for Image Retrieval

For a given query, the retrieval system returns initial results based on predefined similarity metrics. In order to improve the effectiveness of the retrieval system, one way is that the user provides feedback regarding the retrieval results by qualifying images returned as either "relevant" or "irrelevant" so that the retrieval system can identify what the user is really looking for. With feedback, the retrieval system learns the visual features of the images and returns improved results to the user.

The problem of incorporating prior experience of the retrieval system is addressed to improve the performance on future queries in (Bhanu and Dong, 2001 & 2002). A semi-supervised fuzzy clustering method is proposed to learn class distribution (meta knowledge) in the sense of high-level concepts from retrieval experience. Using fuzzy rules, the meta knowledge is incorporated into a probabilistic feature relevance feedback approach to improve the retrieval performance.

In (Zhou, Zhang, Lin, Deng and Wu, 2003), an image retrieval method based on the accumulated user relevance feedback records is presented. The semi-supervised fuzzy clustering on the records is conducted, and the subsequent information filtering within the target cluster is performed to guide the refinement of query parameters. During information filtering, both the user's relevance evaluation and the corresponding query image of the records are used to predict the semantic correlation between the current retrieval query sample and the database images.

Yap and Wu (2005) presents a framework called fuzzy relevance feedback in interactive content-based image retrieval (CBIR) systems based on soft-decision. They propose a learning approach using a fuzzy radial basis function network (FRBFN) and integrate the users' fuzzy interpretation of visual content into the notion of relevance feedback. Based on the users' feedbacks, an FRBFN is constructed, and the underlying parameters and network structure are optimized using a gradient-descent training strategy.

In (Yager and Petry, 2005), an approach to relevance feedback in content-based image retrieval is developed to capture more of the users' relevance judgments by allowing the use of natural language like comments on the retrieved images.

These comments can be reflected into new targets for searching the image database by using methods from fuzzy logic and computational intelligence. Such enhanced information is utilized to develop a system that can provide more effective and efficient retrieval.

Banerjee and Kundu (2007) propose a relevance feedback frame work, which evaluates the features, from fuzzy entropy based feature evaluation index (FEI) for optimal retrieval by considering both the relevant as well as irrelevant set of the retrieved images marked by the users. The results obtained using their algorithm are compared with the agreed upon standards for visual content descriptors of MPEG-7 core experiments.

In (Javidi, Pourreza and Yazdi, 2010), a system of fuzzy relevance feedback for image retrieval is introduced, in which a soft feedback model is used to construct Fuzzy Transaction Repository (FTR) based on user interactions. FTR records the user's intent and, therefore, in terms of the semantic meanings, provides a better representation of each image in the database. The semantic similarity between the query and each database image can then be computed using the current feedback and the semantic values in the FTR. Furthermore, feature re-weighting is applied to the session-term feedback in order to learn the weight of low-level features. These two similarity measures are normalized and combined together to form the overall similarity measure.

Widyanto and Maftukhah (2010) propose fuzzy relevance feedback using Query Vector Modification (QVM) method in image retrieval. They propose six relevance levels are: "very relevant", "relevant", "few relevant", "vague", "not relevant", and "very non relevant" for feedback. For computation of user feedback result, QVM method is proposed to repeatedly reformulate the query vector through user feedback. The system derives the image similarity by computing the Euclidean distance and computation of color parameter value by Red, Green, and Blue (RGB) color model. Five steps for fuzzy relevance feedback are: image similarity, output image, computation of membership value, feedback computation, and feedback result.

Fuzzy Logic in CBIR Systems

Combining the applications of fuzzy sets in feature extractions and representations, similarity measures and indexing, and relevance feedback for image retrieval, some fuzzy content-based image retrieval systems have been developed in the literature.

In (Chen and Wang, 2002), a fuzzy logic approach named UFM (unified feature matching) is proposed for region-based image retrieval. In the retrieval system, an image is represented by a set of segmented regions, each of which is characterized by a fuzzy feature (fuzzy set) reflecting color, texture, and shape properties. As a result, an image is associated with a family of fuzzy features corresponding to regions. Fuzzy features naturally characterize the gradual transition between regions (blurry boundaries) within an image and incorporate the segmentation-related uncertainties into the retrieval algorithm. The resemblance of two images is then defined as the overall similarity between two families of fuzzy features and quantified by a similarity measure, UFM measure, which integrates properties of all the regions in the images.

Huang, Chang and Huang (2003) present a region-based prototype image retrieval system named FuzzyImage. An image is segmented into regions depending on clustering similar feature vectors by fuzzy c-means. Then a similar measurement is used to evaluate the similarity between the query image and incorporated regions. The users can select the most interesting regions from 5 sample images that pop-up, and by feedback to the system. Based on the selected individual regions of query images, the overall similarity helps filter out irrelevant images in a database after relevance feedback and enables a simple user-oriented query interface for a region-based image retrieval system.

In (Krishnapuram *et al*, 2004), an image retrieval system called FIRST (Fuzzy Image Retrieval SysTem) is described. FIRST uses Fuzzy Attributed Relational Graphs (FARGs) to represent images, where each node in the graph represents an image region and each edge represents a relation between two regions. FIRST supports exemplar-based, graphical-sketch-based, as well as linguistic queries involving region labels, attributes, and spatial relations. The given query is converted to a FARG, and a fuzzy graph matching algorithm is used to compare the query graph with the FARGs in the database.

Chiu, Lin and Yang (2003) propose a fuzzy logic framework to realize a personalized CBIR system, and define a query description language to unify the query expression of textual descriptions, visual examples, and relevance feedbacks. In their CBIR system, the proposed unsupervised fuzzy clustering algorithm builds a mapping from low-level image features (Tamura features) to high level human concepts (linguistic terms) in a fully automated way to alleviate the semantic gap problem; the proposed framework captures the user's preference on retrieval and retains it in his/her personal profile to alleviate the perception subjectivity problem.

Kulkarni (2004) proposes a neural-fuzzy based approach for retrieving a specific video clip from a video database. Fuzzy logic is used for expressing queries in terms of natural language and a neural network is designed to learn the meaning of these queries. The queries are designed based on features such as color and texture of shots, scenes and objects in video clips. An error back propagation algorithm is proposed to learn the meaning of queries in fuzzy terms such as very similar, similar and some-what similar.

DATABASE SUPPORT FOR FUZZY IMAGE RETRIEVAL

Image databases can be viewed as controlled collections of images. Concurrently image databases are used by many users, managing a great amount of data, and requiring fast query resolution. This fact leads to the need for database management systems (DBMS) in image management to ensure high performance, scalability, availability with fault tolerance and distribution. While some work has been done on fuzzy content-based retrieval systems, there are few studies working on fuzzy query processing based on a defined database model and fuzzy image database models.

Fuzzy Queries for Image Databases

In image databases with complex structures, images are retrieved and selected not only from their contents, but also from users' descriptions of their appearance through queries specified in terms of user's criteria. It is well known that fuzzy logic can provide a convenient tool for interfacing linguistic categories and expressing user's preference in a gradual and qualitative way. Fuzzy logic methods have been already applied in databases systems and information retrieval to represent flexible queries. In a typical content-based image retrieval (CBIR) system, image databases would also need to handle the vagueness in the user queries.

Fagin (1998) surveys some issues that arise for multimedia queries, and particularly studies fuzzy queries in multimedia database systems. The uncertainty is only allowed at attribute level. The comparison of values at different levels of uncertainty is not considered.

Focusing on image classification and retrieval, Shahabi and Chen (2000) extend an object-relational database system, namely Informix Universal Server, to support soft query. Towards this end, they propose a united model to support soft querying and classification on image databases. The model borrows heavily from the meld of fuzzy logic. The model maintains a profile for each user, which contains the membership value for every image-class pair. For the cases where values for some of these pairs are missing, the model provides estimation based on the level of confidence that this user has on other users. To support a user query, the model combines the profile information with conventional feature similarity algorithms, in a united manner.

Based on the ODMG Object Query Language (OQL), Nepal, Ramakrishna and Thom (1999) propose a Fuzzy Object Query Language (FOQL). The syntax and semantics of a few FOQL constructs are described using an example image database by example queries. Also they describe how the FOQL constructs help the users to formulate queries and handle the underlying problems in CBIR systems such as mapping low level features to high level concepts. Since FOQL is based on ODMG standard, FOQL can be easily mapped into the ODMG-compliant visual query languages.

Dubois, Prade and Sedes (2001) provide a preliminary investigation of the potential applications of fuzzy logic in multimedia databases. The emphasis is on querying issues: detecting similar semistructured documents, intending to extend SQL/OQL-like queries, and querying by examples. They suggest two types of applications of fuzzy-set-based methods in relation with specificities of multimedia systems: the extensions of SQL-like query language and an approach to querying by examples.

Fuzzy Conceptual Data Models for Image Databases

In general image understanding is context-dependent and very subjective. As a result, it is not always possible to express the semantic image content in a precise way. Conceptual data modeling is the first step of semantic image modeling and the uncertain information should be taken into account in order to build a more expressive conceptual data model and be able to handle queries involving in some form of uncertainty.

A conceptual data model is presented in (Aygun and Yazici, 2004) for multimedia database applications based on ExIFO$_2$ model. ExIFO$_2$ proposed originally in (Yazici, Buckles and Petry, 1999) is a fuzzy object-oriented conceptual data model based on IFO data model, which is a mathematically defined conceptual data model that incorporates the fundamental principles of semantic database modeling within a graph-based representational framework (Abiteboul and Hull, 1987). ExIFO$_2$ data model in (Aygun and Yazici, 2004) is enhanced in order to meet the multimedia data requirements, and supports the representation of uncertainty at the attribute level, object/class level and class/subclass level. In addition to uncertain and imprecise information, A way of handling relationships among objects of multimedia database applications is presented also. The conceptual model is finally mapped to a logical model, in which the fuzzy object-oriented data (FOOD) model is chosen, for storing and manipulating the multimedia objects. This mapping is done in a way that it preserves most of the information represented at the conceptual level.

Video can basically be regarded as a consecutive sequence of images ordered in time. Also video data may contain uncertainty due to their complex and subjective semantic content. In order to manage fuzzy video data in multimedia databases, UML (unified modeling language) is extend in (Ozgur, Koyuncu and Yazici, 2009) to represent complex and rich semantic content and knowledge of video data with uncertainty. The fuzzy conceptual model UML is used finally to map to FOOD, a fuzzy object-oriented database. Also in (Kucuk, Burcuozgur, Yazici and Koyuncu, 2009), the fuzzy UML, a fuzzy conceptual data model, is used for multimedia data and its application to news video domain. The proposed model takes an object oriented approach with the ability to handle fuzziness at the attribute, object/class and class/superclass levels. Also the model handles its hierarchical structure and the spatial and temporal relations among the data. In order to apply the model to the domain of news videos, they define several new classes inheriting from the classes in the model to add domain-specific attributes.

Fuzzy Database Models for Image Databases

Storing images in an image database can provide a natural and effective way to access image data. Some work has been done on fuzzy content-based image retrieval systems, but few of them rely on a defined database model. In order to model imprecision and uncertainty of images in databases, the fuzzy databases have been applied as image databases for image storage and retrieval (query). The fuzzy databases include the fuzzy extended relational databases (fuzzy extended RDBs), fuzzy nested relational databases, fuzzy object-oriented databases and fuzzy object-relational databases. Since image data are generally complex, generally the fuzzy relational databases are not used to represent image data. With the fuzzy databases, the imprecise descriptions of image characteristics such as color, shape, texture and semantics are represented and the queries are carried out.

The relational database model is extended in (Wu and Nerasimhalu, 1998) to accommodate facial images and their fuzzy descriptions by allowing ADTs (abstract data types) in the relation tables. Based on the extension of the relation model for fuzzy image database, a tuple relation calculus is extended for content-based fuzzy query processing. Then a concept of fuzzy space is proposed and fuzzy query processing in fuzzy space and fuzzy indexing on complex fuzzy vectors are described. An example image database, the computer-aided facial image inference and retrieval system (CAFIIR), is used to test the content-based fuzzy retrieval of images.

Chianese *et al.* (2004) present a fuzzy approach for image databases. They exploit the fuzzy NF^2 relational model as a foundation for building image catalogues containing the semantic description of a given image database. In order to capture the fuzziness related to the semantic descriptors of an image, the algebraic operators are defined in the proposed model. From the operational point of view, the NF2 relational model is considered being equivalent to the First Normal Form annotated relation model, and can provide a suitable framework for dealing with uncertainties in image databases.

The Object Model of ODMG is extended in (Nepal, Ramakrishna and Thom, 1999) to include fuzzy data types, which are necessary to handle the fuzzy information encountered in the image databases, and the Fuzzy Object Model is hereby proposed. The Object Definition Language (ODL) is extended to Fuzzy Object Definition Language (FODL) to enable users to define fuzzy data in the schema specification. The Fuzzy Object Model extends the built-in types to support fuzzy data, including the fuzzy literal types (Fuzzyboolean atomic literal and Fuzzy collection literal) and the fuzzy collection object types (Fuzzyset, Fuzzybag and Fuzzylist).

Using the fuzzy object-oriented database (FOOD) model, Gokcen, Yazici and Buckles (2000) present an approach for fuzzy content-based retrieval in image databases. For that purpose, the histogram value is considered and a way of calculating the histogram value for each tile is given. Note that the feature included in (Gokcen, Yazici and Buckles, 2000) is only the histogram value, and more complex queries retrieving images are generally based on not only color but also the other features (e.g., cloud pixels, texture, shape etc.). The fuzzy object-oriented data (FOOD) model is chosen in (Aygun and Yazici, 2004) to store and manipulate the multimedia objects. Here the multimedia objects and the relationships among objects of multimedia database applications may contain uncertain and imprecise information and are modeled first in the ExIFO2 data model, a conceptual model which can deal with complex objects along with their uncertain and imprecise properties in order to meet the multimedia data requirements. The ExIFO2 data model is then is mapped to the FOOD model. Based on the FOOD model, videos of football (soccer) games is selected as the multimedia database application to show how they handle crisp and fuzzy querying and retrieval of fuzzy and crisp data from the database. Also Ozgur, Koyuncu and Yazici (2009) introduce an intelligent fuzzy object-oriented database framework (IFOOD), which mainly consists of two parts: a fuzzy object-oriented database (FOOD) and a fuzzy knowledge base (FKB), to represent fuzzy video data in database and to represent complex relationships and knowledge in the form of temporal, spatial and fuzzy semantic rules in knowledge base. Complex and rich semantic content and knowledge of video data with uncertainty are represented first in the fuzzily extended UML. Then the fuzzy conceptual model UML is used to map to the FOOD. Based on the introduced IFOOD, various flexible queries, including (fuzzy) semantic, temporal and (fuzzy) spatial queries, are investigated.

Uysal and Yarman Vural (2005) concentrate on finding a discriminative feature set for each class. For this purpose, Fuzzy ARTMAP architecture is utilized to learn the relevance of each feature for each query class by identifying the weight vectors for features. The weight vector for features is used to label the database, which is used for querying. The proposed system uses the fuzzy object-oriented databases.

In (Chamorro-Martíneza *et al.*, 2005; Barranco *et al.*, 2006; Chamorro-Martíneza *et al.*, 2007), a fuzzy approach for image retrieval on the basis of color features is presented, which deals with vagueness in the color description. The concept of dominant fuzzy color is proposed for the color description, using linguistic labels for representing the color information in terms of hue, saturation and intensity. The use of fuzzy object-relational database model is introduced to store and retrieve imprecise data. In order to deal with fuzzy data in the proposed database model, a general approach supporting the manipulation of fuzzy objects in an object-relational database system is applied, which allows the retrieval of images by performing flexible queries on the database. In (Medina *et al.*, 2009), a fuzzy object-relational database management system (FORDBMS) is used for X-Ray image storage. The system stores X-Ray images along with a set of parameters describing their content, where parameter curves are obtained from X-Ray images of patients suffering from scoliosis. When looking for images with a determined curve pattern, queries can be performed over these parameters to retrieve images matching visually.

It is shown above that the fuzzy extended relational databases, fuzzy nested relational databases, fuzzy object-oriented databases, and fuzzy object-relational databases have been applied for modeling the imprecision and uncertainty in image databases. In addition to these fuzzy database models mentioned above, there are some other types of fuzzy data models that are proposed for image databases. In (Majumdar, Bhattacharya and Saha, 2002), an object-oriented graph theoretic model is proposed to represent an image, which may have uncertainty in the context of spatial and topological relations existing among the objects in the image. With the proposed model, it is allowed to assess the similarity between images using the concept of (fuzzy) graph matching and then flexibility is provided in the similarity algorithm.

CONCLUSION

In this chapter, we review fuzzy set theoretic approach for dealing with uncertainty in image retrieval. The focus is mainly on two aspects of existing work: the first one is research work about the application of fuzzy sets in the extraction and representation of visual (colors, shapes, textures) features, similarity measures and indexing, relevance feedback, and retrieval systems; the second one is research work about the application of fuzzy sets in fuzzy image query processing based on a defined database models and research work about various fuzzy database models in image data management.

The problem of fuzzy image search is a large problem with many aspects. There is a large number of interesting research problems where fuzzy logic can be applied to image search. While work has begun on many of these problems, the area is still wide open for new results. It is especially true when user issue semantic image search. The chapter does not review the research work on this topic. It can be believed that fuzzy logic can play an important role in image search.

ACKNOWLEDGMENT

The work is supported in part by the *National Natural Science Foundation of China* (60873010 and 61073139) and the *Fundamental Research Funds for the Central Universities* (N090504005, N090604012 and N090104001).

REFERENCES

Abiteboul, S., & Hull, R. (1987). IFO: A formal semantic database model. *ACM Transactions on Database Systems*, *12*(4), 525–565. doi:10.1145/32204.32205

Aygun, R. S., & Yazici, A. (2004). Modeling and management of fuzzy information in multimedia database applications. *Multimedia Tools and Applications*, *24*(1), 29–56. doi:10.1023/B:MTAP.0000033982.50288.14

Banerjee, M., & Kundu, M. K. (2007). Image retrieval using fuzzy relevance feedback and validation with MPEG-7 content descriptors. *Proceedings of the 2007 International Conference on Pattern Recognition and Machine Intelligence . Lecture Notes in Computer Science*, *4815*, 144–152. doi:10.1007/978-3-540-77046-6_18

Barranco, C. D., Medina, J. M., Chamorro-Martinez, J., & Soto-Hidalgo, J. M. (2006). Using a fuzzy object-relational database for colour image retrieval. *Proceedings of the 7th International Conference on Flexible Query Answering Systems . Lecture Notes in Computer Science*, *4027*, 307–318. doi:10.1007/11766254_26

Bhanu, B., & Dong, A. L. (2001). Concepts learning with fuzzy clustering and relevance feedback. *Proceedings of the Second International Workshop on Machine Learning and Data Mining in Pattern Recognition . Lecture Notes in Computer Science*, *2123*, 102–116. doi:10.1007/3-540-44596-X_9

Bhanu, B., & Dong, A. L. (2002). Concepts learning with fuzzy clustering and relevance feedback. *Engineering Applications of Artificial Intelligence*, *15*, 123–138. doi:10.1016/S0952-1976(02)00026-X

Bhoyar, K. K., & Kakde, O. G. (2009). Image retrieval using fuzzy and neuro-fuzzy approaches with fuzzy color semantics. *Proceedings of the 2009 International Conference on Digital Image Processing*, (pp. 39-44).

Bosc, P., & Prade, H. (1993). An introduction to fuzzy set and possibility theory based approaches to the treatment of uncertainty and imprecision in database management systems. *Proceedings of the Second Workshop on Uncertainty Management in Information Systems: From Needs to Solutions*.

Chaira, T., & Ray, A. K. (2005). Fuzzy measures for color image retrieval. *Fuzzy Sets and Systems*, *150*(3), 545–560. doi:10.1016/j.fss.2004.09.003

Chamorro-Martínez, J., Galán-Perales, E., Sánchez, D., & Prados-Suarez, B. (2006). A fuzzy approach to image texture representation applied to visual coarseness description. *Proceedings of the 2006 IEEE International Conference on Fuzzy Systems*, (pp. 6019-6024).

Chamorro-Martínez, J., & Martínez-Jiménez, P. (2010). An adaptive fuzzy approach for texture modelling. *Proceedings of the 2010 IEEE World Congress on Computational Intelligence*, (pp. 624-629).

Chamorro-Martinez, J., Medina, J. M., Barranco, C., Galan-Perales, E., & Soto-Hidalgo, J. M. (2005). An approach to image retrieval on fuzzy object-relational database using dominant color descriptors. *Proceedings of the 4th Conference of the European Society for Fuzzy Logic and Technology*, (pp. 676-684).

Chamorro-Martínez, J., Sánchez, D., Prados-Suarez, B., & Soto-Hidalgo, J. M. (2006). A fuzzy approach to dominant color description for image retrieval. *Proceedings of the 2006 International Conference on Information Processing and Management of Uncertainty*, (pp. 1564-1569).

Chamorro-Martínez, J., Sánchez, D., & Soto-Hidalgo, J. M. (2008). A novel histogram definition for fuzzy color spaces. *Proceedings of the 2008 IEEE International Conference on Fuzzy Systems*, (pp. 2149-2156).

Chamorro-Martíneza, J., Medinaa, J. M., Barrancob, C. D., Galán-Peralesa, E., & Soto-Hidalgoa, J. M. (2007). Retrieving images in fuzzy object-relational databases using dominant color descriptors. *Fuzzy Sets and Systems*, *158*, 312–324. doi:10.1016/j.fss.2006.10.013

Chanussot, J., Nystrom, I., & Sladoje, N. (2005). Shape signatures of fuzzy star-shaped sets based on distance from the centroid. *Pattern Recognition Letters*, *26*, 735–746. doi:10.1016/j.patrec.2004.09.025

Chen, Y. X., & Wang, J. Z. (2002). A region-based fuzzy feature matching approach to content-based image retrieval. *IEEE Transactions on Pattern Analysis and Machine Intelligence*, *24*(9), 1252–1267. doi:10.1109/TPAMI.2002.1033216

Chianese, A., Picariello, A., Sansone, L., & Sapino, M. L. (2004). Managing uncertainties in image databases: a fuzzy approach. *Multimedia Tools and Applications*, *23*, 237–252. doi:10.1023/B:MTAP.0000031759.22145.5d

Chien, B.-C., & Cheng, M.-C. (2002). A color image segmentation approach based on fuzzy similarity measure. *Proceedings of the 2002 IEEE International Conference on Fuzzy Systems*, 1, (pp. 449-454).

Chiu, C.-Y., Lin, H.-C., & Yang, S.-N. (2003). A fuzzy logic CBIR system. *Proceedings of the 12th IEEE International Conference on Fuzzy Systems*, 2, (pp. 1171-1176).

Dalvi, N., & Suciu, D. (2007). Management of probabilistic data: Foundations and challenges. *Proceedings of the 2007 ACM SIGACT-SIGMOD-SIGART Symposium on Principles of Database Systems*, (pp. 1-12).

Datta, R., Joshi, D., Li, J., & Wang, J. Z. (2008). Image retrieval: Ideas, influences, and trends of the new age. *ACM Computing Surveys*, *40*(2), 1–60. doi:10.1145/1348246.1348248

DeMichiel, L. G. (1989). Resolving database incompatibility: An approach to performing relational operations over mismatched domains. *IEEE Transactions on Knowledge and Data Engineering*, *1*(4), 485–493. doi:10.1109/69.43423

Dubois, D., Prade, H., & Sedes, F. (2001). Fuzzy logic techniques in multimedia database querying: A preliminary investigation of the potentials. *IEEE Transactions on Knowledge and Data Engineering*, *13*(3), 383–392. doi:10.1109/69.929896

Fagin, R. (1998). Fuzzy queries in multimedia database systems. *Proceedings of the 1998 ACM Symposium on Principles of Database Systems*, (pp. 1-10).

Fonseca, M. J., & Jorge, J. A. (2003). Indexing high-dimensional data for content-based retrieval in large database. *Proceedings of the Eighth International Conference on Database Systems for Advanced Applications*, (pp. 267-274).

Gadi, T., Benslimane, R., Daoudi, M., & Matusiak, S. (1999). Fuzzy similarity measure for shape retrieval. *Proceedings of the 1999 Canadian Conference in Computer Vision, Signal and Image Processing and Pattern Recognition*, (pp. 386-389).

Gokcen, I., Yazici, A., & Buckles, B. P. (2000). Fuzzy content-based retrieval in image databases. *Proceedings of the First International Conference on Advances in Information Systems . Lecture Notes in Computer Science, 1909*, 226–237. doi:10.1007/3-540-40888-6_21

Han, J., & Ma, K. K. (2002). Fuzzy color histogram and its use in color image retrieval. *IEEE Transactions on Image Processing, 11*(8), 944–952. doi:10.1109/TIP.2002.801585

Huang, Y.-P., Chang, T.-W., & Huang, C.-Z. (2003). A fuzzy feature clustering with relevance feedback approach to content-based image retrieval. *Proceedings of 2003 IEEE International Symposium on Virtual Environments, Human-Computer Interfaces and Measurement Systems*, (pp. 57-62).

Javidi, M., Pourreza, H. R., & Yazdi, H. S. (2010). A semantic feedback framework for image retrieval. *International Journal of Computer and Electrical Engineering, 2*(3), 1793–8163.

Konstantinidis, K., Gasteratos, A., & Andreadis, I. (2005). Image retrieval based on fuzzy color histogram processing. *Optics Communications, 248*(4-6), 375–386. doi:10.1016/j.optcom.2004.12.029

Krishnapuram, R., Medasani, S., Jung, S.-H., Choi, Y.-S., & Balasubramaniam, R. (2004). Content-based image retrieval based on a fuzzy approach. *IEEE Transactions on Knowledge and Data Engineering, 16*(10), 1185–1199. doi:10.1109/TKDE.2004.53

Kucuk, D., Burcuozgur, N., Yazici, A., & Koyuncu, M. (2009). A fuzzy conceptual model for multimedia data with a text-based automatic annotation scheme. *International Journal of Uncertainty fuzziness and Knowledge-based Systems, 17*, 135-152.

Kulkarni, S. (2004). *Neural-fuzzy approach for content-based retrieval of digital video*. Canadian Conference on Electrical and Computer Engineering, 4, (pp. 2235–2238).

Kulkarni, S., & Verma, B. (2003). Fuzzy logic based texture queries for CBIR. *Proceedings of the 2003 International Conference on Computational Intelligence and Multimedia Applications*, (pp. 223-228).

Liang, Y. M., Zhai, H. C., & Chavel, P. (2002). Fuzzy color-image retrieval. *Optics Communications, 212*(4-6), 247–250. doi:10.1016/S0030-4018(02)02011-4

Majumdar, A. K., Bhattacharya, I., & Saha, A. K. (2002). An object-oriented fuzzy data model for similarity detection in image databases. *IEEE Transactions on Knowledge and Data Engineering, 14*(5), 1186–1189. doi:10.1109/TKDE.2002.1033783

Medina, J. M., Jaime-Castillo, S., Barranco, C. D., & Campana, J. R. (2009). Flexible retrieval of x-ray images based on shape descriptors using a fuzzy object-relational database. *Proceedings of the Joint 2009 International Fuzzy Systems Association World Congress and 2009 European Society of Fuzzy Logic and Technology Conference*, (pp. 903-908).

Morrissey, J. M. (1990). Imprecise information and uncertainty in Information Systems. *ACM Transactions on Information Systems*, *8*(2), 157–180. doi:10.1145/96105.96113

Müller, H., Michoux, N., Bandon, D., & Geissbuhler, A. (2004). A review of content-based image retrieval systems in medical applications – Clinical benefits and future directions. *International Journal of Medical Informatics*, *73*(1), 1–23. doi:10.1016/j.ijmedinf.2003.11.024

Nepal, S., Ramakrishna, M. V., & Thom, J. A. (1999). A fuzzy object query language (FOQL) for image databases. *Proceedings of the 6th International Conference on Database Systems for Advanced Applications*.

Omhover, J.-F., Detyniecki, M., Rifqi, M., & Bouchon-Meunier, B. (2004). Ranking invariance between fuzzy similarity measures applied to image retrieval. *Proceedings of the 2004 IEEE International Conference on Fuzzy Systems, 3*, (pp. 1367-1372).

Ozgur, N. B., Koyuncu, M., & Yazici, A. (2009). An intelligent fuzzy object-oriented database framework for video database applications. *Fuzzy Sets and Systems*, *160*, 2253–2274. doi:10.1016/j.fss.2009.02.017

Parsons, S. (1996). Current approaches to handling imperfect information in data and knowledge bases. *IEEE Transactions on Knowledge and Data Engineering*, *8*(2), 353–372. doi:10.1109/69.506705

Seaborn, M., Hepplewhite, L., & Stonham, J. (1999). Fuzzy colour category map for content based image retrieval. *Proceedings of the Tenth British Machine Vision Conference*, (pp. 103-112).

Shahabi, C., & Chen, Y.-S. (2000). Soft query in image retrieval systems. *Proceedings of the 2000 SPIE Internet Imaging, Electronic Imaging, 3964*, (pp. 57-68).

Shandilya, S. K., & Singhai, N. (2010). A survey on content based image retrieval systems. *International Journal of Computers and Applications*, *4*(2), 22–26. doi:10.5120/802-1139

Tolias, Y., Panas, S., & Tsoukalas, L. H. (1999). FSMIQ: Fuzzy similarity matching for image queries. *Proceedings of the 1999 International Conference on Information Intelligence and Systems*, (pp. 249-254).

Uysal, M., & Yarman Vural, F. T. (2005). A content-based fuzzy image database based on the fuzzy ARTMAP architecture. *Turk J Elec Engin*, *13*(3), 333–342.

Vereb, K. (2003). On a hierarchical indexing fuzzy content-based image retrieval approach. *Proceedings of the VLDB 2003 PhD Workshop*.

Vertan, C., & Boujemaa, N. (2000). Embedding fuzzy logic in content-based image retrieval. *Proceedings of the 2000 International Conference of the North American Fuzzy Information Processing Society*, (pp. 85-89).

Wei, C.-H., Li, C.-T., & Wilson, R. (2005). A content-based approach to medical image database retrieval . In Ma, Z. (Ed.), *Database modeling for industrial data management: Emerging technologies and applications*. Hershey, PA: Idea Group Publishing. doi:10.4018/978-1-59140-684-6.ch009

Widyanto, M. R., & Maftukhah, T. (2010). Fuzzy relevance feedback in image retrieval for color feature using query vector modification method. *Journal of Advanced Computational Intelligence and Intelligent Informatics*, *14*(1), 34–38.

Wu, J. K., & Nerasimhalu, D. (1998). Fuzzy content-based retrieval in image databases. *Information Processing & Management*, *34*(5), 513–534. doi:10.1016/S0306-4573(98)00017-X

Yager, R. R., & Petry, F. E. (2005). A framework for linguistic relevance feedback in content-based image retrieval using fuzzy logic. *Information Sciences*, *173*(4), 337–352. doi:10.1016/j.ins.2005.03.004

Yap, K.-H., & Wu, K. (2005). Fuzzy relevance feedback in content-based image retrieval systems using radial basis function network. *Proceedings of the 2005 IEEE International Conference on Multimedia and Expo*.

Yazici, A., Buckles, B. P., & Petry, F. E. (1999). Handling complex and uncertain information in the ExIFO and NF^2 data models. *IEEE Transactions on Fuzzy Systems*, *7*(6), 659–676. doi:10.1109/91.811232

Younes, A., Truck, I., & Akdag, H. (2005). Color image profiling using fuzzy sets. *Turk J Elec Engin*, *13*(3), 343–359.

Younes, A., Truck, I., & Akdag, H. (2007). Image retrieval using fuzzy representation of colors. *Soft Computing*, *11*(3), 287–298. doi:10.1007/s00500-006-0070-x

Zadeh, L. A. (1965). Fuzzy sets. *Information and Control*, *8*(3), 338–353. doi:10.1016/S0019-9958(65)90241-X

Zadeh, L. A. (1978). Fuzzy sets as a basis for a theory of possibility. *Fuzzy Sets and Systems*, *1*(1), 3–28. doi:10.1016/0165-0114(78)90029-5

Zhang, R., Zhang, Z., & Yao, J. (2003). A unified fuzzy feature indexing scheme for region based online image querying. *Proceedings of the 2003 IEEE/WIC International Conference on Web Intelligence*, (pp. 421-424).

Zhou, X. D., Zhang, Q., Lin, L., Deng, A. L., & Wu, G. (2003). Image retrieval by fuzzy clustering of relevance feedback records. *Proceedings of the 2003 International Conference on Multimedia and Expo*, 1, (pp. 305-308).

Chapter 14
EDUPMO:
A Framework for Multimedia Production Management

Joni A. Amorim
Universidade Estadual de Campinas (UNICAMP), Brazil

Rosana G. S. Miskulin
Universidade Estadual Paulista "Júlio de Mesquita Filho" (UNESP), Brazil

Mauro S. Miskulin
Universidade Estadual de Campinas, Brazil

ABSTRACT

Engineering is seen today as a synonym of innovation, especially for providing technological solutions that affect not only daily work and entertainment, but education as well. Project portfolio management of multimedia production and use emerges today as a challenge both for the enrichment of traditional classroom based teaching and for distance education offering. In this way, this chapter intends to answer the following question: Which are the fundamental aspects to be considered in the management of projects on educational multimedia production and use? This research presents a proposal of a project management model for digital content production and use. The model, the methodology and the implementation will be named EduPMO, an abbreviation of Educational Project Management Office. Therefore, the model, the methodology, and the implementation should be understood as related but independent entities. This interdisciplinary investigation involves different topics, going from metadata and interoperability to intellectual property and process improvement.

DOI: 10.4018/978-1-61350-126-9.ch014

INTRODUCTION

Digital convergence is finally happening (Amorim & Silva, 2009): all separate media now become digital and come to be delivered via global network, improving education quality. In this new context, Management of Change (MoC) comes into play (Bates, 1999; Conner, 1993; Frame, 1994): teachers demand both digital content and training in order to incorporate multimedia in their daily practice. After considering topics such as accessibility, MoC and multimedia, this chapter presents a initiative from the Universidade Estadual de Campinas (UNICAMP), Brazil, that involves large-scale multimedia production for teaching (MEC, 2007). This chapter discusses the use of multimedia but focuses on its production while presenting a Brazilian perspective on the many challenges and opportunities experienced in real world technology projects.

In education, digital technologies are becoming increasingly important. The use of multimedia can combine text, images, full-motion video, and sound into an integrated package. The authoring process grows in complexity with time due to the increasing multitude of possibilities available: from traditional hypertext to Web-based audio broadcast via really simple syndication (RSS) feed. This growing complexity of modern educational projects and the need for a more efficient production of quality courses stimulates the development of new instructional design approaches.

Improving quality in distance, flexible and ICT-based education turned out to be a priority for most institutions in developing countries, where the digital divide is just one of the many challenges. UNICAMP was established in 1966, as a public university funded by the State of São Paulo, Brazil, and today 87% of its 1,736 professors are full time and 96% have at least a doctoral degree. The University has the largest percentage of graduate students in Brazil and is responsible for 12% of the master's and doctoral theses in the country. UNICAMP is one of the most distinguished Brazilian academic institutions and seeks to contribute to solving social problems, through education and research, as well as through services to the community at large. The University accounts for 15% of the total scientific production in Brazil and manages projects both in technology development and in technology education. In the last years, the Graduate Programs obtained the best evaluation among Brazilian universities by the National Coordination for the Improvement of Graduate Professionals (CAPES).

The incorporation of the best methods and practices is now mandatory in order to achieve a balance among time, cost, scope, quality, risk and customer satisfaction (Mulcahy, 2006). Improving quality and productivity standards in an organization is a difficult challenge; especially because it is also difficult for people to accept changes.

Change is a transformation, a modification, an alteration, a variation or a deviation. It is a transition from one state, condition, or phase to another. Never before the world has changed so fast with such a continuous intensification. In the field of education, massive change comes from ever-advancing technology such as personal digital assistants (PDAs) and interactive digital television (iDTV), suggesting that learning how to better manage change is an important goal to be achieved. A better MoC would enhance the chances of increasing organizational efficiency and effectiveness even when changes are attempted.

The literature on MoC (Bates, 1999; Conner, 1993; Frame, 1994) indicates that there is a basic axiom according to which individuals operate: life is most effective and efficient when people move at a speed that allows them to appropriately incorporate changes, absorbing them with minimum dysfunctional behavior. In education, what happens when teachers are overwhelmed by more change than they can absorb? The answer could be fatigue, frustration, or apathy resulting from prolonged stress, overwork, or intense activity. This phenomenon is referred to as Burnout Syndrome (Carlotto, 2002). The seriousness of this syndrome tends to get higher in the field of education as additional pressure is put on teachers to learn how to teach under new paradigms such as those of technology-based education without appropriate preparation through specific training. The unsuccessful management of change may cause the display of dysfunctional behavior, a fact that may bring a decrease in the quality of education.

This way, this study also discusses how to apply the concept of change to projects involving multimedia use and/or production. The many changes under consideration when the focus is the massive use of technology could be too drastic or too threatening to institutions and individuals, demanding the determination of the level of resilience that exists among the key people involved. The main intent of such approach would be the application of correct resilience principles to build up the basic strength in individuals, thus preventing problems rather than dealing with them after they arise. In other words, steps taken early in the project prevent problems later on (Mulcahy, 2006).

According to Wirick (2009), traditional project management has its roots in Engineering and it was originally viewed as a discipline useful for large-scale projects with many details to be organized and tracked. Engineering is seen today as a synonym of Innovation, in special for providing technological solutions that affect not only daily work and entertainment, but education as well. Project portfolio management of multimedia production and use emerges today as a challenge both for the enrichment of traditional classroom based teaching and for distance education offering. In this way, this chapter intends to answer the following question: "Which are the fundamental aspects to be considered in the management of projects on educational multimedia production and use?"

A possible solution for the central question mentioned above is expressed by the following proposition: "A scientifically studied set of management tools and techniques may be identified as a central element to be considered in the management of projects of multimedia production and/ or use, in this way increasing the success odds of educational projects." As a consequence, this research presents a proposal of a project management model for digital content production and use. The model, the methodology and the implementation will be named EduPMO, an abbreviation of "Educational Project Management Office". Therefore, the model, the methodology and the implementation should be understood as related but independent entities. This interdisciplinary investigation involves different topics, going from metadata and interoperability to intellectual property and process improvement.

After a brief literature review on background topics, this study presents some aspects of a large-scale educational multimedia production project (MEC, 2007). The project is presented in a scenario where the authors recognize the significant interplay between the fields of project management (PM) and knowledge management (KM). This scenario suggests a potential synergy (Regsdell, 2006) between project teams and social networks derived from the KM arena, known as communities of practice (CoPs). Based on this scenario, a framework is presented and discussed.

BACKGROUND

A framework for multimedia production management should be based on different methods and practices in an interdisciplinary perspective that may include: (1) business analysis and requirements engineering; (2) pedagogy and instructional design; (3) technical aspects of multimedia production; (4) project management (PM); (5) program and portfolio management; (6) knowledge management; (7) management of change (MoC); (8) maturity models and process improvement; and (9) intellectual property and innovation. In this way, a brief literature review on part of the background topics is presented in this section.

Greenfield (2004) defines a software factory as a "development environment configured to support the rapid development of a specific type of application" (p. 1). As this author proposes, software factories promise to change the characteristics of the software industry by introducing patterns of industrialization. In the same way, a multimedia factory would be a development environment configured to support the rapid development of different types of digital media, which may include audio, video, software or hypertext, among others. While a mature software factory would intend to have high levels of code reuse, a mature digital multimedia factory would intend to reuse as many parts of products as possible. As a tendency, future may present increasing cases of systematic family-based product development, with product line practices getting better understood both in the software industry and in the educational digital multimedia industry.

Previous works discussed the specificities of new tools for multimedia use on e-learning (Amorim & Machado & Miskulin & Miskulin, 2009) and presented potential advantages and disadvantages of multimedia usage in Brazilian education (Amorim & Silva, 2009; Amorim & Pires & Ropoli & Rodrigues, 2004). The following paragraphs intend to form a basis from which to start a discussion that involves multimedia production and/or use.

New tools for e-learning require the production of educational multimedia. For many reasons, this production is still a challenge in developing countries. As to people with accessibility needs, the occasional use of assistive technologies and adaptive strategies to access the Web, for example, is an additional challenge that cannot be ignored while producing multimedia products to users geographically dispersed in a continental country like Brazil. As a consequence, the production of audio, video, software and hypertext to be published on and used via Internet portals has to consider metadata standards like the IEEE Standard for Learning Object Metadata or the Dublin Core Metadata Standard. In this study, metadata should be understood as data describing data, resources or multimedia content. From this perspective, the Resource Description Framework, which uses the eXtensible Markup Language (XML) as its encoding syntax, is of special relevance since it intends to be a foundation for processing metadata while stimulating interoperability among applications on the Web.

The need for representing and transporting metadata in a manner that maximizes the interoperability of independently developed web servers and clients is evident and brings additional steps to the production of multimedia. Due to that, the educational multimedia production process in large-scale projects must properly define quality standards to be reached that involve not only pedagogical, but also technical aspects that interfere with the project management (Mulcahy, 2006).

In large-scale PM with people who communicate electronically, the use of the best methods and practices for communication management in virtual groups turns out to be of great importance. While considering the role of ICT (Hustad & Munkvold, 2006), a comparison of different organizational groups, like Community of Practice, Knowledge Network, Workgroup and Team, would suggest that the former supports the creation and maintenance of distributed communities, and is the choice of ICT because it is user-friendly and efficient. For a Knowledge Network, the occasional linking of different knowledge networks together, implementing boundary practices through ICT initiated by management, would contrast with a Workgroup. In a Workgroup, characterized by a high degree of formality and a membership mandated from job descriptions and organizational hierarchy, the distributed workgroups depend on ICT for interaction purposes aiming at fulfilling organizational objectives. For a Virtual Team, where the degree of formality is high, there is a dependency on ICT for creating a shared space and for coordinating and performing common tasks with team members selected by management.

Since a Community of Practice (CoP) tends to be informal, or to have a low degree of formality, in a context of self-selected assignment and voluntary participation, it tends to be the best option for educational multimedia production groups that necessarily consist of professionals with complementary profiles. On the other hand, joint enterprises and the subsequent mutual engagement are not necessarily in favor of a shared repertoire or a common vocabulary for communication (Mulcahy, 2006), which intensifies the interplay between the fields of PM and KM. According to Regsdell (2006), the reference material to compare CoPs and project teams should be taken from the Second-Generation Knowledge Management Movement, which emphasizes the discussion of human and social factors with special interest in the generation of new knowledge. This perspective would contrast with the so-called First-Generation, for which the focus would be technological issues related to knowledge management. In the production of educational multimedia, where there is a need for transcending disciplines and bring in different perspectives, resources should be used to cope with new situations and to create new knowledge.

With the objective of communicating electronically in virtual groups, it is necessary to move into a new way of interacting to better use ICT. This transition would be just one more stressing factor in a world where changes are more and more dynamic (Bates, 1999; Frame, 1994). A discussion on the intensification of change would involve, according to Conner (1993), seven fundamental issues: faster communication and knowledge acquisition; a growing worldwide population; increasing interdependence and competition; limited resources; diversifying political and religious ideologies; constant transitions of power; and ecological distress. Due to this intensification, the ability to successfully manage change has become one of the most important skills needed for personal happiness and organizational prosperity. The negative response to change may come in the form of resistance. Different models exist in the literature (Conner, 1993). The emotional response may go from a passive to an active state, from stability to immobilization, to denial and to anger. Other phases may include bargaining, depression, testing and acceptance. On the other hand, the positive response to change may involve at least five phases: uninformed optimism, informed pessimism, hopeful realism, informed optimism, and completion.

While considering the intensification of change not only in the world in general, but in education as well (Bates, 1999), resilience may be understood as the ability to recover readily from illness, depression, adversity, or the like. One can enhance resilience (Conner, 1993) by understanding the basic mechanisms of individuals resistance, viewing resistance as a reaction to the disruption of expectations, interpreting resistance as a deficiency of either ability or willingness, encouraging and participating in open expressions of resistance and understanding that reactions to change may be managed. This study argues for applying the concepts of MoC to projects in order to better prepare the stakeholders involved for the innumerous transitions to happen.

The training of teachers is quite fundamental in a context where their students would be getting prepared to deal with a dynamic environment while taking advantage of mechanisms that would boost resilience from a micro to a macro environment. A more detailed study on teacher training in educational technology in the context of large scale projects may be found on Amorim & Machado & Miskulin & Miskulin (2009).

LARGE SCALE MULTIMEDIA PRODUCTION

In order to make it easier for people with disabilities to use the Web, some organizations have developed guidelines, like the World Wide Web Consortium's Web Accessibility Initiative. As far as education is concerned, guidelines for accessibility of Web sites, browsers, and authoring tools should receive special attention due to the need for including students with disabilities in the Information Society. There are general requirements for Web access by people with physical, visual, hearing, and cognitive or neurological disabilities to be considered. As to the production of multimedia for public High Schools in Brazil, to be discussed in this section, the requirements for Web access, prioritized by the government, were related to visual and hearing disabilities.

In 2007, there was a request from the Brazilian government for large-scale research project proposals for the production of educational multimedia (MEC, 2007), involving different Brazilian organizations, especially Universities. In UNICAMP, proposals in three different fields were approved and the projects planned the creation of 875 multimedia products of four types: audio for digital radio, video for digital TV, educational experiments based on hypertext and software with animations and simulations. Researchers in UNICAMP saw these projects as a way to influence High School teaching in Brazil with potential pedagogical innovation stimulated by accompanying teachers' guide for each product. According to the original request for proposals, with a total budget of 75 million reais, approximately 40 million dollars, the guides should consider the possibility of having students with visual and/or hearing impairment in the classroom, a fact that could make the production of this material even more challenging.

Large-scale projects on educational multimedia production are especially important to a public institution like UNICAMP, since it represents a way to involve both graduate and undergraduate students in multidisciplinary groups where new knowledge may be created while considering the characteristics of the Brazilian population. The experience is a way to develop human resources in new professional areas and to conduct interdisciplinary research, which includes aspects of management, technology and pedagogy as well. The content would come from the three different High School teaching subjects, in previously approved proposals, namely: Biology, Mathematics and Portuguese. The technology for the production of material, on the other hand, would come from the research areas of arts, languages, semiotics, audio, video, software, and many others. As to management, research turned out to be necessary on how to properly plan, execute, monitor and control the project process, with an integrated change control that should compile data from many sources to generate spreadsheets with budget control and timetables. The multitude of professional profiles turned the interaction into a defying time-consuming objective.

The need for transferring information and knowledge while carrying out the project was an additional aspect to be considered in the formation of a scenario where the authors identified the relevant interplay involving the fields of PM and KM. As mentioned before, this scenario suggested a potential synergy (Regsdell, 2006) between project teams and CoPs. According to Kisielnicki (2006), the communication system within the team significantly influences its effectiveness, with the key question to be answered being: "What conditions does the project leader need to create in order to maximize the positive and minimize the negative aspects of teamwork?" Without presenting decisive conclusions, the author advocates the hypothesis that the network communication system, where the communication among all members is direct and cross-divisional, provides the most effective solution for the management of information technology projects. The author also expresses that the ideal research would require the same team to replicate the same project twice with the only difference being the communication method. Since all projects are unique, the conclusions of this and related research should be based on estimates.

Among the many challenges for this project, the first one was related to the proposals themselves, since the group of researchers at UNICAMP involved in the projects had almost no previous experience in preparing project proposals. Another challenge would be the possibility of extending the 18-month duration, originally stated in this request for proposals (MEC, 2007), to more than two years, without increasing the budget. In this case, human resources management asked for additional monthly incomes that were planned for eighteen months only, a situation where the desired increase in duration was limited by the budget constraint. One of the challenges was the integration of subprojects on Biology, Mathematics and Portuguese, a difficult task that would eventually bring benefits, such as the transfer of knowledge (Paquette, 2006) across these three communities that should respect the same technological requirements, to say the least.

Paquette (2006) defines a community of creation as: "a community of practice where members mainly focus on the sharing and generation of new knowledge for the purpose of creating new ideas, practices, and artifacts (or products). They can be legitimized through involvement in a company-sponsored product development effort, or may be informal through various practitioners with similar experience and knowledge meeting, and new innovations arise from this interaction" (p. 73). The author also indicates that technologies may expand the horizon of observation that a participant can monitor by allowing for the identification of additional knowledge sources. For the author, sharing asks for the flow of knowledge to be two-way through process, structural, or social means.

From the perspective that an organization is a community made up of smaller communities, the close alignment of CoPs with organizational strategies may increase their functional contributions. Understanding safe enclaves as being shared electronic and non-electronic social spaces that allow for underlying views to be expressed, Paquette (2006) suggests that CoPs may provide safe enclaves from organizational social-political pressures, a fact that would eventually encourage further knowledge sharing. This additional way of sharing is fundamental in a large-scale educational multimedia production project since the many smaller communities must interact somehow to find better solutions to problems at hand.

Ensuring the presence of a truly collaborative culture brings many challenges in terms of communication management, KM and MoC with virtual group building. Smith (2006) believes in a people-centered approach to KM in which CoPs provide a practical solution for the nurturing of collaborative relationships. With the intention of guaranteeing a greater chance of success on large-scale projects for educational multimedia production, where there may be conflicting demands of cost, scope, quality, etc., establishing, facilitating and supporting CoPs is a relevant topic to be researched. Based on this scenario, a framework is proposed in the next section.

FRAMEWORK PROPOSAL

According to Archer (2006), the growing complexity in products, services, and processes requires more specialization and collaboration among the people involved. At the same time, orchestrating the involvement of groups asks for equilibrium in differentiation and integration. The author believes that CoPs "can create both codification and personalization channels to distribute knowledge and support learning" (p. 22) once they have a defined objective and scope. This way, tacit knowledge that is personal, context-specific, and hard to formalize and communicate would eventually be transformed into documents that could be replicated in order to benefit all those involved in a certain project. The author also confirms that KM is related to management in general, in activities like learning and innovation, benchmarking and best practice, strategy, culture, and performance measurement.

Thus, this chapter suggests a framework for the management of projects on educational multimedia production and use that may benefit on the use of Internet based CoPs. The framework will be named EduPMO, an abbreviation of "Educational Project Management Office". It has three components, the model, the methodology and the implementation. The components should be understood as related but independent entities. In this way, in order to create a system of classification, the fundamental aspects to be considered in the model were divided in nine dimensions, as follows.

In such a model, the dimensions are divided in two categories: implicit and explicit. The explicit dimensions are directly expressed, in total or in part, to the different people participating on projects. The implicit dimensions, on the other hand, still affect the work of the teams, but they are not directly expressed to them since these dimensions represent a set of strategies used by the managers and the educational project management office to manage projects. Despite the obvious interrelationship between the nine dimensions, they were divided into four explicit dimensions and five implicit dimensions in order to facilitate the understanding and the use of the processes involved.

The first dimension, or D1, is the content dimension, and refers to the appropriate understanding of the fundamental project requirements involved, in special in terms of the content to be considered on multimedia production and/or use (IIBA, 2009; IEEE, 1990). The second dimension, or D2, is the pedagogical dimension, and refers to the teaching and learning aspects involved (Lee & Owens, 2000; Lynch & Roecker, 2007; IEEE, 2001). The third dimension, or D3, is the technological dimension, and refers mainly to the processes related to the technical requirements of products to be produced and/or used (Fernandes & Teixeira, 2004; Porto & Souza & Ravelli & Batocchio, 2002; Trindade & Ochi, 2006). The fourth dimension, or D4, is the management dimension, and refers to knowledge areas known as project integration management, project scope management, project time management, project cost management, project quality management, project human resource management, project communications management, project risk management and project procurement management (PMI[a], 2008; Kerzner, 2006). The implicit dimensions go from D5 to D9, as follows.

The fifth dimension, or D5, is the strategic dimension, and refers to meeting the specific strategic objectives through the centralized management of several portfolios and programs, which may include identification, prioritization, authorization, management and control of the projects (PMI[b], 2008; PMI[c], 2008). The sixth dimension, or D6, is the knowledge dimension, and refers to essential aspects to produce an effective management of knowledge, like harvesting, selection, configuration, dissemination and application (Nonaka, 1998; Hansen & Nohria & Tierney, 1999). The seventh dimension, or D7, is the change dimension, and usually refers to the management of transitions related to the project itself or in the way in which the teams work (Bates, 1999; Conner, 1992). The eighth dimension, or D8, is the maturity dimension, and refers to process improvement (Harrington & Conner & Horney, 1999; Harmon, 2007). The ninth dimension, or D9, is the rights dimension, and refers to aspects involving innovation management and intellectual property (Moskowitz, 2006; Brasil, 2008).

For each dimension, processes may be presented through a description and/or a diagram depicting the activities and/or tasks to be performed, with indications of inputs and outputs of the processes together with tools and techniques useful to the implementation of the process. Template documents focused on multimedia production and/or use may be presented for the processes, in a way that six artifacts would be available to managers and/or to the management team for each process: (1) description; (2) diagram; (3) inputs; (4) outputs; (5) tools and techniques; and (6) template documents. In general, the processes would be generic but the template documents would be specific to the type of project under consideration.

In the proposed framework, there are 199 processes to the nine dimensions: 32 processes for D1, 6 processes for D2, 8 processes for D3, 42 processes for D4, 64 processes for D5, 5 processes for D6, 5 processes for D7, 31 processes for D8 e 6 processes for D9.

The methodology from the framework refers to the implementation of the model and has three phases per D-I-A cycle: (1) "D", or Design; (2) "I", or Implementation; and (3) "A", or Assessment. The methodology may be applied for one or more projects of the organization. The design phase should consider the context of the project in order to determine what is possible to be implemented in the short, medium and long terms. After the design, the implementation phase will implement the short term plan and then assess the results in order to bring about elements for the next D-I-A cycle. In an under graduation course of eight semesters, for example, at least eight D-I-A cycles would be possible, with assessment phases at the end of each semester in order to propel continuous improvement.

The first phase, "D", or Design, would have the following fundamental activities: (i) identification by the educational project management office of the methodology components to be implemented in the organization while considering the context of the moment, which may include the definition of the relevant dimensions and the development of glossaries, guides, etc., as a way to define standards and practices; (ii) plan the life cycle processes, an activity that implies on defining the useful processes for each dimension, with description, diagram, inputs, outputs, template documents, tools and techniques to be used; (iii) select the platform that will facilitate the methodology implementation; (iv) if needed, elaborate a formal written document detailing the management office operation during the specified cycle, with objectives, cost, scope, schedule, etc.

The second phase, "I", or Implementation, would have the following fundamental activities: (i) training of the project manager by the management office; (ii) plan in detail of the transition (change) in the way of working in order to improve the management of the project under consideration; (iii) training of the project team by the project manager or by the management office, in this way facilitating the transition (change) in the way of working in order to improve the management of the project under consideration; and (iv) execution, which may include actions going from starting the use of new software to the implementation of a series of processes of a specific dimension.

The third phase, "A", or Assessment, would have the following fundamental activities: (i) assess the implementation while considering the detailed planning of the transition (change) in the way of working in order to improve the management of the project under consideration; (ii) suggest possible actions for the next D-I-A cycle in the specific project being considered; (iii) search for improvement opportunities on the methodology based on the assessment of the implementation; and (iv) suggest possible reviews on the life cycle processes, which implies on possible reviews on descriptions, diagrams, inputs, outputs, template documents, tools and techniques.

In this perspective, the D-I-A cycle will be used continuously as a way to allow the improvement of the methodology based on the different assessments happening in each project. In parallel, different cycles could happen in the same project in the perspective of improving its management during its execution. As a consequence, the improvements tend to happen more often and according to a planed schedule. This context tends to favor the use of contributions from both the managers and the teams with the potential to affect the organization as a whole.

As previously stated, the suggested framework for the management of projects on educational multimedia production and use may benefit on the utilization of Internet based CoPs. In order to create a platform for the educational project management office that incorporates Internet based CoPs, it will be presented an implementation proposal focused on the use of free software and free Internet services like portal hosting. Despite the fact that a free portal hosting sometimes comes with limitations of disk space and data transfer, this platform could be an appropriate starting point for the development of the educational project management office in an organization.

The implementation, in this perspective, refers to the orchestration of the use of different kinds of free software through an Internet portal that represents the platform of the management office. The intent is to have an alternative solution based on the Web for situations in which there is no budget available for infrastructure, in special software and hardware. This solution may work as a support system for anyone interested on the management of educational projects since it would allow the access both to the EduPMO Framework and to related CoPs. This environment may be useful for the exchange of experiences between its users and for the collection of important information on how to improve the framework.

An additional objective refers to the discussion of the results of the utilization of free software and free Internet services in different kinds of projects. In this way, for each dimension a set of Web pages would be needed for the artifacts of the processes: descriptions, diagrams, inputs, outputs, template documents, tools and techniques. Due to the fact that the proposed framework should be useful for different kinds of projects related to multimedia production and/or use, the processes tend to be generic while the template documents would be more focused. It's important to emphasize that the template documents should be properly adapted according to the specificities of the project being considered.

Considering a total of 199 processes for the nine dimensions, the portal would need a minimum of 199 Web pages. The platform should also have specific forums to discuss the applicability of the dimensions of the model. In special, the Portuguese language should be preferred for a Brazilian audience but the English language could be used in a version of the platform focused on the international audience. The free access should be preferred and the creation of similar platforms could be suggested to the users.

FUTURE TRENDS

Dagger et al. (2007) discuss core challenges to achieve information interoperability in next-generation Web based platforms. For greater interoperability, environments must exchange both the information's syntax and its semantics while creating frameworks and standards to support plugability. The authors believe that "service composition will let these e-learning platforms dynamically discover and assemble e-learning services to achieve a given user's specific purpose" (p. 30). This way, next generation systems will support targeted personalization, with services interoperating to contextualize the content and activities of an e-learning experience in which multimedia will be available on demand.

Artificial intelligence based performance support systems, in a context of digital convergence and ubiquitous computing, may allow greater customization of the interface and easier communication for virtual groups. Electronic Performance Support Systems (EPSS) will have their importance increased with time since knowledge workers need access to data, information and knowledge all the time and everywhere (Rossett & Schafer, 2006). It is expected that an LMS will interface with the EPSS to supply the knowledge base and/or multimedia content.

For students with disabilities, the potential customization of multimedia products according to the student profile may enhance the access to these products, bringing education to a new standard of more democratic access. Due to the fact that technologies like the Internet provide the access to portals for an international audience, research is needed on metadata solutions for the automation of translation of interface and documents, eventually allowing teachers and students from one country to access products of other countries even when the original language of the product is another one. An example of a Dublin Core metadata based portal with international content is the "Banco Internacional de Objetos Educacionais" (http://objetoseducacionais2.mec.gov.br/), or "International Bank Educational Objects", the same one where the 875 multimedia products will be from 2010 on. This portal uses the DSpace open source platform which is available for free and can be downloaded from the sourceforge open source software repository.

While discussing software mass customization and supply chain formation, Greenfield (2004) suggests that the software factory vision will be developed gradually within several years. One of the reasons would be that software factories are based on the "convergence of key ideas in systematic reuse, model driven development, development by assembly and process frameworks" (p. 1). The synthesis into an integrated approach is new, but may benefit organizations in different ways. The multimedia factory, as a proposal based on the concept of software factory, is a new paradigm that demands further research; particularly, if the characteristics of the educational field are considered.

CONCLUSION

The production of quality educational multimedia content involves considering both its publication and its use, keeping in view aspects ranging from metadata standards to teachers' guides. The complexity of large-scale projects demands methods to bring order through planning while avoiding the turbulence (Wirick, 2009) propelled by the combination of the speed at which projects are required to produce results and the many obstacles that managers have to deal with.

This chapter presented part of the behind-the-scenes work of a large-scale project on the production of educational multimedia. The scenario showed a significant interplay between the fields of PM and KM, which suggests a potential synergy between project teams and CoPs. Based on this scenario, a framework was discussed while a computational implementation based on free software and the Web was proposed.

Researchers on issues and trends in technology project management in education organizations may benefit from the perspective presented in this chapter, which considered a project in a Brazilian University, faced with many challenges while producing quality educational multimedia. The implications for technology in education easily justify the research on this interdisciplinary research field.

ACKNOWLEDGMENT

The authors would like to thank Professor Renato Pavanello from GGPE (Grupo Gestor de Projetos Educacionais), UNICAMP (Universidade Estadual de Campinas), for fostering research to advance the state of the art of the knowledge of project management.

REFERENCES

Amorim, J. A., Machado, C., Miskulin, R. G. S., & Miskulin, M. S. (2009). Production, publication, and use of educational multimedia content in Brazil: Challenges and opportunities in real world technology projects . In Kidd, T. T. (Ed.), *Handbook of research on technology project management, planning, and operations* (pp. 406–418). Hershey, PA: IGI Global. doi:10.4018/978-1-60566-400-2.ch026

Amorim, J. A., Pires, D. F., Ropoli, E. A., & Rodrigues, C. C. (2004). O Professor e sua Primeira Página na Internet: Uma Experiência de Uso do Ambiente TelEduc. *Revista Brasileira de Informática na Educação, 12*(1), 37-42. ISSN 14145685

Amorim, J. A., & Silva, M. R. C. (2009). Multimedia production and accessibility on distance learning courses. *Educação Temática Digital (Online), 10*, 355-372. ISSN 1676-2592

Archer, N. (2006). A classification of communities of practice . In Coakes, E., & Clarke, S. (Eds.), *Encyclopedia of communities of practice in information and knowledge management* (pp. 21–29). Hershey, PA: Idea Group Publishing. doi:10.4018/978-1-59140-556-6.ch005

Bates, A. W. (1999). *Managing technological change*. San Francisco, CA: Jossey-Bass.

Brasil. (2008). *Guia de Depósito de Patentes. Ministério do Desenvolvimento, Indústria e Comércio Exterior*. Instituto Nacional da Propriedade Industrial - INPI. Diretoria de Patentes – DIRPA. Retrieved September 10, 2009, from http://www.inpi.gov.br/

Brennan, K. (2009). *A guide to the business analysis body of knowledge* (2nd ed.). International Institute of Business Analysis.

Carlotto, M. S. (2002). A síndrome de Burnout e o trabalho docente. *Psicologia em Estudo, 7*(1), 21-29. ISSN 1413-7372

Conner, D. R. (1993). *Managing at the speed of change*. New York, NY: Random House.

Dagger, D., O'Connor, A., Lawless, S., Walsh, E., & Wade, V. P. (2007). *Service-oriented e-learning platforms: From monolithic systems to flexible services. IEEE Internet Computing, 11*(3), 28-35. ISSN 10897801

Fernandes, A. A., & Teixeira, D. S. (2004). *Fábrica de Software: Implantação e Gestão de Operações*. Editora Atlas.

Frame, J. D. (1994). *The new project management: tools for an age of rapid change, corporate reengineering, and other business realities*. San Francisco, CA: Jossey-Bass.

Greenfield, J. (2004). *Software factories: Assembling applications with patterns, models, frameworks, and tools.* Microsoft Corporation MSDN Architecture Center Portal. Retrieved May 13, 2008, from http://msdn.microsoft.com/ en-us/ library/ ms954811.aspx

Hansen, M. T., Nohria, N., & Tierney, T. (1999). *What's your strategy for managing knowledge?* Harvard Business Publishing. ISSN 00178012

Harmon, P. (2007). *Business process change: A guide for business managers and BPM and six sigma professionals* (2nd ed.). MK/OMG Press.

Harrington, H. J., Conner, D., & Horney, N. L. (1999). *Project change management*. McGraw-Hill Companies.

Hustad, E., & Munkvold, B. E. (2006). Communities of practice and other organizational groups . In Coakes, E., & Clarke, S. (Eds.), *Encyclopedia of communities of practice in information and knowledge management* (pp. 60–62). Hershey, PA: Idea Group Publishing. doi:10.4018/978-1-59140-556-6.ch012

IEEE. (1990). *IEEE standard glossary of software engineering terminology*. IEEE Std 610.121990. Retrieved November 15, 2009, from http://standards.ieee.org/

IEEE. (2001). *Reference guide for instructional design and development*. Retrieved September 7, 2001, from http://webstage.ieee.org/ organizations/eab/tutorials /refguideForPdf/mms01.htm

Kerzner, H. (2006). *Gestão de Projetos: As Melhores Práticas*. Bookman Editora. 2006. ISBN 9788536306186

Kisielnicki, J. (2006). Transfer of information and knowledge in the project management . In Coakes, E., & Clarke, S. (Eds.), *Encyclopedia of communities of practice in information and knowledge management* (pp. 544–551). Hershey, PA: Idea Group Publishing. doi:10.4018/978-1-59140-556-6.ch091

Lee, W. W., & Owens, D. L. (2000). *Multimedia-based instructional design: Computer-based training, Web-based training, distance broadcast training, performance-based solutions*. Pfeiffer.

Lynch, M. M., & Roecker, J. (2007). *Project managing e-learning: A handbook for successful design, delivery and management*. Routledge.

MEC. (2007). *Chamada Pública para Produção de Conteúdos Educacionais Digitais Multimídia.* Portal do Ministério da Educação, Secretaria de Educação a Distância, Departamento de Produção e Capacitação em Programas de EAD. Retrieved December 30, 2007, from http://portal.mec.gov.br/seed/

Moskowitz, S. (2006). Introduction - Digital rights management . In Zeng, W., Yu, H., & Lin, C. (Eds.), *Multimedia security technologies for digital rights management*. Academic Press. doi:10.1016/B978-012369476-8/50003-8

Mulcahy, R. (2006). *PM crash course: Premier edition*. Minneapolis, MN: RMC Publications, Incorporated.

Nonaka, I. (1998). The knowledge-creating company. In *Harvard Business Review on Knowledge Management*, 6th ed. Harvard Business Review Paperback Series. Harvard Business School Press (Compiler). ISBN 0875848818

Paquette, S. (2006). Communities of practice as facilitators of knowledge exchange . In Coakes, E., & Clarke, S. (Eds.), *Encyclopedia of communities of practice in information and knowledge management* (pp. 68–73). Hershey, PA: Idea Group Publishing. doi:10.4018/978-1-59140-556-6.ch015

PMIa. (2008). *A guide to the project management body of knowledge (PMBOK guide)* (4th ed.). Project Management Institute.

PMIb. (2008). *The standard for program management* (2nd ed.). Project Management Institute.

PMIc. (2008). *The standard for portfolio management* (2nd ed.). Project Management Institute.

Porto, A. J. V., Souza, M. C. F., Ravelli, C. A., & Batocchio, A. (2002). Manufatura Virtual: conceituação e desafios. *Gest. Prod. São Carlos, 9*(3). Retrieved October 11, 2009, from http://www.scielo.br/

Ragsdell, G. (2006). The contribution of communities of practice to project management . In Coakes, E., & Clarke, S. (Eds.), *Encyclopedia of communities of practice in information and knowledge management* (pp. 104–107). Hershey, PA: Idea Group Publishing.

Rossett, A., & Schafer, L. (2006). Job aids and performance support: The convergence of learning and work. *International Journal of Learning Technology, 2*(4), 310-328. Inderscience Enterprises Limited. ISSN 1753-5263

Smith, P. A. C. (2006). *Organisational change elements of establishing, facilitating, and supporting CoPs. Encyclopedia of communities of practice in information and knowledge management* (pp. 400–406). Hershey, PA: Idea Group Publishing.

Trindade, A. R., & Ochi, L. S. (2006). Um algoritmo evolutivo híbrido para a formação de células de manufatura em sistemas de produção. Pesqui. Oper., 26(2). Retrieved October 11, 2009, from http://www.scielo.br/

Wirick, D. (2009). *Public-sector project management: Meeting the challenges and achieving results*. New Jersey: Wiley. ISBN 0470487313

KEY TERMS AND DEFINITIONS

Community of Practice (CoP): KM social network that tends to be informal, or to have a low degree of formality, in a context of self-selected assignment and voluntary participation.

Framework: a basic conceptual structure used to solve or address complex issues; values, assumptions, concepts, and practices that constitute a perspective of viewing reality.

Management of Change (MoC): management methodologies to prevent, predict, track, estimate impacts of changes on a system.

Metadata: may be understood as data describing data, resources or multimedia content.

Multimedia Factory: based on the concept of software factory, it would be a development environment configured to support the rapid development of different types of digital media, which may include audio, video, software or hypertext, among others; while a mature software factory would intend to have high levels of code reuse, a mature digital multimedia factory would intend to reuse as many parts of products as possible.

Project Management Office (PMO): an organizational entity that performs certain project-focused functions like resource allocation, administrative support, control, and project management methodology development and training.

Resilience: may be understood as the ability to recover readily from illness, depression, adversity, or the like in a context of impacting change.

Software Factory: development environment configured to support the rapid development of a specific type of application.

Chapter 15
Latent Semantic Analysis for Text Mining and Beyond

Anne Kao
Boeing Research & Technology, USA

Steve Poteet
Boeing Research & Technology, USA

Jason Wu
Boeing Research & Technology, USA

William Ferng
Boeing Research & Technology, USA

Rod Tjoelker
Boeing Research & Technology, USA

Lesley Quach
Boeing Research & Technology, USA

ABSTRACT

Latent Semantic Analysis (LSA) or Latent Semantic Indexing (LSI), when applied to information retrieval, has been a major analysis approach in text mining. It is an extension of the vector space method in information retrieval, representing documents as numerical vectors but using a more sophisticated mathematical approach to characterize the essential features of the documents and reduce the number of features in the search space. This chapter summarizes several major approaches to this dimensionality reduction, each of which has strengths and weaknesses, and it describes recent breakthroughs and advances. It shows how the constructs and products of LSA applications can be made user-interpretable and reviews applications of LSA beyond information retrieval, in particular, to text information visualization. While the major application of LSA is for text mining, it is also highly applicable to cross-language information retrieval, Web mining, and analysis of text transcribed from speech and textual information in video.

DOI: 10.4018/978-1-61350-126-9.ch015

INTRODUCTION

A vast amount of information exists in text form, such as free (unstructured) or semi-structured text, including many database fields, reports, memos, email, web sites, blogs, and news articles. Various web mining and text mining methods have been developed to analyze textual resources. *Latent Semantic Analysis (LSA)* (Deerwester, Dumais, Furnas, Landauer, & Harshman, 1990), or Latent Semantic Indexing (LSI) when it is applied to document retrieval, has been a major approach in text mining. It is an extension of the *vector space method* in Information Retrieval (Salton, Wong, & Yang, 1975), using a mathematical approach to represent documents as numerical vectors but with a more sophisticated means of characterizing the essential features of documents and reducing the number of dimensions needed to describe documents to a manageable size. There have been several major approaches to address this *dimensionality reduction*, each of which has strengths and weaknesses. A major challenge in using LSA is that it is typically considered a black box approach that makes it difficult to understand or interpret the results. However, more recent research has not only overcome this challenge, but also demonstrates that the use of LSA extends beyond information retrieval and text document clustering to become a major player in the area of text information visualization. This chapter will summarize the major approaches to LSA, their strengths and weakness, as well as recent breakthroughs and advances and applications beyond information retrieval.

Text mining has adopted certain techniques from the more general field of data analysis, including sophisticated methods for analyzing relationships among highly formatted data, such as numerical data or data with a relatively small fixed number of possible values. Such techniques can expose patterns and trends in this type of data. Text mining can identify relationships between individual unstructured or semi-structured text documents, as well as more general semantic patterns across large collections of such documents. Latent Semantic Analysis, like many other methods of text mining, depends on the twin concepts of "document" and "term." As used in this chapter, a "document" refers to any body of unstructured or semi-structured text. The text may include the entire content of a document in the general sense, such as a book, an article, a paper, or the like -- or only a portion of a document, such as an abstract, a paragraph, a sentence, or a title. Ideally, a "document" describes a coherent topic. In addition, a "document" can be the text field of a database, or encompass text generated from an image or graphic, or it may be text recovered from audio or video formats. We will use the term "document" in this general sense.

A document can be represented as a collection of "terms," each of which can appear in multiple documents. Typically, a "term" consists of an individual word used in the text. However, a "term" can also include multiple words that are commonly used together, for example, "landing gear", or even consist of a string that need not appear explicitly in the text but rather result from token normalization or standardization. Token normalization will be discussed further below.

In vector-based methods of text data analysis, after a suitable set of terms has been defined for a document collection, the collection can be represented as a set of vectors. With traditional vector space methods, individual documents are treated as vectors in a high-dimensional vector space in which each dimension corresponds to some feature of a document, typically a term. A collection of documents can thus be represented by a two-dimensional matrix $A_{(t,d)}$ of features (terms) and documents. In the typical case, the value of each matrix entry is the number of occurrences of that term in the specified document, or some weighting or principled transformation of that number. LSA, as an extension of the vector space method, involves methods of transforming A by various means, e.g. *singular value decomposition*

(SVD) in the case of '*classical*' LSA, which typically attempt to provide a more sophisticated set of features that better capture the latent semantics of the documents. We discuss various such matrix decomposition techniques below in much more detail.

In the rest of this chapter, we begin with a more in-depth discussion of the vector space method as background to LSA. In the main body, we describe the various mathematical approaches to the dimensionality reduction that is the core of LSA, followed by a discussion of how to deal with the addition of new documents and the removal (archival) of old documents (*subspace* updating and downdating). Then we address the problem of providing user interpretable semantics to the constructs of LSA, and we survey several major application areas using LSA. In the last section, we point out what we see as the future work in LSA which would most likely have the highest impact in practical applications.

BACKGROUND

As noted above, the vector space model of text that underlies LSA requires that documents be converted into sets of discrete features, typically words or some word-like unit. This requires parsing of the text string into tokens (tokenization), followed by normalizing tokens (optional), and finally selection of the final features from the results. A "token" identifies a basic unit of text, e.g. a word or term. A token will typically include letters, numbers, hyphens, periods (e.g. "3.5", "boeing.com"), apostrophes (e.g. "N'Djamena"), slashes (e.g. "a/c" for "aircraft"), or "@", which would be part of email addresses. Normalizing tokens is the process of unifying variants of the same term. Normalization of tokens can include lower or upper case, hyphenation ("database", "data-base", "data base"), numbers ("1,000" and "1000"), abbreviation/acronym expansion, known synonym substitution, stemming or lemmatization (e.g. unifying singular and plural nouns or various verb forms by reducing them all to their stem or basic form), spelling normalization, thesaurus- or ontology-based substitutions (e.g. generalizations like "car" to "vehicle"), multiword terms ("landing gear", "New York"), or named entity normalization (e.g. "L.A."/"Los Angeles", "President William J. Clinton"/"Bill Clinton"). Finally, there may be some selection of the normalized tokens, typically in the form of removal of what are called stopwords (e.g. prepositions, pronouns, and exclamations) which typically contribute little or no information about the topics of the documents. Selecting the best set of "terms" to represent a given document generally will depend upon the particular document, or a collection to which the document belongs, as well as the specific goals of the text analysis activity.

The tokenization phase generates a list of terms for each document which will serve as features representing the document. These features need to be assigned numerical values. The initial values are typically the frequency of a token in a document or text unit. These values are usually normalized or weighted. They are frequently divided by the length of the document and may be multiplied by a weight reflecting the importance of the token in the entire document set (e.g. inverse document frequency). A vector is then constructed for each document or text unit whose elements are the weighted frequencies of all the terms that have been selected for the entire document collection. Note that any given document will only contain a fraction of those terms, therefore, at least before weighting, the vector will be very sparse (contain mostly zeros). A term-by-document (*t*-by-*d*) matrix A is then formed with the document vectors as the columns. (see Figure 1a).

The number of terms for even a small corpus of documents will be very large, in the thousands or tens of thousands. The first step toward making this manageable for computation and analysis is to reduce the number of features (the dimensions of the vector space). In the traditional vector space

Figure 1. a) Illustrative example of "vector space method" b) Matrix in a projected to the top two dimensions found by SVD and projected back into word or term space

Term-Doc Matrix A_0

	DOC1	DOC2	DOC3	DOC4	DOC5	DOC6	QUERY
Apache	15	0	10	0	12	0	1
AH-64	0	10	20	0	11	0	0
Eagle	0	0	0	15	0	12	0
Rotorcraft	25	22	10	0	15	0	0
F15	0	0	0	12	0	9	0
	☒	?	☒		☒		

Term-Doc Matrix B_0

	DOC1	DOC2	DOC3	DOC4	DOC5	DOC6	QUERY
Apache	10.98	9.12	8.57	0	9.02	0	1
AH-64	11.08	9.21	8.65	0	9.11	0	0
Eagle	0	0	0	15.14	0	11.82	0
Rotorcraft	.31	17.71	16.64	0	17.52	0	0
F-15	0	0	0	11.82	0	9.2	0
	☒	☒	☒		☒		

model this amounts to making a radical reduction in the number of terms used. This reduction is accomplished by ranking the terms by their likely importance in information retrieval, for example by term frequency times inverse document frequency (tf-idf) or by information gain (Salton & McGill, 1986). Only the top few hundred terms are retained.

By representing documents as vectors in a feature space, similarities between documents can be evaluated by computing the distance between the vectors representing the documents. A cosine measure is commonly used for this purpose, but other distance measures can be used.

Figure 1a is a simple example of a "vector space" representation of a small document collection to illustrate information retrieval using the vector space method. We have deliberately simplified the example for the purpose of illustration, treating each document as if it contained only two or three terms. In this example, the whole collection contains a total of five distinct terms or words. Each document is represented as a vector of term frequencies of these five terms. For example, the term "Apache" occurs 15 times in Document 1, 10 times in Document 3, and 10 times in Document 5, but does not occur in Document 2, 4 and 6 (i.e. 0 times). The collection as a whole is represented as a matrix whose columns are the document vectors and whose rows represent the terms. In a real application, it is common to apply additional "statistical transformations" to accentuate the importance of certain terms while downplaying others based on the distribution of term frequencies, but we will ignore that here. After the document set is represented as a term frequency matrix, the query is also represented as a vector. In this example, the query term is "Apache", so the query vector has a 1 in the entry corresponding to that term, and 0 everywhere else. The distance (e.g. cosine) is then calculated between the query vector and each of the document vectors. In this case, Documents 1, 3 and 5 will be picked out as 'close' to the query. However, we would miss Document 2, since it does not contain the term "Apache", even though it contains the term "AH-64" which is another name for the Apache. If we have that knowledge beforehand, we could make them synonyms. However, in many cases, we do not have that information a priori, and sometimes terms can be ambiguous and the meaning is only clear in context. These are some of the biggest challenges the vector space method faces.

The advantages of the vector space method are that it provides a simple and principled representation of documents and queries, can accommodate many variations appropriate to different document collections, and has been shown to perform relatively well in information retrieval applications.

Unfortunately, by radically reducing the number of terms used, the vector space method throws away a great deal of information that differentiates documents; and, in addition, it ignores the fact that some of the words that are retained may be highly correlated with each other; so keeping them all as separate features is redundant and inefficient. These are some of the weaknesses that the LSA method addresses. In addressing these, it goes beyond the mere comparison of documents with respect to the words they contain and, at least to a certain degree, characterizes the underlying, or "latent", semantics of the documents.

LSA: EXTENDING THE VECTOR SPACE MODEL

LSA takes a different approach to dimensionality reduction. Instead of simply eliminating some of the terms, it transforms them, creating new dimensions by combining terms. It does this in such a way that terms that tend to occur in similar contexts (e.g. synonyms) will tend to be mapped to the same dimension in the new space. The effects of a term in a document is moderated by the other terms that it occurs with, to some degree mapping different senses of the same term to different dimensions and helping to solve the problem of term ambiguity.

More generally, the approaches used for this type of dimensionality reduction usually generate dimensions or features that better represent the meaning of the document than the original terms, going beyond the problems of term synonymy and ambiguity. Whole clusters of semantically related words will tend to get mapped to the same dimension. For example, not only will "car" and "automobile" tend to be mapped to the same dimension, but "wheel", "brake", "driver", "steering" etc. will similarly tend to be mapped to this dimension. Therefore, the end product of the dimension reduction is a reduced vector space model of a text collection that captures much of the conceptual structure underlying the terminological variability present in the source documents. After the initial dimensionality reduction operations, typically on the order of 50 to several hundred dimensions are retained and the text documents are represented in terms of these. In this form, they are suitable for a number of useful applications, including document search and clustering, term clustering, text visualization, and a number of specialized applications.

To illustrate how LSA works, consider Figure 1b, the result of applying SVD (a type of LSA transformation) to the matrix in Figure 1a and then selecting the top two dimensions. To illustrate the effect on the terms, we have projected the result back into word-space. You will notice that the second document no longer has a zero in the cell for Apache but rather 9.1242. This is because it shares words with other documents that have large values for Apache, i.e. "AH-64" and "rotorcraft". Now a query with the term "Apache" will also retrieve the second document, even though the word, "Apache" does not actually occur in that document.

Different Approaches

Next, we survey some of the different mathematical approaches that have been proposed to perform the transformation and combination of dimensions that capture the latent semantics. The basic idea is to approximate the larger space defined by the full set of terms and documents with a much smaller space that preserves the essential characteristics of the full space. This will allow us to perform analyses on very large document collections with reasonable response times on readily available computers.

Singular Value Decomposition

The traditional LSI uses singular value decomposition (SVD) to obtain these dimensions. First, a term-by-document matrix A is composed whose columns consist of all the document vectors constructed as described above. SVD is based on the fact that any matrix A can be decomposed into the product of three matrices:

$$A=U\sum V^{r},$$

where U, whose rows represent the terms, and V, whose rows represent the documents, are orthonormal (that is, the columns of U and V, the left and right singular vectors, respectively, are of length 1 and are mutually orthogonal), and Σ is a diagonal matrix whose elements are weighting factors (called the singular values) in decreasing order. The number of nonzero singular values in Σ is the rank of A. Since the singular values are ranked in decreasing order, Σ can be truncated to just the top k singular values, which will effectively reduce the dimensionality of the space that the document vectors occupy to k (typically 50 to a few hundred). The resulting matrix is called A_k:

$$A_K = U_K \sum_k V_k^r,$$

where U_k and V_k consist of the first k columns of U and V, respectively and Σ_k is the k-by-k diagonal matrix containing just the top k singular values. A_k has the property of being the best possible k-dimensional match to the original matrix A, in the sense that it minimizes the sum of the squared errors. That is, it minimizes the Frobenius norm of the difference between the original matrix A and its approximation $A_{k:}$

$$\left\| A - A_k \right\|_F$$

where the Frobenius norm is the square root of the sum of the squares of the elements of the matrix (at least for real-valued matrices).

The matrix U_k can serve as a basis of a k-dimensional subspace, with the columns of U_k serving as the *basis vectors* of that space. Therefore, all documents can be projected onto this reduced vector space, and a new k-by-d document matrix $\tilde{A}$ be defined as

$$A = U_k^r A$$

SVD produces a result essentially identical to *Principal Components Analysis (PCA)* (Jolliffe, 2002), except that the latter presupposes that the document vectors are centered on the origin (i.e. that the column average is subtracted from the value of each cell).

Bartell, Cottrell, & Belew (1992) point out that LSA using SVD is a special case of Multidimensional Scaling.

Text Representation Using Subspace Representation (TRUST)

Most LSA applications do not really make reference to the principal components as such, but rather to the subspace that the top principal components span or determine. In fact, some applications, such as visualization, really need to provide the user with more flexibility in choosing the basis vectors used to display the documents.

Emphasizing the importance of subspace rather than the particular basis chosen to represent it, TRUST proposes to use a two-sided orthogonal decomposition which produces left and right orthogonal matrices similar to an SVD, but the remaining middle matrix is no longer required to be diagonal (Booker, Condliff, Greaves, Holt, Kao, Pierce, Poteet, & Wu, 1999).

Two common algorithms for computing such a factorization are the rank-revealing URV and ULV decompositions (R is upper triangular and L is lower triangular). In particular, the rank-revealing URV decomposition of a matrix A has the form

$$A=URV^{r},$$

where U and V have orthogonal columns, and R is upper triangular and has the same numerical rank (the maximal number of linearly independent rows or columns in the matrix) as matrix A (i.e. rank(R) = rank(A)). The algorithm consists of an initial triangular factorization (such as the QR decomposition from linear algebra) followed by a rank-revealing post-processing step. These decompositions resemble SVD that provide reliable estimates for the numerical rank and the desired subspaces, and are often used in solving rank-deficient least-squares problems. Then, a rank-k approximation of A, A_k, is defined as:

$$A_K = U_K R_K V_k^r,$$

where U_k and V_k consist of the first k columns of U and V, respectively and R_k is the k-by-k sub-matrix of R consisting of the first k elements of the first k columns. Therefore, all documents can be projected onto the reduced vector space formed by U_k. That is, a new k-by-d matrix $\tilde{A}$ (with the documents represented in terms of the k dimensions rather than the original t terms) can be obtained as

$$A = U_k^T A.$$

Semi-Discrete Decomposition (SDD)

There are also methods that will form a subspace based on a set of non-orthogonal vectors, each with their own advantages. The semi-discrete decomposition (SDD) (Kolda & O'Leary, 1998) was first introduced for image processing applications. The SDD approximates a matrix as a weighted sum (all positive weights) of outer products of a set of vectors whose components only consist of -1, 0, and 1. The k-term SDD of the term-by-document matrix has the form:

$$A_k = \left[x_1\, x_2 \cdots x_k\right] \begin{bmatrix} d_1 & 0 & \cdots & 0 \\ 0 & d_2 & \cdots & 0 \\ \vdots & \vdots & \ddots & \vdots \\ 0 & 0 & \cdots & d_k \end{bmatrix} \begin{bmatrix} y_1^T \\ y_2^T \\ \vdots \\ y_k^T \end{bmatrix} = X_k D_k Y_k^T = \sum_{i-1}^{k} d_i x_i y_i^T,$$

where the components of x_i and y_i all belong to the set {-1, 0, 1}, and d_i is a positive number for all i. The vectors x_i and y_i and scalars d_i are chosen to minimize the Frobenius norm deviation of A_k from A:

$$\left\|A - A_k\right\|_F.$$

Since there is no guarantee of linear independence of x_i and y_i, the rank of A_k might be less than k, thus it is called a k-term approximation. There are no reduced document vectors formed explicitly, but the memory space required for saving x_i and y_i is relatively small compared to the original matrix A. The information retrieval task is performed directly on A_k. Since the components of x_i and y_i are either -1, 0, or 1, SDD requires little memory space to save the matrices X_k and Y_k, using bits rather than the double-precision data type.

Concept Decomposition

The concept decomposition method (Dhillon & Modha, 2001) assumes all documents can be partitioned into k disjoint clusters using the spherical k-means algorithm, which is based on cosine similarity, rather than Euclidean distance. For each cluster, its concept vector is computed by normalizing the centroid or mean vector of the cluster. For example, let m_j be the centroid of the cluster S_j, and $n(S_j)$ be the number of documents in cluster S_j, thus

$$m_j = \frac{1}{n(S_j)} \sum_{a \in S_j} a$$

The concept vector of this cluster is obtained as

$$c_j = \frac{m_j}{\left\| m_j \right\|_2},$$

so c_j is of unit length. Since all clusters are disjoint and decided by the angles between document vectors, their centroids are linearly independent of each other. Therefore, the t-by-k concept matrix $C = [c_1 c_2 \ldots c_k]$ is of rank k. There is no guarantee that this set of basis vectors is orthogonal, but it tends toward orthogonality. In addition, unlike the case of SVD, the concept vectors are usually sparse.

The concept decomposition is a rank k least-squares approximation of A onto the column space of the matrix C. It is defined as

$$A_K = C\tilde{A},$$

where the k-by-d matrix $\tilde{A}$ minimizes $\left\| A - A_k \right\|_F^2$.

It is well-known that there is a close-form solution to this problem and

$$A = (C^T C)^{-1} C^T A$$

The matrix $\tilde{A}$ is a new representation of all documents in a reduced-dimension space.

Random Projection (RP)

The theory (Johnson & Lindenstrauss, 1984) behind the random projection method maintains that if points in a vector space are projected onto a randomly selected subspace of suitably high dimension, the distances between the points are approximately preserved (Hecht-Nielsen, 1994; Kaski, 1998; Papadimitriou, Raghavan, Tamaki, & Vempala, 2000). Let the matrix A be the original term-by-document, $t \times d$ matrix. Then the projected matrix $\tilde{A}$ is defined as

$$\tilde{A} = RA,$$

where R is a rank-k random matrix with unit-length columns and $k \ll t$.

The columns of R are not required to be orthogonal. Therefore, the choice of the random matrix R is one of the key points of interest. The elements r_{ij} of R are often Gaussian distributed or in much simpler distribution such as (Achlioptas, 2001)

$$r_{ij} = \sqrt{3} \cdot \begin{Bmatrix} +1 \text{ with probability } 1/6 \\ 0 \text{ with probability } 2/3 \\ -1 \text{ with probability } 1/6 \end{Bmatrix}.$$

This simpler form results in further computational savings for practical applications.

The main advantage of applying random projection in dimensionality reduction processing is that its computation is relatively simple but still preserves the distance between original data. However, it should be noted that random projection is only useful in situations where the distances in the original high dimensional data are meaningful. Furthermore, its performance can be highly unstable (Bingham & Mannila, 2001). As the high dimensional data are projected to a low dimensional subspace, different random projectors may project data onto different subspaces. This may lead to different clustering results, and sometimes the differences between results can be very dramatic.

It is noted that the text retrieval performance of RP in the reduced subspace was always inferior to that in the original space. In contrast, the retrieval effectiveness of LSI is often better in the projected subspace. In (Vinay, Cox, Wood, & Milic-Frayling, 2005), Vinary et al. showed that despite the attention random projection has received in other applications, in the case of text mining it is outperformed by PCA (which is essentially the same as SVD).

Non-Negative Matrix Factorization (NMF)

Non-negative Matrix Factorization (Paatero & Tapper, 1994; Lee & Seung, 1999; Pauca, Shahnaz, Berry, & Plemmons, 2004; Berry, Browne, Langville, Pauca, & Plemmons, 2006; Shahnaz, Berry, Pauca, & Plemmons, 2006) has recently been shown to be a very useful technique in approximating high dimensional data where the data are comprised of non-negative components, and the low rank approximations are further required to be comprised of non-negative values in order to avoid contradicting physical realities. Given the original non-negative term-by-document matrix A and a positive integer $k<min\{t,d\}$, NMF is to find two reduced-dimensional non-negative matrices W and H of dimension $t\times k$ and $k\times d$, respectively, to solve the optimization problem

$$\min \left\| A - WH \right\|_F^2 .$$

The product of W and H is an approximate factorization of rank at most k, and is called a non-negative matrix factorization of A, although A is not necessarily equal to the product WH. Each column of W contains a basis vector while each column of H contains the weights needed to approximate A.

The NMF problem can also be formulated as a minimum I-divergence problem (O'Sullivan, 2000)

$$\min \sum_{i=1}^{t} \sum_{j=1}^{d} A_{ij} \log \frac{A_{ij}}{(WH)_{ij}} - A_{ij} + (WH)_{ij}$$

that can be solved by alternating minimization procedures (Finesso & Spreij, 2006).

Since the term frequencies in text mining are non-negative, the NMF gives a more direct interpretation than PCA due to non-subtractive combinations of non-negative basis vectors. The strengths of NMF also include better scalability as m, n, k increase, and possibly faster computation time than SVD.

Important challenges affecting the numerical minimization of NMF include the existence of local minima, and perhaps more importantly the lack of a unique solution which can be easily seen by considering $WXX^{-1}H$ for any non-negative invertible matrix X. Since XX^{-1} is the identity matrix, $WXX^{-1}H$ is the same as WH; however, WX is not the same as W nor is $X^{-1}H$ the same as H. Moreover, the optimization formulation of NMF does not guarantee sparsity in the factors of A and the sparsity depends on specific NMF algorithms that impose additional constraints to the optimization problem (Kim & Park, 2006).

Probabilistic LSA

Probabilistic latent semantic analysis (PLSA) introduces a probabilistic model for the analysis of documents. PLSA was developed by Hofmann (1999, 2001) to introduce a more principled statistics based approach to document analysis. In contrast to LSA which decomposes the term-by-document matrix using SVD, PLSA uses a mixture decomposition derived from a latent class model.

The mixture components are multinomial random variables that can be thought of as concepts or topics. This probabilistic model can be used as the basis for information retrieval, clustering, and classification of documents.

Beginning with a term-by-document matrix, PLSA introduces hidden (or latent) class variables in modeling the joint probability distribution of terms and documents. Hofmann estimates the conditional probabilities of the latent classes using the Expectation Maximization (EM) algorithm and calls these class-conditional multinomial distributions "factors" (Hofmann, 1999, 2001). The conditional probabilities of terms given documents can be expressed as convex combinations of the factors (i.e. a weighted sum of the factors, where the weights are non-negative and sum to 1). Advantages of this approach include clear probabilistic meanings of the factors and the ability to use statistical theory in selecting the dimensionality of the model space. Disadvantages include increased computational complexity and that the EM algorithm may find only a local maximum of the likelihood function.

PLSA reveals groups of related terms that describe factors and can distinguish between different meanings or senses of the terms, thus the factors represent concepts. The factors also allow for identification of concepts in documents using synonyms based on similar term correlations. In this framework, each word is generated by a single topic, and documents are collections (mixtures) of topics. This framework does allow for multiple concepts to be assigned to documents.

Blei, Ng, & Jordan (2003) point out that this representation is incomplete in that it provides no probabilistic model at the level of documents and that the number of parameters in the model grows linearly as the number of documents increases, which is prone to overfitting. It also does not provide a clear way to assign probabilities to new documents. They point to latent Dirichlet allocation (LDA) as a way to overcome these limitations.

LSA Using Lanczos Vectors

Implementations of LSA mainly rely on matrix decompositions, predominantly the truncated SVD described above. This computation becomes infeasible for large document collections since it is very demanding both in terms of floating-point arithmetic operations and computer memory requirement. In (Chen, & Saad, 2009), two divide and conquer strategies were proposed to alleviate these difficulties. The algorithms recursively divide the data set using spectral bisection techniques, separately perform relevance analysis on each subset, and merge the partial analysis results to form the query response. The two strategies differ in how the data set (the term-document matrix) is partitioned. In addition, the relevance analysis on each subset is performed with the Lanczos vectors instead of singular vectors to reduce the computational cost. It is well known that the Lanczos procedure is often preferred for computing the SVD of a large sparse matrix, and it is shown in (Chen & Saad, 2009) that using Lanczos vectors is an effective replacement of the singular vectors for dimensionality reduction. Since all computations and relevance analysis can be performed in parallel, the divide and conquer approaches are attractive for analyzing large problem in a parallel computation environment.

Combining LSA with the Vector Space Model

Choosing an optimal dimensionality reduction parameter k for each application remains elusive. Optimal k value is typically in the range of 100-310 (Deerwester et al., 1990, Dumais, 1992). In (Kontostathis, 2007), Kontostathis reported that the SVD exploits higher order term co-occurrence in a collection and the term relationship information can be found within the first few dimensions of the SVD. It was demonstrated that good query performance on a variety of collections can be achieved by using only the first 10 dimensions, if it is combined with a standard vector space query. A convex combination of LSA and vector space model, named EDLSI, was proposed and query's relevance analysis was computed by

$$\alpha q^r A_k + (1-\alpha) q^r A,$$

where $0 \leq \alpha \leq 1$ and q is the query vector.

Discussion of Various Approaches

Since PCA is a cornerstone of most of the LSA approaches, we will use Figure 2 to further illustrate how PCA works. Imagine a document collection with only three terms and each document is plotted in this 3-D term space based on each document's term frequencies. The First Principal Component is the line (or the direction) that accounts for the most variability in the data set. The Second Principal Component is the line (or the direction) that accounts for the second most variability in the data and is orthogonal (i.e. perpendicular) to the First Principal Component. In this illustration, we project the data set from 3-D to the top 2-D principal component space. In a real data set, we typically project from tens of thousands of dimensions (the number of terms) down to about 100 dimensions. Here is an analogy. If we want to project the shadow of an outstretched 3-D human hand on the wall (which would make it a 2-D object) in a way that preserves the most information about the shape of the hand, the shadow (projection) would preserve the length and width of the hand at the expense of the thickness in order to show the fingers and thumb. Intuitively, what PCA does is to automatically and mathematically identify how we can make a projection of a high dimensional data set that preserves most of the information while leaving out most of the 'noise' or minor variation in the data. In a text data set, the 'noise' is the variation in the user's choice of words to express the same concepts. One could call the same helicopter "Apache" or "AH-64", but the context provided by the rest of the words in the documents would allow us to identify these related terms mathematically through PCA.

Most of the discussions of various matrix decompositions tend to focus on the mathematical and computational features of each decomposition or on how well it approximates PCA. For example, SDD tends to use a lot less storage space than SVD, whereas SVD is the only algorithm that accurately reproduces Principal Component Analysis. However, Principal Component Analysis assumes the underlying data distribution to be Gaussian, and term frequency distributions in document collections clearly do not follow a Gaussian distribution. Therefore, there is no theoretical reason to believe that SVD would necessarily provide the best solution.

There have been a couple of attempts to provide a generative probabilistic model of natural language semantics or topics that would explain why LSI works so well. Papadimitriou, Raghavan, Tamaki, & Vempala (2000) model a topic as a probabilistic distribution over words and provide a rigorous proof that LSI will find these (in the limit). However, their model has several unrealistic constraints, such as that each document be only about a single topic and that topics be characterized by non-overlapping sets of words. Ding (2005) proposes a model where the probability of a document is based on its similarity to k "characteristic documents" and with a few assumptions about the shape of the distribution (including one that makes it look rather like a mixture of Gaussians), they show that LSI with SVD produces the optimal Maximum Likelihood solution for parameters for the model. They avoid some of the restrictions of Papdimitriou et al. (1997), but make a number of assumptions in constructing their model, including the quasi-Gaussian assumption.

Ultimately, the best choice is the one that best matches one's application requirements. Given the variation among document collections in terms of size and number of documents and variability in vocabulary and style and the lack of a model

Figure 2. Illustrative example of "Principal Component Analysis"

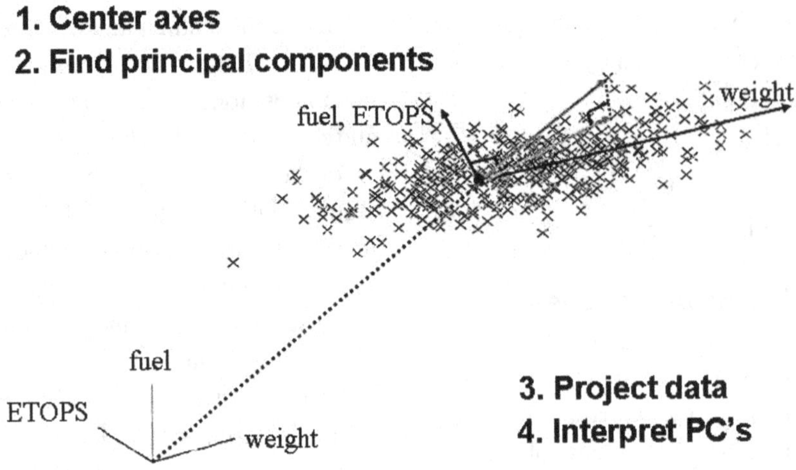

describing these different features, any benchmark test of these different matrix decomposition methods using a standard data set (e.g., the Reuters data set (Lewis, 1997)) can at best only be suggestive about performance on one's own data. On the other hand, if visualization is an important application requirement, it is likely that an orthogonal decomposition would be preferable because otherwise the visualization would mislead the user regarding distances between documents in different locations in the subspace.

Updating and Downdating

Many applications need to work with non-static data sets. New data comes in, sometimes needing to be represented in near real time, and old data may need to be archived. In situations like this, there is a need to modify the subspace that has been generated based on an initial set of data. While one can always rerun the whole decomposition and thus incorporate the new data into the subspace representation, this is impractical when the application needs to work with changes in the data in near real time. A subfield of LSA has come into existence to solve exactly this problem (Berry & Fierro, 1996; Simon & Zha 1997; Cho, Pierce, & Wu, 2000).

First, we will discuss a special case. In some situations, the new data are on topics similar to those of the existing text collection. We can treat each of the new documents in the same way we process a query-by-example: simply project the new document onto the existing subspace and then add the projected information to the existing collection.

$$U_k^T \left[A \ \ a\right] = \left[U_k^T A \ \ U_k^T a\right]$$

This method is called *folding-in*.

Folding-in is computationally efficient; however its accuracy may degrade very quickly. In the adaptive folding-up algorithm (Mason & Spiteri, 2008), a measure of the accumulated error based on the loss of orthogonality in the right singular vector is monitored to determined when the folding-in process has lost the accuracy so that a more accurate updating algorithm should be applied.

It is also possible to use this approach to measure how well the new document fits into the existing subspace. For example, if the new document vector is almost orthogonal to the existing subspace (which we determine by comparing it to its projection in the subspace), we would know that it does not share the major topics of the original document collection.

When it is determined that many new documents do not fit into the existing subspace, it is necessary to run an updating algorithm. What an updating algorithm needs to do is to represent the new features resulting from the new documents in the existing k-dimensional subspace without adding any more dimensions. In order to do this, the algorithm will have to adjust all the dimensions of the subspace and still maintain orthogonality. Mathematically, the algorithm needs to run fast in order to meet the near real time requirements. However, there are a couple of major challenges that make this task very difficult. (1) The matrices representing the documents and terms in the subspace (U and V) are both dense. Many of the nice features that sparse matrix computation can take advantage of are no longer available (or at least not in a straightforward way.) (2) From the application's point of view, it is not usually easy to determine how to add in the new information. For example, new documents can be added in one at a time, or they can be added in as a group (or, mathematically, as a block) of n at a time. The decision could have a profound impact on the new subspace representation. When they are added in one at a time, the algorithm is trying to adjust the subspace based on the new features of each new document, and in essence gives each individual new document a lot of 'weight' in changing the subspace. On the other hand, when they are added in as a group of n at a time, all the features in each group of documents will be 'synthesized' and looked at together, and thus make a different level of contribution to the new subspace. Usually, there is no easy way to determine which is better, or the proper size of the block.

Downdating deals with the reverse situation, when we want to archive documents, the subspace needs to be modified to represent a subset of the original documents collection. Intuitively, it would seem that this is an easier task than updating. However, in fact, it is just the opposite. Not only would downdating need to face the same challenges updating would, as described above, it has an even harder challenge. We need to remove the features representing the set of documents we intend to archive from the subspace, but maintain the number of dimensions and, at least in the cases where orthogonal decomposition is used, maintain their orthogonality. If this is to be done purely on the k-dimensional representation, without additional information from the original data set, it in essence requires us to uncover new features from the already compressed representation. This makes it an even harder task than updating. On the other hand, if the algorithm needs to revert to additional information saved during the initial subspace representation process, or the updating process, it would be challenging to make the algorithm faster than a complete re-run of the subspace representation. It is also not clear what information should be saved by the original decomposition or the updating process that is the most useful and most condensed in order to successfully fill this gap. The subject of downdating thus still remains an open research topic.

LSA and User-Interpretable Meaning

As noted above, one of the criticisms of LSA approaches was that the semantics was all "latent": the user was unable to interpret what the various constructs meant or why it was returning a particular response to a query. In this section we begin to address solutions to this problem, and further extensions are addressed in the application sections on Text Summarization and Text Visualization.

Booker et al. (1999) have pointed out that each dimension in the *latent semantic space* generated by URV corresponds to a weighted average of the frequencies of all the terms in the data set (or some weighted or transformed version of those frequencies), and therefore give the importance of those terms in that dimension. Documents containing words with large positive weights on that dimension will tend to fall toward one end of the dimension and documents containing words with large negative weights will tend to fall near the other end. Note that whether a set of words is at the negative pole or the positive pole of a particular dimension does not mean anything other than they form contrasting sets for that dimension. Although all terms are involved in the weighted average for each dimension, only a handful of terms account for much of the variability. Therefore, a few terms with large positive or negative weights essentially characterize the contrast expressed by that dimension. So the semantics of each basis vector generated by URV (or SVD or, in fact, any orthogonal decomposition) can be characterized semantically as expressing a continuum between two poles, with each pole represented by a set of words. This ability to determine the meaning of the basis vectors becomes especially important in visualization applications, where the user may want to know more than which documents are similar or dissimilar, but also how they are dissimilar. The section on Text Visualization below elaborates on this, suggesting how the user can not only select from the basis vectors provided by TRUST as dimensions of visualization, but also create new axes for the visualization system based on the latent semantic space.

Subsequently, other work has used a similar approach; for example, both work on probabilistic LSA (Hoffman, 1999, 2001) and Non-Negative Matrix Factorization (Amy Langville, personal communication) have suggested that, since all document vectors in those two approaches are non-negative, the basis vectors can be characterized by a single set of words rather than multiple sets of words in the opposite poles in SVD or TRUST, where vectors can have both positive and negative components. On the other hand, the PLSA and NMF approaches do not result in orthogonal basis vectors which may impede the user's interpretation of the relationships between documents in a visualization system.

Documents and clusters of documents can also be characterized by the words (or, more correctly, terms) of natural language. Booker et al. (1999) point out that the document vectors in the latent semantic space with reduced dimensionality can be projected back into the original term space, where the dimensions correspond to the terms in the original document set (see Figure 1b for an example of this projection and back-projection). They refer to the terms with the largest weights as *topic words*, since they will characterize the topics of the documents. Depending on the length of the document, and the centrality of its terms to the topics of the whole collection, many of these terms may actually occur in the document. However, their weights will be modified (up or down) depending on the other words in the document, and words that do not occur in the document will also show up as topic words if the terms it is correlated with appear in the document. For example, in an analysis of comments in an employee survey, a short comment "Give more COLA" (where "COLA" means "Cost of Living Adjustment") the topic word assigned by TRUST was "benefits". This way of assigning natural language terms in the form of topic words to documents can serve as a useful summarization and can be leveraged into more extended sentence or paragraph based summarization, as discussed in the section on Text Summarization below.

Finally, topic words are especially useful in summarizing groups of documents, in particular groups that form convex clusters in the latent semantic space (Booker et al., 1999). In this case, the centroid of the cluster can be treated as a pseudo-document and its topics words extracted just as if it were an actual document. This set of topic words will characterize the set as a whole, since only words that tend to be associated with all of the documents in the latent semantic space will have a large weight; those that only characterize a few of the documents will be cancelled out by the low or negative value those words have for the other documents. An added advantage of this is that the centroid of a cluster is often a by-product of the clustering algorithm and need not be calculated separately, as for example in k-means (Hartigan & Wong, 1979).

APPLICATIONS

Information Retrieval

One of the primary goals of any representation of a corpus is that it be searchable. We would like to submit a query and have returned to us those documents which are most relevant to the given query. In traditional vector space and LSI methods, a query is treated as a pseudo-document and can be represented as a vector q of length t. Like columns of the term-by-document matrix A, each component of query vector q records the occurrence of the corresponding term in the query. Then, an *information retrieval* system will assign a score between the query vector and each of the document vectors and retrieve the set of documents which are closest to the query. A common method used to compute the score vector (of length d) is to measure the Euclidian distance or the cosine of the angle between the query and document vectors.

However, in some cases, a query could be another document like those in the original corpus (you may wish to retrieve similar documents), while in other cases, the query may only consist of a few terms (keywords). An information retrieval system can be undermined by naively treating a query with keywords as a pseudo-document. For example, a query vector resulting from a few keywords contains only a few nonzero components; hence, distance calculations may be polluted by each document's entries for terms that are not of interest. When a user queries by terms, the terms in the documents that are not present in the queries should be treated as "don't care"; we would like the distance metric to be less influenced by these terms. On the other hand, when queries are treated as pseudo-documents, it is assumed that the proportion of term frequencies in the query is significant, and the absence of certain terms means those terms should occur at a lower-than-average frequency in the returned documents. Also, if there is more than one keyword, the distance calculations may penalize a document for disproportionate use of the keywords. Therefore, it is important to distinguish these two types of queries: query-by-example and query-by-term (keywords), and associate them with different scoring methods (Holt & Wu, 2001).

A query-by-example (or document-query) ranks the columns of A_k by a score which reflects each column's proximity to a given query vector in term space. It focuses on document-document comparison and analysis. The query vector needs to be processed in the same way as the documents used to generate the original subspace, including the same normalization weighting. While a document-query requires a document-document comparison, a term-query focuses on term-document relationships. Note that the approximation A_k has already accounted for the semantics latent in the document collection. Thus, if we want a score vector for a term-query consisting of a single term, we could directly pick out the corresponding row of A_k and read off the entries as scores for the documents. This process suggests a different scoring formula from the traditional LSI approach that treats all queries as pseudo-documents since we do not apply preprocessing to the query vector. The term-query is treated as a selection of terms rather than as a document. For queries with multiple keywords, those rows of A_k corresponding to the keywords are picked out and synthesized into a score vector, typically using a weighted sum, where the weights reflect the importance of the term in the whole set of documents (e.g. tf-idf).

Document Classification

Text classification is one of the major applications of text mining. Some view Information Retrieval as a sub-case of text classification, with two classes – relevant and not relevant to the query. However, while in text classification it is usually required to identify what class or classes each text document belongs to, in information retrieval, only a certain number of relevant documents are required to be identified and returned to the user.

LSA has not enjoyed tremendous success in the text classification area. The general approach of LSA is to represent each document in the collection with respect to its relationship to the overall most dominant topics in the collection. Individual details and variations are treated as 'noise' and are not represented. If the text classification task is to identify what classes each document belongs to, based on the overall dominant topics of each document, LSA would provide a good representation for this task. However, in most applications, the requirement is rather different; it is important to identify a document as belonging to a class even when only a relatively small portion of the document contains information related to this class. In the latter case, LSA would be a poor fit.

In terms of text classification algorithms, *k*-nearest neighbors (*k*-NN) (Dasarathy, 1991) is likely the most natural choice. Text classification is a form of supervised learning. Typically, it requires sample data representing instances of each class. Using the combination of an LSA representation and *k*-NN, we can simply find the *k* documents in the subspace that are closest to the document in question, and calculate a 'vote' from the *k* nearest documents. If a certain number of them within a certain distance belong to Class C1, this document will be assigned as belonging to Class C1. The distance calculation is identical to how LSA would handle a query. *k*-NN itself, unlike other classification algorithms, does not require a training phase (the phase where the machine learning program figures out what features to use and how to combine them to predict each class based on the sample data). However, in practice, there are serious challenges in applying this combination of LSA and *k*-NN as a text classifier. One major challenge is its ability to handle high dimensional data. Text data inherently has very high dimensionality, even working in the reduced LSA subspace (typically 50 to several hundred dimensions). Two documents can be close in some of the dimensions while not close in other dimensions in the same subspace. The search space for the *k*-NN algorithm can be very large when the document collection is sizable, and there is no known greedy algorithm or indexing procedure that can speed up the search.

Others have attempted to combine LSA with Support Vector Machines (SVMs) for text classification. SVMs (Vapnik, 1995) perform classification by finding a hyperplane that maximally separates members of a class from non-members in another, typically high-dimensional, feature space. There are two important aspects to SVMs: the hyperplane is as far from the closest members and non-members as it can be (it creates a maximum margin between them) and the high-dimensional feature space is generated using a kernel. A kernel is a function of the two input elements that directly calculates their similarity (inner product) in the higher dimensional space without explicitly transforming them into the higher dimensional vectors. Joachims (1998) suggests that SVMs are a good fit for text classification, because, text has a large number of features (words) and SVMs implicitly avoid overfitting, a common problem when using a large number of features. Joachims just uses words as the features and does not take advantage of LSA. Cristianini, Shawe-Taylor, & Lodhi (2002) show how LSA can motivate a "latent semantic kernel" that takes advantage of word correlations and can be used in SVMs as well as be combined with other kernels (e.g. polynomial or radial basis function). While their theoretical work is very clear, the empirical results are not overly impressive. Gliozzo & Strapparava (2005) discuss Domain Kernels that use the strength of association of words with different semantic domains to enhance text classification with SVMs. Although word-to-domain mapping can be done manually, they propose to use LSA to do it, resulting in something very similar to Cristiani et al.'s latent semantic kernels. Asservatham (2008) further proposes a "weighted semantic kernel" with a global semantic space defined from local concepts by extracting the co-occurrence relations between words by employing LSA locally within each class. Compared to the Domain Kernel which uses a global LSA approach, his kernel shows potential improvement in classification accuracy with the price of additional cost in computing each local LSA.

Document Clustering

Clustering, unlike classification, is a type of unsupervised learning. It does not include a training phase and does not use sample data to identify features which best represent each class and separate this class from other classes. Text clustering aims to identify the natural groupings (i.e. clusters) in the document collection, this is particularly useful where there are no predefined classes (or categories) or samples for each class. Even when there are existing classes with sample data, they often are incomplete. For example, in viewing an actual document collection, one class may contain too many instances and would need to be further broken down. In cases like these, text clustering is very useful way to get information organized. However, as an unsupervised learning method, there is no standard to evaluate the results against. There is a wide array of clustering algorithms, each with its particular behavior to capture specific kinds of "nearness". The choice of a clustering algorithm will depend on the users specific analysis needs and the nature of their data. Text clustering allows users to identify groups of documents that are close to each other. Combined with summarization techniques, it allows users to identify what topics are being discussed in the document collection and which documents are similar to each other. In the rest of this section, we will not go into further discussions on various clustering algorithms. Readers are encouraged to consult various books on clustering such as (Kaufman & Rousseeuw, 2005; Hartigan & Wong, 1979). We will focus on the interaction between LSA and text clustering.

Given there are no pre-identified classes and no sample data for each class, and no clear way of identifying features in the document collection, LSA becomes a natural choice to provide a principled and condensed representation of the text data. LSA does not require users to preselect the words of interest (which are features for clustering algorithms to consider), and it does not require a 'training phase' to identify the correct features. It can automatically find a lower dimension projection (which means fewer features for clustering algorithms to consider), and it provides a good representation of the major topics of the document collection. Once the data is represented using LSA, different clustering algorithms can be used to do the text clustering, flat partitioning algorithms such as *k*-means, or hierarchical clustering algorithms such as S-Link, or density-based clustering algorithm (Hinneburg & Keim, 2002) are all potentially good choices. The decision as to which one to use should be based on the nature of the text collection. For example, *k*-means is known not to handle outliers well, nor to work well when the data set has a crescent or other non-convex shape. However, there is no known theory that can help us determine what clustering algorithm would work best on an arbitrary text collection, whether it is represented by either the original terms or by the LSA representation. Text visualization (described in another section of this chapter) may not shed much light on this issue either, because techniques such as LSA or Multidimensional Scaling (Cox & Cox, 2001) need to be applied to make visualization possible and these could obscure the true nature of the document collection.

Text Clustering itself would not be useful if no additional insight can be provided for each of the clusters identified. Text Summarization plays a crucial role here. If the resulting clusters are convex, LSA techniques described in the Text Summarization section of this chapter can be used to summarize each of the clusters.

Text Summarization

Text summarization methods are used to provide a summary view of one text document or a collection of text documents. There are several ways this can be accomplished using LSA. One approach is to summarize a single text document by providing topic words. These topic words can either be based on the most important topics in the whole document collection, or be based on a user's specific query. A second approach is to identify one or more segments of a document (where a segment is typically a phrase, sentence, or paragraph) which best describe the document. Since this depends on the topic words that have been found in the document, there are two variants depending on whether the topic words are obtained from the document collection or from a user's specific query. A third approach is to summarize a group of documents which have similar topics, typically obtained as a result of text clustering, by providing topic words. All of these approaches can be accomplished using TRUST. In an application, it allows a user to add the individual term weights based on the user's interest, and it supports highlighting of the relevant terms or most important segments of the documents in the text display.

To summarize a text document based on the overall topics in a document collection is a straightforward process. We mathematically identify which terms contribute most to the document projection in the reduced subspace (i.e. find the topic words of the document as discussed in the section on LSA and User-Interpretable Meaning above). We can use all of these topic words as a summarization of the document or, if we want to use just words that are found in the document (for example, if we want to highlight the words in the document), we can use the intersection of these terms and the terms in the document provide a summary of the document.

To summarize a text document based on a user's query, a different algorithm is used depending on whether the query is by-example (another document) or by-term (one or more keywords; see section on Information Retrieval above). If it is query-by-example, we find the topic words of the query document, in the same way we did with the document to be summarized in the previous paragraph, and then use those which also occur in the retrieved document as the summary words for that document.

If the query is a query-by-term, we will examine the term-by-term symmetrical matrix, $U_kU_k^T$, which represents term-term relationships in the document set and identify the terms that are most highly related to those terms that appear in the query. If there is more than one term in our query, these related terms can be combined by summing their weights together, possibly with some kind of weighting like tf-idf that reflects the differing importance of the various query terms. The resulting terms with the largest weights which also occur in the retrieved document constitute the summary of the document with respect to the query-by-term.

Once the most important terms of a document have been identified, summarizing the document by one or a few segments of the document is a straightforward extension. Those segments which include a preponderance of important terms (whether measured by the number of topic words or by the total weight of the topic words, either directly or relative to the size of the segment) would be the most central to the document and therefore provide a reasonable summary.

While in theory, one can summarize any arbitrary collection of documents by simply adding all of the term weights for the individual documents obtained using the method described above, this would be very time consuming and not very practical. LSA can be best used to summarize a set of documents with similar topics, especially when the set is generated by a text clustering algorithm which produces 'convex clusters' in the subspace. The *k*-means algorithm (Hartigan & Wong, 1979) is a typical clustering algorithm that is used for this purpose. When the clusters are convex, LSA can be used to summarize the centroid of the cluster, which is a by-product of the *k*-means clustering algorithm, in terms of topic words. Although the centroid may not be an actual document in the collection, it can be treated as a pseudo-document in the subspace. We can apply the same algorithm we use to summarize a document to this pseudo-document and obtain the summary of the cluster. When the clusters are not convex (e.g. a crescent shape) the centroid may be outside of the actual cluster, which would not work very well as a summarization of the cluster.

Text Visualization

Text Visualization has the advantage of incorporating a user's world knowledge at crucial decision points in conducting analyses without requiring that knowledge to be added to the system in advance. It takes advantage of the human cognitive ability to actively use visual cues to guide the mining process as well as form a quick and active view of the text collection. In this section, we describe how Boeing's text mining algorithm, TRUST, and *Starlight* (an information visualization system developed at the Pacific Northwest National Laboratory that employs the TRUST engine (Risch, Rex, Dowson, Walters, May, & Moon, 1999)) can be used for text visualization and analysis.

TRUST's orthogonal decomposition process provides a set of orthogonal bases which spans an *n*-dimensional subspace, where *n* is a number usually between 50 and a few hundred, with the remaining dimensions eliminated as noise. The document sets can be projected into this subspace. Since human eyes can only visualize data in 2D or 3D, two or three of these n dimensions can be used as axes for visualization. In our discussion, we will mostly focus on 3D visualization. However, most of the technical points we address here apply more-or-less equally to both 2D and 3D visualization. Each document can be viewed as a point in this 3D space, where closeness in the 3D space shows the closeness of the topics covered in these documents (Booker et al., 1999). [1] In this section, we discuss specific features of visualization using TRUST.

Visualization with Labeled Axes

Traditional LSA is performed using PCA. The natural choice of axes for 3D visualization would be the top three principal components. Unfortunately, traditional LSA generates features whose meaning is not very clear. This drawback becomes especially pertinent in the case of visualization, which traditional LSA did not focus on. Compare the following two diagrams, Figure 3a without axis labels and Figure 3b with labels automatically generated by TRUST. TRUST's representation supports visualization well.

To accomplished this labeling, each dimension is generated by URV corresponding to a weighted average of the frequencies of all the terms in the data set. Documents containing words with large positive weights will tend to fall toward one end of the dimension and documents containing words with large negative weights will tend to fall near the other end. Although all terms are involved in the weighted average for each dimension, only a handful of terms account for much of the variability. Therefore, a few terms with large positive or negative weights essentially characterize the contrast expressed by that dimension. So we visually represent the dimensions as axes in the visualization space and label each end of each axis with a small set of the highest weighted terms, positive or negative, respectively.[2]

Thus, TRUST provides a means for representing the semantics of the various dimensions, thereby, aiding the analyst in the interpretation of the visual representation of the documents and in selecting alternate views. This is one of the ways TRUST differs from traditional LSA. Due to limitations in the display here, Figure 3a and Figure 3b show only one term each for each end of each axis. In the actual representation, on each end of each axis, there is a group of terms with weights associated, as seen in Figure 3b below (generated with a different set of parameters). The axis with the label *navigation* at one end and *inspection* at the other indicates that documents located further in the *navigation* direction are more related to the topic 'navigation' and less related to the topic 'inspection'.

The labeling helps the users in two ways. First, it helps them understand the meaning of widely separated items in the default view consisting of the top principal components (or approximation thereof[3]). Second, with information on each of the top principal components available to the user, they have a principled means of selecting other components as axes of visualization, since the semantics of the components are provided and allow them to select axes which will give them the most insight for their task.

Starlight also uses TRUST to label clusters, according to the method described above in the section on Text Summarization. Figure 4 shows a screendump of Starlight's representation of a set of documents with topic words assigned to the clusters.

Visualizing with User Defined Axes

Because text visualizations in 2-D or 3-D are projections of a higher dimensional space, it is possible that none of the principal components may provide the best view to separate the data. Viewing alternate projections may reveal important patterns in the data. However, while the top principal components capture the maximum differences among all the data points, they do not necessarily show all the relevant structure in the data.

TRUST addresses this problem by allowing the user to "customize" his or her own dimensions to be used for visualization. This is another major feature of TRUST which has gone beyond traditional LSA. Even with this ability to intelligently choose which dimensions to use in visualization, there is still another problem: the most useful semantic dimension may not be any single dimension provided by the original matrix operation, but rather some combination of several of these. Consider the data set displayed in Figure 3b. The labeled axes are very useful in helping the analyst get some idea of the information in the collection. However, the analyst may wish to look at the data from some other point of view (e.g., systems on the airplane). By specifying the desired axes in terms of three contrasting pairs of words, Figure 3c is obtained.

Mathematically, once the subspace is defined through the two-sided orthogonal decomposition, there is more than one set of bases or axes that can uniquely define the same subspace. In visualization, this means we can use different axes to represent the same set of documents in the same subspace, and for each set of axes, each document will be represented by a different set of coordinates. Using this property TRUST further allows users to input topics of interest which can then be used as the axes of the visualization.

First, the coordinates of projected documents based on the original term space are computed. Then, a desired axis can be specified as a word or set of words to characterize one end of the axis, as two contrasting sets of words to characterize the opposite ends of the axis, or, more generally, as any weighted set of words, with both positive and negative weights. The only restriction

Figure 3. a) Projection onto top 3 principal components without labels b) Projection onto top 3 principal components with labels. c) Projection onto user selected dimensions

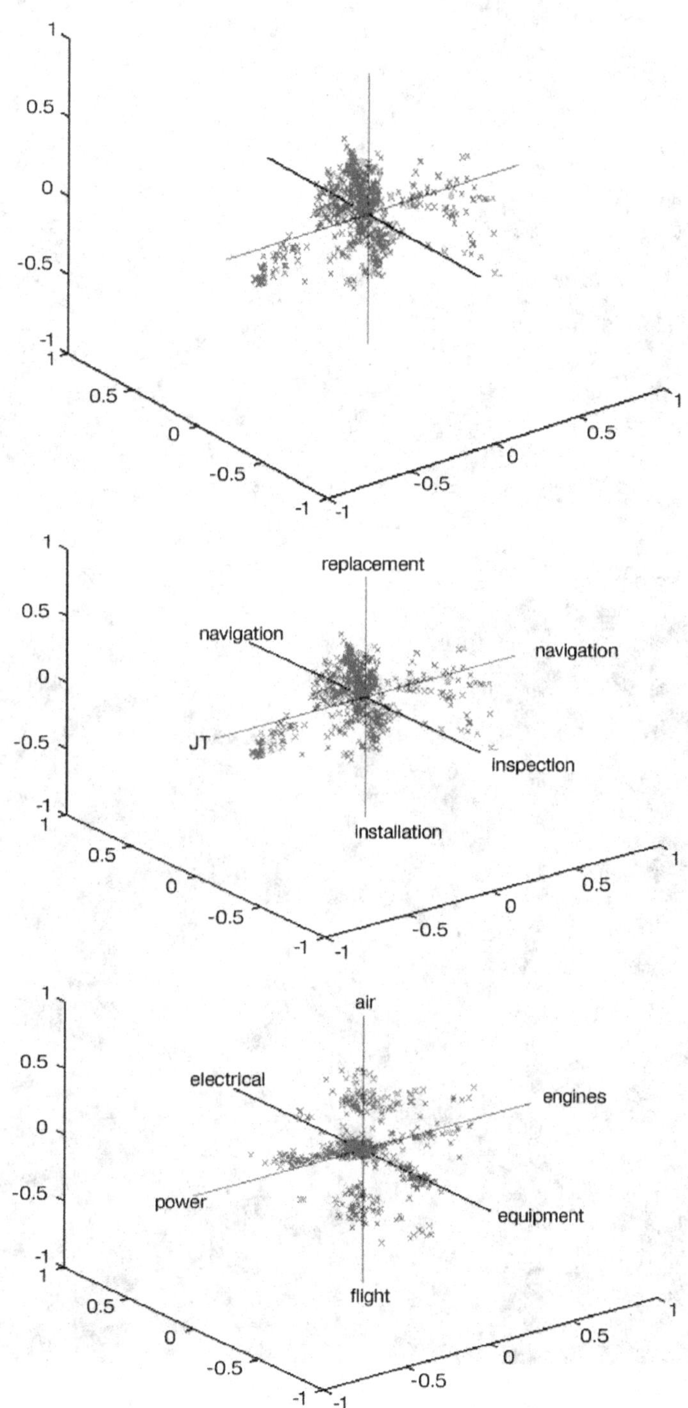

Figure 4. Starlight uses TRUST to generate summary terms for the documents and clusters

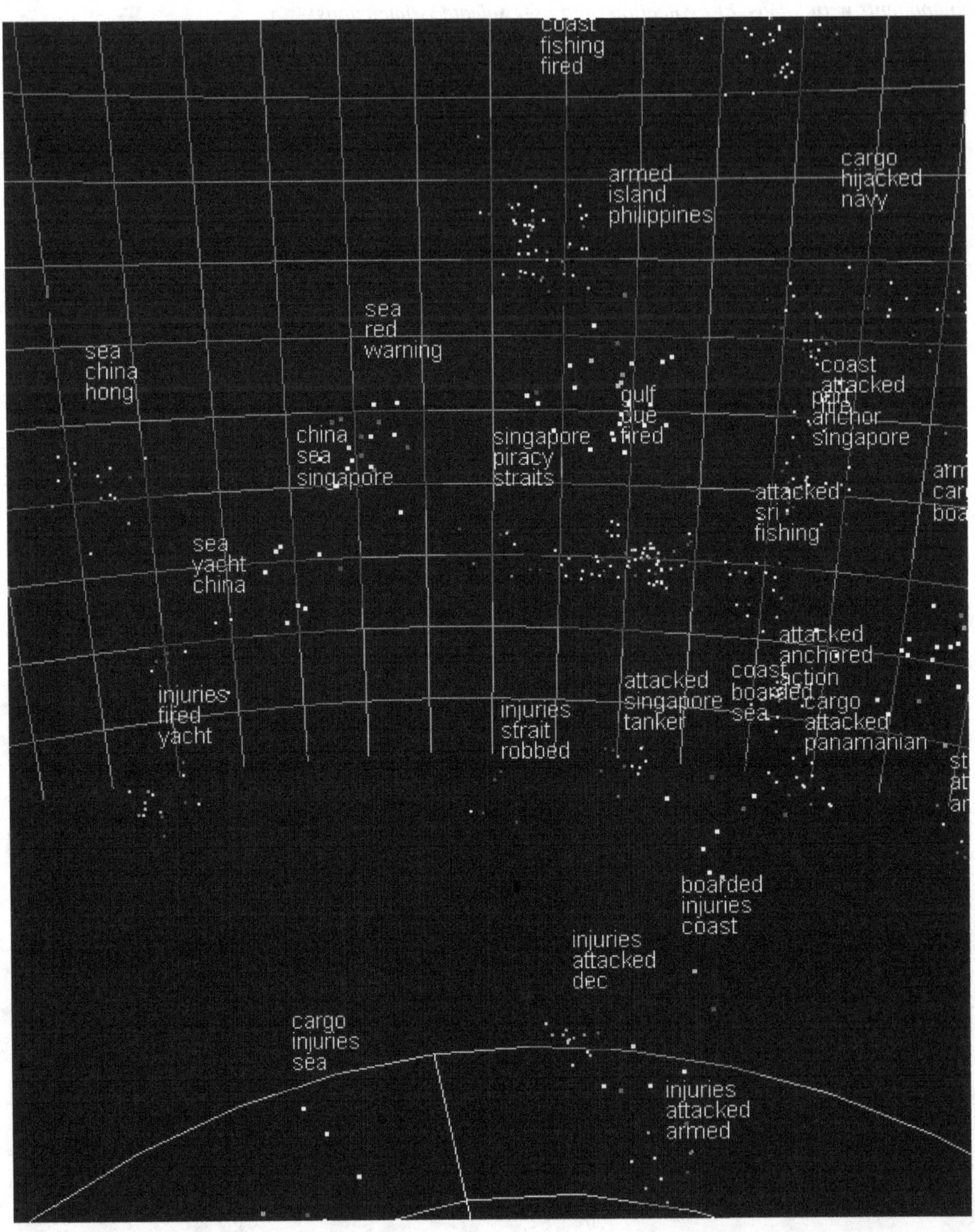

is that the words must come from the original set of terms. A vector is then formed from these words and weights. For example, in Figure 3c, the vertical vector consists of a "+1" in the component corresponding to "air" and a "–1" in the component corresponding to "flight", with the rest of the components implicitly assigned a "0". The resulting vector is then projected into the 100-200 dimensional space of the original URV decomposition, and the documents projected onto the resulting dimensions.

Cross-Language Information Retrieval

LSA in conjunction with a multilingual parallel aligned corpus is a common approach for cross-language information retrieval (Berry, et al., 1994, Littman, et al., 1997). A term-by-document matrix of weighted frequencies is formed from the corpus; each document consists of the concatenation of all the languages, so terms from all languages will appear in any given document. This approach has been shown to be useful in identifying similar documents across languages in the sense of retrieving the most similar document in one language to a query in another language. However this approach has limitations and drawbacks. LSA has no way to distinguish between homographs from different languages, and in some cases this could be problematic, especially when the homographs have very different meanings in the different languages. In addition, under LSA all languages are mixed together in the bag-of-words approach, languages which have more terms overall generally account for a higher percentage of the information in each document.

In (Chew et al., 2007), Chew et al. proposed a tensor (multi-way array) model and PARAFAC2 factorization as an alternative to vector space model and SVD-type factorizations in LSA. PARAFAC2 (Harshman, 1972) is a variant of PARAFAC (Harshman, 1970) which is a multi-way generalization of the SVD. In their approach, an irregular three-way array is formed, each slice of which is a separate term-by-document matrix for a single language in the parallel corpus. The number of documents in each slice will be the same, but the number of terms will vary by language. Let A_k denote the term-by-document matrix for the kth language in the parallel corpus with M_k terms and N documents. The PARAFAC2 algorithm computes the following decomposition:

$$A_k=U_kHS_kV^T.$$

Here, U_k is an orthonormal $M_k \times R$ factor matrix for the slice A_k, and H is a nonsingular matrix of size $R \times R$. A constraint that $(U_kH)^T(U_kH)$ is constant over k is also imposed to ensure uniqueness. Conceptually, the goal is to compute something like an SVD for each language such that V is the same across all languages, although for each language k there will be a separate U_k and S_k (analogous to singular values).

The experimental results that PARAFAC2 outperforms standard LSA by a significant margin by ensuring that the 'concepts' of the difference languages are aligned with one another, and by factoring out some of the statistical differences between languages that caused problems for LSA. Chew et al. concluded that the tensor model and PARAFAC2 is a superior alternative and a good step forward from LSA for multilingual information retrieval.

FUTURE TRENDS / CONCLUSION

LSA originated in the late 1980s and early 1990s as a new method for information retrieval, before the rise of the Internet Age. Its introduction was a landmark in that it applied linear algebra to a seemingly unrelated field, information retrieval. On the algorithm side, various researchers from the linear algebra community proposed improvements on the decomposition or the subspace representation of the text data, including Semi-Discrete Decomposition and Non-Negative Decomposition. Additional research also has been done on the improvements of the representation for dynamic sets of data, i.e. updating and downdating of the subspace representation. While these advancements are mathematically interesting, they are not widely cited academically by work outside of this area, nor used in major information retrieval products. The computational and memory size requirements of internet search or large database search makes LSA impractical even with its recent mathematical improvements.

Most of the research that has originated on the linear algebra side focuses on improvements and variations after the text data is represented by a matrix, and has little to offer beyond the original approach of Deerwester et al. (1990). Not only does this initial step of representation play an important role in the outcome of subspace representation of the text data, it also side-steps the uneasiness that text data inherently do not conform to Gaussian distributions and are thus not suited for PCA-based LSA. Probabilistic LSA attempts to provide a transformation of the original text data into a representation based on a multinomial model. Possibly due to the complexity of the algorithm, this approach is not gaining major ground in the realm of LSA.

Another major criticism of LSA is that it is a "black box" approach that makes it difficult to understand the results. TRUST has successfully disputed this challenge, especially through its implementation as the text mining engine in the text visualization product Starlight. This tool allows users to readily understand and use the results in their analysis tasks.

On the application side, LSA has extended its coverage to many areas such as text visualization, text clustering, and text summarization. There are also attempts to use LSA representation to support text classification. These applications beyond information retrieval continue to make LSA a viable approach beyond a mere historical landmark in information retrieval. While variations on keyword search and web page link mining provide powerful Internet search algorithms, they do not provide a useful method for text visualization. For text data without URL-type links, e.g. text in databases, LSA is playing a major role in content clustering. Probabilistic modeling also does not provide a good answer for text visualization and text clustering.

Moving forward, it is likely that LSA related methods will find new niche areas, in addition to making improvements on its existing strengths in application areas such as text visualization. For example, with its strength in topic relatedness, LSA should be able to make a contribution in the area of distillation (e.g. as in the DARPA sponsored Global Autonomous Language Exploitation program) which goes beyond current text summarization. Further research is needed on the strengths and weakness of different variations of LSA with regard to different analysis applications. Research beyond pure algorithmic variations, can provide a focus in identifying areas where LSA can continue to improve and flourish to become part of mainstream web mining and text mining products. With the growing need for multimedia mining and cross-language information retrieval and processing, LSA's ability to address cross-language and mine textual information in a multimedia (e.g. transcription from speech, caption in video) makes LSA a competitive force in multimedia mining.

REFERENCES

Achlioptas, D. (2001). Database-friendly random projections. In *Proceedings of ACM Symposium on the Principles of Database Systems* (pp. 274-281).

Asservatham, S. (2008). *A local latent semantic analysis-based kernel for document similarities.* IEEE International Joint Conference on Neural Networks.

Bartell, B. T., Cottrell, G. W., & Belew, R. K. (1992). Latent semantic indexing is an optimal special case of multidimensional scaling. *Proceedings of the Fifteenth Annual International ACM SIGIR Conference on Research and Development in Information Retrieval* (pp. 161-167).

Berry, M., Browne, M., Langville, A., Pauca, P., & Plemmons, R. J. (2006). Algorithms and applications for approximate nonnegative matrix factorization. *Computational Statistics & Data Analysis, 52*(1), 155–173. doi:10.1016/j.csda.2006.11.006

Berry, M., Dumais, S., & O'Brien, G. (1994). Using linear algebra for intelligent information retrieval. *SIAM Review, 37*, 573–595. doi:10.1137/1037127

Berry, M. W., & Fierro, R. D. (1996). Low-rank orthogonal decompositions for information retrieval applications. *Numerical Linear Algebra with Applications, 3*(4), 301–328. doi:10.1002/(SICI)1099-1506(199607/08)3:4<301::AID-NLA84>3.0.CO;2-S

Bingham, E., & Mannila, H. (2001). Random projection in dimensionality reduction: Applications to image and text data. In *Proceedings of the 7th International Conference on Knowledge Discovery and Data Mining* (pp. 245-250).

Blei, D. M., Ng, A. Y., & Jordan, M. I. (2003). Latent dirichlet allocation. *Journal of Machine Learning Research, 3*, 993–1022.

Booker, A., Condliff, M., Greaves, M., Holt, F. B., Kao, A., & Pierce, D. J. ... Wu, Y.-J. J. (1999). Visualizing text data sets. *IEEE Computing in Science & Engineering* (pp. 26-35).

Chen, J., & Saad, Y. (2009). Divide and Conquer Strategies for Effective Information Retrieval. *Proceedings of the Ninth SIAM International Conference on Data Mining, 1*(4), 449-460.

Chew, P., Bader, B., & Kolda, T. (2007). Cross-language information retrieval using PARAFAC2. *Proceedings of the 13th ACM SIGKDD International Conference on Knowledge Discovery and Data Mining* (pp. 143-152).

Cho, G., Pierce, D. J., & Wu, Y.-J. J. (2000). *Downdating and mean-correction algorithms for truncated URV. (Mathematics & Computing Technology Report M&CT-TECH-00-012)*. Boeing Company.

Cox, M. F., & Cox, M. A. A. (2001). *Multidimensional scaling*. London, UK: Chapman & Hall.

Cristianini, N., Shawe-Taylor, J., & Lodhi, H. (2002). Latent semantic kernels. *Journal of Intelligent Information Systems, 18*(2-3), 127–152. doi:10.1023/A:1013625426931

Dasarathy, B. V. (1991). *Nearest neighbor (NN) norms: NN pattern classification techniques*. IEEE Computer Society Press.

Deerwester, S., Dumais, S., Furnas, G., Landauer, T., & Harshman, R. (1990). Indexing by latent semantic analysis. *Journal of the American Society for Information Science American Society for Information Science, 41*(6), 391–40. doi:10.1002/(SICI)1097-4571(199009)41:6<391::AID-ASI1>3.0.CO;2-9

Dhillon, I. S., & Modha, D. S. (2001). Concept decomposition for large sparse text data using clustering. *Machine Learning, 42*(1), 143–175. doi:10.1023/A:1007612920971

Ding, C. H. Q. (2005). A probabilistic model for latent semantic indexing. *Journal of the American Society for Information Science and Technology, 56*(6), 597–608. doi:10.1002/asi.20148

Dumais, S. T. (1992). *LSI meets TREC: A status report.* In The First Text Retrieval Conference (TREC-1), NIST Special Publication, (pp. 105-116).

Finesso, L., & Spreij, P. (2006). Nonnegative matrix factorization and I-divergence alternating minimization. *Linear Algebra and Its Applications*, *416*, 270–287. doi:10.1016/j.laa.2005.11.012

Gliozzo, A., & Strapparava, C. (2005) Domain kernels for text classification. In *Proceedings of the Ninth Conference on Computaional Natural Language Learning (CoNLL-2005)*, (pp. 56-63). Association for Computational Linguistics.

Harshman, R. A. (1970). Foundations of the PARAFAC procedure: Models and conditions for an explanatory multi-modal factor analysis. *UCLA Working Papers in Phonetics, 16,* 1-84.

Harshman, R. A. (1972). Foundations mathematical and technical notes. *UCLA Working Papers in Phonetics, 22,* 30-47.

Hartigan, J. A., & Wong, M. A. (1979). Algorithm AS136: A k-means clustering algorithm. *Applied Statistics*, *28*, 100–108. doi:10.2307/2346830

Hecht-Nielsen, R. (1994). Context vectors: General purpose approximate meaning representations self-organized from raw data.

Hinneburg, A., & Keim, D. (2002). A general approach to clustering in large databases with noise. *J. Knowledge and Information System,* *5*(4). Springer.

Hofmann, T. (1999). Probabilistic latent semantic indexing. *In Proceedings of the Twenty-Second Annual International SIGIR Conference on Research and Development in Information Retrieval.*

Hofmann, T. (2001). Unsupervised learning by probabilistic latent semantic analysis. *Machine Learning Journal*, *42*(1), 177–196. doi:10.1023/A:1007617005950

Holt, F., & Wu, Y.-J. J. (2001). Information retrieval and classification with subspace representations. In *Proceedings of CIR 2000, SIAM Proceedings in Applied Mathematics,* SIAM, Philadelphia.

Joachims, T. (1998). Text categorization with support vector machines: Learning with many relevant features. *Proceedings of the European Conference on Machine Learning*. Springer.

Johnson, W. B., & Lindenstrauss, J. (1984). *Extensions of Lipschitz mapping into Hilbert space*. In Conference on Modern Analysis and Probability, 26 (pp. 189-206).

Jolliffe, I. (Ed.). (2002). *Principal component analysis*. Springer-Verlag.

Kaski, S. (1998). Dimensionality reduction by random mapping. In . *Proceedings of International Joint Conference on Neural Networks*, *1*, 237–288.

Kaufman, L., & Rousseeuw, P. J. (2005). *Finding groups in data: An introduction to cluster analysis (Wiley Series in Probability and Statistics)*. Wiley-Interscience.

Kim, H., & Park, H. (2006). *Sparse non-negative matrix factorizations via alternating non-negativity-constrained least squares. (CSE Technical Reports GT-CSE-06-20)*. Georgia Institute of Technology.

Kolda, T. G., & O'Leary, P. D. (1998). A semi-discrete matrix decomposition for latent semantic indexing in information retrieval. *ACM Transactions on Information Systems, 16*, 322–346. doi:10.1145/291128.291131

Kontostathis, A. (2007). Essential dimensions of latent semantic indexing. *Proceedings of the 40th Hawaii International Conference on System Science.*

Landauer, T. K., Foltz, P. W., & Laham, D. (1998). Introduction to latent semantic analysis. *Discourse Processes, 25*, 259–284. doi:10.1080/01638539809545028

Lee, D., & Seung, H. (1999). Learning the parts of objects by non-negative matrix factorization. *Nature*, *401*, 788–791. doi:10.1038/44565

Lewis, D. (1997). *Reuters-21578 text categorization test collection*. Retrieved from http://kdd.ics.uci.edu/ databases/reuters21578/ README.txt

Littman, M., Dumais, S., & Landauer, T. (1997). *Automatic cross-language information retrieval using latent semantic indexing*. AAAI-97 Spring Symposium Series: Cross-Language Text and Speech Retrieval (pp. 18-24).

Mason, J. E., & Spiteri, R. (2008). *A new adaptive folding-up algorithm for information retrieval.* Text Mining Workshop in the Eighth SIAM International Conference on Data Mining.

O'Sullivan, J. A. (2000). Properties of the information value decomposition. *Proceedings IEEE International Symposium on Information Theory* (pp. 491).

Paatero, P., & Tapper, U. (1994). Positive matrix factorization: A non-negative factor model with optimal utilization of error estimate of data values. *Environmetrics*, *5*, 111–126. doi:10.1002/env.3170050203

Papadimitriou, C. H., Raghavan, P., Tamaki, H., & Vempala, S. (2000). Latent semantic indexing: A probabilistic analysis. *Journal of Computer and System Sciences*, *61*(2), 217–235. doi:10.1006/jcss.2000.1711

Pauca, V. P., Shahnaz, F., Berry, M. W., & Plemmons, R. J. (2004). Text mining using non-negative matrix factorizations. In *Proceedings of SIAM International Conference on Data Mining.*

Risch, J., Rex, D. B., Dowson, S. T., Walters, T. B., May, R. A., & Moon, B. D. (1999). The starlight information visualization system . In Card, S., Mackinlay, J., & Shneiderman, B. (Eds.), *Readings in information visualization: Using vision to think*. Morgan Kaufmann.

Salton, G., & McGill, M. (1986). *Introduction to modern information retrieval*. New York, NY: McGraw-Hill, Inc.

Salton, G., Wong, A., & Yang, C. S. (1975). A vector space model for automatic indexing. *Communications of the ACM*, *18*, 613–620. doi:10.1145/361219.361220

Schütze, H., & Pedersen, J. (1993). A vector model for syntagmatic and paradigmatic relatedness. In *Proceedings of the Ninth Annual Conference of the UW Centre for the New OED and Text Research* (pp. 104–113).

Shahnaz, F., Berry, M., Pauca, P., & Plemmons, R. (2006). Document clustering using non-negative matrix factorization. *Information Processing & Management*, *42*, 373–386. doi:10.1016/j.ipm.2004.11.005

Simon, H., & Zha, H. (1997). *On updating problems in latent semantic indexing*. (Technical Report No. CSE-97-011). Department of Computer Science and Engineering, Pennsylvania State University.

Vapnik, V. N. (1995). *The nature of statistical learning theory*. Springer.

Vinary, V., Cox, I., Wood, K., & Milic-Frayling, N. (2005). A comparison of dimensionality reduction techniques for text retrieval. In *Proceedings of Fourth International Conference on Machine Learning and Applications*, 2005.

KEY TERMS AND DEFINITIONS

Basis Vectors (for a given space): A set of linearly independent vectors that define a space in that any vector in that space can be defined as a linear combination (a weighted sum) of those vectors. Linearly independent means that none of them can be defined as a linear combination (or weighted sum) of the others.

Dimensionality Reduction: The process of taking high dimensional data (data represented by a large number of features) and representing it with different and fewer features or dimensions (which may be combinations of the old features) in a principled fashion that preserves some properties of the original space.

Information Retrieval (IR): The process of searching for documents or pieces of text to fulfill a user's information needs.

Latent Semantic Analysis (LSA): A method of representing text documents in terms of features that are weighted combinations of the frequencies words or terms in the documents that makes the "latent semantics" or topics treated in the documents more computationally accessible.

Latent Semantic Space: The subspace of term space whose dimensions correspond to the features uncovered by Latent Semantic Analysis for representing documents in a more semantically useful form.

Principal Components Analysis (PCA): A statistical method for discovering the dimensions that maximize variability in high dimensional data. Mathematically equivalent to SVD, except that it requires that the data all be centered.

Singular Value Decomposition (SVD): A linear algebra method of decomposing an arbitrary matrix into three matrices, two of which are orthonormal (the columns, the left and right singular vectors, respectively, are orthogonal and have length1) and the third is a diagonal matrix whose diagonal values are the singular values of the matrix.

Subspace: A vector space with a lower dimensionality that is wholly contained in a larger vector space.

Tensor model: a multidimensional array representation of an object (e.g., document, network, etc.).

Topic Words: Words that summarize the important topics of a document or piece of text that are automatically assigned based on the representation of that document in latent semantic space.

Vector Space Methods: A method of representing documents as numerical vectors, where the values represent the frequencies of the words or terms in the documents, or some weighting of these to represent their importance in the document set.

ENDNOTES

1. In visualization, documents can be displayed with different shapes and different colors etc. These provide additional information about the documents, and are often thought of as displaying the documents in more than 3 dimensions.
2. Note that the positive and negative signs on the weights merely imply a contrast between documents containing one set of words and documents containing the other set. It is to some degree an artifact of numeric representation which end of the dimension gets labeled as negative and which as positive; in another run on the same data on a different platform, the signs could be reversed. For this reason, the end user would normally not be shown the numerical scales on the axes.
3. Since we only use principal components as a starting point for user exploration, we can choose to use other more efficient approximation methods such as URV instead of SVD as the two-sided orthogonal decomposition method.

Compilation of References

Abiteboul, S., & Hull, R. (1987). IFO: A formal semantic database model. *ACM Transactions on Database Systems*, *12*(4), 525–565. doi:10.1145/32204.32205

Achlioptas, D. (2001). Database-friendly random projections. In *Proceedings of ACM Symposium on the Principles of Database Systems* (pp. 274-281).

Advanced Distributed Learning (ADL) Technical Team. (2004). *Sharable content object reference model (SCORM)*. Retrieved April 2004, from http://www.adlnet.org/ Technologies/scorm/ default.aspx

AForge. (n.d.). *Framework*. Retrieved from http://code.google.com/p/aforge/

Agosti, M., & Smeaton, A. (1996). *Information retrieval and hypertext*. New York, NY: Kluwer.

Agrawal, R., & Srikant, R. (1994). Fast algorithms for mining association rules. In *Proceedings of International Conference on Very Large Data Bases* (pp. 487-499). VLDB.

Agrawal, R., Imielinski, T., & Swami, A. (1993). Mining association rules between sets of items in large databases. In *Proceedings of the International Conference on Management of Data* (pp. 207–216). ACM Press.

Aït Younes, A., Truck, I., & Akdag, H. (2007). Image retrieval using fuzzy representation of colors. *Soft Computing - A Fusion of Foundations . Methodologies and Applications*, *11*(3), 287–298.

Albano, A., Bergamini, R., Ghelli, G., & Orsini, R. (1993). An object data model with roles. In *Proceedings of the 19th International Conference on Very Large Data Bases (VLDB)*, Dublin, Ireland. (pp. 39–51).

Albuz, E., Kocalar, E., & Khokhar, A. A. (2001). Scalable color image indexing and retrieval using vector wavelets. *IEEE Transactions on Knowledge and Data Engineering*, *13*(5), 851–861. doi:10.1109/69.956109

Alsabti, K., Ranka, S., & Singh, V. (1998). An efficient K-means clustering algorithm. *In Proc. 1st Workshop on High Performance Data Mining.*

American College of Radiology. (2003). *The ACR Breast Imaging Reporting and Data System (BI-RADS)* (4th ed.). Reston, VA: American College of Radiology.

Amir, S., Bilasco, I. M., & Djeraba, C. (2009). *A semantic approach to metadata management in sensor systems* (pp. 112–119). Paris, France: Cognitive Systems with Interactive Sensors.

Amir, S. (2009). Un système d'intégration de métadonnées dédiées au multimédia. *In Informatique des Organisations et Systèmes d'Information et de Décision* (pp. 490-492). Toulouse, France.

Amorim, J. A., Machado, C., Miskulin, R. G. S., & Miskulin, M. S. (2009). Production, publication, and use of educational multimedia content in Brazil: Challenges and opportunities in real world technology projects . In Kidd, T. T. (Ed.), *Handbook of research on technology project management, planning, and operations* (pp. 406–418). Hershey, PA: IGI Global. doi:10.4018/978-1-60566-400-2.ch026

Amorim, J. A., & Silva, M. R. C. (2009). Multimedia production and accessibility on distance learning courses. *Educação Temática Digital (Online), 10*, 355-372. ISSN 1676-2592

Amorim, J. A., Pires, D. F., Ropoli, E. A., & Rodrigues, C. C. (2004). O Professor e sua Primeira Página na Internet: Uma Experiência de Uso do Ambiente TelEduc. *Revista Brasileira de Informática na Educação, 12*(1), 37-42. ISSN 14145685

Androutsos, D., Plataniotis, K. N., & Venetsanopoulos, A. N. (1999). A novel vector-based approach to color image retrieval using a vector angular-based distance measure. *Computer Vision and Image Understanding, 75*(1-2), 46–58. doi:10.1006/cviu.1999.0767

Antani, S., Kasturi, R., & Jain, R. (2002). A survey on the use of pattern recognition methods for abstraction, indexing and retrieval of images and video. *Pattern Recognition, 35*(4), 945–965. doi:10.1016/S0031-3203(01)00086-3

Antoniou, G., & Harmelen, F. V. (2008). *A Semantic Web primer* (2nd ed.). Cambridge, MA: The MIT Press.

Archer, N. (2006). A classification of communities of practice . In Coakes, E., & Clarke, S. (Eds.), *Encyclopedia of communities of practice in information and knowledge management* (pp. 21–29). Hershey, PA: Idea Group Publishing. doi:10.4018/978-1-59140-556-6.ch005

Arenas, M., & Libkin, L. (2004). A normal form for XML documents. *ACM Transactions on Database Systems, 29*(1), 195–232. doi:10.1145/974750.974757

Arivazhagan, S., Ganesan, L., & Priyal, S. P. (2006). Texture classification using Gabor wavelets based rotation invariant features. *Pattern Recognition Letters, 27*(16), 1976–1982. doi:10.1016/j.patrec.2006.05.008

Arndt, T., Cafiero, A., & Guercio, A. (1997). Multimedia languages for teleaction objects. *Proceedings of the IEEE Symposium on Visual Languages, VL97*, Capri Isle, Italy, (pp. 322-331).

Arthur, D., & Vassilvitskii, S. (2007). K-means++: The advantages of careful seeding. *Proceedings of the Eighteenth Annual ACM-SIAM Symposium on Discrete Algorithms,* (pp. 1027-1035).

Ashley, K. (2004). The preservation of databases. *Vine, 34*, 66–70. doi:10.1108/03055720410551075

Aslandogan, Y. A., Their, C., Yu, C. T., Zou, J., & Rishe, N. (1997). *Using semantic contents and Wordnet in image retrieval. SIGIR* (pp. 286–295). ACM.

Asservatham, S. (2008). *A local latent semantic analysis-based kernel for document similarities.* IEEE International Joint Conference on Neural Networks.

Auer, S., Bizer, C., Kobilarov, G., Lehmann, J., Cyganiak, R., & Ives, Z. (2008). DBpedia: A nucleus for a Web of open data. In *International Semantic Web Conference: LNCS 4825,* (pp. 722-735).

Aygun, R. S., & Yazici, A. (2004). Modeling and management of fuzzy information in multimedia database applications. *Multimedia Tools and Applications, 24*(1), 29–56. doi:10.1023/B:MTAP.0000033982.50288.14

Baader, F., Calvanese, D., McGuinness, D. L., Nardi, D., & Patel-Schneider, P. (2003). *The description logic handbook, theory, implementation, and applications.* Cambridge University Press.

Baader, F., & Sattler, U. (2001). An overview of tableau algorithms for description logics. In *Studia Logica, 69*(1), 5-40. Springer.

Bach, J., Fuller, C., Gupta, A., Hampapur, A., Gorowitz, B., & Humphrey, R. ... Shu, C. (1996). Virage image search engine: An open framework for image management. In *Proceedings of the SPIE Conference on Storage and Retrieval for Image and Video Databases IV*, (pp. 76–87).

Baeza-Yates, R., & Ribeiro-Neto, B. (1999). *Modern information retrieval.* ACM Press.

Baker, J. A., Kornguth, P. J., & Floyd, C. E. Jr. (1996). Breast imaging reporting and data system standardized mammography lexicon: Observer variability in lesion description. *AJR. American Journal of Roentgenology, 166*, 773–778.

Ballard, D. H., & Brown, C. M. (1982). *Computer vision.* Englewood Cliffs, NJ: Prentice-Hall, Inc.

Banerjee, M., & Kundu, M. K. (2007). Image retrieval using fuzzy relevance feedback and validation with MPEG-7 content descriptors. *Proceedings of the 2007 International Conference on Pattern Recognition and Machine Intelligence . Lecture Notes in Computer Science, 4815*, 144–152. doi:10.1007/978-3-540-77046-6_18

Baral, C., Gonzalez, G., & Son, T. (1998). Conceptual modeling and querying in multimedia databases. *Multimedia Tools and Applications, 7*(1), 37–66. doi:10.1023/A:1009670119569

Barla, A., Odone, F., & Verri, A. (2003). Histogram intersection kernel for image classification. *Proceedings of the International Conference on Image Processing (ICIP03),* (pp. 513-516).

Barranco, C. D., Medina, J. M., Chamorro-Martinez, J., & Soto-Hidalgo, J. M. (2006). Using a fuzzy object-relational database for colour image retrieval. *Proceedings of the 7th International Conference on Flexible Query Answering Systems . Lecture Notes in Computer Science, 4027*, 307–318. doi:10.1007/11766254_26

Bartell, B. T., Cottrell, G. W., & Belew, R. K. (1992). Latent semantic indexing is an optimal special case of multidimensional scaling. *Proceedings of the Fifteenth Annual International ACM SIGIR Conference on Research and Development in Information Retrieval* (pp. 161-167).

Bates, A. W. (1999). *Managing technological change.* San Francisco, CA: Jossey-Bass.

Battle, S. (2004). *Round-tripping between XML and RDF.* In the 3rd International Semantic Web Conference.

Belongie, S., Carson, C., Greenspan, H., & Malik, J. (1997). *Recognition of images in large databases using a learning framework* (Tech. Rep. No. CSD-97-939), University of California, Berkeley, CS Dept.

Belongie, S., Malik, J., & Puzicha, J. (2001). Matching shapes. *Proceedings of the IEEE International Conference on Computer Vision*, Vancouver, Canada, (pp. 454-461).

Benjamins, V. R., Centreras, J., Corcho, O., & Gomez-Perez, A. (2002). *Six challenges for the Semantic Web.* ISWC2002

Benn, W., & Radig, B. (1984). Retrieval of relational structures for image sequence analysis. *Proceedings of the 10th International Conference on Very Large Data Bases*, Singapore, (pp. 533-536).

Berens, J., Finlayson, G. D., & Gu, G. (2000). Image indexing using compressed colour histogram. *IEE Proceedings. Vision Image and Signal Processing, 147*(4), 349–353. doi:10.1049/ip-vis:20000630

Berg, W. A., Campassi, C., Langenberg, P., & Sexton, M. J. (2000). Breast imaging reporting and data system: Inter- and intraobserver variability in feature analysis and final assessment. *AJR. American Journal of Roentgenology, 174*, 1769–1777.

Berners-Lee, T. (1998). *Semantic Web road map.* World Wide Web consortium. Retrieved from http://www.w3.org/ DesignIssues/ Semantic.html

Berners-Lee, T., Hendler, J., & Lassila, O. (2001). The Semantic Web. *Scientific American.*

Berry, M., Browne, M., Langville, A., Pauca, P., & Plemmons, R. J. (2006). Algorithms and applications for approximate nonnegative matrix factorization. *Computational Statistics & Data Analysis, 52*(1), 155–173. doi:10.1016/j.csda.2006.11.006

Berry, M., Dumais, S., & O'Brien, G. (1994). Using linear algebra for intelligent information retrieval. *SIAM Review, 37*, 573–595. doi:10.1137/1037127

Berry, M. W., & Fierro, R. D. (1996). Low-rank orthogonal decompositions for information retrieval applications. *Numerical Linear Algebra with Applications, 3*(4), 301–328. doi:10.1002/(SICI)1099-1506(199607/08)3:4<301::AID-NLA84>3.0.CO;2-S

Bhanu, B., & Dong, A. L. (2001). Concepts learning with fuzzy clustering and relevance feedback. *Proceedings of the Second International Workshop on Machine Learning and Data Mining in Pattern Recognition . Lecture Notes in Computer Science, 2123*, 102–116. doi:10.1007/3-540-44596-X_9

Bhoyar, K. K., & Kakde, O. G. (2009). Image retrieval using fuzzy and neuro-fuzzy approaches with fuzzy color semantics. *Proceedings of the 2009 International Conference on Digital Image Processing*, (pp. 39-44).

Bilasco, I. M., Amir, S., Blandin, P., Djeraba, C., Laitakari, J., Martinet, J., … Zhou, J. (2010). Semantics for intelligent delivery of multimedia content. *SAC ACM.*

Bilasco, I. M., Gensel, J., Villanova-Oliver, M., & Martin, H. (2005). On indexing of 3D scenes using MPEG-7. *Proceedings of the 13th ACM Conference on Multimedia,* (pp. 471-474).

Bimbo, A. D. (1999). *Visual information retrieval.* San Francisco, CA: Morgan Kaufmann.

Bingham, E., & Mannila, H. (2001). Random projection in dimensionality reduction: Applications to image and text data. In *Proceedings of the 7th International Conference on Knowledge Discovery and Data Mining* (pp. 245-250).

Blei, D. M., Ng, A. Y., & Jordan, M. I. (2003). Latent dirichlet allocation. *Journal of Machine Learning Research, 3*, 993–1022.

Blei, D. M., & Jordan, M. I. (2003). Modeling annotated data. In *Proceedings of the 26th Annual International Conference on Research and Development in Information Retrieval* (pp. 127-134). SIGIR '03. ACM Press.

Blostein, D., & Ahuja, N. (1989). Shape from texture: Integrating texture-element extraction and surface estimation. *IEEE Transactions on Pattern Analysis and Machine Intelligence, 11*(12), 1233–1251. doi:10.1109/34.41363

Blum, D. W. (1992). *Method and apparatus for identifying and eliminating specific material from video signals.* (US patent 5,151,788).

Bohring, H., & Auer, S. (2005). Mapping XML to OWL ontologies. *LeipzigerInformatik-Tage, volume 72 of LNI,* (pp. 147-156). GI Publisher.

Booker, A., Condliff, M., Greaves, M., Holt, F. B., Kao, A., & Pierce, D. J. ... Wu, Y.-J. J. (1999). Visualizing text data sets. *IEEE Computing in Science & Engineering* (pp. 26-35).

Bosc, P., & Prade, H. (1993). An introduction to fuzzy set and possibility theory based approaches to the treatment of uncertainty and imprecision in database management systems. *Proceedings of the Second Workshop on Uncertainty Management in Information Systems: From Needs to Solutions.*

Bosch, A., Zisserman, A., & Munoz, X. (2006). Scene classification via pLSA. In *Proceedings of European Conference on Computer Vision* (pp. 517-530).

Bouchon-Meunier, B. (1995). *La Logique Floue et ses Applications*. Addison Wesley.

Bouchon-Meunier, B., & Marsala, C. (2001). Linguistic modifiers and measures of similarity or resemblances. *Proceedings of IFSA/NAFIPS 2001,* (pp. 2195-2199), Vancouver, Canada.

Bouquet, P., Serafini, L., & Zanobini, S. (2003). Semantic coordination: A new approach and an application. *International Semantic Web Conference, LNCS 2870,* (pp. 130-145).

Bourghorbel, S., Boujemaa, N., & Vertan, C. (2002). Histogram-based color signatures for image indexing. *Proceedings of Information Processing and Management of Uncertainty in Knowledge-Based Systems,* IPMU 2002.

Boust, C., Chahine, H., Vièenot, F., Brettel, H., Ben Chouikha, M., & Alquié, G. (2003). Color correction judgments of digital images by experts and naive observers. *Proceedings of PICS, 2003*, 4–9.

Bowers, S., & Delcambre, L. (2000). Representing and transforming model-based information. *First Workshop on the Semantic Web at the Fourth European Conference on Digital Libraries.* (pp. 18-20). Lisbon, Portugal.

Bradshaw, B. (2000). Semantic based image retrieval: A probabilistic approach. *Proceedings of ACM Conference on Multimedia,* (pp. 167-176).

Brasil. (2008). *Guia de Depósito de Patentes. Ministério do Desenvolvimento, Indústria e Comércio Exterior*. Instituto Nacional da Propriedade Industrial - INPI. Diretoria de Patentes – DIRPA. Retrieved September 10, 2009, from http://www.inpi.gov.br/

Brennan, K. (2009). *A guide to the business analysis body of knowledge* (2nd ed.). International Institute of Business Analysis.

Brickley, D. (2004). *RDF vocabulary description language 1.0: RDF schema.* Retrieved February 10, 2004, from http://www.w3.org/TR/ rdf-schema/

Cabot, J., & Ravent'os, R. (2004). Roles as entity types: A conceptual modelling pattern. In *Proceedings of the 23rd International Conference on Conceptual Modeling(ER),* Shanghai, China. 69–82

Canny, J. (1986). A computational approach to edge detection. *IEEE Transactions on Pattern Analysis and Machine Intelligence, 8*(6), 679–698. doi:10.1109/TPAMI.1986.4767851

Carlotto, M. S. (2002). A síndrome de Burnout e o trabalho docente. *Psicologia em Estudo, 7*(1), 21-29. ISSN 1413-7372

Carneiro, G., & Jepson, A. (2004). Flexible spatial models for grouping local image features In *Proceedings of the Conference on Computer Vision and Pattern Recognition* (pp. 747-754). IEEE Computer Society.

Carneiro, G., & Vasconcelos, N. (2005). A database centric view of semantic image annotation and retrieval. *Proceedings of ACM Conference on Research and Development in Information Retrieval.*

Carron, T. (1995). *Segmentations d'images couleur dans la base Teinte-Luminance-Saturation: Approche numérique et symbolique*. Thèse de Doctorat, Université de Savoie.

Carson, C., Thomas, M., Belongie, S., Hellerstein, J., & Malik, J. (1999). *Blobworld: A system for region-based image indexing and retrieval.* In Third International Conference on Visual Information Systems. Springer.

Cees, G., Snoek, M., & Worring, M. (2005). Multimodal video indexing: A review of the state-of-the-art. *Multimedia Tools and Applications, 25*(1), 5–35. doi:10.1023/B:MTAP.0000046380.27575.a5

Chaira, T., & Ray, A. K. (2005). Fuzzy measures for color image retrieval. *Fuzzy Sets and Systems, 150*(3), 545–560. doi:10.1016/j.fss.2004.09.003

Chakrabarti, S., Porkaew, K., & Mehrotra, S. (2000). Efficient query refinement in multimedia databases. *Proceedings of the IEEE International Conference on Data Engineering*, San Diego, California, USA, (p. 196).

Chamorro-Martinez, J., Medina, J. M., Barranco, C., Galan-Perales, E., & Soto-Hidalgo, J. M. (2005). An approach to image retrieval on fuzzy object-relational database using dominant color descriptors. *Proceedings of the 4th Conference of the European Society for Fuzzy Logic and Technology*, (pp. 676-684).

Chamorro-Martínez, J., Galán-Perales, E., Sánchez, D., & Prados-Suarez, B. (2006). A fuzzy approach to image texture representation applied to visual coarseness description. *Proceedings of the 2006 IEEE International Conference on Fuzzy Systems*, (pp. 6019-6024).

Chamorro-Martínez, J., & Martínez-Jiménez, P. (2010). An adaptive fuzzy approach for texture modelling. *Proceedings of the 2010 IEEE World Congress on Computational Intelligence*, (pp. 624-629).

Chamorro-Martínez, J., Sánchez, D., Prados-Suarez, B., & Soto-Hidalgo, J. M. (2006). A fuzzy approach to dominant color description for image retrieval. *Proceedings of the 2006 International Conference on Information Processing and Management of Uncertainty*, (pp. 1564-1569).

Chamorro-Martínez, J., Sánchez, D., & Soto-Hidalgo, J. M. (2008). A novel histogram definition for fuzzy color spaces. *Proceedings of the 2008 IEEE International Conference on Fuzzy Systems*, (pp. 2149-2156).

Chamorro-Martíneza, J., Medinaa, J. M., Barrancob, C. D., Galán-Peralesa, E., & Soto-Hidalgoa, J. M. (2007). Retrieving images in fuzzy object-relational databases using dominant color descriptors. *Fuzzy Sets and Systems, 158*, 312–324. doi:10.1016/j.fss.2006.10.013

Chan, C. K., & Sandler, M. D. (1992). A neural network shape recognition system with Hough transform input feature space. *Proceedings of the International Conference on Image Processing and its Applications*, Maastricht, The Netherlands, (pp. 197-200).

Chang, T., & Jay Kuo, C. C. (1993). Texture analysis and classification with tree structured wavelet transform. *IEEE Transactions on Image Processing, 2*(3), 429–441. doi:10.1109/83.242353

Chang, S. K., & Liu, S. H. (1984). Picture indexing and abstraction techniques for pictorial databases. *IEEE Transactions on Pattern Analysis and Machine Intelligence, 6*, 475–484. doi:10.1109/TPAMI.1984.4767552

Chang, S. F., Puri, A., Sikora, T., & Zhang, H. J. (2001). Introduce to the special issue on MPEG-7. *Circuits and Systems for Video Technology, 11*, 685–687. doi:10.1109/TCSVT.2001.927419

Chang, S. F., Smith, J. R., Beigi, M., & Benitez, A. (1997). Visual information retrieval from large distributed on-line repositories. *Communications of the ACM, 40*, 63–71. doi:10.1145/265563.265573

Chang, S. K. (1996). Extending visual languages for multimedia. *IEEE MultiMedia, 3*(3), 18–26. doi:10.1109/93.556536

Chang, S. K., Polese, G., Orefice, S., & Tucci, M. (1994). A methodology and interactive environment for iconic language design. *International Journal of Human-Computer Studies, 41*, 683–716. doi:10.1006/ijhc.1994.1078

Chang, S. F., Sikora, T., & Puri, A. (2001). Overview of the MPEG-7 standard. *IEEE Transactions on Circuits and Systems for Video Technology, 11*, 688–695. doi:10.1109/76.927421

Chang, P., Han, M., & Gong, Y. (2002). *Extract highlights from baseball game video with hidden Markov models*. International Conference on Image Processing, (pp. I-609-I-612).

Chang, S. F., Chen, W., Meng, H. J., Sundaram, H., & Zhong, D. (1997). Videoq: An automated content based video search system using visual cues. *Proceedings of the 5th ACM International Multimedia Conference*, Seattle, USA, (pp. 313-324).

Chanussot, J., Nystrom, I., & Sladoje, N. (2005). Shape signatures of fuzzy star-shaped sets based on distance from the centroid. *Pattern Recognition Letters, 26*, 735–746. doi:10.1016/j.patrec.2004.09.025

Chao, C. Y., Shih, H. C., & Huang, C. L. (2005). *Semantics-based highlight extraction of soccer program using DBN*. International Conference on Acoustics, Speech, and Signal Processing, (pp. 1057-1060).

Chaudhri, V. K., Farquhar, A., Fikes, R., Karp, P. D., & Rice, J. P. (1998). OKBC: A programmatic foundation for knowledge base interoperability. In *Proceedings of the 15th National Conference on Artificial Intelligence and of the 10th Conference on Innovative Applications on Artificial Intelligence*, (pp. 600-607). AAAI Press.

Chen, Y., & Wang, J. Z. (2002). A region-based fuzzy feature matching approach to content-based image retrieval. *IEEE Transactions on Pattern Analysis and Machine Intelligence, 24*(9), 1252–1267. doi:10.1109/TPAMI.2002.1033216

Chen, Y. X., & Wang, J. Z. (2002). A region-based fuzzy feature matching approach to content-based image retrieval. *IEEE Transactions on Pattern Analysis and Machine Intelligence, 24*(9), 1252–1267. doi:10.1109/TPAMI.2002.1033216

Chen, J., & Saad, Y. (2009). Divide and Conquer Strategies for Effective Information Retrieval. *Proceedings of the Ninth SIAM International Conference on Data Mining, 1*(4), 449-460.

Cheng, C. C., & Hsu, C. T. (2006). Fusion of audio and motion information on HMM-based highlight extraction for baseball games. *Multimedia, 8*, 585–599. doi:10.1109/TMM.2006.870726

Cheung, V., Frey, B. J., & Jojic, N. (2005). Video epitomes. In [Los Alamitos, CA: IEEE Computer Society.]. *Proceedings of the Conference on Computer Vision and Pattern Recognition, 1*, 42–49.

Chew, P., Bader, B., & Kolda, T. (2007). Cross-language information retrieval using PARAFAC2. *Proceedings of the 13th ACM SIGKDD International Conference on Knowledge Discovery and Data Mining* (pp. 143-152).

Chianese, A., Picariello, A., Sansone, L., & Sapino, M. L. (2004). Managing uncertainties in image databases: a fuzzy approach. *Multimedia Tools and Applications, 23*, 237–252. doi:10.1023/B:MTAP.0000031759.22145.5d

Chien, B.-C., & Cheng, M.-C. (2002). A color image segmentation approach based on fuzzy similarity measure. *Proceedings of the 2002 IEEE International Conference on Fuzzy Systems*, 1, (pp. 449-454).

Chiu, C.-Y., Lin, H.-C., & Yang, S.-N. (2003). A fuzzy logic CBIR system. *Proceedings of the 12th IEEE International Conference on Fuzzy Systems*, 2, (pp. 1171-1176).

Cho, G., Pierce, D. J., & Wu, Y.-J. J. (2000). *Downdating and mean-correction algorithms for truncated URV. (Mathematics & Computing Technology Report M&CT-TECH-00-012)*. Boeing Company.

Chrisa, T., & Stavros, C. (2007). Interoperability of XML schema applications with OWL domain knowledge and Semantic Web tools. In *On the Move to Meaningful Internet Systems, OTM 2007, Part I, LNCS 4803*, (pp. 850–869).

Chu, W. T., & Wu, J. L. (2008). Explicit semantic events detection and development of realistic applications for broadcasting baseball videos. *Multimedia Tools and Applications, 38*, 27–50. doi:10.1007/s11042-007-0145-4

Chu, W. T., Wang, C. W., & Wu, J. L. (2006). *Extraction of baseball trajectory and physics-based validation for single-view baseball video sequences*. International Conference on Multimedia and Expo, (pp. 1813-1816).

Chuang, G. C. H., & Kuo, C. C. J. (1996). Wavelet descriptors of planar curves: Theory and applications. *IEEE Transactions on Image Processing, 5*(1), 56–70. doi:10.1109/83.481671

Codd, E. F. (1970). A relational model of data for large shared data banks. *Communications of the ACM, 13*(6), 377–397. doi:10.1145/362384.362685

Codd, E. F. (1972). Further normalization of the database relational model . In Rusum, R. (Ed.), *Data base systems* (pp. 33–64). Prentice Hall.

Cominiciu, D., & Meer, P. (2002). Mean shift: A robust approach towards feature space analysis. *IEEE Transactions on Pattern Analysis and Machine Intelligence*, *24*(5), 603–619. doi:10.1109/34.1000236

Commission Internationale de l'Eclairage (CIE). (1986). *Colorimetry*, 2nd ed. Vienna, Austria: CIE Publication.

Conner, D. R. (1993). *Managing at the speed of change*. New York, NY: Random House.

Costa, P. C. G., Laskey, K. B., & Laskey, K. J. (2005). *PR-OWL: A Bayesian ontology language for the Semantic Web*. URSW`05

Couwenbergh, J. P. (2003). *Guide complet et pratique de la couleur*. Paris, France: Eyrolles.

Cox, M. F., & Cox, M. A. A. (2001). *Multidimensional scaling*. London, UK: Chapman & Hall.

Cristianini, N., Shawe-Taylor, J., & Lodhi, H. (2002). Latent semantic kernels. *Journal of Intelligent Information Systems*, *18*(2-3), 127–152. doi:10.1023/A:1013625426931

Dagger, D., O'Connor, A., Lawless, S., Walsh, E., & Wade, V. P. (2007). *Service-oriented e-learning platforms: From monolithic systems to flexible services. IEEE Internet Computing, 11*(3), 28-35. ISSN 10897801

Dahchour, M., Pirotte, A., & Zim'anyi, E. (2002). A generic role model for dynamic objects. In *Proceedings of the 10th International Conference on Advanced Information Systems Engineering(CAiSE),* Toronto, Ontario, Canada (pp. 643–658).

Dalvi, N., & Suciu, D. (2007). Management of probabilistic data: Foundations and challenges. *Proceedings of the 2007 ACM SIGACT-SIGMOD-SIGART Symposium on Principles of Database Systems*, (pp. 1-12).

Dasarathy, B. V. (1991). *Nearest neighbor (NN) norms: NN pattern classification techniques*. IEEE Computer Society Press.

Datta, R., Joshi, D., Li, J., & Wang, J. Z. (2008). Image retrieval: Ideas, influences, and trends of the new age. *ACM Computing Surveys*, *40*(2), 1–60. doi:10.1145/1348246.1348248

Datta, R., Li, J., & Wang, J. Z. (2005). Content-based image retrieval: Approaches and trends of the new age. In *MIR '05: Proceedings of the 7th ACM SIGMM International Workshop on Multimedia Information Retrieval*, (pp. 253-262). New York, NY: ACM Press.

Davies, J., Fensel, D., & Harmelen, F. V. (2003). *Towards the Semantic Web - Ontology-driven knowledge management*. Wiley.

Davis, J. (1999). *IBM/DB2 universal database: Building extensible, scalable business solutions*. Retrieved from http://www.software.ibm.com/data/pubs/papers

Deerwester, S., Dumais, S., Furnas, G., Landauer, T., & Harshman, R. (1990). Indexing by latent semantic analysis. *Journal of the American Society for Information Science American Society for Information Science*, *41*(6), 391–40. doi:10.1002/(SICI)1097-4571(199009)41:6<391::AID-ASI1>3.0.CO;2-9

DeMichiel, L. G. (1989). Resolving database incompatibility: An approach to performing relational operations over mismatched domains. *IEEE Transactions on Knowledge and Data Engineering*, *1*(4), 485–493. doi:10.1109/69.43423

Deng, Y., Manjunath, B. S., Kenney, C., Moore, M. S., & Shin, H. (2001). *An* efficient color representation for image retrieval. *IEEE Transactions on Image Processing*, *10*(1), 140–147. doi:10.1109/83.892450

Deruyver, A., Hode, Y., Leammer, E., & Jolion, J. M. (2005). Adaptive pyramid and semantic graph – Knowledge driven segmentation . In Brun, L., & Vento, M. (Eds.), *Lecture Notes in Computer Science, 3434* (pp. 213–222).

Deselaers, T., Deserno, T. M., & Muller, H. (2007). Automatic medical image annotation in ImageCLEF 2007: Overview, results, and discussion. *Pattern Recognition Letters*, *29*, 1988–1995. doi:10.1016/j.patrec.2008.03.001

Dhillon, I. S., & Modha, D. S. (2001). Concept decomposition for large sparse text data using clustering. *Machine Learning*, *42*(1), 143–175. doi:10.1023/A:1007612920971

DIG35. (2002). *Metadata standard for digital images*. Retrieved June 2002, from http://xml.coverpages.org/dig35.html

Ding, C. H. Q. (2005). A probabilistic model for latent semantic indexing. *Journal of the American Society for Information Science and Technology*, *56*(6), 597–608. doi:10.1002/asi.20148

Ding, Z., & Peng, Y. (2004). A probabilistic extension to ontology language OWL. *Proceedings of the 37th Hawaii International Conference on System Sciences*.

Diplaros, A., Gevers, T., & Patras, I. (2006). Combining color and shape information for illumination-viewpoint invariant object recognition. *IEEE Transactions on Image Processing*, *15*(1), 1–11. doi:10.1109/TIP.2005.860320

Djeraba, C., Hadouda, K., & Briand, H. (1997). Management of multimedia scenarios in an object-oriented database system. *Multimedia Tools and Applications*, *4*(2), 97–114. doi:10.1023/A:1009634430444

Doan, A. H., Domingos, P., & Levy, A. (2000). *Learning source descriptions for data integration*. In the Workshop at the Conference of the American Association for Artificial Intelligence, (pp. 81–92).

Doan, A., Madhavan, J., Domingos, P., & Halevy, A. (2002). *Learning to map between ontologies on the Semantic Web*. In the 11th International World Wide Web Conference, (pp. 662-673), Hawaii, USA.

Doerr, M., Hunter, J., & Lagoze, C. (2003). Towards a core ontology for information integration. *Journal of Digital Information*, *4*(1).

Doller, M., Renner, K., & Kosch, H. (2007). *Introduction of an MPEG-7 query language*. International Conference on Digital Information Management, 1, (pp. 92-97).

Duan, L. Y., Xu, M., Chua, T. S., Tian, Q., & Xu, C. S. (2003). *A mid-level representation framework for semantic sports video analysis*. ACM International Conference on Multimedia, (pp. 33-44).

Dubois, D., Prade, H., & Sedes, F. (2001). Fuzzy logic techniques in multimedia database querying: A preliminary investigation of the potentials. *IEEE Transactions on Knowledge and Data Engineering*, *13*(3), 383–392. doi:10.1109/69.929896

Dumais, S. T. (1992). *LSI meets TREC: A status report*. In The First Text Retrieval Conference (TREC-1), NIST Special Publication, (pp. 105-116).

Duygulu, P., & Vural, F. (2001). Multi-level image segmentation and object representation for content based image retrieval. *Proceedings of SPIE Electronic Imaging, Storage and Retrieval for Media Databases*, San Jose, USA, (pp. 460-469).

Duygulu, P., Barnard, K., de Freitas, N., & Forsyth, D. (2002). Object recognition as machine translation: Learning a lexicon for a fixed image vocabulary. *Proceedings of European Conference on Computer Vision* (ECCV), Copenhagen, Denmark, (pp. 97-112).

Duygulu, P., Chen, M.-Y., & Hauptmann, A. (2004). *Comparison and combination of two novel commercial detection methods*. International Conference on Multimedia and Expo, (pp. 27-30).

Elmasri, R., & Navathe, S. B. (2003). *Fundamentals of database systems* (4th ed.). Addison-Wesley.

El-Naqa, I., Yang, Y., Galatsanos, N. P., Nishikawa, R. M., & Wernick, M. N. (2004). A similarity learning approach to content-based image retrieval: Application to digital mammography. *IEEE Transactions on Medical Imaging*, *23*, 1233–1244. doi:10.1109/TMI.2004.834601

El-Zakhem, I., Aït Younes, A., Truck, I., Greige, H., & Akdag, H. (2007). *Color image profile comparison and computing*. ICSOFT 2007 2nd International Conference on Software and Data Technologies, (pp. 228-231), Barcelona, Spain.

El-Zakhem, I., Aït Younes, A., Truck, I., Greige, H., & Akdag, H. (2008). *Mapping personal perception into user profiles for image retrieving*. 8th International FLINS Conference on Computational Intelligence in Decision and Control, (pp. 393-398). Madrid, Spain.

Enser, P. G. B., Sandom, C. J., & Lewis, P. H. (2005). Surveying the reality of semantic image retrieval . In Bres, S., & Laurini, R. (Eds.), *Lecture Notes in Computer Science, 3736* (pp. 177–188).

Fagin, R. (1996). Combining fuzzy information from multiple systems. In *Proc. 15th ACM Symp. Principles of Database Systems*, Montreal, Canada (pp. 216-226).

Fagin, R. (1998). Fuzzy queries in multimedia database systems. *Proceedings of the 1998 ACM Symposium on Principles of Database Systems*, (pp. 1-10).

Fellbaum, C. (1998). *WordNet: An electronic lexical database*. Cambridge: The MIT Press.

Feng, D., Siu, W. C., & Zhang, H. J. (2003). *Multimedia information retrieval and management: Technological fundamentals and applications*. Berlin, Germany: Springer.

Fernandes, A. A., & Teixeira, D. S. (2004). *Fábrica de Software: Implantação e Gestão de Operações*. Editora Atlas.

Finesso, L., & Spreij, P. (2006). Nonnegative matrix factorization and I-divergence alternating minimization. *Linear Algebra and Its Applications*, *416*, 270–287. doi:10.1016/j.laa.2005.11.012

Flickner, M., Sawhney, H., Niblack, W., Ashley, J., Huang, Q., & Dom, B. (1995). Query by image and video content: The QBIC system. *IEEE Computer . Special Issue on Content Based Retrieval*, *28*(9), 23–32.

Fonseca, M. J., & Jorge, J. A. (2003). Indexing high-dimensional data for content-based retrieval in large database. *Proceedings of the Eighth International Conference on Database Systems for Advanced Applications*, (pp. 267-274).

Foulloy, L. (1990). *Du contrôle symbolique des processus: Démarche, outils, exemples*. Ph.D. Thesis, Université Paris XI.

Frame, J. D. (1994). *The new project management: tools for an age of rapid change, corporate reengineering, and other business realities*. San Francisco, CA: Jossey-Bass.

Freeborough, P. A. (1997). A comparison of fractal texture descriptors. Proceedings of the 8th British Machine Vision Conference, Essex, UK.

Fu, K. S. (1982). *Syntactic pattern recognition and applications*. New Jersey: Prentice-Hall.

Gadi, T., Benslimane, R., Daoudi, M., & Matusiak, S. (1999). Fuzzy similarity measure for shape retrieval. *Proceedings of the 1999 Canadian Conference in Computer Vision, Signal and Image Processing and Pattern Recognition*, (pp. 386-389).

Garcia, R., & Celma, O. (2005). *Semantic integration and retrieval of multimedia meta-data*. In the 5th International Workshop on Knowledge Markup and Semantic Annotation (pp. 69-80).

Gebara, D., & Alhajj, R. (2007). *Waveq: Combining wavelet analysis and clustering for effective image retrieval*. 21st International Conference on Advanced Information Networking and Applications Workshops, 1, (pp. 289–294).

Gevers, T., & Stokman, H. (2003). Classifying color edges in video into shadow-geometry, highlight, or material transitions. *IEEE Transactions on Multimedia*, *5*, 237–243. doi:10.1109/TMM.2003.811620

Gevers, T., & Smeulders, A. W. M. (2000). PicToSeek: Combining color and shape invariant features for image retrieval. *IEEE Transactions on Image Processing*, *9*, 102–119. doi:10.1109/83.817602

Gevers, T., & Smeulders, A. (1998). Image indexing using composite color and shape invariant features. *Proceedings of the 6th International Conference on Computer Vision*, Bombay, India, (pp. 576-581).

Ghoshal, A., Ircing, P., & Khudanpur, S. (2005). Hidden Markov models for automatic annotation and content-based retrieval of images and video. In *Proceedings of the 28th International ACM SIGIR Conference on Research and Development in Information Retrieval* (pp. 544-551).

Gliozzo, A., & Strapparava, C. (2005) Domain kernels for text classification. In *Proceedings of the Ninth Conference on Computaional Natural Language Learning (CoNLL-2005)*, (pp. 56-63). Association for Computational Linguistics.

Gokcen, I., Yazici, A., & Buckles, B. P. (2000). Fuzzy content-based retrieval in image databases. *Proceedings of the First International Conference on Advances in Information Systems . Lecture Notes in Computer Science*, *1909*, 226–237. doi:10.1007/3-540-40888-6_21

Gonzalez, R. C., & Woods, R. E. (2002). *Digital image processing*. Upper Saddle River, NJ: Prentice Hall.

Google. (2004). *Google achieves search milestone with immediate access to more than 6 billion items*. Retrieved from http://www.google .com/ press/ pressrel/ 6billion.html

Gool, L., Tuytelaars, T., & Turina, A. (2001). Local features for image retrieval . In Veltkamp, R. C., Burkhardt, H., & Kriegel, H. P. (Eds.), *State-of-the-art in content-based image and video retrieval* (pp. 21–41). Kluwer Academic Publishers.

Greenfield, J. (2004). *Software factories: Assembling applications with patterns, models, frameworks, and tools.* Microsoft Corporation MSDN Architecture Center Portal. Retrieved May 13, 2008, from http://msdn.microsoft.com/en-us/library/ ms954811.aspx

Guan, H., & Wada, S. (2002). Flexible color texture retrieval method using multi-resolution mosaic for image classification. In *Proceedings of the 6th International Conference on Signal Processing* (pp. 612-615).

Haddad, H., Chevallet, J.-P., & Bruandet, M.-F. (2000). *Relations between terms discovered by association rules.* In 4th European Conference on Principles and Practices of Knowledge Discovery in Databases PKDD'2000, Workshop on Machine Learning and Textual Information Access.

Hafner, J., Sawhney, H. S., Equitz, W., Flickner, M., & Niblack, W. (1995). Efficient color histogram indexing for quadratic form distance functions. *IEEE Transactions on Pattern Analysis and Machine Intelligence, 17*(7), 729–736. doi:10.1109/34.391417

Hammami, M., Chen, L., Zighed, D., & Song, Q. (2002). Définition d'un modèle de peau et son utilisation pour la classification des images. *Proceedings of MediaNet, 2002*, 187–198.

Hammouda, K. M., & Kamel, M. S. (2004). Efficient phrase-based document indexing for web document clustering . In *IEEE Trans. on Knowledge and Data Engineering* (pp. 1279–1296). IEEE Computer Society.

Han, J., & Ma, K. K. (2002). Fuzzy color histogram and its use in color image retrieval. *IEEE Transactions on Image Processing, 11*(8), 944–952. doi:10.1109/TIP.2002.801585

Han, J., Koperski, K., & Stefanovic, N. (1997). GeoMiner: A system prototype for spatial data mining. In *Proceedings of International Conference on Management of Data* (pp. 553–556). ACM SIGMOD'97, ACM Press.

Hanjalic, A. (2003). *Multimodal approach to measuring excitement in video* (pp. 289–292). International Conferences on Multimedia and Expo.

Hanjalic, A., & Zhang, H. J. (1999). An integrated scheme for automated video abstraction based on unsupervised cluster-validity analysis. *Circuits and Systems for Video Technology, 9*, 8. doi:10.1109/76.809162

Hanjalic, A. (2003). *Generic approach to highlights extraction from a sport video.* International Conference on Image Processing, (pp. 1-4).

Hansen, M. T., Nohria, N., & Tierney, T. (1999). *What's your strategy for managing knowledge?* Harvard Business Publishing. ISSN 00178012

Haralick, R., Shanmugan, K., & Dinstein, I. (1973). Texture feature for image classification. *IEEE Transactions on Systems, Man, and Cybernetics, SMC-3*(6), 610–621. doi:10.1109/TSMC.1973.4309314

Harmon, P. (2007). *Business process change: A guide for business managers and BPM and six sigma professionals* (2nd ed.). MK/OMG Press.

Harrington, H. J., Conner, D., & Horney, N. L. (1999). *Project change management.* McGraw-Hill Companies.

Harris, C., & Stephens, M. (1988). A combined corner and edge detector. *Proceedings of the 4th Alvey Vision Conference*, Manchester, UK, (pp. 147-151).

Harshman, R. A. (1970). Foundations of the PARAFAC procedure: Models and conditions for an explanatory multi-modal factor analysis. *UCLA Working Papers in Phonetics, 16,* 1-84.

Harshman, R. A. (1972). Foundations mathematical and technical notes. *UCLA Working Papers in Phonetics, 22,* 30-47.

Hartigan, J. A., & Wong, M. A. (1979). Algorithm AS136: A k-means clustering algorithm. *Applied Statistics, 28,* 100–108. doi:10.2307/2346830

Hashizume, C., Vinod, V. V., & Murase, H. (1998). Robust object extraction with illumination-insensitive color descriptions. *Proceedings of the IEEE International Conference on Image Processing*, Chicago, USA, (pp. 50-54).

Hausenblas, M. (2007). *Multimedia vocabularies on the Semantic Web*. Retrieved July 2007, from http://www.w3.org/2005/ Incubator/mmsem/ XGR-vocabularies-20070724/

Hecht-Nielsen, R. (1994). Context vectors: General purpose approximate meaning representations self-organized from raw data.

Henrich, A., & Robbert, G. (2001). POQLMM: A query language for structured multimedia documents. In *Proceedings 1st International Workshop on Multimedia Data and Document Engineering*, (pp. 17–26).

Herrera, F., Herrera-Viedma, E., & Martinez, L. (2008). A fuzzy linguistic methodology to deal with unbalanced linguistic term sets. *IEEE Transactions on Fuzzy Systems*, *16*(2), 354–370. doi:10.1109/TFUZZ.2007.896353

Herrera, F., & Martinez, L. (2001). A model based on linguistic two-tuples for dealing with multigranularity hierarchical linguistic contexts in multiexpert decision-making. *IEEE Transactions on Systems, Man and Cybernetics . Part B*, *31*(2), 227–234.

Hersh, W. (2009). *Information retrieval: A health and biomedical perspective*. New York, NY: Springer.

Hinneburg, A., & Keim, D. (2002). A general approach to clustering in large databases with noise. *J. Knowledge and Information System, 5*(4). Springer.

Hofmann, T. (2001). Unsupervised learning by probabilistic latent semantic analysis. *Machine Learning Journal*, *42*(1), 177–196. doi:10.1023/A:1007617005950

Hofmann, T. (1999). *Probabilistic latent semantic indexing*. In 22nd Annual International SIGIR Conference on Research and Development in Information Retrieval (SIGIR '99) (pp. 35-44)

Hoiem, D., Sukthankar, R., Schneiderman, H., & Huston, L. (2004). Object-based image retrieval using the statistical structure of images. *Proceedings of the IEEE Computer Society Conference on Computer Vision and Pattern Recognition*, Washington DC, USA, (pp. 490-497).

Holt, F., & Wu, Y.-J. J. (2001). Information retrieval and classification with subspace representations. In *Proceedings of CIR 2000, SIAM Proceedings in Applied Mathematics,* SIAM, Philadelphia.

Hong, P., Qi, T., & Huang, T. S. (2000). Incorporate support vector machines to content-based image retrieval with relevance feedback. *Proceedings of IEEE International Conference on Image Processing,* (pp. 750-753).

Hough, P. V. C. (1962). *Method and means for recognizing complex patterns*. (U.S. Patent: 3069654).

Howarth, P., & Ruger, S. (2004). Evaluation of texture features for content-based image retrieval. In *Proc. of International Conference on Image and Video Retrieval*, (pp. 326–334).

Hsu, W., Chua, T. S., & Pung, H. K. (2000). Approximating content based object level image retrieval. *Multimedia Tools and Applications*, *12*, 59–79. doi:10.1023/A:1009692213403

Hu, M. (1962). Visual pattern recognition by moment invariants. *IEEE Transactions on Information Theory*, *8*(2), 179–187. doi:10.1109/TIT.1962.1057692

Hua, X.-S., Lu, L., & Zhang, H.-J. (2005). *Robust learning-based TV commercial detection*. International Conference on Multimedia and Expo.

Huang, P. W., & Jean, Y. R. (1996). Spatial reasoning and similarity retrieval for image database-systems based on RS-Strings. *Pattern Recognition*, *29*(12), 2103–2114. doi:10.1016/S0031-3203(96)00048-9

Huang, J., Kumar, S. R., Mitra, M., Zhu, W. J., & Zabih, R. (1997). Image indexing using color correlograms. *Proceedings of the 1997 Conference on Computer Vision and Pattern Recognition (CVPR '97),* pp. 767.

Huang, T. S., Mehrotra, S., & Ramchandran, K. (1996). Multimedia analysis and retrieval system (mars) project. In *Proceedings of 33rd Annual Clinic on Library Application of Data Processing - Digital Image Access and Retrieval*.

Huang, Y.-P., Chang, T.-W., & Huang, C.-Z. (2003). A fuzzy feature clustering with relevance feedback approach to content-based image retrieval. *Proceedings of 2003 IEEE International Symposium on Virtual Environments, Human-Computer Interfaces and Measurement Systems*, (pp. 57-62).

Hubel, D. H., & Wiesel, T. N. (1974). Sequence regularity and geometry of orientation columns in the monkey striate cortex. *The Journal of Comparative Neurology*, *158*(3), 267–293. doi:10.1002/cne.901580304

Hull, R., & King, R. (1987). Semantic database modeling: Survey, applications, and research issues. *ACM Computing Surveys*, *19*(3), 201–260. doi:10.1145/45072.45073

Hung, M. H., & Hsieh, C. H. (2008). Event detection of broadcast baseball videos. *Circuits and Systems for Video Technology*, *18*, 1713–1726. doi:10.1109/TCSVT.2008.2004934

Hunter, J. (2003). Enhancing the semantic interoperability of multimedia through a core ontology. *IEEE Trans. on Circuits and Systems for Video Technology*, *13*, 49–58. doi:10.1109/TCSVT.2002.808088

Hunter, J. (2001). Adding multimedia to the Semantic Web: Building an MPEG-7 ontology. In I. F. Cruz, S. Decker, J. Euzenat, & D. L. McGuinness (Eds.), *Proceedings of the International Semantic Web Working Symposium*, (pp. 261-283).

Hustad, E., & Munkvold, B. E. (2006). Communities of practice and other organizational groups. In Coakes, E., & Clarke, S. (Eds.), *Encyclopedia of communities of practice in information and knowledge management* (pp. 60–62). Hershey, PA: Idea Group Publishing. doi:10.4018/978-1-59140-556-6.ch012

Hyvonen, E., Saarela, S., & Viljanen, K. (2003). *Intelligent image retrieval and browsing Semantic Web techniques – A case study*. The International SEPIA Conference.

IBM. (1995). *DATABASE 2 SQL reference - For common servers*. (Part No. S20H-4665-00).

ID3. (1999). *Developer information*. Retrieved September 2007, from http://www.id3.org/ Developer_Information

Idris, F., & Panchanathan, S. (1997). Review of image and video indexing techniques. *Journal of Visual Communication and Image Representation*, *8*(2), 146–166. doi:10.1006/jvci.1997.0355

IEEE. (1990). *IEEE standard glossary of software engineering terminology*. IEEE Std 610.121990. Retrieved November 15, 2009, from http://standards.ieee.org/

IEEE. (2001). *Reference guide for instructional design and development*. Retrieved September 7, 2001, from http://webstage.ieee.org/ organizations/eab/tutorials / refguideForPdf/mms01.htm

IPTC. (2008). *Standard photo metadata*, June 2008. Retrieved June 2008, from http://www.iptc.org/ std/ photometadata/2008/ specification/ IPTC-PhotoMetadata-2008.pdf

Iqbal, Q., & Aggarwal, J. K. (2002). Retrieval by classification of images containing large manmade objects using perceptual grouping. *Pattern Recognition*, *35*, 1463–1479. doi:10.1016/S0031-3203(01)00139-X

Iqbal, Q., & Aggarwal, J. (2002). CIRES: A system for content-based retrieval in digital image libraries. *Proceedings of the International Conference on Control, Automation, Robotics and Vision*, Singapore, (pp. 205-210).

ITEA2-CAM4Home. (2008). *Collaborative aggregated multimedia for digital home*. Retrieved May 2008, from http://www.cam4home-itea.org/

Jacobs, C. E., Finkelstein, A., & Salesin, D. H. (1995). Fast multiresolution image querying. *Proceedings of the 22nd Annual Conference on Computer Graphics*, Los Angeles, USA, (pp. 277-286).

Jain, A. K., & Vailaya, A. (1996). Image retrieval using color and shape. *Pattern Recognition*, *29*(8), 1233–1244. doi:10.1016/0031-3203(95)00160-3

Jain, R. (2008). Multimedia information retrieval: Watershed events. *Proceedings of the ACM First International Conference on Multimedia Information Retrieval*, (pp. 229-236).

James, Z., & the Wang Research Group. (n.d.). *Research on intelligent media annotation*. Pennsylvania State University. Retrieved from http://wang.ist.psu.edu/ IMAGE/

Javidi, M., Pourreza, H. R., & Yazdi, H. S. (2010). A semantic feedback framework for image retrieval. *International Journal of Computer and Electrical Engineering*, *2*(3), 1793–8163.

Jensen, F. V., Lauritzen, S. L., & Olesen, K. G. (1990). *Bayesian updating in causal probabilistic network by local computation.*

Jeon, J., & Manmatha, R. (2004). Using maximum entropy for automatic image annotation. In *Proceedings of the Third International Conference Image and Video Retrieval* (pp. 24-32). CIVR. Springer.

Jhanwar, N., Chaudhuri, S., Seetharaman, G., & Zavidovique, B. (2004). Content based image retrieval using motif cooccurrence matrix. *Image and Vision Computing*, *22*(14), 1211–1220.

Jianfeng, Y., Yang, Z., & Zhanhuai, L. (2003). *A hierarchical method to describe multimedia content.* In 5th International Conference on Computational Intelligence and Multimedia Applications (pp. 413-418).

Jianfeng, Y., Yang, Z., & Zhanhuai, L. (2004). *A multimedia document database model based on multi-layered description supporting complex multimedia structural and semantic contents.* In 10th International Multimedia Modelling Conference (pp. 33-39).

Jiang, S., Ye, Q., Gao, W., & Huang, T. (2004). *A new method to segment playfield and its applications in match analysis in sports video.* ACM International Conference on Multimedia, (pp. 292-295).

Jing, Y., & Croft, B. W. (1994). An association thesaurus for information retrieval. In *Proceedings of RIAO-94, 4th International Conference Recherche d'Information Assistee par Ordinateur* (pp. 146-160). New York, US.

Joachims, T. (1998). Text categorization with support vector machines: Learning with many relevant features. *Proceedings of the European Conference on Machine Learning*. Springer.

Johnson, W. B., & Lindenstrauss, J. (1984). *Extensions of Lipschitz mapping into Hilbert space.* In Conference on Modern Analysis and Probability, 26 (pp. 189-206).

Jojic, N., Frey, B. J., & Kannan, A. (2003). Epitomic analysis of appearance and shape. In *Proceedings of the Conference on Computer Vision and Pattern Recognition.* IEEE Computer Society.

Jolliffe, I. (Ed.). (2002). *Principal component analysis.* Springer-Verlag.

Kalfoglou, Y., & Schorlemmer, M. (2003). Ontology mapping: The state of the art. *The Knowledge Engineering Review*, *18*(1), 1–31. doi:10.1017/S0269888903000651

Kalfoglou, Y., & Schorlemmer, M. (2002). *Information-flow-based ontology mapping.* In the 1st International Conference on Ontologies, Databases and Application of Semantics, (pp. 98-127). Irvine, CA.

Kant, S., & Mamas, E. (2005). *Statistical reasoning – A foundation for Semantic Web reasoning.* URSW`05.

Kaski, S. (1998). Dimensionality reduction by random mapping. In . *Proceedings of International Joint Conference on Neural Networks*, *1*, 237–288.

Kaufman, L., & Rousseeuw, P. J. (2005). *Finding groups in data: An introduction to cluster analysis (Wiley Series in Probability and Statistics).* Wiley-Interscience.

Kauppinen, H., Seppanen, T., & Pietikainen, M. (1995). An experimental comparison of autoregressive and Fourier-based descriptors in 2D shape classification. *IEEE Transactions on Pattern Analysis and Machine Intelligence*, *17*(2), 201–207. doi:10.1109/34.368168

Kender, J. (1976), *Saturation, hue and normalized color: Calculation, digitization effects, and use.* Master's Thesis, Dept. of Computer Science, Carnegie-Mellon University.

Kender, J., & Yeo, B. (1998). Video scene segmentation via continuous video coherence. *Proceedings of the IEEE Computer Society Conference on Computer Vision and Pattern Recognition*, Santa Barbara, USA, (pp. 367-373).

Kerzner, H. (2006). *Gestão de Projetos: As Melhores Práticas.* Bookman Editora. 2006. ISBN 9788536306186

Kim, H., & Park, H. (2006). *Sparse non-negative matrix factorizations via alternating non-negativity-constrained least squares. (CSE Technical Reports GT-CSE-06-20).* Georgia Institute of Technology.

Kisielnicki, J. (2006). Transfer of information and knowledge in the project management. In Coakes, E., & Clarke, S. (Eds.), *Encyclopedia of communities of practice in information and knowledge management* (pp. 544–551). Hershey, PA: Idea Group Publishing. doi:10.4018/978-1-59140-556-6.ch091

Klyne, G., Reynolds, F., Woodrow, C., Ohto, H., Hjelm, J., Butler, M. H., & Tran, L. (2004). *Composite capability/preference profiles (CC/PP): Structure and vocabularies 1.0.* W3C recommendation. Retrieved January 2004, from http://www.w3.org/ TR/ CCPP-struct-vocab/

Kolda, T. G., & O'Leary, P. D. (1998). A semi-discrete matrix decomposition for latent semantic indexing in information retrieval. *ACM Transactions on Information Systems*, *16*, 322–346. doi:10.1145/291128.291131

Konstantinidis, K., Gasteratos, A., & Andreadis, I. (2005). Image retrieval based on fuzzy color histogram processing. *Optics Communications*, *248*(4-6), 375–386. doi:10.1016/j.optcom.2004.12.029

Kontostathis, A. (2007). Essential dimensions of latent semantic indexing. *Proceedings of the 40th Hawaii International Conference on System Science.*

Kosch, H. (2003). *Distributed multimedia database technologies supported by MPEG-7 and MPEG-21*. CRC Press. doi:10.1201/9780203009338

Kosch, H., Böszörmenyi, L., Döller, M., Libsie, M., Kofler, A., & Schojer, P. (2005). The life-cycle of multimedia metadata. *IEEE MultiMedia*, *12*(1), 80–86. doi:10.1109/MMUL.2005.13

Kosch, H., Tusch, R., Boszormenyi, L., Bachlechner, A., Hofbauer, C., Riedler, C., et al. Hanin, C. (2001). *SMOOTH - A distributed multimedia database system*. In 27th International VLDB Conference, (pp. 713-714).

Krishnapuram, R., Medasani, S., Jung, S.-H., Choi, Y.-S., & Balasubramaniam, R. (2004). Content-based image retrieval based on a fuzzy approach. *IEEE Transactions on Knowledge and Data Engineering*, *16*(10), 1185–1199. doi:10.1109/TKDE.2004.53

Kubo, M., Aghbari, Z., & Makinouchi, A. (2003). Content-based image retrieval technique using wavelet-based shift and brightness invariant edge feature. *International Journal of Wavelets, Multresolution, and Information Processing*, *1*(2), 163–178. doi:10.1142/S0219691303000141

Kucuk, D., Burcuozgur, N., Yazici, A., & Koyuncu, M. (2009). A fuzzy conceptual model for multimedia data with a text-based automatic annotation scheme. *International Journal of Uncertainty fuzziness and Knowledge-based Systems*, *17*, 135-152.

Kulkarni, S. (2004). *Neural-fuzzy approach for content-based retrieval of digital video*. Canadian Conference on Electrical and Computer Engineering, 4, (pp. 2235–2238).

Kulkarni, S., & Verma, B. (2003). Fuzzy logic based texture queries for CBIR. *Proceedings of the 2003 International Conference on Computational Intelligence and Multimedia Applications*, (pp. 223-228).

Kumar, A., & Zhang, D. (2006). Personal recognition using hand shape and texture. *IEEE Transactions on Image Processing*, *15*(8), 2454–2461. doi:10.1109/TIP.2006.875214

Kunttu, I., Lepistö, L., Rauhamaa, J., & Visa, A. (2006). Multiscale Fourier descriptors for defect image retrieval. *Pattern Recognition Letters*, *27*(2), 123–132. doi:10.1016/j.patrec.2005.08.022

Kuo, C. M., Hung, M. H., & Hsieh, C. H. (2008). *Baseball playfield segmentation using adaptive Gaussian mixture models*. International Conference on Innovative Computing Information and Control.

Landauer, T. K., Foltz, P. W., & Laham, D. (1998). Introduction to latent semantic analysis. *Discourse Processes*, *25*, 259–284. doi:10.1080/01638539809545028

Laws, K. I. (1980). *Textured image segmentation*. Ph.D. dissertation, Department of Engineering, University of Southern California.

Le Saux, B. (2003). *Classification non exclusive et personnalisation par apprentissage: Application à la navigation dans les bases d'images*. Ph.D. Thesis, INRIA, France.

Lee, W. W., & Owens, D. L. (2000). *Multimedia-based instructional design: Computer-based training, Web-based training, distance broadcast training, performance-based solutions*. Pfeiffer.

Lee, D., & Seung, H. (1999). Learning the parts of objects by non-negative matrix factorization. *Nature*, *401*, 788–791. doi:10.1038/44565

Lew, M. S., Sebe, N., Djeraba, C., & Jain, R. (2006). Content-based multimedia information retrieval: State of the art and challenges. *ACM Trans. Multimedia Comput. Commun. Appl.*, *2*(1), 1–19. doi:10.1145/1126004.1126005

Lewis, D. (1997). *Reuters-21578 text categorization test collection*. Retrieved from http://kdd.ics.uci.edu/databases/reuters21578/ README.txt

Li, Z., Zayane, O. R., & Tauber, Z. (1999). Illumination invariance and object model in content-based image and video retrieval. *Journal of Visual Communication and Image Representation*, *10*, 219–244. doi:10.1006/jvci.1998.0403

Li, J., & Wang, J. (2004). Studying digital imagery of ancient paintings by mixtures of stochastic models. *IEEE Transactions on Image Processing*, *13*(3), 340–353. doi:10.1109/TIP.2003.821349

Li, J., & Wang, J. Z. (2003). Automatic linguistic indexing of pictures by a statistical modeling approach. *IEEE Transactions on Pattern Analysis and Machine Intelligence*, *25*(9), 1075–1088. doi:10.1109/TPAMI.2003.1227984

Li, C. (1998). Multimedia and imaging databases. *IEEE Communications Magazine*, *36*(2), 28–30. doi:10.1109/MCOM.1998.648745

Li, Y., Lee, S. H., Yeh, C. H., & Kuo, C.-C. J. (2006). Techniques for movie content analysis and skimming. *IEEE Signal Processing Magazine*, *23*, 79–89. doi:10.1109/MSP.2006.1621451

Li, C. C., Chou, S. T., & Lin, C. W. (2008). Statistical pitch type recognition in broadcast baseball videos. *Proceedings of the International Conference of Computer Vision & Graphic Image Processing.*

Li, J., Ozsu, M., & Szafron, D. (1997). MOQL: A multimedia object query language. In *Proceedings of the 3rd International Workshop on Multimedia Information Systems*, (pp. 19-28). Como, Italy.

Li, Q., Yang, J., & Zhuang, Y. (2002). MediaView: A semantic view mechanism for multimedia modeling. *IEEE Pacific Rim Conference on Multimedia, LNCS 2532,* (pp. 61-68).

Liang, Y. M., Zhai, H. C., & Chavel, P. (2002). Fuzzy color-image retrieval. *Optics Communications*, *212*(4-6), 247–250. doi:10.1016/S0030-4018(02)02011-4

Lienhart, R., Kuhmnch, C., & Effelsberg, W. (2001). *On the detection and recognition of television commercials*. International Conference on Multimedia Computing and Systems, (pp. 509-516).

Lim, J.-H., Tian, Q., & Mulhem, P. (2003). Home photo content modeling for personalized event-based retrieval. *IEEE MultiMedia*, *10*, 28–37. doi:10.1109/MMUL.2003.1237548

Lim, J.-H. (1999). *Learnable visual keywords for image classification*. In 4th ACM International Conference on Digital Libraries, (pp.139-145)

Littman, M., Dumais, S., & Landauer, T. (1997). *Automatic cross-language information retrieval using latent semantic indexing*. AAAI-97 Spring Symposium Series: Cross-Language Text and Speech Retrieval (pp. 18-24).

Liu, C. J., & Wechsler, H. (2001). A shape- and texture-based enhanced fisher classifier for face recognition. *IEEE Transactions on Image Processing*, *10*(4), 598–608. doi:10.1109/83.913594

Liu, S., Chia, L. T., & Chan, S. (2004). Ontology for nature scene image retrieval. *Lecture Notes in Computer Science*, *3291*, 1050–1061. doi:10.1007/978-3-540-30469-2_14

Liu, Y., Zhang, D., Lu, G., & Ma, W. Y. (2007). A survey of content-based image retrieval with high-level semantics. *Journal of the Pattern Recognition Society*, *40*, 262–282. doi:10.1016/j.patcog.2006.04.045

Liu, C. C., Hsu, J. L., & Chen, A. L. (2001). Efficient near neighbour searching using multi-indexes for content-based multimedia data retrieval. *Multimedia Tools and Applications*, *13*(3), 235–254. doi:10.1023/A:1009601513674

Liu, M., & Hu, J. (2009). Information networking model. *Proceedings of the 28th International Conference on Conceptual Modeling.* Gramado, Brazil, LNCS, Springer 2009.

Long, F., Zhang, H., & Feng, D. D. (2003). Fundamentals of content-based image retrieval . In Feng, D., Siu, W. C., & Zhang, H. J. (Eds.), *Multimedia information retrieval and management-Technological fundamentals and applications*. Springer.

Lowe, D. (2004). Distinctive image features from scale-invariant keypoints. *International Journal of Computer Vision*, *60*(2), 91–110. doi:10.1023/B:VISI.0000029664.99615.94

Lowe, D. G. (1999). Object recognition from local scale-invariant features. *Proceedings of the 7th International Conference on Computer Vision*, Kerkyra, Greece, (pp. 1150-1157).

Luo, J., & Savakis, A. (2001). Indoor versus outdoor classification of consumer photographs using low-level and semantic features. In *Proceedings of International Conference ion Image Processing,* vol. 2, (pp. 745–748). ICIP'01. IEEE Computer Society.

Lynch, M. M., & Roecker, J. (2007). *Project managing e-learning: A handbook for successful design, delivery and management*. Routledge.

Ma, W. Y., & Manjunath, B. S. (1999). NeTra: A toolbox for navigating large image databases. *Multimedia Systems*, *7*, 184–198. doi:10.1007/s005300050121

Madhavan, J., Bernstein, P. A., & Rahm, E. (2001). *Generic schema matching with Cupid.* In the 27th International Conference on Very Large Data Bases, (pp. 49-58).

Mahmoudi, F., Shanbehzadeh, J., Eftekhari-Moghadam, A. M., & Soltanian-Zadeh, H. (2003). Image retrieval based on shape similarity by edge orientation autocorrelogram. *Pattern Recognition*, *36*, 1725–1736. doi:10.1016/S0031-3203(03)00010-4

Majumdar, S., Kothari, M., Augat, P., Newitt, D. C., Link, T. M., & Lin, J. C. (1998). High-resolution magnetic resonance imaging: Three dimensional trabecular bone architecture and biomechanical properties. *Bone*, *22*, 445–454. doi:10.1016/S8756-3282(98)00030-1

Majumdar, A. K., Bhattacharya, I., & Saha, A. K. (2002). An object-oriented fuzzy data model for similarity detection in image databases. *IEEE Transactions on Knowledge and Data Engineering*, *14*(5), 1186–1189. doi:10.1109/TKDE.2002.1033783

Manjunath, B. S., Ohm, J. R., Vasudevan, V. V., & Yamada, A. (2001). Color and texture descriptors. *Transactions on Circuits and Systems for Video Technology*, *11*(6), 703–715. doi:10.1109/76.927424

Manjunath, B. S., Wu, P., Newsam, S., & Shin, H. D. (2000). A texture descriptor for browsing and similarity retrieval. *Signal Processing Image Communication*, *16*(1-2), 33–43. doi:10.1016/S0923-5965(00)00016-3

Manjunath, B. S., Huang, T., Teklap, A. M., & Zhang, H. J. (2000). Guest editorial introduction to the special issue on image and video processing for digital libraries. *Image Processing*, *9*, 1–2. doi:10.1109/TIP.2000.817594

Manjunath, B. S., Salembier, P., & Sikora, T. (2002). *Introduction to MPEG-7. John Wiley & Sons*. England: LTD.

Marlow, S., Sadlier, D. A., McGerough, K., O'Connor, N., & Murphy, N. (2001). *Audio and video processing for automatic TV advertisement detection.* Irish Signals and Systems Conference, (pp. 25-27).

Marshall, S. (1989). Review of shape coding techniques. *Image and Vision Computing*, *7*(4), 281–294. doi:10.1016/0262-8856(89)90032-2

Martinet, J., & Satoh, S. (2007). *A study of intra-modal association rules for visual modality representation.* In International Workshop on Content-Based Multimedia Indexing, (pp. 344–350). CBMI. IEEE Computer Society.

Mason, J. E., & Spiteri, R. (2008). *A new adaptive folding-up algorithm for information retrieval.* Text Mining Workshop in the Eighth SIAM International Conference on Data Mining.

Matas, J., Chun, O., Urban, M., & Pajdla, T. (2002). Robust wide baseline stereo from maximally stable extremal regions. *Proceedings of the British Machine Vision Conference*, Cardiff, UK.

Materka, A., & Strzelecki, M. (1998). *Texture analysis methods-a review (Tech. Rep. No. COST B11)*. Brussels, Belgium: Technical University of Lodz, Institute of Electronics.

Matthias, F., Christian, Z., & David, T. (2004). *Lifting XML schema to OWL*. In the 4th International Conference of Web Engineering, (pp. 354-358).

McBride, B. (2001). *Jena: Implementing the RDF model and syntax specification*. Retrieved from http://www.hpl.hp.com/ personal/ bwm/ papers/ 20001221-paper

McGuinness, D. L., & Harmelen, F. V. (2004). *OWL Web ontology language overview*. W3C. Retrieved from http://www.w3.org/ TR/ owl- features/

MEC. (2007). *Chamada Pública para Produção de Conteúdos Educacionais Digitais Multimídia.* Portal do Ministério da Educação, Secretaria de Educação a Distância, Departamento de Produção e Capacitação em Programas de EAD. Retrieved December 30, 2007, from http://portal.mec.gov.br/seed/

Medina, J. M., Jaime-Castillo, S., Barranco, C. D., & Campana, J. R. (2009). Flexible retrieval of x-ray images based on shape descriptors using a fuzzy object-relational database. *Proceedings of the Joint 2009 International Fuzzy Systems Association World Congress and 2009 European Society of Fuzzy Logic and Technology Conference*, (pp. 903-908).

Melton, J., & Eisenberg, A. (2001). SQL multimedia and application packages (SQL/MM). *SIGMOD Record*, *30*(4), 97–102. doi:10.1145/604264.604280

Microsoft. (n.d.). *Bayesian network toolkit*. Retrieved from http://research.microsoft.com/ adapt/ MSBNx/

Mikolajczyk, K., & Schmid, C. (2002). An affine invariant interest point detector. *Proceedings of the 6th European Conference on Computer Vision*, Copenhagen, Denmark, (pp. 128-142).

Mindru, F., Tuytelaars, T., Gool, L., & Moons, T. (2004). Moment invariants for recognition under changing viewpoint and illumination. *Computer Vision and Image Understanding*, *94*, 3–27. doi:10.1016/j.cviu.2003.10.011

Mindru, F., Moons, T., & Gool, L. (1998). Color-based moment invariants for the viewpoint and illumination independent recognition of planar color patterns. *Proceedings of International Conference on Advances in Pattern Recognition*, (pp. 113-122).

Mitra, M., Huang, J., & Kumar, S. R. (1997). Combining supervised learning with color correlograms for content-based image retrieval. *Proceedings of Fifth ACM Multimedia Conference.*

Mizutani, M., Ebadollahi, S., & Chang, S.-F. (2005). *Commercial detection in heterogeneous video streams using fused multi-modal and temporal features*. International Conference on Acoustics, Speech, and Signal Processing, (pp. 157-160).

Moghaddam, H. A., Khajoie, T. T., & Rouhi, A. H. (2003). A new algorithm for image indexing and retrieval using wavelet correlogram. In . *Proceedings of the International Conference on Image Processing*, *2003*, 497–500.

Mokhtarian, F., & Bober, M. (Eds.). (2003). *Curvature scale space representation: Theory, applications, and Mpeg-7 standardization*. Norwell, MA: Kluwer Academic Publishers.

Monay, F., & Perez, D. G. (2003). *On image auto-annotation with latent space models*. In 11th ACM International Conference on Multimedia, (pp. 275-278)

Mori, G., Belongie, S., & Malik, J. (2001). Shape contexts enable efficient retrieval of similar shapes. *Proceedings of the IEEE Computer Society Conference on Computer Vision and Pattern Recognition*, Hawaii, USA, (pp. 723-730).

Morrissey, J. M. (1990). Imprecise information and uncertainty in Information Systems. *ACM Transactions on Information Systems*, *8*(2), 157–180. doi:10.1145/96105.96113

Moskowitz, S. (2006). Introduction - Digital rights management. In Zeng, W., Yu, H., & Lin, C. (Eds.), *Multimedia security technologies for digital rights management*. Academic Press. doi:10.1016/B978-012369476-8/50003-8

Muhimmah, I., Oliver, A., Denton, E. R. E., Pont, J., Perez, E., & Zwiggelaar, R. (2006). Comparison between Wolfe, Boyd, BI-RADS and Tabar based mammographic risk assessment. In *Proceedings of the 8th International Workshop on Digital Mammography* (pp. 407-415).

Mulcahy, R. (2006). *PM crash course: Premier edition.* Minneapolis, MN: RMC Publications, Incorporated.

Muller, H., Michoux, N., Bandon, D., & Geissbuhler, A. (2004). A review of content-based image retrieval systems in medical applications – Clinical benefits and future directions. *International Journal of Medical Informatics*, *73*(1), 1–23. doi:10.1016/j.ijmedinf.2003.11.024

Munsell, H. (1912). A pigment color system and notation. *The American Journal of Psychology*, *23*, 236–244. doi:10.2307/1412843

Mylonas, P., Spyrou, E., & Avrithis, Y. (2007). High-level concept detection based on mid-level semantic information and contextual adaptation. In *Proceedings of the Second International Workshop on Semantic Media Adaptation and Personalization* (SMAP), (pp. 193-198). Washington, DC: IEEE Computer Society.

Narasimhalu, A. D. (1996). Multimedia databases. *Multimedia Systems*, *4*(5), 226–249. doi:10.1007/s005300050026

Nelson, S. J., Johnston, D., & Humphreys, B. L. (2001). Relationships in medical subject headings . In Bean, C. A., & Green, R. (Eds.), *Relationships in the organization of knowledge* (pp. 171–184). New York, NY: Kluwer Academic Publishers.

Nepal, S., Ramakrishna, M. V., & Thom, J. A. (1999). A fuzzy object query language (FOQL) for image databases. *Proceedings of the 6th International Conference on Database Systems for Advanced Applications.*

Nepal, S., Srinivasan, U., & Reynolds, G. (2001). Automatic detection of "Goal" segments in basketball. *Proceedings of the 9th ACM International Conference on Multimedia*, (pp. 261-269).

Niblack, W., Barber, R., Equitz, W., Flickner, M., Glasman, E., & Petkovic, D. ... Taubin, G. (1993). The qbic project: Querying images by content using color, texture, and shape. In *Proceedings of the SPIE Conference on Storage and Retrieval for Image and Video Databases*, (pp. 173–187).

Nishibori, M., Tsumura, N., & Miyake, Y. (2004). Why multi-spectral imaging in medicine? *Journal of Imaging Science and Technology*, *48*, 125–129.

Nishibori, M. (2000). Problems and solutions in medical color imaging. In *Proceedings of the Second International Symposium on Multi-Spectral Imaging and High Accurate Color Reproduction* (pp. 9-17).

Nonaka, I. (1998). The knowledge-creating company. In *Harvard Business Review on Knowledge Management*, 6th ed. Harvard Business Review Paperback Series. Harvard Business School Press (Compiler). ISBN 0875848818

O'Sullivan, J. A. (2000). Properties of the information value decomposition. *Proceedings IEEE International Symposium on Information Theory* (pp. 491).

Obdrzalek, S., & Matas, J. (2002). Local affine frames for image retrieval. *Proceedings of the International Conference on Image and Video Retrieval*, London, UK, (pp. 318-327).

Omhover, J. F., Detyniecki, M., & Bouchon-Meunier, B. (2004). A region-similarity-based image retrieval system. [Perugia, Italy.]. *Proceedings of IPMU*, *04*, 1461–1468.

Omhover, J.-F., Detyniecki, M., Rifqi, M., & Bouchon-Meunier, B. (2004). Ranking invariance between fuzzy similarity measures applied to image retrieval. *Proceedings of the 2004 IEEE International Conference on Fuzzy Systems, 3*, (pp. 1367-1372).

Oomoto, E., & Tanaka, K. (1993). OVID: Design and implementation of a video-object database system. *IEEE Transactions on Knowledge and Data Engineering*, *5*(4), 629–643. doi:10.1109/69.234775

Oracle. (1999). *Oracle 8iTM release 2 features overview*. November 1999. Retrieved from http://www.oracle.com

Ouyang, A., & Tan, Y. P. (2002). A novel multi-scale spatial-color descriptor for content-based image retrieval. In *Proceedings of the 7th International Conference on Control, Automation, Robotics and Vision* (pp. 1204-1209).

Ozgur, N. B., Koyuncu, M., & Yazici, A. (2009). An intelligent fuzzy object-oriented database framework for video database applications. *Fuzzy Sets and Systems*, *160*, 2253–2274. doi:10.1016/j.fss.2009.02.017

Paatero, P., & Tapper, U. (1994). Positive matrix factorization: A non-negative factor model with optimal utilization of error estimate of data values. *Environmetrics*, *5*, 111–126. doi:10.1002/env.3170050203

Papadimitriou, C. H., Raghavan, P., Tamaki, H., & Vempala, S. (2000). Latent semantic indexing: A probabilistic analysis. *Journal of Computer and System Sciences*, *61*(2), 217–235. doi:10.1006/jcss.2000.1711

Paquette, S. (2006). Communities of practice as facilitators of knowledge exchange . In Coakes, E., & Clarke, S. (Eds.), *Encyclopedia of communities of practice in information and knowledge management* (pp. 68–73). Hershey, PA: Idea Group Publishing. doi:10.4018/978-1-59140-556-6.ch015

Parsons, S. (1996). Current approaches to handling imperfect information in data and knowledge bases. *IEEE Transactions on Knowledge and Data Engineering*, *8*(2), 353–372. doi:10.1109/69.506705

Pass, G., & Zabih, R. (1999). Comparing images using joint histograms. *Multimedia Systems*, *7*(3), 234–240. doi:10.1007/s005300050125

Pass, G., & Zabih, R. (1996). Histogram refinement for content-based image retrieval. *Proceedings of the 3rd IEEE Workshop on Applications of Computer Vision*, (p. 96).

Patel-Schneider, P. F., Hayes, P., & Horrocks, I. (2004). *OWL Web ontology language semantic and abstract syntax.* W3C recommendation. Retrieved February 2004, from http://www.w3.org/ TR/owl-semantics/

Pauca, V. P., Shahnaz, F., Berry, M. W., & Plemmons, R. J. (2004). Text mining using non-negative matrix factorizations. In *Proceedings of SIAM International Conference on Data Mining.*

Pearl, J. (1998). *Probabilistic reasoning in intelligent systems: Networks of plausible inference* (pp. 1–20). Morgan Kaufmann.

Peckham, J., & Maryanski, F. J. (1988). Semantic data models. *ACM Computing Surveys, 20*(3), 153–189. doi:10.1145/62061.62062

Peng, Z., & Kambayashi, Y. (1995). Deputy mechanisms for object-oriented databases. In *Proceedings of the Eleventh International Conference on Data Engineering (ICDE),* Taipei, Taiwan, (pp. 333–340).

Pentland, A., Picard, R. W., & Sclaroff, S. (1996). Photobook: Content-based manipulation of image databases. *International Journal of Computer Vision, 18*(3), 233–254. doi:10.1007/BF00123143

Pentland, A., Picard, R., & Sclaroff, S. (1994). Photobook: Tools for content based manipulation of image databases. In *Proceedings of the SPIE Conference on Storage and Retrieval for Image and Video Databases II.*

Pereira, F. (2001). The MPEG-21 standard: Why an open multimedia framework? Springer . *Interactive Distributed Multimedia Systems, LNCS, 2158,* 219–220. doi:10.1007/3-540-44763-6_23

Petkov, N., & Kruizinga, P. (1997). Computational models of visual neurons specialized in the detection of periodic and aperiodic oriented visual stimuli: Bar and grating cells. *Biological Cybernetics, 76*(2), 83–96. doi:10.1007/s004220050323

Petkovic, M., & Jonker, W. (2003). Content-based video retrieval: A database perspective. *Proceedings of the First ACM Conference on Multimedia Systems and Applications.* Springer.

PMIa. (2008). *A guide to the project management body of knowledge (PMBOK guide)* (4th ed.). Project Management Institute.

PMIb. (2008). *The standard for program management* (2nd ed.). Project Management Institute.

Ponte, J., & Croft, W. B. (1998). A language modeling approach to information retrieval. In *Proceedings of the 21st Annual International ACM SIGIR Conference on Research and Development in Information Retrieval* (pp. 275-281). SIGIR'98. ACM Press.

Porto, A. J. V., Souza, M. C. F., Ravelli, C. A., & Batocchio, A. (2002). Manufatura Virtual: conceituação e desafios. *Gest. Prod. São Carlos, 9*(3). Retrieved October 11, 2009, from http://www.scielo.br/

Quelhas, P., Monay, F., Odobez, J.-M., Gatica-Perez, D., & Tuytelaars, T. (2007). A thousand words in a scene. [IEEE Computer Society.]. *Transactions on Pattern Analysis and Machine Intelligence, 29*(9), 1575–1589. doi:10.1109/TPAMI.2007.1155

Quelhas, P., Monay, F., Odobez, J. M., Gatica-Perez, D., Tuytelaars, T., & Van Gool, L. (2005). Modeling scenes with local descriptors and latent aspects. *In Proceedings of the Tenth IEEE International Conference on Computer Vision.* IEEE Computer Society.

Ragsdell, G. (2006). The contribution of communities of practice to project management. In Coakes, E., & Clarke, S. (Eds.), *Encyclopedia of communities of practice in information and knowledge management* (pp. 104–107). Hershey, PA: Idea Group Publishing.

Rahm, E., & Bernstein, P. A. (2001). A survey of approaches to automatic schema matching. *The VLDB Journal, 10*(4), 334–350. doi:10.1007/s007780100057

Rennhackkamp, M. (1997). Extending relational DBMSs. *DBMS Online, 10*(13).

Ribeiro-Neto, B., Silva, I., & Muntz, R. (2000). Bayesian network models for information retrieval. In Crestani, F., & Pasi, G. (Eds.), *Soft computing in information retrieval: Techniques and applications* (pp. 259–291). Springer.

Ricardo, B. Y., & Berthier, R. N. (1999). *Modern information retrieval. ACM Press.* Addison-Wesley.

Risch, J., Rex, D. B., Dowson, S. T., Walters, T. B., May, R. A., & Moon, B. D. (1999). The starlight information visualization system . In Card, S., Mackinlay, J., & Shneiderman, B. (Eds.), *Readings in information visualization: Using vision to think.* Morgan Kaufmann.

Ro, Y. M., Kim, M., Kang, H. K., Manjunath, B. S., & Kim, J. (2001). MPEG-7 homogeneous texture descriptor. *ETRI Journal*, *23*(2), 41–51. doi:10.4218/etrij.01.0101.0201

Roire, J. (2000). *Les noms des couleurs*. Pour la science, Hors série, no. 27.

Rossett, A., & Schafer, L. (2006). Job aids and performance support: The convergence of learning and work. *International Journal of Learning Technology*, *2*(4), 310-328. Inderscience Enterprises Limited. ISSN 1753-5263

Rui, Y., Huang, T. S., & Chang, S. F. (1999). Image retrieval: Current techniques, promising directions, and open issues. *Journal of Visual Communication and Image Representation*, *10*(1), 39–62. doi:10.1006/jvci.1999.0413

Rui, Y., Huang, T. S., & Chang, S. F. (1999). Image retrieval: Current techniques, promising directions and open issues. *Journal of Visual Communication and Image Representation*, *10*, 39–62. doi:10.1006/jvci.1999.0413

Rui, Y., Huang, T. S., & Mehrotra, S. (1998). Constructing table-of-content for video. *ACM Journal of Multimedia Systems*, *7*, 359–368. doi:10.1007/s005300050138

Rui, Y., Gupta, A., & Acero, A. (2000). Automatically extracting highlights for TV baseball programs. *Proceedings of the ACM International Conference on Multimedia*, (pp. 105-115).

Rui, Y., Huang, T., Ortega, M., & Mehrotra, S. (1998). Relevance feedback: A power tool for interactive content-based image retrieval. *IEEE Trans. On Circuit and Systems for Video Technology*, *5*, 644-656.

Rui, Y., She, A. C., & Huang, T. S. (1996). Modified Fourier descriptors for shape representation – A practical approach. *Proceedings of the 1st International Workshop on Image Databases and Multimedia Search*, Amsterdam, The Netherlands.

Sacks-Davis, R., Kent, A., Ramamohanarao, K., Thom, J., & Zobel, J. (1995). Atlas: A nested relational database system for text applications. *IEEE Transactions on Knowledge and Data Engineering*, 7(3), 454–470. doi:10.1109/69.390250

Salton, G., & McGill, M. J. (1983). *Introduction to modern information retrieval*. McGraw-Hill.

Salton, G., Wong, A., & Yang, C. S. (1975). A vector space model for automatic indexing. *Communications of the ACM*, *18*, 613–620. doi:10.1145/361219.361220

Sampat, M. P., Whitman, G. J., Stephens, T. W., Broemeling, L. D., Heger, N. A., & Bovik, A. C. (2006). The reliability of measuring physical characteristics of spiculated masses on mammography. *The British Journal of Radiology*, *79*, S134–S140. doi:10.1259/bjr/96723280

Santini, S., & Gupta, A. (2002). Principles of schema design for multimedia databases. *IEEE Transactions on Multimedia*, *4*(2), 248–259. doi:10.1109/TMM.2002.1017737

Santini, S., & Jain, R. (1999). Similarity measures. *IEEE Transactions on Pattern Analysis and Machine Intelligence*, *21*(9), 871–883. doi:10.1109/34.790428

Schmid, C., & Mohr, R. (1997). Local greyvalue invariants for image retrieval. *IEEE Transactions on Pattern Analysis and Machine Intelligence*, *19*(5), 530–535. doi:10.1109/34.589215

Schober, J., Hermes, T., & Herzog, O. (2005). PictureFinder: Description logics for semantic image retrieval. *Proceedings of the IEEE International Conference on Multimedia and Expo*, Amsterdam, Netherlands, (pp. 1571-1574).

Schütze, H., & Pedersen, J. (1993). A vector model for syntagmatic and paradigmatic relatedness. In *Proceedings of the Ninth Annual Conference of the UW Centre for the New OED and Text Research* (pp. 104–113).

Seaborn, M., Hepplewhite, L., & Stonham, J. (1999). Fuzzy colour category map for content based image retrieval. *Proceedings of the Tenth British Machine Vision Conference*, (pp. 103-112).

Sebe, N., & Lew, M. S. (2002). Texture features for content-based retrieval . In Lew, M. S. (Ed.), *Principles of visual information retrieval* (pp. 51–85). London, UK: Springer.

Sebe, N., Lew, M. S., Zhou, X., Huang, T. S., & Bakker, E. (2003). The state of the art in image and video retrieval. In *Proceedings of the International Conference on Video Retrieval (CIVR)*.

Sethi, I. K., & Coman, I. L. (2001). Mining association rules between low-level image features and high-level concepts. *Proceedings of the SPIE Data Mining and Knowledge Discovery*, *3*, 279–290.

Shafer, G. R., & Shenoy, P. P. (1990). Probability propagation. *Annals of Mathematics and Artificial Intelligence*, *2*(1-4), 327–351. doi:10.1007/BF01531015

Shahabi, C., & Chen, Y.-S. (2000). Soft query in image retrieval systems. *Proceedings of the 2000 SPIE Internet Imaging, Electronic Imaging, 3964,* (pp. 57-68).

Shahnaz, F., Berry, M., Pauca, P., & Plemmons, R. (2006). Document clustering using non-negative matrix factorization. *Information Processing & Management*, *42*, 373–386. doi:10.1016/j.ipm.2004.11.005

Shandilya, S. K., & Singhai, N. (2010). A survey on content based image retrieval systems. *International Journal of Computers and Applications*, *4*(2), 22–26. doi:10.5120/802-1139

Shao, L., & Brady, M. (2006). Specific object retrieval based on salient regions. *Pattern Recognition*, *39*(10), 1932–1948. doi:10.1016/j.patcog.2006.04.010

Shao, L., & Brady, M. (2006). Invariant salient regions based image retrieval under viewpoint and illumination variations. *Journal of Visual Communication and Image Representation*, *17*(6), 1256–1272. doi:10.1016/j.jvcir.2006.08.002

Shao, L., Kadir, T., & Brady, M. (2007). Geometric and photometric invariant distinctive regions detection. *Information Sciences*, *177*(4), 1088–1122. doi:10.1016/j.ins.2006.09.003

Sharma, G. (2003). *Digital color imaging handbook*. CRC Press.

Shi, Z. P., Hu, H., Li, Q. Y., Shi, Z. Z., & Duan, C. L. (2005). Texture spectrum descriptor based image retrieval. *Journal of Software*, *16*(6), 1039–1045. doi:10.1360/jos161039

Shi, D. C., Xu, L., & Han, L. Y. (2007). Image retrieval using both color and texture features. *Journal of China University of Posts and Telecommunications*, *14*(1), 94–99. doi:10.1016/S1005-8885(08)60020-5

Shih, T. Y. (1995). The reversibility of six geometric color spaces. *Photogrammetric Engineering and Remote Sensing*, *61*(10), 1223–1232.

Shvaiko, P., & Euzenat, J. (2005). A survey of schema-based matching approaches. *Journal on Data Semantics*, *5*(1), 146–171.

Simon, H., & Zha, H. (1997). *On updating problems in latent semantic indexing*. (Technical Report No. CSE-97-011). Department of Computer Science and Engineering, Pennsylvania State University.

Sivic, J., & Zisserman, A. (2004). Video data mining using configurations of viewpoint invariant regions. *Proceedings of the IEEE Conference on Computer Vision and Pattern Recognition*, Washington DC, USA, (pp. 488-495).

Sivic, J., Russell, B. C., Efros, A. A., Zisserman, A., & Freeman, W. T. (2005). Discovering object categories in image collections. In *Proceedings of the International Conference on Computer Vision*. (pp. 370-377). ICCV. IEEE Computer Society.

Sivic, J., Schaffalitzky, F., & Zisserman, A. (2004). Efficient object retrieval from videos. *Proceedings of the 12th European Signal Processing Conference*, Vienna, Austria.

Sklansky, J. (1978). Image segmentation and feature extraction. *IEEE Transactions on Systems, Man, and Cybernetics*, *8*, 237–247. doi:10.1109/TSMC.1978.4309944

Smeulders, A. W. M., Worring, M., Santini, S., Gupta, A., & Jain, R. (2000). Content-based image retrieval at the end of the early years. *IEEE Transactions on Pattern Analysis and Machine Intelligence*, *22*(12), 1349–1380. doi:10.1109/34.895972

Smith, A. R. (1978). Color gammet transform pairs. *Computer Graphics*, *12*(3), 12–19. doi:10.1145/965139.807361

Smith, P. A. C. (2006). *Organisational change elements of establishing, facilitating, and supporting CoPs. Encyclopedia of communities of practice in information and knowledge management* (pp. 400–406). Hershey, PA: Idea Group Publishing.

Smith, J. R., & Chang, S. F. (1997). Querying by color regions using the VisualSEEK content based visual query system . In Maybury, M. (Ed.), *Intelligent multimedia information retrieval* (pp. 23–41). CA: AAAI Press.

Smith, J. R., & Chang, S. F. (1996). VisualSEEk: A fully automated content-based image query system. *ACM International Conference Multimedia*, (pp. 87–98).

Sobel, I., & Feldman, G. (1973). A 3x3 isotropic gradient operator for image processing . In Duda, R., & Hart, P. (Eds.), *Pattern classification and scene analysis* (pp. 271–272). John Wiley and Sons.

Sonka, M., Hlavac, V., & Boyle, R. (1998). *Image processing, analysis and machine vision*. International Thomson Computer Press.

Stonebraker, M., & Kemnitz, G. (1995). The POSTGRES next-generation database management system. *Communications of the ACM*, *34*, 78–92. doi:10.1145/125223.125262

Su, J. (1991). Dynamic constraints and object migration. In *Proceedings of the 17th International Conference on Very Large Data Bases (VLDB)*, Barcelona, Catalonia, Spain, (pp. 233–242).

Suchanek, F., Kasneci, G., & Weikum, G. (2008). Yago - A large ontology from Wikipedia and WordNet. *Elsevier Journal of Web Semantics*, *6*(3), 203–217. doi:10.1016/j.websem.2008.06.001

Sumengen, B., & Manjunath, B. S. (2006). Graph partitioning active contours (GPAC) for image segmentation. *IEEE Transactions on Pattern Analysis and Machine Intelligence*, *28*(4), 509–521. doi:10.1109/TPAMI.2006.76

Sun, Y., & Ozawa, S. (2003). Semantic-meaningful content-based image retrieval in wavelet domain. In *Proc. of the 5th ACM SIGMM International Workshop on Multimedia Information Retrieval*, (pp. 122–129).

Swain, M. J., & Ballard, D. H. (1991). Color indexing. *International Journal of Computer Vision*, *7*(1), 11–32. doi:10.1007/BF00130487

Tamai, S. (1999). The color of digital imaging in pathology and cytology. In *Proceedings of the First Symposium of the "Color" of Digital Imaging in Medicine* (pp. 61-66).

Teague, M. R. (1980). Image analysis via the general theory of moments. *Journal of the Optical Society of America*, *70*(8), 920–930. doi:10.1364/JOSA.70.000920

Terdiman, D. (2009). Tagging gives Web a human meaning. *CNET News*. Retrieved from http://news.cnet.com/ Tagging- gives- Web- a- human- meaning/ 2009- 1025_ 3- 5944502.html

Thompson, H. S., Mendelsohn, N., Beech, D., & Maloney, M. (2009). *W3C xml schema definition language (XSD) 1.1 part 1: Structure*. W3C candidate recommendation, April 2009. Retrieved April 2009, from http://www.w3.org/ TR/xmlschema11-1/

Tirilly, P., Claveau, V., & Gros, P. (2008). Language modeling for bag-of-visual words image categorization. In *Proc. Int. Conf. on Content-based Image and Video Retrieval*.

Tolias, Y., Panas, S., & Tsoukalas, L. H. (1999). FSMIQ: Fuzzy similarity matching for image queries. *Proceedings of the 1999 International Conference on Information Intelligence and Systems*, (pp. 249-254).

Torralba, A., & Oliva, A. (1999). *Semantic organization of scenes using discriminant structural templates*. In International Conference on Computer Vision (pp. 1253-1258).

Tourassi, G. D. (1999). Journey toward computer-aided diagnosis: Role of image texture analysis. *Radiology*, *213*(2), 407–412.

Trindade, A. R., & Ochi, L. S. (2006). Um algoritmo evolutivo híbrido para a formação de células de manufatura em sistemas de produção. Pesqui. Oper., 26(2). Retrieved October 11, 2009, from http://www.scielo.br/

Troncy, R. (2003). *Integrating structure and semantics into audio-visual documents*. In the 2nd International Semantic Web Conference, (pp. 566-581).

Truck, I., Akdag, H., & Borgi, A. (2001). A symbolic approach for colorimetric alterations. [Leicester, England.]. *Proceedings of EUSFLAT*, *2001*, 105–108.

Truck, I., Akdag, H., & Borgi, A. (2001). Using fuzzy modifiers in colorimetry. *Proceedings of the 5th World Multiconference on Systemics, Cybernetics and Informatics, SCI 2001*, (pp. 472-477), Orlando, Florida, USA.

Tsai, C.-F., & Hung, C. (2008). Automatically annotating images with keywords: A review of image annotation systems. *Recent Patents on Computer Science*, *1*, 55–68. doi:10.2174/1874479610801010055

Tsinaraki, C., Polydoros, P., & Christodoulakis, S. (2004). *Integration of OWL ontologies in MPEG-7 and TVAnytime compliant semantic indexing*. In the 16th International Conference on Advanced Information Systems Engineering, (pp. 299 - 325).

TV-Anytime Forum, Metadata Working Group. (2003). *Metadata specification version 1.3*. Retrieved March 2003, from ftp://tva:tva@ftp.bbc.co.uk/Specifications/COR3_SP003v13.zip

Uysal, M., & Yarman Vural, F. T. (2005). A content-based fuzzy image database based on the fuzzy ARTMAP architecture. *Turk J Elec Engin, 13*(3), 333–342.

Vailaya, A., Figueiredo, A. T., Jain, A. K., & Zhang, H.-J. (2001). Image classification for content-based indexing. *IEEE Transactions on Image Processing, 10*, 117–130. doi:10.1109/83.892448

Vailaya, A., Figueiredo, M. A. T., Jain, A. K., & Zhang, H. J. (1999). *Content based hierarchical classification of vacation images*. In IEEE Conference on Multimedia Computing and Systems: vol. 1, (pp. 518-523).

van Kaick, O., & Mori, G. (2006). *Automatic classification of outdoor images by region matching*. In 3rd Canadian Conference on Computer and Robot Vision, (pp. 9-16)

Vapnik, V. (1998). *Statistical learning theory*. New York, NY: John Wiley and Sons.

Vapnik, V. N. (1995). *The nature of statistical learning theory*. Springer.

Varela, C., Timp, S., & Karssemeijer, N. (2006). Use of border information in the classification of mammographic masses. *Physics in Medicine and Biology, 51*, 425–441. doi:10.1088/0031-9155/51/2/016

Veenland, J. F., Grashuis, J. L., Weinans, H., Ding, M., & Vrooman, H. A. (2002). Suitability of texture features to assess changes in trabecular bone architecture. *Pattern Recognition Letters, 23*, 395–403. doi:10.1016/S0167-8655(01)00172-6

Veltkamp, R. C., & Tanase, M. (2002). Content-based image retrieval systems: A survey. (Technical Report, UU-CS-2000-34), Department of Computer Science, Utretch University.

Veltkamp, R., & Tanase, M. (2000). Content-based image retrieval systems: A survey. (Technical Report UU-CS-2000-34), Utrecht University.

Vereb, K. (2003). On a hierarchical indexing fuzzy content-based image retrieval approach. *Proceedings of the VLDB 2003 PhD Workshop*.

Vertan, C., & Boujemaa, N. (2000). Embedding fuzzy logic in content-based image retrieval. *Proceedings of the 2000 International Conference of the North American Fuzzy Information Processing Society*, (pp. 85-89).

Vetro, A., & Timmerer, C. (2005). Digital item adaptation overview of standardization and research activities. *IEEE Transactions on Multimedia, 7*(3), 418–426. doi:10.1109/TMM.2005.846795

Viitaniemi, V., & Laaksonen, J. (2006). Techniques for still image scene classification and object detection . In Kollias, S. (Eds.), *Lecture Notes in Computer Science, 4132* (pp. 35–44).

Vinary, V., Cox, I., Wood, K., & Milic-Frayling, N. (2005). A comparison of dimensionality reduction techniques for text retrieval. In *Proceedings of Fourth International Conference on Machine Learning and Applications*, 2005.

Vincent, M. W., Liu, J., & Liu, C. (2004). Strong functional dependencies and their application to normal forms in XML. *ACM Transactions on Database Systems, 29*(3), 445–462. doi:10.1145/1016028.1016029

Vocabulary Workspace, E. X. I. F. (2004). *RDF schema*. Retrieved December 2003, from http://www.w3.org/2003/12/exif/

Vogel, J., & Schiele, B. (2004). Natural scene retrieval based on a semantic modeling step. *Proceedings of Conference on Image and Video Retrieval* (CIVR), Dublin, Ireland, (pp. 207-215).

Voorhees, H., & Poggio, T. (1987). Detecting textons and texture boundaries in natural images. *Proceedings of the 1st International Conference on Computer Vision*, London, UK, (pp. 250-258).

Wallace, M., Atahnasiadis, T., Avrithis, Y., Delopoulus, A. N., & Kollias, S. (2006). Integrating multimedia archives: The architecture and the content layer. *IEEE Transactions on Systems, Man, and Cybernetics, 36*(1), 34–52. doi:10.1109/TSMCA.2005.859184

Wang, J., Li, J., & Wiederhold, G. (2001). Simplicity: Semantics-sensitive integrated matching for picture libraries. *IEEE Transactions on Pattern Analysis and Machine Intelligence, 23*(9), 947–963. doi:10.1109/34.955109

Wang, B., Li, L., Li, M., & Ma, W.-Y. (2006). Large-scale duplicate detection for Web image search. In *Proceedings of International Conference on Multimedia and Expo* (pp. 353-356). IEEE Computer Society.

Wang, J. Z., & Du, Y. (2001). Scalable integrated region-based image retrieval using IRM and statistical clustering. *Proceedings of the ACM and IEEE Joint Conference on Digital Libraries,* (pp. 268-277), Roanoke, VA.

Weber, R., Schek, H., & Blott, S. (1998). A quantitative analysis and performance study for similarity search methods in high-dimensional spaces. *Proceedings of 24th VLDB, 1998,* (pp. 194–205).

Wei, C.-H., Li, C.-T., & Wilson, R. (2005). A content-based approach to medical image database retrieval . In Ma, Z. (Ed.), *Database modeling for industrial data management: Emerging technologies and applications.* Hershey, PA: Idea Group Publishing. doi:10.4018/978-1-59140-684-6.ch009

Wei, C.-H., & Li, C.-T. (2006). Calcification descriptor and relevance feedback learning algorithms for content-based mammogram retrieval. In *Proceedings of the 8th International Workshop on Digital Mammography 2006* (pp. 307-314).

Weibel, S. Kunze, J., Lagoze, C., & Wolf, M. (1998). *Dublin Core metadata for resource discovery.* Retrieved April 1998, from http://www.ietf.org/ rfc/rfc2413.txt

WG12: Learning Object Metadata. (2002). *Learning object metadata standard.* Retrieved December 2002, from http://ltsc.ieee.org/wg12/

Widyanto, M. R., & Maftukhah, T. (2010). Fuzzy relevance feedback in image retrieval for color feature using query vector modification method. *Journal of Advanced Computational Intelligence and Intelligent Informatics, 14*(1), 34–38.

Wieringa, R. J., Jonge, W. D., & Spruit, P. (1995). Using dynamic classes and role classes to model object migration. *Theory and Practice of Object Systems, 1*(1), 61–83.

Wirick, D. (2009). *Public-sector project management: Meeting the challenges and achieving results.* New Jersey: Wiley. ISBN 0470487313

Won, C. S., Park, D. K., & Park, S. J. (2002). Efficient use of Mpeg-7 edge histogram descriptor. *ETRI Journal, 24*(1), 23–30. doi:10.4218/etrij.02.0102.0103

Won Suk, L., Burger, T., Sasaki, F., & Malaise, V. (2009). *Use cases and requirements for ontology and API for media object 1.0.* W3C Working Group.

Wong, R. (1999). Heterogeneous multifaceted multimedia objects in DOOR/MM: A role-based approach with views. *Journal of Parallel and Distributed Computing, 56*(3), 251–271. doi:10.1006/jpdc.1998.1522

WordNet. (n.d.). *Software.* Retrieved from http://www.cogsci. princeton.edu/ ~wn/

Worring, M., & Gevers, T. (2001). Interactive retrieval of color images. *International Journal of Image and Graphics, 1*(3), 387–414. doi:10.1142/S0219467801000244

Wu, H., Lu, H. Q., & Ma, S. D. (2005). A survey of relevance feedback techniques in content-based image retrieval. *Chinese Journal of Computers, 28*(12), 1969–1979.

Wu, P., Manjunath, B. S., Newsam, S., & Shin, H. D. (2000). A texture descriptor for browsing and similarity retrieval. *Signal Processing Image Communication, 16*(1-2), 33–43. doi:10.1016/S0923-5965(00)00016-3

Wu, J. K., Narasimhalu, A. D., Mehtre, B. M., Lam, C. P., & Gao, Y. J. (1995). CORE: A content-based retrieval engine for multimedia Information System. *Multimedia Systems, 3*(1), 25–41. doi:10.1007/BF01236577

Wu, J. K., & Nerasimhalu, D. (1998). Fuzzy content-based retrieval in image databases. *Information Processing & Management, 34*(5), 513–534. doi:10.1016/S0306-4573(98)00017-X

Wu, L., Li, M., Li, Z., Ma, W., & Yu, N. (2007). Visual language modeling for image classification. In *Proceedings of the International Workshop on Workshop on Multimedia Information Retrieval* (pp. 115-124). MIR '07. ACM Press.

Wu, X., Zhao, W.-L., & Ngo, C.-W. (2007). *Near-duplicate keyframe retrieval with visual keywords and semantic context.* In 6th ACM International Conference on Image and Video Retrieval (CIVR 2007) (pp.162-169)

Wyatt, J. C., & Sullivan, F. (2005). E-health and the future: Promise or peril? *British Medical Journal, 331,* 1391–1393. doi:10.1136/bmj.331.7529.1391

Xie, L., Xu, P., Chang, S. F., Divakaran, A., & Sun, H. (2004). Structure analysis of soccer video with domain knowledge and hidden Markov models. *Pattern Recognition Letters, 25,* 767–775. doi:10.1016/j.patrec.2004.01.005

Xin, Y. Q., Pawlak, M., & Liao, S. (2007). Accurate computation of zernike moments in polar coordinates. *IEEE Transactions on Image Processing*, *16*(2), 581–587. doi:10.1109/TIP.2006.888346

Xiong, Z., Radhakrishnan, R., Divakaran, A., & Huang, T. S. (2005). *Highlights extraction from sports video based on an audio-visual marker detection framework*. International Conference on Multimedia and Expo, (pp. 29-32).

XMP. (2008). *Specification, part 2.* Retrieved January 2008, from http://www.adobe.com/devnet/ xmp/pdfs/ XMPSpecificationPart2.pdf

Xu, C., Wang, J., Li, Y., & Duan, L. (2006). Live sports event detection based on broadcast video and Web-casting text. *Proceedings of the ACM International Conference on Multimedia*, (pp. 221-230).

Yager, R. R., & Petry, F. E. (2005). A framework for linguistic relevance feedback in content-based image retrieval using fuzzy logic. *Information Sciences*, *173*(4), 337–352. doi:10.1016/j.ins.2005.03.004

Yahoo. Media RSS Module. (2008). *RSS 2.0 module*. Retrieved January 2004, from http://video.search.yahoo.com/ mrss

Yang, B., & Hurson, A. (2005). Ad hoc image retrieval using hierarchical semantic-based index. *Proceedings of IEEE International Conference on Advanced Information Networking and Applications*, Taiwan, (pp. 629-634).

Yang, J., Wang, W., Wang, H., & Yu, P. (2002). Delta-clusters: Capturing subspace correlation in a large data set. *Proceedings of the 18th International Conference on Data Engineering,* (p. 517).

Yap, K.-H., & Wu, K. (2005). Fuzzy relevance feedback in content-based image retrieval systems using radial basis function network. *Proceedings of the 2005 IEEE International Conference on Multimedia and Expo.*

Yazici, A., Buckles, B. P., & Petry, F. E. (1999). Handling complex and uncertain information in the ExIFO and NF^2 data models. *IEEE Transactions on Fuzzy Systems*, *7*(6), 659–676. doi:10.1109/91.811232

Yeh, C. H., Kuo, C. H., & Liou, R. W. (2009). Movie story intensity representation through audiovisual tempo analysis. *Multimedia Tools and Applications*, 205–228. doi:10.1007/s11042-009-0278-8

Yeh, C. H., & Teng, C. H. (2009). *Statistical understanding of broadcast baseball videos from the perspective of semantic shot distribution*. Computer Vision & Graphic Image Processing.

Yeh, C. H., Lee, S. H., & Kuo, C.-C. J. (2005). Content-based video analysis for knowledge discovery . In Chen, C. H., & Wang, P. S. P. (Eds.), *Handbook of pattern recognition and computer vision* (3rd ed.). World Scientific Publishing Co.doi:10.1142/9789812775320_0029

Yoshitaka, A., & Ichikawa, T. (1999). A survey on content-based retrieval for multimedia databases. *IEEE Transactions on Knowledge and Data Engineering*, *11*(1), 81–93. doi:10.1109/69.755617

Younes, A., Truck, I., & Akdag, H. (2005). Color image profiling using fuzzy sets. *Turk J Elec Engin*, *13*(3), 343–359.

Younes, A., Truck, I., & Akdag, H. (2007). Image retrieval using fuzzy representation of colors. *Soft Computing*, *11*(3), 287–298. doi:10.1007/s00500-006-0070-x

Yu, H., Li, M., Zhang, H.-J., & Feng, J. (2002). Color texture moments for content-based image retrieval. In . *Proceedings of the International Conference on Image Processing, 2002*, 929–932. doi:10.1109/ICIP.2002.1039125

Yu, X., Xu, C., Leong, H. W., Tian, Q., Tang, Q., & Wan, K. W. (2003). *Trajectory-based ball detection and tracking with applications to semantic analysis of broadcast soccer video*. ACM International Conference on Multimedia, (pp. 11-20).

Zachary, J. M., & Iyengar, S. S. (1999). Content based image retrieval systems. In *Proceedings of the IEEE Symposium on Application-Specific Systems and Software Engineering and Technology*, (pp. 136–143).

Zadeh, L. A. (1965). Fuzzy sets. *Information and Control*, *8*(3), 338–353. doi:10.1016/S0019-9958(65)90241-X

Zadeh, L. A. (1978). Fuzzy sets as a basis for a theory of possibility. *Fuzzy Sets and Systems*, *1*(1), 3–28. doi:10.1016/0165-0114(78)90029-5

Zeitouni, K. (2002). *A survey of spatial data mining methods databases and statistics point of views*. Hershey, PA: IRM Press.

Zhang, D. S., & Lu, G. J. (2002). Shape-based image retrieval using generic Fourier descriptor. *Signal Processing Image Communication, 17*(10), 825–848. doi:10.1016/S0923-5965(02)00084-X

Zhang, D. S., & Lu, G. J. (2003). A comparative study of curvature scale space and Fourier descriptors for shape-based image retrieval. *Journal of Visual Communication and Image Representation, 14*(1), 41–60. doi:10.1016/S1047-3203(03)00003-8

Zhang, D. S., & Lu, G. J. (2004). Review of shape representation and description techniques. *Pattern Recognition, 37*(1), 1–19. doi:10.1016/j.patcog.2003.07.008

Zhang, Z. Y., Shi, Z. P., Shi, Z. W., & Shi, Z. Z. (2008). Image retrieval based on contour. *Journal of Software, 19*(9), 2461–2470. doi:10.3724/SP.J.1001.2008.02461

Zhang, M., & Alhajj, R. (2010). Effectiveness of naq-tree as index structure for similarity search in high-dimensional metric space. *Knowledge and Information Systems, 22*(1). doi:10.1007/s10115-008-0190-y

Zhang, D., & Chang, S. F. (2002). Event detection in baseball video using superimposed caption recognition. *ACM International Conference on Multimedia*, (pp. 315-318).

Zhang, D., & Lu, G. (2001). A comparative study on shape retrieval using Fourier descriptors with different shape signatures. *Proceedings of the Second IEEE Pacific Rim Conference on Multimedia: Advances in Multimedia Information Processing,* (pp. 855-860). October 24-26.

Zhang, G., Ma, Z. M., & Deng, L. G. (2007). Directed filter for dominant direction fuzzy set in content-based image retrieval. In *Proceedings of the 2007 ACM Symposium on Applied Computing*. (pp. 76-77). Seoul, Republic of Korea: ACM Press.

Zhang, G., Ma, Z. M., & Deng, L. G. (2008). Texture feature extraction and description using fuzzy set of main dominant directions of variable scales in content-based medical image retrieval. In *Proceedings of the 2008 ACM Symposium on Applied Computing* (pp. 1760-1761). Fortaleza, Brazil: ACM Press.

Zhang, G., Ma, Z. M., Tong, Q., He, Y., & Zhao, T. N. (2008). Shape feature extraction using Fourier descriptors with brightness in content-based medical image retrieval. In *Proceedings of the Fourth International Conference on Intelligent Information Hiding and Multimedia Signal Processing*. (pp. 71-74). Harbin, China: IEEE Computer Society.

Zhang, R., Zhang, Z., & Qin, Z. (2004). Semantic repository modeling in image database. *Proceedings of IEEE International Conference on Multimedia and Expo*, Taipei, Taiwan, (pp. 2079-2082).

Zhang, R., Zhang, Z., & Yao, J. (2003). A unified fuzzy feature indexing scheme for region based online image querying. *Proceedings of the 2003 IEEE/WIC International Conference on Web Intelligence*, (pp. 421-424).

Zhao, T., Tang, L. H., Ip, H. H. S., & Qi, F. (2001). Visual keyword image retrieval based on synergetic neural network for Web-based image search. *Real-Time Systems, 21*, 127–142. doi:10.1023/A:1011147421401

Zheng, Q. F., Wang, W. Q., & Gao, W. (2006). Effective and efficient object-based image retrieval using visual phrases. In *Proceedings of the 14th Annual ACM International Conference on Multimedia* (pp. 77-80). ACM Press.

Zhou, X. D., Zhang, Q., Lin, L., Deng, A. L., & Wu, G. (2003). Image retrieval by fuzzy clustering of relevance feedback records. *Proceedings of the 2003 International Conference on Multimedia and Expo*, 1, (pp. 305-308).

Zhou, X., Zhuang, X., Yan, S., Chang, S. F., Johnson, M. H., & Huang, T. S. (2008). SIFT-bag kernel for video event analysis. In *Proceeding of the 16th ACM International Conference on Multimedia*, (pp. 229-238). MM '08. ACM Press.

Zhu, G., Xu, C., Zhang, Y., Huang, Q., & Lu, H. (2008). *Event tactic analysis based on player and ball trajectory in broadcast video*. International Conference on Content-based Image and Video Retrieval, (pp. 515-524).

Ziou, D., Hamri, T., & Boutemedjet, S. (2009). A hybrid probabilistic framework for content-based image retrieval with feature weighting. *Pattern Recognition, 42*(7), 1511–1519. doi:10.1016/j.patcog.2008.11.025

About the Contributors

Li Yan received her Ph.D. degree from Northeastern University, China. She is currently an Associate Professor of the School of Software at Northeastern University, China. Her research interests include database modeling, XML data management, as well as imprecise and uncertain data processing. She has published papers in several journals such as Data and Knowledge Engineering, Information and Software Technology, International Journal of Intelligent Systems and some conferences such as WWW and CIKM.

Zongmin Ma (Z. M. Ma) received the Ph. D. degree from the City University of Hong Kong in 2001 and is currently a Full Professor in College of Information Science and Engineering at Northeastern University, China. His current research interests include intelligent database systems, knowledge representation and reasoning, the Semantic Web and XML, knowledge-bases systems, and semantic image retrieval. He has published over 80 papers in international journals, conferences and books in these areas since 1999. He also authored and edited several scholarly books published by Springer-Verlag and IGI Global, respectively. He has served as member of the international program committees for several international conferences and also spent some time as a reviewer of several journals. Dr. Ma is a senior member of the IEEE.

* * *

Amine AÏT YOUNES is an Associate Professor of computer science at Reims University, France, since 2004. He is also a researcher in the CReSTIC laboratory (Centre de Recherche en Sciences et Technologies de l'Information et de la Communication) with the SIC team (Signal Image et Connaissance). He got his Master degree in Industrial Engineering from the National Polytechnic School of Algiers, Algeria, in 1995. He got his PhD on Decision Aiding from the University Paris Dauphine, France in 2001. He has several publications in international journals and conferences in different fields of multicriteria decision aiding and cognitive modeling via fuzzy logic.

Herman AKDAG is presently Professor of computer science at Reims University. He is also Senior Researcher in the LIP6 laboratory (Laboratoire d'Informatique de Paris VI) with the MaLIRE team. Initially focused on Information Theory and Knowledge Representation, his scientific orientations evolved to Machine Learning and Cognitive Modeling via Fuzzy Logic. Herman Akdag published more than 100 papers in conferences proceedings, journals and books. Brief Biographical Story: -1976: Senior Engineer, INSA de Lyon, France; -1980: PhD on Information Theory, Paris VI, France; -1980: Associate

Professor, University of Reims, France, -1992: HDR on Multi-Valued Logics, Paris VI, France, -1995: Full Professor, University of Reims, France. Membership in Learned Societies: IEEE, AFIA (French Artificial Intelligence Society), President of Eïdétique Society (France), Member of Saint Joseph College Society (Turkey).

Reda Alhajj received his B.Sc. degree in Computer Engineering in 1988 from Middle East Technical University, Ankara, Turkey. After he completed his BSc with distinction from METU, he was offered a full scholarship to join the graduate program in Computer Engineering and Information Sciences at Bilkent University in Ankara, where he received his M.Sc. and Ph.D. degrees in 1990 and 1993, respectively. Currently, he is Professor in the Department of Computer Science at the University of Calgary, Alberta, Canada. He published over 275 papers in refereed international journals and conferences. He served on the program committee of several international conferences including IEEE ICDE, IEEE ICDM, IEEE IAT, SIAM DM; program chair of IEEE IRI 2008, OSIWM 2008, SONAM 2009, IEEE IRI 2009. He is editor in chief of International Journal of Social Networks Analysis and Mining, associate editor of IEEE SMC- Part C and he is member of the editorial board of the Journal of Information Assurance and Security; he has been guest editor for a number of special issues and edited a number of conference proceedings. He recently received the Grad Studies Outstanding Achievement in Supervision Award. Dr. Alhajj's primary work and research interests are in the areas of biocomputing and biodata analysis, data mining, multiagent systems, schema integration and re-engineering, social networks and XML. He currently leads a research group of 7 PhD and 9 MSc candidates. Dr. Alhajj recently received with Dr. Jon Rokne donation of equipment valued at $5 million from RBC and Teradata for their research on Computational Intelligence and Bioinformatics research.

Samir Amir is a PhD student at the University Lille 1 in Lille, France, since September 2009. In 2005, he has received his engineer degree on electronics and telecommunications from Saad Dahleb University of Blida, Algeria. He received his master degree on image and signal processing in 2006 from the University of Rennes 1 in Rennes, France. He integrated LIFL as research engineer in the frame of CAM4Home project. His research interests include multimedia metadata integration, metadata modeling, ontology matching and query rewriting.

Joni A. Amorim has received his undergraduate degree in Mathematics from UNICAMP (Universidade Estadual de Campinas), Brazil. He is a M.Sc. in Engineering and a Ph.D. candidate at FEEC (Faculdade de Engenharia Elétrica e de Computação) at UNICAMP. His research interests involve project management, multimedia production and ICT-based education. He works as a project manager at UNICAMP. He develops research with the Universidad Politécnica de Valencia, Spain.

Görkem Aşılıoğlu obtained his bachelor's degree from the Department of Computer Engineering, TOBB University, Ankara, Turkey (2009). He is currently MSc candidate at TOBB University.

Ioan Marius Bilasco is an Assistant Professor at the University Lille 1 in Lille, France, since 2009. In 2003, he received his MS degree on multimedia adaptation in Computer Science from the University Joseph Fourier of Grenoble. He received his PhD on semantic adaptation of 3D data in 2007 from the University Joseph Fourier. He is a member of the LIFL Laboratory in Lille since 2008. He integrated

LIFL as a PostDoc in the frame of CAM4Home ITEA2-EUREKA project, where he leaded the metadata modeling activity. His research interests also include multimedia semantics, content modeling, user modeling, and user behavior detection (especially eye-gaze detection).

Shi-Kuo Chang received the B.S.E.E. degree from National Taiwan University in 1965, the M.S. and Ph.D. degrees from the University of California, Berkeley, in 1967 and 1969, respectively. He was a research scientist at IBM Watson Research Center, Professor at the Department of Information Engineering, University of Illinois at Chicago, Professor and Chairman of the Department of Electrical and Computer Engineering, Illinois Institute of Technology, Professor and Chairman of the Department of Computer Science, University of Pittsburgh. He is currently Professor and Director of Center for Parallel, Distributed and Intelligent Systems, University of Pittsburgh. Dr. Chang is a Fellow of IEEE. His research interests include image information systems, visual languages and distributed multimedia systems. Dr. Chang is the Editor-in-Chief of the Journal of Visual Languages and Computing published by Academic Press and the Editor-in-Chief of the International Journal of Software Engineering & Knowledge Engineering published by World Scientific Press.

Sherry Y. Chen is a Reader in the School of Information Systems, Computing and Mathematics at Brunel University. She obtained her PhD from the Department of Information Studies, University of Sheffield, UK. Her current research interests include human-computer interaction, data mining and e-business.

Vincenzo Deufemia graduated in Computer Science (cum laude) in 1999. He received the PhD degree in Computer Science from the University of Salerno in 2003. Since March 2006 he is assistant professor in the Department of Mathematics and Informatics at Salerno University. His main research focuses on software engineering, sketch understanding, visual languages, parsing technologies, and multimedia databases. On these topics he published several peer-reviewed articles in international journals, books, conference and workshop proceedings. He has served as program committee member for several international conferences. He was Publicity Chair of the 14th International Conference on Software Engineering and Knowledge Engineering (SEKE'02).

Chabane Djeraba is a Professor of computer science at University of Sciences and Technologies of Lille (USTL), France, since 2003. He is a member of LIFL laboratory which is a join research unit of both French Scientific Research National Center (CNRS) and USTL, where he heads a research team on Mining, indexing and recognition of multimedia and complex data. He had been an associate professor of computer science in Nantes University, 1994-2003. He obtained a PhD in Computer Science from Claude Bernard University of Lyon, France, 1993; a master degree from Pierre Mendes France University, France, 1990; and an engineer degree from Computer National Institute (INI), Algiers, Algeria, 1989. He organized major multimedia conferences and being co-chair of workshops such as ACM Multimedia Information Retrieval, and ACM Multimedia Data Mining. He has been the guest editor of special issues on top multimedia journals (ex. IEEE Multimedia). During the last fifteen years, he published a hundred scientific publications in the areas of multimedia indexing and retrieval and mining, including one leading book in multimedia data mining, and he participated to several program committees of major conferences and journals (ex. International journal of Multimedia Tools and Applications, Springer-Kluwer).

Ismail Elsayad is pursuing his doctoral studies in the University of Lille, France, that he joined in 2008. He holds a Master of Science in Computer Engineering from Duisburg-Essen University, Germany, and a Bachelor of Science in Computer Engineering from the Lebanese International University in Beirut, Lebanon. His research interests focus on image descriptors and content-based image retieval.

Imad EL-ZAKHEM is currently an assistant professor at the University of Balamand, Lebanon. He got his Master degree in Electrical and Computer Engineering from the National Technical University of Athens, Greece, in 1999. He worked as a senior developer and later held a position of an IT manager. He has been a lecturer in the University Of Balamand since 2003. At 2009 Imad El-Zakhem got his PhD degree from the University of Reims, France. His research is focused on Machine Learning and Cognitive Modeling via Fuzzy Logic.

Lisa Fan is an associate professor at Department of Computer Science, Faculty of Science, University of Regina. She received her Ph.D. from the University of London, U.K. Dr. Fan's main research areas include Web Intelligence, Intelligent Learning Systems, Web-based Adaptive Learning, Cognitive Modeling. She is also interested in intelligent systems applications in engineering (intelligent manufacturing system and intelligent transportation system).

William Ferng is a mathematician with extensive experience in matrix computations and in applying analytical methods in industrial applications. He received a Ph.D. degree in applied mathematics from North Carolina State University. He has published several papers in prestigious journals in areas ranging from numerical algorithms to parallel computing. He joined The Boeing Company in 2001. Since then he has led many Boeing collaboration efforts with internationally recognized mathematicians. His current work includes social networks analysis using mathematical approaches, data and text mining, and information assurance.

Shang Gao received his BSc in Computer Science from the University of Waterloo in 2006, and MSc in Computer Science from the University of Calgary in 2009. He is currently a PhD candidate in the Department of Computer Science at the University of Calgary under the supervision of Prof. Reda Alhajj. He received a number of prestigious awards and scholarships including iCore graduation studies scholarship, Department of Computer Science research award and University of Calgary Queen Elizabeth II Scholarship. He published over 10 papers in fully refereed conferences and journals. His research interests cover data mining, financial data analysis, social networks, bioinformatics and XML.

Hanna Greige is currently the chairman of the Department of Mathematics at the University of Balamand, Lebanon. He got his PhD from the University Pierre et Marie Curie, Paris in 1980. He worked as a researcher for 15 years in Paris on various mathematical modeling projects. He Joined the University of Balamand in 1994. He served as the chairman of the computer science department for 10 years. Also, he established the mathematics department which he headed since he joined the university. He has several publications in international journals and conferences in different fields of mathematical modeling, statistics, and image processing.

Dawen Jia received his BEng degree from Wuhan University, China, in 2004. He began his successive postgraduate and doctoral program in 2004 at Wuhan University. He was awarded a scholarship under the State Scholarship Fund to further his studies in Canada as a joint PhD candidate in 2007. His research interests include database modeling techniques, metadata management and multimedia information management.

Jamal Jida received Maitrise of applied Mathematics from Lebanese University in 1981, Diploma of Deep studies Mathematics & Informatics (DEA) from University of Montpellier II, USTL – FRANCE in 1985, PhD in Mathematics & Informatics from University of Nice – FRANCE in 1987. Since 1992 He is professor lecturer of mathematics and informatics at the Lebanese University, Tripoli Lebanon. His main areas of research include XML, image processing, data mining and web optimization.

Dr. **Anne Kao** is a Technical Fellow in Boeing. She has been leading Text Mining projects since 1991. The wide range of applications she has worked on includes survey comments analysis, airplane safety, airplane maintenance and reliability, Network Centric Operations and Homeland Security. She is the co-editor of a book on Natural Language Processing and Text Mining published by Springer in 2007, as well as a reviewer for major ACM and IEEE conferences and major journals on data mining, visual analytics and social network analysis. Dr. Kao has a Ph.D. in Philosophy, specializing in philosophy of language, as well as an MS in Computer Science.

Botang Li is a graduate student at Department of Computer Science, University of Regina. He received his bachelor degree in Guangdong, China and has more than two year industry experiences in software development. Image Retrieval, Web Mining, and Intelligent System Applications are his current research areas and interests.

Yu-Dun Lin was born in Chiayi, Taiwan in 1985. He received the B.S. degree from the Department of Electronics Engineering, National Changhua University of Education, Changhua, Taiwan, in 2008. His research interests include abnormal events detection and video content analysis.

Mengchi Liu is a full professor of Computer Science at Carleton University, Canada. He received his Ph.D and M.Sc in Computer Science from University of Calgary in Canada in 1992 and 1990 respectively, and M.Eng and B.S in Computer Science from Wuhan University in China in 1986 and 1983 respectively. His research interests include information modeling techniques, database system, knowledge-based systems, and their implementation techniques.

Emine Merve Kaya obtained her bachelor's degree from the Department of Computer Engineering, TOBB University, Ankara, Turkey (2009). She is currently PhD candidate at the Department of Electrical and Computer, Engineering, Johns Hopkins University, Maryland, USA.

Jean Martinet has joined the University of Lille, France, in 2008, where he is Assistant Professor in Computer Sciences. He has visited the National Institute of Informatics (NII), Japan, for a two-year postdoctoral research fellowship. He joined the video processing project at NII in 2005 after being awarded a fellowship from the Japan Society for the Promotion of Science (JSPS). He was formerly a

Ph.D. student during 3 years at Universit?Joseph Fourier, Grenoble France. He received his B.Sc. and M.Sc. degrees in 1999 and 2001 from Universit?Joseph Fourier. His research interests include image and video analysis, indexing and retrieval.

Rosana G. S. Miskulin has a Doctor's degree in Education and is a researcher at IGCE (Instituto de Geociências e Ciências Exatas) at UNESP (Universidade Estadual Paulista), Brazil. Her research interests involve teacher training, mathematics education and ICT-based education.

Mauro S. Miskulin has a Doctor's degree in Engineering and is a researcher at FEEC (Faculdade de Engenharia Elétrica e de Computação) at UNICAMP (Universidade Estadual de Campinas), Brazil. His research interests involve distance and ICT-based education. He is the president of the Ibero-American Science and Technology Education Consortium.

Tansel Özyer obtained his bachelor's degree and M.Sc. degree from the Department of Computer Engineering, Bilkent, Ankara (1996) and Middle East Technical University, Ankara (2000). After spending several years in the industry in North America, he joined the PhD program in the Department of Computer Science at the University of Calgary, Canada in 2002 and received his PhD degree in 2006. He published over 50 refereed conference papers and journal articles at prestigious venues. Currently he is assistant professor TOBB University, Ankara, Turkey. His research interests are data mining, bioinformatics, social networks and XML.

Ranjan Parekh is a faculty at the School of Education Technology, Jadavpur University, Calcutta, India, the same University from where he has obtained his B.E. and Ph.D. (Engineering) degrees. He is involved in teaching subjects related to Multimedia and Web technologies at the postgraduate level, both in the conventional classroom mode and the distance education mode. His research interests include multimedia databases, distributed multimedia presentations, scripting representations and uses of multimedia in health informatics. He has collaborative research ties with academic institutions in UK, USA, Singapore and Australia. Before moving to academics he had worked for 8 years with the supermini / mainframe maintenance industry. He is the author of the book entitled "Principles of Multimedia" published by McGraw Hill, (www.mhhe.com/parekh/multimedia) which is being used as text/reference book in a number of institutions in India and abroad.

Giuseppe Polese received the Laurea degree in Computer Science from the University of Salerno, Italy, in 1989, the M.S. degree in Computer Science from the University of Pittsburgh, PA, in 1994, and the Ph.D. in Computer Science & Applied Mathematics from the University of Salerno, in 1998. He was a Software Engineer and Project Manager at the italian airspace company (Alenia) from 1989 to 1991. He has been a consultant for several software firms, including Siemens, Olivetti, and Telecom Italia. He is currently Associate Professor with the Department of Mathematics & Computer Science at the University of Salerno. His research interests include databases, multimedia software engineering, and visual languages.

Stephen R. Poteet is a computational linguist with over twenty years of experience in both artificial intelligence and statistical approaches to text mining. He has designed and implemented systems for aviation maintenance and prognostics, safety, business intelligence, political intelligence, and battlefield management using various text mining technologies including text classification and clustering, trend analysis, latent semantic analysis, and information extraction. He holds five US patents and has four patents pending. He co-edited a book on "Natural Language Processing and Text Mining" and has co-authored a number of papers and book chapters on text mining, latent semantic analysis, specialized entity extraction, and knowledge management using text classification.

Lesley Quach holds a B.S. in Computer Science from the University of Washington and has joined Boeing's Phantom Works Mathematics and Computing Technology since 1997. She has been involved in a number of projects related to web technology, text mining, knowledge management, and product lifecycle management. She submitted one patent and published several papers related to knowledge management.

Duygu Sarıkaya obtained her bachelor's degree from the Department of Computer Engineering, TOBB University, Ankara, Turkey (2009). She is currently MSc candidate at TOBB University.

Ling Shao received the B.Eng. degree in Electronic Engineering from the University of Science and Technology of China (USTC), the M.Sc. degree in Medical Image Analysis and the Ph.D. (D.Phil.) degree in Computer Vision at the Robotics Research Group from the University of Oxford. His Ph.D. thesis was about invariant salient regions detection and the application of detected salient regions on specific object and object category retrieval. Dr. Ling Shao is currently a Senior Lecturer (Associate Professor) in the Department of Electronic and Electrical Engineering at the University of Sheffield. Before joining Sheffield University, he worked for 4 years as a Senior Research Scientist in the Video Processing and Analysis Group, Philips Research Laboratories, The Netherlands. Prior to that, he worked shortly as a Senior Research Engineer at the Institute of Electronics, Communications and Information Technology, Queen's University of Belfast. His research interests include Multimedia Signal Processing, Video Search and Mining, Human Action/Activity Recognition, Content Based Multimedia Retrieval, Human-Computer Interaction, etc. He has published over 50 academic papers in refereed journals and conference proceedings and has filed 9 patent applications. Ling Shao is the Editor-in-Chief of the Journal of Advances in Multimedia, an associate editor of the International Journal of Image and Graphics and the EURASIP Journal on Advances in Signal Processing, and serves on the editorial boards of Journal of Electrical and Computer Engineering and The Open Signal Processing Journal. He has been serving as Program Committee member for many international conferences, including ICIP, ICASSP, ICCE, EUSIPCO, CIVR, etc., and as reviewer for many journals, such as IEEE Trans. Image Processing, Image and Vision Computing, and Pattern Recognition.

Nalin Sharda gained B.Tech. and Ph.D. degrees from the Indian Institute of Technology, Delhi. Presently he teaches and leads research in mobile multimedia communications at Victoria University, Australia. He has held visiting positions at Aachen University -Germany, Karlstad University -Sweden, Jaypee University of Information Technology -India, and Florida Atlantic University -USA. His publications include the Multimedia Information Networking textbook published by Prentice Hall, and over 120 articles, papers and handbook chapters. He has been invited to present lectures and seminars in the Distinguished Lecturer series of the European Union's Prolearn program. He has presented over 60 seminars, lectures, and Keynote addresses in Austria, Australia, Finland, Germany, Hong Kong, India, Macau, Malaysia, Pakistan, Japan, Singapore, Slovenia, Sweden, Switzerland, UAE, and USA. For further details visit http://sci.vu.edu.au/~nalin/

Md. Haidar Sharif was born in a city in Bangladesh named Jessore on the 31st December, 1977. In 2001, he received his BSc degree in Electronics and Computer Science from Jahangirnagor University, Bangladesh. Afterwards, nearly five years, he was involved in a project concerning computer architecture at Max Planck Institute of Colloids and Interfaces, Golm, Germany. In 2006, he received his MSc degree in Computer Engineering from Duisburg-Essen University, Germany. Since 2007, he has been working under the supervision of Prof. Chabane Djeraba. His research interests include abnormal event and/or behavior detection, object tracking, visual computing, and high-performance distributed computing.

Wen-Yu Tseng was born in Yunlin, Taiwan, in 1985. He received the B.S. degree from the Department of Automatic Control Engineering, Feng Chia University, Taichung, Taiwan, in 2008. His research interests include surveillance system and scalable video coding.

Chih-Chung Teng was born in Taichung in 1984. He receives the B.S. degree from the Department of Electronics Engineering, Chunghua University, Hsinchu, Taiwan, in 2007, and the M.S. degree from the Department of Electrical Engineering, National Sun Yat-Sen University, Kaohsiung, Taiwan, in 2009. His research topics include image/audio/video signal processing.

Rodney Tjoelker is a statistician with extensive experience in applying analytical methods to solve complex industrial problems. He joined The Boeing Company in 1990 and has been recognized as a Boeing Associate Technical Fellow for his work and leadership of a cross-functional team in developing innovative data mining solutions for a variety of aerospace applications. He is the manager of the Cyber Analytics group in Boeing's Networked Systems Technology research and development organization. He earned a master's degree in statistics from the University of Washington, Seattle.

Chia-Hung Wei is currently an assistant professor of the Department of Information Management at Ching Yun University, Taiwan. He obtained his Ph.D. degree in Computer Science from the University of Warwick, UK, and Master's degree from the University of Sheffield, UK, and Bachelor degree from the Tunghai University, Taiwan. His research interests include content-based image retrieval, digital image processing, medical image processing and analysis, machine learning for multimedia applications and information retrieval.

Jason Wu is an Associate Technical Fellow at The Boeing Company. He received a Ph.D. degree in applied mathematics from the University of Maryland at College Park. His research interests include numerical linear algebra, digital signal processing, and parallel computation. He has been a lead in the development of mathematical methods and process automation in many applications including text and data mining, visual analytics, model correlation, structural optimization, reduced order modeling, inverse problems, and implicit geometry. He holds five US patents and is co-author of several journal papers and book chapters on text mining related topics.

Chia-Hung Yeh received the B.S. and Ph.D. degrees from National Chung Cheng University (CCU), Chiayi, Taiwan, in 1997 and 2002, respectively, all from the Department of Electrical Engineering. He received postdoctoral research fellowship from Prof. C.-C. Jay Kuo's group at the Department of Electrical Engineering-Systems, University of Southern California in 2002-04. He was an assistant professor at the Department of Computer Science and Information Engineering, National Dong-Hwa University in 2006-07. Since Aug. 2007, he joins the Department of Electrical Engineering, National Sun Yat-Sen University (NSYSU). His research interests include multimedia communication and multimedia database management. He served the Editorial Board of the *Journal of Multimedia* in 2006-08, and has been on the Editorial Board of *Recent Patents on Signal Processing* since 2009. He has also been an invited speaker at conferences, a reviewer, and researcher, who (co)-authored two book chapters and more than 90 technical international conferences and journal papers. He received the outstanding student award from CCU in 2002, and distinguished assistant professor award of NSYSU in 2007 and outstanding mentor award of College of Engineering, NSYSU, in 2009.

Gang Zhang was born in China in 1973. He received the B.S. degree from Northeastern University in 2000, and the M.S. degree in Northeastern University in 2004. Now he is a Ph.D candidate in Northeastern University and a teacher in Shenyang University of Technology. His research interests include content-based image retrieval, image analysis and understanding, artificial intelligence, etc.

Index

E

F

G

H

I

J

K

L

M

N

O

P

Q

R

S

T

U

V

W

X

Y